OStdWnds

The OStdWnds unit defines two standard types of windows: TEditWindow and TFileWindow. A TEditWindow provides a simple text-editing window. A TFileWindow also provides a simple text-editing window, but one that can read from and write to files.

WinCRT

The WinCRT unit makes it possible for standard DOS Borland Pascal programs to run as Windows applications. Of course, it's really more accurate to call these programs "Windows-compatible" applications, since they don't really take advantage of any of Windows' special features. You can use the WinCRT unit any time you need to port a DOS-based Borland Pascal program to Windows and have to do it with a minimum of recoding.

System

The System unit provides basic Borland Pascal procedures, functions, and definitions that are used by virtually all programs. It is automatically linked to every BPW program when it is compiled, so you never need to explicitly name the System unit in a USES clause.

WinDOS

The WinDOS unit provides a variety of routines for working with MS-DOS and handling files; it corresponds to the DOS unit in standard Turbo Pascal. When using BPW you should provide for as many of these operations as possible to be handled by calls to Windows functions instead of directly through the DOS unit.

Strings

The Strings unit provides support for the use of null-terminated strings, a string type that is required by the Windows API. In Borland Pascal for DOS, a string is normally treated as an array of characters with the first position (array[0]) containing the current length of the string. It has a maximum size of 255 characters and can occupy from 1 to 256 bytes of PC memory. A null-terminated string, on the other hand, has no length byte to indicate where the string ends. Instead, it indicates the end of the string with a NULL (#0) character. This means that it can contain up to 65,535 characters, much more than a standard string.

Computer users are not all alike.
Neither are SYBEX books.

We know our customers have a variety of needs. They've told us so. And because we've listened, we've developed several distinct types of books to meet the needs of each of our customers. What are you looking for in computer help?

If you're looking for the basics, try the **ABC's** series. You'll find short, unintimidating tutorials and helpful illustrations. For a more visual approach, select **Teach Yourself,** featuring screen-by-screen illustrations of how to use your latest software purchase.

Running Start books are really two books in one—a tutorial to get you off to a fast start and a reference to answer your questions when you're ready to tackle advanced tasks.

Mastering and **Understanding** titles offer you a step-by-step introduction, plus an in-depth examination of intermediate-level features, to use as you progress.

Our **Up & Running** series is designed for computer-literate consumers who want a no-nonsense overview of new programs. Just 20 basic lessons, and you're on your way.

We also publish two types of reference books. Our **Instant References** provide quick access to each of a program's commands and functions. SYBEX **Encyclopedias** and **Desktop References** provide a *comprehensive reference* and explanation of all of the commands, features, and functions of the subject software.

Our **Programming** books are specifically written for a technically sophisticated audience and provide a no-nonsense value-added approach to each topic covered, with plenty of tips, tricks, and time-saving hints.

Sometimes a subject requires a special treatment that our standard series doesn't provide. So you'll find we have titles like **Advanced Techniques, Handbooks, Tips & Tricks,** and others that are specifically tailored to satisfy a unique need.

We carefully select our authors for their in-depth understanding of the software they're writing about, as well as their ability to write clearly and communicate effectively. Each manuscript is thoroughly reviewed by our technical staff to ensure its complete accuracy. Our production department makes sure it's easy to use. All of this adds up to the highest quality books available, consistently appearing on best-seller charts worldwide.

You'll find SYBEX publishes a variety of books on every popular software package. Looking for computer help? Help Yourself to SYBEX.

For a brochure of our best-selling publications:
SYBEX Inc. 2021 Challenger Drive, Alameda, CA 94501
Tel: (510) 523-8233/(800) 227-2346 Telex: 336311
Fax: (510) 523-2373

SYBEX

PROGRAMMING IN

BORLAND PASCAL

PROGRAMMING IN
BORLAND PASCAL®

Scott D. Palmer

SYBEX®

San Francisco • Paris • Düsseldorf • Soest

Acquisitions Editor: David Clark
Developmental Editor: Gary Masters
Editor: Jon Britton
Technical Editor: Amrik Dhillon
Project Editors: Barbara Dahl, Michelle Nance
Book Designer and Chapter Artist: Suzanne Albertson
Production Artist: Lisa Jaffe
Screen Graphics: John Corrigan
Typesetter: Thomas Goudie
Proofreader/Production Assistant: Janet MacEachern
Indexer: Nancy Anderman Guenther

Cover Designer: Ingalls + Associates
Cover Illustrator: David Bishop

Screen reproductions produced with Collage Plus.
Collage Plus is a trademark of Inner Media Inc.

SYBEX is a registered trademark of SYBEX Inc.

TRADEMARKS: SYBEX has attempted throughout this book to distinguish proprietary trademarks from descriptive terms by following the capitalization style used by the manufacturer.

SYBEX is not affiliated with any manufacturer.

Every effort has been made to supply complete and accurate information. However, SYBEX assumes no responsibility for its use, nor for any infringement of the intellectual property rights of third parties which would result from such use.

Library of Congress Card Number: 92-63264
ISBN: 0-7821-1151-3

Manufactured in the United States of America
10 9 8 7 6 5 4 3 2 1

Dedicated to my father, and to all the other men who risked their lives for the cause of freedom during World War II. We, your sons and grandsons, will not forget your courage, your honor, your example.

Scott

ACKNOWLEDGMENTS

Because this book combines and adds to the contents of two earlier books, *Mastering Turbo Pascal 6* and *Programmer's Introduction to Turbo Pascal for Windows*, many people contributed to its creation. At Sybex, Managing Editor Barbara Gordon, project editors Barbara Dahl and Michelle Nance, and Editor-in-Chief Dr. Rudolph Langer were all a great help; acquisitions editor David Clark helped launch the project. Technical reviewer Amrik Dhillon was a tremendous help, as was copy editor Jon Britton, who caught many errors in the text. Developmental editor Gary Masters was also a great help in the early stages of the project. And the Sybex credits would not be complete without a grateful nod toward Sybex's original editor of the "Turbo Pascal for Windows" book, Doug Robert.

Valuable feedback on technical aspects of parts of the book was also provided by Prof. Kenneth Epstein of Gallaudet University, Prof. David Maharry of Wabash College, and Harold Oginz of Texas Instruments Corporation. Special thanks must go to Prof. Bernard V. Liengme of St. Francis Xavier University in Nova Scotia, who sent a careful page-by-page analysis of *Mastering Turbo Pascal 6* and went far "beyond the call of duty" in offering his advice.

At Borland International, Nan Borreson, Karen Giles, and Cindy DeMartini were all helpful in obtaining copies of the software and answers to questions.

At Waterside Productions, I must thank my literary agents Bill Gladstone and Amy Davis for helping to launch the project and keep things on track; Margo Maley, Chris Randall, Carolyn Underwood, and Dawn Carlen also helped with some of the details.

As usual, my family was an invaluable source of encouragement while I was working on this project.

CONTENTS AT A GLANCE

TABLE OF CONTENTS

PART II   DOS Programming with Turbo Pascal 7

PART IV   Cross-Platform Programming Issues

INTRODUCTION

First, congratulations on choosing Borland Pascal or Turbo Pascal! You now have one of the most powerful and flexible programming tools ever created for any computer. Whether you're still learning the basics or are an experienced programmer, this book will help you get the most out of your investment.

You can write programs for DOS real mode, for DOS protected mode, or for Microsoft Windows, and build on any Pascal knowledge you already have. And because this book teaches standard Pascal as well as Borland/Turbo Pascal, you can learn techniques useful in Pascal programming on any computer—not just on PCs!

With Borland/Turbo Pascal, you'll have the advantage of Pascal's easy-to-understand language features, but you'll also have access to the most advanced and sophisticated programming techniques, including object-oriented programming, "embedded" assembly language, and Microsoft Windows functions.

Borland Pascal as a Learning Tool

Borland Pascal 7 (just like Turbo Pascal 7 and Turbo Pascal for Windows) provides an ideal way to learn both "the basics" and the most advanced techniques of Pascal programming for DOS and Windows. Pascal keywords, comments, strings, and other program elements are all displayed in different colors and type fonts on the screen. Extensive help is available on almost any Borland Pascal or Windows programming feature, including both explanations and tutorial code examples.

The DOS versions of Borland Pascal have integrated source-code debugging, which helps you find most program bugs easily. If you need help tracking down more subtle problems, the separate Turbo Debuggers (for DOS real mode and DOS protected mode) can help you identify them, and Turbo Profiler can help make your programming more efficient. For debugging Windows applications, you can use Turbo Debugger for Windows, as well as (if you have Borland Pascal 7) other Windows debugging tools that are included with the package.

Borland Pascal for Professional Programming

Don't be fooled by the tutorial features: Borland Pascal gives you the power to do anything you can do in C, C++, or any other programming tool. Although Borland Pascal shields you from the details of the Windows Application Programming Interface (API) when you *don't* need them, you have full access to even the most low-level functions whenever you *do* need them. You can use the same object-oriented features found in Borland C++, and for the most low-level hardware manipulations, you can embed assembly language into your Borland Pascal programs.

You get the best of both worlds: the ease and familiarity of Pascal, the power and flexibility of C/C++ and assembly language!

Program Listings on Disk

The companion disk included with this book contains all the program listings presented in the examples. Use the disk to get started with your own applications or simply to save typing as you follow along with the examples.

To install the files on the listings disk, follow these steps:

1. Make sure that your hard disk has at least 450K of free disk space. If you don't have at least 450K of free disk space, you cannot install the listings disk.

2. Put the listings disk in your 5¼-inch floppy drive (probably drive A).

3. Make the drive with the disk in it the default drive—that is, if the disk is in drive A, type **A:** and press *Enter*.

4. Type **install** and press *Enter*. The install program will create the required directories on your hard disk, then will copy the files into the appropriate directories. The files are now installed.

How This Book Is Structured

To help you use it most efficiently, this book is divided into four Parts. The first Part discusses general issues of programming and Pascal, including correct program design and the features of the Pascal language. If you're just starting out in programming, this is the place to begin.

Part II provides an in-depth tutorial on the features of Borland Pascal 7 and the Pascal language in general. It shows you how to create simple and complex data structures, evaluate the efficiency of your code, find and correct program bugs, create graphics and sound effects, use object-oriented techniques, and use Turbo Vision, the Borland application framework for DOS programs.

Part III discusses the Windows environment and how to create Windows programs with Borland Pascal for Windows. It shows you how to use ObjectWindows, the powerful library of object types that makes Windows programming a breeze. You'll also see how to create Windows menus, dialog boxes, and graphics, and how to exchange data between programs by using the Clipboard and dynamic data exchange (DDE).

Part IV shows how to create portable programs in Borland Pascal: programs that you can move to almost any Pascal compiler on almost any computer, and run with a minimum of changes. You'll also learn how to create DOS protected-mode programs that can use up to 16 megabytes of PC memory, and how to create dynamic link libraries that can be used by either DOS protected-mode or Windows programs.

Let's Get Started!

The most important thing in programming is to have fun. You've taken the first step by purchasing this book and Borland Pascal. Now, take the next step—sit down at your PC and get ready for an adventure. This book is your guide. The rest is up to you.

PART I

General Programming Issues

CHAPTER ONE

A Quick Tour of Borland Pascal

- **What Is Borland Pascal?**

- **Installing Borland Pascal**

- **A Simple Pascal Program**

Borland Pascal is, quite simply, the most powerful and comprehensive Pascal programming package ever created for any computer. It comes with three separate programming platforms: Turbo Pascal 7, for "real mode" MS-DOS programming; Borland Pascal for Windows, for Microsoft Windows programming; and Borland Pascal, which can generate protected-mode MS-DOS programs, real mode MS-DOS programs, and Microsoft Windows programs.

In addition to its three programming platforms, Borland Pascal includes several utilities that help you produce the most efficient programs possible:

- The Borland Resource Workshop, which makes it easy for you to create Windows resources such as menus, icons, and dialog boxes

- Turbo Debugger, which helps you find errors in your DOS, Windows, and DPMI (DOS protected-mode interface) programs

- WinSight and WinSpector, two more tools for debugging Windows programs

- Turbo Profiler, which helps you locate inefficient or time-wasting sections of program code

- Turbo Assembler, which lets you create assembly-language routines that can either run on their own or be embedded in your Turbo Pascal code

- An integrated Object Browser that lets you view the lineage of variables in object-oriented programs

This chapter gives a "bird's-eye view" of Borland Pascal. The specific techniques for using Borland Pascal's programming platforms are discussed in the chapters that follow.

Installing Borland Pascal or Turbo Pascal

Installing Borland Pascal or Turbo Pascal is very easy. Just take the installation disk from your disk set, put it in your floppy drive, and switch to that drive. Then type **install** and press *Enter*. The installation program will take you step-by-step through setting up Borland Pascal or Turbo Pascal for your computer.

Although Borland Pascal comes with three different programming platforms, you might not want to install all of them. Unless you say otherwise, however, the installation program will copy all three to your hard disk—Turbo Pascal 7 (for DOS real-mode programming), Borland Pascal (for both real mode and DOS protected-mode programming), and Borland Pascal for Windows (for Windows programming)—requiring almost 30 megabytes of disk space!

You can save a substantial amount of disk space by only installing the Turbo Pascal IDEs (integrated development environments) that you need. For DOS programming, it's a good idea to choose the DPMI (protected-mode) IDE, which is BP.EXE. This development environment can do everything that TURBO.EXE can do, but it also has object browsing and the ability to create DPMI and Windows applications. If you're going to do mainly Windows programming, of course, the Windows IDE is the one you want.

If you need to, you can also save disk space by not copying Turbo Assembler, Turbo Profiler, and some of the run-time libraries unless you really need them. The days when Turbo Pascal could fit on a single 360K floppy disk are gone forever, but you can still get by with only a few megabytes of disk space.

Creating and Using a Data Directory

It will make your life a lot easier if, before creating your first program, you set up a data directory to hold the programs you write. That way, your own Pascal programs won't be in the same directory as Borland Pascal itself and will be easier to find when you need them.

To create and use a data directory, follow these steps. If there's anything you don't understand, consult your MS-DOS manual.

1. If you're in one of the Borland Pascal IDEs, exit to DOS by pressing *Alt+F* and then "X".

2. At the DOS prompt, make sure that you're in the root directory by typing **cd** and pressing *Enter*.

3. From the root directory, type **md\bp\myfiles** and press *Enter*.

4. With a text editor such as the Turbo Pascal editor (don't use a word processor!), load your AUTOEXEC.BAT file from the root directory.

5. If AUTOEXEC.BAT does not have a statement beginning with the word PATH, then add this statement on a separate line: PATH=C:\BP\BIN. (Don't include the period.)

6. If AUTOEXEC.BAT does have a path statement, then add the BP\BIN directory to the end of it. For example, if the path statement reads PATH=C:\;C:\DOS, then change it to PATH=C:\;C:\DOS;C:\BP\BIN. Don't include the period at the end, and be sure to proofread your changes.

7. Save the new version of the AUTOEXEC.BAT file and reboot your PC.

Turbo Pascal 7

The most familiar element of Borland Pascal is Turbo Pascal 7, the latest incarnation of Borland's top-selling Pascal development environment. On the surface, it hasn't changed much since Turbo Pascal 6 (see Figure 1.1).

But the surface similarity is deceptive, because there's a lot more power under the hood. The most visible advance is the fact that the Turbo Pascal editor now highlights Pascal keywords, comments, and other program code in different colors so

FIGURE 1.1:
The Turbo Pascal 7 integrated development environment

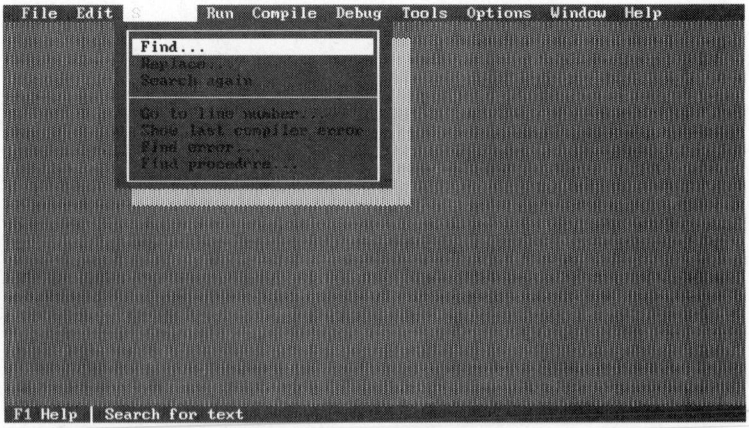

that your programs are easier to read and debug. There are also enhancements in the Turbo Vision application framework, which lets you add drop-down menus, dialog boxes, and mouse support to your programs with a minimum of effort.

Turbo Pascal 7 itself—the familiar TURBO.EXE—can be used to develop real-mode programs that run under MS-DOS. These programs have access to the normal DOS 640K of standard memory. But the Borland Pascal 7 package and the Turbo Pascal 7 package also come with "Borland Pascal," BP.EXE, an integrated development environment just like Turbo Pascal except that it has integrated object browsing and can produce programs for DOS real mode, Windows, and DOS protected mode (see Figure 1.2).

With Borland Pascal (BP.EXE), your applications can work with the DPMI to use all available PC memory, even that beyond 640K. You can also use Borland Pascal to create dynamic link libraries (DLLs) with routines that can be used by both DOS DPMI and Windows applications, no matter what language was used to create them.

Creating a Simple Pascal Program

Let's use Turbo Pascal to look at the steps in creating a simple program—the HELLO program. Listing 1.1 shows this program written in Turbo Pascal.

FIGURE 1.2:
Borland Pascal includes integrated object browsing

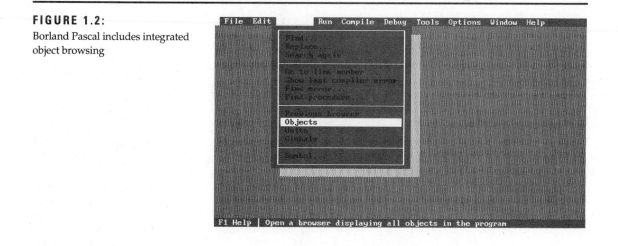

Listing 1.1

```
PROGRAM Listing1_1;

BEGIN
    WRITELN('Hello, world!')
END.
```

The HELLO program is popular because it illustrates the basic elements of a Pascal program. The first line is the PROGRAM statement: this tells Turbo Pascal that the file is meant as a program, not as some other type of file. Just like all statements in a Pascal program, the PROGRAM statement ends with a semicolon.

The next line is the word BEGIN. This is not a Pascal statement: instead, it marks the beginning of a statement. END marks the end of the statement. Every Pascal program must have at least one BEGIN..END pair. In this case, the BEGIN..END is the main body, or the "action part," of the program. The program will carry out whatever commands appear between the BEGIN and END.

The only thing this program does is display a message on the PC's screen: "Hello, world!"

To create this program, switch to your MYFILES directory and start Turbo Pascal or Borland Pascal. Then do the following:

1. Open the File menu by pressing *Alt+F* or using the mouse to click on the word "File" at the top of the screen.

2. From the File menu, select New. An empty file window will appear on the screen.

3. Type Listing 1.1 into the empty file window. Make sure that you've typed it exactly as it appears in the book.

4. From the File menu, select Save. (A shortcut is to press the *F2* function key.)

5. In the dialog box that appears, type **list1_1** as the file name and press *Enter*. That saves the file to disk under the name LIST1_1.PAS.

Compiling and Running the HELLO Program

That creates the program. Now, let's change it into a form that the PC can run: that's called "compiling" it. (Another step, linking the program, is done automatically by Turbo Pascal.) Follow these steps to compile and run the program:

6. Open the Compile menu by pressing *Alt+C* or by clicking with the mouse on Compile at the top of the screen.

7. Press C to select Compile. If you've typed in the listing correctly, a message box should appear that says "Success, press any key."

8. Open the Run menu and select Run. (A shortcut that lets you bypass the Run menu is simply to press *Ctrl+F9*.) The program will display "Hello, world!" on your screen, but it will go by so fast that you won't be able to see much. To see it, press *Alt+F5*; then press any key to get back to Turbo Pascal.

Borland Pascal for Windows

Borland Pascal for Windows is the other "big gun" included with Borland Pascal. It lets you write sophisticated applications for Microsoft Windows but shields you from much of the complexity involved in dealing with Windows itself.

Here, we're only taking a quick tour, so we'll do the HELLO program to show you what it looks like as a Windows application. If you aren't using Borland Pascal for Windows, you can skip this section.

To start Borland Pascal for Windows, just switch to the Windows Program Manager and click on the BPW icon in the Borland Pascal program group. Borland Pascal for Windows will open.

We're not going to do anything fancy here: just write a minimal HELLO program that will run as a Windows application. To do that, we're going to use one of Borland Pascal for Windows' neatest features: the *WinCRT* unit, which lets you run most DOS Turbo Pascal programs as Windows applications. To do this, type in Listing 1.2. Notice that the only difference between Listing 1.1 and Listing 1.2 is that the latter has an extra line: *USES WinCRT*. This line tells Borland Pascal for Windows that you want to run a standard Pascal program as a Windows application. The details are handled for you automatically.

Listing 1.2

```
PROGRAM Hello2;

USES WinCRT;

BEGIN
   WRITELN('Hello, world!')
END.
```

First, select Save from the File menu. Save the program in your MYFILES directory as LIST1_2.PAS (Borland Pascal for Windows will add the ".PAS".)

To compile and run Listing 1.2, select Compile from the Compile menu and then Run from the Run menu. The program will run in its own window, as shown in Figure 1.3. To close the program window, just click on the control button at the top left corner of the window and select Close from the menu.

That's enough for a quick tour. We'll cover each of these tools in more depth later in the book. In the next chapter, let's turn to consider how a program should be designed: that's one of the most important lessons that Turbo Pascal has to teach.

FIGURE 1.3:

The HELLO program running as a Windows application

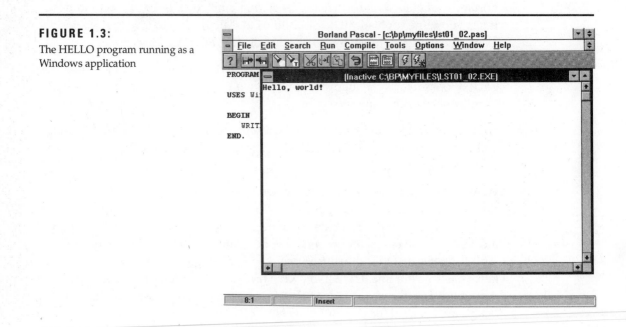

CHAPTER

TWO

Programming and Program Design

- Structured Programming Concepts

- Understanding and Debugging Structured Programs

- Using Program Comments

Essentially, a computer program is very simple. It takes data (input), manipulates it in some way (processing), and then returns the processed data back to you (output). Apart from the fact that it *does* something, the main difference between a computer program and a few paragraphs of ordinary English prose is that the program must be far more precise than the prose.

For example, if you ask a human being "Do you know what time it is?," he or she is likely to respond by telling you the current time. However, that *wasn't* what you asked for: humans, who are much smarter than the most powerful computers, normally look beyond what is *said* and try to infer what is *meant*. Computers, on the other hand, understand only what is *said*. They can't "fill in the blanks" the way a person can. If (using a programming language) you ask a computer "Do you know what time it is?" it most likely will answer with a simple "Yes." Because human beings communicate in so many nonverbal ways (gestures, expressions, intonations, and the contexts in which we speak), English and other human languages are ill-equipped for talking with a computer.

What Is a Computer Program?

Basically, a computer program is a sequence of instructions that tells the computer *precisely* what to do and when to do it. To achieve this level of precision, we use specially designed computer languages such as Pascal.

Although the details are complex, a computer is fundamentally a simple device. Just as Morse Code uses combinations of short and long signals to represent letters, the computer uses ons and offs to represent letters, numbers, and special characters. The capital letter "A", for example, is on-off-off-off-off-off-on, and the period (.) is off-on-off-on-on-on-off.

The computer's CPU has certain built-in operations that it can perform. These operations are called its *instruction set*. The operations must be very simple, for example, comparing two numbers, moving a tiny piece of information from one part of the computer to another, or checking whether a switch is on or off. Each type of processor has its own unique instruction set. The IBM PC and compatible computers, for which Turbo Pascal is designed, are based on the Intel 80x86 family (8086, 80286, 80386, and 80486) of processors, which has a rich instruction set.

Although computers work very well with sequences of ons and offs, represented in machine language (the computer's internal lingo) as sequences of zeroes and ones, people find it difficult to work at this level. It's not that easy for a person to see the difference between 00111010 and 00110010 at a glance, particularly when dealing with page after page of zeros and ones. For this reason, *high-level languages* were invented.

Programming Languages

A high-level language consists of words that are easier for a human being to recognize and remember than sequences of zeroes and ones. It consists of words (source code) like those we've already seen in Chapter 1, such as WRITE, PROGRAM, BEGIN, and END. When a program is compiled, each high-level word is translated into many strings of zeroes and ones, which represent both instructions and data. In fact, that's basically all a compiler really does. Today, the ons and offs are electronic switches that the computer sets by itself in response to the statements in your program.

High-level languages vary greatly in just how "high" they are—that is, in how much they insulate you from the details of your PC's operations. At the lowest level is assembly language, each word of which corresponds to just one instruction in the PC's processor. Assembly language is useful when you need to manipulate the computer directly and when you know *exactly, precisely* what you want to do. If you don't, you can get into real trouble.

A bit higher up are languages such as C, which are sometimes used (to the outrage of assembly-language programmers) for writing compilers and operating systems. C provides more shorthand than assembly language, but it gives a significant amount of access to the PC's low-level functions. And, like assembly language, C has few "guard rails" to keep you from getting into trouble if you don't know what you are doing.

Still higher are languages like Pascal, which combine easy-to-remember shorthand, some low-level access, and at least a few safety features for the novice programmer. Turbo Pascal provides the best of both worlds by letting you include assembly-language routines in your Pascal programs whenever you need sophisticated low-level access, and by extending the Pascal language to support graphics and object orientation. The Pascal language itself was designed by Niklaus Wirth in the early 1970s as a way to teach structured programming ideas to students of computer science, and to this day, it still exhibits that tutorial heritage.

At the highest level are languages such as Paradox and dBASE, which provide little if any low-level access but offer powerful shorthand for specialized functions such as data management and graphics.

The vocabulary of a particular high-level language is referred to as its set of "reserved words." Because these words have a very precisely defined meaning in the language itself, they cannot be used for anything else in your program.

BASIC, Pascal, and Structured Programming

Because it is included with the PC's operating system, many more people know how to write programs in BASIC than in any other language. BASIC and Pascal share a common purpose—to teach people how to program. The crucial difference between them is that BASIC (Beginners' All-Purpose Symbolic Instruction Code) is designed simply to teach programming, while Pascal is designed to teach *structured* programming. BASIC allows you "to get away with" some bad programming practices that you'll need to unlearn as a Pascal programmer.

In particular, Pascal requires you to declare all identifiers before using them, while BASIC allows you to make up new variables anywhere, without ever having to explicitly define them. In some versions of BASIC, such as GW-BASIC, there is very limited support for separate subroutines to which you can pass variables. These subroutines are a key feature of Pascal. And while BASIC encourages you to sit down and start coding, Pascal almost *requires* a separate step to design your program before you ever write a line of code.

Structured vs. Unstructured Programming

The vast difference between structured and unstructured ("spaghetti") programming is shown clearly in Listings 2.1 and 2.2. Listing 2.1 shows an unstructured GW-BASIC program that makes change for a purchase, somewhat like a cash register. When the user first starts the program, a screen is displayed that explains how the program works; then the program pauses. After the pause, it asks the user to enter the amount owed and the amount paid. By subtracting the amount owed from the amount paid, it computes the change, and then asks the user if he or she wants to go again. It then pauses and either goes again or terminates, depending on the user's answer.

Listing 2.1

```
10 REM Program MakeChange, coded in GW-BASIC.
20 CLS
30 PRINT "This is a program to make change. You will"
40 PRINT "enter two integers: the first is the amount due,"
50 PRINT "while the second is the amount paid."
60 PRINT
70 PRINT "Press any key to continue ..."
80 WHILE INKEY$ = ""
90 WEND
100 PRINT
110 INPUT "Enter the amount due in cents (an integer): ",AMOUNTDUE
120 PRINT
130 INPUT "Enter the amount paid in cents (an integer): ",PAYMENT
140 PRINT
150 CHANGE = PAYMENT - AMOUNTDUE
160 PRINT "Your change is "; CHANGE; " cents."
170 PRINT "Have a nice day."
180 INPUT "Do you want to go again (Y/N)? ", DOANOTHER$
190 CLS
200 IF DOANOTHER$ = "Y" OR DOANOTHER$ = "y" THEN GOTO 100
210 PRINT "Press any key to continue ..."
220 WHILE INKEY$ = ""
230 WEND
240 CLS
250 END
```

Listing 2.2

```
PROGRAM Listing2_2;

    { This program illustrates how structured programming makes
      a program easier to understand than a "spaghetti" approach. }

USES CRT;  { for CLRSCR }

VAR
    Payment,
    Change  : integer;
```

```
PROCEDURE Pause;
   VAR
      proceed : char;
   BEGIN
      WRITELN;
      WRITE(' Press the Enter key to continue ...');
      READ(proceed)
   END;

PROCEDURE ExplainProgram;
   BEGIN
      CLRSCR;
      WRITELN(' This is a program to make change.  You will be prompted');
      WRITELN(' to enter two integers: the first represents the amount');
      WRITELN(' due, while the second represents the amount paid.');
      pause;
      WRITELN
   END;

PROCEDURE CountMoney(var Payment, Change : integer);
   VAR
      AmountDue : integer; { declare private variables for }
      DoAnother : char;{ the CountMoney routine       }
   BEGIN
      DoAnother := 'Y';  { put the letter 'Y' into DoAnother }
      WHILE UPCASE(DoAnother) = 'Y' DO{ set up a loop }
         BEGIN
         WRITELN;
         WRITE(' Please enter the amount due in cents (an integer): ');
         READLN(AmountDue);
         WRITELN;
         WRITE(' Please enter the amount paid in cents (an integer): ');
         READLN(Payment);
         Change := Payment - AmountDue;{ calculate change }
         WRITELN;
         WRITELN(' Your change is ', Change, ' cent(s).');
         WRITELN(' Have a nice day.');
         WRITE(' Do you want to go again (Y/N)? ');{ exit from loop? }
         READLN(DoAnother);
         CLRSCR
         END          { of the WHILE .. DO loop }
   END;            { of the CountMoney procedure }
```

```
BEGIN
    ExplainProgram;
    CountMoney(payment, change);
    pause
END.
```

There are two things to note about Listing 2.1. First, it's confusing; lines of code are jumbled together, making it harder to understand what the program does. Second, each time we wanted to pause the program, we ended up writing the same code all over again. (This case is slightly artificial, but if we wanted to pass some variables to the pause routine, we really *would* be forced to repeat the code.)

The program in Listing 2.1 is a very short and simple one; but if you can imagine trying to understand a 100-page program written in the same unstructured way, it's clear that the "spaghetti" approach can cause some real problems.

Compare this to Listing 2.2, which illustrates a structured Pascal program that does the same thing. The program in Listing 2.2 is harder to write in the first place than the unstructured version, which starts at the beginning and runs straight through to the end. The Pascal program uses the quirky kind of Chinese puzzle-box thinking that is the hallmark of structured programming, and you simply *must* plan the program before you write it.

The benefits of this extra initial effort are considerable. The program in Listing 2.2 is far easier to *understand, debug,* and *modify* than the unstructured program in Listing 2.1. It is even easier to fine-tune a structured program to make it run faster. Let's examine each of these points in turn.

Understanding the Program

It is true that for a 25-line program such as the one shown in Listing 2.1, understanding the program is a fairly trivial matter. However, note that even in this short program, all the different tasks that the program performs are jumbled together. You have to look carefully to be sure where the pause lines end and the prompt-the-user lines begin. If the program were even a few pages long, this could become a significant problem. With a real-world program, which could run to 100 or more pages, you'd be in deep trouble—as, indeed, some old COBOL programmers are today.

In Listing 2.2, however, each specific job is handled by a separate subroutine, and each subroutine has a name that describes what it does. To achieve this separation of program tasks you must carefully think through your program before you start to code, and you must decide beforehand what the basic subparts of the program should be. The end result, however, is that you will easily understand what each part of the program does, even if it is 100 pages long. Note that although parts of the structured program are indented, Pascal itself pays no attention to indenting. The indentation is there simply to make the program easier for humans to read.

There is a trick to understanding structured programs. Instead of starting at the beginning and reading to the end, you start at the end and work your way back to the beginning. At the end of the code listing, the action part of the program shows you the main outline of how the program works—a sort of bird's-eye view. The first line of the action part is almost always a call to a subroutine (a procedure or function) defined earlier in the program, so you go back and examine how that subroutine works. That routine itself may call earlier routines (such as pause), and you look at them, too. Finally, when you have a good understanding of what is done by the first line of the program's action part, then you can go on to the second line.

In the case of Listing 2.2, there are only three lines in the action part. The first line calls the *ExplainProgram* procedure, which in turn calls the *pause* procedure. The second line calls the *CountMoney* procedure, passing two variables to that procedure (see Chapter 9 for passing variables to procedures). The third line calls the *pause* routine directly. And that's all there is to the program. The overall structure of the program in Listing 2.2 is shown in Figure 2.1.

Debugging the Program

Structured design is a tremendous help in debugging any program of more than trivial complexity. In Listing 2.1, a bug could occur anywhere in the program. A minor change in a variable, a change in an arithmetic statement, and kaboom! The program crashes and you don't know why. In a long unstructured program, the crash could occur at a place in the code listing some distance away from the actual source of the trouble. When the program crashes on line 2550, but the cause of the problem is on line 830, you can have an extraordinarily difficult time trying to find out what's wrong.

FIGURE 2.1:

Structure of MakeChange
program (Listing 2.2)

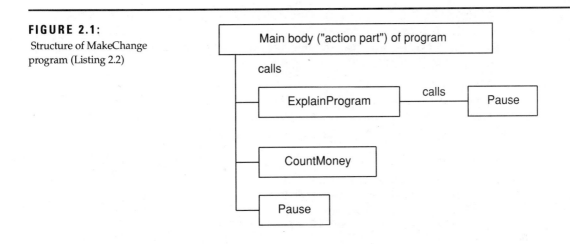

In Listing 2.2, however, you can localize bugs by treating each different routine as a "black box" whose content is hidden from the rest of the program. The conceptual notion of a black box is like a compartment in a submarine: each compartment is sealed off from all the others. If one compartment springs a leak and floods with water, all the other compartments stay dry. That way, the damage is contained and it's easier to find which compartment is leaking.

Structured programming works the same way to localize bugs and to limit the mischief they can create. Listing 2.3 shows how you might write the first code for the MakeChange program in Listing 2.2.

Listing 2.3

```
PROGRAM Listing2_3;

    { Listing 2.3. This illustrates top-down design and debugging,
      using "stubs" for the program's subroutines. }

USES CRT;   { for CLRSCR }

VAR
    Payment,
    Change  : integer;

PROCEDURE Pause;
    VAR
        proceed : char;
```

```
    BEGIN
       WRITELN;
       WRITE(' Press the Enter key to continue ...');
       READ(proceed)
    END;

PROCEDURE ExplainProgram;
    BEGIN
       WRITELN(' The ExplainProgram procedure has run.');
       pause
    END;

PROCEDURE CountMoney(var Payment, Change : integer);
    BEGIN
       WRITELN(' The CountMoney procedure has run.');
       pause
    END;



BEGIN          { main body of program }
    ExplainProgram;
    CountMoney(payment, change);
END.
```

Top-Down and Bottom-Up Debugging

Listing 2.3 illustrates two features of developing structured programs that are tremendously helpful in debugging: top-down and bottom-up development. You start with the main part of the program as a framework on which to place your (as yet empty) subroutines. Each subroutine performs an essentially vacuous task, displaying a message that it has run. You then develop the subroutines one at a time, debugging them separately before adding them to the main program.

Because each subroutine is a black box as far as the main program is concerned, nothing that happens inside a subroutine should have any direct effect on either the main program or the other subroutines. The only things that are visible to the main program and the other subroutines are (a) what *goes into* a given subroutine, and (b) what *comes out of* a given subroutine. And the items that go in and out of a subroutine should always go through the "front door" as "parameters." See Chapter 9 for a discussion of parameters.

This means that if a bug does occur in a subroutine, it is easy to isolate. You know exactly what is going in and what is coming out. To develop a subroutine separately from the main program, you need to write a *driver* to assign input values to the subroutine. When you think the subroutine has been coded correctly, you run the test program (like that shown in Listing 2.4) and try one set of values after another to see if the subroutine works correctly.

Listing 2.4

```
PROGRAM Listing2_4;

    { This program illustrates how to use subroutine drivers
        to develop a subroutine separately from the main program. }


USES CRT;   { for CLRSCR }

VAR
    AmountDue,
    Payment,
    Change  : integer;
    Proceed : char;

PROCEDURE Driver(var Payment, AmountDue : integer);
    BEGIN
        CLRSCR;
        WRITE(' Initial value for payment? ');
        READLN(payment);
        WRITE(' Initial value for amount due? ');
        READLN(AmountDue)
    END;

PROCEDURE CountMoney(var Payment, AmountDue, Change : integer);
    BEGIN
        Change := Payment - AmountDue;    { calculate change }
        WRITELN;
        WRITELN(' Your change is ', Change, ' cent(s).');
        WRITELN(' Have a nice day.')
    END;             { of the CountMoney procedure }


BEGIN
    proceed := 'Y';
    WHILE UPCASE(proceed) = 'Y' DO
```

```
      BEGIN
      Driver(payment, amountdue);
      CountMoney(payment, amountdue, change);
      WRITE(' Do another (Y/N)? ');
      READLN(proceed)
      END
END.
```

In addition to ordinary values (such as 25 or 100 in the case of CountMoney), you should try very large and very small values (for example, 1,000,000 and 0); values that don't make sense (for example, a payment of 75 when the amount due is 100); and values that are the wrong type (for example, "F" or "&" instead of integers). The goal is to ensure the following:

1. The subroutine runs correctly when it receives the sort of input it expects (in this case, integers where the payment is greater than the amount due).

2. The subroutine has ways to handle input that it doesn't expect (such as receiving letters instead of numbers for the amount due, or receiving an amount due of zero). This is called bulletproofing the routine.

Modifying the Program

Structured design is also very helpful when you need to modify a program. You may need a new feature, or need a change in an existing feature, or you may find, long after the program is in use, a subtle bug that you'd like to fix.

With an unstructured program, making changes can be a nightmare, because any part of the program can have unexpected effects on any other part of the program. You can make a change on page 19 and then, suddenly, the code on page five won't work right anymore—and you won't have the faintest idea why.

With structured programming, each part of the program is a black box whose internal features are hidden from the rest of the program, and whose interactions with other parts of the program are tightly controlled *by you*. Changes in the internal structure of a routine should have no effect on its work with other parts of the program. As long as it takes the expected input values and returns the correct output values, that's all the rest of the program is concerned with.

Moreover, to add a new feature, you need to make only minor changes either in the main program or in one of the main subroutines, so that the subroutine for the new feature will be called when needed.

Today there is an entire discipline called software maintenance that is devoted to rescuing people from unstructured code written in the 1960s and 1970s. Fortunately, you'll never have to worry about this. With Pascal, you'll learn how to do it right the first time.

Using Program Comments

Program comments can clarify a program. You can create a comment in one of the following two ways:

- By enclosing the comment material in left and right curly brackets, { and }.
- By enclosing the comment material in a left comment bracket, (*, and a right comment bracket, *).

Either combination of symbols will cause Pascal to ignore anything that's between the two brackets. You must be careful, however, not to combine the two types of brackets into a single comment. When Pascal sees a {, it will ignore everything until it comes to the next }. Likewise, when Pascal sees a (*, it ignores everything until it comes to a *). Thus, the following piece of code will cause an error:

```
BEGIN
   WRITELN(' Comments are beautiful.')
   { Our opinion. *)
END;
```

In the case above, the first comment bracket does not match the second. In any single comment, both comment brackets must be of the same type.

What Comments Are Good For

In addition to explaining particular parts of your code, comments are used in two other ways. The first is to "comment out" the parts of your program that are still under development. Once you have part of your program working, you can tell Turbo Pascal to ignore any new, untested code by enclosing it in comment brackets until you're sure that it works right. Generally, it's a good idea to use one type of comment bracket for explanations and the other for "commenting out" sections of code. If you use the same type for both jobs, you run the risk that a stray unmatched comment bracket will cause your program to go haywire.

The other use of comment brackets is to insert *compiler directives* into your program. These tell the Pascal compiler to do things it would not ordinarily do, such as to add some extra error checking to your program. See Chapter 7 for details on compiler directives.

Object-Oriented Programming

The most exciting developments in recent Pascal history have been Turbo Pascal's development of support for object-oriented programming, and the "Turbo Vision" object library that is included with Turbo Pascal 7.

Here, we want to take a quick look at how object-oriented programming naturally evolved from—and differs from—structured programming.

Object-oriented programming, like structured programming, uses the idea that the internal features of each program part should be hidden from all the other parts. Where object-oriented programming differs from structured programming is in the notion that program parts are not subroutines, but intelligent data that have their own subroutines; data that know how to do things for themselves.

Most programming languages (such as BASIC) still do not provide direct support for object-oriented programming. However, for languages that have procedure and function data types (such as standard Pascal), object orientation can be simulated.

CHAPTER THREE

An Overview of Pascal Programming

- **Designing Your Program**

- **Overview of Pascal**

Regardless of the programming language you use, you must spend some time at the beginning to plan and design your program. This requires more than just knowing that you should split the program into subroutines. The question is, *which* subroutines? How should different tasks be divided so that the chief goals of the program are achieved efficiently, with clear, easy-to-understand code?

Designing Your Program

I don't want to give you the idea that this is a simple problem. Many books have been written about program design, but people are still arguing about the best ways to do it. Nevertheless, there are a few simple rules that you can follow to create a good design without having to become a master theoretician. These rules are similar to remembering "control the center" and "castle early" in the game of chess, in that they are basic principles you should observe to create efficient, easy-to-understand programs.

State What the Program Should Do

The first step for planning a program design is to summarize in one sentence what the program is supposed to do. For a music composition program, which we might call "Turbo Tunemaker," this sentence would be something like the following:

```
Allow the user to play music on his or her PC.
```

That is, of course, very general. It does not tell us anything about where the music comes from, how it is to be selected by the user, or if it can be edited by the user, but it does state the main task that the program must accomplish.

Divide the Main Task into Subtasks

As a second step, we will make our problem definition somewhat more specific by dividing the main task into several subtasks.

```
Allow the user to play music on his or her PC, meaning that the
program should
```

- Explain itself to the user

- Let the user enter tunes from the keyboard

- Let the user save tunes to a disk file
- Let the user load tunes from a disk file
- Let the user play tunes
- Let the user edit existing tunes

Notice that I have not said anything about Pascal in this design; I've simply identified the major tasks that the program has to perform. In this case, the major tasks divide rather neatly, and each receives its own subroutine. At this stage, there are three main principles to follow:

1. Subdivide the program's tasks in outline form until each subroutine performs a clear logical step, such as playing a tune or saving a tune to a disk file.

2. Avoid becoming involved in language details. Keep your focus on what the program is supposed to accomplish.

3. Attend to housekeeping details such as setting up the program to run and explaining the program to the user. Each of these may need its own subroutine.

Decide on Broad Implementation

Once you have created a usable outline of the tasks that the program must perform and how they are to be divided into subroutines, you need to consider some of the specifics of how to implement the program. If you ask yourself the following three questions, the answers should provide some of these specifics.

1. *What must be global and what can be local?* Remember that the code inside each subroutine is hidden both from the main program and from the other subroutines. Parts of the program that are hidden inside a subroutine are local to that subroutine, because they are not accessible to other parts of the program. Parts that are not in a subroutine, on the other hand, are called global. One programming principle is so important it deserves special emphasis as a rule of thumb: *Within reason, hide everything you can.*

   This means that the main structure of the program should not be cluttered up with a lot of details about how various parts of the program work. Those details should be hidden inside subroutines, which can contain their own variables, data structures, and local subroutines.

Some parts, however, do need to be global. If a variable is shared by several subroutines, such as the variable for a tune in Turbo Tunemaker, then it must be global so that it is accessible to all those subroutines. Hiding it inside one of the subroutines would not make sense. Similarly, a subroutine to pause the program, which will be called by many other subroutines, must be global. Anything that doesn't really need to be global, however, should be hidden inside a subroutine.

2. *Which data structures will work best?* The parts of your program that hold data are called *data structures,* and you design many of these structures yourself. At this stage, you simply need to decide what the data structures must do— never mind how they will be coded in a particular language. In Turbo Tunemaker, we will need some kind of list to hold the notes of the tune being played. Because some tunes are longer than others, ideally it should be the type of list whose length can vary while the program is being run.

3. *Which language is best suited for the program at hand?* In some ways, it would be easier to code Turbo Tunemaker in Microsoft QuickBASIC than Turbo Pascal, because QuickBASIC has a built-in music Play command. QuickBASIC, however, lacks support for object-oriented programming and other Turbo Pascal features that we'll be using.

Starting to Write Code

At this stage of program development, you have two options. First, you can do as many people advise and write the program in *pseudocode,* which means, essentially, that you code it in English. For example:

```
start program
clear the screen
display on screen "Welcome to Turbo Tunemaker!"
pause

subroutine to set up a tune list
   initialize the list
   end of subroutine
...etc
```

There's no question that this extra step will give you a more detailed understanding of your program, but what you end up with is in English, not in Pascal. If you do your design work properly, then you don't need pseudocode. If you haven't done your design work properly, then the additional pseudocode is not that helpful. For small programs particularly, pseudocode is redundant; however, for larger programs, it may help you gain a better understanding of your program. To me, however, it makes more sense to go directly to your second option, which is to start coding your program in the language you've chosen.

Specific Features of Pascal

If you are like me, you've probably been chomping at the bit, wondering when we are going to start talking about Pascal. Well, chomp no more: we have arrived.

Pascal Identifiers

The fundamental building blocks of a Pascal program are called *identifiers*, which are essentially just names for different parts of the program. Each part of the program must have its own identifier, and, with a few key exceptions, no two parts of a program can have the same identifier. Thus, the following code will cause an error if you try to compile it:

```
PROGRAM ClientNames; { same name as variable, below }
USES CRT,            { for CLRSCR }
CONST
    NumberOfClients = 5;
VAR
    ClientNames : ARRAY[1..NumberOfClients] of STRING[15];
    Counter : integer;
PROCEDURE Pause;
    VAR
       ch : CHAR;
    BEGIN
       WRITE ('Press any key...');
       REPEAT UNTIL Keypressed;
       Ch:= READKEY
    END;
BEGIN
    CLRSCR;
    FOR Counter := 1 to NumberOfClients DO
       BEGIN
       WRITE(' Enter a client name: ');
       READLN(Clients[Counter])
```

```
        END;
    pause
END.
```

The reason, as shown in Figure 3.1, is that two parts of the program have the same name—that is, both the program name and one of the variables are called *ClientNames*. Remember that it would not make any difference if one were called *ClientNames* and the other were called *CLIENTNAMES* or *clientnames*, because Pascal does not distinguish between upper- and lowercase letters.

I know I have introduced some things in this short program that you have not seen before. Don't worry: you will get to them very soon. In the meantime, you can learn a lot by trying to figure them out on your own. If you want to enter and run the program, just change one of the *ClientNames* identifiers to another legal identifier, such as *Clients*.

Reserved Words

Turbo Pascal's vocabulary constitutes its own built-in set of identifiers called *reserved words*. These are words such as BEGIN, PROCEDURE, TYPE, UNIT, and VAR. In addition to reserved words, there are also *standard identifiers* such as WRITELN and READLN. You should not use either reserved words or standard identifiers to name parts of the program that you create. If you do try to use

FIGURE 3.1:

Compile-time error because of duplicate identifiers

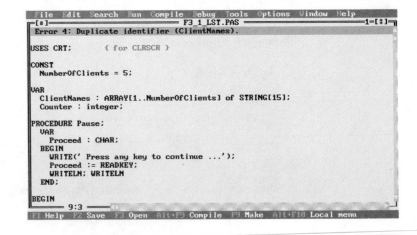

reserved words, your program won't compile. If you use standard identifiers, your program probably will compile, but most likely it won't run correctly because you've redefined one or more of Pascal's key words.

Rules for Identifiers

You cannot use just any old word or string of characters as an identifier. You have to follow certain rules. A Pascal identifier must observe the following conventions:

1. It must begin with a letter or an underline character ("_").

2. It cannot contain any spaces or other special characters such as ., !, ?, #, or -.

3. It can have any combination of letters, digits, and underline characters after the first character.

4. It can be as long as you like, but Turbo Pascal pays attention only to the first 63 characters.

Thus, the following are legal, user-defined identifiers:

ClientRecord	**COUNTER**
_AnyOldThing	file2read
Number_Of_Loops	NumberOfLoops
mrspeel	general_george_s_patton

The following list contains some *illegal* identifiers that will cause an error when you try to compile the program:

Identifier	**Mistake**
Client Record	contains a space
2motleycrue	doesn't start with a letter or underline
Number-Of-Loops	contains illegal characters ("-")
Begin	same as a Pascal reserved word
data.txt	contains illegal character (".")

Overall Program Structure

Unlike spaghetti code, Pascal programs have a very definite structure that has to be followed. Each program is broken up into sections. The main sections of a Pascal program (demonstrated in Listing 3.1) are as follows:

Listing 3.1

```
PROGRAM Listing3_1;

    { This listing demonstrates how to use an array to
      hold multiple variables in a list structure—in
      this case, a client list. The maximum number of
      clients in the list is declared as a constant in
      the constant section; the advantage of doing this
      is that you can change every occurrence of this
      number in the program simply by changing the value
      declared for NumberOfClients in the CONST section.
      Notice also how we set up a FOR loop to load the
      client names into the array. }


USES CRT;      { for CLRSCR }

CONST
    NumberOfClients = 5;

VAR
    Clients : ARRAY[1..NumberOfClients] of STRING[15];
    Counter : integer;

PROCEDURE Pause;
    VAR
        Proceed : CHAR;
    BEGIN
        WRITE(' Press any key to continue ...');
        Proceed := READKEY;
        WRITELN; WRITELN
    END;

BEGIN
    CLRSCR;
    FOR Counter := 1 to NumberOfClients DO
        BEGIN
        WRITE(' Enter a client name: ');
```

```
        READLN(Clients[Counter])
        END;
    pause
END.
```

- **The PROGRAM statement.** This gives the name of the program and marks
  the official beginning of the program for your Pascal compiler. In standard
  Pascal (though this is not required in Turbo Pascal), the program statement
  also has to identify any files that the program will be using, such as a data
  file containing a list of names and addresses.

- **The USES clause.** This tells Turbo Pascal what units the program uses. *Units*
  are separately compiled libraries of routines and/or object types. By naming
  a unit in your USES clause, you can use material from the unit without
  having to include it in your program. If Turbo Pascal cannot find a given subroutine (or object type) in the current program, it looks in the units named by
  the USES clause to find them. This feature is not supported by standard Pascal, but many versions (such as Microsoft QuickPascal and DEC Vax Pascal)
  have similar features.

- **The LABEL section.** This is a section that your computer science professor
  might not tell you about, because it involves the hated GOTO statement.
  With a GOTO statement, you jump from one place in your program to
  another, and structured-programming purists maintain that you should
  never, ever use GOTOs.

  In the LABEL section, you list labels for program lines that are GOTO destina-
  tions. In standard Pascal, labels must be integers that range from 0..9999, and
  leading zeroes don't count (for example, 000125 and 125 are considered the
  same label). Turbo Pascal also lets you use ordinary identifiers for labels,
  such as *DestinationLine*, though of course they must be unique within your
  program (or at least within a subroutine).

- **The CONST (constant) section.** In this section, you declare any constants
  used by your program. Constants can be either simple or complex expressions, such as the following:

```
10
'stockfile'
CHR(13)
1000 div 5
```

Each constant receives its own identifier. The number 10, for example, could be *NumberOfClients*. In this section, you also can declare typed constants, which are not really constants, but are variables whose initial values are preset in the constant section. You declare constants as follows:

```
Name = 'stockfile';
MaximumNumberofRecords = 100;
Company : STRING[20] = ";  {a typed constant}
```

Except for typed constants, which are really variables, the values you set in the CONST section cannot be changed during the program run.

- **The TYPE section.** In this section, you can create and declare your own data types beyond those supported by Pascal. While Turbo Pascal supports data types of numbers, text, and so forth, you can use the TYPE section to create data types that are tailored to your own needs, such as the following:

```
TYPE
    String10 = STRING[10];      { needed for passing  }
    String15 = STRING[15];      { string variables to }
    String20 = STRING[20];      { subroutines         }
    DaysOfWeek = (Sunday, Monday, Tuesday, Wednesday,
                  Thursday, Friday, Saturday);
    Digits = 0..9;
    FirstSixLetters = 'A'..'F';
    Weekdays = Monday..Friday; {uses "DaysOfWeek" type}
    WorkDays = ARRAY[Monday..Friday] of String20;
    Client = RECORD
               Firstname,
               Lastname  : string[15];
               Address   : string[30];
               City      : string[15];
               State     : string[2];
               Zipcode   : string[5];
               Balance   : real;
               PaidUp    : Boolean  { True or False }
    END;
```

It is important to understand that merely defining a data type in the TYPE section does not automatically put that type to use in your program. The above section does not, for example, give you a variable named Client into which you can start loading clients' names, addresses, and other information. In order to do that, you have to declare a variable of the Client data type—a job you can do in the VAR section, which follows next.

Remember that you do not have to declare any simple Pascal types in this section—only types that you create.

- **The VAR (variable) section.** In this section, you declare the names and data types of variables that you use in the program. A variable name can be any legal identifier, and the data type can be a standard Turbo Pascal data type or a data type you defined in the TYPE section. The only variables not declared in this section are a special type called dynamic variables, which are created while the program is actually running. (See Chapter 11 for a discussion of dynamic variables.)

- **The procedures and functions section.** This is the section for your program's subroutines, and it is the only section of the program that does not begin with an explicit section label. As soon as you declare a procedure or a function, Turbo Pascal knows that you've started this section. If you are writing a medium-sized program with many subroutines, you should use comments to break up this section into subsections such as utility routines, input routines, help routines, and so forth. (In a very large program, you should create some units and put as many subroutines as possible into them.)

- **The main body of the program.** In a well-designed program, this part is usually only a few lines long. The main body of the program should show only the overall structure of what happens in the program, leaving all the details to the subroutines.

Statements and Data Types

Now that you have seen the overall structure of a Pascal program, we are ready to delve deeper into how that structure is implemented. In the following sections, I will present an overview of the specifics of writing Pascal code. If and when you need complete details, you should look ahead to the appropriate chapters in Part II.

Begin and End

In order to understand the functions of BEGIN and END in a Pascal program, you must grasp an odd idea: *a Pascal program is just a single big statement.* Think of it in terms of the English language for a moment. The following is a legal sentence in English:

```
Go to the grocery store.
```

So is this:

```
Go to the grocery store and
pick up the kids after school.
```

The second example is not *two* sentences, but one sentence with two subsentences as its component parts. It is, of course, called a compound sentence.

In the same way, a Pascal program is a big compound statement composed of simpler statements. By using BEGIN and END, you signal to Pascal where a compound program statement is supposed to begin and end. Semicolons are used in the same way that the word "and" is used in English: to tie two simpler statements together into a compound statement. Thus, you must use BEGIN and END to show the start and finish of a compound statement. Here are some legal Pascal statements:

```
WRITELN(' This is a simple statement.');  { simple }
IF a = 1 THEN DoOneThing ELSE DoAnotherThing; { simple }

IF a = 1  { simple IF..}
   THEN BEGIN  { THEN which }
      WRITELN(' a = 1');  {contains a }
      pause { compound   }
      END  {THEN clause }
   ELSE WRITELN(' a doesn''t equal 1');

BEGIN { compound   }
   WRITELN(' Block is a compound statement.');
   WRITELN(' Substatements linked by semicolons.');
   WRITELN(' No semicolon right before the END');
   WRITELN(' There's no next statement from');
   WRITELN(' the last line must be separated.') END;
```

The bottom line is that any time you are constructing a compound statement from simpler statements, you should start with BEGIN, separate the simpler statements with semicolons, and finish with END. Moreover, because each BEGIN..END sequence is itself a statement, it must be separated from other statements by a semicolon after the word END. The only exception occurs at the very end of the entire program, when you must put a period after END (see Listing 3.2).

Listing 3.2

```
PROGRAM Listing3_2;

   { This program illustrates how BEGIN, END, and semicolons
     are used to define and separate program statements. }


USES CRT;


PROCEDURE Pause;
   VAR
        Proceed : CHAR;
   BEGIN
      WRITELN(' Press any key to continue ...');
      Proceed := READKEY;
      WRITELN; WRITELN
   END;


PROCEDURE ExplainProgram;
   BEGIN
      WRITELN;
      WRITELN(' This program shows how compound statements');
      WRITELN(' are formed with BEGIN, END, and semicolons.');
      pause
   END;

PROCEDURE ExplainPunctuation;
   BEGIN
      WRITELN;
      WRITELN(' Note that each simple statement within a');
      WRITELN(' compound statement is separated from the');
      WRITELN(' others by a semicolon, except for the very');
      WRITELN(' last one before the END.');
      pause
   END;

PROCEDURE ExplainENDs;
   BEGIN
      WRITELN;
      WRITELN(' Furthermore, each END in the program has a');
      WRITELN(' semicolon after it to separate it from the rest');
      WRITELN(' of the program unless (a) it comes just before');
```

```
   WRITELN(' another END, or (b) it comes at the end of the');
   WRITELN(' program, in which case it has a period after it.');
   pause
END;

{ ------------------------------------------------------------ }
{                     MAIN BODY OF PROGRAM                     }
{ ------------------------------------------------------------ }
BEGIN
   CLRSCR;
   ExplainProgram;
   ExplainPunctuation;
   ExplainENDs;
END.
```

Simple Data Types

The idea behind data types is a fairly commonsensical one. In the real world, there are, of course, many different types of things, such as gases, solids, colors, people, minerals, and diskettes. Because computer programs are ultimately about the real world, a programming language uses different data types so that it can manipulate information about the many different types of things in the real world more efficiently.

Pascal supports both simple and complex data types. You can use the simple data types as building blocks to define your own complex data types. Essentially, Pascal's simple data types break down into numbers, text, truth values, and pointers.

Numeric Data Types

Numeric data types are divided into integers (whole numbers) and real numbers (numbers with a decimal point). Turbo Pascal's integer type ranges from –32,768 to 32,767, so some examples of Pascal integers would be 123, 5, 30000, and –555. Real numbers in Turbo Pascal range from 2.9 times 10^{-39} to 1.7 times 10^{38}, which is an astronomical range.

Each type has several subtypes (see Chapter 5). For the time being, you need to be aware only of the following:

- If you do an arithmetic calculation with integers and real numbers, the result will be a real number—a fact which can occasionally get you into trouble. In Listing 3.3, we multiplied an integer (3) by a real number (2.00) and tried to put the result in an integer-type variable (c). The result is a compile-time error, as shown in Figure 3.2.

Listing 3.3

```
PROGRAM Listing3_3;

    { This program demonstrates how mixing numeric types in an
      arithmetic operation can lead to trouble. Multiplying an
      integer by a real number gives a real number. }


USES CRT;

VAR
    a, c : integer;
    b : real;

PROCEDURE Pause;
    VAR
        Proceed : CHAR;
    BEGIN
        WRITELN(' Press any key to continue ...');
        Proceed := READKEY;
        WRITELN; WRITELN
    END;

BEGIN
    a := 3;               { assign integer value to a }
    b := 2.00;            { assign real value to b     }
    c := a*b;             { assign a times b to c      }
    WRITELN(' The value of c is ', c, '.');
    pause
END.
```

FIGURE 3.2:

Compile-time error because of
incompatible data types

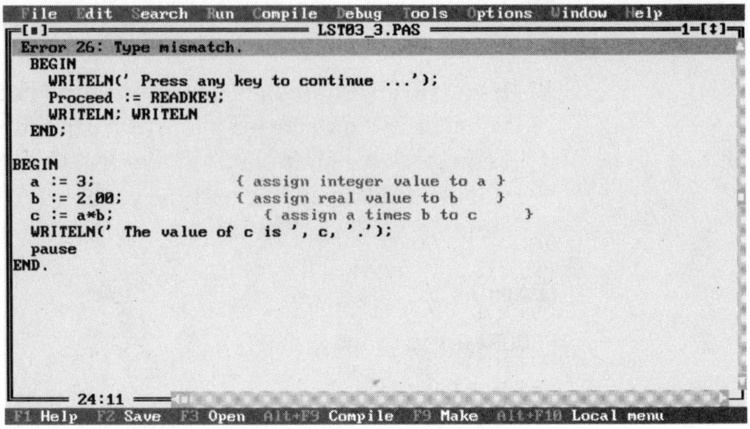

```
 File  Edit  Search  Run  Compile  Debug  Tools  Options  Window  Help
┌─[■]──────────────────── LST03_3.PAS ───────────────────1─[↕]─┐
│ Error 26: Type mismatch.                                      │
│  BEGIN                                                        │
│    WRITELN(' Press any key to continue ...');                │
│    Proceed := READKEY;                                        │
│    WRITELN; WRITELN                                           │
│  END;                                                         │
│                                                               │
│ BEGIN                                                         │
│   a := 3;                      { assign integer value to a }  │
│   b := 2.00;                   { assign real value to b    }  │
│   c := a*b;                    { assign a times b to c     }  │
│   WRITELN(' The value of c is ', c, '.');                     │
│   pause                                                       │
│ END.                                                          │
│                                                               │
│                                                               │
│                                                               │
│                                                               │
│──── 24:11 ═══════                                            │
 F1 Help  F2 Save  F3 Open  Alt+F9 Compile  F9 Make  Alt+F10 Local menu
```

- Your real numbers will look extremely odd unless you format them. Turbo Pascal displays real numbers in scientific notation, which means that they are displayed in terms of powers of 10. Thus,

$$12.5 = 1.25 = 10^1 \text{ is displayed as } 1.2500000000E+01$$

You can put a stop to this by telling Turbo Pascal how many digits you want in your real number. For instance, if the real-number variable **a** has a value of 12.5, then you can make it show up as 12.5 (and in other formats) like this:

```
WRITELN(' The value of a is ', a:0:1, '.');
WRITELN(' The value of a is ', a:0:5, '.'); {with five decimal places}
WRITELN(' The value of a is ', a:10:1, '.'); {in a 10-character-wide column}
```

Putting the *:0:1* after the name of the variable does the trick. The number after the first colon denotes the total number of digits you want in the number; if you make this 0 (zero), then the length stretches to fit the actual number. The number after the second colon is the number of digits that you want to the right of the decimal point.

Text Data Types

There are two text data types in Turbo Pascal—characters (called CHAR) and strings. A character is any single letter, digit, or special symbol, such as 'g', 'P', '5', '&', or '+'; and it must be enclosed in single-quote marks. A string is an ordered sequence of characters, such as 'U.S.S. Enterprise' or 'Pascal', and must also be enclosed in single-quote marks.

You will use characters often to get user's answers to on-screen prompts, such as "Proceed (Y/N)?" You will use strings most often to display text and to give text input, such as

```
WRITE(' Enter your name: ');   { displays a string }
READLN(Name);                  { gets input string }
```

Standard Pascal does not have a string data type. It treats strings as packed arrays of characters. (See "Arrays" below.) If you have to do a program in standard Pascal, use packed arrays instead of strings. Turbo Pascal will ignore the packed part, which it does not support, and will handle arrays of characters in much the same way that it handles strings. The only problem is that it is much harder to read strings into and out of arrays, but don't worry—we will develop some routines for that later.

There is also a data type called *text* that is used to represent unstructured disk files. See Chapter 12 for a discussion of this data type.

Truth-Value Data Types

In standard logic, there are two truth values, true and false, and a factual statement is either one or the other. The same conditions apply in programming languages. In Pascal, truth values are denoted by the words true and false; the true/false data type is called Boolean, named after the English mathematician George Boole (1815-1864). The reason for calling truth value statements "factual" (Boolean) statements is that most program statements are not factual; instead, they are imperatives, such as "shut the door" or "put this value in variable x," which are neither true nor false.

You can use Boolean variables and expressions to control the flow of your program. For example, if *PaidUp* is a Boolean variable, then you could write

```
IF PaidUp = TRUE
   THEN SendThankYou
   ELSE BugForMoney;
```

Because factual statements are true or false, you can use them to set the truth values of Boolean variables, as follows:

```
PaidUp := (CustomerBalance = 0.00)
```

Because the statement *CustomerBalance = 0.00* makes an assertion, it is either true or false. Its value therefore can be assigned to a Boolean variable. You can combine factual statements or Boolean variables with logical operators such as AND, OR, and XOR to form more complex expressions. See Chapter 5 for a discussion of the Boolean type.

Pointer Data Type

The pointer data type differs markedly from the types that I have discussed so far. Instead of holding something ordinary, like a number or a text string, a pointer holds the memory address of a variable. Pointers are used to keep track of dynamic variables. (See Chapter 11.) For the time being, do not try to do anything with pointers unless you are sure that you understand them.

Structured Data Types

There are three structured data types to be discussed here: arrays, records, and objects. Arrays are used to hold static lists of data, while records and objects can be used to create your own customized data types.

Arrays

You can think of an array as a row of slots into which you can fit data items of a single type. Thus, an array can hold numbers, text items, truth values, pointers, and even user-defined types such as records and objects.

To declare an array, you must specify three main things: the name of the array, the number of slots it will have, and the type of data item that the slots will need to hold. Note, however, that because ARRAY is a built-in data type, you do not strictly have to declare it in the type section. Either of the following will do fine:

```
TYPE
    Enrollment = ARRAY[1..100] of Student;
{ Where Student is a previously defined data type }
VAR
    StudentList : Enrollment;
{ Declares variable to be of enrollment data type }
```

or, more economically,

```
VAR
    StudentList : ARRAY[1..100] of Student;
```

You do need to declare an array type in the TYPE section if you intend to pass variables of that array type into subroutines. Therefore, even though the second method is easier, it's usually better to declare array types in the TYPE section.

You refer to the individual items in an array by using the name of the array variable combined with its array index. To refer to the fifth element in an array named *TextList*, which holds text strings, for example, we would write *TextList[5]*. With the *StudentList* array, which holds records, it is more complicated: to refer to the name part of the student record in position 5, we would write *StudentList[5].Name*.

Records

Records are used in Pascal to hold together different pieces of information that can be of different types. For example, a student record would hold name and address (strings), grade-point average (a real number), and whether or not the student was on academic probation (a Boolean value). A record is defined in the TYPE section by naming the record type, defining its data slots, called fields, and ending the definition with END:

```
TYPE
   Student = RECORD
             Name      : STRING[20];
             Address   : STRING[30];
             City      : STRING[10];
             State     : STRING[2];
             Zipcode   : STRING[5];
             GPA       : real;
             Probation : Boolean
             END;
```

You then can create variables of this type and use them as follows:

```
VAR
   Pupil : Student;
{ declares individual variable} { of Student record type }
   StudentList : ARRAY[1.100] of Student;
```

```
                  { declares an array of student }
                  { records }
BEGIN
   Pupil.Name := 'Gerald Ford';
   Pupil.Address := '30 Rockefeller Center'

   StudentList[1].Name := 'Jimmy Carter';
   StudentList[1].Address := '10 Maple Street';
   StudentList[1].City := 'Plains'
   StudentList[1].State := 'California'
   StudentList[1].Zipcode := '90069'
   StudentList[1].GPA := 4.00;
   StudentList[1].Probation := false
END;
```

There are also some special tricks that you can do with records, such as using them to hold arrays of records (see Chapter 9).

Objects

Objects are the central data type used by Turbo Vision. They look similar to records, but they have very special properties:

- Object types include their own subroutines (procedures and functions).

- They can be derived from previously defined object types (ancestor types) and inherit the features of those types.

- They can override the features of their ancestor types and add their own new features, including new data fields and subroutines.

Constants and Variables

Constants and variables are pretty much self-explanatory. A constant is a data item that never changes its value during a program run, while a variable can have new values assigned to it at any time. Both can be any legal Pascal data type. It is best to think of a variable as a kind of "box" that can hold data of a certain type.

Declaring Constants

You declare constants in your program as we've already seen, by assigning values to them in the CONST section of your program. Some typical constant declarations might be the following:

```
CONST
   MaxCount = 100;
   Interest = 0.18;
   Space    = ' ';
```

One question that frequently arises is: Why do we need to declare constants in the first place? What's the point of declaring

```
NumberOfCustomers = 100;
```

when we could simply insert 100 at any place where we use the constant *Number-OfCustomers*?

The answer is that by declaring constants, we make a program easier to understand and modify than it would be otherwise. For example, after declaring *NumberOf-Customers* as a constant at the start of your program, you might in a later procedure define a variable as the following:

```
CustomerList = ARRAY[1..NumberOfCustomers] of Customer
```

The use of a named constant has two benefits. First, it makes the code easier to understand than *ARRAY[1..100]*. Calling the upper limit of the list *NumberOfCustomers* makes it clear what's going on. Second, if you later want to *change* the number of customers in your program, you need to change only the constant declaration at the very beginning, instead of having to search through the program for every instance where you referred to the number of customers.

Declaring Variables

Before a normal variable can be used in a program, it has to be named and its type has to be declared. A variable can be any data type, whether a built-in type or a user-defined type that's been declared in the TYPE section. To declare a variable, you simply give its name, a colon, and then its type:

```
VAR
   Counter       : INTEGER;
   StudentList   : ARRAY[1..100] of Student;
   String20      : STRING[20];
   YesNo         : CHAR;
```

Pascal Statements

There are several different types of statements in Pascal. The most important are *assignment* statements, *input/output* (I/O) statements, and *control* statements. We've already seen examples of all three types in the program listings, but let's take an "official" look at them now.

Assignment Statements

Assignment statements assign a value to a variable. If a variable is a kind of box that can hold data of a certain type, then an assignment statement essentially takes an item of that type and puts it into the box. There is one thing to be careful about, however, especially if you've done programming in BASIC. Pascal uses a combination of the colon and the equal sign to make its assignment operator :=, while BASIC uses the equal sign by itself, =. If you use an equal sign by itself in Pascal, the program interprets it as a Boolean operator to compare two values; at best, your program won't compile.

Some examples of assignment statements are the following:

```
counter := 15;
Name := 'Zardoz';
PaidUp := TRUE;
StudentList[5].Name := 'Frank Borland';
```

Input/Output Statements

Input/output (I/O) statements are used to transfer data from one place to another: for example, to get it from the keyboard, display it on the screen, write it to a disk file, or print it on a printer. We've already seen several of these. Examples are:

```
WRITELN(' This displays text on the screen.');
READLN(Name);    { Gets a string from the keyboard }
WRITELN(myfile, 'This writes text to a disk file.');
```

There are two things to notice in these examples. First, you can use I/O statements to assign values to variables. In line 2 of the example, the READLN statement not only gets a string from the keyboard, but puts that string into the variable *Name*.

Second, the WRITELN statement at the bottom writes a line of text to a disk file that's denoted by the file variable *myfile*. WRITELN and READLN can take the name of a file as either the destination (with WRITELN) or the source (with READLN) of the information they use. Note that if you don't specify a file name,

Pascal assumes that you want to *read* from the keyboard and *write* to the screen. If you want to read from or write to a disk file, you must first associate it with a file variable and then open the file (see Chapter 12).

Control Statements

Control statements are used to direct the flow of your program in one direction or another based on the value of some variable. We've already seen examples of IF..THEN..ELSE, which is one of the most common control statements. Others set up loops or test for a variety of values. We'll just summarize them below.

IF..THEN..ELSE   You use IF..THEN..ELSE (or just IF..THEN when you don't need an ELSE) when you want the program to go in one of two directions based on an either/or situation. For example:

```
IF PaidUp
    THEN SendThankYou
    ELSE BugForMoney;

IF GPA < 2.00
    THEN SendProbationLetter
    ELSE BugForMoney;
```

In this case, *PaidUp* is either true or it isn't; there is no third alternative. (Well, it could be undefined, but in that case, your program won't compile in the first place.) You don't strictly need an ELSE clause; you might not want the program to do anything about late bill-payers, so you would write simply:

```
IF PaidUp = true
    THEN SendThankYou;
```

FOR Loops   Sometimes, you simply want to repeat an operation a certain number of times. In that case, you would use a FOR loop. A good example of using a FOR loop would be to assign initial values to the slots in an array:

```
VAR
    Letters = ARRAY[1..50] of char;
    Counter : integer;
BEGIN
    FOR counter := 1 to 50 DO
        Letters[counter] := ' '
END;
```

This assigns initial values to the Letters array so that each slot has a space in it. Notice that we used an integer-type counter variable. In the FOR statement itself, we used the assignment operator and not the equal sign. The DO part of the statement can be any legal Pascal statement, whether simple (as in the example) or compound (a BEGIN..END statement).

Other Control Statements   There are several other types of control statements (CASE, WHILE..DO, REPEAT..UNTIL), but we'll defer our discussion of these until Chapter 7.

Procedures and Functions

You have already seen several examples of procedures. Functions are similar to procedures except that they actually have a data type. A good analogy is to think of procedures as being like complete sentences, while functions are like nouns. A function is simply an operator that takes a value of a certain type and gives back another value—a value that is normally, but does not need to be, different from the original value. That is why functions are usually written with parentheses after them; the parentheses indicate that the function "has a hole" in it that must be filled by a value of a certain type. An example of a function might be the following:

```
FUNCTION PaidUp (balance: real) : Boolean;
   BEGIN
      IF balance <= 0.00
         THEN PaidUp := TRUE
         ELSE PaidUp := FALSE
   END;

BEGIN            { main body of program }
   IF PaidUp(215.00)
      THEN SendThankYou(Customer)
      ELSE BugForMoney(Customer)
END;
```

When you pass the value *215.00* to the function *PaidUp*, it returns a value of false, which you can then use in an IF..THEN statement.

Parameters and Scope

The above example also shows another new idea: the idea of passing values to a subroutine. Because each subroutine (whether it is a procedure or a function) is a "black box," you want to maintain complete control over what goes into it and what comes out of it. Therefore, if the subroutine will handle any values from outside, they should be declared as "parameters" when you define the subroutine in the procedures and functions section of the program. Listing 3.4 is an example.

Listing 3.4

```
PROGRAM Listing3_4;

   { Illustrates a subroutine to add two integers. }


USES CRT;

VAR
   a,b,c : integer;

PROCEDURE AddTwoNumbers(a,b : integer; var c: integer);
   BEGIN
     c := a + b
   END;


BEGIN            { main body of program }
   a := 1;
   b := 2;
   AddTwoNumbers(a,b,c)
END.
```

Notice that in Listing 3.4, you declare each type of value that goes into and comes out of the procedure when you first define the procedure. You then pass the values (integers) to the procedure as parameters by calling the procedure and listing the appropriate variables in parentheses after the procedure name.

Three variables are passed to the procedure. The first two, a and b, already have values and won't be changed by the procedure. Therefore, we simply make a copy of their values (1 and 2) and pass those values to the procedure. Variable c, however, will be changed by the procedure; that's why there is a *var* before it in the parameter list when we defined the *AddTwoNumbers* procedure.

There's one other interesting thing to note—perhaps you've caught it already. The parameter names are the same as the names of the variables we passed to the procedure, but this did not cause a "duplicate" identifier error when you compiled

Listing 3.4. This is an exception to the rule that identifiers must be unique. An even more important exception is shown in Listing 3.5.

Listing 3.5

```
{ Illustrates the meaning of "scope." The global variable
  MyName is a string variable outside of the AddTwoNumbers
  subroutine. However, a new, local variable called MyName
  is declared inside the AddTwoNumbers subroutine. Inside
  the subroutine, this integer variable overrides the global
  MyName variable, but is invisible everywhere outside the
  subroutine. }


USES CRT;

VAR
   a,b,c : integer;
   MyName : string[5];

PROCEDURE Pause;
   VAR
      Proceed : CHAR;
   BEGIN
      WRITELN(' Press any key to continue ...');
      Proceed := READKEY;
      WRITELN; WRITELN
   END;

PROCEDURE AddTwoNumbers(a,b : integer; var c: integer);
   VAR
      MyName : integer;
   BEGIN
      c := a + b;
      MyName := 10;
      WRITELN(' Inside the procedure, MyName is ', MyName, '.');
   END;


BEGIN            { main body of program }
   clrscr
   a := 1;
   b := 2;
   MyName := 'Scott';
   WRITELN(' Outside the procedure, MyName is ', MyName, '.');
```

```
      pause;
      AddTwoNumbers(a,b,c);
      pause;
      WRITELN(' Outside again, Myname is ', MyName, '.');
      pause
END.
```

At the global level of Listing 3.5, outside the *AddTwoNumbers* procedure, we defined *MyName* as a string variable and assigned it the value 'Scott'. Inside the *AddTwoNumbers* procedure, however, we created an integer variable with the same name and assigned it the value *10*. Not only do we *not* get a "duplicate identifier" error message when we compile Listing 3.5, but the value of *MyName* is one thing outside the procedure and something else inside the procedure!

The reason for this strange situation is that, as you'll remember, each subroutine is a black box whose content is hidden from the outside world. When we declare a new variable inside the *AddTwoNumbers* procedure, it is not visible to anything outside the procedure. Inside the procedure, it simply replaces the global variable, so there's no conflict between the two variable names. We really have two different variables: one that exists at the global level, and another that exists only inside the *AddTwoNumbers* procedure.

It is important to realize, however, that it is just the inside of each subroutine that is hidden from the global level and from other subroutines. The global level of the program is visible everywhere else in the program, including from inside the subroutines. If we had not declared a new, local variable inside the *AddTwoNumbers* procedure, we would have had a completely different result, as in Listing 3.6.

Listing 3.6

```
PROGRAM Listing3_6;

    { Unlike the AddTwoNumbers routine in Listing 3.5, the
      routine in this listing does NOT declare a local integer
      variable to override the global string variable MyName.
      Therefore, the program won't compile because the global
      variable MyName is visible inside the AddTwoNumbers
      routine, and the routine tries to assign an integer to
      it -- in spite of the fact that MyName is a string
      variable. }
```

```
USES CRT;

VAR
    a,b,c : integer;
    MyName : string[5];

PROCEDURE Pause;
    VAR
        Proceed : CHAR;
    BEGIN
        WRITELN(' Press any key to continue ...');
        Proceed := READKEY;
        WRITELN; WRITELN
    END;

PROCEDURE AddTwoNumbers(a,b : integer; var c: integer);
    BEGIN
        c := a + b;
        MyName := 10;
        WRITELN(' Inside the procedure, MyName is ', MyName, '.');
    END;


BEGIN            { main body of program }
    a := 1;
    b := 2;
    MyName := 'Scott';
    WRITELN(' Outside the procedure, MyName is ', MyName, '.');
    pause;
    AddTwoNumbers(a,b,c);
    pause;
    WRITELN(' Outside again, Myname is ', MyName, '.');
    pause
END.
```

In Listing 3.6, we did not declare a local variable inside the procedure, so when we tried to assign the integer value 10 to the *MyName* variable, the program thought we were talking about the global *MyName* variable. Because this is a string variable instead of an integer variable, Listing 3.6 won't compile. To correct the error, simply take out the line that says *MyName := 10;* and run the program. This time, *MyName* remains 'Scott' all through the program.

There is an important lesson in Listing 3.6. The lesson is that even though you should "never say 'never'," you should *never, ever directly change global variables from within a subroutine.* If a subroutine is going to deal with a global variable, the variable should be passed to the subroutine as a parameter—never sneaked "through the back door" as in Listing 3.6. There are exceptions to this rule, but they are few and you should stick to the rule until you get some more programming experience.

PART II

DOS Programming with Turbo Pascal 7

CHAPTER FOUR

The Turbo Pascal Development Environment

- The Turbo Pascal Integrated Development Environment

- Using the Turbo Pascal Edition

- Using Multiple Windows

- Menus and Speed Keys

In Chapter 1, we took a a quick look at the Turbo Pascal integrated development environment, called the IDE. Now, we return for a more detailed look at the different parts of the IDE and will discuss how to put them to work. If you are already comfortable using the IDE, you might want to browse through this chapter and come back to it for reference as needed, or, if you wish, you can work through it. Either way, you will see that there are some neat new features in Turbo Pascal 7.

Main Parts of the IDE

When you first start Turbo Pascal, you see the Turbo Pascal desktop on the screen, as in Figure 4.1. Across the top line of the screen is the menu bar, from which Turbo Pascal's menus pull down. Across the bottom line is help information about operations you can perform with various key combinations. No matter what you are doing in the IDE, the bottom line always displays some relevant help information for the current window.

You can activate the menu bar and open menus in any of the following three ways:

- Press *F10* to activate the menu bar, use the arrow keys to highlight the menu you want, and then press *Enter* to open the menu.

FIGURE 4.1:
The Turbo Pascal desktop

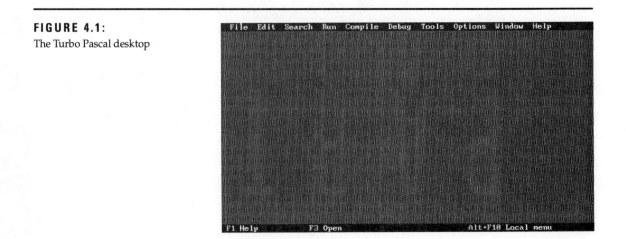

- Hold down the *Alt* key and press the highlighted letter in the menu name—for example, *Alt+F* to open the File menu.

- If you are using a mouse, click on the name of the menu that you want to open.

Once you've opened a menu, you can choose menu options in much the same way: by highlighting the option you want and pressing *Enter*, by pressing the highlighted letter (if any) in the menu choice, or by clicking on the menu choice with the mouse. Table 4.1 shows how to activate the different pull-down menus. Table 4.2 summarizes the jobs performed by the different function keys and function key combinations. Note that some of these jobs, such as using *F8* to "step current subroutine" (used in debugging), won't become clear until you have more programming experience.

TABLE 4.1: Menu Activation Keys

Key	Result
F10	Activate menu bar (use arrow keys to highlight menu name, then press Enter)
Alt+F	Open File menu
Alt+E	Open Edit menu
Alt+S	Open Search menu
Alt+R	Open Run menu
Alt+C	Open Compile menu
Alt+D	Open Debugging menu
Alt+T	Open Tools menu
Alt+O	Open Options menu
Alt+W	Open Window menu
Alt+H	Open Help menu

TABLE 4.2: Tasks Performed by Function Keys

Function Key	Alone	Alt	Shift	Control
F1	Activate help	Prev. help	Help index	Find help
F2	Save File	-	-	Reset program
F3	Open file	Close file	-	Call stack
F4	Run to cursor	-	-	Evaluate expr.
F5	Zoom /Unzoom	User screen	-	Size/move window
F6	Next window	-	Previous window	-
F7	Trace into subroutine	-	-	Add watch
F8	Step over current subroutine	-	-	Toggle breakpoint
F9	Make	Compile	-	Run program
F10	Open menu bar	-	-	-

Using the IDE Windows

Opening an IDE window lets you enter a program or view information about that program. When you are in a particular window, it's called the *active* window, and any commands or text that you enter will be directed to that window. In previous versions of Turbo Pascal, you could have only one file window open at a time, but Turbo Pascal 7 lets you have as many open windows as can fit into your PC's available memory.

The active window has several features that provide information and let you manipulate the window with a mouse. If you do not have a mouse, you can do the same things using the menus or speed keys. Here, we're going to look at file windows containing Turbo Pascal program listings. However, most of the features we will discuss apply to all on-screen windows, including other types of windows. Table 4.3 shows the most important windowing commands and speed keys.

TABLE 4.3: Windowing Commands and Keys

Key	Result
Alt+W	Opens Window menu. Can also be done by clicking on Window with the mouse.
Alt+0	Opens dialog box with window list. You then use the arrow keys to highlight the window you want and press Enter to move to that window.
Alt+N	Jumps directly to window number N. The window number (N) is displayed at the top right of the window frame. Can also be done by clicking on the window frame of the desired window with the mouse.
Alt+F3	Closes current window or file. This applies to all windows, not just file windows. Can also be done by clicking on the Close button with the mouse.
F5	Zoom a window to take up the entire screen, or unzoom a window that's already been zoomed. Can also be done by clicking on the Zoom button with the mouse.
Control+F5	Move/resize current window (arrow keys to move, Shift+arrow keys to resize). To resize with the mouse, grab onto the lower right corner of the window and drag. To move with the mouse, grab onto the top edge of the frame and drag.
F6	Jump to next window (e.g., from No. 3 to No. 4).
Shift+F6	Jump to previous window (e.g., from No. 4 to No. 3).

Opening a Window

Let's open a window that will contain Listing 3.1 from the previous chapter. You can open a file window in two ways: first, by choosing Open or New from the File menu, or second, by pressing the *F3* key. Either method opens up the Open File dialog box, as shown in Figure 4.2.

There are a few other things to notice about the Open File dialog box. At the top, it has a blank that shows the name of the currently highlighted file or directory in the file list. The file list, below, is in a miniwindow and shows all the files and subdirectories that are in the current directory. Across the bottom of the file list window is a scroll bar.

At the bottom of the Open File dialog box is detailed information about the currently highlighted file or directory, including file size and the date it was created.

FIGURE 4.2:

The Open File dialog box

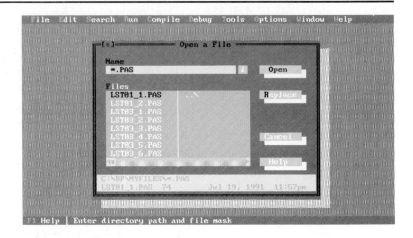

Finally, on the right side of the box, there are four push buttons that you use to tell Turbo Pascal to perform different actions.

- Open: This opens a new file window and loads the highlighted file into that window.

- Replace: If you already have a file open in a file window, this loads the highlighted file into the current window—replacing the file that was already there. If you have changed the already opened file, you will be prompted to save your changes before the new file is loaded.

- Cancel: This button, which appears in all dialog boxes, lets you cancel the current operation if you change your mind. Pressing *Escape* will also cancel the current operation.

- Help: This button, which also appears in all dialog boxes, opens up a screen of help information and provides information about the various operations you can perform with it.

If you have been saving your program files in the BP\MYFILES subdirectory, then press the *Tab* key once to move to the file list, highlight BP\MYFILES, and press *Enter* to open that directory. Move the highlight to LIST3_1.PAS and press *Enter* to open the file. (If you have a mouse, you can do the same sequence by double-clicking on BP\MYFILES to open the directory and double-clicking on LIST3_1.PAS to open the file.)

Parts of a Screen Window

Because there is only one file open, the window we opened is automatically the active window. At the top left of the frame is the close button. You click on this button with the mouse cursor to close the active window. Or, if you are not using a mouse, you press *Alt+F3* to close the window. Either way, if you've made changes in the current file, you will be prompted to save the file before closing the window.

In the middle of the top line is the name of the file that is in the current window. In Figure 4.3, this file is LIST3_1.PAS. At the top right is the number of the current window (useful if you have more than one window open) and the zoom arrow, which lets you zoom and unzoom a window with your mouse to occupy the entire screen, or only a part of the screen. You can also zoom and unzoom the current window by pressing the *F5* key.

At the lower left of the frame are two numbers separated by a colon; here, they are 1:1. These numbers give the current location of the regular cursor (not the mouse cursor): the first number shows the current line, and the second number shows the current column. Thus, if the cursor were on line 25 and in column 15, the frame would show 25:15.

FIGURE 4.3:

Parts of file window

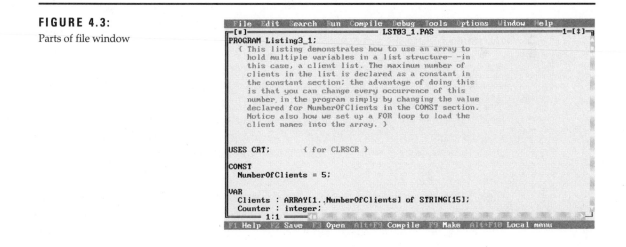

Scroll Bars

On the right edge of the frame and the right part of the bottom edge are two shaded areas called scroll bars. If you have a mouse, you can use these bars to move instantly around your file. Looking closely at the vertical scroll bar, you can see that it has an up arrow and a down arrow. To move up in your file, you move the mouse cursor to the up arrow and either click on it with the left mouse button (to move one line at a time) or hold down the left mouse button (to move continuously). The little square inside the scroll bar shows your current position in the file: when it is at the top of the scroll bar, you are at the top of the file; when it is in the middle, you are in the middle of your file, and so forth. The scroll bar in the bottom edge of the frame works the same way, except that it moves you left and right instead of up and down.

If you are not using a mouse, you can use the *PgUp*, *PgDn*, *Home*, *End*, and arrow keys to move around your file. In this particular case, it is often easier than using a mouse.

Resizing and Moving Windows

At the bottom right-hand corner of the window is the resize button. You grab this button by highlighting it with the mouse cursor and holding down the left mouse button. You then can resize the current window by dragging the bottom right corner. You also can move the window by grabbing and dragging the top edge of the frame around the screen.

You also can resize or move a window by using menus and speed keys. To resize a window, select Size/Move from the Window menu or press *Ctrl+F5*, the corresponding speed key for that menu choice. Then, you can resize the window by holding down the *Shift* key and pressing the arrow keys, or you can move it by pressing the arrow keys alone, as shown in Figure 4.4. After moving and resizing the windows, restore them to their original full-screen condition.

Note two other things about Figure 4.4. First, you can tell if the window is in Size/Move mode because the frame looks different. When you press *Enter* to tell Turbo Pascal that you are finished, it goes back to looking normal. Second, the bottom line of the screen—as usual—displays help information for whatever you are doing at the moment.

FIGURE 4.4:
Moving and resizing a window

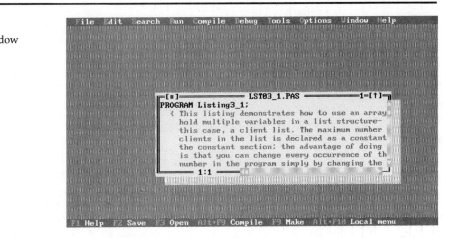

Working with Multiple Windows

Now that you are familiar with the parts of a screen window, let's see how Turbo Pascal allows you to work with several windows open at once. We've already got a window open with Listing 3.1 in it; now, use the Open File dialog box as before to open new windows with Listings 3.2 and 3.3 in them. Your screen should look like the screen shown in Figure 4.5.

FIGURE 4.5:
Cascading file windows

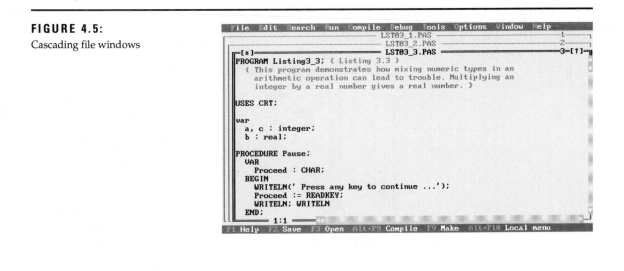

What we have here is called *cascading* windows. Each new window is below and to the right of the previous window, so that the top edge of each window is visible, showing the file name and window number.

Jumping between Windows

Currently, the active window is window number 3. You can switch to a different window in one of the four following ways:

1. Press *F6* to go to the "next" window and *Shift+F6* to go to the "previous" window. In this case, pressing *F6* would take you to window number 1, then to number 2, and finally back to number 3. *Shift+F6* would take you back to window number 2, then 1, then back to 3 again.

2. Choose List from the Window menu or press *Alt+0* (Alt+zero, not Alt+O) to open up a list of open windows, as shown in Figure 4.6. In the list, move the highlight to the window you want and press *Enter*.

3. Use the mouse to click on the frame of the window you want (or click inside the window, if it is visible). This will move you directly to that window.

4. Press *Alt+n* to move to window number *n*.

Unless you are a hardcore mouse user, or you have a lot of windows open, methods 1 and 2 are generally the most efficient.

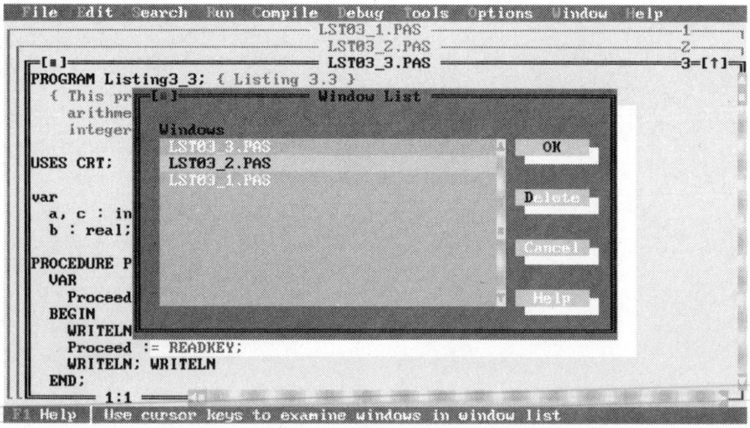

FIGURE 4.6:
The List Windows dialog box

Tiled Windows

At the moment, only one window is really visible, with the others peeking out from behind it. There are many situations, however, where you will want to see two or more windows simultaneously. That's when tiled windows are used. To display your three windows in tiled format, open the Window menu and select Tile. Your windows should now be displayed as shown in Figure 4.7.

With the windows tiled, you now have the opportunity to try out some of the windowing commands discussed earlier. To see how these commands work, do the following:

- Press *F6* a few times to jump forward between windows; then press *Shift+F6* a few times to jump backward.

- Press *F5* to zoom one of the windows to full screen size; then press *F5* again to return it to its previous size.

- With window 3 as the current window, press *Ctrl+F5* and move the window around some; then change its size. Finally, return it to its original size and position on the screen.

- If you have a mouse, try these same operations with the mouse. Click in a window to jump to that window; zoom a window by clicking on the zoom arrow at the top right of the frame; resize and move the window by grabbing the appropriate part of the frame with the mouse cursor. Remember to return the window to its original size and position when you're finished.

FIGURE 4.7:

Tiled file windows

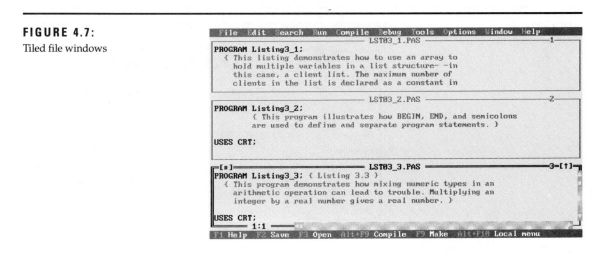

Closing a Window

To prepare to close a window, choose Cascade from the Window menu and return the windows to cascading format.

Closing a window is even easier than opening it. Make sure that window 3 (with Listing 3.3) is the current window. Then either press *Alt+F3* or click on the close button at the top left of the frame. Window 3 and the file with Listing 3.3 will close, leaving the other two windows still on-screen. You can use these methods to close any on-screen window, not just file windows. If you have changed your file since the last time you saved it, Turbo Pascal will prompt you to save your changes.

Using Dialog Boxes

Dialog boxes are very similar to windows. The difference is that although windows allow you to write programs or see information about your programs, dialog boxes are designed specifically to let you give commands to Turbo Pascal itself. Let's look at a typical dialog box. From the Options menu, select Environment, then choose Preferences from the submenu that opens up. Your screen should look like the one in Figure 4.8.

Along the top edge of the dialog box you will see the close button and the name of the dialog box, just as with a regular window. However, the zoom button, scroll

FIGURE 4.8:

The Preferences dialog box

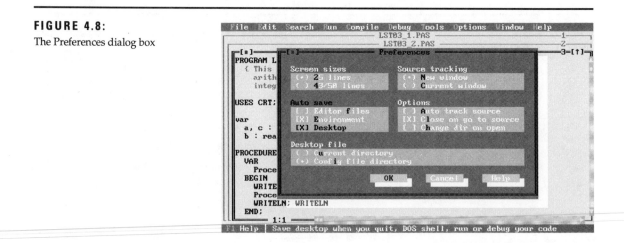

bars, cursor position, and move/resize buttons are missing. This is because you must work with a dialog box in a more structured way than an ordinary window. To move from one section of the box to another, or from one button to another, you must do the following:

- To move from one section of the box to another, for example, from the Screen sizes to the Source tracking section, press the *Tab* key, or press the highlighted key letter for the option you want. For example, while the cursor is in Screen sizes, press "f" to toggle the AutoSave option for Editor files, and move to that box. To move backward, press *Shift+Tab*. You can move directly to a section by clicking in it with the mouse.

- To move from one radio button or checkbox to another, use the arrow keys or the mouse.

- To move from one push-button to another, use *Tab/Shift+Tab*. Clicking on a push-button with the mouse will cause its command to be executed instantly.

Types of Buttons in a Dialog Box

There are three types of buttons in a dialog box, though not all three types are in every dialog box. In Figure 4.8, the buttons are divided into five groups; you move from one group to another by using *Tab* (forward) and *Shift+Tab* (backward), or by using the mouse. The different types of buttons are as follows:

- **Radio buttons**. These let you select only one option out of several. In Figure 4.8, the Screen sizes, Source tracking, and Desktop file options have radio buttons. Screen size, for example, must be either 25 lines or 43/50 lines; it cannot be both. You select one of the radio buttons by moving the highlight with the arrow keys. (Do not do this right now.)

- **Checkboxes**. These let you select as many of the options as you want. In Figure 4.8 under Auto save, for example, you can tell Turbo Pascal to automatically save just the Editor files, or the Environment files, or the Desktop files, or any combination of the three options. In Figure 4.8, all three options are chosen. You select (or deselect) a checkbox by moving the cursor to the box and pressing the spacebar; alternatively, you can click inside the box's brackets with the mouse.

- **Push-buttons**. These buttons, along the bottom of the dialog box in Figure 4.8, tell Turbo Pascal what to do with the options you've selected via radio buttons and checkboxes. The OK button means go ahead, the Cancel button means cancel the operation, and the Help button calls up an explanation of how to use this particular dialog box.

We will not do anything with the Preferences dialog box right now, so close it by pressing *Alt+F3*. You can also close dialog boxes by pressing *Escape*, although this will not close a regular window.

Reopening a File

We closed the window with Listing 3.3 to show you how to use the buttons in dialog boxes. Reopen the Open File dialog box by pressing *F3*. Now, instead of tabbing to the file list to select LIST3_3.PAS, just press the down arrow key. A list of the files you've recently opened, with the highlight on LIST3_3.PAS, will pop up, as shown in Figure 4.9. To reload this file, press *Enter* twice; to load any other recently used file, highlight the file name and press *Enter* twice.

The list of recently used files is called a *pick list*. If you look at Figure 4.2 again, you can see that the blank (called an input box) above the file list has a down arrow on its right end. This means it has a pick list and that you can open the pick list by pressing the down arrow. Pick lists are used in several different dialog boxes, not just the Open File box.

FIGURE 4.9:

A pick list in the Open File dialog box

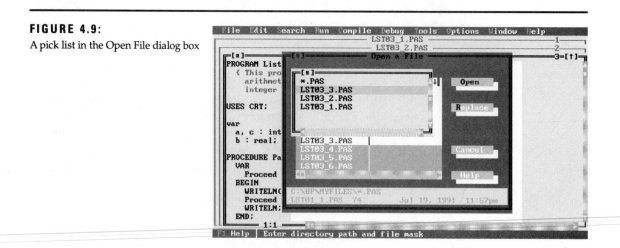

One thing can go wrong here: the file you pick *must* be in the current directory. If you saved LIST3_3.PAS to the \TP\FILES directory, and you are currently in the \TP directory, then all you will get on your screen is an empty file window. To reload the file, you must select Change Dir from the File menu to switch to the directory where the file is located.

Using the Turbo Pascal Editor

The editor in Turbo Pascal 7 does pretty much anything you need. It is not as powerful as some stand-alone editors, such as Brief and Multi-Edit, but these editors owe their enormous power to the expense of great complexity. The Turbo Pascal editor, on the other hand, is relatively easy to learn and use. Tables 4.4 through 4.6 list some miscellaneous editor commands that you may find helpful.

TABLE 4.4: Opening and Closing File Commands

Command	Method
Open file	Press F3 or select Open from File menu. Then highlight file in dialog box and press Enter; with mouse, double-click on filename in list.
Close file window and file	Press Alt+F3 or, with mouse, click on Close button at top left of window frame.
Close file but keep file window open	Press F3 or select Open from File menu. Then type new file name or highlight file in list; select Replace push-button instead of Open.
Save file and continue editing	Press F2 or select Save from File menu.
Save file under a different name	Select Save as from File menu. Then type in the new file name in the dialog box and press Enter.
Abandon changes to file	Press Alt+F3 or click on Close button; then answer no when prompted to save changes.

TABLE 4.5: Insert/Delete Commands

Result	Key Command
Toggle between insert and overstrike	Press Ctrl+V or Insert key
Insert new line at cursor position	Press Ctrl+N or Enter
Delete line at cursor position	Ctrl+Y
Restore line just deleted	Select Restore Line from Edit menu
Delete from cursor position to end of line	Ctrl+Q+Y
Delete character to left of cursor	Backspace or Ctrl+H
Delete character at cursor position	Del or Ctrl+G
Delete word at cursor position	Ctrl+T
Delete selected block	Ctrl+K+Y

TABLE 4.6: Cursor Movement Commands

Result	Key Command
Go to top of file	Ctrl+PgUp
Go to bottom of file	Ctrl+PgDn
Go to top of current screen	Ctrl+Home
Go to bottom of current screen	Ctrl+End
Go up one screen	PgUp
Go down one screen	PgDn
Go to beginning of line	Home
Go to end of line	End
Go right one word	Ctrl+Right Arrow
Go left one word	Ctrl+Left Arrow
Go right one column	Right Arrow
Go left one column	Left Arrow
Go up one line	Up Arrow
Go down one line	Down Arrow
Create bookmark (mark cursor position for instant return)	Ctrl+K+n, where n is an integer from 0 to 9
Jump back to bookmark	Ctrl+Q+n, where n is the number of the bookmark

Using Copy and Paste

From the File menu, select New. In the empty file window, enter the program shown in Listing 4.1. Don't try to compile or run it just yet. If and when it works, Listing 4.1 will ask "What is programming?" and will keep displaying the answer, "It's a GAS!!!!" until the user presses *Escape.*

Listing 4.1

```
PROGRAM Listing4_1;

USES CRT;


CONST
   Escape = CHR(27);          { 'Escape' = the Escape key, ASCII 27 }

VAR
   YesNo,
   Proceed : char;


BEGIN
   CLRSCR;

   gotoXY(20,5);
   WRITELN('What is programming?');

   WRITELN; WRITELN;
   DELAY(1000);
   Proceed := ' '; YesNo := 'Y';
   window(8, 8, 80, 21);
   WHILE Proceed <> Escape DO
      BEGIN
      WRITELN('It''s a GAS!!!!!');
      WRITELN;
      DELAY(1000);
      IF KEYPRESSED then Proceed := READKEY;
      END;
   window(1,1,80,24);
   gotoXY(1,24);
   pause
END.
```

If you looked carefully at Listing 4.1 after you entered it, you saw that there's a key element missing. We used the *pause* routine at the end of the program, but we didn't declare it anywhere!

The reason was that there is absolutely no necessity to retype the *pause* routine into every program. There are two ways to make retyping unnecessary. One is to create a separate unit to hold utility routines such as the *pause* routine. (For a discussion about this method see Chapter 10.) The other, simpler way is to use Turbo Pascal's copy-and-paste feature to copy the routine from one window into another. And that's what we will do here.

At the moment, you should have Listings 3.1 through 3.3 and Listing 4.1 in separate windows on-screen. Press *F6* to move from Listing 4.1 to one of the other windows; it doesn't really matter which one, since the *pause* routine is in all of them. Using the arrow keys or the mouse, move the cursor down to the first *P* in *PROCEDURE Pause;*. Then, do one of the following:

- Hold down one of the *Shift* keys and tap the down arrow key until the entire *pause* routine is highlighted.

- Hold down the left mouse button and drag the cursor down until the entire *pause* routine is highlighted.

Your screen should now look like Figure 4.10. The *pause* routine is ready to copy to the clipboard, from which we can then paste it into Listing 4.1.

FIGURE 4.10:

Copying a selected block

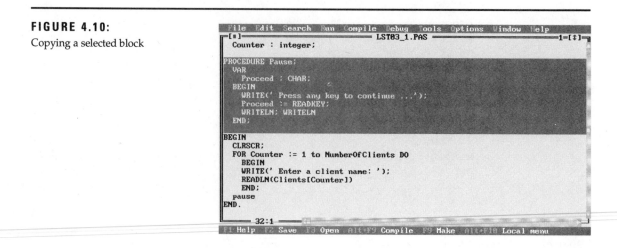

Open the Edit menu and select Copy; or you could use the *Ctrl+Insert* speed key to do the same thing. This copies the highlighted text to the clipboard. Now, press *Shift+F6* to jump back to the window with Listing 4.1. Move the cursor down so that it is one line above the *BEGIN* that starts the main body of the program; press the *Enter* key a few times to open up some space. Then, with the cursor two lines above *BEGIN*, reopen the Edit menu and select Paste. Presto! The *pause* routine is now pasted into Listing 4.1. To remove the highlight, press *Ctrl+K+H*, then save your file. (Instead of opening the Edit menu and selecting Paste, you can also use the Paste speed key, *Shift+Insert*.)

There are some other interesting things in Listing 4.1. In fact, it demonstrates some pretty special Turbo Pascal features. Here is a quick summary of some of these features:

- It shows how to define a constant as a certain key being pressed, in this case the *Escape* key.

- It shows how to use *gotoXY* to move the cursor directly to a given screen location. The two numbers in *gotoXY(x,y)* are the x and y coordinates on the screen.

- It shows how to use the Window command to create a screen window (without visible borders) in a program. The numbers in Window(x1, y1, x2, y2) are the coordinates of the top right and lower left corners of the window on the screen.

- It shows how to use *delay(n)* to pause the program momentarily; the number in the parentheses is in milliseconds (thousandths of a second), so DELAY(1000) causes the program to pause for one second.

- It shows how to set up a WHILE loop, which is discussed in detail in Chapter 7.

- Finally, it shows how to use KEYPRESSED and READKEY to get input from the user without requiring the user to press the *Enter* key.

Block Operations

Copy and paste is one of the most useful examples of a block operation, in which you select a block of text and perform some operation on it. There are different ways to select a block in Turbo Pascal 7. The easiest way is to position the cursor at the beginning of the block, hold down the *Shift* key, and press the down-arrow key until the entire block is highlighted. You can do the same thing with the mouse by positioning the mouse cursor at the beginning of the block, holding down the left mouse button, and dragging the cursor downward until the whole block is selected.

Finally, there's the traditional method: you mark the beginning of the block with *Ctrl+K+B* and the end of the block with *Ctrl+K+K*. If you're using an earlier version of Turbo Pascal, this is the method you'll have to use. Table 4.7 summarizes the different block operations that you can perform.

Creating and Jumping to Bookmarks

One of the most useful features of Turbo Pascal's editor is its ability to create up to 10 bookmarks that let you instantly return to a particular place in your program. In the listings we've developed up to this point, this feature may not seem very valu-

TABLE 4.7: Block Commands

Result	Key Commands
Mark beginning of selected block*	Ctrl+K B
Mark ending of selected block	Ctrl+K K
Select a single word	Ctrl+K T
Copy selected block to current cursor position	Ctrl+K C
Move selected block to current cursor position	Ctrl+K V
Delete selected block	Ctrl+K Y
Read file from disk into current file	Ctrl+K R
Write selected block to disk as a text file	Ctrl+K W
Highlight/dehighlight selected block	Ctrl+K H
Print selected block	Ctrl+K P
Indent selected block	Ctrl+K I
Unindent selected block	Ctrl+K U

* Blocks also can be selected by one of the following two methods: You can position the cursor at the beginning of the block. Hold down the Shift key and tap the appropriate arrow key (down, right, etc.) until the entire block is highlighted. Or you can use a mouse and position the mouse cursor at the beginning of the block. Hold down the left mouse button and drag the cursor to the end of the block so that the entire block is highlighted.

able. Real-life programs, however, can be over 1,000 lines long. The main program of a fairly small PC game I once wrote is 1,677 lines long, and that *doesn't* count the other parts of the program that were in separate units. When you have a very long program, bookmarks can make it a lot easier to find your way around.

To create a bookmark, you move the cursor to the place you want to mark, then press *Ctrl+K+n*, where *n* is an integer from 0 to 9. To return to a bookmark from anywhere else in the program, press *Ctrl+Q+n*, where *n* is the number of the bookmark to which you want to return. At any one time, as the numbering indicates, you can have up to 10 different bookmarks in a program. About the only thing Turbo Pascal does not do for you is keep track of which bookmark is which; you have to remember that on your own.

The Turbo Pascal 7 IDE supports the following <Ctrl>Q keys:

A   Search and Replace

B   Move the cursor to the beginning of the selected block

C   Move to the end of the file

D   Move to the end of the line (<End> key)

E   Move to the top of the screen

F   Forward search

K   Move the cursor to the end of the selected block

L   Restore line

R   Move to the start of the file

S   Move to the beginning of the line

X   Move to the bottom of the screen

Y   Delete to the end of the line, from the cursor

[Find matching delimiter

]   Find matching delimiter (backward search)

Using Search and Replace

If you have used a word processor, then you have a good idea of how search and search-and-replace features work. In Turbo Pascal, you can use search to find the first (or every) occurrence of a particular subroutine or other identifier. Search and replace is most useful when you must make a global change in a piece of text; for example, you might change a variable name at the top of your program, and need to hunt down and change every occurrence of the old name to change it to the new one.

Turbo Pascal 7 has a Find menu that takes care of everything for you. Also, instead of having to remember what the search options are (g for global, u for ignore uppercase/lowercase, and so on.), you can specify them in a dialog box. Figure 4.11 shows the dialog box for Find, while Figure 4.12 shows the dialog box for Find and Replace.

FIGURE 4.11:

The Find dialog box

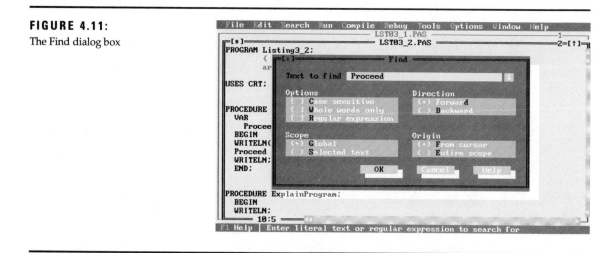

FIGURE 4.12:

The Find and Replace dialog box

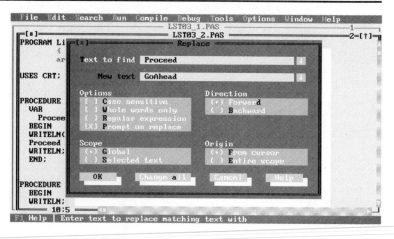

Turbo Pascal Menus

Turbo Pascal 7 provides full menu support for almost everything you need in program development. Here, we will take a step-by-step tour of each menu in the IDE. Some of the menu choices will not be completely explained until later chapters, because they deal with issues that haven't been covered yet. In this chapter, I will indicate what each menu choice does; if further explanation is needed, I will provide it in the appropriate chapter.

The File Menu (Alt+F)

The following options are available in the File menu:

- New: This opens an empty file window into which you can enter a new program file. There is no speed key.

- Open: This opens a new file and file window by going through the Open File dialog box. The speed key for this menu choice is *F3*.

- Save: This saves the file in the active file window to disk in the current default directory, though you are given the option of saving it in a different directory. If you haven't yet named your file, you will be prompted for a file name. The speed key is *F2*.

- Save As: This lets you save the file under a different file name, which you are prompted to enter. This is most useful when you are developing a medium-to-large program and need to keep copies of the program at different stages of development and debugging.

- Save All: This saves all files in all open file windows, not just the file in the active window.

- Change Dir: This lets you change the default directory where files will be saved. The Change Directory dialog box is shown in Figure 4.13. The current directory is shown in the input box at the top. You can change to a different directory by pressing *Tab* once to get to the directory tree, using the arrow keys to highlight the directory you want, and pressing *Enter*. When the tree changes to show that the directory you want is selected, then tab to the OK button and press *Enter* again. Or, if you're using a mouse, you can skip all the tabbing and just double-click on the directory you want, then single-click on the OK button. There are two other things to note about the Change Directory dialog box. First, observe that there's a down arrow at the right end of the input box; this means that there's a pick list of recently used directories.

Second, be careful: all files are saved to the current directory, not just program files. If you change your Turbo Pascal options and save them while the directory is changed to something other than the Turbo Pascal program directory, then Turbo Pascal will not be able to find your changed options the next time you start the program. If you need to use the Options menu during a session, be sure to switch back to the \TP directory first.

- Print: This prints the file in the active file window. The speed key, *Ctrl+K+P*, also can be used to print a selected block of text.

- Printer Setup: This lets you set printer control codes if needed.

- DOS Shell: This lets you suspend Turbo Pascal and temporarily exit to MS-DOS, where you can run DOS commands such as dir and rename, as well as other programs. When you are ready to go back to Turbo Pascal, simply type **exit** at the DOS prompt. You'll return to Turbo Pascal at the exact place where you were when you suspended work—for example, on line 10 of Listing 4.2.

FIGURE 4.13:
File menu—Change Directory dialog box

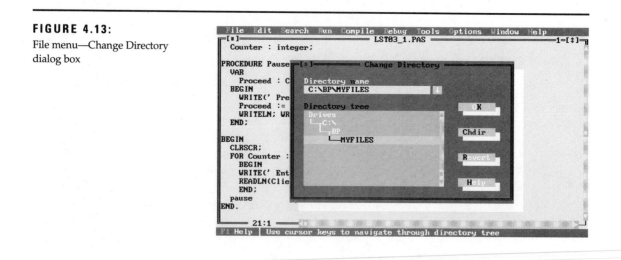

- Exit: This quits Turbo Pascal completely. If you've set the Options menu to save your file and desktop configuration, Turbo Pascal will remember what files were open when you quit and reopen them when you start it up again. The speed key is *Alt+X*.

- Pick List: A list of recently used files.

The Edit Menu (Alt+E)

Most of the options on this menu have to do with manipulating selected blocks of text.

- Undo: Undo the last editing operation.

- Redo: Undo the last "Undo."

- Cut: This deletes a highlighted block of text from your file and copies it to the clipboard, from where it can be copied elsewhere in the same file or to a different file. The speed key is *Shift+Delete*.

- Copy: This copies a highlighted block of text to the clipboard without deleting the original highlighted block. You can then copy the text from the clipboard in the same way as with the Cut menu choice. The speed key is *Ctrl+Insert*.

- Paste: This copies text from the clipboard to the current cursor position (the text cursor, *not* the mouse cursor). The speed key is *Shift+Insert*.

- Clear: This deletes highlighted text from your file *without* copying it to the clipboard, so that it can't be copied elsewhere. You also can use this to clear the clipboard itself by selecting the text in the clipboard window from Show Clipboard. The speed key is *Ctrl+Delete*.

- Show Clipboard: This opens a window that displays the current text contained in the clipboard.

The Search Menu (Alt+S)

The following options are available in the Search menu.

- Find: This searches your file for a text string that you specify in the Find dialog box, mentioned earlier in this chapter. The speed key is *Ctrl+Q+F*.

- Replace: This searches your file for a text string and replaces it with another text string; you specify both strings in the Replace dialog box mentioned earlier in this chapter. The speed key is *Ctrl+Q+A*.

- Search again: Repeats the last Find or Replace that you did. This is useful for finding multiple occurrences of a text string in a file.

- Go to Line Number: This is a quick way of jumping around in a large program file without having to do a lot of paging up and down.

- Find Procedure: This lets you search for a procedure or function during a debugging session. This menu choice is not available at other times, but when it is not, you can use the standard Find menu choice.

The Run Menu (Alt+R)

The Run menu lets you run your programs from within the IDE so that you can test and fine-tune them before you compile them to stand-alone program files.

- Run: This menu choice compiles, links, and runs the program in the active file window. Whether it compiles the program to memory or to a disk file depends on how the Destination menu choice is set in the Compile menu. The speed key is *Ctrl+F9*.

- Step Over: This steps through your program line by line, but jumps over any subroutines without stepping through them. (Normally, you'll use *both* tracing into and stepping over.) The speed key is *F8*.

- Trace Into: This lets you run your program one line at a time, which is called *stepping through* the program. It differs from Step Over, the next menu choice, in that it *always* goes one line at a time. For example, if you are tracing and come to the *pause* routine, you will go through the routine line by line. Step Over, on the other hand, will execute the *pause* routine as a single line in your program, because that's all that the subroutine call, *pause;*, takes. The speed key is *F7*.

- Go to Cursor: This runs the program but makes it stop at the line where the cursor is located. For example, if the cursor were on line 556, the program would stop on line 556. Remember, however, that a structured program typically does *not* start on line 1 of the code and run to the end, so there will be a few twists and turns along the way. The speed key is *F4*.

- Program Reset: When you are debugging a program, you will frequently step through it a line at a time, or have it run to a specified point in the program (called a *breakpoint*). When you do this, the program is ready to start running again at the *next line* after the place that it is currently stopped. Using this menu choice lets you reset the program run, so that when you restart the program, it will run from the beginning. The speed key is *Ctrl+F2*.

- Parameters: This lets you give your programs command-line parameters while running them in the IDE. A command-line parameter is something that comes after the name of a program when you start the program. When you select this menu choice, you enter command-line parameters in a dialog box for your IDE program.

The Compile Menu (Alt+C)

The Compile menu gives you various options for compiling your program in the IDE.

- Compile: This compiles and links your program to the currently selected destination (memory or disk) that you chose with the Destination menu choice in the Compile menu. The speed key is *Alt+F9*.

- Make: This compiles and links not only the primary file (the file in the current editor window if you haven't specified a different file), but all other files that are used by the primary file. This includes units and object files; units are recompiled only if they have been changed since the previous compilation. The speed key is *F9*.

- Build: This is similar to Make except that *all* files are recompiled, whether they've changed or not since the previous compilation.

- Destination: This tells Turbo Pascal whether the result of a compile, make, or build operation should be sent to memory or to a disk file. If it is sent to a disk file, then the file name is the same as the primary file, except that it has an .EXE extension instead of a .PAS extension.

- Primary File: This tells Turbo Pascal which file should be the master program file. If you do not use this option, the file is automatically the file in the current file window.

- Clear Primary File: If you have designated a primary file with the Primary File menu choice, this clears your selection.

- Information: This shows information about the currently compiled program, such as program size, number of lines compiled, and so on.

The Debug Menu (Alt+D)

The Debug menu provides various features to help you find any problems in your programs and correct them.

- Breakpoints: This displays a list of current "breakpoints" in your program, as shown in Figure 4.14. A breakpoint lets you stop your program in the middle so you can inspect the values of variables, registers, and so on.

- Call stack: This displays a list of currently active procedures and functions, along with the order in which they were called by the program.

- Register: This displays the current values held in PC's processor registers. You will rarely use this except for low-level system programs.

- Watch: This opens the "Watch Window" and lists variables that are being "watched." When you step through a program one line at a time (see below), you can put a "watch" on variables to see how their values change as the program executes.

FIGURE 4.14:

The Breakpoints window

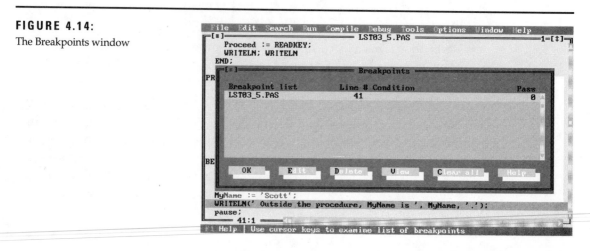

- Output: This displays any text output from your program.

- User screen: This is similar to the output window, but it displays your program's output on the full PC screen instead of in a window in the IDE.

- Evaluate/Modify: When your program is stopped at a breakpoint, this lets you inspect the values of variables, as shown in Figure 4.15. You can also change variable values to see how certain values will affect the program.

- Add watch: This lets you specify a variable whose value you want to watch as you step through the program. The speed key is *Ctrl+F7*.

- Add breakpoint: This lets you set a breakpoint to stop the program at the currently highlighted line in the source code. The speed key is *Ctrl+F8*.

FIGURE 4.15:
The Evaluate/Modify dialog box

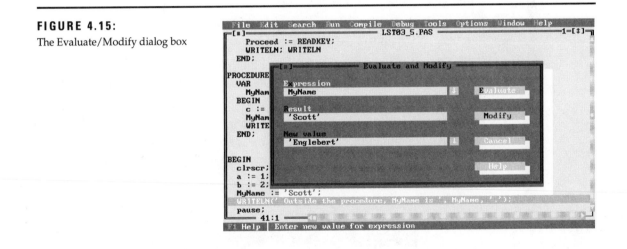

The Tools Menu (Alt+T)

This menu has additional tools for use with Turbo Pascal programs, including Turbo Assembler (for use with assembly-language files), Turbo Debugger (for more sophisticated debugging than you can do from the IDE), and Turbo Profiler (for analyzing the efficiency of your programs). By selecting "Tools" from the Options menu, you can customize the Tools menu, deleting menu choices you don't need and adding menu choices for your own programs, such as an external program editor like Brief.

The Options Menu (Alt+O)

This menu lets you set various options for the Turbo Pascal IDE, including how much error checking it does on your programs, how the editor acts, and what colors the IDE uses (if any) on your PC's screen.

- Compiler: This lets you set compilation options in the IDE, as shown in Figure 14.6. Most of these are for advanced programming and debugging, but for now, let's note that while you're developing your program, it's a good idea to have the IDE trap all the run-time errors it can, so that Range Checking, Stack Checking, and I/O Checking should all be turned on. When you are sure that your program works right, you should turn these options off before your final compilation; this will reduce the size of your compiled program file.

- Memory Sizes: This lets you manipulate the amount of memory reserved for the stack and the heap. (See Chapter 11.)

- Linker: This lets you change options for linking your programs. Because Turbo Pascal automatically takes care of linking your program, you will seldom have to worry about this option.

- Debugger: This lets you tell Turbo Pascal whether you will be using the integrated IDE debugging capabilities alone, or if you will also be using Turbo Debugger, a stand-alone program that works with Turbo Pascal.

FIGURE 4.16:

Options menu—Compile Options dialog box

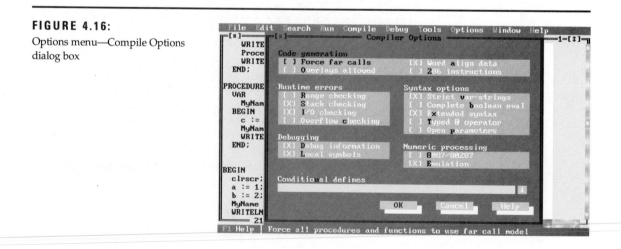

- Directories: This opens a dialog box that lets you specify where Turbo Pascal should look for programs, units, and other files if it can't find them in the current directory (see Figure 4.17).

- Tools: This enables you to customize the Tools menu.

- Environment: This takes you to a submenu from which you can set options for global preferences (shown in Figure 4.18), and for the editor, the mouse (if you have one), startup options, and screen colors. The two most important options are these: (1) in the Preferences dialog box, where you can tell Turbo Pascal to remember the files and IDE configuration whenever you quit the program, so it can reload them when you start Turbo Pascal again; and (2) in the Startup dialog box, where you can tell Turbo Pascal to use expanded (EMS) memory, if you have it, for faster performance.

- Open: This lets you open a different options file than TURBO.TP.

- Save: This lets you save the current Turbo Pascal options. If you want the options used as the default, then you can save them in a file called TURBO.TP; otherwise, you can save them in a different file.

- Save As: This lets you save current option settings in a file other than TURBO.TP.

FIGURE 4.17:

Options menu—Directories

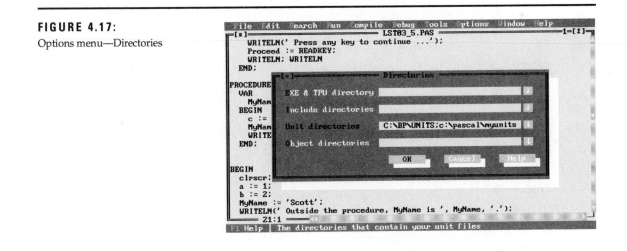

FIGURE 4.18:

Options
menu—Environment/Preferences

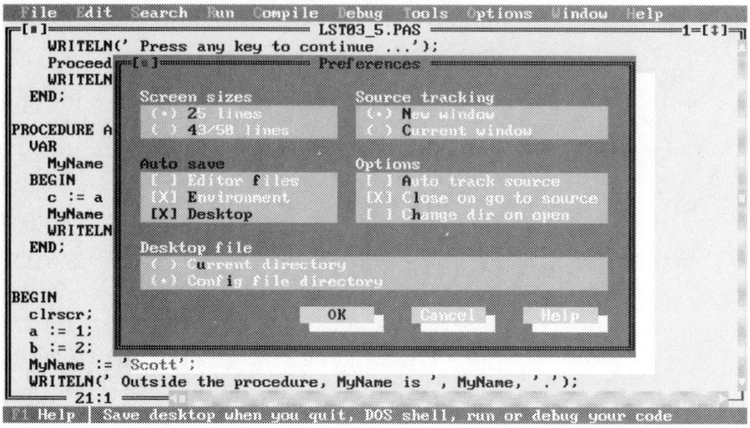

The Window Menu (Alt+W)

We've already seen several uses of the Window menu, such as to zoom, tile, and resize windows. Here are the menu choices:

- Tile: This arranges multiple screen windows so that they don't overlap and at least part of each window is visible.

- Cascade: This arranges multiple screen windows so that they overlap, with each window slightly below and to the right of the previous window. Only the active window is fully visible.

- Close all: This closes all currently open screen windows.

- Refresh display: This redraws the screen.

- Size/move: This lets you resize or move a screen window, either with the keyboard or the mouse.

- Zoom: If a window only occupies part of the screen, this "zooms" it to fill the entire screen. If a window has already been zoomed, this restores it to its original size and position. The speed key is *F5*.

- Next: If there are multiple screen windows, this moves the cursor into the next screen window. The speed key is *F6*.

- Previous: If there are multiple screen windows, this moves the cursor into the previous screen window. The speed key is *Shift+F6*.

- Close: This closes the current screen window. The speed key is *Alt+F3*.

- List: This displays a list of the current screen windows. You can select from the list by choosing a window number or by clicking on the appropriate item in the list.

The Help Menu (Alt+H)

The following options are available in the Help menu.

- Contents: This lists the different general topics for which help is available.

- Index: This displays an alphabetical list of specific help topics, such as the use of particular Turbo Pascal commands.

- Topic search: This lets you search for help on a particular keyword, such as WRITELN. The speed-key method is to position the cursor on the word for which you want help, then press *Ctrl+F1*.

- Previous topic: This takes you back to the previous help screen you looked at.

- Using help: This provides general information about how to use Turbo Pascal's help system.

- Files: This lets you delete help files if you don't need them.

- Compiler directives, Procedures and functions, Reserved words, Standard units, Turbo Pascal language, Error messages, and About...: These take you directly to help information on specific topics.

CHAPTER FIVE

Simple Data Types

- Ordinal Types

- Nonordinal Types

- String Types

- Typed Constants

In Chapter 3, we introduced the idea of a data type and showed you some simple examples. Now, we're ready to go into the subject in greater depth. In this chapter, we'll discuss simple data types. Normally, when programmers use one of these types, we are talking about a single thing—such as a number, a letter, or a piece of text—and not a collection of things. This is in contrast to structured data types. As a rule, structured data items are complex, made up of collections of other items. An array of integers, for example, is a structured data item that can hold more than one integer.

From our previous discussion, recall that a variable is like a box that can hold a certain kind of thing: an integer, a piece of text, or a truth value (true or false). Just as you cannot put a square peg into a round hole, so you cannot put a truth value into a box designed to hold a number, any more than you can put a text string into a box designed to hold a truth value. With very few exceptions, a Pascal variable will accept and hold only items of the correct type.

This kind of restriction on what-can-go-into-what is called *strong typing*. Essentially, strong typing is a safeguard to prevent the programmer from accidentally doing things that would make the program blow up, and Pascal is a strongly typed language.

Some languages, such as C, are weakly typed, which means that often you can mix different data types and have them automatically converted into a compatible type. Turbo Pascal stands somewhere in between, letting you do some type mixing but stopping anything that looks too dangerous. We'll see some examples of both in this chapter.

Ordered (Ordinal) Data Types

Although the commonsense division of data types is into numbers, text, and "other," there is a more useful way to classify simple data types in Pascal: as ordinal and nonordinal types.

An *ordinal type* is a type whose members come in a certain order, such as 1,2,3,4,5 or a,b,c,d,e. Moreover, the members of the type must be discrete and not continuous. Integers, for example, are an ordinal type because

- They come in a definite order, that is, 1,2,3,4,5,....

- Between any two adjacent members of the type, there are no other members of the type. For example, between the integers 1 and 2, there are no other integers; this is what is meant by calling the type discrete and not continuous.

Real numbers, on the other hand, are *not* an ordinal type because even though they are in order, they are continuous. Between any two real numbers, there is always an infinite number of other real numbers. For example, between the real numbers 2.141 and 2.142, there's 2.1411, 2.1412, 2.1413, and so forth. Similarly, pebbles on the seashore are not an ordinal type, because they're discrete but not in any kind of order.

The point of all this is that ordinal types let us do some fairly interesting operations, which depend on being able to pick out the *next* or *previous* member of the type. For any integer, no matter how large or how small, we can pick out the next or previous integer. With real numbers, on the other hand, there is *no* definable "next" or "previous" number to choose. For example, no matter how precisely we pick out the next real number after 2.1413, we can always find a slightly smaller next number between 2.1413 and the number we picked.

Because members of ordinal types have definite successors and predecessors, they are often used as loop counters. Listing 5.1 illustrates the use of a subrange of the CHAR type as a loop counter.

Listing 5.1

```
PROGRAM Listing5_1;

    { Shows how any ordinal type can be used as a counter, as
      long as the inherent limitations of the type are not
      exceeded. Here, we use a subset of the ASCII characters
      as values for a loop counter. }

uses crt;

const
```

```
    space = ' ';

var
    counter : char;

procedure pause;
    var
        ch : char;
    begin
    writeln;
    writeln('Press any key to continue ...');
    repeat until keypressed;
    ch := readkey;
    writeln
    end;


begin
    clrscr;
    writeln(' List of letters from "a" to "z":');
    writeln(' -----------------------------');
    for counter := 'a' to 'z' do
        write(space, counter);
    pause
end.
```

Integer Types

Turbo Pascal has two basic numeric types: integers (whole numbers) and real numbers (those with decimal points). Each basic type is subdivided into several subtypes used for different purposes. Here, I'll discuss integer types.

One of the most important features of all of Turbo Pascal's numeric types is that they take up different amounts of space in your PC's memory. Remember the on/off switches discussed in Chapter 2? Well, each on/off switch can hold a single binary digit (*bit*) of information, which means it holds either a zero or a one. Put eight of those bits together and you have a byte, which is the smallest meaningful piece of information (for example, a letter, digit, or other symbol) in the computer.

With an ordered sequence of eight zeroes and ones, you can represent 256 different symbols: enough for all 26 letters of the alphabet (upper- and lowercase), 10 digits (zero through nine), and special characters such as carriage returns and linefeeds.

At any rate, sometimes you may write programs where the amount of memory needed is critical, and this is precisely when you can reap benefits from some of the more unusual number types in Turbo Pascal. In most situations, however, it's probably better to stick with the ordinary integer type: it uses more PC memory, but it is less likely to cause problems than some of the other types. This illustrates the general principle that you should keep your code as simple as possible. Doing so makes your programs more reliable and easier to understand.

Integers

Integers are whole numbers (for example, 1, −15, 207, and 60) and can range from a low value of −32,768 to a high value of 32,767, for a total range of 65,536. Integers cannot have a decimal point, and each integer requires 16 bits (two bytes or one "word") of memory to hold it. (See Table 5.1.) This two-byte memory requirement is much less than that required by real numbers, which need three times as much memory (six bytes per real number), so whenever you can get by with integers instead of real numbers, do it.

TABLE 5.1: Integer Data Types

Type	Range	Memory Required (Bytes)
Shortint	−128..+127	1
Integer	−32,768..+32,767	2
Longint	−2,147,483,648 .. +2,147,483,647	4
Byte	0..255	1
Word	0..65,535	2

Note that although I am using commas to make it easier for you to read numbers in the text, you should *never* use commas when typing numbers into a Pascal program. Thus, if you want to declare a constant A whose value is 1,500, you would write it in the program as $A = 1500$.

You declare a variable to be of type integer in the following way:

```
VAR
    Counter : INTEGER; {Counter is an integer variable}
```

It is worth noting that when you declare constants in a Pascal program, generally, you do not need to declare the data type. The constant declaration itself, for example, *Maximum = 100*, makes it clear what type the constant is, and Turbo Pascal will automatically select the most appropriate data type.

Bytes

The Turbo Pascal byte data type is different from the generally understood meaning of byte as the smallest meaningful piece of information in your PC. In Turbo Pascal, bytes simply are a more economical version of integers, taking up only eight bits of your PC's memory—that is, one byte's worth.

Bytes pay for this reduced memory requirement, however, with a more limited range than integers. A byte can be any integer from 0 to 255, which is a range of only 256 numbers, instead of the integer type's range of 65,536 numbers. The reason for the range limitation is that there are only 256 different ordered combinations of eight bits (zeroes and ones), so that is the largest number of symbols that is possible to represent with eight bits. (Similarly, integers have a range of 65,536 numbers because there are 65,536 ordered combinations of 16 bits.) Also, unlike integers, bytes can represent only positive numbers. To see some of the difficulties that can occur with bytes, enter and run Listing 5.2.

Listing 5.2

```
PROGRAM Listing5_2;

USES CRT;

VAR
   a, b, c : BYTE;

PROCEDURE Pause;
   VAR
      Proceed : char;
   BEGIN
      WRITELN;
      WRITE(' Press any key to continue ...');
      REPEAT UNTIL KeyPressed;
         Proceed := Readkey;
      WRITELN; WRITELN;
   END;
```

```
BEGIN
   CLRSCR;

   a := 10;
   WRITELN(' The value of a is ', a, '.');
   pause;

   b := 15;
   WRITELN(' The value of b is ', b, '.');
   pause;

   c := (a-b);
   WRITELN(' C = a - b, so ', a, ' - ', b, ' equals ', c, '.');
   pause
END.
```

If you look at the code for Listing 5.2, it is fairly obvious that our point is to generate an error by assigning a value of −5 to *c*, which is a byte-type variable. When you compile the program, however, you might think that everything is fine, because it compiles with no error messages.

However, this is the most dangerous type of error, because it sneaks up on you after the program is running. When you actually run Listing 5.2, you'll be amazed to learn that 10 minus 15 is 251! Of course, that's actually a run-time error caused by trying to assign a negative value to a byte-type variable.

A More Sophisticated Pause Routine

Listing 5.2 also introduces a more sophisticated version of the *Pause* procedure. Instead of requiring you to press the *Enter* key, now you can simply press any key as in commercially developed programs such as Turbo Pascal itself. This requires just a few tricks, which will become clearer as we go along. This routine has definite advantages over the previous *Pause* routine, which can require the user to press the *Enter* key more than once, if used more than once in a program.

Short Integers

Like bytes, short integers are more economical with your PC's memory than ordinary integers, but they pay for it with a more limited range. Because short integers use only eight bits of memory, we know at the outset that the overall range is going to be 256 different numbers; the only question is, which 256 numbers? Although characters (discussed later in this chapter) and short integers both take up eight bits, short integers are *numbers* and can be used in arithmetic calculations, while characters cannot be used for arithmetic.

Short integers differ from bytes in that they are *signed* numbers, that is, they can be either positive or negative. This means that one bit out of the eight has to show whether the number is positive or negative—leaving seven bits, with 128 possible combinations, left for the numbers themselves. Therefore, short integers have a range of −128 to +127. You declare a short integer variable as follows:

```
VAR
    MinutesLeft : SHORTINT;
```

Just as with bytes, you should only use short integers when you really need to economize on memory. Otherwise, you can get into the sort of trouble illustrated by Listing 5.3, which generates an error because the loop counter must go up to 150 while a short integer's maximum value is 127.

Listing 5.3

```
PROGRAM Listing5_3;

    { Illustrates potential problems with "shortint" and other
      fancy integer types. In this case, the loop counter variable
      NumberOfLoops needs to go up to 150, but the maximum value
      of a shortint variable is 127. }


VAR
    NumberOfLoops : shortint;
    { Make loop counter a short integer }

PROCEDURE Pause;
    VAR
        Proceed : CHAR;
    BEGIN
        WRITE(' Press any key to continue ...');
        Proceed := READKEY;
        WRITELN; WRITELN
    END;


BEGIN     { main body of program }
    FOR NumberOfLoops := 1 TO 150 DO
```

```
    WRITELN(' Don''t promiscuously use short integers!');
    pause
END.
```

Words

Words are unsigned, like bytes, and take up 16 bits of memory, like standard integers. Their 16-bit status means that they have a range of 65,536; in this case, the range is 0..65,535. This type does not save any memory over integers; its only advantage is when you need to deal with positive numbers greater than 32,767. As with the other special integer types, you should use the word type only when you're very sure that it is appropriate. You declare a word as follows:

```
VAR
    RecordCounter : WORD;
```

Long Integers

Long integers are the "big gun" of whole numbers: big not only in the huge range of integers they can handle, but also in the amount of PC memory required—a whopping 32 bits, twice as much as standard integers. Because they use 32 bits, long integers can represent a total range of 4,294,967,296 different numbers; and because LONGINT is a signed type, including both positive and negative numbers, the range is from -2,147,483,648 to +2,147,483,647: over four billion integers.

You declare a long integer variable as follows:

```
VAR
    ReallyBigCounter : LONGINT;
```

Characters

"Characters" in Pascal refers not merely to the letters A to Z, but to all the characters of the extended ASCII character set. ASCII, which stands for American Standard Code for Information Interchange, defines the set of characters that your PC can handle. It includes letters (upper- and lowercase), digits (0..9), punctuation, and special characters such as the *Enter* key. In all, there are 256 ASCII characters. A character variable takes up eight bits of memory.

The ASCII Character Set

The order of ASCII characters is determined by the ASCII number of the character. For example, the first 32 ASCII characters (that is, 0 to 31) are nonprinting control characters, such as the *Enter* character (ASCII 13) and the *Escape* key (27). The rest of the ASCII characters are as follows:

- ASCII 32-47, 58-64, 91-96, and 123-127: Various punctuation and other special characters, such as the spacebar, parentheses, brackets, at sign (@), and question mark.

- ASCII 48-57: The ten digits 0 to 9, treated as characters instead of being treated as numbers. I'll come back to what this means in the section "Treating Digits as Characters" below.

- ASCII 65-90: The uppercase letters A through Z.

- ASCII 97-122: The lowercase letters a through z. Notice that the number of each lowercase letter is 32 more than its corresponding uppercase letter: for example, the number of "A" is 65 and the number of "a" is 97.

- ASCII 128-255: Various foreign-language and box-drawing characters.

For many ordinary operations, you can ignore all the ASCII numbers and simply work with the characters themselves. For example, the next character after A is B, the next character after 5 is 6, and so on. The ASCII numbers become important when you want to do something with a nonprinting character, such as the *Enter* key, the *Escape* key, or one of the arrow keys.

Treating Digits as Characters

It may seem puzzling that we include the digits 0 through 9 in the set of characters. The fact is that there are two ways of looking at these digits. Viewed as numbers, they can be used in arithmetic operations. Viewed as characters, they cannot be used for arithmetic: in this case, they're simply more letters displayed on the screen. Note, however, that you can't put a character digit such as 5 into an integer variable, because the character 5 is not an integer.

There are times when it is advantageous to treat digits as characters: for instance, when you're setting up a list of numbered menu choices. There is a slight decrease in memory requirements and code size because integers take 16 bits and characters only 8. There is also a slight increase in safety because you cannot accidentally do an arithmetic calculation with characters. Listing 5.4 shows how to use digits as characters.

Listing 5.4

```
PROGRAM Listing5_4;

USES CRT;


CONST
    a = '5';                { 'a' = the character '5'  }
    Escape = CHR(27);    { 'Escape' = the Escape key, ASCII 27 }

VAR
    Proceed : char;

BEGIN
    CLRSCR;
    Proceed := ' ';
    WHILE Proceed <> Escape DO
        BEGIN
            WRITELN(' There''s no place like home.');
            WRITELN;
            DELAY(1000);
            IF KEYPRESSED THEN Proceed := READKEY
        END
END.
```

The Boolean Data Type (Truth Values)

Remember that every factual statement has a Boolean value (a truth value) of either true or false. The two values of true and false are an ordinal type. In the ordering, false comes first and is represented by 00. True comes next and is represented by 01, so the order is *False, True*.

Normally, you'll use Boolean values to control the flow of your program. Any time you see an IF..THEN, CASE, WHILE..DO, or other statement that makes your program go in one direction or another, you're using Boolean values. Consider, for example:

```
IF Name = 'Sledge Hammer'
   THEN WRITELN(' What a nice name.')
   ELSE WRITELN(' Well, that''s a nice name, too!');
```

The IF clause of this statement is not really about anybody's name: it's about a truth value. What it says is that IF this statement is true (that is, has the Boolean value of true), THEN do one thing; otherwise, do something else.

Boolean Ordering

Listing 5.5 illustrates the ordering of the two Boolean values, and also gives us our first look at two of the functions we can use with ordinal types: the predecessor function *PRED()* and the successor function *SUCC()*. These two functions work pretty much as you'd expect: whatever ordinal value you put between the parentheses, *PRED()* returns the previous value, while *SUCC()* returns the next value. For example, if you ever got tired of the day being Monday, you could apply the *PRED()* function to it and get

```
PRED(Monday) = Sunday
```

or the *SUCC()* function and get

```
SUCC(Monday) = Tuesday
```

Listing 5.5

```
PROGRAM Listing5_5;

    { Illustrates the use of Booleans to control the flow of the
      program, and introduces PRED and SUCC functions.}


USES CRT;

VAR
    Statement1,
    Statement2,
    Statement3,
    Statement4      : BOOLEAN;
```

```
      FirstNumber,
      SecondNumber   : INTEGER;

PROCEDURE Pause;
   VAR
      Proceed : char;
   BEGIN
      WRITELN;
      WRITELN(' Press any key to continue ...');
      Proceed := READKEY;
      WRITELN
   END;


{ Main body of program }
BEGIN
   CLRSCR;
   FirstNumber := 100;
   SecondNumber := 200;

   IF FirstNumber = 100
      THEN Statement1 := (FirstNumber > SecondNumber)
      ELSE Statement1 := (FirstNumber <= SecondNumber);
   WRITELN(' The truth-value of Statement1 is ', Statement1, '.');
   pause;

   { ------------------------------------------ }
   { Use the Predecessor function to assign     }
   { the "previous" boolean value to Statement2 }
   { ------------------------------------------ }
   Statement2 := PRED(Statement1);
   WRITELN(' The truth-value of Statement2 is ', Statement2, '.');
   pause;

   { ----------------------------------------- }
   { Use the Successor function to assign       }
   { the "next" boolean value to Statement3 }
   { ----------------------------------------- }
   Statement3 := SUCC(Statement1);
   WRITELN(' The truth-value of Statement3 is ', Statement3, '.');
   pause;

   Statement4 := SUCC(statement3);
```

```
    WRITELN(' The truth-value of Statement4 is ', Statement4, '.');
    pause
```

`END.`

There is another neat trick in Listing 5.5. Notice that we never specifically assigned a truth value to *Statement1*. Instead, it looks as though we assigned a statement to it. What happened is that because *FirstNumber > SecondNumber* makes a factual assertion, it has a truth value of true or false. As it happens, this value is false, so that is the truth value that was assigned to *Statement1*. We also covered ourselves by putting in an ELSE clause to take care of all the other possibilities.

Finally, Listing 5.5 illustrates a problem you can run into frequently with certain ordinal types. Sometimes, when you get to the end of an ordinal type, you want the *SUCC()* function to cycle back to the beginning; in this case, you want *SUCC(True)* to be False. Similarly, at the beginning, you want *PRED()* to cycle to the end, which would make *PRED(False) = True*. In Listing 5.5, *PRED(False)* is true, as it should be, but *SUCC(True)* is incorrectly evaluated as true. You will learn how to solve this problem in the following section, where enumerated types are discussed.

Enumerated-Data Types

An enumerated-data type is a type you define by enumerating its members; the order in which you list the members becomes their order in the type. Thus, for example,

```
TYPE
    Stooges = (Larry, Moe, Curly);
```

defines a perfectly good enumerated-data type in Pascal. You can apply the *SUCC()* and *PRED()* functions to get things like *SUCC(Moe) = Curly*. A more useful enumerated type would be something like:

```
TYPE
    DaysOfWeek = (Mon, Tue, Wed, Thu, Fri);
```

Usually, enumerated types are used for indexing arrays. Arrays are a structured type that we discussed briefly in Chapter 3 and to which we'll return in Chapter 8 to explore fully. For the time being, note that enumerated types can make the structure and purpose of arrays a little clearer:

```
TYPE
    DaysOfWeek = (Sun, Mon, Tue, Wed, Thu, Fri, Sat);
```

```
VAR
    ThingsToDo : ARRAY[Mon..Fri] of STRING[20];
```

By using the enumerated type *DaysOfWeek* to index the array *ThingsToDo*, you can refer to individual slots in the array by the name of a particular day, such as *ThingsToDo[Wed]*. It makes no difference to Pascal whether you use *Mon..Fri* or *1..5*; this is just somewhat easier to read and understand. Also, note that you don't have to use everything in your enumerated type to index the array; if you wish, you can use only part of it, in this case, Monday to Friday.

Another use for enumerated types is as loop counters, for example:

```
TYPE
    DaysOfWeek = (Sun, Mon, Tue, Wed, Thu, Fri, Sat);
VAR
    Day = DaysOfWeek;  { loop counter }

BEGIN
    ..
    FOR Counter := Mon TO Fri DO     { loop five times }
    WRITELN(' Another workday!');  { do this each time }
    ..
END;
```

Displaying Enumerated-Data Type

It is important to understand that the members of an enumerated type are not text strings. You cannot, for example, use a line of code like the following:

```
WRITELN(' The next stooge after Moe was ', SUCC(Moe), '.');
```

If you do, you'll get an error message that says "Cannot read or write variables of this type," meaning that you cannot print an enumerated data item to the screen. To display or print the words in an enumerated type, you have to set up some text items (strings) that contain the names of the type's members. The best way to do this is to use an array, as follows:

```
TYPE
    Stooges = (Larry, Moe, Curly);
VAR
    StoogeNames : ARRAY[Larry..Curly] of STRING[5];
BEGIN
    StoogeNames[Larry] := 'Larry';
```

```
StoogeNames[Moe]   := 'Moe';
StoogeNames[Curly] := 'Curly';

{ And then print the strings in the array }
WRITELN('The first stooge was ',StoogeNames[Larry],'.');

{ .. and so on }
END;
```

Cycling Back in Enumerated Types

Sometimes, you have an ordinal type in which applying *SUCC()* to the last member of the type should take you back to the first member of the type, and applying *PRED()* to the first member should take you to the last member. Usually, this happens with enumerated types, but it can be applied generally to other ordinal types.

A typical example of this situation would be the days of the week. Sunday is the first day of the week, and *PRED(Sunday)* should give a value of Saturday; likewise, Saturday is the last day, and *SUCC(Saturday)* should give a value of Sunday. However, if you simply code it like this, you'll get an error, because *SUCC(Saturday)* is undefined.

```
TYPE
    DaysOfWeek =
    (Sunday,Monday,Tuesday,Wednesday,Thursday,Friday);
VAR
    Day1,
    Day2 : DaysOfWeek;
BEGIN
    Day1 := Saturday;
    Day2 := SUCC(Day1)
END;
```

The solution to this problem is to anticipate the possibility of calls to *SUCC(Saturday)* or *PRED(Sunday)* and write your assignment statements to account for those situations. An example of how to do this is shown in Listing 5.6.

Listing 5.6

```
PROGRAM Listing5_6;

TYPE
    DaysOfWeek = (Sunday, Monday, Tuesday, Wednesday, Thursday,
                  Friday, Saturday);
```

```
VAR
   Day1,
   Day2,
   Day3 : DaysOfWeek;

BEGIN
   Day1 := Sunday;
   IF Day1 = Sunday
      THEN Day2 := Saturday
      ELSE Day2 := PRED(Day1);
   IF Day1 = Saturday
      THEN Day3 := Sunday
      ELSE Day3 := SUCC(Day1)
END.
```

Subrange Types

With any ordinal type, it is also possible to create a *subrange type*. To create a subrange type, you simply take part of the original ordinal type (the *base type*) and declare it as its own type. For example, with the character type as the base type, you could declare subrange types as follows:

```
TYPE
   UpperCaseLetters = 'A'..'Z';
```

With integers as the base type, you could declare

```
TYPE
   OneToAHundred = 1..100;
```

Note that if the base type is a built-in Turbo Pascal type (such as characters or integers), you don't have to declare it. On the other hand, if it is an enumerated type, you must declare it:

```
TYPE
   DaysOfWeek =
(Sunday,Monday,Tuesday,Wednesday,Thursday,Friday,Saturday);
   WorkDays = Monday..Friday;
```

Because the *WorkDays* type is a subrange of the *DaysOfWeek* type, the *DaysOfWeek* type has to be declared first. Otherwise, Turbo Pascal will not recognize *Monday..Friday* as a legitimate type. And because subrange data types are derived from ordinal data types, the subrange types themselves are *also* ordinal data types.

Functions That Work with Ordinal Data

We have already seen a few examples of applying the successor and predecessor functions to members of ordinal data types. Now, I'll explain ordinal functions a little more completely.

- The value that a function takes is called its *argument*. Thus, in *SUCC(Saturday)* and *PRED(15)*, the arguments are Saturday and 15, respectively.

- Normally, a function can take only arguments of a certain type or group of types. Thus, for example, *SUCC()* can take only arguments of an ordinal type.

- The value returned by the function does not have to be of the same data type as the argument. For example, as we'll see in a moment, the *ORD()* function takes a base ordinal type and returns a number, as in *ORD(Saturday) = 7*.

SUCC(), PRED(), and Other Ordinal Routines

Now that we've seen some examples of how *SUCC()* and *PRED()* work, here is a summary of the functions and procedures you can apply to ordinal data types:

- *ORD()*: This function returns the position of an ordinal data item in the ordinal type. In the *DaysOfWeek* type, *ORD(Sunday) = 1*, *ORD(Tuesday) = 3*, and *ORD(Saturday) = 7*. Likewise, in the set of ASCII characters, *ORD('A') = 65*, *ORD('B') = 66*, which are the numbers of *'A'* and *'B'* in the order of ASCII characters. (For the character data type, the opposite of *ORD()* is *CHR()*, which takes an ASCII number and returns a character, for example, *CHR(65) = 'A'*.)

- *SUCC()*: This function returns the next member of an ordinal data type—for example, *SUCC('B') = 'C'*.

- *PRED()*: This function returns the previous member of an ordinal data type— for example, *PRED('C') = 'B'*.

- *DEC()*: This decreases an ordinal value by one position, and is a procedure rather than a function. For example, if the variable *letter* has a value of *'C'*, then *DEC(letter)* changes its value to *'B'*.

  Notice that we didn't say *DEC(letter) = 'B'*: this is because *DEC()* and *INC()* are procedures, not functions. You can think of *DEC()* as the "complete sentence" counterpart of "*PRED()*". Although you can use *PRED()* and *SUCC()* as words in a sentence, as shown in Listing 5.7 and Figure 5.1, you can use procedures such as *DEC()* and *INC()* only as whole statements that stand on their own. When you try to compile Listing 5.7, you get an error message because you're trying to use *INC()* as a function. If you delete the last two lines of the program (not *END*), the program will compile and run properly.

- *INC()*: This increases an ordinal value by one position, and works in the same way as *DEC()*.

Listing 5.7

```
PROGRAM Listing5_7;

USES CRT;

VAR
    RegLtr : char;

PROCEDURE Pause;
    VAR
        Proceed : char;
    BEGIN
        WRITE(' Press any key to continue ...');
        Proceed := Readkey;
        WRITELN; WRITELN
    END;

BEGIN
    CLRSCR;
    WRITELN;
    WRITELN(' The third capital letter is ', SUCC('B'), '.');
    pause;

    RegLtr := 'B';
    WRITELN(' The RegLtr variable now holds ', RegLtr, '.');
    pause;

    INC(RegLtr);
    WRITELN(' The RegLtr variable now holds ', RegLtr, '.');
    pause;

    WRITELN(' The fourth letter is ', Inc('C'), '.'); { Error! }
    pause;

END.
```

FIGURE 5.1:
PRED() and SUCC() are functions, similar to words in English.

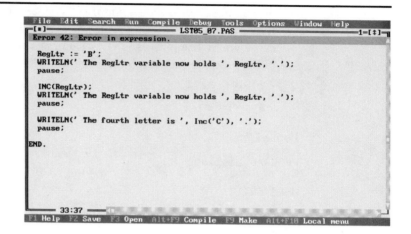

Nonordinal Types

As we have seen, members of ordinal data types are simple data items that come in a specific order, and each ordinal data item has an identifiable successor and predecessor. Members of nonordinal data types have little in common except that they fail to satisfy at least one of the requirements for being an ordinal type. Either they lack a specific order (for example, text strings), or they fail to have identifiable successors and predecessors (for example, real numbers).

The two nonordinal types are real numbers and strings. The real number type is further subdivided into types REAL, SINGLE, DOUBLE, EXTENDED, and COMP.

Real Numbers

Real numbers differ from the other numeric types we've been discussing because, as noted earlier, real numbers are not an ordinal type. No matter which real number we pick, it is impossible to pick out the next or previous real number; neither is it possible to figure out where our chosen real number stands in the order of all real numbers. Examples of real numbers are 2.0, 3.15, 1.414, and 6.023.

In Turbo Pascal, real numbers are expressed in scientific notation, that is, as powers of 10. This means, for example, that the real numbers:

$$2.2 = 2.2 \times 10^0 = 2.2000000000E+0$$

$$3,456.75 = 3.45675 \times 10^3 = 3.4567500000E+3$$

$$100 = 1.00 \times 10^2 = 1.0000000000E+2$$

Because most PC screens cannot display exponents (at least not when they are running in character mode), Turbo Pascal uses a modified scientific notation to handle the exponents, with E and a plus or minus sign showing which power of 10 the number should be raised to. To bypass this, you must specify the total number of digits and decimal places in your number. You do it by adding a format after the Pascal identifier which represents the number, as shown in Listing 5.8.

Listing 5.8

```
PROGRAM Listing5_8;

   { This program shows how to format real numbers. }


USES CRT;

VAR
   a,b,c : REAL;

PROCEDURE Pause;
   VAR
      Proceed : CHAR;
   BEGIN
      WRITE(' Press any key to continue ... ');
      Proceed := READKEY;
      WRITELN; WRITELN
   END;

PROCEDURE SetValues(VAR a,b,c : REAL);
   BEGIN
      a := 1.1;
      b := 21.59;
      c := 350.1167
   END;
```

```
PROCEDURE DisplayWithNoFormat(a,b,c : REAL);
   BEGIN
      WRITELN;
      WRITELN(' List of real number variables "a" to "c" with no format');
      WRITELN(' -------------------------------------------------------');
      WRITELN(' ',a);
      WRITELN(' ',b);
      WRITELN(' ',c);
      WRITELN;
      pause
   END;



PROCEDURE DisplayFirstFormat(a,b,c : REAL);
   BEGIN
      WRITELN;
      WRITELN(' List of real number variables "a" to "c" with formatting');
      WRITELN(' ---------------------------------------');
      WRITELN(' ',a:0:1);
      WRITELN(' ',b:0:2);
      WRITELN(' ',c:0:4);
      WRITELN;
      pause
   END;

PROCEDURE DisplayColumnFormat(a,b,c : REAL);
   BEGIN
      WRITELN;
      WRITELN(' List of real number variables in column format');
      WRITELN(' ------------------------------------------------');
      WRITELN(' ',a:8:4);
      WRITELN(' ',b:8:4);
      WRITELN(' ',c:8:4);
      WRITELN;
      pause
   END;


{ ---------------------------------------------------------------- }
{                       MAIN BODY OF PROGRAM                       }
{ ---------------------------------------------------------------- }
BEGIN
   CLRSCR;
   SetValues(a,b,c);
```

```
    DisplayWithNoFormat(a,b,c);
    DisplayFirstFormat(a,b,c);
    DisplayColumnFormat(a,b,c)
END.
```

The first digit after the identifier indicates the total number of spaces that you want your number to take up; the second tells how many decimal places you want in your number, that is, how many digits should be to the right of the decimal point.

If you specify *0* for the total number of digits, then Turbo Pascal automatically expands the format to fit the number. You can specify other total numbers of digits when you want to line up columns of numbers as shown in Listing 5.8.

Listing 5.8 also provides several examples of passing variables as parameters to subroutines. When you define a subroutine, you must include in the definition the number, type, and order of any variables that the subroutine will need to get from outside itself. Then, when you call the subroutine, you can simply include the names of the appropriate variables in parentheses after the name of the subroutine. Any variables to be changed by the subroutine *must* be declared as VAR parameters when you first define the subroutine. We will examine subroutines and parameters more thoroughly in Chapter 9.

Types of Real Numbers

Just as with integers, real number types differ primarily in their range and in the amount of PC memory that they require. The different types are shown in Table 5.2. As with integers, it's better to use the plain "real" data type unless you have a special reason for needing one of the others. Even with the plain "real" data type, you get an almost unimaginably large range of numbers, quite large enough to count all the stars in our galaxy and several other galaxies, as well.

Using Fancy Real Types

If you ever need to use Turbo Pascal's specialized real-number types (single, double, extended, and comp), there are two ways to do it. Technically, these data types require an 80x87 (8087, 80287, or 80387) math coprocessor in your PC in order to work, and if you have some extra money, that is the best solution.

On the other hand, for a cheaper solution that's almost as good, use Turbo Pascal's built-in library of routines for handling real numbers and turn on 80x87 software emulation, which tells Turbo Pascal to use 80x87 instructions to handle the fancy

TABLE 5.2:   Real Number Data Types

Type	Range	Significant Digits	Memory Required (Bytes)
Real	$2.9 \times 10^{-39} .. 1.7 \times 10^{38}$	11-12	6
Single	$1.5 \times 10^{-45} .. 3.4 \times 10^{38}$	7-8	4
Double	$5.0 \times 10^{-324} .. 1.7 \times 10^{308}$	15-16	8
Extended	$3.4 \times 10^{-4932} .. 1.1 \times 10^{4932}$	19-20	10
Comp*	$-2^{63} + 1 .. 2^{63} - 1$	19-20	8

*The Comp type holds integers between -9.2×10^{18} and $+9.2 \times 10^{18}$.

real-number types. This is slower and slightly less powerful than using an 80x87 math coprocessor, but you can use this method on all PCs—most of which are not 80x87-equipped.

There are two ways to do this. The first is to use the Compiler Options dialog box (opened from the Options menu) to turn on 80x87 emulation as the default. (If you choose this method, then 80x87 emulation will be used in all of your programs.)

Numeric Processing Compiler Directives

The second way is to put two "compiler directives" at the beginning of your program that tell Turbo Pascal to turn on 80x87 emulation. A compiler directive is a special kind of program comment that tells Turbo Pascal (or any other Pascal compiler) how to handle certain situations when it compiles your program. We'll discuss compiler directives in detail in Chapter 7, but for the time being, here are instructions on how to use them to handle precise real numbers.

Usually, a compiler directive is a *toggle*, which means that it works like a light switch. Flip it up, and the light is turned on; flip it down, and the light is turned off. The equivalent of up for most compiler directives is the plus sign, while the equivalent of down is the minus sign.

There are two numeric processing compiler directives that you can use for floating-point arithmetic—that is, with real numbers:

- {$N+} and {$N-}, which turn 80x87 code generation on and off, respectively. When 80x87 code generation is on, Turbo Pascal generates floating-point instructions that take advantage of your math coprocessor's arithmetic capabilities. If you don't have a math coprocessor, you also must have *80x87 emulation* turned on; otherwise, you will get a compilation error message that says you need a math coprocessor.

- *{$E+}* and *{$E-}*, which turn 80x87 emulation on and off, respectively. When emulation is turned on, Turbo Pascal links your program with a run-time library of routines that handle floating-point arithmetic in approximately the same way as the 80x87 does. It is slower than having an extra processor in your PC, but it works.

You should use both of these compiler directives if your program must handle precise floating-point arithmetic but you do not know if your PC has a math coprocessor. This program will use a math coprocessor if one is present; and will use 80x87 emulation routines if one is not present.

```
PROGRAM VeryPreciseNumbers;

{$N+}            { turns on 80x87 code generation }

{$E+}            { links 80x87 emulation routines
                   in case 80x87 not present      }

{...details of program }
```

Of course, there's no point in using either of these compiler directives if you are only using integers and real numbers without many digits. They will make your compiled program slightly bigger.

Notice one unusual thing about compiler directives. I said earlier that Pascal ignores anything between two comment brackets. Compiler directives are the single exception to this rule. When Turbo Pascal encounters a left comment bracket that is immediately followed by a dollar sign, as in the example above, it knows it is dealing with a compiler directive instead of an ordinary comment. As a result, it carries out the directive's instructions on how the program is to be compiled.

Cautions about Real Numbers

One point that needs to be made is that although integers are handled by Turbo Pascal as exact values, *real numbers* are handled only as approximate values. This results more from the limitations of the PC's processor (8086, 80286, 80386, or 80486) than it does from Turbo Pascal itself, but it must be reckoned with if you are using real numbers with many digits.

In most situations, this won't cause you any trouble. Turbo Pascal has no problem distinguishing between 1.00 and 0.99, or between 1000.151 and 1000.152. The real-number data type has 11 to 12 significant digits, depending on the circumstances, and so as long as you are within that limit, you are fairly safe.

When you are doing calculations that require a high degree of precision, however, you should bear in mind that real numbers (and other real types) have a limited number of "significant digits." This means that only the significant digits (from left to right) count as part of the number. If you need greater precision than is provided by standard real numbers, you can use a double-precision or an extended data type, which provides 15-16 and 19-20 significant digits, respectively. Remember that to use these types, you must have 80x87 code generation turned on and either 80x87 emulation or a math coprocessor.

Arithmetic Operations with Integers and Real Numbers

Most of Turbo Pascal's arithmetic operations are quite ordinary: addition, subtraction, and multiplication work just as you would expect. There are, however, a few special points of which you need to be aware.

Integer and Real Division

First, there are two kinds of division in Pascal: integer division and real-number division. Integer division is denoted by the word *div*, while real-number division is denoted by the forward slash ("/"). When you use integer division, both of the numbers involved must be integers, and the result is also an integer, as in:

    6 div 3 = 2

    20 div 4 = 5

    15600 div 15 = 1040

    11 div 3 = 3

That last result might have surprised you. Eleven divided by three is *three*? However, we are using *integer division*, which is a special kind of division that only handles whole numbers—and the number of times that three will *evenly* divide eleven is indeed three. It is wise to remember this potential pitfall whenever you use integer division: the result is always an integer, and any fractions are discarded.

Real division, on the other hand, is exactly what you would expect. It takes two real numbers or integers, divides one into the other, and gives back a third real number as the result. For example,

7.50 / 3.0 = 2.50

12.25 / 2 = 6.125

6 / 3 = 2.0

The result of real division is a real number even if the operands are both integers and there is no remainder: for example, *6 / 3 = 2*, but the 2 that is the solution is a real number. If you try to assign it to an integer variable, you will get a compile-time error because the data types do not match. Thus, the following code will not compile:

```
PROGRAM MisMatch;

VAR
    WholeNum : integer;

BEGIN
    WholeNum := 6 / 3        { type mismatch }
END.
```

The MOD Operator

The other arithmetic operator that might be unfamiliar is the *mod* (modulus) operator, which returns the *remainder* of an integer division. Thus,

15 mod 2 = 1; { two divides 15 7 times, remainder = 1 }

12 mod 12 = 0; { 12 divides 12 once, remainder = 0 }

The *mod* operator is often used to set up loops in which a variable cycles from a low value to a high value and then starts again at the low value. The North American clock, for example, gives the hour of day as *mod 12*:

7th hour of the day = 7 mod 12 = 7 o'clock

15th hour of the day = 15 mod 12 = 3 o'clock

24th hour of the day = 24 mod 12 = 0 o'clock

As the third time indicates, normally, you need to set up a separate statement to handle the maximum value in the range that you are using: the 24th hour of the day is not zero o'clock, but 12 o'clock.

Turbo Pascal's arithmetic operators are summarized in Table 5.3.

TABLE 5.3:   Arithmetic Operations with Integers and Real Numbers

Operator	Operation	Data Type of Operands	Data Type of Results
+	Addition	Integer or real	Integer or real
−	Subtraction	Integer or real	Integer or real
* (asterisk)	Multiplication	Integer or real	Integer or real
div	Integer division	Integer	Integer
/ (slash)	Real division	Real or integer	Real
mod	modulus	Integer	Integer

Evaluating Arithmetic Expressions

Sometimes, the exact meaning of an arithmetic expression is ambiguous. For example, does *120 div 3 + 5* mean that you should

divide 3 into 120 and then add 5 to the result, or

add 5 to 3 and then divide the sum into 120?

Parentheses are the main tool for eliminating this kind of ambiguity. By grouping parts of an expression in parentheses, you indicate which operations are to be performed first. Operations inside parentheses are done first, then at the next level out of the parentheses, and so forth. Thus,

$(120 \text{ div } 3) + 5 = 40 + 5 = 45$

$120 \text{ div } (3 + 5) = 120 \text{ div } 8 = 15$

$120 \text{ div } (3 + (5 * 3)) = 120 \text{ div } (3 + 15) = 120 \text{ div } 18 = 6$

If parentheses do not resolve the issue, then operations are done in the following order: multiplication, division, modulus, addition, and subtraction. And, if there is still an ambiguity, any operations equal in priority are done from left to right.

The String Data Types

Strings, as pieces of text, are the most familiar type to human beings. Unfortunately, Standard Pascal (as defined by the International Organization for Standardization) provides no string data type; instead, you have to treat strings as packed arrays of characters, which can be quite tedious.

Fortunately, Turbo Pascal 7 provides not just one but *two* string data types. Turbo Pascal does see strings as arrays of characters but for most purposes we can ignore this and allow Turbo Pascal to handle it for us. When we need to think of a string as an array, we can do it (as, for example, when we want to pick out the *n*th character in a string by using the array index).

It is worth noting that in most of the cases where we have had to deal with strings, we have not had to worry about declaring a string data type. The program statement

```
WRITELN(' This is a string.');
```

automatically displays a string on the screen for us. It is only when we want to create string variables and/or constants that we have to worry about string types.

Even so, there is little to worry about except for how much memory the string will require. You declare a string variable as follows:

```
VAR
   Firstname : STRING[10];
```

You can also, of course, declare string constants if you want. The number between the square brackets in *STRING[10]* indicates how long the string is supposed to be; the length can be anything from 1 to 255. If you do not include a length, as in

```
VAR
    Firstname : STRING;
```

Turbo Pascal assigns a default length of 255 characters.

Now, there is a puzzle here: what happens if you assign a length of 10 to a string, but use only five characters, as in *Firstname := 'Steve'*? The answer is that Turbo Pascal keeps track of the actual length (called the *logical length*) of the string as well as its physical length, which is the amount of PC memory it requires, determined by the number you put between the brackets. A string, remember, is really an array of characters; Turbo Pascal keeps the logical length of the string in a special 0 slot at the very beginning of the array.

Thus, while a program is running, the logical length of a string can vary from zero (the minimum) to its physical length (the maximum) as it receives new pieces of text assigned to it.

```
VAR
    Firstname : STRING[10];      { physical length 10 }

BEGIN
    Firstname := 'Joe' { logical length 3, physical
                                length 10 }

    Firstname := 'Philippe' { logical length 8,
                                   physical length 10 }
    { ... etc. }
END;
```

Apostrophes in Quoted Strings

By now, you may be wondering: what happens if you want to include an apostrophe in the middle of a quoted string? Since Turbo Pascal uses the apostrophe character to mark the beginning and end of a string, how can you use the same character in a string without causing problems?

The answer is simply to use a double-apostrophe, as in

```
WRITELN('Don''t look back.');
```

The double apostrophe tells Turbo Pascal that the apostrophe is meant as an apostrophe instead of as a string delimiter.

Null-Terminated Strings

Borland Pascal and Turbo Pascal 7 support a new string type: null-terminated strings. Standard Turbo Pascal strings, as noted above, have a "length bit" in the zero position of the string. The length bit tells Turbo Pascal how many characters are in the string—or, what is the same thing, the memory address of the last character in the string.

The main disadvantage of this approach is that it limits the length of strings to 255 characters. Of less importance for standard Turbo Pascal programs is that this method of handling strings is incompatible with Microsoft Windows and the C programming language, both of which require the use of null-terminated strings.

So what is a null-terminated string? Simply, it's an array of characters that ends with a null character, '\0'. The null character marks the end of the string, making it unnecessary to use a length bit in position zero of the string. Null-terminated strings can be up to 65,535 characters in length, and this limit is imposed by DOS, not by Turbo Pascal.

We won't discuss null-terminated strings any further here, other than to note a few things about using them:

1. For most DOS programs, use the standard Turbo Pascal string type.

2. If you want to use null-terminated strings, you must turn on "extended syntax" with the Options/Compiler menu choice or put a {$X+} at the top of your program file. You must also name the STRINGS unit in your USES clause. This unit contains a variety of functions for manipulating null-terminated strings. If you've programmed in C, the functions and their names are very similar to those in the C string-handling library.

3. If you're using null-terminated strings, you must be sure to allow an extra slot in the array for the null terminator at the end. And remember that null-terminated strings begin at array slot 0, so you can't number the string slots like you can with a normal Turbo Pascal array, for example, [5..75].

4. Many operations that work with standard strings don't work with null-terminated strings. If your program has inexplicable bugs, that may be the cause.

We'll return to null-terminated strings in the section on Borland Pascal for Windows.

Passing Strings to Subroutines

Ordinarily, you do not have to declare string types in the TYPE section of your program, because STRING is a built-in data type in Turbo Pascal. You will need to declare strings in the TYPE section whenever you need to pass string variables as parameters to subroutines (procedures and functions). Turbo Pascal will not allow you to declare a subroutine with a standard string type, such as in

```
PROCEDURE DisplayYourName(Name : STRING[20]);
```

This program line will not compile because Turbo Pascal won't accept *STRING[20]* or any similar expression *(STRING[5], STRING[255])* in a subroutine definition. To pass a string as a parameter to a subroutine, you have to declare a string type in the TYPE section and use that type in defining your subroutine:

```
TYPE
    String20 = STRING[20];

{ ... etc. }

PROCEDURE DisplayYourName(Name : String20);

{ ... etc. }
```

Typed Constants

Typed constants suffer from a seriously misleading name. First, all constants have a data type. Second, typed constants are not constants: they are variables that you declare in the TYPE section of your program. A typed constant declaration includes the name, data type, and *the initial value* of the variable you are declaring.

Thus, in spite of their name, typed constants do have a role of sorts. You can use typed constants to declare variables and set their initial values at the same time. For example, the following two code fragments are equivalent:

```
TYPE
   Distance : integer = 600;
```

does the same job as

```
VAR
   Distance : integer;
BEGIN
   Distance := 600;
{ ... etc. }
END;
```

CHAPTER
SIX

Simple Pascal Statements

- Simple vs. Compound Statements

- Types of Simple Statements

Fundamental Types of Statements

At the highest level there are only two fundamental kinds of statements in any Pascal program: first, statements that move *data* to one place or another, and second, statements that move *the program* in one direction or another.

Examples of statements that move data to one place or another are *assignment statements,* which move a value into a variable; *I/O (input/output) statements,* which move data from your PC's memory to the screen, disk drive, printer, or some other device; and *definitional statements,* which set the values of constants. Thus, the following are *data moving* statements:

- *Counter := 1;* { assignment statement; moves a value into a variable }

- *WRITELN(' This is displayed on the screen.');* { I/O statement; moves a text string from memory to the PC's screen }

- *Pi = 3.1415927;* { definitional statement; defines Pi as the real number specified }

- *Name : STRING[10];* { definitional statement; defines the Name variable as being of type STRING with physical length 10 }

Examples of statements that move the program in one direction or another (officially called *control statements*) are *looping statements,* which make the program repeat a sequence of operations until a certain condition is fulfilled; and *branching statements,* which, based on the value of some control variable, make the program take one path instead of another. Thus, the following are *program moving* statements:

- *FOR counter := 1 TO 10 DO WRITELN(' This is loop number ', counter, '.');* {looping statement; causes the program to execute an I/O statement (display a text string) 10 times }

- *IF PaidUp THEN SendThankYou ELSE BugForMoney;* { branching statement; causes the program to go in one direction or another based on the truth value of the Boolean variable "PaidUp" }

Serving in support of these two official kinds of statements is a third kind of statement, which *asserts* some fact or another. Examples of this kind of statement are *Boolean statements,* such as those involving NOT, and OR; and *arithmetic comparisons,* such as those involving the relational operators >, <, and =. Thus, the following are assertion statements:

- *Counter = 10 OR Name = 'Smith'* { asserts that either the counter variable equals 10 or the name variable = 'Smith' }

- *Balance >= 100.00* { asserts that the balance variable is greater than or equal to the real number 100.00 }

Observe that neither of these examples would qualify by itself as a legal statement in Pascal. Assertion statements in Pascal are used exclusively to help program-moving statements direct the program into one path or another. Ironically, this is exactly the opposite of how humans talk. As a rule, most of our statements assert something, like "There's a camel in the kitchen." The type of statement that Pascal uses, called an *imperative,* is used less frequently in English; for example, "Call the zoo!" The reason for this is that human communication is fact-oriented, and program statements are almost exclusively action-oriented.

Simple and Compound Statements

Pascal statements can be either simple or compound. A simple statement performs a single Pascal action, while a compound statement does several actions in sequence. Some examples of simple statements are the following:

- *WRITELN(' This is a simple statement.');*
- *Counter := Counter + 1;*
- *IF Counter = 10 THEN Finish ELSE KeepOnTruckin;*

A compound statement is composed of simple statements. You might have looked at the third example, above, and wondered why it is not a compound statement. To see why it is a simple statement, remember the definition: a simple statement performs a single Pascal action. Depending on the value of *Counter,* the IF..THEN..ELSE statement performs a single program action. That is why it is a simple statement.

Compound statements use BEGIN, END, and the semicolon (;) to show Pascal where they begin and end. The following are examples of compound statements:

```
BEGIN
   WRITE(' Enter your name: ');
   READLN(Name)
END;

BEGIN
   IF Name = 'Albert Einstein'
      THEN BEGIN
            WRITELN(' E = mc2 ');
            END
      ELSE WRITELN(' That's a nice name!');
   Counter := Counter + 1
END;
```

Notice that we enclosed a compound statement within one of the simple statements of the second example. You can do this to as many levels as you like, enclosing statements within statements, within other statements, although it is generally a good idea to keep things as simple as you can.

Indentation and Lines Do Not Matter

You should realize that the indentation and separate lines of a Pascal program are there entirely for the benefit of the programmer. Pascal is a statement-oriented language, not a line-oriented one. How your program code indents and divides into different lines makes no difference to Pascal. A line-oriented language, such as BASIC, executes a program one *line* at a time, while a statement-oriented language, such as Pascal, executes a program one *statement* at a time. This is why, for example, a Pascal statement can be split into two or more program lines, while a BASIC statement (even in Microsoft QuickBASIC) cannot. Thus, the following two code fragments are equivalent:

```
BEGIN
   IF Counter = 10
      THEN BEGIN
            WRITELN(' End of list.');
            WRITE(' Do another (Y/N): '):
            READLN(YesNo);
            IF UPCASE(YesNo) = 'Y'
            THEN DoAnother
            ELSE Quit
```

```
        END;
    pause
END;
```

is the same as

```
BEGIN IF Counter = 10 THEN BEGIN
WRITELN(' End of list.');
WRITE(' Do Another (Y/N): ');
READLN(YesNo); IF UPCASE(YesNo) = 'Y' THEN DoAnother
ELSE Quit END; pause END;
```

It is important to understand this, particularly because many beginning programmers think that structured programming means simply indenting your code. It is true that most structured programs are indented, but indenting and other devices that make code more readable have no necessary connection with structured programming.

To convince yourself, enter and run Listing 6.1, which is hard to read but runs just fine. Actually, Listing 6.1 includes some formatting, which makes it easier to read than some professionally written Pascal programs that have no formatting at all.

Listing 6.1

```
PROGRAM Listing6_1;

USES CRT; VAR Counter : integer; YesNo : char;

PROCEDURE Pause;
    VAR Proceed:char; BEGIN WRITE(' Press a key to continue ...');
    Proceed := READKEY; WRITELN; WRITELN END;

PROCEDURE DoAnother;
    BEGIN WRITELN(' The DoAnother routine has run.'); pause END;

PROCEDURE Quit;
    BEGIN WRITELN(' The Quit Routine has run.'); pause END;

BEGIN CLRSCR; Counter := 10; IF Counter = 10 THEN BEGIN
WRITELN(' End of list.'); WRITE(' Do Another (Y/N): ');
READLN(YesNo); IF UPCASE(YesNo) = 'Y' THEN DoAnother
ELSE Quit END END.
```

The idea that Pascal is statement-oriented is usually explained by saying that semi-colons are statement *separators,* not statement *terminators.* If that idea seems unclear, just remember the following rules:

1. A simple program statement performs a single Pascal action.

2. All statements in a Pascal program must be separated by semicolons.

3. Compound statements are made up of one or more simple statements.

4. Compound statements start with BEGIN and end with END. BEGIN and END are not themselves statements; rather, they mark the beginning and ending of a compound statement.

5. If a compound statement contains more than one component statement, you must use semicolons to separate its component statements.

6. You do not need to put a semicolon before an END or before a THEN or ELSE in an IF..THEN..ELSE statement.

The only situation when Pascal is somewhat line oriented occurs in handling text strings: you cannot break a string across more than one line. If we were to write

```
IF Counter = 10 THEN WRITELN(' End oflist.');
```

then the program would not compile and we would get the error message, "String constant exceeds line."

Specific Types of Simple Statements

Now that we've discussed the general ideas, let's move on to look at the general types of simple statements in Pascal. The basic types are assignment state-ments, definition statements, I/O statements, and control statements, such as IF..THEN..ELSE.

Assignment Statements

We have seen several examples of assignment statements already. An assignment statement takes a value and puts it into a variable. To do this, Pascal uses the assign operator, which consists of a colon and an equal sign, as in the following:

```
Counter := 10;
Name := 'Smith';
Students[55].GPA := 3.21;
Area := Height * Width;
SuccessfulRead := IORESULT;
```

If you need a nickname for the assignment operator, it is best to think of it as "gets" so you don't accidentally confuse it with "equals." For example, think of it as "Counter gets 10" instead of "Counter equals 10." Another reason to think of the assignment operator as "gets" is to remind you that you're not in BASIC, which uses the equals sign as its assignment operator.

There are two things to watch out for when using assignment statements. First, the expressions on the left and right of the assignment operator must be compatible. This means that they must either be of the same type (for example, character) or that they can be converted easily between the two types; for example, integer and short-int, and so forth.

Second, the item on the right side of the assignment operator must *already be defined*. In other words, you can't assign the value of variable *a* to variable *b*, as in

```
b := a;
```

unless you have previously assigned a value to *a*.

Definition Statements

Definition statements occur mainly in the TYPE, CONST, and VAR sections of your program and its subroutines (procedures and functions). These tell Pascal that, for the duration of your program, a certain identifier is either

- A name for a certain value declared in the CONST section, or

- Of a certain built-in or user-defined data type.

We've seen many examples of definition statements. Here are a few more:

```
CONST
   Pi = 3.14159;

TYPE
   StudentPtr = ^Student;
   Student = RECORD
             Firstname,
             Lastname : STRING[15];
             GPA       : REAL;
             Probation: BOOLEAN;
             Next      : StudentPtr
             END;
VAR
   StudentList : StudentPtr;
   Counter     : INTEGER;
   YesNo       : CHAR;
```

Just in case you're wondering what *StudentPtr* means, it is a pointer that points to variables of the "user-defined type Student." Of course, it is also a teaser, meant to spark your curiosity about pointers, which will be covered in Chapter 11.

I/O Statements

Input/output, or I/O, statements move data between your PC's memory and input/output devices, such as the PC's screen, the disk drives, the printer, or the modem. At the moment, we are going to look at two ways to exchange data with the PC screen and with the disk drives.

WRITELN and WRITE

The most familiar I/O statements are the WRITELN and WRITE statements. These take a sequence of printable values (strings, characters, numbers, and so on) and "write" them to an I/O device. You might think that WRITELN and WRITE are only for displaying things on screen; but as we will see, they do a lot more than that.

WRITELN and WRITE differ in that WRITELN displays whatever you want and then adds an end-of-line marker (a carriage return and linefeed) at the end of the line. The result is that after displaying what it is supposed to display, WRITELN moves you down to the next line. WRITE, on the other hand, simply displays what it is supposed to display and then leaves the cursor wherever it is.

This makes WRITE ideal for on-screen prompts and for displaying sequences of values on the same line. Listing 6.2 shows how to use WRITE for both of these tasks.

Listing 6.2

```
PROGRAM Listing6_2;

USES CRT;

VAR
    Counter,
    NumberOfLoops : INTEGER;

PROCEDURE Pause;
    VAR
        Proceed : CHAR;
    BEGIN
        WRITE(' Press any key to continue ...');
        Proceed := READKEY;
        WRITELN; WRITELN
    END;

BEGIN
    CLRSCR;
    WRITE(' Please enter the number of loops you want: ');
    READLN(NumberOfLoops);
    WRITELN;
    FOR Counter := 1 TO NumberOfLoops DO
        BEGIN
        WRITE(' ',counter);
        DELAY(500)                  { delay writing next for 1/2 second }
        END;
    WRITELN; WRITELN;
    pause
END.
```

Note that in Listing 6.2, the cursor pauses on the same line as the *Please enter the number of loops you want* prompt. Similarly, all the numbers are displayed on the same line. The two WRITELN statements after the loop are there to move the cursor down two lines on the screen.

Files in WRITELN and WRITE: Although it is not obvious from what you have seen so far, both WRITELN and WRITE are designed to send output to disk files. If you do not specify a file name, then they assume that you want to use the standard out-put file—OUTPUT, which is just the PC's screen. Thus, a WRITELN statement such as *WRITELN('Display on screen')* will send its output to the screen. Turbo Pascal's printer unit also defines a standard output file called "LST" that allows you to send output to the printer.

You can, however, specify other file names with WRITELN and WRITE. To il-lustrate this, examine Listing 6.3. (See Chapters 12 and 13 for working with disk files.)

Listing 6.3

```
PROGRAM Listing6_3;

USES CRT;

TYPE
   String20 = STRING[20];

VAR
   Name     : String20;
   Namefile : TEXT;    { "text" is a type of file variable }
   YesNo    : CHAR;


PROCEDURE Pause;
   VAR
      Proceed : CHAR;
   BEGIN
      WRITE(' Press any key ... ');
      Proceed := READKEY;
      WRITELN; WRITELN
   END;


PROCEDURE Init(VAR YesNo : CHAR; VAR Namefile : text);
   BEGIN
      YesNo := 'Y';
      ASSIGN(Namefile, 'Names.txt');
      REWRITE(Namefile)
   END;


PROCEDURE Shutdown(VAR Namefile : text);
```

```
BEGIN
   CLOSE(Namefile)
END;

PROCEDURE ReadInNames(VAR Name : string20;
                      VAR YesNo : CHAR;
                      VAR Namefile : text);
BEGIN
   WHILE UPCASE(YesNo) = 'Y' DO
      BEGIN
      WRITELN;
      WRITE(' Enter a name for the file: ');
      READLN(Name);
      WRITELN(Namefile, Name);
      WRITE(' Add another name (Y/N)? ');
      READLN(YesNo)
      END
END;


BEGIN
   CLRSCR;
   Init(YesNo, Namefile);
   ReadInNames(Name, YesNo, Namefile);
   Shutdown(Namefile);
   pause
END.
```

The program in Listing 6.3 prompts the user for information by writing text strings to the standard output file (the screen). It then gets the information the user enters by reading it from the standard input file (the keyboard). Finally, it writes the information to a text file, NAMES.TXT, on disk.

Notice that the key difference from what we have seen before occurs in the *ReadInNames* procedure, where the second WRITELN statement includes the name of a file variable as well as the text string that is supposed to be written. Before you can use this file variable, you must associate it with a DOS file name through the ASSIGN statement, then open the file with REWRITE (if you want to write to the file) or RESET, if you want to read from the file. Finally, at the end of the program, you must CLOSE the file.

By using Turbo Pascal's built-in Printer unit, you also could have sent the names to your printer. To send text to the printer using the Printer unit, you use the unit's predefined file variable *LST*, which automatically sends output to the printer, as in

```
USES CRT, Printer;
   CONST
      FormFeed = #12;   { to make printer eject page }
   BEGIN
      WRITELN(LST,' This goes to the printer.');
      WRITELN(LST, formfeed)
   END.
```

READLN and READ

READLN and READ work in exactly the same way as WRITELN and WRITE, except that they get input from some file (normally the keyboard) and put it into a variable. Listing 6.2 shows an example of READLN, and we've seen many others. Listing 6.4 shows how READLN can be used to display the names that we entered in the disk file from Listing 6.3.

Listing 6.4

```
PROGRAM Listing6_4;

USES CRT;

TYPE
   String20 = STRING[20];

VAR
   Name : String20;
   NameFile : text;

PROCEDURE Pause;
   VAR
      Proceed : CHAR;
   BEGIN
      WRITE(' Press any key ... ');
      Proceed := READKEY;
      WRITELN; WRITELN
   END;


PROCEDURE Init(VAR Namefile: text);
```

```
   BEGIN
      ASSIGN(Namefile, 'names.txt');
      RESET(Namefile)
   END;

PROCEDURE Shutdown(VAR Namefile : text);
   BEGIN
      CLOSE(Namefile)
   END;

PROCEDURE DisplayNames(VAR Namefile : text;
                       VAR Name : string20);
   BEGIN
      CLRSCR;
      WHILE NOT EOF(Namefile) DO
      { has end of file been reached ? }
         BEGIN
            READLN(Namefile, Name);
            WRITELN(Name);
            WRITELN;
            pause
         END
   END;

BEGIN
   Init(Namefile);
   DisplayNames(Namefile, Name);
   Shutdown(Namefile)
END.
```

Evaluating Assertion Statements

As I noted earlier, statements that assert something is true or false are "second-class citizens" in Pascal, because the only official program statements are commands. However, assertive statements do have an important role to play in directing the flow of a Pascal program. Based on whether an assertion statement is true or false, Pascal control statements move the program in one direction or another. Statements like *IF Balance = 0.0 THEN SendThanks* depend on the evaluation of the truth value of an assertion statement.

Boolean Operators

Sometimes, you will encounter statements that are not quite as simple as *Balance = 0.0*. For example, suppose that you had a statement like the following:

```
IF (WaterLevel > 25 AND NoLifeJacket) OR Temperature < 30
    THEN YellForHelp
    ELSE TakeASwim;
```

It is not quite as obvious how to evaluate whether the IF statement is true or false. AND and OR are Boolean operators, meaning that they take truth values and, based on what the truth values are, determine whether the entire statement is true or false. If there is any ambiguity about what goes with what, you should use parentheses to make things clear. In the example above, we used parentheses to make it clear that the statement breaks up into

```
(WaterLevel > 25 AND NoLifeJacket) OR Temperature < 30,
```

instead of using

```
WaterLevel > 25 AND (NoLifeJacket OR Temperature < 30)
```

Beyond that, there are some simple rules for figuring out this type of statement. These rules are shown in Tables 6.1 through 6.4.

TABLE 6.1: Truth Table for a Statement P Used with NOT

P	NOT P
TRUE	FALSE
FALSE	TRUE

TABLE 6.2: Truth Table for Two Statements P and Q Connected by AND

P	Q	P AND Q
TRUE	TRUE	TRUE
TRUE	FALSE	FALSE
FALSE	TRUE	FALSE
FALSE	FALSE	FALSE

TABLE 6.3:   Truth Table for Two Statements P and Q Connected by AND

P	Q	P OR Q
TRUE	TRUE	TRUE
TRUE	FALSE	TRUE
FALSE	TRUE	TRUE
FALSE	FALSE	FALSE

TABLE 6.4:   Truth Table for Two Statements P and Q Connected by XOR

P	Q	P XOR Q
TRUE	TRUE	FALSE
TRUE	FALSE	TRUE
FALSE	TRUE	TRUE
FALSE	FALSE	FALSE

Tables 6.1 through 6.4 are known as truth tables. They show how you can determine the truth values of statements that use Boolean operators. The statements P and Q are components of the statements constructed with the Boolean operators. On each line of the truth table, you see the truth value of the compound statement if P and Q have the values shown. For example,

P	Q	P OR Q
-----	------	-------
TRUE	FALSE	TRUE

means that if P is true and Q is false, then P OR Q will be true. Likewise, Table 6.2 shows that whenever P is true, NOT P is false, and whenever P is false, then NOT P is true; NOT simply reverses whatever truth value it is applied to.

Other Relational Operators

In addition to the Boolean operators, Turbo Pascal has a large number of other operators that are used in assertion statements. These operators are shown in Table 6.5.

TABLE 6.5:   Relational Operators for Assertion Statements

Operators	Meaning	Takes What Types as Arguments?	Result
=	Equals	Compatible simple, pointer, set, string, and array types	Boolean
<>	Does not equal	Same	Boolean
<	Less than	Same	Boolean
>	Greater than	Same	Boolean
>=	Greater than or equal to	Same	Boolean
<=	Less than or equal to	Same	Boolean
Set Operator			
>=	Superset of	Compatible set types	Boolean
<=	Subset of	Same	Boolean
in	Member of	Same	Boolean

Order of Evaluation

Turbo Pascal uses precedence rules to decide which expressions are evaluated first. For example, expressions containing NOT are evaluated before expressions containing OR. If you forget to include parentheses in your assertion statement, Turbo Pascal will figure out its truth value by (1) applying precedence rules, and (2) reading and evaluating the statement from left to right.

However, it is easy to make a mistake in remembering or applying the precedence rules, so I strongly recommend that you rely on parentheses instead.

Even if you do use parentheses, it's essential that you understand the precedence rules for Boolean expressions. The precedence levels of Boolean operators, which are referred to informally above, are summarized in Table 6.6.

TABLE 6.6: Precedence of operators in Turbo Pascal

Operators	Precedence
@@, NOT	first
, * /, div, mod, AND, shl, shr	second
+, −, OR, XOR	third
=, <>, <, >, <=, >=, IN	fourth

Let's look at a few examples of how these rules apply. Where p, q, and r are Boolean statements, the following expressions are equivalent:

- NOT p OR q is equivalent to (NOT p) OR q, because NOT has a higher precedence level than OR.

- p AND NOT q OR r is equivalent to (p AND (NOT q) OR r). NOT q is evaluated first because NOT has a higher precedence level than both AND and OR. Moreover, AND has a higher precedence level than OR, so NOT q goes with the AND p instead of with the OR r.

- p AND q AND r is equivalent to (p AND q) AND r, because when operators are equivalent in precedence level, Turbo Pascal evaluates the expression from left to right. (In fact, because AND is commutative, you can group this expression any way you like and it will come out the same.)

Table 6.6 also shows some other operators that you may find in Boolean expressions, including arithmetic operators. Just like Boolean operators, these are evaluated according to their level of precedence.

Short-Circuit Boolean Evaluation

Sometimes, it is not necessary for Turbo Pascal to read an entire Boolean expression to know if it is true or false. For example, in

```
(6 < 5) AND (Name = 'Sam');
```

Turbo Pascal could conclude that the entire expression is false as soon as it reads the first statement, which says that six is less than five. Because AND statements evaluate to true if and only if both of the statements connected by AND are true, and six is *not* less than five, the overall expression is obviously false as soon as you read the first statement.

Normally, however, some versions of Pascal read Boolean expressions in their entirety before evaluating them as true or false—even if, as in our example, they do not need to do so. Usually, this will simply slow down your program and result in a slightly larger compiled program file, but there are a few cases in which it will actually cause a run-time error. The most common situation for an actual error is in searching a *linked* list (a topic covered in detail in Chapters 11 and 18). For example, you might have a search statement that says the following:

```
WHILE currptr <> nil
AND currptr^.keyfield <> searchkey
{...continue the search }
```

This tells Pascal that if you haven't reached the end of the list (that is, *currptr* doesn't equal *nil*) and the current item's key field does not contain what you are searching for, then it should continue the search. However, if you *have* reached the end of the list and Pascal tries to look at the key field of the current item, the program will crash because there *is* no current item. It is trying to look for something that is not there.

To avoid this problem, Turbo Pascal's default setting uses what is called *short-circuit* Boolean evaluation, which stops evaluating a Boolean expression as soon as the truth value of the expression is clear. The second part of the AND statement above—the part that causes the run-time error—would never be evaluated if the first part turned out to be false.

Because it is the default setting, you need not do anything to make Turbo Pascal use short-circuit evaluation. In rare cases, you may want to turn off this option so that Turbo Pascal does a full evaluation of Boolean expressions. In such cases, you can use the complete evaluation compiler directive, *{$B+}*, to turn on full Boolean evaluation. When full evaluation is no longer needed in your program, you can turn complete evaluation off with the *{$B-}* compiler directive so that Turbo Pascal will resume doing short-circuit evaluations.

Simple Control Statements

In this chapter, we will look at two kinds of simple control statements: IF..THEN..ELSE statements and FOR statements. Both of these statements direct the flow of your program: IF..THEN..ELSE statements into one branch or another, and FOR statements into a loop that will execute a predetermined number of times.

In Chapter 7, we will look at more complex and powerful control statements that build on the basic concepts introduced in this section.

IF..THEN..ELSE Statements

We've already seen many IF..THEN..ELSE statements in our program examples. Normally, this type of statement is most useful when you want the program to go in one direction or another based on a single value that either *is* or *is not* a certain value. This means that IF statements are good to test single conditions, such as whether or not a statement is true.

Where IF statements are not quite as good is in making the program branch in one of several directions based on one of several possible values. For example, in an on-screen menu that has six choices, you cannot simply say

```
IF Menuchoice = 1
   THEN OpenFile
   ELSE Quit;
```

That gives you only two possibilities. In such situations, you would use a CASE statement, which will be discussed in Chapter 7.

FOR.. Statements

There are really only two varieties of FOR statements: FOR..TO and FOR..DOWNTO. As is probably obvious, FOR..TO counts upward and FOR..DOWNTO counts downward.

The counter variable in a FOR statement can be any ordinal type, including integers, characters, or enumerated types. Thus, a perfectly good FOR statement would be

```
FOR Counter := 10 DOWNTO 1 DO
   WRITELN(' Counting down, count ', Counter, '.');
```

Note two key differences between Pascal's FOR statement and FOR statements in BASIC. First, you use the assignment operator, not the equal sign, in setting up your counter loop. Second, the counter variable is automatically increased or decreased with each pass through the loop; there is no need for a NEXT statement.

You must be careful about how you set up FOR statements (and most others, for that matter). FOR takes a single statement and repeats it in the loop. Thus, if you wrote the code in Listing 6.5, the first line after the FOR statement would repeat five times, but the second line would display only once. That's because the FOR statement repeats only the first statement after it; to include multiple statements in the loop, you must use BEGIN and END to combine them into a single statement, as shown in Listing 6.6.

Listing 6.5

```
PROGRAM Listing6_5;

USES CRT;

VAR
    Counter : INTEGER;

PROCEDURE Pause;
    VAR
        Proceed : CHAR;
    BEGIN
        WRITE(' Press any key ... ');
        Proceed := READKEY;
        WRITELN; WRITELN
    END;


BEGIN
    CLRSCR;
    FOR Counter := 1 TO 5 DO
        WRITELN(' Ho, ho, ho!');
        WRITELN(' This one doesn''t repeat!');
    pause
END.
```

Listing 6.6

```
PROGRAM Listing6_6;

USES CRT;

VAR
    Counter : INTEGER;

PROCEDURE Pause;
    VAR
        Proceed : CHAR;
    BEGIN
        WRITE(' Press any key ... ');
        Proceed := READKEY;
        WRITELN; WRITELN
    END;


BEGIN
    CLRSCR;
    FOR Counter := 1 TO 5 DO
        BEGIN
        WRITELN(' Ho, ho, ho!');
        WRITELN(' This one does repeat!')
        END;
    pause
END.
```

More Advanced Pascal Statements

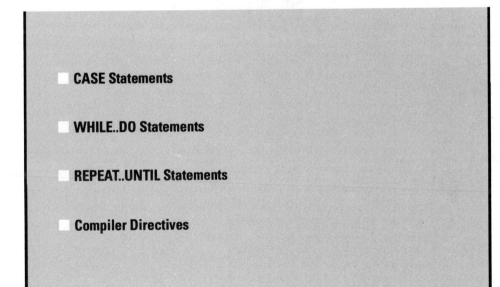

- CASE Statements

- WHILE..DO Statements

- REPEAT..UNTIL Statements

- Compiler Directives

In the previous chapter, we looked at some fairly simple Pascal statements—from WRITELN to the slightly more complex IF..THEN and FOR statements. Here, we'll continue that discussion by examining some more complex statements, as well as when—and when not—to use them.

Case Statements

In the examples we have seen of IF..THEN..ELSE statements, there were only two alternatives in the IF clause: either true or false. Thus, in the following, we are dealing with only two possible branches in the program.

```
IF Name = 'Smith' THEN WRITELN(' Another Smith!');
IF Balance = 0.00
    THEN SendThankYou
    ELSE BugForMoney;
```

In the first case, the program executes an extra statement if the Name is 'Smith', while if the name is not 'Smith', it does not execute the statement. In the second case, if the balance is zero, then the program branches one way and sends a thank you note; otherwise, it branches in a different direction and sends a bill.

Sometimes, however, there are more than two alternatives. In that situation, things can get fairly messy with IF statements, as in Listing 7.1. (Actually, as nested IF statements go, the one in Listing 7.1 is hardly messy at all.) This is a common programming situation in which you are setting up a user menu. Depending on the number that the user enters, you want the program to do one of several different things.

Listing 7.1

```
PROGRAM Listing7_1;

    { Demonstrates the relative inefficiency of nested
      IF..THEN..ELSE statements compared to CASE statements in
      handling several alternatives. }

USES CRT;

CONST
```

```
    Escape = CHR(27);

VAR
   Choice : INTEGER;
   Continue : CHAR;

PROCEDURE Pause;
   VAR
      Proceed : CHAR;
   BEGIN
      WRITE(' Press any key to continue ...');
      Proceed := READKEY;
      WRITELN; WRITELN
   END;



PROCEDURE Init(VAR Choice : INTEGER; VAR Continue : CHAR);
   BEGIN
      Choice := 0;
      Continue := ' '
   END;

PROCEDURE AddRecords;
   BEGIN
      WRITELN('The AddRecords procedure has run.')
   END;

PROCEDURE EditRecords;
   BEGIN
      WRITELN('The EditRecords procedure has run.')
   END;

PROCEDURE DisplayRecords;
   BEGIN
      WRITELN('The DisplayRecords procedure has run.')
   END;

PROCEDURE DeleteRecords;
   BEGIN
      WRITELN('The DeleteRecords procedure has run.')
   END;

PROCEDURE GetMenuChoice(VAR Choice : INTEGER);
   BEGIN
```

```pascal
      WINDOW(26,5,75,24);
      WRITELN('   MASTER MENU');
      WRITELN('-------------------');
      WRITELN('1. Add Records');
      WRITELN('2. Edit Records');
      WRITELN('3. Display Records');
      WRITELN('4. Delete Records');
      WRITELN('5. Quit');
      WRITELN;
      WRITE('Enter your choice (1-5): ');
      READLN(Choice)
   END;

PROCEDURE DoChoice(VAR Choice : INTEGER);
   BEGIN
      WRITELN;
      IF Choice = 1 THEN AddRecords
          ELSE IF Choice = 2 THEN EditRecords
              ELSE IF Choice = 3 THEN DisplayRecords
                  ELSE IF Choice = 4 THEN DeleteRecords
                      ELSE IF Choice = 5 THEN Continue := Escape;
      WRITELN
   END;


{ --------------------------------------------------------------- }
{                        MAIN BODY OF PROGRAM                     }
{ --------------------------------------------------------------- }
BEGIN
   Init(Choice,continue);
   WHILE Continue <> Escape DO
      BEGIN
         CLRSCR;
         GetMenuChoice(Choice);
         DoChoice(Choice);
         window(1,1,80,24);
         GoToXY(1,22);
         pause
      END
END.
```

The nested IF statement, of course, is in the *DoChoice* procedure. In passing, note several other things about Listing 7.1:

- Each subroutine that deals with variables from outside itself declares those variables as parameters.

- A separate subroutine initializes the variables. Strictly speaking, you do not have to initialize the *Choice* variable, because its value is set in the *GetMenu-Choice* subroutine before any action is taken that depends on its value. However, it certainly doesn't hurt to initialize global variables, and it is somewhat safer.

- We set up a WHILE..DO loop to run the main body of the program until you press *Escape*. This is a fairly common approach. WHILE..DO loops are discussed below.

The program in Listing 7.1 does the job, but that series of nested IF..THEN..ELSE statements is messy: and messy code is always more prone to hidden bugs than clear, easy-to-understand code. Situations like this call for using a CASE statement, as shown in Listing 7.2.

Listing 7.2

```
PROGRAM Listing7_2;

    { Demonstrates how to use a CASE statement to handle multiple
      alternatives. }

USES CRT;

CONST
    Escape = CHR(27);

VAR
    Choice : INTEGER;
    Continue : CHAR;

PROCEDURE Pause;
    VAR
        Proceed : CHAR;
    BEGIN
        WRITE(' Press any key to continue ...');
        Proceed := READKEY;
```

```
            WRITELN; WRITELN
        END;
        BEGIN
            Choice := 0;
            Continue := ' '
        END;

PROCEDURE AddRecords;
    BEGIN
        WRITELN('The AddRecords procedure has run.')
    END;

PROCEDURE EditRecords;
    BEGIN
        WRITELN('The EditRecords procedure has run.')
    END;

PROCEDURE DisplayRecords;
    BEGIN
        WRITELN('The DisplayRecords procedure has run.')
    END;

PROCEDURE DeleteRecords;
    BEGIN
        WRITELN('The DeleteRecords procedure has run.')
    END;

PROCEDURE GetMenuChoice(VAR Choice : INTEGER);
    BEGIN
        WINDOW(26,5,75,24);
        WRITELN('   MASTER MENU');
        WRITELN('--------------------');
        WRITELN('1. Add Records');
        WRITELN('2. Edit Records');
        WRITELN('3. Display Records');
        WRITELN('4. Delete Records');
        WRITELN('5. Quit');
        WRITELN;
        WRITE('Enter your choice (1-5): ');
        READLN(Choice)
    END;

PROCEDURE DoChoice(VAR Choice : INTEGER);
    BEGIN
        WRITELN;
```

```
      CASE Choice OF
            1 : AddRecords;
            2 : EditRecords;
            3 : DisplayRecords;
            4 : DeleteRecords;
            5 : Continue := Escape
            END;
        WRITELN
    END;


{------------------------------------------------------------------ }
{                        MAIN BODY OF PROGRAM
}
{------------------------------------------------------------------ }
BEGIN
   Init(Choice,continue);
   WHILE Continue <> Escape DO
      BEGIN
         CLRSCR;
         GetMenuChoice(Choice);
         DoChoice(Choice);
         window(1,1,80,24);
         GoToXY(1,22);
         pause
      END
END.
```

The general form of a Pascal CASE statement is as follows:

```
CASE variable OF
     constantvalue1 : statement1;
     constantvalue2 : statement2;
     constantvalue3 : statement3;
     { ... etc. }
     END;
```

The values in the list must be constants of an ordinal data type, such as CHAR, IN-TEGER, or an enumerated type. They can also be lists or ranges of ordinal values, such as 1,2, 'A'..'Z', or 50..100, so that if *constantvalue1* in the above example were 50..100 and the variable's value were 75, then statement 1 would be carried out. The maximum range of the constant values in the CASE statement is 0..255, so you can use characters, integers, and enumerated types as long as you do not exceed that range. Also, of course, the type of the constant values has to be compatible with the type of the control variable.

Turbo Pascal goes beyond standard Pascal and lets you add an ELSE clause. This is useful in cases where the control variable might not have *any* of the values you listed in the CASE statement:

```
CASE variable OF
        constantvalue1 : statement1;
        constantvalue2 : statement2;
        constantvalue3 : statement3;
        { ... etc. }
        ELSE statement4
        END;
```

This tells Turbo Pascal that if the variable has value 1, it should do statement 1; if it has value 2, do statement 2; and on to the end of the value list. If the variable doesn't have *any* of the values listed, the ELSE clause tells it to do statement 4. The ability to include an ELSE clause is fairly important, because if a control variable did not match any of the values in your CASE statement, your program could crash or, even worse, malfunction in a subtle way that you would not notice.

Listing 7.3 shows how to build some error-checking into your CASE statements, first with an IF..THEN..ELSE clause in standard Pascal, then with a CASE..ELSE clause in Turbo Pascal. When we arrive at the section on sets in Chapter 8, we will show how to create more sophisticated error-checking for *all* values entered by the user.

Listing 7.3

```
PROGRAM Listing7_3;

    { Demonstrates how to use an ELSE clause in a CASE statement. Also
      shows how to use an IF clause in standard Pascal to substitute
      for an ELSE clause. }

USES CRT;

VAR
    Choice1 : INTEGER;
    Choice2 : CHAR;

PROCEDURE Pause;
    VAR
```

```
         Proceed : CHAR;
      BEGIN
         WRITE(' Press any key to continue ...');
         Proceed := READKEY;
         WRITELN; WRITELN
      END;

PROCEDURE NumberChoice(VAR Choice1 : INTEGER);
   BEGIN
      CLRSCR;
      WRITE(' Enter your choice (1-10): ');
      READLN(Choice1);
      IF (Choice1 < 1) OR (Choice1 > 10)
          THEN WRITELN(' You dolt! You didn''t enter a valid choice.')
          ELSE CASE Choice1 OF
             1,2 : WRITELN(' Your choice was 1 or 2.');
             3..9: WRITELN(' Your choice was in the range 3..9.');
             10  : WRITELN(' Your choice was 10.')
             END;
      pause
   END;

PROCEDURE CharacterChoice(VAR Choice2 : CHAR);
   BEGIN
      CLRSCR;
      WRITE(' Enter your choice (A..Z, 0..9): ');
      READLN(Choice2);
      CASE Choice2 OF
         'A'     : WRITELN(' Your choice was the letter A.');
         'B','C' : WRITELN(' Your choice was B or C.');
         'D'..'Z' : WRITELN(' Your choice was in the range D..Z.');
         '0'..'9' : WRITELN(' You chose a digit from 0 to 9.')
         ELSE WRITELN(' You dolt! You didn''t enter a valid choice.')
      END;
      pause
   END;


{ ---------------------------------------------------------------- }
{                     MAIN BODY OF PROGRAM                         }
{ ---------------------------------------------------------------- }
BEGIN
   NumberChoice(Choice1);
   CharacterChoice(Choice2)
END.
```

When Not to Use Case Statements

There is an important fact that you should remember about CASE statements: they are merely a convenient (and somewhat limited) shorthand for a series of nested IF statements. IF statements can do everything CASE statements can do. In fact, IF statements can do things that CASE statements *cannot* do.

For example, the following statements are perfectly legal with IF:

```
IF Name = 'Smith'
   THEN SendSmithLetter
   ELSE IF Name = 'Jones'
      THEN SendJonesLetter
      ELSE IF Name = 'Quayle'
         THEN SendQuayleLetter;

IF (Reading > 100) AND (Reading <= 200)
   THEN SoundAlarm
   ELSE IF (Reading > 200) AND (Reading <= 300)
      THEN Evacuate
      ELSE IF Reading > 300
         THEN Goodbye;

IF number1 = number2           { number1, 2, 3, and 4  }
   THEN DoRoutine1             { are integer variables }
   ELSE IF number1 = number3
      THEN DoRoutine2
      ELSE IF number1 = number4
      THEN DoRoutine3;
```

However, if you tried to code these statements with CASE, your program wouldn't compile. The first statement uses text strings to tell the program which way to go—and text strings *are not* an ordinal data type. The second statement tries to use greater than and less than operators; but > *100* is neither a constant, a finite list of constants, nor a range of constants. The third statement tries to use variables as CASE selectors: however, the CASE selectors (as distinguished from the control variables) have to be constants.

So, in a nutshell, all of the following should be coded with IF..THEN..ELSE instead of CASE. *Do not* use a CASE statement in the following situations:

- When you need to use a nonordinal data type as the CASE selector, such as a text string.

- When you need to make a greater than or less than comparison with the CASE selector.

- When you need to use a variable as a CASE selector.

- When you might need to deal with a range of CASE selectors that is greater than 0..255.

WHILE..DO Statements

Like FOR statements, which were discussed in Chapter 6, WHILE..DO statements set up a loop that carries out a series of statements over and over. The key differences between WHILE and FOR statements are as follows:

- A FOR statement sets up a loop to run for a specified number of times. A WHILE statement, on the other hand, sets up a loop to run only while a certain condition is true. If the loop condition is never true, then the statements in the loop *never* execute at all.

- A FOR statement requires a counter variable. This counter variable has its value set by the FOR statement, so you do not need a separate step to set an initial value for the counter variable. A WHILE statement does not require a counter variable, although it can use one to set the truth value of its loop condition.

- Although a WHILE statement does not require a counter variable, it does depend on the loop condition being true. If the WHILE statement is meant to run at least once, then the condition must be initialized so that it is true when the program arrives at the WHILE statement. In such circumstances, however, it may be better to use a REPEAT..UNTIL statement, which is discussed below.

- If the loop condition in a WHILE statement is initially true and never becomes false inside the loop, the WHILE statement will continue to execute forever unless you break out of the loop (by pressing *Ctrl+Break* or by rebooting your PC).

Thus, you should use a WHILE statement when you want a certain sequence of actions to be performed as long as a certain condition is true, but you are not sure exactly how long that condition will continue to be true. The general form of a WHILE statement is as follows:

```
WHILE (Boolean value of true) DO (loop statement);
```

The Boolean value of true that controls the WHILE loop can be anything that evaluates to a Boolean value of TRUE. This includes equals statements, comparisons, and, of course, the Boolean value of TRUE itself (though you probably would not use a naked Boolean value). Thus, the following are legal WHILE statements:

```
WHILE TRUE DO Readfile;

WHILE NOT EOF(MyFile) DO Readfile;

WHILE Name = 'Smith' DO
   BEGIN
   SmithCounter := SmithCounter + 1;
   READLN(MyFile, Name)
   END;

WHILE (1+5 > 17) DO
   WRITELN(' The laws of arithmetic are suspended.');

WHILE Continue <> Escape DO
DisplayMenu;
```

It is very important to make sure that the Boolean expression (loop condition) used by the WHILE statement is defined and meaningful *before* the program arrives at the WHILE statement. Note that this does not mean it has to be *true*—only that its variables and constants must have values, and that the Boolean expression must have a truth value.

Thus, for instance, if you hadn't assigned any value to *Continue* in the final example above, anything might happen. The memory address reserved for the value of *Continue* would probably contain garbage instead of meaningful information; and with a million-to-one shot, it could even have the exact configuration of garbage to look like *Escape*. In any event, you'd be in trouble. Therefore, it is essential to observe the following procedures:

- Make sure that your program assigns appropriate values to variables used in WHILE statements before the WHILE statements are invoked in the program.

- Make sure that any constants used in the WHILE statement's Boolean expression are defined and of the correct type.

It is perfectly possible, of course, to use a WHILE statement as a substitute for a FOR loop, as shown in Listing 7.4. However, a FOR loop is both more economical (requiring fewer lines of code) and *safer* than a WHILE loop. It is better to reserve WHILE loops (and REPEAT..UNTIL loops) for times when you *are not* sure how long the loop will go on. Listing 7.5 shows how, if you know how many loops to make, a FOR loop needs fewer lines of code than a WHILE loop.

Listing 7.4

```
PROGRAM Listing7_4;

    { Demonstrates use of a WHILE loop as a substitute for a FOR
      loop. In this case, a FOR loop is better. }

USES CRT;

VAR
    Counter : INTEGER;

PROCEDURE Pause;
    VAR
        Proceed : CHAR;
    BEGIN
        WRITE(' Press any key to continue ...');
        Proceed := READKEY;
        WRITELN; WRITELN
    END;

BEGIN
    Counter := 0;
    CLRSCR;
    WHILE Counter <= 15 DO
        BEGIN
        WRITELN(' The counter now equals ', Counter, '.');
        WRITELN;
        Counter := Counter + 1
        END;
        pause
END.
```

Listing 7.5

```pascal
PROGRAM Listing7_5;

    { Demonstrates how a FOR loop requires fewer lines of code than
      a WHILE loop when you know in advance how many loops to
      make. }

USES CRT;

VAR
    Counter : INTEGER;

PROCEDURE Pause;
    VAR
        Proceed : CHAR;
    BEGIN
        WRITE(' Press any key to continue ...');
        Proceed := READKEY;
        WRITELN; WRITELN
    END;

BEGIN
    CLRSCR;
    FOR Counter := 1 TO 15 DO
        BEGIN
        WRITELN(' The counter now equals ', Counter, '.');
        WRITELN;
        END;
        pause
END.
```

Avoiding Endless Loops

We mentioned that FOR loops are safer than WHILE loops. That is because a FOR loop will always terminate eventually; but a WHILE loop can continue forever if you are not careful. Not only will this cause you to miss lunch—and dinner, and breakfast, until you die of starvation at your PC—but it tends to upset your friends, who think you should be out working for a living.

Listing 7.6 shows an unterminating WHILE loop. Look at it, study it, enjoy it, but *do not run it*. It sets up an endless loop because the WHILE condition never becomes false.

Listing 7.6

```
PROGRAM Listing7_6;

   { DO NOT RUN THIS PROGRAM. SIMPLY STUDY IT TO SEE WHY
     THE LOOP NEVER TERMINATES. }


USES CRT;

VAR
   Counter : INTEGER;

BEGIN
   CLRSCR;
   Counter := 0;
   WHILE Counter <= 10 DO
      BEGIN
      WRITELN(' Going through the loop again!');
      WRITELN(' That''s ', Counter, ' times so far!');
      WRITELN;
      WRITELN(' Press Control-Break to exit.');
      DELAY(1000)
      END
END.
```

Getting Out of Endless Loops

If you ever do get stuck in an endless loop, however, there are three different remedies you can apply, in this order:

- Press *Ctrl+Break*; if nothing happens, try it again.

- Try to warm boot your PC by pressing *Ctrl+Alt+Delete*. (If your PC has a warm boot button, press it.)

- Turn your PC off. Wait 30 seconds (allow the hard disk time to stop completely), then turn your PC back on again. At the DOS prompt, key in **chkdsk/f** to check your disk for problems.

When and When Not to Use While

You *should* use a WHILE statement when:

- You want a (simple or compound) statement to execute as long as a certain condition is true, but you are not sure how long that will be.

- You want to allow for the possibility that the loop condition will never be true and, therefore, the DO part of the WHILE statement will never execute.

You should *not* use a WHILE statement when:

- You know in advance (or the program can determine in advance) how many loops are needed. In that case, use a FOR statement.

- You need to make sure that the loop executes at least once. If the loop condition of a WHILE statement is false when the program arrives at the WHILE statement, then the WHILE loop will never execute.

REPEAT..UNTIL Statements

REPEAT..UNTIL statements are very similar to WHILE statements. In both cases, you set up a loop that will run (or not run) depending on whether a loop condition is true or false. The key differences are:

- In a WHILE statement, the loop continues to execute as long as a certain condition (the loop condition) is true. In a REPEAT statement, on the other hand, the loop executes as long as the loop condition is false—that is, *until* it becomes true.

- In a WHILE statement, the loop condition is evaluated *before* you go through the loop, in order to determine whether you should go through the loop. On the other hand, in a REPEAT statement, the loop condition is not tested until *after* you go through the loop. As a result,

- In a REPEAT statement, your program will always go through the loop at least once.

The general form of a REPEAT statement is as follows:

```
REPEAT {loop statements} UNTIL
(Boolean value of true);
```

Unlike a WHILE loop, you can have multiple statements in a REPEAT loop without having to make them into a single compound statement with BEGIN and END. This is because Pascal needs some way to tell where the statements in the WHILE loop are supposed to end, but in a REPEAT statement, the keyword UNTIL marks the end of the loop:

```
WHILE counter <= 10 DO    { incorrect WHILE loop }
   statement;
   statement;
   statement;
   { ... Where does this WHILE statement end? You must
     use BEGIN and END so that WHILE is followed by a
     single statement. }

REPEAT
   statement;
   statement;
   statement
UNTIL Counter > 10;       { marks end of REPEAT loop }
```

The Boolean value that controls the loop can be anything that has a truth value. Thus, the following are legal REPEAT statements:

```
REPEAT UNTIL True;

REPEAT ReadName(MyFile) UNTIL EOF(MyFile);
{ read names until end of file }

REPEAT
NameCounter := NameCounter + 1;
READLN(MyFile, Name)
UNTIL Name = CHR(13);

REPEAT
   WRITELN(' The laws of arithmetic are suspended.')
   UNTIL (1+5 < 17);

REPEAT DisplayMenu UNTIL Continue = Escape;
```

When and When Not to Use Repeat

You *should* use a REPEAT statement when:

- You want a (simple or compound) statement to execute until a certain condition becomes true, but you are not sure how long it will take.

- You want to make sure that your program goes through the loop at least once no matter what.

You should *not* use a REPEAT statement when:

- You know in advance (or the program can determine in advance) how many loops are needed. In that case, use a FOR statement.

- There are circumstances under which the program should *not* go through the loop even one time. In that situation, use a WHILE statement instead of REPEAT.

GOTO Statements

Among structured programming purists, the GOTO statement is the black sheep of Pascal statements. It lets you jump directly from one line of your program to another without using structured programming methods. If you are taking a course in Pascal, you would be well-advised to avoid GOTO statements—they could hurt your grade!

In practical programming situations, however, there are some cases in which GOTO offers a reasonable way to solve a problem. These are usually exit-if-error types of situations. For example, in the middle of its run, your program might find that a necessary file is nowhere to be found! Then, you could (but would not have to) use a GOTO statement to jump to the end and terminate the program or subroutine, as shown in Listing 7.7. Listing 7.8 shows how you would prompt the user for a different file name.

Listing 7.7

```
PROGRAM Listing7_7;

USES CRT;

LABEL GetOut;              { Line label to GOTO in case of error. }

VAR
   Name   : STRING[10];
   MyFile : TEXT;          { Declares a file variable to use in
                             opening a text file. }

PROCEDURE Pause;
   VAR
      Proceed : CHAR;
   BEGIN
      WRITE(' Press any key to continue ...');
      Proceed := READKEY;
      WRITELN; WRITELN
   END;


BEGIN
   ASSIGN(MyFile, 'students.txt');
   {$I-}                    { Turn off input checking. }
   RESET(MyFile);
   {$I+}                    { Turn input checking back on. }
   IF IORESULT <> 0
      THEN GOTO GetOut
      ELSE BEGIN
         WRITELN(' The file is there!');
         READLN(MyFile, Name)
         END;
   pause;

GetOut: END.
```

Listing 7.8

```
PROGRAM Listing7_8;

   { Shows how to prompt the user for a different filename if
     the initial attempt to open a file doesn't work. }

USES CRT;

TYPE
   String10 = STRING[10];
   String12 = STRING[12];

VAR
   Name    : String10;
   NewFileName : String12;
   MyFile : TEXT;          { Declares a file variable to use in
                            opening a text file. }


{ ------------------------------- }
{ MAIN-LEVEL PROCEDURE DECLARATION }
{ ------------------------------- }
PROCEDURE Pause;
   VAR
      Proceed : CHAR;
   BEGIN
      WRITE(' Press any key to continue ...');
    . Proceed := READKEY;
      WRITELN; WRITELN
   END;


{ ------------------------------- }
{ MAIN-LEVEL PROCEDURE DECLARATION }
{ ------------------------------- }
PROCEDURE EnterNewFile(VAR NewFileName : string12;
                       VAR MyFile : text);
   BEGIN
      WRITELN;
      WRITELN(' That file can''t be opened!');
      WRITE(' Please enter a new filename or press <Enter> to exit: ');
      READLN(NewFileName);
      IF NewFileName = ''   { If the user only pressed Enter }
         THEN Halt          { then halt the program.         }
```

```
    ELSE BEGIN
        ASSIGN(MyFile, NewFileName);  { assign new filename }
        {$I-}
        RESET(Myfile);                      { try to open file }
        {$I+}
        IF IORESULT = 0      { was file opened okay? }
            THEN BEGIN
                WRITELN(' File opened successfully!');
                CLOSE(MyFile)  { Must close all open files   }
                END            { before the program ends.     }
            ELSE Halt
        END
END;


{ ------------------------------------------------------------ }
{                    MAIN BODY OF PROGRAM                       }
{ ------------------------------------------------------------ }
BEGIN
    CLRSCR;
    ASSIGN(MyFile, 'students.txt');
    {$I-}                    { Turn off input checking. }
    RESET(MyFile);
    {$I+}                    { Turn input checking back on. }
    IF IORESULT <> 0       { If file-open wasn't a success }
        THEN EnterNewFile(NewFileName, MyFile)
        ELSE BEGIN
            WRITELN(' The file is there!');
            READLN(MyFile, Name);
            CLOSE(MyFile);  { must close file before program ends. }
            END;
    pause;

END.
```

The general form of a GOTO statement, as you can see, is

```
GOTO <label>;
```

where *<label>* is a line identifier that you declared in the LABEL section of the program (see Chapter 3).

There are very definite limitations on GOTO in Turbo Pascal to prevent it from being used indiscriminately. In particular, you cannot use GOTO to jump out of the current code block. This means that if you are inside a subroutine, you can jump only to another place inside that subroutine; you cannot jump out of it to another subroutine, nor can you jump to the main body of the program.

GOTO is pretty much your only option in standard Pascal, but Turbo Pascal provides two other commands that permit you to make jumps: EXIT and HALT. EXIT jumps you out of the current subroutine and returns you to the next line in the calling program or subroutine. HALT, on the other hand, stops the program completely and returns you to DOS. Listing 7.9 shows how you could use HALT instead of GOTO in a situation where you want to password-protect your program.

Listing 7.9

```
PROGRAM Listing7_9;

   { Shows how to use HALT in place of GOTO. }

USES CRT;

TYPE
   String10 = STRING[10];

CONST
   ThePassword = 'frankcapra';

VAR
   Password: String10;

PROCEDURE Pause;
   VAR
      Proceed : CHAR;
   BEGIN
      WRITE(' Press any key to continue ...');
      Proceed := READKEY;
      WRITELN; WRITELN
   END;


PROCEDURE GetPassword(VAR Password : string10);
   BEGIN
      CLRSCR;
      WRITE(' Please enter the password: ');
      READLN(Password);
      IF Password <> ThePassword
```

```
        THEN HALT                       { unauthorized access! }
    END;


BEGIN
    GetPassword(Password);
    WRITELN(' Congratulations! You know the password!');
    pause
END.
```

Compiler Directives

As the name suggests, *compiler directives* are statements in your program that tell the compiler to do things in a certain way. You have already seen one compiler directive in Listing 7.7: there, we used *{$I-}* to turn off input/output (I/O) checking before we tried to open a nonexistent file, and then we used *{$I+}* to turn I/O checking back on again before proceeding with the program.

If we had not turned off I/O checking, then the program would have stopped with a run-time error when it tried to open the file. Turning off I/O checking, however, allowed us to handle the situation in a more controlled way. By checking the built-in variable *IORESULT*, which equals zero if the previous I/O operation was a success, we were able to tell if the file had been opened properly. Then, we either could shut down the program or give the user an opportunity to specify another file.

The compiler directives that you can use, and how you must set them up, are determined by the Pascal compiler you are using. Turbo Pascal, for instance, has different compiler directives than Vax Pascal.

Normally, Turbo Pascal compiles your program with certain default settings: I/O and Stack checking are ON, Range checking is OFF, Debug information is ON, and Complete Boolean evaluation is OFF. Some of these default settings are shown in Figure 7.1, which shows the Compiler Options dialog box from the Options menu. If you change the settings in this dialog box (and save your changes with the Save Options choice in the Options menu), then the new settings will apply to all of your Turbo Pascal programs until you change the settings again.

FIGURE 7.1:

The Compiler Options dialog box

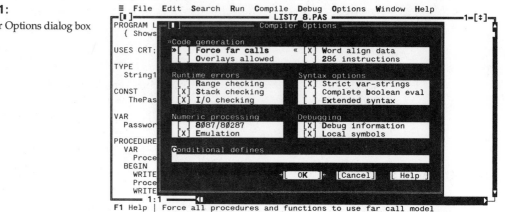

Compiler directives, however, allow you to change the default settings and have your changes apply only to a particular program—even just to one part of a particular program, as shown in Listing 7.7. A compiler directive is a special kind of comment that *is not* ignored by Turbo Pascal. It begins with a left curly bracket, then a dollar sign, then the name of the directive, and finally it closes with a right curly bracket, as we saw in the *{$I-}* and *{$I+}* compiler directives discussed above.

There are three kinds of compiler directives: *switch directives*, which turn a particular compiler option ON or OFF (as with I/O checking); *parameter directives*, which specify values that affect how the program is compiled (such as the size of the heap; see Chapter 11); and *conditional directives*, which tell Turbo Pascal how to handle "conditional compilation" of parts of your program.

There are quite a few compiler directives; here are the ones you are most likely to need often:

- *{$I-}* and *{$I+}*: The first turns input checking off, the second turns it back on again. Input checking will stop your program if it attempts to open a file that is not there, or if it expects a certain kind of input (for example, an integer) but receives something else (such as a letter). Turning off input checking allows you to anticipate these situations and to build some sophisticated error-trapping into your program.

- *{$R-}* and *{$R+}*: The first turns range checking off, the second turns it back on again. When you compile your program, Turbo Pascal normally will not check to see if (for example) you tried to assign a negative number to a BYTE-type variable (legal range 0..255), or if you have referred somewhere to the 101st slot in a 100-slot array variable. This type of error can come out and clobber you (with unpredictable results) when you try to run the program. It is a good idea to turn range checking ON at least while you are developing and debugging your program. You do this by putting the compiler directive *{$R+}* at the beginning of your program. Then, when you are certain that everything is working properly, you can turn it back OFF by deleting the *{$R+}* before your final compilation; this will make your .EXE file slightly smaller.

- *{$S+}* and *{$S-}*: The first turns stack-overflow checking ON, the second turns it OFF. Normally, Turbo Pascal operates with stack-overflow checking ON. The *stack* is an area of your PC's memory that Turbo Pascal uses to store variables and the addresses of subroutines. If you have a lot of subroutine calls and local variables, the amount of memory required can exceed the available stack space—particularly if you have made an error somewhere and your program is spinning out of control. With stack-overflow checking ON, the program will halt with a run-time error if it exceeds the available stack space; with stack-overflow checking OFF, the program will crash, with unpredictable results.

An Error-Checking Substitute for READLN

We've seen in Listing 7.7 that the compiler directive to turn off I/O checking (and turn it on again) can be used to trap errors when opening files. Let's use it to create a generally more useful error-trapping routine: *GetGoodInt*.

It is sad but true that we all make errors at the keyboard. We mean to press one key but press another: a letter instead of a number, for example. Computer programs are extremely unforgiving of even the slightest mistake. Any of the following can cause a run-time error that will halt our program:

- Entering a letter when the program expects a number. For example, we might have an integer variable *Choice* and get input from the keyboard by *READLN(Choice)*. If you enter a number, the program will halt because it expected an integer and it got a letter. I/O checking will not allow this, but at the same time, we cannot simply allow a letter to get through to the program—that could result in consequences that would be even worse!

- Entering a number that is outside the range the program expects. We may have set up a CASE statement that expects to get a number from 1 to 4. We've seen how to build error-checking into a CASE statement with ELSE and IF..THEN..ELSE, but it would be even better if we could trap the errors before they ever get to the CASE statement.

Listing 7.10 shows what can happen when we use a naked READLN statement to get input from the keyboard. Enter and run this program, but instead of keying in a number from 1 to 4 at the menu prompt, type a letter instead. The result is shown in Figure 7.2.

Listing 7.10

```
PROGRAM Listing7_10;

   { Demonstrates potential problems that can arise if we don't
     have an error-trapping input routine. }

USES CRT;

CONST
   Escape = CHR(27);

VAR
   Choice : INTEGER;
   Continue : CHAR;


{ ============== UTILITY ROUTINES FOR THE PROGRAM ============== }

{ ------------------------------- }
{ MAIN-LEVEL PROCEDURE DECLARATION }
{ ------------------------------- }
PROCEDURE Pause;
   VAR
      Proceed : CHAR;
   BEGIN
      WRITE(' Press any key to continue ...');
      Proceed := READKEY;
```

```
      WRITELN; WRITELN
   END;


{ ------------------------------ }
{ MAIN-LEVEL PROCEDURE DECLARATION }
{ ------------------------------ }
PROCEDURE Init(VAR Choice: INTEGER; VAR Continue : CHAR);
   BEGIN
   CLRSCR;
   Choice := 0;
   Continue := ' '
   END;


{ ------------------------------ }
{ MAIN-LEVEL PROCEDURE DECLARATION }
{ ------------------------------ }
PROCEDURE AddRecords;
   BEGIN
   WRITELN;
   WRITELN(' The AddRecords routine has run.');
   WRITELN;
   pause
   END;

{ ------------------------------ }
{ MAIN-LEVEL PROCEDURE DECLARATION }
{ ------------------------------ }
PROCEDURE EditRecords;
   BEGIN
   WRITELN;
   WRITELN(' The EditRecords routine has run.');
   WRITELN;
   pause
   END;

{ ------------------------------ }
{ MAIN-LEVEL PROCEDURE DECLARATION }
{ ------------------------------ }
PROCEDURE DisplayRecords;
   BEGIN
   WRITELN;
   WRITELN(' The DisplayRecords routine has run.');
   WRITELN;
```

```
      pause
      END;


{ ------------------------------- }
{ MAIN-LEVEL PROCEDURE DECLARATION }
{ ------------------------------- }
PROCEDURE Displaymenu(VAR Choice : INTEGER);
   BEGIN
      CLRSCR;
      WRITELN; WRITELN;
      WRITELN('        MAIN MENU');
      WRITELN('        ---------');
      WRITELN('        1. Add Records');
      WRITELN('        2. Edit Records');
      WRITELN('        3. Display Records');
      WRITELN('        4. Quit');
      WRITELN;
      WRITE('        Enter your choice (1-4): ');
      READLN(Choice)
   END;


{ ------------------------------- }
{ MAIN-LEVEL PROCEDURE DECLARATION }
{ ------------------------------- }
PROCEDURE DoChoice(VAR Choice : INTEGER);
   BEGIN
      CASE Choice OF
         1 : AddRecords;
         2 : EditRecords;
         3 : DisplayRecords;
         4 : Continue := Escape
         END
   END;



{ ------------------------------------------------------------ }
{                   MAIN BODY OF PROGRAM                       }
{ ------------------------------------------------------------ }
BEGIN
   Init(choice, continue);
   REPEAT
```

```
        DisplayMenu(choice);
        DoChoice(choice)
    UNTIL Continue = Escape;
    CLRSCR
END.
```

Even if you protect your CASE statement with an ELSE (or IF clause), the program will still stop if you enter something that is the wrong data type for the variable in the READLN statement. To protect against these kinds of errors, we need something more sophisticated—and we need to use the I/O checking compiler directive to let us get the input and to handle it without errors.

Before we start coding, we need to have a clear idea of what we are trying to accomplish. We want to create an input routine that will do the following:

- Get integer input from the keyboard, just like a READLN statement with an integer variable.

- Take *any* input character from the user and inspect it before passing it to the integer variable.

- Check to make sure that the input character is the correct data type; that is, that it is an integer.

- Check to make sure that the input integer is in the acceptable range—in this case, that it is an integer from 1 to 4.

FIGURE 7.2:

Run-time error caused by entering an unexpected data type

- If the input character *is not* the correct data type or *is not* in the acceptable range, then blank the screen where the user typed the character and continue to display the prompt.

This is what the *GetGoodInt* procedure in Listing 7.11 does. It uses a few Turbo Pascal features that we have not covered yet, but here is how it works. After we've used WRITE to prompt the user for a number between 1 and 4, we call *GetGoodInt* just as we would normally call READLN. The difference is that with READLN, we specify only the variable that gets the input value.

Listing 7.11

```
PROGRAM Listing7_11;

USES CRT;

CONST
   Escape = CHR(27);

VAR
   Choice : INTEGER;
   Continue : CHAR;


{ ============== UTILITY ROUTINES FOR THE PROGRAM ============== }

{ -------------------------------- }
{ MAIN-LEVEL PROCEDURE DECLARATION }
{ -------------------------------- }
PROCEDURE Pause;
   VAR
      Proceed : CHAR;
   BEGIN
      WRITE(' Press any key to continue ...');
      Proceed := READKEY;
      WRITELN; WRITELN
   END;


{ -------------------------------- }
{ MAIN-LEVEL PROCEDURE DECLARATION }
{ -------------------------------- }
```

```
PROCEDURE GetGoodInt(MinNum, MaxNum: INTEGER;  VAR InNum: INTEGER);

   { An error-trapping substitute for "readln" to get integer
     input from the keyboard. This procedure takes two parameters:
     a set of "acceptable" integers for input, and a variable
     parameter that is the actual integer input.  If the input
     integer is not in the set of acceptable integers, this
     procedure returns to the original screen position and waits
     for the user to enter an acceptable integer. }

   VAR
      markX, markY  : BYTE;
      LoopControl   : INTEGER;

   BEGIN
      REPEAT
         markX := whereX;    { mark cursor location }
         markY := whereY;

         {$I-}                    { I/O checking off }
         Readln(InNum);          { Get character from keyboard }
         {$I+}                    { I/O checking back on }
         LoopControl := ioresult; { Was input a "Good Integer"? }

         IF (LoopControl <> 0) THEN   { if not integer type }
      BEGIN
      gotoXY(markX, markY);        { return to orig. cursor pos. }
      ClrEOL                       { clear to end of line        }
      END;

         IF (inNum < MinNum) or (inNum > MaxNum) THEN { not in range }
      BEGIN
      gotoXY(markX, markY); { returns to original cursor pos. }
      ClrEOL                { clears to end of line           }
      END

      until (LoopControl = 0) { correct data type entered }
           and (InNum >= MinNum) and (InNum <= MaxNum)
                           { number entered in acceptable range }
      END;


{ ------------------------------- }
{ MAIN-LEVEL PROCEDURE DECLARATION }
{ ------------------------------- }
```

```
PROCEDURE Init(VAR Choice: INTEGER; VAR Continue : CHAR);
    BEGIN
    CLRSCR;
    Choice := 0;
    Continue := ' '
    END;



{ ------------------------------- }
{ MAIN-LEVEL PROCEDURE DECLARATION }
{ ------------------------------- }
PROCEDURE AddRecords;
    BEGIN
    WRITELN;
    WRITELN(' The AddRecords routine has run.');
    WRITELN;
    pause
    END;


{ ------------------------------- }
{ MAIN-LEVEL PROCEDURE DECLARATION }
{ ------------------------------- }
PROCEDURE EditRecords;
    BEGIN
    WRITELN;
    WRITELN(' The EditRecords routine has run.');
    WRITELN;
    pause
    END;


{ ------------------------------- }
{ MAIN-LEVEL PROCEDURE DECLARATION }
{ ------------------------------- }
PROCEDURE DisplayRecords;
    BEGIN
    WRITELN;
    WRITELN(' The DisplayRecords routine has run.');
    WRITELN;
    pause
    END;


{ ------------------------------- }
{ MAIN-LEVEL PROCEDURE DECLARATION }
{ ------------------------------- }
```

```
PROCEDURE Displaymenu(VAR Choice : INTEGER);
   BEGIN
      CLRSCR;
      WRITELN; WRITELN;
      WRITELN('        MAIN MENU');
      WRITELN('        ---------');
      WRITELN('        1. Add Records');
      WRITELN('        2. Edit Records');
      WRITELN('        3. Display Records');
      WRITELN('        4. Quit');
      WRITELN;
      WRITE('        Enter your choice (1-4): ');
      GetGoodInt(1,4,Choice)
   END;



{ ------------------------------- }
{ MAIN-LEVEL PROCEDURE DECLARATION }
{ ------------------------------- }
PROCEDURE DoChoice(VAR Choice : INTEGER);
   BEGIN
      CASE Choice OF
          1 : AddRecords;
          2 : EditRecords;
          3 : DisplayRecords;
          4 : Continue := Escape
          END
   END;



{ --------------------------------------------------------------- }
{                      MAIN BODY OF PROGRAM                        }
{ --------------------------------------------------------------- }
BEGIN
   Init(choice, continue);
   REPEAT
      DisplayMenu(choice);
      DoChoice(choice)
   UNTIL Continue = Escape;
   CLRSCR
END.
```

With *GetGoodInt*, on the other hand, we specify the minimum acceptable value, the maximum acceptable value, and the variable, in that order. If the user tries to enter something that is not an integer, or is not between the minimum and maximum values (inclusive), then *GetGoodInt* will erase what the user typed and sit there, waiting patiently for valid input.

Notice one other important thing about Listing 7.11. As soon as we checked the data type of the input item with IORESULT, we assigned the value of IORESULT to the *LoopControl* variable and used *LoopControl* for all other tests. The reason for doing this is that the value of IORESULT changes as soon as your program does another operation, such as comparing it to zero. Thus, the only way to use the value of IORESULT in successive program statements is to assign it to another variable *immediately* after the I/O operation you are using IORESULT to test.

We will use *GetGoodInt* often in later chapters. In the next chapter, we will create an error-trapping routine for getting character input. It is not easy, but you now possess the knowledge and skills to do it.

CHAPTER
EIGHT

Structured and User-Defined Data Types

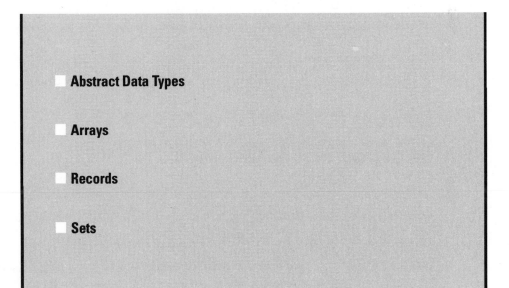

- **Abstract Data Types**

- **Arrays**

- **Records**

- **Sets**

In Chapter 6, we looked at simple data types, such as text strings and numbers. These data types are not only simple, they are also predefined in Turbo Pascal, so you do not need to set them up in each program yourself.

In this chapter, we will discuss some more complex data types. These, in addition to being complex, are data types that you define for yourself. Far from being an extra burden, this gives you a great deal of flexibility to make your Pascal program work the way *you* want it to—whether or not your ideas agree with the ideas that are built into the language.

Abstract Data Types

Before we begin our discussion about particular data types, we need to make a very important point. Pascal lets you create complex data types—often called data structures—in some fairly specific ways. For example, it has a built-in data type called ARRAY that allows you to set up lists and tables (as well as other structures) to hold a fixed number of items of a given type. The items can be integers, characters, strings, records, pointers, objects, or even other arrays.

The important point is that you must keep two concepts separate. There is a clear distinction between an *idea* and its *implementation* as in:

1. The idea of a fixed-length list that holds items of a particular type, and

2. The specific way that fixed-length lists are implemented in Pascal and the specific words used to describe them.

The idea of a fixed-length list is called an *abstract data type*. Fixed-length lists can be implemented in many different ways, not all of them having anything to do with the word ARRAY, which is the data type normally used to create them in Pascal. In Pascal, you can set up a fixed-length list by creating the list type in the TYPE section and then declaring a variable of that type in the VAR section, as in the following:

```
TYPE
   Student = RECORD
             Name : STRING[10];
             GPA  : REAL;
             Probation : BOOLEAN
             END;
```

```
      { creates a data type for student records }

   StudentList = ARRAY[1..100] of Student;
      { creates a data type for listing student records }

   NumberList = ARRAY[1..50] of INTEGER;
      { creates a data type for listing integers }

VAR
   Enrollment   : StudentList;
      { creates a list to hold 100 student records }

   Top50        : NumberList;
      { creates a list to hold 50 integers }
   UnitedStates : ARRAY[1..50] OF STRING[15];
      { creates a list to hold 50 15-character strings }
```

(Note that you don't absolutely have to declare an ARRAY data type in the TYPE section. As with the *UnitedStates* variable above, you can simply declare an ARRAY variable in the VAR section.)

In BASIC, however, you create an array with a DIM (dimension) statement, as in the following:

```
TYPE Student
    Name AS STRING * 10
    GPA AS SINGLE
    Probation AS INTEGER
END TYPE
; Creates a data type for student records

DIM StudentList(1 TO 100) AS STUDENT
; Creates a list variable to hold 100 student records
```

Although these BASIC data structures are usually referred to as arrays, the word ARRAY is not part of the BASIC language. In addition, BASIC allows you to create what are called dynamic arrays that are, in fact, *variable*-length arrays—an idea that is almost a self-contradiction in Pascal.

The bottom line is this: *Do not be misled* into thinking that the way a programming language implements an idea is the only way to do it—or that the *idea* has some necessary connection with the *words* used to describe it in a particular language. By keeping these distinctions in mind, you will gain two important benefits:

1. You will understand what you are *actually doing* when you set up data types, instead of doing everything just by rote. This is more fun, makes you a better programmer, and (in class work) gets you a better grade.

2. You will see that there are different ways to accomplish the same thing. For example, in Chapter 11, we will create variable-length lists by using pointers. However, you also can create a variable-length list by using several arrays. If you think you can only create a variable-length list by using pointers, then you will be helpless if you ever need to create variable-length lists in a language that does not have pointers, such as BASIC or FORTRAN. But if you keep the clear distinction in your mind between an idea and its implementation, then you will be able to handle such situations with the confidence that comes when you know what you are really doing.

Arrays

With that rather philosophical introduction, let's begin with Pascal's ARRAY data type, which is ideally suited to handling fixed-length lists.

The best way to think of an array is as a sort of "rack" having a predetermined number of slots that can hold items of a certain type (see Figure 8.1). It is similar to a compact disc or cassette tape rack. You create an array data type by using the Pascal word ARRAY, indicating the number of slots in the array, and indicating the type of items that will go into the slots of the array. You refer to the individual slots of the array by combining the name of the array variable with the slot index (usually a number).

FIGURE 8.1:

Individual variables vs. arrays

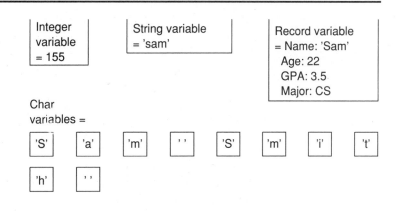

| Integer variable = 155 | String variable = 'sam' | Record variable = Name: 'Sam' Age: 22 GPA: 3.5 Major: CS |

Char variables =

| 'S' | 'a' | 'm' | ' ' | 'S' | 'm' | 'i' | 't' |

| 'h' | ' ' |

Think of an array as a "rack" in which there are slots for a fixed number of variables of a certain type.

Array of six integers

| 20 | 4 | 31715 | -279 | 0 | 4 |

Array of strings

| 'Sam' | 'Jim' | 'Sue' | 'Tom' | 'Deb' | 'Wil' |

Array of 10 characters

| 'S' | 'a' | 'm' | ' ' | 'S' | 'm' | 'i' | 't' | 'h' | ' ' |

Array of records

'Sam'	'Jim'	'Sue'	'Tom'	'Deb'	'Wil'
22	19	17	21	18	17
3.5	4.0	3.8	3.6	3.6	3.9
CS	Phys	Chem	Bus	Engl	Music

You can declare an array type in the TYPE section of your program as follows:

```
TYPE
    MyList = ARRAY[m..n] OF <slot type>
```

where:

- *MyList* is the name of the new data type you are declaring.

- *m* and *n* are members of an ordinal type (called the *index type* for the array), with *m* lower than *n*. They can be any ordinal data type, including characters, integers, and Boolean values. Normally, you will use a subrange of the full data type; for example, instead of using all integers (which is too many), you will use [1..10], [0..999], or [50..59]. Note that [1..10] and [50..59] both define a 10-slot array; the only difference is in the indexes by which you refer to the slots. You also can use enumerated types that you have defined yourself (for example, *ARRAY[Sun..Sat]*).

- *m* and *n* must be constants; they cannot be variables. The size of the array is determined when the program is compiled, and if you try to use a variable as the upper or lower bound of the array indexes, Pascal cannot determine the size of the array.

- The *<slot type>* is the type of item that you intend to hold in the array. This can be any legal data type except a file or a stream (the object-oriented counterpart of a file).

Thus, the following are all valid array types:

```
TYPE
    MyList = ARRAY[1..100] OF STRING[10];

    ToDoItems = ARRAY[1..10] OF STRING[15];
    Days = (Sun, Mon, Tue, Wed, Thu, Fri, Sat);
    Week = ARRAY[Sun..Sat] OF ToDoItems;

    CapLetters = ARRAY['A'..'Z'] OF CHAR;
```

Declaring Array Variables

It is important to remember—and easy to forget—that simply *declaring* an array data type does not create any arrays. Thus, if you attempted to put something into *MyList* (above), such as

```
MyList[55] := 'Sam';
```

your program would not compile, because the *MyList* declaration in the TYPE section only defines a data type: it does not create any members of that type. We can define the *concepts* of unicorns and gryphons, but it doesn't automatically mean that there *are* any of them. In the same way, before you can use an array type, you have to represent the idea as a concrete instance of the variable in the VAR section.

Strictly speaking, with most array variables, you do not have to declare the array type in the TYPE section of your program. This is because ARRAY is a predefined type in Pascal, and you are just specifying how big it is and what it will hold. Thus, the following two code fragments are equivalent:

```
TYPE
    MyList : ARRAY[1..10] of STRING[10];
VAR
    NameList : MyList;
```

and

```
VAR
    NameList : ARRAY[1..10] OF STRING[10];
```

However, if you ever want to pass an array variable to a subroutine (as you will very often need to do), then you *do* have to declare the type in your TYPE section. A parameter that you pass to a subroutine has to be of a predefined type, so you could not write something like

```
PROCEDURE AddName(VAR NameList : ARRAY[1..10] OF STRING[10]);
```

Instead, you have to use a type that is either predefined in Pascal or declared in the TYPE section of your program, as in

```
TYPE
    MyList = ARRAY[1..10] OF STRING[10];
{ ... etc. }

PROCEDURE AddName(VAR NameList : MyList);
{ ... etc. }
```

You refer to individual elements of an array by combining the name of the array with the index of the particular slot, such as

```
VAR
    NameList : ARRAY[1..10] OF STRING[10];
BEGIN
```

```
    NameList[1] := 'Bill';  { assigns 'Bill' to slot 1 }
    WRITELN(' Name in slot 1 is ', NameList[1], '.');
END;
```

Arrays make our programs neater, faster, and easier to understand. For example, we could keep the names of students in a programming class in separate string variables as in Listing 8.1; however, arrays permit us to keep the names all together in a single list, as in Listing 8.2.

Listing 8.1

```
PROGRAM Listing8_1;

    { Using separate string variables for the items in a list.}

USES CRT;

TYPE
    String10 = STRING[10];

VAR
    Student1,
    Student2,
    Student3,
    Student4,
    Student5      : String10;

PROCEDURE Pause;
    VAR
        Proceed : CHAR;
    BEGIN
        WRITE(' Press any key to continue ...');
        Proceed := READKEY;
        WRITELN; WRITELN
    END;



BEGIN
    Student1 := 'Jim';
    Student2 := 'Tammy';
    Student3 := 'Oral';
    Student4 := 'Billy';
```

```
                    Student5 := 'Elmer';

                    CLRSCR;
                    WRITELN(' The name of student # 1 is ', Student1, '.');
                    WRITELN(' The name of student # 2 is ', Student2, '.');
                    WRITELN(' The name of student # 3 is ', Student3, '.');
                    WRITELN(' The name of student # 4 is ', Student4, '.');
                    WRITELN(' The name of student # 5 is ', Student5, '.');
                    pause
                 END.
```

Listing 8.2

```
PROGRAM Listing8_2;

   { Demonstrates use of array type to hold students names. This
     makes the program much more flexible, because if the class
     size changes, all that is required to change the progam
     is to modify the constant "NumberOfStudents." }

USES CRT;

CONST
   NumberOfStudents = 5;

TYPE
   String10 = STRING[10];
   StudentList = ARRAY[1..NumberOfStudents] OF String10;

VAR
   Class : StudentList;
   Continue : CHAR;

PROCEDURE Pause;
   VAR
      Proceed : CHAR;
   BEGIN
      WRITE(' Press any key to continue ...');
      Proceed := READKEY;
      WRITELN; WRITELN
   END;

PROCEDURE Initialize(VAR Class : StudentList;
                     VAR Continue : CHAR);
   VAR
```

```
      Counter : INTEGER;
   BEGIN
      Continue := 'Y';
      FOR Counter := 1 TO NumberOfStudents DO
         Class[Counter] := '              '
   END;

PROCEDURE EnterStudentName(VAR Class : StudentList);
   VAR
      Counter : INTEGER;
   BEGIN
      Counter := 1;              { initialize counter variable }

      WHILE (Class[Counter] <> '              ')      { find first empty slot }
         AND (Counter < NumberOfStudents) DO
            Counter := counter + 1;

      IF (Counter = NumberOfStudents)              { test to see if }
      AND (Class[Counter] <> '              ')         { array is full. }
         THEN WRITELN(' Sorry. The array is full.')
         ELSE BEGIN
            WRITELN;
            WRITE(' Enter the student name: ');
            READLN(Class[Counter]);
            WRITELN;
            WRITELN(' The name you entered was ', Class[Counter], '.');
            pause
            END
   END;                  { of EnterStudentName subroutine }

BEGIN
   CLRSCR;
   Initialize(class, continue);
   REPEAT
      EnterStudentName(class);
      WRITE(' Enter another (Y/N)? ');
      READLN(Continue)
      UNTIL UPCASE(Continue) = 'N'
END.
```

There are several things to notice about Listing 8.2. First, the array should be initialized. Second, because the array will hold only a predetermined number of items, we need to test it to make sure that it is not already full.

Initializing Arrays

When Pascal sets up an array variable, it reserves an area of your PC's memory to hold the variable—that is, the array and the values in its slots. This memory area could contain almost anything, so it is important to initialize an array before you use it. This means putting an *empty* value into all the slots so that you can tell which slots are empty and which are occupied. It doesn't really matter what value you use for empty, as long as (1) it is something that cannot be mistaken for any of the values that eventually will be put into the slots, and (2) it is the right data type to fit into the array's slots.

Thus, in Listing 8.2, the array holds 10-character strings. To initialize the array, we used a FOR loop to assign an empty value of a space character to each slot. This enabled us, in the *EnterStudentName* subroutine, to find the first empty slot for a new student name, or to determine that the array was full. If the array had been set up to hold integers instead of strings, we might have used '0' to fill all the slots—as long as we knew that a zero value would never be assigned as an *actual* value for a slot in the array.

Testing for a Full Array

The other task you have to do, before trying to put data into the array, is to see if it is already full (as in Listing 8.2). If you try to put additional values into an array that is already full, you will either get a run-time error in your program or you will corrupt your data.

In the section of this chapter called "Records," you will learn an easier way to handle this problem.

Traversing an Array

Now that you know how to set up an array, we should discuss a few basic ideas about how to use the data in an array. In Listing 8.3, we will look at how to *traverse* an array, which means starting at the first slot and moving through the array slot-by-slot until we reach the end. After that, we will consider how to search an array for a particular target value, such as a name in a record.

Listing 8.3

```
PROGRAM Listing8_3;

   { Demonstrates how to traverse an array-based list. }

USES CRT;

CONST
   NumberOfStudents = 3;


TYPE
   string10 = STRING[10];

   Student = RECORD
             Fname  : string10;
             GPA    : REAL
             END;

   Roster = ARRAY[1..10] OF Student;

VAR
   SList : Roster;

PROCEDURE Pause;
   VAR
      Proceed : CHAR;
   BEGIN
      WRITE(' Press any key to continue ...');
      Proceed := READKEY;
      WRITELN; WRITELN
   END;

PROCEDURE InitializeList(VAR SList : Roster);
      { Note that because SList is an array of records (explained
        in the next section), each item in SList is itself a
        record. Therefore, we can use the WITH notation (explained
        in the next section) to refer to the fields in the record. }
   VAR
      LoopCounter : INTEGER;
   BEGIN
      FOR LoopCounter := 1 TO 10 DO
         BEGIN
         SList[LoopCounter].Fname := ' ';
```

```
                SList[LoopCounter].GPA := 0.00
                END
        END;

PROCEDURE LoadUpList(VAR SList : Roster);
     VAR
          LoopCounter : INTEGER;
     BEGIN
          CLRSCR;
     FOR LoopCounter := 1 TO NumberOfStudents DO
          WITH SList[LoopCounter] DO
               BEGIN
               WRITE(' Enter name of student number ', LoopCounter, ': ');
               READLN(SList[LoopCounter].Fname);
               WRITELN;
               WRITE(' Enter his/her GPA, from 0.00 TO 4.00: ');
               READLN(GPA);
               WRITELN
               END
END;

PROCEDURE TraverseList(SList : Roster);
     VAR
          Slot : INTEGER;
     BEGIN
          Slot := 1;
          CLRSCR;
          REPEAT
               WRITE(' The name in node ', slot, ' of the list ');
               WRITELN('is ', SList[Slot].fname, ',');
               WRITELN(' with a GPA of ', SList[Slot].GPA:0:2, '.');
               Slot := Slot + 1;
               WRITELN;
               pause
          UNTIL (SList[Slot].Fname = ' ') OR (Slot = 10);
          WRITELN;
          WRITELN(' That''s the end of the list!');
          WRITELN(' There were ', (slot - 1), ' student records counted.');
          WRITELN
     END;
```

```
{ ------------------------------------------------------ }
{                   MAIN BODY OF PROGRAM                  }
{ ------------------------------------------------------ }
BEGIN
    CLRSCR;
    InitializeList(SList);
    LoadUpList(SList);
    TraverseList(SList);
    pause
END.
```

In Listing 8.3, we set up a simple record type called *Student*, which contains the first name and grade-point average of each student. Then, using an array, we set up a list type to hold the student records and, in the VAR section, create a variable of that list type. Then, we created procedures to do the following:

- *InitializeList* enters "blank" values in the fields of every record in the array. When we are traversing the list, this enables us to determine if the end of the list has been reached even when the list does not occupy the entire array.

- *LoadUpList* enables us to load some student names and grade-point averages into the list. When we traverse the list, these names and grade-point averages will be displayed on the screen.

- *TraverseList* visits each record in the array, displays its contents on the screen, and then moves on to the next record. This process continues until the end of the list is reached: the REPEAT statement tells the program to continue moving forward in the list until it reaches either a blank record or the end of the array. Note how, in the program line that begins with UNTIL, we use the "blank" contents of empty records (put there by the *InitializeList* routine) to determine if the end of the list has been reached.

Note that in the *TraverseList* routine, we could have declared *SList* as a VAR parameter even though *TraverseList* is not supposed to make any changes in it. For reasons to be discussed in Chapter 9, this would reduce the memory requirements of the program but would introduce the risk of an accidental change to the *SList* array. Here, for both simplicity and safety, we've chosen not to declare it as a VAR parameter.

The main body of the program, as usual, is only a few lines long and shows the overall structure of the program.

Sequential Search of an Array

Traversing the array in Listing 8.3 is useful if you want to see all the records in the list, but it is an inefficient method to find a specific record. For that task, you need a more specialized routine to search the list until it finds the record you want.

The search routine we will use here is called *sequential search*. It is slower and less sophisticated than some other search routines we will see in Chapter 18, but it does an adequate job. It also works with unsorted lists, while the more sophisticated search routines often require that lists be sorted before they can be searched. Sequential search is illustrated in Listing 8.4.

Listing 8.4

```
PROGRAM Listing8_4;

   { Demonstrates how to search an array-based list. }

USES CRT;

CONST
   NumberOfStudents = 3;


TYPE
   string10 = STRING[10];

   Student = RECORD
             Fname  : string10;
             GPA    : REAL
             END;

   Roster = ARRAY[1..10] OF Student;

VAR
   SList : Roster;

PROCEDURE Pause;
   VAR
      Proceed : CHAR;
```

```
BEGIN
   WRITE(' Press any key to continue ...');
   Proceed := READKEY;
   WRITELN; WRITELN
END;

PROCEDURE InitializeList(VAR SList : Roster);
     { Note that because SList is an array of records (explained
        in the next section), each item in SList is itself a
        record. Therefore, we can use the WITH notation (explained
        in the next section) to refer to the fields in the record. }
   VAR
      LoopCounter : INTEGER;
   BEGIN
      FOR LoopCounter := 1 TO 10 DO
      BEGIN
      SList[LoopCounter].Fname := ' ';
      SList[LoopCounter].GPA := 0.00
      END
   END;

PROCEDURE LoadUpList(VAR SList : Roster);
   VAR
      LoopCounter : INTEGER;
   BEGIN
      CLRSCR;
   FOR LoopCounter := 1 TO NumberOfStudents DO
      WITH SList[LoopCounter] DO
         BEGIN
         WRITE(' Enter the name of student number ', LoopCounter, ': ');
         READLN(SList[LoopCounter].Fname);
         WRITELN;
         WRITE(' Enter his/her GPA, from 0.00 TO 4.00: ');
         READLN(GPA);
         WRITELN
         END
   END;

PROCEDURE SearchList(SList : Roster);
   VAR
      Slot      : INTEGER;
      SearchKey : string10;
      Found     : BOOLEAN;
   BEGIN
      Slot := 1;
```

```
      Found := FALSE;
      CLRSCR;
      WRITE(' Enter the student name for which to search: ');
      READLN(SearchKey);
      WHILE (Found = FALSE) AND (Slot <= 10) DO
         BEGIN
            IF SList[slot].fname = SearchKey
            THEN BEGIN
               WRITELN(' Search target found at slot #', slot, '!');
               Found := TRUE
               END
            ELSE slot := slot + 1
         END;
      IF Found = FALSE THEN WRITELN(' Search string not found.');
      pause
   END;


{ ----------------------------------------------------------------- }
{                      MAIN BODY OF PROGRAM                          }
{ ----------------------------------------------------------------- }
BEGIN
   CLRSCR;
   InitializeList(SList);
   LoadUpList(SList);
   SearchList(SList);
   pause
END.
```

Listing 8.4 is identical to Listing 8.3 except for the fact that we have replaced the *TraverseList* routine with a *SearchList* routine. As expected, *SearchList* takes *SList* as a parameter and has three local variables:

- *Slot*, an integer variable that is used to hold the number of the array slot we are currently inspecting;

- *SearchKey*, a string variable that holds the name for which we are searching; and

- *Found*, a Boolean variable that indicates whether or not the string in *Search-Key* has been found in the *SList* array.

First, the *SearchList* sets the *Slot* and *Found* variables to their initial values. Then, it prompts the user to enter a search string, which is stored in the *SearchKey* variable.

Then, a WHILE loop begins stepping through the array, one slot at a time. At each slot, it compares the *Fname* field of the student record to the *SearchKey* variable.

If the two match, the program displays a message on-screen that the search string has been found. It then sets the *Found* variable to true and drops out of the WHILE loop. If there is not a match, it increases the slot number by one and goes through the loop again, repeating the process until either the *Found* variable becomes true or the end of the array is reached. If the search string is never found, then the program displays a "not found" message on the screen.

The main body of the program matches Listing 8.3 exactly, except for calling *SearchList* instead of *TraverseList*.

Multidimensional Arrays

Although we have used an array to create a list, you also can use arrays to create more complex two- and three-dimensional table structures, as shown in Figure 8.2. You create a multidimensional array by declaring multiple coordinates in your array definition, as in the following:

```
TYPE
   TwoDTable = ARRAY[1..8, 1..4] OF STRING[15];
   ThreeDTable = ARRAY[1..8, 1..4, 1..3] OF STRING[15];
```

You then can refer to slots in variables of these array types by multiple coordinates, as in:

```
MyTwoDTable[3,4]
MyThreeDTable[3,4,2]
```

Internally, Pascal treats all arrays as one-dimensional lists. In your PC's memory, Pascal stores everything in the first slot of the first array (including other array slots), then everything in the second slot, and so forth. But, fortunately, you don't often have to worry about this.

Advantages and Disadvantages of Arrays

The biggest advantage of arrays, in terms of what we have looked at so far, is that they allow us to create a unified list or table of values that we can traverse from one end to the other, as we did in the *EnterStudentName* procedure of Listing 8.2. In a list, there are usually next and previous members of the list, which you reach by

FIGURE 8.2:

Two- and three-dimensional arrays

ARRAY [1..8, 1..4] = ARRAY [1..8] OF ARRAY [1..4]

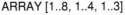

ARRAY [1..8, 1..4, 1..3]
= ARRAY [1..8] OF ARRAY [1..4] OF ARRAY [1..3]

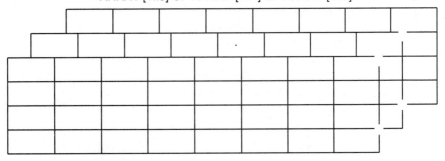

moving forward or backward in the list. With stand-alone variables, however, there is no easy way to create such a unified list. When you need to search for a given value or put a group of values in a certain order, it helps tremendously to have them in a list.

The biggest disadvantage of arrays, in terms of what we have looked at so far, is that they tend to waste memory. When you set up a list or a table with an array, you need to give it the maximum number of slots that you will ever possibly need. This means that most of the time, some—or even a majority—of the slots in the array will be empty. One way is to set up a special index function (called an *access function*) to create triangular, diagonal, or other odd-shaped tables that provide multidimensional arrays but require less memory.

Compared to other ways of setting up lists (for example, with pointers, which will be discussed in Chapter 11), array operations are much faster because all the elements of the array are stored side-by-side in your PC's memory. To find the next element in a list by using a pointer, you first have to look at the pointer, and then you have to go to the memory address to which it points. This two-step process is slower than going directly to the *n*th slot of an array, but it usually requires less memory.

Records

In Pascal, a *record* is simply a way to combine several different data items in the same wrapper. The data items can be of the same or different data types; there can be only one, or there can be many. In a record definition, each slot for a data item is called a *field*.

Therefore, you must be clear at the outset that although you can use Pascal records for what are ordinarily called records (such as student records), there is no necessary connection between the two concepts. Records in Pascal are used for many other things.

To define a record type in your program, you use the reserved word RECORD and then list the field names of the record along with the data type of each field. You finish the record type definition with the word END. Thus, the following are all legal record types:

```
CONST
   NumberStudents = 5;

TYPE
   String2  = STRING[2];
   String5  = STRING[5];
   String10 = STRING[10];
   String20 = STRING[20];

   Students = RECORD
               List : ARRAY[1..NumberStudents] of String10;
               Current : INTEGER
               END;

   StudentRec  = RECORD
```

```
              Fname,
              Lname  : String10;
              Address: String20;
              City   : String10;
              State  : String2;
              Zip    : String5;
              GPA    : SINGLE;
              Class  : INTEGER
              END;
```

```
Enrollment = ARRAY[1..NumberStudents] of StudentRec;
```

Just as with arrays, it is important to remember that simply declaring a record type in the TYPE section of your program does *not* create any records. To do that, you have to declare a variable in the VAR section of your program and specify that it is of the record type you want, as in:

```
VAR
   Class : Students;
   Joe   : StudentRec;
```

You refer to the fields of a record by using the name of the record variable, a period, and the field name. Thus, for example, if we created (as above) a variable called *Class* that is of type *Students,* we could refer to the individual elements of the array in the list field by *Class.list[n],* where *n* is the index of the array slot to which we want to refer. Listing 8.5 shows how to use a record in this way to simplify the *EnterStudentName* procedure in Listing 8.2.

Listing 8.5

```
PROGRAM Listing8_5;

   { Shows how to embed an array inside of a record to make
     list operations easier. }

USES CRT;

CONST
   NumberStudents = 3;

TYPE
   String10 = STRING[10];
   Students = RECORD
               List: ARRAY[1..NumberStudents] OF String10;
```

```
            Current : INTEGER
            END;

VAR
   Class : Students;
   Continue : CHAR;

PROCEDURE Pause;
   VAR
       Proceed : CHAR;
    BEGIN
      WRITE(' Press any key to continue ...');
      Proceed := READKEY;
      WRITELN; WRITELN
    END;

PROCEDURE Initialize(VAR Class : Students;
                     VAR Continue : CHAR);
   VAR
      Counter : INTEGER;
   BEGIN
      Continue := 'Y';
      FOR Counter := 1 TO NumberStudents DO
         Class.List[Counter] := ' ';
      Class.Current := 1
   END;

PROCEDURE EnterStudentName(VAR Class : Students);
   VAR
      Counter : INTEGER;
   BEGIN
      Counter := 1;                { initialize counter variable }

      IF Class.Current <= NumberStudents
         THEN BEGIN
            WRITELN;
            WRITE(' Enter the student name: ');
            READLN(Class.list[Class.current]);
            WRITE(' The name you entered was ');
            WRITELN(Class.list[Class.current]);
            Class.current := Class.current + 1;
            END
         ELSE BEGIN
            WRITELN(' Sorry. The array is full.');
            pause;
```

```
            halt
            END;
   END;                    { of EnterStudentName subroutine }

BEGIN
   CLRSCR;
   Initialize(class, continue);
   REPEAT
      EnterStudentName(Class);
      WRITE(' Enter another (Y/N)? ');
      READLN(Continue)
      UNTIL (UPCASE(Continue) = 'N')
END.
```

Notice that in Listing 8.5, we no longer had to start at the beginning of the list and look for the first open slot. By using a record, we added a slot counter, *Class.Current*, to keep track of which slot we should use next. Each time we added a new item to the array, we added 1 to *Class.Current*. When *Class.Current* finally exceeded the upper limit of the list, we automatically knew that the array was full.

Using a WITH Clause

Of course, if you have many statements with the same record variable, the dot-notation can become pretty tedious. With a student record, for example, we might write the following:

```
Joe.Fname := 'Joe';
Joe.Lname := 'Smith';
Joe.Address := '123 Maple Drive';
Joe.City := 'Delafield';
Joe.State := 'WI';
Joe.Zip := '53018';
Joe.GPA := 3.50;
Joe.Class := 4;
```

Using a WITH clause makes it unnecessary to repeat the name of the record variable each time you want to access its fields. You need to remember, however, that a WITH clause applies only to the very next statement that comes after it. To do the same thing as above by using a WITH clause, you would write

```
WITH Joe DO
BEGIN
   Fname := 'Joe';
   Lname := 'Smith';
```

```
      Address := '123 Maple Drive';
      City := 'Delafield';
      State := 'WI';
      Zip := '53018';
      GPA := 3.50;
      Class := 4
END;
```

If you had an array of records, such as a list of student records, you would use the WITH clause as follows:

```
WITH List[n] DO { List[n] is the record in array slot n }
   BEGIN
      Fname := 'Sue';
      Lname := 'Storm';
      { ... etc. }
   END;
```

Of course, you could set up a loop to increase n to keep adding new records to the array as long as you wanted to (at least until the array was full).

Variant Records

Sometimes, you will need a record type that can use different fields depending on the values of other fields. For example, a university might have some students who live in dormitories on campus, while others live in apartments off-campus. In that case, you can set up your record type to have a "dorm rent" field if the student lives on campus. To do this, you embed a CASE statement in the record definition, as follows:

```
TYPE
   StudentRec  = RECORD
                   Fname,
                   Lname  : String10;
                   Address: String20;
                   City   : String10;
                   State  : String2;
                   Zip    : String5;
                   GPA    : SINGLE;
                   Class  : INTEGER;
                   CASE OnCampus : BOOLEAN of
                      TRUE : (DormRent : SINGLE;
                              RentPaid : BOOLEAN);
                      FALSE: (Age : INTEGER;
```

```
                               ParentPermission : BOOLEAN)
                END;
```

In student records where the *OnCampus* field is true, then the record will also have the *DormRent* and *RentPaid* fields. If the *OnCampus* field is false, then the record will have the *Age* and *ParentPermission* fields.

Sets

A set is just a collection of things. In Pascal, a set is a collection of simple-data-type items. To create a set variable, you declare it in the *VAR* section of your program, as follows:

```
VAR
   GoodChars : SET OF CHAR;   { declares set variable }
BEGIN
GoodChars := ['Y','y','N','n']; {assigns value to set}
```

The specific syntax of a set declaration is as follows, where *BaseType* is the simple data type of the items included in the set:

```
VAR
   MySet : SET OF BaseType;
```

Note that this declaration simply creates *MySet* as a set variable that can hold members of the base type; it does not actually load any members into the set. To do that, you must use an assignment statement, as in the following:

```
MySet := [ element1, element2, ... elementN];
```

where the elements are members of the base type and *N*, of course, is less than or equal to 256, because a Turbo Pascal set cannot have more than 256 elements. Observe also that the members assigned to *MySet* are enclosed in square brackets, not parentheses or curly brackets, and that they are separated by commas.

Sets are obviously quite similar to lists, but there are some very important differences. The main difference is that lists are intrinsically *ordered* data structures, but sets are intrinsically *unordered.* Thus:

- 'A', 'B', 'C' is a different list from 'C', 'B', 'A', but

- ['A', 'B', 'C'] is the same set as ['C', 'B', 'A'].

For the same reason, items can appear more than once in a list, but can appear only once in a set:

- 'A', 'B', 'C', 'A' is different from 'A', 'B', 'C', but

- ['A', 'B', 'C', 'A'] is the *same set* as ['A', 'B', 'C'].

The elements of a set can be of any simple type, as long as the type does not have more than 256 members. Thus, CHAR is a perfectly good base type for a set, because it has 256 members; likewise, the user-defined type *CLASS = 1..4* is a good base type. However, the INTEGER type is not a legal base type for a set, because it has more than 256 members. To use integers, as in the CLASS type example, you have to define a type as a subrange of the integers and use that subrange type. Moreover, only integers from 0 to 255 are allowed.

Limits and Advantages of Turbo Pascal Sets

The reason why Turbo Pascal (unlike some other Pascal compilers) allows only 256 elements in a set, and elements can have ordinal values only from 0 to 255, is that Turbo Pascal uses a special scheme for storing sets in memory. This scheme minimizes the amount of memory that sets require, and maximizes the speed of set operations, but it also imposes the 256-element limit.

Internally, Turbo Pascal handles a set as an array of bits, the maximum size of which is 32 bytes (32 bytes multiplied by 8 bits per byte = 256). Each bit in the array indicates if the corresponding member of the base type is an element of the set or not. Thus, a set of CHAR would be stored as a 32-byte (256-bit) array: In each slot of the array there is a bit (1 or 0) which tells if the corresponding ASCII character is in the set (bit = 1) or not in the set (bit = 0). For example, if Set ARRAY is a set variable of TYPE Char, then:

- If SetArray[65] = 1, then the upper case letter 'A' is in the set, because the ASCII number (ordinality) of 'A' is 65.

- If SetArray[97] = 0, then the lower case letter 'a' is *not* in the set, because the ASCII number (ordinality) of 'a' is 97.

- If SetArray[13] = 1, then the carriage return character (*Enter* key) is in the set, because its ASCII number (ordinality) is 13.

Compatible Set Types

Normally, set operations can be performed only between two or more sets that are "compatible." For instance, you cannot use the union operator to unite two sets with a different base type. Similarly, you cannot use IN to see if an integer is a member of a set whose base type is CHAR, as in Listing 8.7; this causes a compile-time error.

Listing 8.6

```
PROGRAM Listing8_6;

   { Demonstrates the use of "IN" to test for set membership. }

USES CRT;

VAR
   Letters : SET OF CHAR;

PROCEDURE Pause;
   VAR
      Proceed : CHAR;
   BEGIN
      WRITE(' Press any key to continue ...');
      Proceed := READKEY;
      WRITELN; WRITELN
   END;

BEGIN
   CLRSCR;
   Letters := ['A', 'B', 'C'];

   IF 'A' IN Letters
      THEN WRITELN(' The letter "A" is in!');

   IF NOT ('a' IN Letters)
      THEN WRITELN(' The letter "a" is out!');

   IF 5 IN Letters
      THEN WRITELN(' The number 5 is in!');

   pause
END.
```

The base type of a set determines if the set is type-compatible with another set or with a potential set member. Two sets that have the same base type are compatible; a data item is compatible with a set if it is a member of the set's base type.

One of the most obvious uses of sets is to create lists of acceptable values. In Listing 8.7, we create a *GetGoodChar* subroutine that serves as an error-trapping substitute for READLN. It allows us to specify a set of acceptable characters. If the user keys in an unacceptable value (whether it is a letter that is not on the list, or something that is not a letter), then *GetGoodChar* just sits there waiting for valid input—just like the *GetGoodInt* routine we developed in the previous chapter.

Listing 8.7

```
PROGRAM Listing8_7;

   { Demonstrates the use of a set to create a list of
     acceptable values. }

USES CRT;

TYPE
   GoodChars = set of char;   { used with the GetGoodChar procedure }

CONST
   YNchars : GoodChars = ['Y', 'y', 'N', 'n'];
            { set of acceptable characters }

VAR
   YesNo : CHAR;

PROCEDURE Pause;
   VAR
      Proceed : CHAR;
   BEGIN
      WRITE(' Press any key to continue ...');
      Proceed := READKEY;
      WRITELN; WRITELN
   END;

PROCEDURE GetGoodChar(GoodOnes:GoodChars; VAR InChar:char);
   { An error-trapping substitute for "readln" to get character
     input from the keyboard. This procedure takes two parameters:
     a set of "acceptable" characters for input, and a variable
     parameter that is the actual character input.  If the input
```

```
character is not in the set of acceptable characters, this
procedure returns to the original screen position and waits
for the user to enter an acceptable character.}

VAR
    markX, markY  : byte;

BEGIN
    REPEAT
        markX := whereX;
        markY := whereY;
        READLN(InChar);
        IF NOT (InChar IN GoodOnes)
            THEN BEGIN
                    gotoXY(markX, markY);
                    ClrEOL
                 END
    UNTIL InChar IN GoodOnes
END;

BEGIN
    CLRSCR;
    WRITE(' Have you stopped beating your flagellum (Y/N)? ');
    GetGoodChar(YNchars, YesNo);
    WRITELN;
    IF UPCASE(YesNo) = 'Y'
        THEN WRITELN(' Congratulations! You''re promoted to eucaryote!')
        ELSE WRITELN(' I''ve never seen a cilia fellow!');
    pause
END.
```

For any set, it has to be completely clear whether something is in the set or not. You can test for something being in a set, as in Listing 8.4, by using IN:

```
IF InChar IN GoodOnes
    THEN Congratulations;
```

However, to test if something is not in a set, you must use a slightly odd way of phrasing it (see Table 8.1). If you write *IF InChar NOT IN GoodOnes*, then your program won't compile. You have to write

```
IF NOT(InChar IN GoodOnes)
    THEN ToughLuck;
```

TABLE 8.1: Set Operators

Operators	Operation	Operand Types
IN	Set membership: determines if the item on the left of IN is a member of the set on the right. Returns a Boolean value (true or false).	Simple type, set (must be compatible)
+	Union: adds the members of two sets together to produce a new, consolidated set. For two sets A and B, an item is in the union if it is a member of *either* set. If any item is in both original sets, it appears only once in the union set.	Compatible sets
−	Difference: With two sets A and B, *A − B* subtracts from A any members that are also in B. The result is a set containing all those items that were in A but were not also in B.	Compatible sets
*	Intersection: The opposite of union (above). For sets A and B, the intersection *A * B* includes those items that are members of *both* A and B. If any item is in only one of the sets, it is not in the intersection.	Compatible sets

Set Operations

The most common use of sets is to determine if a certain value is acceptable or not by checking to see if it is in the set. In *GetGoodChar*, for example, we specify a set of "good characters" for user input. When the user keys in a value, the routine checks the value against the set of good characters to determine if it is acceptable. If it is, then the value is passed to the program; if not, then the on-screen character is erased and the prompt is redisplayed.

There are, however, several other useful set operations. You may even be familiar with some of them already. They are:

Set union, denoted in Pascal by +. This combines the elements in two sets. For example:

- If set1 = ['a', 'b'] and set2 = ['b', 'c'], then set1 + set2 = ['a', 'b', 'c']. (Remember that ['a', 'b', 'b', 'c'] is the same set as ['a', 'b', 'c'].)
- If set1 = ['a', 'b'] and set2 = ['c', 'd'], then set1 + set2 = ['a', 'b', 'c', 'd'].
- If set1 = ['a', 'b'], set2 = ['c', 'd'], and set3 = ['e', 'f'], then set1 + set2 + set3 = ['a', 'b', 'c', 'd', 'e', 'f'].

Set intersection, denoted in Pascal by *. This produces a set containing only the elements that are in both sets. Stated another way, an item is in the intersection of two or more sets if and only if it is a member of *every* set that is being intersected. For example:

- If set1 = ['a', 'b'] and set2 = ['b', 'c'], then set1 * set2 = ['b'];
- If set1 = ['a', 'b'] and set2 = ['c', 'd'], then set1 * set2 = [] (the empty set).
- If set1 = ['a', 'b'], set2 = ['a', 'c'], and set3 = ['a', 'd'], then set1 * set2 * set3 = ['a'].

Set difference, denoted in Pascal by the minus sign, −. This produces a set containing only the elements that are in the set on the left of the difference sign but not in the set on the right. For example:

- If set1 = ['a', 'b', 'c'] and set2 = ['b', c'], then set1 − set2 = ['a'].
- If set1 = ['a', 'b'] and set2 = ['c', 'd'], then set1 − set2 = ['a', 'b'].
- If set1 = ['a', 'b'] and set2 = ['a', 'b', 'c'], then set1 − set2 = [] (the empty set).

Several other set operators produce Boolean expressions that are true or false. These operators are:

Set equality, denoted in Pascal by the equal sign, =. This produces an expression which is true if and only if the sets being compared have exactly the same elements.

For example:

- If set1 = ['a', 'b'] and set2 = ['a', 'b'], then set1 = set2 is true.
- If set1 = ['a', 'b'] and set2 = ['a', 'b', 'c'], then set1 = set2 is false.

Set inequality, denoted in Pascal by the left and right angle brackets, <>. This produces an expression which is true if and only if the sets being compared do *not* have exactly the same elements. For example:

- If set1 = ['a', 'b'] and set2 = ['a', 'b'], then set1 <> set2 is false.
- If set1 = ['a', 'b'] and set2 = ['a', 'b', 'c'], then set1 <> set2 is true.

Subset, denoted in Pascal by the left angle bracket and the equal sign, <=. This produces an expression which is true if and only if every element in the set on the left of the subset sign is also a member of the set on the right of the subset sign. For example:

- If set1 = ['a', 'b'] and set2 = ['a', 'b', 'c'], then set1 <= set2 is true.
- If set1 = ['a', 'b', 'c'] and set2 = ['a', 'b', 'c'], then set1 <= set2 is true (every set is a subset of itself).
- If set1 = ['a', 'b', 'c'] and set2 = ['a', 'b'], then set1 <= set2 is false ('c' is in set1 but not in set2).
- If set1 = [] (the empty set) and set2 = ['a', 'b'], then set1 <= set2 is true. Note that the empty set is a subset of all other sets, so this expression is true no matter what elements are in set2.

Superset, denoted in Pascal by the right angle bracket and the equal sign, >=. This produces an expression that is true if and only if every element in the set on the right of the superset sign is also a member of the set on the left of the superset sign. For example:

- If set1 = ['a', 'b'] and set2 = ['a', 'b', 'c'], then set1 >= set2 is false.
- If set1 = ['a', 'b', 'c'] and set2 = ['a', 'b', 'c'], then set1 >= set2 is true (every set is a superset of itself).

- If set1 = ['a', 'b', 'c'] and set2 = ['a', 'b'], then set1 >= set2 is true (everything in set2 is also in set1).

- If set1 = [] (the empty set) and set2 = ['a', 'b'], then set1 >= set2 is false. Note that the empty set is only a superset of itself, so this expression is almost always false.

CHAPTER NINE

Procedures and Functions

- **How Procedures and Functions Work**

- **The Idea of Scope**

- **Common Mistakes with Procedures and Functions**

In the previous chapters, we've seen many examples of procedures and functions. In this chapter, we'll go into full details of how to use them. We will find that one of the most important things about them is the part that remains hidden.

What Procedures and Functions Are

Procedures and functions are two different kinds of subroutines—that is, they are named blocks of program code to which you can pass values. Where they differ is that procedures are meant primarily to *do something*, to perform a sequence of actions. On the other hand, functions also may perform actions, but their *main* job is to take one value (or group of values) and return another value. A procedure is like a complete sentence, while a function is like an individual word. Both are like mini-programs in that they can contain their own constants, variables, data types, procedures, and functions.

Of course, if that's *all* they were, then procedures and functions would be a useful but essentially trivial programming tool. But that is not all they are. The most important thing about subroutines is that they embody the very *essence* of structured programming: to separate different tasks into different, "air-tight" compartments of the program; to hide the internal details of each compartment; and to keep total control over how the different compartments interact with each other and with the main body of the program. All this has, of course, several benefits:

- It reduces the number of things you have to worry about. Instead of a disorganized and very large number of interactions between different parts of a mixed-up program, you have to deal only with a small number of interactions between different air-tight compartments—interactions that you define and control.

- Given an overall program design, it allows you to develop and test a program "one piece at a time"—coding and debugging each compartment by itself without requiring you to worry about any of the others. Just like the adage about how to eat an elephant (one bite at a time), this lets you develop large, complex programs without having to think about anything but the part you are doing at that moment.

- It makes your program easier to understand and modify. Because each sub-routine is concerned only with what comes into it and what goes out of it, you can add new subroutines or change the inner workings of existing sub-routines with minimal and easy-to-see impact on the rest of the program.

Sometimes the best way to explain an idea is to point to a simple example. So far, we have seen many examples of procedures and quite a few examples of functions. To spotlight the most basic features, though, let's look at two that are built into the Pascal language: the WRITELN procedure and the *SUCC()* function. (WRITELN is sometimes referred to loosely as a "command," but it actually is a built-in procedure.)

How Procedures Work

WRITELN has the classic features of a procedure. It takes a value (or group of values) that you pass to it, and then it does something with those values: in this case, it sends them to an output device. Usually, the WRITELN output device is the PC's screen, but it also can be a disk file, a printer, or some other device. Thus, for example,

```
WRITELN(' Frank Borland and his burro, Lotus');
```

displays a constant text string on the PC's screen. Similarly,

```
WRITELN(studentlist[n].fname, studentlist[n].lname);
```

displays the first and last names of student number *n* on the screen, where *studentlist* is an array of student records. In this case, however, it uses string *variables* to determine what it should display on the screen. Notice that the WRITELN statement stands by itself; in Pascal, a WRITELN statement, as a procedure, is a "complete sentence."

How Functions Work

Just like procedures, functions start by taking in a value or group of values. What happens then, however, is quite different. Based on the values it has received, the function assigns to *itself* a new value which it then passes back to the program. The *SUCC()* function, for example, takes an ordinal value and returns the next value in order after it, as in:

```
SUCC(5) = 6;
SUCC('a') = 'b';
SUCC(false) = true;
```

Most people have some trouble getting a grip on this idea. Perhaps the plot of the movie *Invasion of the Body Snatchers* offers a good analogy. There, pods from outer space turned themselves into look-alikes of individual Earth people—and then *took the places* of those Earth people in human society. Just like a pod from outer space, a function takes values, does something with them, and then replaces them with itself. Thus, both

```
WRITELN(' The successor of 5 is ', 6, '.');
```

and

```
WRITELN(' The successor of 5 is ', SUCC(5), '.');
```

will display the sentence, "The successor of 5 is 6" on your PC's screen. Listing 9.1 illustrates how a user-defined function can make this sort of transformation take place.

Listing 9.1

```
PROGRAM Listing9_1;

{ Illustrates a simple procedure and a simple function. }

USES CRT;

CONST
Tax = 0.05;

VAR
Amount : REAL;

  { ------------------------------- }
{ MAIN-LEVEL PROCEDURE DECLARATION }
{ ------------------------------- }
PROCEDURE Pause;
VAR
Proceed : CHAR;
```

```
BEGIN
WRITE(' Press any key to continue ...');
Proceed := READKEY;
WRITELN; WRITELN
END;



{ ------------------------------ }
{ MAIN-LEVEL FUNCTION DECLARATION }
{ ------------------------------ }
FUNCTION WithSalesTax (VAR Amount : REAL; TaxRate : REAL) : REAL;
BEGIN
WithSalesTax := Amount + (Amount * TaxRate)
END;



{ ------------------------------- }
{ MAIN-LEVEL PROCEDURE DECLARATION }
{ ------------------------------- }
PROCEDURE GetAmount(VAR Amount : REAL);
VAR
Continue : CHAR;

{ --------------------------- }
{ Local procedure             }
{ --------------------------- }
{ Under GetAmount             }
{ --------------------------- }
PROCEDURE PromptForAmount;
BEGIN
CLRSCR;
WRITELN;
WRITE(' Enter amount of purchase: ');
READLN(Amount);
WRITELN;
WRITELN(' With sales tax, that comes to ',
        WithSalesTax(Amount,Tax):0:2, '.');
WRITELN;
WRITE(' Do Another (Y/N)? ');
READLN(Continue)
END;

{ --------------------------------- }
{ Main body of higher-level procedure }
```

```
{ ----------------------------------- }
{ Procedure name: GetAmount          }
{ ----------------------------------- }
BEGIN
Continue := ' ';
REPEAT PromptForAmount
UNTIL UPCASE(Continue) <> 'Y'
END;



{ ------------------------------------------------------------------ }
{                      MAIN BODY OF PROGRAM                          }
{ ------------------------------------------------------------------ }
BEGIN
GetAmount(Amount);
pause
END.
```

Information Hiding

Here's a trick question: what happens inside the WRITELN procedure and the *SUCC()* function to the values that have been passed to them? If you don't know, don't feel bad—you don't *need* to know, nor should you ever *have* to know. All that matters is that something goes into them (values), and something comes out the way you want it (either text on the screen or an ordinal value).

As far as the rest of the program is concerned, all of its procedures and functions— whether they are built into Pascal or created by you—should be like this. Particular data goes into them, and particular data comes out in the desired way. That's all the rest of the program should ever have to know.

This is a very important structured programming concept: it is called *information hiding.* What that means is, as I've said, the inside of each subroutine is hidden from everything outside itself, both from other subroutines and from the main part of the program. Because of this, you do not have to worry that anything inside a subroutine might have an unexpected effect on anything outside. Information hiding puts *you* in complete control of how your program works.

The Idea of "Scope"

Until this point, we have been using the terms "global" and "local" variables fairly loosely, without discussing what they mean. The central idea that makes it all make sense is the idea of *scope*. And although this is a fairly simple idea, it is easier to understand than it is to explain.

The best way to understand the idea of scope is to consider how a Pascal program is structured. Figure 9.1 shows the overall structure of the program in Listing 9.1. Notice that the main body of the program is at the top, which is only appropriate, since it has the highest level of control over what happens and when. Just below it, on the same level, are the *Pause*, *WithSalesTax*, and *GetAmount* subroutines. On the lowest level is the *PromptForAmount* procedure, which connects directly only to the *GetAmount* routine.

In a way, the hierarchy of a program resembles a company's organization chart. Global identifiers, which are declared at the very top of the hierarchy, are visible from everywhere in the program, just as everyone in a company is likely to know

FIGURE 9.1:
Overall structure of Listing 9.1

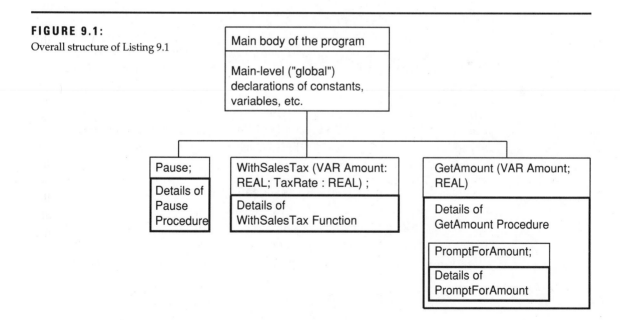

the name of the company president. In Listing 9.1, the constant *Tax* and the variable *Amount* are global in scope; which means that they are visible everywhere in the program, even from inside subroutines.

On the other hand, identifiers declared inside a subroutine are "local" to that subroutine. They are visible everywhere inside the subroutine, but *not* visible outside of the subroutine—just as people who work in one department of a company know everyone in their own department; but people in other departments and in the company's top management might not know *anyone* in that department.

In Figure 9.1 note that if one subroutine is declared inside another (as *PromptForAmount* is declared inside the *GetAmount* procedure), then it, too, is local to the higher-level subroutine. This means two things:

- Because it is inside the higher-level subroutine, it can see everything that is above it in the hierarchy, including local variables (and other identifiers) that are inside the higher-level subroutine.

- Because it is local to the higher-level subroutine, it is hidden from everything outside the higher-level subroutine, just as any other internal detail.

In Figure 9.1, parts of program blocks that are surrounded by single lines are visible to everything underneath them in the tree diagram, as well as to everything on the same level and to the main body of the program. Parts that are surrounded by double lines are hidden from all other program blocks, as well as from the main program.

At the bottom right, the *PromptForAmount* procedure is a special case. It is declared *inside* the *GetAmount* procedure, so it is visible inside *GetAmount* but hidden from everything outside. Even inside the *GetAmount* routine, however, the details of *PromptForAmount* are still hidden.

It all boils down to this: the *scope* of any identifier includes (1) the program block in which it is named and (2) any program block below it in the program's hierarchy tree unless the lower block has a local identifier with the same name. One block is "below" another block if and only if you can follow the tree downward from the upper to the lower block without ever having to move up or move to a different branch of the tree.

Declaring and Using Identifiers

Pascal enforces a rule that is very similar to the idea of scope: *identifiers must be declared before they can be used.* This is why we must declare all our global constants, variables, and data types at the very beginning of the program code: that way, they can be used anywhere else in the program, whether in a subroutine or way down at the bottom in the main body of the program.

Similarly, subroutines must be declared before they are used. If subroutine A is used by subroutine B, then it must be declared *before* subroutine B. Otherwise, when Pascal compiles the program and arrives at the line where subroutine B calls subroutine A, it will stop with an "unknown identifier" error message because subroutine A has not been declared yet.

There are two minor exceptions to this rule. As we'll see in Chapter 11, you can declare a pointer data type before you declare the data type it points to. And, later in this chapter, we'll see how to use "forward declarations" to circumvent the declare-before-use rule with subroutines.

The rule that identifiers must be declared before they are used is a simple one, but it goes to the very heart of structured programming: the idea that you should plan and design your program before you start to write code. The rule is just another way that Pascal teaches you how to create efficient, bug-free programs.

How to Declare Procedures and Functions

Normally, you declare subroutines after the VAR section of your program and before the main body of the program. Remember: the section where you declare subroutines is different from the main body of the program, where the subroutines actually do something. Here, you are just spelling out the details of what they are, what values they use from outside themselves, and how they work. Thus, each procedure or function declaration must contain the following information (see Figures 9.2 and 9.3):

- *The name of the procedure or function.* This follows the standard rules for Pascal identifiers. It must begin with a letter and can be as long as you like. It can have digits and underlines, but no dashes or other special characters. No distinction is made between upper- and lowercase letters, so you can use them to make the purpose of the routine clearer, such as *GetNumberFromUser*. However, the name shouldn't be the same as a Pascal reserved word (such as "case") or standard identifier (such as "writeln").

FIGURE 9.2:

Information in a procedure declaraton

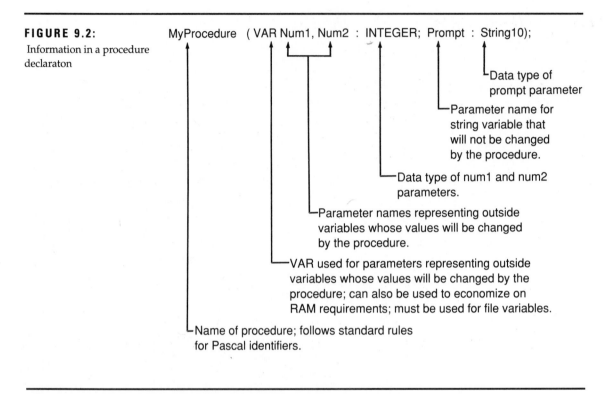

FIGURE 9.3:

Information in a function declaration

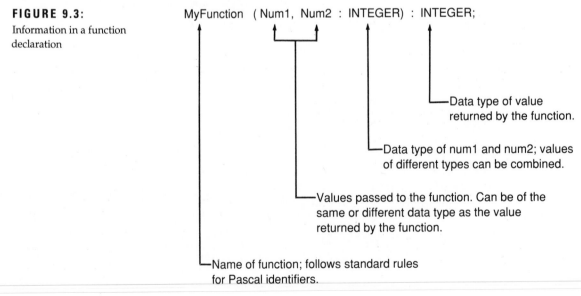

- *The names and data types of parameters.* The parentheses that come after the name of the subroutine make up the "front door" through which values can be passed to the subroutine. Just like a real-life security checkpoint, each item you intend to go in or out the door must be properly identified by name and data type. Any item that tries to enter the subroutine without proper identification papers will be detained by the security guard; that is, Turbo Pascal will stop the program with either a compilation or a run-time error.

- *In a procedure, whether the parameters are value or VAR parameters.* In Figure 9.2, the first two parameters (*num1* and *num2*) are VAR parameters, while the third (*prompt*) is not. Note that you can have any combination of data types and parameter types. Some parameters may be VAR parameters, while others are not; some parameters can be of type INTEGER, while others are CHAR, BOOLEAN, REAL, or structured types such as ARRAY and STRING. For reasons that I'll explain in the next section of this chapter, only VAR parameters can be changed by a subroutine. One of the most common programming mistakes is to forget to use VAR in front of parameters that need to be changed by a subroutine.

- *In a function, the data type of the value returned by the function.* This is the data type of the value that the function itself will assume. Although the *SUCC()* function returns a value that is the same data type as the value it gets, things don't have to be this way. A function can get integer values and return a string, get a character value and return a Boolean, or any other combination. For example, the Turbo Pascal *STR()* function takes an integer and returns the string-type version of the same integer—for example, replacing the integer 1555 with the string '1555'.

Passing Parameters to Subroutines

I've referred several times to the "parameters" used by a subroutine. Here, I'll discuss the meaning of this concept and how it works.

When we're using subroutines, we often need to pass values to the subroutines from outside. Sometimes, these are constant values that won't be changed by the subroutine, such as the text strings (for example, *'This is a string constant'*) that we pass to the WRITELN procedure or the ordinal constants (for example, *15*, *'a'*) we might pass to the *SUCC()* function. At other times, these values will actually be changed by the subroutine, such as when we pass an integer variable to a procedure that adds up numbers and gives us a total.

As we saw in our discussion of scope, two kinds of identifiers are visible from within a subroutine: identifiers that are local to that subroutine, and identifiers that are above that subroutine in the program hierarchy. Thus, in Listing 9.2, both the global variable *TotalStock* and the local variables *InStock*, *NewNum*, and *Continue* are accessible from inside the *GetNumberInStock* subroutine.

Listing 9.2

```
PROGRAM Listing9_2;

USES CRT;

VAR
    TotalStock: INTEGER;


PROCEDURE Pause;
    VAR
        Proceed : CHAR;
    BEGIN
        WRITE(' Press any key to continue ...');
        Proceed := READKEY;
        WRITELN; WRITELN
    END;

PROCEDURE GetNumberInStock;
    VAR
        InStock,
        NewNum    : INTEGER;
        Continue : CHAR;
    BEGIN
        CLRSCR;
        Continue := 'Y';
        InStock := 0;
        WHILE UPCASE(Continue) = 'Y' DO
            BEGIN
            WRITELN;
            WRITE(' Enter number to add to total: ');
            READLN(NewNum);
            InStock := InStock + NewNum;
            WRITE(' Add another (Y/N)? ');
```

```
        READLN(Continue)
      END;
   WRITELN;
   WRITELN(' The total number in stock is ', InStock, '.');
   pause
END;


BEGIN
   TotalStock := 0;
   GetNumberInStock;
   WRITELN(' The total number in stock is ', TotalStock, '.');
   pause
END.
```

However, in Listing 9.2, we've got an obvious problem. The subroutine lets us add up numbers and get a total, but it gives us no way to hook up to the global variable (*TotalStock*) that we want to change. Thus, we are able to get the result we want inside the *GetNumberInStock* routine, but we are cut off from the outside.

For this obvious problem, most people seize upon the obvious solution: just put an extra line into the *GetNumberInStock* procedure to copy the value of the local variable *InStock* to the global variable *TotalStock*, as shown in Listing 9.3. This solution will work, and Turbo Pascal won't stop you from doing it. From a structured programming viewpoint, however, it's just about the worst thing you could do.

Listing 9.3

```
PROGRAM Listing9_3;

   { Shows the WRONG way to change the value of a global
     variable. }

USES CRT;

VAR
   TotalStock: INTEGER;


PROCEDURE Pause;
   VAR
      Proceed : CHAR;
   BEGIN
      WRITE(' Press any key to continue ...');
```

```
      Proceed := READKEY;
      WRITELN; WRITELN
   END;

PROCEDURE GetNumberInStock;
   VAR
      InStock,
      NewNum   : INTEGER;
      Continue : CHAR;
   BEGIN
      CLRSCR;
      Continue := 'Y';
      InStock := 0;
      WHILE UPCASE(Continue) = 'Y' DO
         BEGIN
         WRITELN;
         WRITE(' Enter number to add to total: ');
         READLN(NewNum);
         InStock := InStock + NewNum;
         WRITE(' Add another (Y/N)? ');
         READLN(Continue)
         END;
      WRITELN;
      WRITELN(' The total number in stock is ', InStock, '.');
      TotalStock := InStock;
      pause
   END;


BEGIN
   TotalStock := 0;
   GetNumberInStock;
   WRITELN(' The total number in stock is ', TotalStock, '.');
   pause
END.
```

The reason that it is a bad move is that the inside of each subroutine is supposed to be hidden from the rest of the program. In Listing 9.3, you allow part of the outside program to "break into" the inside of the subroutine, thus violating the principle of information hiding. *TotalStock*, in effect, sneaks into the *GetNumberInStock* routine through a back window. And whether it is a subroutine or your own house, you don't want anybody sneaking in through the windows. Figure 9.4 illustrates the situation.

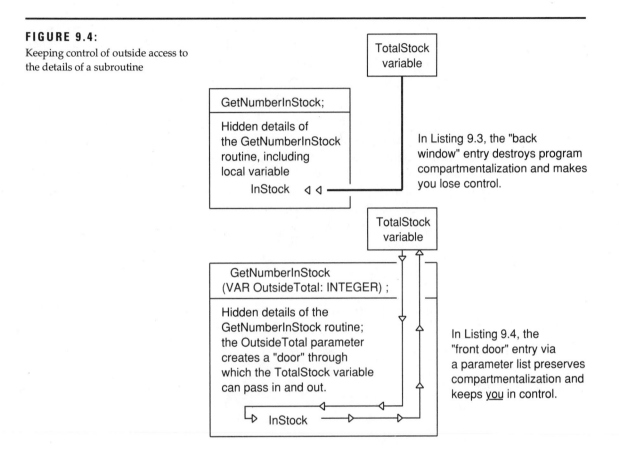

FIGURE 9.4:

Keeping control of outside access to the details of a subroutine

The whole point of structured programming is that it puts you *in control* of your program. You can develop your program one piece at a time and isolate different parts of the program in airtight compartments. When you allow back-window access to subroutines, you give up control of your program and break the airtight seals on the compartments. In a simple program like Listing 9.3, this is not a major problem. If you're developing a medium or large-sized program with dozens of subroutines, however, you'll find that this sort of back-window access makes it almost impossible to keep track of what is interacting with what—which variables are being changed by which subroutines, where your program bugs are coming from, and so on.

The solution is found in the idea of *passing parameters* to your subroutines. Passing parameters is a way of controlling what goes into your subroutines and what comes out of them. It also makes it easier for you to see, at a glance, with which outside variables and values a subroutine is dealing.

To pass parameters to a subroutine, you add a *parameter list* to your original declaration of the subroutine. This list gives the parameter names and data types of each item that needs to go into the subroutine. When you call the subroutine in the main body of the program, you include the names of the items that you want to pass to the subroutine. Thus, in Listing 9.4, we created an *OutsideTotal* parameter through which the *TotalStock* variable is able to enter the *GetNumberInStock* procedure. In this case, the *TotalStock* variable is changed by the procedure, so it has to be a VAR parameter—a concept that I'll explain below.

Listing 9.4

```
PROGRAM Listing9_4;

   { Shows the RIGHT way to change the value of a global variable,
     by declaring it as a parameter in a subroutine. }

USES CRT;

VAR
   TotalStock: INTEGER;


PROCEDURE Pause;
   VAR
      Proceed : CHAR;
   BEGIN
      WRITE(' Press any key to continue ...');
      Proceed := READKEY;
      WRITELN; WRITELN
   END;

PROCEDURE GetNumberInStock(VAR OutsideTotal : INTEGER);
   VAR
      InStock,
      NewNum   : INTEGER;
      Continue : CHAR;
   BEGIN
      CLRSCR;
```

```
         Continue := 'Y';
         InStock := 0;
         WHILE UPCASE(Continue) = 'Y' DO
            BEGIN
            WRITELN;
            WRITE(' Enter number to add to total: ');
            READLN(NewNum);
            InStock := InStock + NewNum;
            WRITE(' Add another (Y/N)? ');
            READLN(Continue)
            END;
         WRITELN;
         WRITELN(' The total number in stock is ', InStock, '.');
         OutsideTotal := InStock;·
         pause
      END;


BEGIN
   TotalStock := 0;
   GetNumberInStock(TotalStock);
   WRITELN(' The total number in stock is ', TotalStock, '.');
   pause
END.
```

When it enters a subroutine via a parameter list, an outside item temporarily takes on the name of the parameter with which it is associated. Thus, in Listing 9.4, the *TotalStock* variable gets into the subroutine via the *OutsideTotal* parameter, and travels under that name while it is inside the subroutine. When it leaves the subroutine, it takes back its original name of *TotalStock*.

In Listing 9.4, we used a parameter name that was different from *TotalStock* because we wanted to make it clear that what was happening inside the procedure was being done *to the parameter,* not directly to the global variable. Whenever possible, however, it is simpler (and easier to remember) if you use the same name for the parameter as for the item it is replacing. Normally, therefore, we would have declared the *GetNumberInStock* procedure as

```
PROCEDURE GetNumberInStock(VAR TotalStock : INTEGER);
```

Because the *TotalStock* parameter is temporarily replacing the global *TotalStock* variable, there is no conflict between the two identifiers.

Creating Parameter Lists

To create a parameter list, you first have to decide which items from outside need to be passed to the subroutine. These can include both constants and variables. Then you should decide:

- What parameter names to use.

- Which outside values need to be changed by the subroutine. These will need to be declared as VAR (variable) parameters. Other parameters can be declared as "value" parameters.

- In what order you will list the parameters. Generally, it saves extra work to list all parameters of the same type together.

Thus, the following are acceptable parameter lists:

```
PROCEDURE MyRoutine1(VAR num1 : INTEGER);
        { one variable parameter of type INTEGER }

PROCEDURE MyRoutine2(num1, num2 : INTEGER;
                  VAR total : INTEGER);
        { two value parameters of type INTEGER and
          one variable parameter of type INTEGER }

PROCEDURE MyRoutine3(Name : String10;

  VAR PaidUp : BOOLEAN);
            { a value parameter of type String10 and a
              variable parameter of type BOOLEAN }

FUNCTION MyRoutine4(num1, num2 : INTEGER;
                  Operation : String10) : INTEGER;
            { two value parameters of type INTEGER and
              one value parameter of type String10. }
```

Rules for Parameter Lists

There aren't many rules for creating parameter lists, but there are a few. First, when you actually call the routine in the action part of your program, the items you pass to it must be of *exactly the same type* as the parameters that you declared, as well as being in the correct order. Thus, for example, if you declared a parameter list as

```
PROCEDURE MyRoutine(num1 : INTEGER; YesNo : CHAR);
```

and tried to call the procedure in your program by writing *MyRoutine('Y', 5)*, then your program wouldn't compile. The first value you passed to the procedure, 'Y', is a different data type from the *num1* parameter that stands in for it inside the procedure. The second value, 5, is also a different data type from the *YesNo* parameter. If you reversed the order of the values in your procedure call, though, and made it *MyRoutine(5, 'Y')*, then everything would work fine.

Identical and Compatible Types   When I said that parameters and the items they receive must be exactly the same type, I meant it in a stronger sense than in most situations. For example, if you have two string variables that are both of type *STRING[10]*, then you can assign the value of one string variable to the other string variable, as shown in Listing 9.5.

Listing 9.5

```
PROGRAM Listing9_5;

   { Illustrates compatible data types. }

USES CRT;

VAR
   name1 : STRING[10];
   name2 : STRING[10];

PROCEDURE Pause;
   VAR
      Proceed : CHAR;
   BEGIN
      WRITE(' Press any key to continue ...');
      Proceed := READKEY;
      WRITELN; WRITELN
   END;

BEGIN
   CLRSCR;
   WINDOW(5,3,75,22);
   name1 := 'Jonas Salk';
   name2 := name1;
   WRITELN(' The name in variable name1 is ', name1, '.');
   WRITELN;
```

```
    WRITELN(' The name in variable name2 is ', name2, '.');
    WRITELN;
    pause
END.
```

Listing 9.5 *looks* a little odd, since there's really no reason to declare *name1* and *name2* in separate statements, but it is perfectly legal. However, because *name1* and *name2* were defined as the *STRING[10]* data type in separate statements, they are only of *compatible*, not *identical*, data types. To be of an *identical* data type, two identifiers must refer to the same type definition statement. If we were to substitute

```
VAR
    Name1, Name2 : STRING[10];
```

in Listing 9.5, then *Name1* and *Name2* would be identical in their data type, not merely compatible. Notice that this is not a problem with built-in Pascal types such as integers and characters.

The reason it is sometimes a problem in declaring parameters is that data types such as strings and arrays are partly defined by you. It is true that both are built-in data types in Turbo Pascal (strings being just a special kind of array), but *you* specify how many slots each string or array type is supposed to have.

This means that when you pass a string to a subroutine, you can end up with two type-declaration statements, as in

```
VAR
    name1 : STRING[10];
PROCEDURE MyRoutine(ParameterName : STRING[10]);
    { ... etc. }
```

Because you declared *name1* to be of *STRING[10]* type in one place and the parameter name to be of *STRING[10]* type in another place, the variable and parameter are merely *compatible*, not identical, in their data type. And a parameter will accept only an item whose data type is identical to its own. Therefore, Listing 9.6 won't compile.

Listing 9.6

```
PROGRAM Listing9_6;

    { Shows how you can't pass an item to a parameter when
      their data types are merely compatible; the types must be
      identical. }

USES CRT;

VAR
    Name1 : STRING[10];

PROCEDURE Pause;
    VAR
        Proceed : CHAR;
    BEGIN
        WRITE(' Press any key to continue ...');
        Proceed := READKEY;
        WRITELN; WRITELN
    END;

PROCEDURE SetName(VAR ParameterName : STRING[10]);
    BEGIN
     ParameterName := 'Sam'
    END;

BEGIN
    CLRSCR;
    SetName(Name1);
    WRITELN(' The name in variable Name1 is ', name1, '.');
    pause
END.
```

The solution to this predicament, when you need to pass a structured type such as a string or an array, is to put a special definition in the TYPE section of your program, as shown in Listing 9.7. Then, the variable or other item you pass to the parameter will have a data type identical to that of the parameter itself, since both will refer to the same type definition statement. This is a small but significant change—which works fine.

Listing 9.7

```
PROGRAM Listing9_7;

   { Shows how to pass an item to a parameter by including a
     special TYPE statement in the program. }

USES CRT;

TYPE
   String10 = STRING[10];

VAR
   Name1 : String10;

PROCEDURE Pause;
   VAR
      Proceed : CHAR;
   BEGIN
      WRITE(' Press any key to continue ...');
      Proceed := READKEY;
      WRITELN; WRITELN
   END;

PROCEDURE SetName(VAR ParameterName : String10);
   BEGIN
      ParameterName := 'Sam'
   END;

BEGIN
   CLRSCR;
   SetName(Name1);
   WRITELN(' The name in variable Name1 is ', name1, '.');
   pause
END.
```

Value and Variable Parameters

Now we have come to a very important distinction: that between value and variable parameters. When you put VAR in front of a parameter name in a subroutine declaration, it means that the item that gets passed to this parameter is passed "by reference." If you do not put VAR in front of the parameter, then the item is passed "by value."

As usual, the technical jargon tends to obscure rather than to clarify what's really happening. Let's take things one at a time. When you first declare a variable in your program, Pascal sets aside a location in your PC's memory to hold that variable. When you pass a variable to a parameter "by reference," it means that you are making that parameter refer to *the same memory address* as the original variable.

Thus, any value that you assign to that parameter will be sent to the memory location for the outside variable that was passed (by reference) to the parameter. This means that anything you do to the parameter is done simultaneously to the outside variable. And this is why VAR parameters are called "variable" parameters: they can actually change the values of the outside variables that they receive.

Contrast this with a parameter that was not declared as a VAR parameter. In this case, the outside item is passed "by value." Instead of making the parameter refer to the same memory location as the item itself, Pascal makes a *copy* of the item's value and passes *that* to the parameter. The parameter does not refer to anything outside the subroutine, and changes made in the parameter can affect only the copied value—*not* the outside variable.

In a nutshell, when you use a VAR parameter, you are passing the *actual outside variable* into the subroutine. When you do not use a VAR parameter, you are passing only a *copy* of the outside variable into the subroutine, and the outside variable itself will not and cannot be changed.

You should use VAR parameters when:

- The item passed to the subroutine needs to have its value changed by the subroutine.

- The item passed to the subroutine is a variable that represents a disk file. In this case, Turbo Pascal requires that you use a VAR parameter because it is impractical to make a copy of the original file.

- You need to economize on the memory used by your program. Because value parameters make copies of the original variables, they require more memory than VAR parameters. When you are passing some very large data items (such as large arrays) to a subroutine, the memory required for making copies can be considerable, so VAR parameters may be a better choice.

You should use value parameters when:

- The item passed to the subroutine does not need to be changed by the subroutine.

- You want a little extra safety against accidental changes to an outside variable.

Forward Declarations

There are many situations in which one subroutine in a program calls another. Because nothing can be used in a Pascal program before it is declared, this means that you have to declare the subroutine that gets called *before* you declare the subroutine that calls it, as in

```
PROCEDURE MyRoutine1(SomeParameter : INTEGER);
   { code for the procedure }
PROCEDURE MyRoutine2(AnotherParameter : CHAR);
   BEGIN
      MyRoutine1(15);
      { ... etc.}
   END;
```

But what happens if sometimes *MyRoutine2* calls *MyRoutine1*, but at other times *MyRoutine1* calls *MyRoutine2*—as in the following:

```
PROCEDURE MyRoutine1(SomeParameter : INTEGER);
   BEGIN
      IF SomeParameter < 10 THEN MyRoutine2('Y');
      { ... etc.}
PROCEDURE MyRoutine2(AnotherParameter : CHAR);
   BEGIN
      MyRoutine1(15);
      { ... etc.}
   END;
```

We seem to be in an impossible situation. If *MyRoutine2* is to be able to call *MyRoutine1*, then *MyRoutine1* has to be declared first. But if *MyRoutine1* has to call *MyRoutine2*, then *MyRoutine2* has to be declared first. But we cannot declare both of them first.

Or can we? The solution to our problem is called a *forward declaration*. Pascal does not care if we spell out all the details of a subroutine before we call it, just so long as we've declared it. A forward declaration tells Pascal that a routine needs to be declared at a certain place, but that the details will be given later. To make a forward declaration, we simply give the first line of the subroutine declaration and, at the end, we add the word FORWARD, as in

```
PROCEDURE MyRoutine2(AnotherParameter : CHAR);
FORWARD;
PROCEDURE MyRoutine1(SomeParameter : INTEGER);
   BEGIN
      IF SomeParameter < 10 THEN MyRoutine2('Y');
      { ... etc.}
PROCEDURE MyRoutine2(AnotherParameter : CHAR);
   BEGIN
      MyRoutine1(15);
      { ... etc.}
   END;
```

Because we've declared *MyRoutine2* before *MyRoutine1* (even though we have not given the details), we can now have *MyRoutine1* call *MyRoutine2* and *MyRoutine2* call *MyRoutine1*.

Common Mistakes with Procedures and Functions

There are three mistakes that beginning programmers make again and again with procedures and functions. These errors are common enough to warrant some discussion. In order of priority, the mistakes are as follows.

Failure to Use VAR When Needed

By far, the most common mistake is failing to put VAR in front of a parameter for an outside variable that needs to be changed by the subroutine. This means that only a *copy* of the outside variable actually will be passed into the subroutine, and the outside variable won't be changed at all. This mistake is illustrated in Listing 9.8.

Listing 9.8

```
PROGRAM Listing9_8;

    { Shows how failure to use VAR when needed to indicate a
      variable parameter will cause a program to malfunction.
      Here, the error is in the AddSalesTax procedure, where
      "OutsideAmount" should be declared as a VAR parameter. }


USES CRT;

VAR
    Amount : REAL;

PROCEDURE Pause;
    VAR
        Proceed : CHAR;
    BEGIN
        WRITE(' Press any key to continue ...');
        Proceed := READKEY;
        WRITELN; WRITELN
    END;

PROCEDURE AddSalesTax(OutsideAmount : REAL);
    CONST
        SalesTax = 0.05;
    BEGIN
        OutsideAmount := OutsideAmount + (OutsideAmount * SalesTax)
    END;

BEGIN
    CLRSCR;
    WRITE(' Enter the amount of purchase: ');
    READLN(Amount);
    WRITELN(' The amount without tax is ', Amount:0:2, '.');
    pause;
    AddSalesTax(Amount);
    WRITELN(' The amount with tax is ', Amount:0:2, '.');
    pause
END.
```

Directly Changing Global Variables

The second most common mistake is directly changing the values of global variables. Beginning programmers often think that they can get away with this practice because, in the simple example programs they are most likely to see, it does no special harm. If you are writing any program of reasonable complexity, however, it will certainly land you in deep trouble. It's better to get into the habit of doing things right from the very beginning.

Parameters in the Wrong Order

The third most common error is passing parameters in the wrong order. Just as parameters are *declared* in a specific order, the items that will be passed to the parameters must be listed in the *same* order when the subroutine is actually used in the program. Otherwise, the program either will not compile at all (if there is a data-type mismatch) or the subroutine will malfunction, as in Listing 9.9.

Listing 9.9

```
PROGRAM Listing9_9;

  { Demonstrates problems that can arise from incorrectly ordered
    values passed to a subroutine. The values must be in the same
    order as the parameter list. }

USES CRT;

VAR
   num1, num2, num3  : INTEGER;

PROCEDURE Pause;
   VAR
      Proceed : CHAR;
   BEGIN
      WRITE(' Press any key to continue ...');
      Proceed := READKEY;
      WRITELN; WRITELN
   END;

PROCEDURE Initialize(VAR a,b,c : INTEGER);
   BEGIN
      CLRSCR;
```

```
      a := 0;
      b := 0;
      c := 0
   END;


PROCEDURE AddTwoNumbers(a,b : INTEGER; VAR c : INTEGER);
   BEGIN
      c := a + b
   END;

BEGIN
   Initialize(num1, num2, num3);
   num1 := 10;
   num2 := 25;
   AddTwoNumbers(num3, num1, num2);
   WRITELN(' The sum of ', num1, ' and ', num2, ' is ', num3, '.');
   pause
END.
```

Although you might think that the error in Listing 9.9 is a harmless one because the program does compile all right, it is, in fact, the *worst* kind of program bug: one that compiles without any error messages but gives you the wrong answers when you run the program. Though anyone can see that 10 + 25 isn't equal to 0, the errors in a complex program are not nearly as obvious—and therefore can be catastrophic.

About Breaking the Rules

Much of this chapter has been an extended sermon on the evils of failing to compartmentalize subroutines properly. In an ideal world, all outside variables used in subroutines would be passed to the subroutines as parameters, and the internal details of each subroutine would be completely sealed off from the rest of the program in which it occurs.

In the real world, however, there is no denying the truth: sometimes, highly skilled programmers fail to declare outside variables as parameters. Instead, they violate the principle of information hiding and pull some global variables directly into their subroutines. And their programs work fine.

In part, they can do this precisely *because* they are highly skilled. Nobody tells Jimmy Connors how to play tennis, Gata Kamsky how to play chess, or Mike Tyson how to throw a punch. (Nobody would dare!) If an expert decides to break the rules, the presumption must be that the expert knows the "correct" method but, based on experience, thinks that a different approach will work better in solving the current problem.

The novice programmer is in a different situation. Lacking the expert's years of experience, he or she should follow the rules whenever possible. Later, after acquiring more experience, he or she will be better equipped to decide if a particular rule can be ignored in a specific case.

At the same time, there are some situations in which it is safer to break the rules than in others. Although I am not saying it is "all right" to use outside variables in a subroutine without declaring them as parameters, here are four situations in which it is less dangerous to do so:

1. *When the program is very simple.* In this case, it's foolish to be a stickler about information hiding. The main purpose of structured programming is to make complex programs easier to code, debug, understand, and modify. If the program is very simple, then structured programming becomes less important.

2. *When you are the one and only programmer.* Another benefit of structured programming is that it allows you to divide a large programming project between the members of a project team. Each subroutine can be coded and tested separately, and because of information hiding, the individual programmer does not need to worry about how other programmers are coding their subroutines. If you are the only programmer working on the project, however, then strict information hiding becomes less important. Note that it does *not* become *un*important. To the extent that your code fails to follow structured methods, it will be more difficult to understand and modify in the future. If you forget how you coded a part of the program, or someone else needs to modify your program in the future, unstructured code will make things more difficult.

3. *When a subroutine is local within another subroutine.* When one subroutine is declared inside another, often it is unnecessary to pass variables as parameters to the local subroutine. Global variables will already have been passed as parameters to the main subroutine, and the level of complexity *within* a subroutine is normally (and should be) quite manageable. Thus, you should pass global variables as parameters to the main subroutine, but if you declare a

local subroutine inside the main subroutine, it can get away with not declaring everything it uses as a parameter.

4. *When a subroutine simply abbreviates code.* Sometimes, you will find that the main body of your program has too many lines in it and would be clearer if you moved some of those lines off into a separate subroutine. These lines of code, as part of the main body of the program, may already have been using global variables. If you create a subroutine simply to abbreviate the main program, particularly if the main program is fairly simple, then it does no great harm to adjust global variables directly, so long as it is very obvious what you did. Nevertheless, it is still a better practice to bring the global variables into the subroutine as parameters.

CHAPTER TEN

Using Turbo Pascal Units

- Why Use Units?

- Parts of a Unit

- Standard Turbo Pascal Units

If units are not a radical novelty, then at the very least they are a useful one. In previous chapters, we have often used the *pause* routine to stop the execution of our programs so that we could look at the output. We have also used *GetGoodInt* and *GetGoodChar* to provide error-trapping input routines. But there is one major problem: we have always had to include the routines we wanted in each new program that used them. This task is made easier by Turbo Pascal's ability to cut and paste between different file windows, but it is still a minor irritation.

In this chapter, we will look at a cure for that irritant: Turbo Pascal units. A *unit* is a separately compiled Pascal file in which you can put frequently used routines. When you need to use one of the routines, you simply name the unit in the USES clause of your program. If Turbo Pascal cannot find the definition of a particular routine in your program itself, it looks for it in the units you have named.

Turbo Pascal comes with several predefined and precompiled units that you can use with your programs. We have used the CRT unit in almost every listing so far to provide routines for clearing the screen and detecting keypresses (in the *pause* procedure). Later in this chapter, we will discuss Turbo Pascal's predefined units.

In addition to its predefined units, Turbo Pascal allows you to create your own units with routines that you develop yourself. These are used in exactly the same way as the predefined units, by including their names in a USES statement after the name of your program:

```
PROGRAM MyProgram;
USES CRT, MyUtils;
```

Parts of a Unit

A unit is divided into two main parts, as shown in Figure 10.1. In Figure 10.1, the publicly accessible part of the unit is surrounded by a single line; the hidden part of the unit is surrounded by a double line.

FIGURE 10.1:

Structure of a unit

Unit MyUnit;	Name of unit
INTERFACE	Start of "public" section of unit
USES CRT;	Other units used by this unit
CONST, TYPE, and VAR declarations	Constant, type, and variables used in this unit
Headers of subroutines in this unit.	Header information of subroutines defined in this unit
IMPLEMENTATION	Start of "private" section of unit
Details of subroutines in this unit.	Code for public subroutines in this unit
Declarations of private subroutines in this unit.	Code for private subroutines in this unit (these not declared in interface section)
Initialization Section (optional) BEGIN..END;	Code to initialize variables used i the unit
END.	End of unit

Single line denotes public, "visible" part of unit. Double line denotes private, "hidden" part of unit.

Interface

The public part of a unit, which is visible to other program modules that use the unit, consists of (1) the name of the unit and (2) the INTERFACE section of the unit. Other program modules that use the unit can use any subroutines, constants, variables, data types, or other program elements that are declared in this section of the program. It begins with the word INTERFACE and ends with the word IMPLEMENTATION, which marks the beginning of the next section of the unit.

It is important to note that this public section contains everything that a user or program needs to know in order to use the routines in the unit. For example, a unit could be declared as shown in Listing 10.1. In the INTERFACE section of the unit, you provide the name of each subroutine, what goes into it, and what comes out of it. And, remember, whether a subroutine is in a unit or not, in structured programming, that information is *all* that the rest of the program should need to be able to use the subroutine.

Listing 10.1

```
Unit MyUtils;   { Listing 10.1: miscellaneous utility routines. }

INTERFACE
{ ==================== PUBLIC section of unit ==================== }

USES CRT, GRAPH;

TYPE
   GoodChars = set of char;    { used with the GetGoodChar procedure }

CONST
   YNchars : GoodChars = ['Y', 'y', 'N', 'n'];



PROCEDURE Pause;    { accepts any key }


PROCEDURE GetGoodChar(GoodOnes:GoodChars; var InChar:char);

PROCEDURE GetGoodInt(MinNum, MaxNum: integer; var InNum:integer);


IMPLEMENTATION
{ ==================== PRIVATE section of unit ==================== }


PROCEDURE Pause; { Pauses the program until user presses a key. }
   VAR
      Proceed : char;
   BEGIN
      Writeln;
      Write(' Press any key to continue ... ');
      Proceed := readkey;
```

```
      Writeln; Writeln
   END;


PROCEDURE GetGoodChar(GoodOnes:GoodChars; var InChar:char);

   {An error-trapping substitute for "readln" to get character
    input from the keyboard. This procedure takes two parameters:
    a set of "acceptable" characters for input, and a variable
    parameter that is the actual character input.  If the input
    character is not in the set of acceptable characters, this
    procedure returns to the original screen position and waits
    for the user to enter an acceptable character.}

   VAR
      markX, markY  : byte;
   BEGIN
      repeat
        BEGIN
           markX := whereX;
           markY := whereY;
           Readln(InChar);
           if not (InChar in GoodOnes) then
           BEGIN
              gotoXY(markX, markY);
              ClrEOL
           END
        END
      until InChar in GoodOnes
   END;



PROCEDURE GetGoodInt(MinNum, MaxNum: integer;   var InNum: integer);

   {An error-trapping substitute for "readln" to get integer
    input from the keyboard. This procedure takes two parameters:
    a set of "acceptable" integers for input, and a variable
    parameter that is the actual integer input.  If the input
    integer is not in the set of acceptable integers, this
    procedure returns to the original screen position and waits
    for the user to enter an acceptable integer.}

   VAR
      markX, markY  : byte;
```

```
    LoopControl   : integer;

BEGIN
    repeat
        BEGIN
            markX := whereX;
            markY := whereY;

            {$I-}
            Readln(InNum);
            {$I+}
            LoopControl := ioresult;

            if (LoopControl <> 0) then
                BEGIN
                    gotoXY(markX, markY);
                    ClrEOL
                END;

            if (inNum < MinNum) or (inNum > MaxNum) then
                BEGIN
                    gotoXY(markX, markY);
                    ClrEOL
                END
        END
    until (LoopControl = 0) and (InNum >= MinNum) and (InNum <= MaxNum)
END;



END.    { of the "MyUtils" unit }
```

Units do have one peculiar aspect. In program listings, it did not matter if the program name declaration matched the file name of the program. If a program was named Register, you could save it just as easily under the name LIST5_X.PAS as you could under the name REGISTER.PAS. With units, however, Turbo Pascal must (1) locate the file on your hard disk and (2) use it by the unit name you have specified in your USES statement. Thus, the name of a unit must match its file name on disk. A unit called MyUtils, for example, must be saved under the name MYUTILS.PAS, not under another name such as LIST10_3.PAS. This limits the names of units to eight characters, but you can always clarify the unit's purpose by inserting a comment under the unit name.

Implementation

The IMPLEMENTATION section of the unit is "private" and is hidden from any other program modules that use the unit. It contains, as shown in Listing 10.1, the details of how subroutines named in the INTERFACE section actually work. It can also contain private declarations of subroutines, variables, constants, data types, and any other identifiers that you want to use in the unit but which should not be visible to anything outside the unit.

This ability to include such private declarations is very important. It lets you avoid some rather tricky bugs that can occur when another program module accidentally uses a variable, constant, or other identifier in a unit when it is not supposed to. Then, when you try to find the bug, you think you are looking at one variable when, in fact, you're looking at a completely different one. When it is appropriate, creating some private declarations in the IMPLEMENTATION section of the unit means that this problem cannot happen—at least not with the private identifiers. Remember the programming maxim: *Hide everything you can.*

The IMPLEMENTATION section begins with the word IMPLEMENTATION and ends with the word END, which marks the end of the unit.

Initialization

The initialization section of the unit allows you to assign values to variables and do other setup work that needs to be done before the subroutines in the unit are actually used. The initialization section, which is just like the main body of a regular program file, carries out its instructions when the unit is called. If you are using multiple units, then their initialization sections (if any) run in the order that they are named in your USES statement. As you can see in Listing 10.1, the initialization section is hidden inside the IMPLEMENTATION section:

```
Unit MyStuff;
INTERFACE
   { public declarations }
IMPLEMENTATION
   { private declarations }
   BEGIN { initialization section }
   { initialization statements }
   END;
END. { of MyStuff unit }
```

Depending on the situation, you also can use the initialization section of a unit to make sure that it is possible for the unit to work. For example, if certain files or memory-resident drivers are needed to run the unit, then the initialization section can determine if these are present. If they are not, then it can take the appropriate action, from warning the user to shutting down the entire program.

If your initialization needs are simple and the variables you are initializing are public, then you can use typed constants in the INTERFACE part of the unit as a simpler alternative to having an initialization section. For example, in Listing 10.1, we used the initialization section only to assign the string 'James' to the public variable *Name*. In this case, it would have been better to declare *Name* as a typed constant (a preinitialized variable) as follows:

```
Unit List10_1;
INTERFACE
TYPE
    String10 = STRING[10];
CONST
    Name : string10 = 'James'
{ ... etc. }
```

This would create *Name* as a public variable and initialize it with the value *'James'*. (If you need to review typed constants, they are discussed in Chapter 5.)

Listing 10.2 demonstrates how to name a unit in a USES statement. Note that the CRT unit is named first. In Turbo Pascal 4.0, if you used multiple units, and unit No.1 used unit No.2 (as Listing10.1 uses the CRT unit), then you had to list unit No.2 first in the USES statement, in accordance with Pascal's general rule that everything must be declared before it is used. Turbo Pascal 5.0 relaxed this rule so for that and later versions, you can list units in any order you desire.

Listing 10.2

```
PROGRAM Listing10_2;

USES CRT, List10_1;

VAR
    NewName : string10;
    NewNumber : INTEGER;

PROCEDURE Pause;
    VAR
```

```
        Proceed : CHAR;
    BEGIN
        WRITELN;
        WRITE(' Press any key to continue ...');
        Proceed := READKEY;
        WRITELN; WRITELN
    END;

BEGIN
    CLRSCR;
    NewNumber := NumberOfNames;
    WRITE(' The current value of "Name" in the List10_1 unit is ');
    WRITELN(Name, '.');
    pause;

    GetName(Name);    { uses Name variable from unit }
    WRITE(' The new value of "Name" in the List10_1 unit is ');
    WRITELN(Name);
    pause;

    GetName(NewName); { uses NewName variable from this program }
    WRITELN(' The current value of "NewName" is ', NewName, '.');
    pause
END.
```

In the main body of Listing 10.2, we first assign the *NumberOfNames* constant from the unit to a *NewNumber* variable in our program, demonstrating that constants in the INTERFACE section are indeed visible to the calling program. Then, we called the *GetName* routine from the unit and let it load a value into the *Name* variable, also from the unit. Finally, we used *GetName* with a variable from the calling program—which is much more common than using it with a variable from the unit. In both cases, it loaded the name you entered into the correct variable.

Why Use Units?

There are three main reasons to use units. The first, as I have already mentioned, is to store frequently used subroutines in a separate file from which they can be called *without* having to include them in the main program each time. The second, which was celebrated as "shattering the 64K barrier" when units were first introduced, provides a practical way to create programs larger than the 64K size limit of Turbo

Pascal 3.0. The third, which makes programming easier in the long run, is "procedural abstraction" that allows you to hide details about how subroutines in a unit actually work.

Packaging Frequently Used Routines

Packaging frequently used subroutines is more than just a matter of saving effort. By keeping subroutines in a separate unit, you can reduce the amount of time needed to compile a large program, because the units do not have to be recompiled each time you recompile your main program. This means that you can make as many changes as you want to in your main program, and not have to worry about those changes having any effect on the units.

If you are developing software for other Turbo Pascal programmers, you can distribute your work in precompiled units, which they can incorporate into their own programs. The people at TurboPower Software and Blaise Computing, two vendors of programming tools for Turbo Pascal, make a very nice living at this. Even if you are developing routines only for use in your own organization, this lets you distribute standardized units without the fear that they will be modified by anyone but you.

Developing Large Programs

One of the greatest benefits of using units is that they provide a practical way to develop programs larger than 64K. The 64K limit on program size is not an arbitrary feature of Turbo Pascal, but results from the limitations of the Intel 8086 processor, which, with its descendants (the Intel 80286, 80386, and 80486), powers virtually all PCs. The 8086, as a 16-bit microprocessor, handles data in 16-bit chunks. This means that it can directly handle 2^{16} (64K) different numbers to stand for memory locations; 64K is the number of different 16-digit combinations of zeroes and ones.

In order to deal with more memory, however—a full one megabyte, or 1,024K—the 8086 divides your PC's memory into 64K *segments*, each of which begins at a paragraph address. To calculate a given memory location, the 8086 combines two 16-bit pieces of information: the paragraph address where the 64K segment starts, and the offset, which gives a specific address within that segment. Thus, through some complex maneuvering, your PC can handle a full megabyte of RAM.

Even with this segmented-addressing scheme, however, the 8086 is still only a 16-bit processor and cannot easily handle information in chunks larger than 64K—the size of a single memory segment. This means that Turbo Pascal cannot compile a program file larger than 64K because all the code has to fit into a single segment. And, although the 80386 and 80486 processors are 32-bit chips that can address 2^{32} memory locations, we still have the 64K limit to keep compatibility with less powerful 8086 and 80286-based PCs.

Units provide a way around this problem. By splitting off groups of subroutines into their own units and then naming them in a USES clause at the beginning of your program, you can evade the 64K size limitation on your programs because no single program file is larger than 64K. You can even do the same trick with units themselves, which can use other units.

Procedural Abstraction

Procedural abstraction is a less obvious, but in the long run, no less important reason for using units. An important feature of subroutines, as you should recall from Chapter 9, is that their details remain hidden from the main part of the program. If you include a subroutine in the main program, then you are able to violate this information-hiding principle—even though it is not a good idea to do so. Units, however, enforce information hiding very strictly: the details of a unit's subroutines are completely invisible to the main program.

As we saw in Figure 10.1, the only public parts of a unit are its name and its INTERFACE section, which gives "headers" of the unit's subroutines without any of their details, for example,

```
PROCEDURE Pause;
```

Everything except the unit's name and its Interface section is hidden from the main program. You can even include private subroutines that are accessible only within the unit by defining them in the IMPLEMENTATION (hidden) section and omitting their headers from the INTERFACE section. Like units themselves, these can make your main program easier to read and provide subroutines that are local to a group of procedures but do not have to be included in each procedure.

Suppose, for example, that you want to use a local subroutine *DoBalance* inside two other subroutines *OnTimePayment* and *LatePayment*, but you do not want it accessible to other parts of the program. If you declared it as follows,

```
{ ... other declarations }
PROCEDURE DoBalance(VAR balance : REAL);
{ details of DoBalance routine}
PROCEDURE OnTimePayment(VAR balance : REAL);
{ details of OnTimePayment routine }
PROCEDURE LatePayment(VAR balance : REAL);
{ details of LatePayment routine }
{ ... the rest of the program }
```

then *DoBalance* would be accessible to both *OnTimePayment* and *LatePayment*, but it would *not* be hidden from the rest of the program as you wish. However, making it local to the two subroutines involves some redundancy, as in

```
{ ... other declarations }
PROCEDURE OnTimePayment(VAR balance : REAL);
     { ... }
     PROCEDURE DoBalance;
     { details of DoBalance }
PROCEDURE LatePayment(VAR balance : REAL);
     { ... }
     PROCEDURE DoBalance;
     { details of DoBalance }
{ ... the rest of the program }
```

Of course, there are other ways around this problem, but using *DoBalance* as a private subroutine in a unit with *OnTimePayment* and *LatePayment* gives you a fairly neat solution. Assuming that *DoBalance* is declared before *OnTimePayment* and *LatePayment* in the implementation section of the unit, it would then be accessible to both subroutines, and would be hidden from the main program.

Setting Up the MyUtils Unit

Now that we have a good idea of what units are and how they work, let's create a new unit called MyUtils to hold frequently used utility routines. In this chapter, we'll add the *Pause*, *GetGoodInt*, and *GetGoodChar* routines to MyUtils. As we develop new utility routines in later chapters, we will add them as well.

To create the MyUtils unit, enter Listing 10.3 and save it under the file name MYUTILS.PAS. If you want to avoid rekeying, you can use Turbo Pascal's paste feature (discussed in Chapter 4) to paste the three routines into the implementation section of the unit. *Pause* can be found in Listing 10.2, *GetGoodInt* in Listing 7.11, and *GetGoodChar* is in Listing 8.4.

Listing 10.3

```
Unit MyUtils;  { Listing 10.3: miscellaneous utility routines. }


INTERFACE
{ ==================== PUBLIC section of unit ==================== }

USES CRT, GRAPH;

TYPE
   GoodChars = set of char;   { used with the GetGoodChar procedure }

CONST
  YNchars : GoodChars = ['Y', 'y', 'N', 'n'];



PROCEDURE Pause;   { accepts any key }

PROCEDURE GetGoodChar(GoodOnes:GoodChars; var InChar:char);

PROCEDURE GetGoodInt(MinNum, MaxNum: integer; var InNum:integer);


IMPLEMENTATION
{ ==================== PRIVATE section of unit ==================== }


PROCEDURE Pause; { Pauses the program until user presses a key. }
   VAR
      Proceed : char;
   BEGIN
      Writeln;
      Write(' Press any key to continue ... ');
      Proceed := readkey;
```

```
    Writeln; Writeln
END;


PROCEDURE GetGoodChar(GoodOnes:GoodChars; var InChar:char);

    {An error-trapping substitute for "readln" to get character
     input from the keyboard. This procedure takes two parameters:
     a set of "acceptable" characters for input, and a variable
     parameter that is the actual character input.  If the input
     character is not in the set of acceptable characters, this
     procedure returns to the original screen position and waits
     for the user to enter an acceptable character.}

    VAR
        markX, markY  : byte;
    BEGIN
        repeat
           BEGIN
              markX := whereX;
              markY := whereY;
              Readln(InChar);
              if not (InChar in GoodOnes) then
                 BEGIN
                    gotoXY(markX, markY);
                    ClrEOL
                 END
           END
        until InChar in GoodOnes
    END;




PROCEDURE GetGoodInt(MinNum, MaxNum: integer;  var InNum: integer);

    {An error-trapping substitute for "readln" to get integer
     input from the keyboard. This procedure takes two parameters:
     a set of "acceptable" integers for input, and a variable
     parameter that is the actual integer input. If the input
     integer is not in the set of acceptable integers, this
     procedure returns to the original screen position and waits
     for the user to enter an acceptable integer.}

    VAR
        markX, markY  : byte;
```

```
    LoopControl   : integer;

BEGIN
   repeat
      BEGIN
         markX := whereX;
         markY := whereY;

         {$I-}
         Readln(InNum);
         {$I+}
         LoopControl := ioresult;

         if (LoopControl <> 0) then
            BEGIN
               gotoXY(markX, markY);
               ClrEOL
            END;

         if (inNum < MinNum) or (inNum > MaxNum) then
            BEGIN
               gotoXY(markX, markY);
               ClrEOL
            END
      END
   until (LoopControl = 0) and (InNum >= MinNum) and (InNum <= MaxNum)
END;
```

```
END.   { of the "MyUtils" unit }
```

There are several things to note about the MyUtils unit. First, like all units, it begins with the reserved word UNIT and the name of the unit. An explanatory comment tells what the unit is to be used for.

Then, in the interface part of the unit, we include the following:

- A USES statement that names other units used by the MyUtils unit. You already know that we use the CRT unit for the CLRSCR routine and several other routines. The GRAPH unit will be used in Chapter 15 for both text and graphics-oriented routines, such as determining the type of video adapter in the user's PC and setting screen colors.

- A TYPE declaration that defines a data type for use with the *GetGoodChar* routine.

- A CONST declaration that sets up a typed constant (a pre-initialized variable) of the data type we just defined. In this case, the type is the set of characters; the typed constant is a set that can include any characters we assign to it. In the typed constant declaration, we load 'Y', 'y', 'N', and 'n' into the set and refer to them by the variable name *YNchars* (for Yes-No characters).

- Headers for the subroutines that are currently defined in this unit. Each header lists the name of the subroutine and the parameters it takes, as well as the data type of each parameter and whether or not it is a VAR parameter.

In the implementation part of the unit, we repeat the header of each subroutine, but this time, we include the full details of how the subroutine works. Note that the header in the interface section must exactly match the header in the implementation section; otherwise, Turbo Pascal will not be able to compile the unit and will give you an "undefined forward" error message. (The headers in the interface section are, in a certain sense, forward declarations of subroutines to come. The only difference is that in the interface part of a unit, you do not have to specify that they are forward declarations, because it is assumed.)

The MyUtils unit ends with the reserved word END and a period. If we had wanted to, we could have declared *YNchars* in the interface section as a variable instead of a typed constant. In that case, we could have included an initialization section to load it with the characters we wanted.

Standard Turbo Pascal Units

Turbo Pascal comes with several predefined and precompiled units that add new features to the Pascal language. We will be using each of these units later, so at this point, let's just take a quick look at what each unit is and what it contains.

System

The system unit provides a wide variety of low-level features, and is automatically linked with every program; therefore, you do not have to specify the system unit in a USES clause. Because of this, you can consider the routines in the system unit to be a built-in part of the Turbo Pascal language.

DOS

The DOS unit, which will be discussed in Chapter 16, has routines that let you call a variety of MS-DOS functions, from reading directories of files on disk to executing outside programs from your Turbo Pascal program.

CRT

The CRT unit contains several useful routines that we have seen already: CLRSCR, WINDOW, GotoXY, KeyPressed, ReadKey, and ClrEOL. Other important routines in the CRT unit are the following:

- TextMode, which allows you to set the screen mode (color or monochrome) with either a 40- or an 80-column screen width and 25-, 43-, or 50-line screen height.

- TextColor and TextBackground, which allow you to set the color of text and the background over which it is displayed.

- AssignCRT, which associates a text file with the screen.

- Sound and NoSound, which we will use in creating Turbo Tunemaker in Chapter 19.

Printer

The printer unit has only one task to carry out, and that is to let your program direct output to a printer. The printer unit automatically assigns the file name LST to your PC's LPT1 printer port, and any output you direct to LST will be sent to the printer, as in

```
WRITELN(LST, 'This will print on your printer.');
```

If your printer is connected to a different port than LPT1, do not despair. You can create your own printer-file variable and assign a different port to it, just as you would assign a DOS name to any other file variable. If your printer is connected to the LPT2 port (or the COM1 or COM2 port), you can direct output to the printer by including the following lines in your program:

```
PROGRAM PrintDemo;
USES PRINTER;
VAR MyPrinter : text;
BEGIN
    ASSIGN(MyPrinter, 'LPT2');
    REWRITE(MyPrinter);
    { ... etc. }
    CLOSE(MyPrinter)
END.
```

Graph

The graph unit allows you to create a wide range of graphics displays, from bar charts and fractals to fancy type styles and sizes. We'll discuss the graph unit in detail in Chapter 15.

Overlay

The overlay unit allows you to develop very large programs whose size exceeds your PC's available DOS memory. Normally, when you start a program, the entire program is loaded into your PC's RAM. With very large programs, however, this is not possible. The overlay unit lets your program swap pieces of itself in and out of memory as they are needed. Pieces that are not currently being used can be held on disk or in expanded memory.

Because of its specialized application for very large programs, we will not discuss the overlay unit any further in this book.

Strings

The strings unit contains special routines for handling null-terminated strings. For most purposes, you won't need this unit. The string-handling functions in this unit are almost identical to those used in the standard C library.

Turbo Vision Units

Borland Pascal and Turbo Pascal 7 come with nine predefined units of objects that you can use to create programs with Turbo Vision. These units include objects that let you add pull-down menus, mouse support, dialog boxes, multiple windows, and memory management to your programs without having to write the extra code yourself.

Special Unit Files

There are four special unit files that you need to know about. The first, TURBO.TPL, contains all the standard Turbo Pascal units except for the graph unit; hence, you won't find separate unit files on disk for the CRT, graph, overlay, or other built-in units: they are all included in the TURBO.TPL file.

Second, if you wish, you can also include your own units in TURBO.TPL by using the TPUMOVER program, which should be in your Turbo Pascal main program directory. However, there isn't much to be gained by this, because you can still use your units whether or not they are in the TURBO.TPL file.

Third and fourth are the Graph3 and Turbo3 units, which you can use to produce programs that are backward-compatible with Turbo Pascal 3.0.

CHAPTER
ELEVEN

Pointers and Dynamic Allocation

- **Pointers and Dynamic Variables**

- **The Stack and the Heap**

- **Creating and Using Linked Lists**

In Chapter 8, we saw how to create fixed-length lists of items by using arrays. This allowed us to put student records, for example, into a single array instead of having to create a separate variable for each record.

This approach has many advantages. Because the elements of an array are stored next to each other in the computer's memory, it takes very little time to go from one record in an array to the next. It is also simple: declare an array variable with a certain number of slots of the appropriate type, and you can then simply "load it up" by putting values into each slot.

Disadvantages of Arrays

There is also a large disadvantage in this approach: Pascal arrays are inflexible and sometimes tend to waste space in your computer's memory. To be certain of having enough space for all the data items you need, you must make the array large enough to contain all the data items that you might ever possibly need. If there are many large items in the array, you could easily run out of available memory. If you try to cut down the size of the array to save memory, however, you run the risk of "overflow"—that is, of having more data items than can fit into the array.

For that reason, arrays (and fixed-length lists in general) can be a bad choice when you are not sure of how many data items you will need. In some obvious cases, this is not a problem: for example, you could create a 50-slot array to hold data about the states in the United States. Or, if the data items are small and there will never be too many of them, you can "overbook" your array with many extra slots and never have any problems.

In some other cases, however, fixed-length lists like those you create with an array just will not do the job. Lists of widely varying lengths waste PC memory if you use arrays to hold them.

There are other problems. Suppose that you have a sorted list in an array and you have to insert a new item into the middle of the list. Even if the array is not full, this can be a major undertaking. First, you must identify the correct place to insert the new item. Then, you must open up that array slot by moving all the items that come after it (each of these items must be moved up one position in the array). Finally, you can insert the new item into the list. Although this is *possible* (unlike the case of trying to insert an item into a full array, which is not possible), it involves a great deal of extra work both for the program and the programmer.

To handle situations like this, we need a way to create variable-length lists and other more flexible data structures. These data structures will use only as much memory as they need on a particular run of the program.

Dynamic Allocation

Dynamic memory allocation is the solution to the problem. Although the name is intimidating, the idea is fairly simple. Consider, first, the case of ordinary, static variables such as array variables. When a program is compiled, Turbo Pascal sets aside (allocates) a certain amount of memory for all the variables and other data items declared in the program. Later, when the program is run by the user, these decisions about memory allocation have already been made and cannot be changed. For that reason, this kind of memory allocation is called *static*.

Dynamic memory allocation, however, takes place after the program is actually running; memory allocation decisions can be made and new variables can be created "on the fly." The feature (in Pascal and many other languages) that makes this possible is the *pointer*. When used in a few clever ways, which we will discuss presently, pointers give us tremendous flexibility for creating new variables whenever we need them, and also for getting rid of old variables when they are no longer needed.

The Idea of Pointers

It is important to understand the problems we meet with in any attempt to create new variables after the program is running. The main problems are (1) keeping track of which variables are being used and (2) locating where each variable is situated in the computer's memory. With static variables, these are not problems at all; these decisions are made at compile time and each variable is declared explicitly and named in the Pascal source code. But to create new variables *after* the program is running, we must determine the following:

- How to refer to each new variable. Although static variables are named in the source code, for example, "Counter," dynamic variables do not have names. If we need to talk about one of them or assign a value to it, how do we accomplish this task?

- How to locate each new variable. Because the memory addresses of dynamic variables are not pre-assigned at compile time, we must have some way to find the dynamic variables when we need them.

A pointer is a special kind of variable that solves these problems for us. Instead of holding an integer, a string, an array, a record, or some other *substantive* item, a pointer holds the *memory address* of another variable—a variable that may or may not exist at the time the program is compiled. After the program is running, we can take a pointer, point it at a memory location (in an area called the *heap*), and create a new dynamic variable in that location.

Normally, a pointer variable, like any other variable, is set up so that it will work only with items of a given type. Just as an integer variable can hold only integers, a string variable can hold only strings, and so forth, each pointer variable is designed to *point to* only one specific type of dynamic variable. As a result, when you use that pointer to create a new dynamic variable, Turbo Pascal knows how much space to reserve in the heap for the new variable: for instance, it must allocate more space for an array variable than for a character variable.

A pointer can point to any data type *except* file types. You declare a pointer data type as follows:

```
TYPE
   MyFirstPointer = ^INTEGER;
   MySecondPointer = ^MyPointerDataItem;
   MyPointerDataItem = RECORD
                       Name : string10;
                       Age  : INTEGER;
                       Paid : BOOLEAN
                       END;
```

The caret (^) in the type declaration indicates that the type being defined is a pointer type. The key to produce the caret is located on the top row of most PC keyboards, and is produced by holding down the *Shift* key and pressing the 6 key. In some mainframe computer versions of Pascal (and many books about Pascal), the up-arrow symbol (↑) is used instead of the caret, but the caret will work fine with the vast majority of Pascal compilers.

The first pointer type we declared will point only to dynamic variables of type INTEGER. The second pointer type, *MySecondPointer*, is designed to point only to items of type *MyPointerDataItem*. If you try to point it at anything else, your program either will not compile or will crash while running. Turbo Pascal does permit the use of untyped pointers (see discussion below), but these require special procedures and extra caution.

If you look carefully at the type declaration above, you will see an apparent paradox. Pascal requires all identifiers to be declared before they are used; however, we used the data type *MyPointerDataItem* in setting up the *MySecondPointer* type one line *before* we declared it in the program code.

This is one of the few exceptions to the rule that all identifiers must be declared before they are used. When we declare a pointer type that points to a user-defined data type, Pascal assumes that we are going to declare the second type before the end of the TYPE section. If we fail to do so, the program will not compile. This exception to the declare-before-use rule becomes very important when we use pointers to create linked data structures, some of which we will see later in this chapter.

One issue has come up previously but is worth repeating. What we have done so far *does not create any dynamic variables;* indeed, it does not even create any pointer variables. All that the TYPE section does is to set up user-defined data types that we can then use for specific data items, that is, variables and constants.

Creating Dynamic Variables

Once we have declared pointer types in the TYPE section of the program, we can proceed to create variables of those types in the VAR section. You declare a pointer variable just as any other:

```
TYPE
    MyFirstPointer = ^INTEGER;
    MySecondPointer = ^MyPointerDataItem;
    MyPointerDataItem = RECORD
                        Name : string10;
                        Age  : INTEGER;
```

```
                        Paid : BOOLEAN
                        END;
VAR
   NumPtr : MyFirstPointer;
   RecPtr : MySecondPointer;
```

Note that both of these pointer variables are *static,* not dynamic, variables: they are embedded in the program code and are fixed at compile-time. They cannot be changed by the user.

This is the normal situation. *Some* variables must always be static so that dynamic variables have a known memory location to which they can be connected. Moreover, although it can point to an integer variable, *NumPtr* itself is not an integer but a pointer. In the same way, *RecPtr* is not a record but a pointer *to* a record. In both cases, the pointers point to dynamic variables, but are themselves static variables.

To create dynamic variables, we use Pascal's built-in *New* procedure with a pointer variable. This procedure allocates a portion of memory for a variable of the appropriate type; then points the pointer at that memory location (that is, it loads that memory address into the pointer variable). The process is shown in Listing 11.1. (Turbo Pascal also extends the *New* procedure with object-oriented features that go beyond standard Pascal, but we will defer our discussion of those features until the chapter on object-oriented programming.)

Listing 11.1

```
PROGRAM Listing11_1;

   { Demonstrates how to set up pointer types and create
     dynamic variables. }

TYPE
   String10 = STRING[10];

   MyFirstPointer = ^INTEGER;

   MySecondPointer = ^MyPointerDataItem;
   MyPointerDataItem = RECORD
                       Name : string10;
                       Age  : INTEGER;
```

```
                  Paid  : BOOLEAN
                  END;

VAR
   NumPtr : MyFirstPointer;
   RecPtr : MySecondPointer;

BEGIN
   NumPtr := NIL;           { Initializes the variable to NIL. }
   RecPtr := NIL;

   New(NumPtr);
   NumPtr^ := 5;            { Refers to the variable that NumPtr points
                             to by "dereferencing" NumPtr. }

   New(RecPtr);
   WITH RecPtr^ DO          { Refers to the variable that RecPtr points
                             to by "dereferencing" RecPtr. }
      BEGIN
         Name := 'Sam';     { Assigns values to the fields in RecPtr^, }
         Age  := 25;        { the dynamic record variable pointed to   }
         Paid := TRUE       { by the pointer RecPtr.                    }
      END

END.
```

Of course, it is very convenient that we have a pointer that tells us where a dynamic variable is located—but how do we refer to the variable itself? *NumPtr* and *RecPtr* refer to pointers, not to the dynamic variables to which they point. Suppose we create a dynamic variable by calling the *New* routine with *NumPtr*, as in Listing 11.1. How do we assign a value to the new variable?

We do it by *dereferencing* the pointer. In the TYPE section, we put a caret *before* the name of a data type. To talk about what a pointer points to, we put a caret *after* the name of the pointer variable, as in *NumPtr*^ and *RecPtr*^. By dereferencing a pointer, we tell Pascal that we are talking about what the pointer points to, just as we do in Listing 11.1. In summary:

- *NumPtr* is a pointer that points to a dynamic integer variable; *NumPtr*^ is a dynamic integer variable.

- *RecPtr* is a pointer that points to a dynamic record variable of type *MyPointerDataItem*; *RecPtr*^ is a dynamic record variable of type *MyPointerDataItem*.

Avoid Dangling Pointers

Note that in Listing 11.1, the *NumPtr* and *RecPtr* variables are declared in the VAR section, just like any other static variables.

In the first two lines of the program body, we set both of these pointers to NIL. NIL is a predefined value that tells Pascal that a pointer does not point to anything. If we leave a pointer undefined—that is, if we do not assign a value to it—then it might contain anything, even a memory address used by the operating system or some other vital piece of software. Such a pointer is called a *dangling pointer*. If it is accidentally used, the results are unpredictable and can be potentially disastrous.

For this reason, it is wise to be very careful with pointers. Any time a pointer does not have a dynamic variable assigned to it, it should be set to the value NIL. You may get away with not doing this, but considering the risks, it is wiser to play it safe.

Linked Data Structures

What we have seen of dynamic variables so far is interesting but not very impressive. In Listing 11.1, we had two static pointer variables and used them to create two dynamic variables: one an integer and one a record. Where is the great flexibility that dynamic allocation was supposed to deliver?

The flexibility appears when we realize that pointers can point to almost any user-defined data element, *including* one that contains more pointers. This means that we can use pointers to create daisy-chained data structures. To create the first item in the daisy chain, we use *New* with the initial, static pointer. The dynamic record variable we create *also* contains a pointer, which we use with *New* again to create a second item in the chain, which has its own pointer we can use with *New* to create a third item, and so forth. A simple example of how this works is given in Listing 11.2.

Listing 11.2

```
PROGRAM Listing11_2;

   { Gives a simple example of a linked data structure
     using pointers. }

TYPE
   String10 = STRING[10];

   NodePtr = ^ListItem;
```

```
ListItem = RECORD
             Number : INTEGER;
             next   : NodePtr
             END;


VAR
    ListHead : nodeptr;

BEGIN
    New(ListHead);                    { creates a new list node }
    ListHead^.Number := 1;            { assigns 1 to the number field }

    New(ListHead^.next);              { creates another new list node }
    ListHead^.next^.Number := 2;  { assigns 2 to the number field }

    New(ListHead^.next^.next);              { creates a third list node }
    ListHead^.next^.next^.Number := 3;  { assigns 3 to the number field }
    ListHead^.next^.next^.next := NIL   { sets the "next" pointer to NIL }
END.
```

Listing 11.2 performs an essentially trivial task, but it demonstrates the basic idea on which all linked data structures are built: a daisy-chain of records, each of which contains one or more pointers that point to other records or to NIL. Using this concept, we start with a single static pointer, *ListHead*, and create a linked list that contains three integers. None of the list's three record variables exist before the program runs: all are created with the *New* procedure at run-time.

Here is how Listing 11.2 works. The *ListItem* record type contains two fields: an integer field and a pointer field that can point to another record of type *ListItem*. When the program first begins to run, there are no variables of this type. There is, however, a static pointer variable *ListHead* that can point to *ListItem-type* records. The details become somewhat complicated, so let's take it line by line:

- Line 1: We call the *New* procedure with the *ListHead* variable. This creates a dynamic record variable of type *ListItem* and points *ListHead* at that variable's memory location.

- Line 2: We dereference the *ListHead* pointer. Remember, what *ListHead* points to is a record, so we can manipulate the dereferenced pointer just as we would any other record variable. Using the dot notation (see the discussion of records in Chapter 8 if you are hazy on this point), we assign the integer *1* to the Number field of the record variable.

- Line 3: The Next field of the *ListHead^* record variable is itself a pointer variable. Therefore, we can use the *New* routine to create another new node in the list and point the Next field of *ListHead^* at the new node.

- Line 4: Because *ListHead^.next* points to a dynamic variable, we can dereference it (*ListHead^.next^*) and put the integer value 2 into the Number field of the dynamic variable.

- Line 5: Because *ListHead^.next^.next* is a pointer, we can use the *New* routine to create another list node and point the pointer at it.

- Line 6: Because *ListHead^.next^.next^* is a dynamic record variable, we can assign the integer value 3 to its Number field.

- Line 7: Because *ListHead^.next^.next^.next* is a pointer that is not going to point to anything, we set it to NIL.

In a certain sense, this is not a fair example, because we will see techniques later in this chapter that make it much easier to refer to items in a list. However, this example presents the basic idea of linked data structures without any extra features to complicate the picture. In fact, a picture makes it much easier to understand linked data structures, as shown in Figure 11.1.

Disposing of Dynamic Variables

So far, we have seen how to use pointers to create new variables while a program is running. Some of these variables, however, may be used in a certain part of the program and then never be needed again. If there were no way to free up the memory used by dynamic variables, then—at least in terms of saving memory—they would be only a slight improvement over static variables.

Fortunately, there is a way to free up the memory used by dynamic variables that are no longer needed: Pascal's *Dispose* procedure. Using the *Dispose* procedure with a pointer variable frees the memory reserved for the variable that the pointer points to, and then disconnects the pointer from that memory address. The memory location that was used for the "disposed" dynamic variable can be used for other dynamic variables, and the pointer's value itself becomes undefined. Listing 11.3 shows how to use the *Dispose* procedure.

FIGURE 11.1:

Linked data structures in Listing 11.1

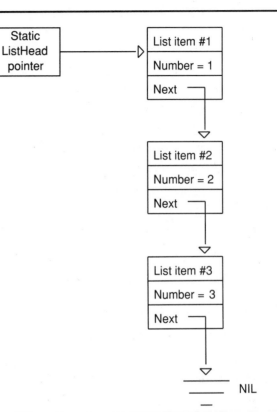

Listing 11.3

```
PROGRAM Listing11_3;

    { Shows how to use the Dispose procedure to free up
      memory used by dynamic variables when they are no
      longer needed. }


TYPE
    String10 = STRING[10];

    NodePtr = ^ListItem;
    ListItem = RECORD
```

```
             Number : INTEGER;
             next   : NodePtr
             END;


VAR
   ListHead : nodeptr;

BEGIN
   New(ListHead);                    { creates a new list node }
   ListHead^.Number := 1;            { assigns 1 to the number field }

   New(ListHead^.next);              { creates another new list node }
   ListHead^.next^.Number := 2;      { assigns 2 to the number field }
   ListHead^.next^.next := NIL;      { end of the list              }

   Dispose(ListHead^.next);    { de-allocates memory }
   ListHead^.next := NIL       { sets undefined pointer to NIL }
END.
```

It is *very important,* when a pointer's value becomes undefined, that it is assigned either a new memory location or a NIL value. As we noted earlier, a "dangling" pointer is like a time bomb waiting to explode. Unless a pointer is going to receive a new value immediately after you use it with *Dispose,* then it should be set to NIL with the program line (for example)

```
ThisPtr := NIL;
```

The Stack and the Heap

We've referred earlier in this chapter to the *heap,* where Turbo Pascal reserves memory for dynamic variables. Another term you will hear frequently is the *stack,* and this is a good place to explain both terms.

The stack is an area of memory that Turbo Pascal reserves for local variables used by subroutines. When a procedure or function is called in your program, Turbo Pascal sets aside space in the stack for the local variables hidden inside that procedure or function. Immediately after that in the stack, Pascal places the "return address" of the line that called the subroutine, so that when the subroutine finishes its work, the program can continue from the exact point at which it called the subroutine.

The default size of the stack is 16,384 bytes (16K). You can use the *{$M}* compiler directive or the Memory Sizes choice on the Options menu to change the amount of memory reserved for the stack. Normally, however, you should not have to increase the amount of stack memory unless you are using many large local variables. *Stack overflow*—running out of stack space—is a common problem for novice programmers, and usually means that some routine is incorrectly designed. If you have this problem, take a careful look at your code before you rush to increase the stack size.

Although the stack has nothing much to do with dynamic allocation, it provides a useful contrast to the heap. The heap is an area of memory that Turbo Pascal uses to store dynamic variables (that is, variables created by your program while it is running). When we say that Turbo Pascal allocates memory on the heap, this simply means that it reserves a certain location where you can store the values of dynamic variables. Because a variable is fundamentally a memory location that can take values of a certain type, allocating the memory is the same thing as creating the variables.

Normally, Turbo Pascal uses all the free memory in your PC for the heap. Suppose that you have 640K in your PC. If your program takes up 200K (including the stack), DOS 50K, and memory-resident programs 100K, then the heap size will be 640K minus (200K + 50K + 100K), or 290K. This is a lot of memory, but if you make extensive use of linked data structures, you will be surprised at how easy it is to fill. Figure 11.2 shows how PC memory is allocated between your program, the stack, and the heap.

Note that Figure 11.2 omits some details that are not relevant to our immediate purpose of understanding the heap, but it is accurate in its essentials.

MemAvail and MaxAvail

Two important functions for using the heap, particularly if you are making extensive use of dynamic variables or are using large dynamic variables, are *Memavail* and *Maxavail*. *Memavail* informs you of the total amount of memory (in bytes) available on the heap, while *Maxavail* informs you of the largest single (contiguous) piece of memory available on the heap.

These two functions are different because the heap allocates memory for dynamic variables wherever it can find some free space, and de-allocates memory in no particular order. This means that you can have the bottom of the heap area, as shown

FIGURE 11.2:

Memory map of the stack and the heap

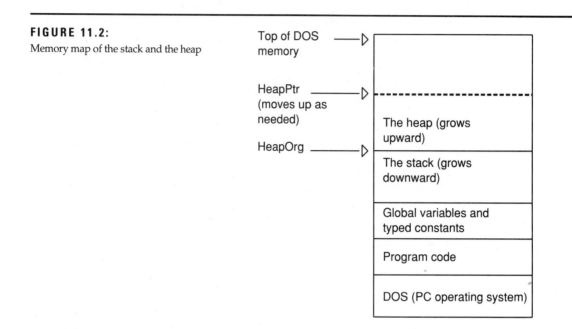

in Figure 11.2, occupied by dynamic variables, have free space above it, and then have still more dynamic variables above the free space. Thus, the available memory on the heap is split into smaller pieces.

When it comes to creating a dynamic variable on the heap, however, the only thing that matters is the size of the pieces—not the total heap memory available. If there is 100K of heap space available but the largest contiguous piece is 25K, then your program will have a run-time error (heap overflow) if you try to create a dynamic variable that requires 30K.

You can use *Memavail* to determine the total amount of free space on the heap, and *Maxavail* as a safety mechanism to prevent heap overflow. Where *SizeOf* is a function that returns the amount of memory needed by a particular variable type, you can use *Memavail* and *Maxavail* as follows:

```
TYPE
    RecPtr = ^StudentRecord;
    StudentRecord = RECORD
                        Name : STRING[10];
                        GPA  : REAL
                        END;
```

```
VAR
    Student : RecPtr;
BEGIN
    { ... program statements }
    WRITELN('Total heap memory available: ', MemAvail);
    IF MaxAvail < SizeOf(StudentRecord)
        THEN WRITELN(' Inadequate heap space.')
        ELSE NEW(Student);
    { ... more program statements }
END.
```

The IF clause checks to make sure that an adequate-sized piece of memory is available on the heap before trying to create a dynamic variable, and thus prevents your program from suffering a heap overflow error.

The best solution, of course, is to prevent the problem from occurring in the first place. Shortages of heap space often can be avoided if you scrupulously dispose of dynamic variables as soon as they are no longer needed. As noted earlier, if you fail to do this, you have lost one of the major advantages that dynamic variables have over static variables. There is an old saying that someone who *does not* read is no better off than someone who *cannot* read. To this, we might add that a programmer who does not use the advantages of dynamic variables is no better off than someone who only knows how to use arrays.

Using Untyped Pointers

Normally, a pointer variable can point only to dynamic variables of a specific type: the type that you declared when you set up the pointer type. Thus, in our previous example,

```
TYPE
    MyFirstPointer = ^INTEGER;
    MySecondPointer = ^MyPointerDataItem;
    MyPointerDataItem = RECORD
                            Name : string10;
                            Age  : INTEGER;
                            Paid : BOOLEAN
                            END;
VAR
    NumPtr : MyFirstPointer;
    RecPtr : MySecondPointer;
```

the pointer variable *NumPtr* can point only to integer variables, and the pointer variable *RecPtr* can point only to variables of the type *MyPointerDataItem*. In these cases, we may not know how many dynamic variables we will need, but we know, at least, what size they will be when we create them.

There are rare occasions, however, when we know that we will need to create dynamic variables, but we do not know at compile time how big they will be during a particular run of the program. For these situations, Turbo Pascal provides an *untyped pointer* type that can point at these unknown-at-compile-time data objects. It is declared as follows:

```
VAR
    MysteryPtr : Pointer;
```

This untyped pointer type is not supported by standard Pascal and is used mainly for low-level system programming, such as to save the contents of video memory to an array for later restoration. Untyped pointers cannot be dereferenced like normal pointers. Because they are not set up to point to variables of a specific type, they cannot be used with the *New* and *Dispose* procedures, which need to know how much heap memory to allocate or release.

GetMem and FreeMem

To allocate and de-allocate memory for untyped pointers, you must use Turbo Pascal's *GetMem* and *FreeMem* procedures. These work exactly like the *New* and *Dispose* procedures, except that in addition to the untyped pointer variable, you must also specify the amount of heap memory to allocate or deallocate:

```
GetMem(MysteryPtr, 4000);
FreeMem(MysteryPtr, 4000);
```

where *MysteryPtr* is an untyped pointer variable and, in our example, 4000 is the number of bytes of memory that *MysteryPtr*'s referent uses on the heap.

Dynamic Data Structures

Now, we arrive at a practical application of dynamic allocation: creating and manipulating a linked list. We will look at other dynamic data structures in Chapter 17, but this should be adequate to demonstrate their power.

It is always important to keep a clear idea of what one is doing, but nowhere is this more important than when handling linked data structures. If you think exclusively in terms of pointers and dereferencing and heap memory, you can become hopelessly confused. On the other hand, if you step back from the technical details and focus on what you are really trying to accomplish, the task of manipulating linked data structures begins to seem almost trivial.

The operations we are going to perform, and the results we will achieve, are illustrated in Figure 11.3.

Creating a Singly Linked List

Given that background, let's "think through" what we need to do to create a linked list. Suppose we have the following:

```
TYPE
    RecPtr = ^StudentRec;
    StudentRec = RECORD
                    Name  : STRING[10];
                    GPA   : REAL;
                    Next  : RecPtr
                    END;
VAR
    ListHead,
    ListTail  : RecPtr;
```

This type of list is called *singly linked* because there is only one pointer link between each record and the next. Another kind of list, called *doubly linked,* offers some advantages but it is slightly more complicated to manipulate. Instead of having only a *next* pointer in each record, it also has a *previous* pointer that points to the previous record in the list. In this chapter, we will demonstrate only singly linked lists.

To add an item to the list, we must first determine where to add it. If the list is empty, we simply use the *New* procedure with the *ListHead* pointer; this creates a dynamic variable of the type *StudentRec* and points the *ListHead* pointer at its memory location in the heap. We then assign values to the record and set its Next field to NIL because, in a one-record list, there is no "next" record.

If the list is not empty, then our task is slightly more complicated. First, assuming that we are simply adding records as they come along (not in any sorted order), we have to find the end of the list. We could do this by starting at the *ListHead* record and moving down the list until we arrived at a record whose Next field was NIL,

FIGURE 11.3:

Adding items to a singly linked list

Case #1: Adding to an empty list

Initial situation:

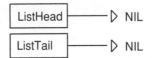

Desired result after adding an item:

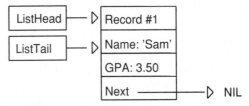

Case #2: Adding to a nonempty list

Initial situation (list could contain any number of items):

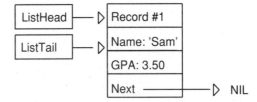

Desired result after adding an item:

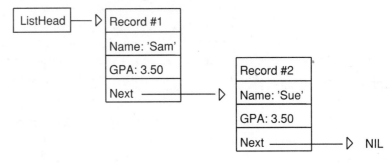

but there is an easier way. We can declare an extra pointer of the same type as *List-Head* to keep track of the end of the list. This means that in a list with only one item, both the *ListHead* and the *ListTail* pointers will point at the same record.

To add a new item to the end of the list, we call the *New* procedure with the Next pointer of the *ListTail* record. This creates a new dynamic record and points the Next pointer of the *ListTail* record at that record. We then assign values to the new record, set its Next field to NIL, and repoint the *ListTail* pointer so that it now points at the new end of the list.

This process of adding a node to a list is demonstrated in Listing 11.4.

Listing 11.4

```
PROGRAM Listing11_4;

    { Shows how to create a linked list of student names and GPAs.
      Uses the MyUtils unit created in Chapter 10. }


USES CRT, MyUtils;

TYPE
    string10 = STRING[10];

    RecPtr = ^StudentRec;
    StudentRec = RECORD
                    Name : string10;
                    GPA : real;
                    Next : RecPtr
                    END;
VAR
    ListHead,
    ListTail : RecPtr;
    proceed  : CHAR;

PROCEDURE init(VAR ListHead, ListTail : RecPtr; VAR proceed : CHAR);
    BEGIN
        ListHead := NIL;
        ListTail := NIL;
        proceed := 'Y'
    END;

PROCEDURE addname(VAR ListHead, ListTail : RecPtr);
    BEGIN
    CLRSCR;
    IF ListHead = NIL
        THEN BEGIN
```

```
      NEW(ListHead);
      WRITE(' Enter name: '); READLN(ListHead^.name); WRITELN;
      WRITE(' Enter GPA: '); READLN(ListHead^.GPA);
      ListHead^.next := NIL;
      ListTail := ListHead;
      pause
      END
 ELSE BEGIN
      NEW(ListTail^.next);
      IF ListHead = ListTail
         THEN ListHead^.next := ListTail^.next;
      ListTail := ListTail^.next;
      WRITE(' Enter name: '); READLN(ListTail^.name); WRITELN;
      WRITE(' Enter GPA: '); READLN(ListTail^.GPA); WRITELN;
      ListTail^.next := NIL;
      pause
      END
   END;


BEGIN
   init(ListHead, ListTail, proceed);
   REPEAT
      addname(ListHead, ListTail);
      WRITE(' Do another (Y/N)? ');
      READLN(proceed)
   UNTIL UPCASE(proceed) <> 'Y';
   pause
END.
```

Traversing a Linked List

Compared to creating a singly linked list, traversing the list is a fairly simple exercise. We create a new *current item pointer* to keep track of where we are in the list, along with a counter to keep track of the item number. Then we simply tell Pascal that until the current pointer is NIL—that is, until the end of the list has been reached—to visit each list item, report its contents, and then move on to the next item in the list. The process of traversing a linked list is demonstrated in Listing 11.5.

Listing 11.5

```
PROGRAM Listing11_5;

   { Shows how to traverse a linked list of student names and
     GPAs. Uses the MyUtils unit created in Chapter 10. }


USES CRT, MyUtils;

TYPE
   string10 = STRING[10];

   RecPtr = ^StudentRec;
   StudentRec = RECORD
                   Name : string10;
                   GPA : real;
                   Next : RecPtr
                   END;
VAR
   ListHead,
   ListTail : RecPtr;
   proceed  : CHAR;

PROCEDURE init(VAR ListHead, ListTail : RecPtr; VAR proceed : CHAR);
  BEGIN
      ListHead := NIL;
      ListTail := NIL;
      proceed := 'Y'
  END;

PROCEDURE addname(VAR ListHead, ListTail : RecPtr);
   BEGIN
   CLRSCR;
   IF ListHead = NIL
      THEN BEGIN
           NEW(ListHead);
           WRITE(' Enter name: '); READLN(ListHead^.name); WRITELN;
           WRITE(' Enter GPA: '); READLN(ListHead^.GPA);
           ListHead^.next := NIL;
           ListTail := ListHead;
           pause
           END
      ELSE BEGIN
           NEW(ListTail^.next);
```

```
            IF ListHead = ListTail
                THEN ListHead^.next := ListTail^.next;
            ListTail := ListTail^.next;
            WRITE(' Enter name: '); READLN(ListTail^.name); WRITELN;
            WRITE(' Enter GPA: '); READLN(ListTail^.GPA); WRITELN;
            ListTail^.next := NIL;
            pause
            END
    END;

PROCEDURE TraverseList(ListHead : RecPtr);
    VAR
        currptr : RecPtr;
        counter : integer;
    BEGIN
        currptr := ListHead;
        counter := 0;
        if currptr = NIL then WRITELN(' The list is empty.');
        while currptr <> NIL do
                BEGIN
                counter := counter + 1;
                WRITELN;
                WRITE(' The name in StudentRec number ', counter);
                WRITELN(' is ', currptr^.name, '.');
                WRITE(' The GPA of ', currptr^.name, ' is ');
                WRITELN(currptr^.GPA:0:2, '.');
                WRITELN;
                WRITELN(' So far, ', counter, ' records have been visited.');
                currptr := currptr^.next;
                pause
                END;
        currptr := NIL;     { not strictly needed }
    END;

BEGIN
    init(ListHead, ListTail, proceed);
    REPEAT
        addname(ListHead, ListTail);
        WRITE(' Do another (Y/N)? ');
        READLN(proceed)
    UNTIL UPCASE(proceed) <> 'Y';
    pause;
    TraverseList(ListHead);
END.
```

Sequential Searching of a Linked List

Doing a sequential search of a linked list is quite similar to the search of an array-based list that we saw in Chapter 8. The main difference is that, instead of combining an *empty value* with a slot counter to tell us when we have reached the end of the list, we simply search the list until we find the searched-for value or run into the value NIL.

We traverse the list in the same way as shown in Listing 11.5, and at each list item, we compare the name field with the search target. If the name field equals the search target, then we set the Boolean *found* variable to true and drop out of the WHILE loop that does the search. If the name field does not match the search target, we then move ahead one item until we find the search target or reach the end of the list, either of which will cause us to drop out of the loop. This process is demonstrated in Listing 11.6.

Listing 11.6

```
PROGRAM Listing11_6;

   { Demonstrates a simple sequential search of a list containing
     student names and GPAs. Uses the MyUtils unit created in
     Chapter 10. }

USES CRT, MyUtils;

TYPE
   string10 = STRING[10];

   RecPtr = ^StudentRec;
   StudentRec = RECORD
                   Name : string10;
                   GPA : real;
                   Next : RecPtr
                END;
VAR
   ListHead,
   ListTail : RecPtr;
   proceed  : CHAR;

PROCEDURE init(VAR ListHead, ListTail : RecPtr; VAR proceed : CHAR);
   BEGIN
      ListHead := NIL;
```

```
        ListTail := NIL;
        proceed := 'Y'
    END;

PROCEDURE addname(VAR ListHead, ListTail : RecPtr);
    BEGIN
    CLRSCR;
    IF ListHead = NIL
        THEN BEGIN
            NEW(ListHead);
            WRITE(' Enter name: '); READLN(ListHead^.name); WRITELN;
            WRITE(' Enter GPA: '); READLN(ListHead^.GPA);
            ListHead^.next := NIL;
            ListTail := ListHead;
            pause
            END
        ELSE BEGIN
            NEW(ListTail^.next);
            IF ListHead = ListTail
                THEN ListHead^.next := ListTail^.next;
            ListTail := ListTail^.next;
            WRITE(' Enter name: '); READLN(ListTail^.name); WRITELN;
            WRITE(' Enter GPA: '); READLN(ListTail^.GPA); WRITELN;
            ListTail^.next := NIL;
            pause
            END
    END;

procedure SearchList(ListHead : RecPtr);
    VAR
        currptr : RecPtr;
        target  : string10;
        found   : BOOLEAN;
        counter : INTEGER;

    BEGIN
        currptr := ListHead;
        counter := 0;
        found := FALSE;
        WRITE(' Enter a name for which to search: ');
        READLN(target);
        if currptr = NIL then WRITELN(' Sorry. The list is empty.');
        while (currptr <> NIL) AND (NOT Found) DO
            BEGIN
            counter := counter + 1;
```

```
        IF currptr^.name = target
          THEN BEGIN
                 Found := TRUE;
                 WRITE(' Search target found at list item # ');
                 WRITELN(counter, '.')
                 END
            ELSE currptr := currptr^.next;
        END;
      IF found = FALSE THEN WRITELN(' Sorry. Target not found.');
      pause
   END;

BEGIN
   init(ListHead, ListTail, proceed);
   REPEAT
     addname(ListHead, ListTail);
     WRITE(' Do another (Y/N)? ');
     READLN(proceed)
   UNTIL UPCASE(proceed) <> 'Y';
   pause;
   SearchList(ListHead);
END.
```

Freeing Up Heap Memory

In the program examples we have seen so far, we have assumed that we have unlimited memory available for our dynamic data structures. Often, this assumption is justified, because all DOS memory not occupied by the program is used for the heap, which holds dynamic variables (see Figure 11.2).

However, it is also possible to run out of heap space; this occurs, for example, when you run a routine repeatedly that creates new dynamic variables on each run, or when you use large dynamic arrays. Recall that each time you create a new dynamic variable, Pascal reserves space for it on the heap. If you do not have a way to free up heap memory when you are finished with your dynamic variables, then eventually you can run out of heap memory.

There are two ways that this can happen. As noted earlier in this chapter, Pascal allocates space on the heap wherever it can find a block of free memory. This means that (a) the *total* amount of memory (as reported by *MemAvail*) can be inadequate for the dynamic variables you want to create, or (b) the *largest single (contiguous) block* of memory can be smaller than an individual dynamic variable that you want to create.

As an example of the first problem, you might need to create 1000 dynamic variables with each dynamic variable taking up 100 bytes. Even if you had blocks of heap memory that were larger than 100 bytes, you would still run out of space if there were less than 1000 such blocks. As an example of the second problem, you might want to create a dynamic array that requires 50K of heap memory. However, if you had blocks of only 45K, 30K, 40K, and 35K, it would not matter that the *total* is more than 50K; you need a single block (as reported by *MaxAvail*) that is 50K or larger.

Pascal's *Dispose* procedure provides only a partial solution to these problems. It is very good for freeing up heap space that is reserved for a single variable, but it cannot be applied directly to a linked data structure. Remember, when you call the *Dispose* procedure with a dynamic variable, as in

```
Dispose(ThisDynamicVariable)
```

it frees up (deallocates) the heap memory occupied by the dynamic variable and points the corresponding pointer to NIL.

Suppose, however, that this dynamic variable is the first item in a linked list. Our call to the *Dispose* procedure does indeed free up the heap memory occupied by the first item, but the memory for the other items is still officially *occupied*, even if we can no longer do anything with it.

What we need is a way to free up the memory occupied by a variety of dynamic variables: some of which are easily accessible, others not so easily. Furthermore, there will be times when we simply want to clear the entire heap and start afresh. Turbo Pascal has two built-in procedures, *Mark* and *Release*, that provide us with a way to free up heap memory. These procedures, however, are not supported by standard Pascal and other versions of Pascal, so we will also discuss a more generalized way to clear heap memory.

Using the Mark and Release Procedures

With the *Mark* procedure, you put a "bookmark" at a certain point in the heap; then you simply go about your business creating dynamic variables. Later, when you call the *Release* procedure, all the dynamic variables that you created since inserting the bookmark are destroyed, and the memory they occupied becomes free for use by other dynamic variables.

As an analogy, suppose that you have a short stack of papers on your desk. You want to keep the papers that you already have, but any new papers that come in should be thrown away at the end of the day. To handle this situation, you might put a large, brightly colored piece of cardboard on top of the original stack. Then, when any new papers come in, they are put on top of the colored piece of cardboard. When you need to throw new papers out at the end of the day, you just pick up the piece of cardboard (with the new papers on top) and dump them into the wastebasket.

Calling the *Mark* procedure is like putting that piece of cardboard on top of the original stack of papers. Calling the *Release* procedure is like picking up the cardboard and dumping any new papers into the wastebasket.

Mark and *Release* provide one of the few occasions to use untyped pointers. You call *Mark* and *Release* with an untyped pointer as follows:

```
Mark(UntypedPointerVariable)
Release(UntypedPointerVariable)
```

The pointer variable is the bookmark that you insert into the heap; it is declared simply as a pointer type, as shown in Listing 11.7.

Listing 11.7

```
PROGRAM Listing11_7;

    { Demonstrates the use of Mark and Release to free up heap
      memory. In this case, we mark a place in the heap at the
      beginning of the program. We then create a dynamic array
      which takes up some heap memory. Finally, we use Release
      to free up the memory occupied by the array. In a case
      like this, of course (with only one dynamic variable),
      Dispose would work just as well as Release. See Listing
      11.8 for a case in which Release provides a much easier
      solution than Dispose. }

USES CRT, MyUtils;

TYPE
    MyArray = ARRAY[1..100] of CHAR;
```

```
    arrayptr = ^MyArray;

VAR
    i        : INTEGER;
    mainptr  : arrayptr;
    heapmark : POINTER;

PROCEDURE LoadUpArray(VAR thisarray : myarray);
    VAR i : INTEGER;
    BEGIN
    FOR i := 1 TO 100 DO thisarray[i] := 'a'
    END;

BEGIN
    CLRSCR;
    mainptr := NIL;
    MARK(heapmark);
    WRITELN(' There are now ', memavail, ' free bytes on the heap.');
    WRITELN;
    pause;

    NEW(mainptr);
    loaduparray(mainptr^);
    WRITELN(' There are now ', memavail, ' free bytes on the heap.');
    WRITELN;
    pause;

    RELEASE(heapmark);
    mainptr := NIL;     { being a stickler for safety }
    WRITE(' After using release, there are now ', memavail);
    WRITELN(' free bytes on the heap.');
    pause

END.
```

In Listing 11.7, we declare a *heapmark* pointer variable in the VAR section; because this is an untyped pointer, we do not have to declare it in the TYPE section.

As the action part of the program begins, it uses the untyped pointer to mark the top of the heap; then it displays a message about the current heap space available. After that, it creates and loads a 100-slot dynamic array. (Strictly speaking, we do not have to load it, but arrays usually have something in them.) After creating the array, the program again displays a message about the current heap space available. Finally, it calls *Release* with the same untyped pointer. Presto! All the heap space occupied by the array has been freed.

You can use the same method to deallocate memory that is being used by the items in a linked list, as shown in Listing 11.8. There are situations, however, in which *Mark* and *Release* are not appropriate: for instance, when you need to free up space used by a linked data structure but do not want to disturb other dynamic variables on the heap. Also, *Mark, Release,* and untyped pointers are not supported by most versions of Pascal, so it is essential to learn the normal method to free up memory. This method is discussed in the following section.

Listing 11.8

```
PROGRAM Listing11_8;

   { Works in the same way as Listing 11.7. The key difference
     is that in this listing, the heap memory freed by Release
     is occupied by a dynamically linked list instead of an
     array. }

USES CRT, MyUtils;

CONST
   maxitems = 100;

TYPE
   nodeptr = ^node;
   node    = RECORD
                item : CHAR;
                next : nodeptr
                END;

VAR
   i           : INTEGER;
   listhead,
   listtail    : nodeptr;
   heapmark    : POINTER;
   free1,
   free2,
   difference : LONGINT;

PROCEDURE init(VAR listhead, listtail : nodeptr;
               VAR heapmark : POINTER;
```

```
                 VAR free1 : LONGINT);
   BEGIN
      listhead := NIL;
      listtail := NIL;
      MARK(heapmark);
      CLRSCR;
      WRITE(' Before creating the list, there are ', memavail);
      WRITELN(' bytes available on the heap.');
      free1 := MEMAVAIL;
      pause
   END;

PROCEDURE LoadUpList(VAR listhead, listtail : nodeptr);
   VAR i : INTEGER;
   BEGIN
   FOR i := 1 TO MaxItems DO
      BEGIN
         IF listhead = NIL
            THEN BEGIN
                 NEW(listhead);
                 listhead^.item := 'a';
                 listhead^.next := nil;
                 listtail := listhead
                 END
            ELSE BEGIN
                 NEW(listtail^.next);
                 listtail := listtail^.next;
                 listtail^.item := 'a';
                 listtail^.next := NIL
                 END
      END  { of FOR statement }
   END;  { of PROCEDURE }

BEGIN
   CLRSCR;
   init(listhead, listtail, heapmark, free1);
   WRITELN;

   loaduplist(listhead, listtail);

   WRITELN(' After creating a ', maxitems, '-node list, there are now');
   WRITELN(' ', memavail, ' free bytes on the heap.');
   free2 := (free1 - memavail);
```

```
WRITELN;
WRITELN(' This indicates the the list is taking up ', free2);
WRITELN(' bytes of heap space.');
pause;

RELEASE(heapmark);
WRITELN(' After executing the release procedure with the heapmark,');
WRITELN(' available heap memory is now ', memavail, ' bytes.');
WRITELN;
difference := (MEMAVAIL - free1);
WRITELN(' The difference between the original amount of heap memory');
WRITELN(' available and the current amount is ', difference,' bytes.');

pause

END.
```

Deallocating a Linked List

The great virtue of the *Mark* and *Release* procedures is that they are fairly easy to apply. They cannot, however, remove a single dynamic data structure from the middle of the heap. For that, you have to know how to use the *Dispose* procedure with linked data structures. In this section, we will see how to do this with a singly linked list.

The method takes a little thought. The head item in a singly linked list contains the pointer to the next item. If we simply use *Dispose* on the head item in the list, we will have no way to find the next item in the list, because the pointer to it will have been destroyed when we disposed of the head item. What we need is a way to free up the memory used by a list, item by item, while at each point keeping track of the next item in the list. This is provided by the method shown in Listing 11.9.

Listing 11.9

```
PROGRAM Listing11_9;

  { This listing demonstrates a method for deallocating
    the memory used by a singly linked list. At each
    step, a temporary pointer keeps track of the next
    item in the list while the current item is disposed
```

```
      of. This process continues until the end of the list
      is reached. }

USES CRT, MyUtils;

CONST
   maxitems = 5;

TYPE
   nodeptr = ^node;
   node    = RECORD
                item : CHAR;
                next : nodeptr
                END;

VAR
   i           : INTEGER;
   listhead,
   listtail    : nodeptr;
   free1,
   free2,
   difference : LONGINT;

PROCEDURE init(VAR listhead, listtail : nodeptr;
               VAR free1 : longint);
   BEGIN
      listhead := NIL;
      listtail := NIL;
      CLRSCR;
      WRITE(' Before creating the list, there are ', MEMAVAIL);
      WRITELN(' bytes available on the heap.');
      free1 := MEMAVAIL;
      pause
   END;

PROCEDURE LoadUpList(VAR listhead, listtail : nodeptr);
   VAR i : INTEGER;
   BEGIN
   FOR i := 1 to maxitems do
      BEGIN
         IF listhead = NIL
            THEN BEGIN
                 new(listhead);
                 listhead^.item := 'a';
                 listhead^.next := NIL;
```

```
                    listtail := listhead
                    END
                ELSE BEGIN
                    new(listtail^.next);
                    listtail := listtail^.next;
                    listtail^.item := 'a';
                    listtail^.next := NIL
                    END
        END   { of FOR statement }
    END;   { of PROCEDURE }

PROCEDURE DeallocateList(VAR listhead : nodeptr);
    VAR
        tempptr1,
        tempptr2 : nodeptr;
    BEGIN
        tempptr1 := listhead;
        while tempptr1 <> NIL do
            BEGIN
            tempptr2 := tempptr1;
            tempptr1 := tempptr1^.next;
            DISPOSE(tempptr2)
            END
        END;

BEGIN
    CLRSCR;
    init(listhead, listtail, free1);
    WRITELN;

    loaduplist(listhead, listtail);

    WRITELN(' After creating a ', maxitems, '-node list, there are now');
    WRITELN(' ', MEMAVAIL, ' free bytes on the heap.');
    free2 := (free1 - MEMAVAIL);
    WRITELN;
    WRITELN(' This indicates the the list is taking up ', free2);
    WRITELN(' bytes of heap space.');
    pause;

    DeallocateList(listhead);
    WRITELN(' After using the DeallocateList routine to dispose of list');
    WRITELN(' nodes, available heap memory is now ', MEMAVAIL, ' bytes.');
    WRITELN;
    difference := (MEMAVAIL - free1);
```

```
WRITELN(' The difference between the original amount of heap memory');
WRITELN(' available and the current amount is ', difference,' bytes.');

pause;

END.
```

In Listing 11.9, we declare a simple node type for the items in the linked list: each node will contain only a character and a pointer to the next item. Then, in the VAR section, we declare head and tail pointers for the list, along with an integer-type counter variable and three *longint*-type variables for reporting the free heap memory with the *Memavail* function.

The *Init* procedure initializes all the variables and reports the starting amount of heap memory. We then create the linked list, using the *New* procedure to create new, dynamic nodes for the list. After the list has been created, we again use *Memavail* to check the available heap space.

Now comes the interesting part. In the *Deallocatelist* procedure, we declare two local pointer variables that can point to items in the list. We then point the first local pointer at the head of the list and set up a WHILE loop to traverse the list. In each pass through the loop, we point the second local pointer at the current node, repoint the first pointer at the next node, and then dispose of the current node, freeing up the heap memory that it occupies. Unlike using the *Mark* and *Release* procedures, this method applies to any version of Pascal.

Static vs. Dynamic Data Structures

Many people, when they first encounter dynamic linked lists, think that using dynamic variables is always a better approach than using static variables such as arrays. It is true that dynamic allocation offers many advantages in some situations. When correctly implemented, however, each approach has both strong and weak points in particular cases.

The strong point of using arrays is that they are slightly faster than dynamically linked data structures. Because all the elements of an array are located next to each other in the PC's memory, you can go directly to any array element in a one-step process. With a dynamically linked list, you have a two-step process: first, you look at the pointer to find the memory address of the variable you need, and second, you go to that address. So, in situations where speed is more important than memory economy, arrays and other static data structures have an edge over dynamically linked data structures.

Another factor to take into consideration with static data structures is flexibility. If you are creating a list in which new items must often be inserted and deleted in the middle of the list, then an array-based list will be terribly inefficient. Remember, to insert an item in the middle of an array, you must move many items over to open up a slot for the new item; the process is similar when deleting an item. This is terribly inefficient compared to inserting or deleting an item from the middle of a linked data structure, which simply involves rearranging a few pointers.

This leads us to the strong point of using dynamically linked structures: their immense flexibility and memory economy. If you need to maintain lists whose size is unpredictable, or whose size varies widely from one program run to another, then linked data structures are probably better; likewise if you must insert and delete many items in the middle of a list. You will have to make a small sacrifice in terms of speed, but it will be more than offset by the flexibility that dynamic structures provide.

It is true that in these days of faster and faster PCs, people tend to think that program efficiency does not matter—that sloppy program code can be compensated for by incredibly efficient hardware. Although this idea has a grain of truth to it, that is no reason to use an inferior solution for a particular problem when a superior solution is available. You should analyze the situation carefully before deciding to use one type of data structure or another.

Handling Text Files

- **Different File Types**

- **Writing and Reading with Text Files**

- **Closing Files**

In previous chapters, we have seen several ways to create variables and lists. However, all of these approaches suffered from one major shortcoming: our data was always lost as soon as we turned off the computer. In this chapter, we will look at how to remedy that shortcoming by creating and using files.

Different File Types

Although the usual idea of a file is that it is a collection of information (such as text, records, and the like), Pascal uses the idea in a somewhat broader sense. In Turbo Pascal, files fall into one of two main categories:

- **Device files**, which are I/O devices in the computer, such as the keyboard, the screen, the printer port, and the modem; and

- **Disk files**, which are collections of related data on the computer's disk drives. The category of disk files is further subdivided into *text files, typed files,* and *untyped files*. We will show how to use text files in this chapter; typed and untyped files will be discussed in Chapter 13.

Turbo Pascal (and other implementations of the Pascal language) can read data from or write data to files in any of these categories. However, there is an important problem in doing so. Each different kind of computer and operating system has its own rules for naming and accessing different types of devices and disk files. Under MS-DOS, for instance, PC file names can be up to 11 characters long (8 characters plus a 3 character extension). On the other hand, under VMS, Vax minicomputer file names can be up to 39 characters long, not counting additional information that can be included on the version number of the file and where the file is located in a computer network.

In this chapter, of course, our primary focus will be on text files, even though we must first introduce some general methods for handling any kind of file. The greatest advantage of text files is that they are simple and involve familiar ideas—an advantage that should not be ignored even by experienced programmers. Writing data to a text file is just like typing text on a page: you start at the top of the page and enter text one line at a time. Reading data from a text file is similar: start at the top line and read line-by-line until you arrive at the end. If you wish, you can send a text file to the printer or, with the DOS Type command, you can display it on-screen.

It is important to understand that although text files are easier to understand and work with than typed files, they are fundamentally similar. Any type of file is a sequence of items of a particular kind. In text files, the items in question are lines of text, while in typed files, the items are records, arrays, integers, or some other nontext data items. Untyped files, which are often discussed as if they were a third type of file, represent less a distinct file type than a special way to handle text and typed files.

File Names and File Variables

If Pascal had to incorporate all the different file and I/O conventions into the Pascal language itself, there would have to be a radically different version of Pascal for each different computer and operating system. Instead, Pascal uses *file variables* to insulate the programmer from having to worry about such details. A file variable is a Pascal identifier that serves inside a program as an "alias" for a disk file or an I/O device in the underlying computer hardware and operating system.

Before a file or device can be used in a Pascal program, it must be associated with a file variable that will be its name inside the program. Thus, for example, 'students.txt' is a legal file name in DOS, but it is illegal as a Pascal identifier because it contains a period. To use this DOS disk file in a program, we must first associate it with a file variable that *is* a legal Pascal identifier. To do this, Turbo Pascal uses its built-in *Assign* procedure:

```
ASSIGN(numberfile, 'numbers.txt');
```

Notice that just as 'numbers.txt' is illegal in Pascal, 'numberfile' would not be a legal file name in DOS because it is too long. The name of the file variable is part of a Pascal program, and follows the rules for Pascal identifiers.

Anytime the program writes data to or reads data from the file variable *numberfile*, Pascal directs the operation through the appropriate operating system services in DOS, which passes data to and from the associated disk file or device. Listing 12.1 illustrates the use of the *Assign* procedure with a file variable.

Listing 12.1

```
PROGRAM Listing12_1;

    {  This listing shows how to use the ASSIGN command to
       associate a file variable with an external disk file
       or device. Note that ASSIGN takes two parameters: a
       file variable, which in this case is numberfile, and
       a text string that is the name of the disk file or
       device. REWRITE opens the file for writing, which
       means that you can send data to the file but, with
       text files, cannot at the same time read data from
       the file. Finally, CLOSE closes the file; this is a
       very important step that is sometimes forgotten by
       novice programmers. }


VAR
    numberfile : TEXT;
    counter : INTEGER;

BEGIN
    ASSIGN(numberfile, 'numbers.txt');
    REWRITE(numberfile);
    WRITELN(numberfile, 'List of integers from 1 to 50:');
    WRITELN(numberfile, '------------------------------');
    FOR counter := 1 TO 50 DO
        WRITELN(numberfile, counter);
    CLOSE(numberfile)
END.
```

The VAR section of Listing 12.1 declares two variables: *numberfile*, which is a text file variable, and *counter*, a variable that we will use to control a loop. In the main body of the program, ASSIGN links the file variable with a disk file named *'numbers.txt'*, and REWRITE opens the file so the program can write data to it. Notice that to write data to the file, the WRITELN statements have the name of the file variable, a comma, and the names of the items to be written to the file.

After you enter and run the program in this listing, you can look at the file *'numbers.txt'* in the same directory as the listing itself. Your program created the file, opened it, wrote the integers from 1 to 50 in it, and then closed the file.

When you pass a file variable to a subroutine, you *must* pass it as a VAR parameter. The reason is simple. When you pass a variable to a subroutine without using VAR, the variable is passed "by value," meaning that Pascal makes a copy of the variable and passes the copy to the subroutine. When you pass a variable as a VAR parameter, however, the variable is passed "by reference": instead of a copy, the subroutine receives a pointer to the actual variable that the parameter represents. It is not practical to pass files by value—that is, to make a copy of a file any time you pass it to a subroutine. For that reason, files (of any type) can be only passed to subroutines as VAR parameters.

It is worth noting that even with the use of file variables, file operations (and other I/O operations) tend to vary from one implementation of the Pascal language to another. Sometimes, the differences are merely terminological: Vax Pascal has a command called *Open*, which works the same as Assign, except that it offers a large number of options for opening a file in different ways. At other times, the differences are more substantive: most mainframe and minicomputer Pascals use GET and PUT commands that are not in Turbo Pascal.

If you are writing a program that has to be moved to a different Pascal compiler, then you should try to group all I/O operations into a few separate compartments of your program. When you move your program to the other compiler, the areas most likely to need modification will be easier to find.

Prompting the User for a File Name

In Listing 12.1, the actual name of the disk file is embedded in the program code itself. Of course, if this were the only way to use files in Turbo Pascal, it would create terrible problems. Any time the user had to work with a different file, we would have to produce a different version of our program.

Turbo Pascal (and Pascal in general) offers a simple solution to this problem. Instead of embedding the file name in the code, as is done in Listing 12.1, the user is prompted for a file name. This file name is then stored in a string variable whose contents—the name of the disk file—is then loaded into the file variable by the AS-SIGN command. Listing 12.2 illustrates how to do this.

Listing 12.2

```
PROGRAM Listing12_2;

    { Shows how to prompt the user for a file name. The file
      name is then loaded into the file variable with the ASSIGN
      comand. }

USES CRT;

VAR
    NameOfFile : STRING[12];
    numberfile : TEXT;
    counter    : INTEGER;

BEGIN
    CLRSCR;
    WRITE(' Please enter the name of the file you want to use: ');
    READLN(NameOfFile);
    ASSIGN(numberfile, NameOfFile);
    REWRITE(numberfile);
    WRITELN(numberfile, 'List of integers from 1 to 50:');
    WRITELN(numberfile, '------------------------------');
    FOR counter := 1 TO 50 DO
        WRITELN(numberfile, counter);
    CLOSE(numberfile)
END.
```

Listing 12.2 is basically the same as Listing 12.1 except that it creates and uses a new string variable, *NameOfFile*, to hold the file name entered by the user. We prompt the user to enter a file name with a WRITE statement; notice that there is no file name included in this statement because the output is going to the PC's screen. (The screen is denoted by the default output file variable, *output*. If you do not specify a file name, Turbo Pascal assumes that you want output directed to the screen.)

After the user enters a file name, ASSIGN links the file name with the file variable, REWRITE opens the file for writing, and the user is in business. Everything else works exactly the same as in Listing 12.1.

DOS Device Files

As noted above, a file variable can denote either a disk file or a device in the computer. Turbo Pascal has standard names for the various devices in your PC. To use one of these devices—for example, to direct output to the printer—you simply use the ASSIGN command to link the standard device name with a file variable. Then, exactly the same as with a disk file, any action performed on the file variable will apply to the device. The standard device names are shown in Table 12.1.

TABLE 12.1:   Standard DOS Device Names in Turbo Pascal

Name	Function	Input	Output
CON	Screen, keyboard	Yes	Yes
LPT1	Printer port #1	No	Yes
LPT2	Printer port #2	No	Yes
LPT3	Printer port #3	No	Yes
LST	Printer port #1*	No	Yes
PRN	Printer port #1	No	Yes
COM1	Communications port #1	Yes	Yes
COM2	Communications port #2	Yes	Yes
NUL	Wastebasket	Yes	Yes

* Note: Defined in the Printer unit.

You use the names in Table 12.1 just as you would the names of disk files, except that some of the devices (for example, the printer ports) are write-only: you can send data to them, but you cannot read data from them.

A typical application of these device names is to send output to the printer. This is shown in Listing 12.3.

Listing 12.3

```
PROGRAM Listing12_3;

  { Demonstrates how to use a standard device name with a
    file variable. The device name is treated just as if it
    were the name of a disk file. In this case, the device
    name stands for printer port #1. Instead of being written
    to a disk file, as in Listings 12.1 and 12.2, this list
    of integers is sent to the printer. Notice that after the
```

```
        list is sent to the printer, we send a "form feed" character
        (ASCII number 12) to advance the paper in the printer. }
VAR
   MyPrinter : TEXT;
   counter   : INTEGER;

BEGIN
   ASSIGN(MyPrinter, 'PRN');   { link printer with file variable }
   REWRITE(MyPrinter);         { open file for output }

   WRITELN(MyPrinter, 'List of integers from 1 to 50:');
   WRITELN(MyPrinter, '-----------------------------');

   FOR counter := 1 TO 50 DO        { write integers 1..50 }
   WRITELN(MyPrinter, counter);

   WRITELN(MyPrinter, chr(12));  { Send form feed to printer. }

   CLOSE(MyPrinter)     { close file }
END.
```

You declare the printer device PRN just like any other file, by using ASSIGN with the file variable and putting the name of the device within single quotes. After that, any output sent to the *MyPrinter* text file variable is routed to your PC's printer port #1. (A printer port is a device by which your PC can be connected to a printer.) If your printer is connected to one of the other ports, such as printer port #2 (LPT2) or a serial port (COM1 or COM2), you can send output to the printer by substituting the appropriate device name for 'PRN' in the ASSIGN statement.

The devices in Table 12.1 are pretty much what you would expect them to be. CON takes input from the keyboard and directs output to the screen. LPT1, LPT2, LPT3, LST, and PRN are names for printer ports. COM1 and COM2 are the names of communication ports; generally, you will use these for communicating with a modem. In certain situations, printers can also be connected to these COM ports.

The only device that may seem a little puzzling is NUL, which the table describes as a "wastebasket." NUL ignores anything that is sent to it. If you attempt to read from the NUL device, it tells your program that the end of the file has been reached. You will not use this frequently, but it can be helpful when you need to include an input or output file name in your program but do not want to deal with an actual file or device.

Opening Files

Once you have associated a device or disk file with a file variable in your Pascal program, you are almost ready to use the file. First, however, the file must be opened. A text file can be opened for (1) reading data from the file or (2) writing data to the file, but not both at the same time.

The attempt to write data to a text file open for reading or to read data from a text file open for writing is a very common error. If you want to write data to a text file that is open for reading, you must first reopen it for writing by using REWRITE or APPEND. Likewise, if you want to read data from a file that is open for writing, you must first reopen it for reading by using RESET. You do not have to close the file before reopening it in either case.

Typed and untyped files, which will be discussed in Chapter 13, do not suffer from this limitation. No matter how typed and untyped files are opened, they are available for both reading and writing.

Turbo Pascal offers the three commands just mentioned for opening files: REWRITE, APPEND, and RESET. It has one command for closing files: CLOSE.

REWRITE

As we have already seen in the listings, REWRITE opens a file for writing—that is, it opens a file in such a way that you can put data into it. It also positions the *file pointer*—the location where the next line of text will be entered—at the very beginning of the file. The first use of WRITE or WRITELN with the file variable will write text to this line in the file.

If you use REWRITE with a name of a disk file that does not yet exist, REWRITE will create the file for you. However, if you use REWRITE with a file that *already* exists, it will wipe out the existing file and replace it with a new, empty file that is ready for you to enter data into. The use of REWRITE is illustrated in Listings 12.1 through 12.3, so it won't be repeated here.

APPEND

To add new data to an existing text file, you must open the file with APPEND. Instead of creating a new file or wiping out the old file, as REWRITE does, APPEND opens an existing file for writing and positions the file pointer at the current end of the file. Any new uses of WRITE or WRITELN with the file variable will add new text to the end of the file. The use of APPEND is illustrated in Listing 12.4.

Listing 12.4

```
PROGRAM Listing12_4;

    { Demonstrates how to add new material to an existing text
      file by opening the file with APPEND instead of REWRITE. }

VAR
    numberfile : TEXT;
    counter : INTEGER;

BEGIN
    ASSIGN(numberfile, 'numbers.txt');
    APPEND(numberfile);
    WRITELN(numberfile);
    WRITELN(numberfile, 'List of integers from 51 to 100:');
    WRITELN(numberfile, '--------------------------------');
    FOR counter := 51 TO 100 DO
    WRITELN(numberfile, counter);
    CLOSE(numberfile)
END.
```

Listing 12.4 is identical to Listing 12.1 except that (a) it opens the file *'numbers.txt'* with APPEND instead of REWRITE, and (b) it appends the numbers *51* to *100* to the bottom of the file. If you look at the file *'numbers.txt'* after running this program, you will see that the new numbers have been added at the end.

RESET

So far, we have seen several examples of writing to text files, but no examples of reading from them. To read from a text file, you open it with RESET. This opens the file for reading and positions the file pointer at the very beginning of the file. The first use of READ or READLN will read text from the first line of the file. Additional READs and READLNs after that will read from succeeding lines of the file, depending on whether you use READ or READLN. (See "Reading from Text Files" below.) Listing 12.5 demonstrates the use of RESET.

Listing 12.5

```
PROGRAM Listing12_5;

    { Demonstrates the use of RESET to open a file for reading. }

USES CRT, MyUtils;

VAR
    numberfile : TEXT;
    counter    : INTEGER;
    line       : STRING[80];

BEGIN
    CLRSCR;
    ASSIGN(numberfile, 'numbers.txt');
    RESET(numberfile);
    WHILE NOT EOF(numberfile) DO
        BEGIN
        FOR counter := 1 TO 20 DO
            BEGIN
            READLN(numberfile, line);
            WRITELN(line);
            END;
        pause
        END;
    CLOSE(numberfile)
END.
```

In addition to the file and counter variables, Listing 12.5 creates a new *line* variable. This is a text string that holds the contents of each line as it is read in from the file. After opening the file for reading with RESET, we do a few things that are relatively complex—at least compared to what we have seen so far.

- The line *WHILE NOT EOF(numberfile) DO* uses the end-of-file function (discussed in "The EOF and EOLN Functions" section below) to tell the program that it should continue executing the WHILE loop until the end of the file is reached.

- Embedded in the WHILE loop is a FOR loop. If we did not include this extra loop, then the program would simply read the file from start to finish without any pauses. By using the FOR loop, we tell the program to read 20 lines from the file, display each line on the screen, and then pause so that we can look at what has been displayed. After the user presses a key, the FOR loop executes again, bringing in another 20 lines from the file, and pauses again. This process continues until the end of the file is reached, at which point we drop out of the WHILE loop.

- Finally, after all the lines in the file have been read and displayed on-screen, the file is closed and the program ends.

These embellishments aside, the main point is that we opened the file for reading with RESET, read from it, and closed it. If you look at the *'numbers.txt'* file itself, you will see that it was completely unchanged by this operation.

There are two other tricks you can do with RESET. First, there may be times when you want to add data to a text file, but you are not sure if the text file already exists and holds data or not. Using REWRITE in this situation won't work, because if the file currently exists, REWRITE will wipe out the data it already contains. But APPEND won't work either, because if the file does *not* exist, then your program will have a run-time error because APPEND, unlike REWRITE, will not create a new file.

By using RESET, however, we can devise a *safe* way to open text files for writing, as shown in Listing 12.6.

Listing 12.6

```
PROCEDURE OpenFileForWriting(VAR thisfile : text);

   { Provides a safe way to open text files for writing. }

   VAR
      FileExists : INTEGER;
   BEGIN
      {$I-}
      RESET(thisfile);      { try to open the file }
      {$I+}
      FileExists := IORESULT; { file opened successfully? }
      IF FileExists = 0
         THEN APPEND(thisfile)
         ELSE REWRITE(thisfile)
   END;
```

Listing 12.6 is not a full program; it is a routine procedure that you can use in any program that manipulates text files. It takes the text file itself as a parameter and declares a local integer variable *FileExists*. It then turns off input checking and tries to open the file with RESET. (We had to turn off input checking, because if the file doesn't exist and input checking is on, then we'll get a run-time error.) After the call to RESET, we immediately turn input checking back on.

If the call to RESET was a success, then the file was opened and IORESULT = 0, indicating that the file already exists. If the call to RESET was not a success, then IORESULT <> 0 and we have learned that the file does not yet exist. With that information, it is a simple matter to set up an IF statement that uses APPEND if the file already exists, and REWRITE if it does not.

The second trick is also quite useful. There may be times when you need to read from a text file, return to the beginning of the file, and start reading all over again. The simplest way to achieve this is to reopen the file by calling RESET again. Remember, in addition to opening the file for reading, RESET positions the file pointer at the very beginning of the file.

Writing to Text Files

We have already seen the basics of writing to text files. There are just a few other things that you should know to be able to write to text files. None is particularly mysterious, and to help achieve efficiency they are worth pointing out.

First, there is the difference between WRITE and WRITELN. You have already seen this as it applies to the computer screen, and it has the same effect when you WRITE or WRITELN to a file. The following code will write a single integer on each line:

```
FOR counter := 1 TO 5 DO
     WRITELN(thisfile, counter);
```

The result is a file that contains five lines:

```
1
2
3
4
5
```

WRITE, on the other hand, does not add an end-of-line character (ASCII 13) after each operation. Thus,

```
FOR counter := 1 TO 5 DO
     WRITE(thisfile, counter);
```

will produce a file with a single line:

```
12345
```

You should also realize that though there are many times when you need to use separate WRITE statements, it is not always necessary. WRITE and WRITELN can take multiple parameters, so

```
WRITE(thisfile, 1, 2, 3, 4, 5);
```

will produce a file with the same single line containing '12345'.

Just as you would use WRITELN when you are sending text to the screen, you can insert a blank line in a file with a plain WRITELN statement and no parameters.

Reading from Text Files

Most of the operations for reading from text files are similar to those for writing to text files. A READ statement reads one or more items without moving the file pointer down to the next line. READLN also reads one or more items, but it *does* move the file pointer down to the next line. If you want to move the file pointer without reading anything, you use a READLN statement with no parameters.

Thus, suppose that you had a text file called *NumFile* with the following contents:

```
11 2 20 43 5
225 2 67 4 7
```

If you had some integer variables *a* through *j*, you could read these two lines in two different ways. First, you could use READ and insert an empty READLN statement at the end, as in

```
READ(numfile, a, b, c, d, e);
READLN(numfile);
READ(numfile, f, g, h, i, j);
READLN;
```

Alternatively, you could simply use two READLN statements, as in

```
READLN(numfile, a, b, c, d, e);
READLN(numfile, f, g, h, i, j);
```

That seems easy enough, but it becomes a little trickier if you are reading in a line of characters. To see why, enter and run Listing 12.7.

Listing 12.7

```pascal
PROGRAM Listing12_7;

   { Illustrates a potential problem reading characters
     from a text file. There are two different solutions. }

USES CRT, MyUtils;

VAR
   a, b, c, d, e : CHAR;
   CharFile      : TEXT;

BEGIN
   CLRSCR;
   ASSIGN(charfile, 'chars.txt');
   REWRITE(charfile);
   WRITELN(charfile, 'a', ' ', 'b', ' ', 'c', ' ', 'd', ' ', 'e');
   pause;

   RESET(charfile);
   READLN(charfile, a, b, c, d, e);
   WRITELN(a, b, c, d, e);
   pause;

   CLOSE(charfile)
END.
```

Instead of displaying the line's contents as 'a b c d e', as it should, this program displays the line's contents as 'a b c'. The problem with Listing 12.6 does not occur when you are reading in a line of numbers separated by spaces. The problem is that the space character is itself a character, so instead of reading 'abcde', as you want it to, the READLN statement reads in 'a', space, 'b', space, 'c'—for five characters.

What you need is a way to filter out the characters (called *delimiters*) that separate the characters you want, whether the delimiters are spaces, commas, or some other ASCII character.

One way to do this is by using *dummy* character variables. If you know (as you normally will) the exact format of the lines you will be reading from the file, you can include separate READ statements with dummy variables to advance the file pointer past the spaces. A somewhat more elegant solution is to set up an IF statement that executes an extra READ statement if the last character read from the file was a space (or any other delimiter character). This approach is shown in Listing 12.8.

Listing 12.8

```
PROGRAM Listing12_8;

    { Illustrates one solution to the problem of reading characters
      from a line in a text file. }

USES CRT, MyUtils;

CONST
    space = ' ';

TYPE
    SomeLetters = ARRAY['a'..'e'] OF CHAR;

VAR
    letters    : SomeLetters;
    CharFile   : TEXT;
    counter    : CHAR;

BEGIN
    CLRSCR;
    ASSIGN(charfile, 'chars2.txt');
    REWRITE(charfile);
    FOR counter := 'a' TO 'e' DO
        BEGIN
            WRITE(charfile, counter);
            WRITE(charfile, space)
        END;
    pause;

    RESET(charfile);
    FOR counter := 'a' TO 'e' DO
        IF NOT EOLN(charfile) THEN
            REPEAT
                READ(charfile, letters[counter])
            UNTIL letters[counter] <> space;

    FOR counter := 'a' TO 'e' DO
        BEGIN
        WRITE(letters[counter]);
        WRITE(space)
```

```
        END;
    pause;

    CLOSE(charfile)
END.
```

The EOF and EOLN Functions

There are two important Boolean-type functions that give you control over how long your program reads from or writes to a file. These are the EOF (end of file) and the EOLN (end of line) functions. When Pascal creates a text file, it ends each line with an end-of-line marker (ASCII 13), which corresponds to the *Enter* key on your PC keyboard. In addition, Pascal marks the end of the file with a *Ctrl+Z* character.

Listing 12.7 illustrates the use of the EOLN function. After the file is reopened for reading with RESET, the statement *WHILE NOT EOLN(charfile)* ... tells Pascal to keep on performing the read operation until it arrives at the end of the line, where EOLN becomes true and, therefore, NOT EOLN becomes false.

Likewise, Listing 12.5 illustrates the use of the EOF function to read a file until the end. This is a very typical example of setting up a loop to execute WHILE the end of the file has not yet been reached.

Closing Files

We have already seen how to close a file by using the CLOSE procedure with the file variable. There are two aspects of this, however, that we have not yet discussed.

The first is to understand that disk I/O operations (such as reading data from a file or writing data to a file) are usually the slowest processes that your program performs. This is because such operations depend on mechanical components in the disk drives that are much slower than the electronic components in your computer's processor and memory. If your program had to do a disk access every time you wrote data to a file, it would seriously degrade the program's performance.

Pascal solves this problem by trying to minimize the number of times your program must physically access the disk drive. When a file is opened with RESET or REWRITE, Pascal sets aside an area of memory to hold data that is read from or written to the file. This area of memory is called the *file buffer*, and when you write data to a file in your program, normally, it goes into the file buffer rather than to the disk file itself.

Turbo Pascal periodically *flushes* the file buffer to the disk file and actually writes its contents to the disk file. This is why, if you forget to close a file at the end of your program, at least some of the things you wrote to the file will actually be there— some, but *not* all. Using the CLOSE procedure executes a final flush and writes all remaining data to the file. If you forget to close the file, data that is still in the file buffer will be lost.

The second thing to understand is that if you ever need to force the file buffer to flush, but do not want to close the file, you can use Turbo Pascal's FLUSH procedure. Its syntax is identical to that of CLOSE:

```
FLUSH(file variable);
```

This will cause all data currently written to the file buffer to be written to the disk file itself.

CHAPTER
THIRTEEN

Typed and Untyped Files

- **Advantages and Disadvantages of Typed Files**

- **Typed Files vs. Text Files**

- **Using SEEK**

In the previous chapter, we looked at some ways to use text files. The principal advantage of text files is that they are the computer equivalent of printed pages and, hence, are very easy to understand and manipulate. Also, they are highly portable between different versions of Pascal, most of which handle text files in about the same way. Finally, of course, they can be used to send text-format data to other programs or to a printer for reports.

In this chapter, we will look at typed and untyped files. Unlike text files, which consist (obviously) of text, typed files consist of items of a particular data type. And though the name "untyped files" suggests a third kind of file, untyped files are, in fact, a fast and powerful way to use both text and typed files.

Typed Files

In text files, the fundamental unit is the line of text—or, depending on your preference, the text character. In typed files, the fundamental unit is not a line of text but items of a specific data type. The items can be integers, real numbers, strings, characters, arrays, and other built-in Pascal types, as well as user-defined types such as records and objects.

In fact, the units in a typed file are commonly referred to as *records,* but you must be careful to avoid confusion on this point. The "records" in a typed file can indeed be items of the record data type, but they can also be integers, strings, or any other legal Pascal type except a file type. Thus, a file "record" might or might not be a Pascal record-type data item.

Unlike the lines in text files, the units in a typed file must all be of the same size. (The only exception is the unusual case of a typed file that contains variant records.) You declare a typed file as follows:

```
VAR
    ThisFile : FILE OF <type>
```

where <type> can be any built-in or user-defined data type except another file type. Thus, you could have the following as a typed file:

```
TYPE
    string15 = STRING[15];
    studentrec = RECORD
```

```
                       fname,
                       lname : string15;
                       GPA   : REAL
                       END;
VAR
    numfile : FILE OF INTEGER;
    ltrfile : FILE OF CHAR;
    strfile : FILE OF string15;
    stdfile : FILE OF studentrec;
```

A typed file can contain only items of the appropriate type: for example, if a file is declared as a FILE OF INTEGER, it cannot have real numbers, characters, or any other noninteger value. In a certain sense, this is no different from text files, which also can contain only text items. With text files, however, text is also the *only* type that they can contain, requiring Pascal (or the programmer) to convert text file items to other types as needed by the program. Listings 13.1 and 13.2 illustrate two programs for storing integers in a file; the only difference between them is that Listing 13.1 uses a text file and Listing 13.2 uses a typed file.

Listing 13.1

```
PROGRAM Listing13_1;

   { This program uses a text file to store integers, in contrast
     with Listing 13.2, which uses a typed file. The purpose of this
     listing is to illustrate some of the differences between text
     and typed files. }

USES CRT, MyUtils;

VAR
   Numfile : TEXT;
   counter,
   HowMany : INTEGER;

BEGIN
   ASSIGN(numfile, 'numfile.txt');
   REWRITE(numfile);
   CLRSCR;
   WRITE(' How many integers to store in file? ');
   READLN(HowMany);

   { Now we write some numbers to the text file. }
   FOR counter := 1 TO HowMany DO
```

```
    WRITELN(numfile, counter);

{ ---------------------------------------------------------- }
{ Now we use RESET to reopen the text file for reading. }
{ ---------------------------------------------------------- }
RESET(numfile);
FOR counter := 1 TO 4 DO READLN(numfile);

READLN(numfile, HowMany);  { the HowMany variable is available }
WRITELN;
WRITELN(' The number on line 5 is ', HowMany, '.');
pause;

    CLOSE(numfile)
END.
```

Listing 13.2

```
PROGRAM Listing13_2;

    { Demonstrates a very simple typed file. This stores the same
      data as the text file in Listing 13.1, and shows some of the
      differences between text and typed files. }

USES CRT, MyUtils;

VAR
    Numfile : FILE OF INTEGER;
    counter,
    HowMany : INTEGER;

BEGIN
    ASSIGN(numfile, 'numfile.dat');
    REWRITE(numfile);
    CLRSCR;
    WRITE(' How many integers to store in file? ');
    READLN(HowMany);

    FOR counter := 1 TO HowMany DO
        WRITE(numfile, counter);


    { ---------------------------------------------------------- }
    { Observe what we have NOT done: we have not reopened the    }
    { file for reading, as we had to do in Listing 13.1 with the }
```

```
{ text file. When open, a typed file is available for both   }
{ reading and writing, regardless of how it was opened.      }
{ --------------------------------------------------------- }
SEEK(numfile, 4);
READ(numfile, HowMany);
WRITELN(' The number in record #5 is ', HowMany, '.');
pause;

CLOSE(numfile)
END.
```

The first difference between Listing 13.1 and Listing 13.2 appears, as expected, in the VAR section when we declare the file variable *Numfile*. In 13.1, this is declared as a text file, while in 13.2 it is declared as a file of integers (a typed file).

Linking the file variable with a disk file and opening the file for writing also work the same way, using ASSIGN and REWRITE. In fact, almost everything is the same until we arrive at the last part of the program, where we read a number from the file.

In Listing 13.1, the text file was opened for writing with the REWRITE procedure. Before we can read from it, we must reopen it with RESET. We then execute four empty READLN statements to move the file pointer down to the fifth line, where we read the number on the file's fifth line and display it on the screen.

In Listing 13.2, however, we did not need to reopen the file with RESET. This is because an open typed file is available for both reading and writing, *regardless* of how it was opened.

The next difference in Listing 13.2 occurs when we move the file pointer down to the fifth record in the file. Because a typed file consists of records instead of lines, we use the SEEK procedure with a record number to move the file pointer to that record in the file. The first record in the file is always record number 0; therefore, to see the fifth number in the file, we seek record number 4. There are no other differences between Listings 13.1 and 13.2: in both, the files are closed in the same way.

Comparative Size of Typed Files

Listings 13.1 and 13.2 illustrate another important point: sometimes a typed file will be smaller than a text file with the same data, and sometimes it will not. If you run Listing 13.1 and tell it to produce a file containing 50 integers, the file will take up 191 bytes of disk space. The typed file with 50 integers produced by Listing 13.2, however, takes up only 100 bytes of disk space. (These values are approximate; the size of the files on your machine will depend on your DOS version and how your disk is configured.)

To determine if a typed file will take up less disk space than a text file, a rule of thumb is this: if the data items to be stored are all the same size or very nearly so, then a typed file probably will take up less disk space than a text file. On the other hand, if the data items to be stored vary widely in their actual size, then a text file probably will be smaller.

That rule is still fairly abstract, so let's look at a concrete example. Listings 13.1 and 13.2 produced two files of integers, all of which were about the same size. That is, when considered as two characters in a text file, '20' takes up eight bits (one byte) for each character, for a total of two bytes. In a typed file, the same number stored *as an integer* takes up two bytes because that's how much space integers take up. But when you add in the overhead (end-of-line markers, and so on) of the text file, the text file ends up being bigger.

Listings 13.3 and 13.4 create files that hold text strings. Both use a string variable 15 characters long, and both write the names to a file. In Listing 13.3, the names are written to a text file, in which each name occupies only the number of characters it actually needs. This amount of space, plus the end-of-line characters and so forth, adds up to the amount of space required by the text file.

Listing 13.3

```
PROGRAM Listing13_3;

USES CRT;

CONST
    continue : CHAR = 'Y';     { a "typed constant" }

VAR
    namefile : TEXT;
    student  : STRING[15];

BEGIN
    ASSIGN(namefile, 'names.txt');
    REWRITE(namefile);
    CLRSCR;
    WHILE UPCASE(continue) = 'Y' DO
```

```
      BEGIN
      WRITELN;
      WRITE('Enter a student''s first name: ');
      READLN(student);
      WRITELN(namefile, student);
      WRITELN(namefile);
      WRITELN;
      WRITE(' Add another (Y/N)? ');
      READLN(continue)
      END;
   CLOSE(namefile)
END.
```

Listing 13.4

```
PROGRAM Listing13_4;

USES CRT;

CONST
   continue : CHAR = 'Y';     { a "typed constant" }

TYPE
   string15 = STRING[15];

VAR
   namefile : FILE OF string15;
   student : string15;

BEGIN
   ASSIGN(namefile, 'names.dat');
   REWRITE(namefile);
   CLRSCR;
   WHILE UPCASE(continue) = 'Y' DO
      BEGIN
      WRITELN;
      WRITE('Enter a student''s first name: ');
      READLN(student);
      WRITE(namefile, student);
      WRITELN;
      WRITE(' Add another (Y/N)? ');
      READLN(continue)
      END;
   CLOSE(namefile)
END.
```

Listing 13.4, however, creates a file of 15-character strings. In the typed file that this program creates, each data item takes up 15 characters of space—*whether or not* the actual name is 15 characters long. This means that, because most names are shorter than 15 characters, a text file probably will be smaller than a typed file for this kind of information.

To test this theory, run Listing 13.3 and Listing 13.4, entering the following names in each: Rebecca, Sam, Nick, Susan, and George. This will produce (subject to the conditions noted earlier) a text file that requires 45 bytes of disk space and a typed file that requires 80 bytes of disk space.

Advantages and Disadvantages

As the joke says, there is good and bad news about typed files. ("Take my file— please!") The good news is that typed files can help your program run faster than it would if it used text files. Depending on the situation, typed files also can make it easier for you to program file I/O operations.

The bad news is that you've just heard all the good news. Typed files are not necessarily smaller than text files, nor are they always easier to handle. Moreover, different Pascal compilers handle typed files in far more varied ways than the ways in which they handle text files; so typed files and programs that use them are far less portable from one Pascal to another.

Typed files are faster than text files because typed files store data in Turbo Pascal's native format for that data type. Consider a simple example: a file of integers, with one integer on each line. You can store the same group of integers in a text file or a typed file. In the text file, however, the integers are stored as ASCII character representations of integers—that is, Turbo Pascal sees the file as containing text items such as '1543', '5', and '21', instead of the integers 1543, 5, and 21. When a program reads the content of each text line into an integer variable, Pascal must convert each text item from the file into an integer type.

File I/O is already the slowest operation that your program performs, and this extensive type conversion just adds one more operation for your program to do when it reads from or writes to a text file. The extra work becomes even more obvious when you store the contents of complex data items (such as records) in a text file. In this case, you have to write the type-conversion routines into your program, converting values as needed and loading them one-by-one into your program's data structures.

Handling complex data elements is, in fact, the main area where typed files excel—not only in terms of speed, but also in terms of programming simplicity. For ease of programming, there is no difference between a text file containing numbers (actually, of course, representations of numbers as ASCII characters) and a typed file containing the same numbers. But when you have a complex type, matters become quite a bit easier with typed files.

Suppose you had the following record type in your program:

```
TYPE
   student = RECORD
             fname,
             lname : string15;
             GPA   : REAL
             END;
```

With a text file, you could store the information for each field of the record on a separate line, with a blank line between records. But reading the information from the file into a program's record variables is somewhat laborious, as shown by this code fragment:

```
READLN(class, studentvariable.fname);
READLN(class, studentvariable.lname);
READLN(class, studentvariable.GPA);
READLN(class); { skips blank line between records }
```

That is four lines of code to read a single record: three lines actually to read the record, and the fourth line to move the file pointer ahead to the start of the next record. A typed file, however, stores each student record in exactly the same format as a variable of the student data type, so your code is much simpler:

```
READ(class, studentvar);
```

Because the file record is the same data type as the student variable, you can skip the process of reading information line-by-line and field-by-field; instead, you just pop the file record into the student variable with a single operation. Also, there's no need to move the file pointer to the next record, because a typed file is designed to be easy for Turbo Pascal (not people) to read, and the records are packed together. In this case, you end up with less work for Turbo Pascal (no type conversion) and less work for you, the programmer (fewer lines of code to write). The cost is that you lose the intuitive familiarity of text files and the portability that they provide.

Writing and Reading Data

You write data to typed files in almost exactly the same way that you write data to text files. Using the WRITE procedure with the file variable for the typed file, you can write variables to the file. Similarly, you use the READ procedure to read data from typed files. Because typed files do not have lines, however, you cannot use WRITELN or READLN with typed files. The formal syntax of WRITE and READ statements with typed files is as follows:

```
WRITE(typedfile, variable1, variable2, … );
READ(typedfile, variable1, variable2, … );
```

Here, *typedfile* is the file variable that stands for the typed file, while *variable1*, *variable2*, and so forth are variables of the data type that the file is set up to hold. This points up another difference between typed and text files: you can only write variables, not constants, to a typed file. With a text file, it is perfectly legal to write

```
WRITE(filename, 5);
```

where *filename* stands for a text file and *5* is the number 5. If you try to use the same statement with a typed file, however, your program will not compile, because 5 is a constant, not a variable.

Using SEEK

After you have written data to a typed file, sometimes you need to pluck data from somewhere in the middle of the file. To do this, you can use Turbo Pascal's SEEK procedure to find data if you have the record number. The SEEK procedure is not implemented in many versions of Pascal, but it makes things a little easier for the Turbo Pascal programmer.

SEEK and similar routines are the reason that typed files are sometimes referred to as *random-access* files. To see why this is so, consider what you would have to do to read a data item on line 25 of a text file. From the beginning of the file, you would have to execute 24 empty READLN statements to move the file pointer to the 25th line. This is called *sequential access* because you have to go through all the lines in sequence until you arrive at the one you want.

With the SEEK procedure, however, you can go directly to any record in the file, and you do not have to cycle past the preceding records in order to get to it. This is called random access. A more familiar example of random access is provided by a compact disc, which allows you to go directly to any song at random without having to play through the preceding songs first. A cassette tape, on the other hand, is a sequential-access device. If you want to listen to a song in the middle of the tape, you must fastforward through the other songs first.

Thus, typed files are random-access files in that they *permit* random access of the records they contain. However, they have no necessary connection with random access; if you prefer, you can go through a typed file's records in sequence just as easily, from the first record to the last.

You use the SEEK procedure with a typed-file variable and a record number, as in

```
SEEK(numfile, 5);
```

SEEK, however, must be used with caution; if there are only 10 records in a file and you try to seek record number 11 (or any other record number beyond the last record in the file), your program will halt with a run-time error. To avoid this, it is a good idea to use Turbo Pascal's *FileSize* function before using SEEK; this will tell the user how many records are in the file. *FileSize* takes a typed-file variable as an argument and returns an integer, which is the number of records in the file. You use *FileSize* as follows:

```
WRITELN(' File contains ', FileSize(numfile), 'records.');
```

Editing and Adding Records

With typed files, you can also change data in the middle of a file or add new data to the end of the file. It's not always completely straightforward, but it's not that difficult, either. To change a record in the middle of a file, you use the SEEK procedure to find the record number you want, and then write new data into it.

Adding data to an existing typed file is a little more difficult than adding data to an existing text file. You may recall that with text files, we can use the APPEND procedure to open the file for writing, and we position the file pointer at the end of the file—precisely where we want to add new data. Unfortunately, we cannot use APPEND with typed files. Instead, we must set up a three-step process: (1) determine the number of records with the *FileSize* function; (2) use SEEK to move the file pointer to the last record in the file; and (3) execute an empty READ statement to move the file pointer past the last record to the very end of the file.

Methods for editing current records and adding new records are demonstrated in Listing 13.5.

Listing 13.5

```
PROGRAM Listing13_5;

{ This listing illustrates how to change a value in the middle
  of a typed file and how to add a new value to the end of a
  typed file. More sophisticated operations, such as sorting the
  elements of a file or inserting a new item between two current
  items, would normally be handled by reading the file into a
  data structure, such as an array or linked list, performing
  the desired operation, and then writing the new data back to
  the disk file. Note that a special procedure is needed to add
  data at the end of a typed file because APPEND will not work
  with typed files as it will with text files. }



USES CRT, MyUtils;

TYPE
   NumberFile = FILE OF INTEGER;

VAR
   Numfile : NumberFile;


{ -------------------------------- }
{ MAIN-LEVEL PROCEDURE DECLARATION }
{ -------------------------------- }
PROCEDURE CreateAndLoadFile(VAR numfile : numberfile);
   VAR
      counter,
      SizeNum : INTEGER;
   BEGIN
      CLRSCR;
      ASSIGN(numfile, 'numbers.dat');
      REWRITE(numfile);
      WRITE(' How many integers do you want in the file? ');
      READLN(SizeNum);
      WRITELN;
      FOR counter := 1 TO SizeNum DO
          WRITE(numfile, counter);
```

```
      CLOSE(numfile)
   END;

{ ------------------------------ }
{ MAIN-LEVEL PROCEDURE DECLARATION }
{ ------------------------------ }
PROCEDURE ChangeRecord(VAR numfile : NumberFile);
   VAR
      NumberOfRecords,
      RealRecNum,
      RecNum,
      RecVal1,
      RecVal2  : INTEGER;
   BEGIN
      RESET(numfile);
      CLRSCR;
      NumberOfRecords := filesize(numfile);
      WRITE(' The current size of the file is ');
      WRITELN(NumberOfRecords, ' records.');
      WRITELN;
      WRITE(' Which record do you want to change? ');
      READLN(recnum);
      RealRecNum := recnum - 1;
      WRITELN;
      WRITE(' What integer do you want to change it to? ');
      READLN(RecVal2); WRITELN;

      SEEK(numfile, RealRecNum);
      READ(numfile, recval1);
      WRITE(' The old value of record #',recnum);
      WRITELN(' is ', recval1, '.');
      delay(1500);

      SEEK(numfile, RealRecNum);
      WRITELN(' Now writing a new value to record #', recnum, '.');
      WRITE(numfile, recval2);

      SEEK(numfile, RealRecNum);
      READ(numfile, recval2);
      WRITE(' The new value of record #', recnum);
      WRITELN(' is ', recval2, '.');
      pause;
```

```
        CLOSE(numfile)
    END;


{ -------------------------------- }
{ MAIN-LEVEL PROCEDURE DECLARATION }
{ -------------------------------- }
PROCEDURE AddNewRecord(VAR numfile : NumberFile);
    VAR
        NumberOfRecords,
        LastRecord,
        LastRecordValue,
        NewValue    : INTEGER;
    BEGIN
        RESET(numfile);
        NumberOfRecords := FileSize(numfile);
        LastRecord := NumberOfRecords - 1;
        WRITE(' There are now ', NumberOfRecords);
        WRITELN(' records in the file.'); WRITELN;
        WRITE(' Enter a new integer to add at end of file: ');
        READLN(newvalue);
        SEEK(numfile, lastrecord);
        READ(numfile, lastrecordvalue);
        WRITE(numfile, newvalue);
        NumberOfRecords := FileSize(numfile);
        WRITELN;
        WRITE(' There are now ', NumberOfRecords);
        WRITELN(' records in the file.');
        pause;
        CLOSE(numfile)
    END;

BEGIN
    CreateAndLoadFile(numfile);
    ChangeRecord(numfile);
    AddNewRecord(numfile)
END.
```

Inside Listing 13.5

Listing 13.5 demonstrates several techniques and tricks that you can use when working with typed files. The listing does the following things:

- It creates a file of integers, referred to in the program by the file variable *numfile*.

- It asks the user how many integers should be entered into the file, and then writes the integers in sequence from 1 to the number the user chooses.

- After closing the file variable to make sure that all records (integers) have been written to the disk file, it reopens the file and changes a record in the middle of the file.

- It also finds the end of the file and adds a new record at the end.

The *ChangeRecord* procedure takes the typed file as a VAR parameter (remember that files can be passed to subroutines only as VAR parameters). After reopening the file, it uses the *FileSize* function to determine the number of records in the file, then prompts the user for the number of a record to be changed.

Here is where the routine may look a little odd: we use an additional variable, *RealRecNum*, which is assigned a value one less than the record number that the user specified. This is because, in typed files, records are numbered not from 1, but from zero. Thus, the first record is record 0, the fifth record is record 4, and so forth. To insulate the user from this complication, we use the *RealRecNum* variable for all program references to record numbers. Thus, when the user asks for record number five, he or she expects it to contain the integer 5; we do some behind-the-scenes manipulation to satisfy this expectation and thereby avoid confusing the user.

After converting the user's requested record number to a "real" record number, we use SEEK to position the file pointer at the correct record and inspect the value of that record. However, this READ operation causes the file pointer to move ahead to the *next* record, so before we can change the selected record, we must use SEEK again to reposition the file pointer. This WRITE operation, just like the preceding READ operation, again causes the file pointer to move ahead, so we use SEEK a third time to move the file pointer back to where we want it and inspect the new value of the chosen record. We then close the file to make sure that all the values are written to disk.

The *AddNewRecord* routine uses some similar tricks. It uses the *FileSize* function to determine the number of records, and a *Lastrecord* variable to hold the number of the last record. Recall that because the record numbering starts with zero, if there are 25 records in a file, then the last record is record number 24. The *AddnewRecord* routine uses SEEK to go directly to the last record; executes a READ statement to move the file pointer past the last record, to the end of the file; and then writes a new record at the end of the file. It uses *FileSize* again to find the new number of records in the file; displays the number on the screen; and closes the file.

If you wanted to add a new record in the middle of the file, you could do that, although it would be a fairly slow and fairly complicated process. A better solution, and one that is normally used, is to read the contents of the file into a linked list or other data structure, do any manipulations in the computer's RAM, and then write the revised list back to the file. This is faster and more flexible than trying to manipulate the file directly.

Untyped Files

In spite of its name, the *untyped file* is not a third type of file: instead, it is a way of handling any DOS file without regard for the structure of the data it contains—even without regard for its origin. You can treat any file as an untyped file (whether or not it is wise to do so) by associating it with an untyped file variable, as in:

```
VAR
    ThisFile,
    ThatFile : FILE;    { untyped file variable }
    Buffer   : ARRAY[0..1024] OF BYTE;
BEGIN
    ASSIGN(ThisFile, 'miscfile.dat');
    RESET(ThisFile, 1);
    REWRITE(ThatFile, 1);
    REPEAT
    BLOCKREAD(ThisFile, Buffer, SizeOf(Buffer), Num);
    BLOCKWRITE(ThatFile, Buffer, Num, NumToFile);
    UNTIL (Num = 0) OR (NumToFile <> Num);
    CLOSE(ThisFile);
    CLOSE(ThatFile)
END.
```

Applications for untyped files do exist, but they are fairly uncommon. Their great advantage is that because they treat files without any regard for their structure, they provide a very fast way of reading and writing files.

The example above illustrates the main operations that are done with untyped files. First, the file is associated with an untyped–file variable—*that is*, a file variable that is neither declared as a text nor as a typed file, but simply as a "file." Then, you need to create some storage in the computer's memory for the data that is read from the file. Normally, this will be an array, because this is the fastest form of storage and, after all, speed is a major reason for using untyped files.

RESET and REWRITE have an added feature when used with untyped files. Because data is read from and written to untyped files in blocks, you should specify the size of the blocks to be used. One byte is ideal as a block size because it divides evenly into a file of any size, whether the file is 128 bytes or 17. If you do not specify a block size when you open the file with RESET or REWRITE, then Turbo Pascal uses the default block size of 128 bytes, which may cause problems with files whose size is not evenly divisible by 128.

As is evident from the example, you cannot use READ and WRITE with untyped files. Instead, you need to use *BlockRead* and *BlockWrite*, which are discussed below.

BLOCKREAD and BLOCKWRITE

BLOCKREAD reads data from the untyped file into the storage area you have set up in the computer's memory. Its basic use is as follows:

```
BLOCKREAD(VAR f:FILE; VAR Buffer:ARRAY; Count:WORD;
 VAR Result:WORD);
```

The first parameter in BLOCKREAD is the untyped file variable. The second is the variable representing the storage area for the data from the file, which is usually, but not necessarily, an array; the third is the maximum number of blocks to be read from the file; and the fourth is a variable that returns the actual number of blocks read in the BLOCKREAD operation.

BLOCKWRITE is similar. Its first parameter, as in the example, is an untyped file variable for the file that will be *written to;* second is the variable for the storage area; third is the maximum number of blocks to be written; and fourth is the actual number of blocks that are written in the operation.

One potential pitfall, if you do use BLOCKWRITE, is that it inserts an end-of-file character (*Ctrl+Z*) at the end of a block. This means that if a block ends in the middle of an existing file and you look for the end of the file by using the EOF function, your program will stop at the end of the block. BLOCKWRITE and BLOCKREAD should both be used with caution.

CHAPTER FOURTEEN

Debugging Your Programs

- General Debugging Techniques

- Common Program Bugs

- Using the Turbo Pascal Integrated Debugger

In this chapter, we will look at the bane of programmers everywhere: the omnipresent, impossible-to-exterminate program "bugs." A bug is anything in your code that prevents a program from compiling and running correctly, *whether or not the cause is technically an "error."* Some program bugs are catastrophic in their effects, while others are innocuous and still others are so obscure that no one will ever discover them.

First, we will look at general methods for avoiding bugs and for dealing with them when they occur. Though Borland Pascal and Turbo Pascal 7 have powerful integrated debugging capabilities, the methods discussed in this section of the chapter can be applied with any version of Pascal, including Turbo Pascal versions 4 and earlier, which did not have integrated debugging. Moreover, ideas not specifically tied to Pascal can be applied in any programming language.

Second, we will look at a rogues' gallery of common program bugs—what they are, how they occur, and what to do about them. Like the first section, this material applies to any version of Pascal and, to a large extent, to programming in any language.

Third, we will look at the specific integrated debugging capabilities provided by Borland Pascal and Turbo Pascal 7, and show how these can help you debug your programs faster and more easily.

General Debugging Issues

Many people, especially novice programmers, have the wrong idea about debugging. They think that debugging is something you do at the end of the program development process: first you write the program, then you debug it, then it sells a million copies and you retire to Bora Bora.

Retire to Bora Bora you might, but a comfortable retirement will be a lot more likely if you realize that debugging is an on-going process that begins with correct program design and careful coding. Far from treating debugging as a separate step, you should design your program with ease of debugging in mind. You should also develop it one subroutine at a time and debug each subroutine as it is completed, before "hooking it up" to the main program.

The truth is that in any program of more than minimal complexity, it is probably impossible to eliminate all bugs. The most popular PC database manager of the 1980s, Ashton-Tate's dBASE, had hundreds of documented bugs. *TechNotes*, the Ashton-Tate magazine, devoted an entire section each month to newly discovered "anomalies," which is a euphemism for bugs. A recent version of Lotus 1-2-3, a popular spreadsheet program, was reported to have over 10,000 bugs before it went through testing and debugging.

dBASE, 1-2-3, and other commercial software packages (including Turbo Pascal itself) are developed by top-notch programmers who have many years of experience. If even *they* can't totally eliminate bugs from their programs, then you shouldn't feel too bad if you have trouble eliminating bugs from yours.

Experienced programmers are also familiar with another painful truth: whatever the user *perceives* as a bug *is* a bug. Eliminating bugs is not simply a matter of making your program run correctly. It is also a matter of making your program run the way the user *expects* it to run—a task that is sometimes much more difficult because it involves a certain amount of mind reading.

There are eight different levels of *program correctness* that we work to achieve through the design and debugging process. These levels are shown in Table 14.1.

Most beginners think that compile-time errors are the most serious—that going from level 1 to level 2 is the most important hurdle. However, all that it means when a program compiles is that the source code follows the rules of Pascal. It does not

TABLE 14.1: Levels of Program Correctness

Level	Correctness
1	Does not compile.
2	Compiles without errors.
3	Starts to run but halts with a run-time error.
4	Runs but produces incorrect results.
5	Produces correct results for small set of "normal" input data.
6	Produces correct results for large set of "normal" input data under all normal or expected run-time conditions.
7	Produces correct results for extreme, abnormal, and incorrect input data under normal, expected, and unexpected run-time conditions.
8	Produces correct results for any possible data and run-time conditions.

mean that the program is error-free, or that it will produce correct results, or even that it will produce any results at all. Compile-time errors are the least serious and easiest to correct of program errors. Also, because you literally *cannot* run a program that won't compile, such errors pose no threat to your data.

Run-time errors are almost in the same class as compile-time errors. Most common run-time errors are easy to identify because the program halts when it encounters them (for example, a missing file) or the program does something else fairly obvious (for example, going into an endless loop). Uncommon run-time errors usually result from running the program under unusual or unexpected conditions, such as with inadequate memory or disk space; these can be identified, if at all, only through exhaustive testing.

Virtually all other errors are *logic errors,* which result from the programmer's mistaken analysis of the problem he or she is trying to solve. Sometimes, the code is so intricate that getting the solution *right* is almost a matter of luck, such as trying to run a loop inside an IF statement inside another loop. It's in these situations that careful thought prior to coding is even more important than usual, and extra efforts should be made to produce the simplest, clearest code possible.

The Connection between Design and Debugging

Another thing that makes debugging easier is to be a fanatic about structured design and compartmentalization. In a 1,000-line unstructured program, each line could conceivably interact with 999 other lines, meaning that there are 999! (999 factorial, or $999 \times 998 \times 997 \times \ldots 1$) possible interactions between different parts of the program: a level of complexity beyond any human mind's ability to grasp. In reality, of course, you would never have this many interactions, but you can see the problem.

Even when you divide the program into 30-line subroutines, you are still faced (inside each subroutine) with 29! possible interactions, and although this is still a large number, it is far more manageable than before. When one considers that the actual number of interactions is much lower than this, and that 30 lines will fit easily on a single page, it seems *very* manageable.

Achieving this reduction in complexity, however, requires strict adherence to structured programming methods. Any outside data items manipulated by a subroutine must be passed to it as parameters; otherwise, the compartmentalization of the subroutine is breached and it can no longer be treated as a black box. Its internal features could then interact in an uncontrolled way with any other part of the program—in which case, we might as well be writing unstructured "spaghetti" code.

General Debugging Methods

The most important weapon in debugging your program is to understand both the broad outlines of how the program works and the details of how each subroutine processes the parameters that are passed to it. With this in mind, you will see how the parts of your program fit together and why each part behaves in the way that it does.

Creating the Main Program First

The first step is to create a framework that eventually will become the main program. On this framework you will hang the individual subroutines that, eventually, will work together to make a complete program. Notice that, strictly speaking, this is a design method; however, design and debugging are so intimately connected that it must be discussed here.

The overall framework (sometimes called the *main control program* because it determines when subroutines are called and what values are passed to them) should contain as little detail as possible. It is all right to include a loop here or an IF..THEN statement there, but as much detail as possible should be hidden inside the subroutines. Naturally, at the start of the process, you cannot be sure that this detail-hiding will always work: you might need to bring some details out of a subroutine and keep them in the main program. The presumption, however, should always be in favor of hiding details inside subroutines. Listing 14.1 shows a program at this stage of development; however, don't try to run this listing, because although the incomplete program will compile, it will go into an endless loop.

Listing 14.1

```pascal
PROGRAM Listing14_1;


    { Illustrates how to create an empty "main program framework,"
      which is filled in as subroutines are completed. }

USES CRT;

VAR
    Continue : CHAR;
    a, b,
    Result   : INTEGER;


PROCEDURE AddTwoNumbers(a, b: INTEGER; VAR result: INTEGER);
    BEGIN
    END;

PROCEDURE MultiplyTwoNumbers(a, b: INTEGER; VAR result: INTEGER);
    BEGIN
    END;

PROCEDURE Quit;
    BEGIN
    END;

PROCEDURE DisplayMenu;
    BEGIN
    END;

PROCEDURE GetMenuChoice;
    BEGIN
    END;


{ main body of program }
BEGIN
    Continue := 'Y';
    WHILE UPCASE(Continue) = 'Y' DO
        DisplayMenu
END.
```

You can see that at this stage, we have simply decided on the main tasks that the program should perform. Each of those tasks has been delegated to a subroutine, leaving very little in the main program framework itself. This is as it should be: the less detail that is included in the main framework, the fewer things that can go wrong without being noticed by the programmer.

Testing Each Subroutine Separately

Once you have decided what the subroutines should be, you should develop and debug each one separately before you plug it into the main program. This involves two basic steps: first, to define the initial and ending conditions for the subroutine; and second, to use a *driver program* to test the subroutine with a wide range of input values.

Define Initial and Final Conditions   Defining initial and final conditions for a subroutine involves specifying exactly what output values the subroutine should produce for each set of input values. For example, in the subroutine *AddTwoNumbers*, we would specify that the subroutine should accept integers and return an integer as a result. Note that it is possible for the sum of two integers to exceed the limits of the integer data type, which ranges only from −32,768 to +32,767: for example, 25,000 + 25,000 would generate an error. Depending on the situation, we could design the subroutine either to handle such situations or to refuse to input numbers whose sum exceeds the integer data type, but, in any case, we need to be aware of this limitation and decide how to deal with it.

Create a Driver Program   The next step is to develop each subroutine inside a driver program that will let you test a wide range of different input values. A simple driver program (all driver programs should be as simple as possible) is shown in Listing 14.2. This driver program works with the *AddTwoNumbers* procedure from Listing 14.1.

Listing 14.2

```
PROGRAM Listing14_2;

    { Illustrates a simple driver program for developing and
      testing the AddTwoNumbers subroutine in Listing 14.1. }
```

```
USES CRT, MyUtils;

VAR
    continue : CHAR;
    a, b,
    result   : INTEGER;

PROCEDURE AddTwoNumbers(a, b: INTEGER; VAR result: INTEGER);
    BEGIN
    result := a + b;
    WRITELN;
    WRITELN(' The sum of ', a, ' and ', b, ' is ', result, '.');
    pause
    END;

{ main body of driver program }
BEGIN
    CLRSCR;
    continue := 'Y';
    REPEAT
        WRITELN;
        WRITE(' Enter the first number to add: ');
        READLN(a);
        WRITE(' Enter the second number to add: ');
        READLN(b);
        AddTwoNumbers(a,b,result);
        WRITE(' Do another (Y/N)? ');
        READLN(continue);
    UNTIL UPCASE(continue) <> 'Y'
END.
```

Listing 14.2 sets up a REPEAT loop that allows you to feed one pair of integers after another into the *AddTwoNumbers* routine to make sure that it works properly. Remember that to test the routine fully, you should try not only expected input such as 15 and 100, 2 and 2, or 40 and 10, but zero, negative, and very large values such as 0 and 0, −1000 and 85, or 30,000 and 30,000.

This last pair of integers, in fact, will reveal that, as suspected, the routine has a weak spot: it is possible for two integers to add up to a number that exceeds the range of the integer data type. In this case, the program will not stop on a run-time error, but will give a wildly erroneous result (between the two, a run-time error is infinitely preferable). Depending on how ambitious you are, you can include code to handle situations like that one, as well as to trap incorrect data type input such as 'c' and 'x'. A driver program will help you identify where these traps need to be placed.

Tracing Code Blocks

Tracing code blocks is also an important debugging method. When your code reaches a certain level of complexity, it is hard to determine what goes with what: which END goes with which BEGIN or CASE statement, which ELSE goes with which IF, and so forth. This is one of the most common sources of programming errors. When you have one too few (or one too many) ENDs, a left comment bracket that isn't matched by a right bracket, or a REPEAT loop that goes who-knows-where, your program probably won't compile. Moreover, the error message you receive in this case is likely to be unhelpful. "Error in statement" is the usual error message, and it tells you only that there is probably an unterminated BEGIN somewhere above the line where you got the error message.

Tracing code blocks can help you master this complexity. To use this method, simply print out a listing of your program code (in Turbo Pascal, use the Print option in the File menu). Then start at the deepest level of nested statement and use a pencil to connect each BEGIN with its corresponding END, each REPEAT with its corresponding UNTIL, and so forth. Ultimately, this can lead you to bugs that would, otherwise, be very difficult to find.

Let's look at an example of this process. Consider the following code block:

```
BEGIN
    CASE num of
        1: BEGIN
            { ... details }
            END;
        2: BEGIN
            { ... details }
            END;
        3: BEGIN
                IF num > 5
                THEN BEGIN
                        { ... details }
                ELSE BEGIN
                        { ... details }
                        END
            ELSE BEGIN
```

```
        { ... details }
        END
    END
```

Although this code may seem messy and confusing, it is far less so than much of the code you will see in actual programming. Situations where you have END, END, ENDs stacked on top of each other are prime targets for bug-hunting. Let's see how tracing can help us find the errors in this block. We start at the deepest level of nesting: in this situation, that means the different BEGIN..END pairs in the CASE statement.

The reason for starting at the deepest level is that is where Pascal starts putting together (parsing) the statements. Each BEGIN or CASE at the deepest level takes the first END that it encounters; then the next BEGIN or CASE takes the next END, and so forth. This process continues until Pascal works its way though to the outer-most level.

In this case, tracing reveals what was not apparent at a glance. The very first BEGIN is never terminated; as a result, it will probably grab hold of another section of code's END further down in the program. At that point, the compiler will stop and give you an "Error in statement" error message, but the real error is here at the very beginning. In fact, the END taken by the CASE was probably the END that was meant to go with the first BEGIN; the programmer forgot to include an END for the CASE statement. To complicate matters further, two BEGINs nested inside the CASE statement are never terminated, and will probably cause a compilation error as well.

```
    BEGIN
        CASE num of
        1:    BEGIN
                { ... details }
                END;
        2:    BEGIN
                { ... details }
                END;
        3:    BEGIN
                IF num > 5
                THEN    BEGIN
                        { ... details }
                ELSE    BEGIN
                        { ... details }
                        END
                ELSE    BEGIN
```

```
                                { ... details }
                             END
             END
```

You can do the same thing as we've done here with loops, comment brackets, and any other program structure that starts on one line and should terminate on another.

Inserting Debug Code

Another general debugging technique is to insert *debug code* at various places in your program. Debug code allows you to monitor the values of variables as your program runs. It is not really needed in the Turbo Pascal IDE (for versions 5 and later), which lets you put *watches* on variables. However, if you are developing a Pascal program with version 3 or 4 of Turbo Pascal, with the Turbo Pascal command-line compiler, or with a different Pascal compiler, debug statements can be very helpful.

The most basic kind of debug statement simply displays the current value of a variable on the screen. If your program runs but gives incorrect results or behaves oddly, it may be that a variable is not getting the values you expected it to. Listing 14.3 shows a classic application of a debugging statement.

Listing 14.3

```pascal
PROGRAM Listing14_3;

   { Illustrates the use of debug statements to track the
     values of variables. }

USES CRT, MyUtils;

VAR
   counter,
   a, b,
   result  : INTEGER;
   debugging: BOOLEAN;

PROCEDURE AddTwoNumbers(a, b: INTEGER; VAR result: INTEGER);
   BEGIN
   result := a + b;
   WRITELN;
   WRITELN(' The sum of ', a, ' and ', b, ' is ', result, '.');
```

```
    pause
    END;


BEGIN
    CLRSCR;
    counter := 0;
    debugging := TRUE;
    WHILE counter <= 10 DO
        BEGIN
        WRITE(' Enter the first number to add: ');
        READLN(a);
        WRITELN;
        WRITE(' Enter the second number to add: ');
        READLN(b);
        AddTwoNumbers(a,b,result);
        IF debugging
        THEN WRITELN(' Counter value is now ', counter, '.')
        END;
    pause
END.
```

The error in Listing 14.3 may seem contrived (and remember that you should use FOR instead of WHILE when you have a loop counter variable), but it is a typical error made by beginning programmers. The program sets up a loop that is to execute 10 times, using a counter variable to keep track of how many times it has gone through the loop so far. However, the programmer forgot to include a statement in the loop that will increase the value of the counter variable, so the counter stays at zero and the loop executes over and over unto eternity.

Without the debugging statement, it might take a while to identify the problem, even in a simple case like this one. With the debugging statement, however, the problem is immediately apparent because the value of the counter never changes.

Note that we used a Boolean variable to determine if the debugging statement executes or not. If there are many debugging statements scattered throughout a routine (or an entire program), then this provides an easy way to turn all of them on or off by adjusting the value of a single variable. Make "debugging" true and the debugging statements all go to work; make it false, and they become invisible. One caution: if you use this method, you should remove (or comment out) the debugging statements before you do the final compilation of your debugged program. Otherwise, the debugging statements (which no longer serve a purpose) will be included in the compiled version of your program, resulting in a larger .EXE file than necessary.

Test Under Different Conditions

The fact that a program runs properly on one computer under one set of conditions does not mean that it will run on another computer under a different set of conditions. A final step in debugging your program is to test it under a variety of different conditions. Try running it with less memory available, or with memory-resident utility packages such as Borland's Sidekick. If your program uses graphics or special effects such as reverse video, try it out on different types of monitors with different types of video adapters. A program that uses graphics may run fine with a VGA adapter and a color monitor, but it may behave oddly or not work at all with a Hercules adapter and a monochrome monitor.

Whether you do this level of testing, of course, will depend on the purpose of your program, who will be using it, and how ambitious you are. If you have a text-only program that will be run only on standard PCs, then it is a waste of effort to test it on a variety of machines. It's all up to you.

Give Your Program to a Kid

You might think that this is a frivolous suggestion, but it's quite serious. Kids (1) are imaginative, (2) have lots of free time, (3) love to "show up" adults, and (4) will conduct a bug hunt with the sort of fanatical devotion that you could never get even from the most conscientious adult programmer.

A Demonology of Common Bugs

On the theory that "forewarned is forearmed," in this section we will look at some of the most common programming errors with Pascal and discuss what to do about them. Many of these errors also apply to programming in languages other than Pascal.

Compile-Time Errors

Compile-time errors are the most innocuous of bugs, principally because they are caught by the compiler and therefore pose no threat to your data. However, they can be maddening for beginners, particularly when the error messages they generate are less helpful than they might be—even in Turbo Pascal, which is far better than many other compilers in this area.

Unknown Identifier

This bug means that Turbo Pascal cannot find a certain identifier that you have used in your program—whether it is a name for a variable, constant, subroutine, or some other program element. It is normally caused by one of three things:

1. A typing error when you keyed in the program. In this case, you simply misspelled the identifier when you attempted to call it in your program. This is a trivial mistake and is always easy to correct.

2. Forgetting to name a unit in the USES clause of your program; for example, forgetting to name the CRT unit in a program that uses the CLRSCR procedure. (This error cannot occur in versions of Turbo Pascal before version 4, which was the first to support units.) Like error No. 1, this is easily corrected.

3. An error in structuring your program. This is the most difficult type of "unknown identifier" bug to correct. It means that for some reason, the identifier you used is inaccessible at the place in the code where you used it. In hunting for this kind of error, you should remember the following:

    a Identifiers must be declared before they are used. If subroutine X uses subroutine Y, then Y must be defined in the code *before* subroutine X. Make sure that general routines used by several other routines are either toward the beginning of the program code or are in their own unit; in either case, they will be accessible to routines that are declared later in the program code.

    b Identifiers inside subroutines are hidden from everything outside of the subroutine.

    c Even inside a subroutine, an identifier must be declared before it is used, so even local subroutines must be declared in the proper order.

";" Expected

This is a trivial but fairly common bug. As you will recall, semicolons are used to separate statements in a Pascal program from other statements. To correct this bug, just add a semicolon at the end of the line from which it is missing. Normally, the compilation error occurs on the line immediately after the line without the semicolon.

Missing END or Comment Bracket

The error message "Error in statement" is usually a dead giveaway for this kind of bug. When you get this error message, first check the highlighted statement to make sure that it is not the source of the trouble. If it isn't, then all you really know at the beginning is that *somewhere* in the code above that statement, another statement or a comment is not terminated properly: you may have too few ENDs, mixed-up comment brackets, or some variation on those errors.

The first and best weapon against this type of error is to have a firm knowledge of the rules for constructing statements and expressions in Pascal (the syntax of Pascal). Armed with this knowledge, you should trace through the code with a pencil, as we described above in the section on general debugging methods.

The best way to avoid this type of error in the first place is to stick religiously with the proper methods for structured design, compartmentalization, and code testing. When such bugs do pop up, as inevitably they will from time to time, this will help localize them within a small block of code, making them much easier to find and correct.

Mixed-Up IFs and ELSEs

This bug is most likely to occur when you have two or more nested IF..THEN..ELSE and CASE statements. Remember that unless you tell it otherwise, an IF statement will try to grab the closest THEN and/or ELSE statement that it can find that isn't separated from it by a semicolon. Thus, the following code will cause a compile-time error:

```
CASE choice of
    1 : AddNewRecord;
    2 : EditCurrentRecord;
    3 : IF RecordsOpen
        THEN CloseRecords
ELSE WRITELN(' You must enter a choice from 1 to 3.')
    END;
```

In this situation, the ELSE clause is intended to cover the situation in which the user enters a choice that does not match any of the items in the CASE statement. However, because the IF statement in case 3 is not terminated with a semicolon, it grabs onto the ELSE clause, which as a result will execute only if CASE 3 is chosen—*not* if the user's choice fails to match any of the choices in the CASE statement.

This kind of error may not stop the program, but may result in unexpected and incorrect program behavior. Like the missing END or comment bracket, the main remedy for this kind of error is to trace through your code with a pencil. It also helps to proofread your code.

Run-Time Errors

Run-time errors, as the name implies, get past the compiler and pop up only when someone tries to run your program. Some run-time errors will pop up immediately and on every program run; others will occur only under special conditions. Obviously, the first category of run-time errors is more important, but proper defensive programming should try to anticipate all but the most remote possibilities for run-time errors.

Failure to Initialize Variable Before Use

Some variables need to be initialized (set to initial values) at the beginning of a program or subroutine; other variables do not. The problem is that you often don't know which is which until you run into a bug. Variables that are used as counters in FOR loops do not have to be initialized, but variables used to control WHILE and REPEAT loops should be initialized. Likewise, expressions and variables that control IF and CASE statements may or may not need to be initialized.

The safest course is, at the beginning of a program or subroutine, to initialize all variables at that level with a separate subroutine, just as we have done in several of the program listings. You initialize a variable simply by assigning it a known initial value, as in *counter := 0*.

The only type of variable that absolutely *must* be initialized is the pointer. An uninitialized pointer variable conceivably could contain the memory address of part of the operating system, part of Turbo Pascal, or of some vital piece of data: the potential results are catastrophic. All pointer variables should be set to NIL at the beginning of a program or subroutine, and should be set to NIL again as soon as they are disposed of and are no longer needed.

Attempt to Assign Out-of-Range Value

This error can occur when you are using "fancy" numeric types such as bytes, which have a fairly limited range of values. It also can occur with integers, enumerated types, and subrange types. A typical example of this error would be an attempt to assign the integer 500 to a variable of type byte, which can take only values in the range 0 to 255.

It pays to anticipate and take steps to cope with the possibility that the user might enter some off-the-wall value. This is the purpose of using error-trapping input routines such as *GetGoodChar* and *GetGoodInt*.

Use of Out-of-Range Array Index

This error is most likely to occur when you are using an array to hold a list. If the array is full and the user tries to enter another item into the list, then this error might pop up. The solution is to include code to keep track of how much space is left in the array and, if appropriate, to refuse the new input and inform the user of the array's full condition.

To trap this sort of error, it helps to test your program with range-checking turned on (use the Compiler options dialog box from the Options menu or insert a {$R+} compiler directive at the top of your program code).

Failure to Handle Nonmatch in CASE Statement

In standard Pascal (and many real-world implementations of the standard), your program will stop with a run-time error if the user enters a choice for a CASE statement that doesn't match any of the choices included in the CASE statement. For example, consider the following code:

```
CASE choice of
      1 : DoThis;
      2 : DoThat;
      3 : DoSomethingElse
      END;
```

As long as the user enters a value from 1 to 3, everything is fine. However, if the user enters 4, then the program will stop with a run-time error. In Chapter 7, we saw how to defend against this possibility in standard Pascal by using an IF statement with the CASE statement.

Turbo Pascal provides two levels of protection against this kind of error. First, as we saw in Chapter 7, it allows you to use an ELSE clause with a CASE statement, thereby making an extra IF..THEN..ELSE statement unnecessary. Second, even if you don't use an ELSE clause, Turbo Pascal programs will not stop with a run-time error if the user's choice fails to match any of the CASE choices. On the one hand, this is good, because it prevents the program from stopping when it might not really need to stop. On the other hand, it's bad, because a nonmatching CASE could indicate a subtle error in the logic of the routine. The moral is, simply, that you should be careful in coding CASE statements.

Reading Incompatible Value into Variable

This is a fairly straightforward error. Your code contains a variable of one data type; the user is prompted to enter a value for the variable but mistakenly enters a value of the wrong data type or a value that is not in the acceptable range of values. For example, you might ask the user how old he or she is; instead of entering an integer, the user might enter a letter; or instead of entering an integer that makes sense, he or she might enter a number such as 181 or 20,015.

The only defense against these errors is to replace Pascal's READ and READLN procedures with your own error-trapping input routines, such as *GetGoodInt* and *GetGoodChar*.

File Not Found

When this error occurs, usually you are trying to RESET or APPEND a file that isn't there. Of course, "isn't there" can mean two different things: either the file doesn't exist at all, or the file exists but is in a directory other than the one in which your program is looking for it. There is no simple solution for this problem; probably the most straightforward solution is to make sure that all the files needed to run the program are in the same directory on disk. Another solution is to include the directory path in the file name, as shown in the code fragment below:

```
VAR
   MyFile : TEXT;
BEGIN
   ASSIGN(MyFile, 'c:\bp\oldfiles\data.txt');
   REWRITE(MyFile);
   WRITELN(MyFile, 'Uses a path in the file name.');
   close(MyFile)
END.
```

Turbo Pascal offers some more elegant ways to achieve the same result, but this solution is fairly portable across different Pascal compilers. When the "file not found" is a unit file, you need to make sure that Turbo Pascal's Directory Options dialog box includes the unit's home directory in its list of unit directories.

File Not Closed

Usually, this error pops up when you think you have written some data to a disk file. After your program runs, you check the file and discover that some (or all) of the data you entered is missing. This is a clue that your program did not close the file before finishing its run. Remember that any data written to a file is normally stored in a *file buffer* in your computer's memory before being physically written to the file. This speeds up your program, but it also means that if you fail to close the file at the end of the program, then some data may be left in the file buffer without having been written to the disk file.

Thus, when you find that data is missing from a disk file, the first thing to check is whether the file was closed properly in your program.

Logic Errors

Logic errors are the most difficult kind of errors to debug. They don't cause compilation errors; they don't cause run-time errors; they just cause programs to crash or produce incorrect results. It's important to understand that logic errors have nothing to do with Pascal. Logic errors occur when the programmer analyzes a problem incorrectly and comes up with the wrong solution, which is then written into Pascal program code. To debug a logic error requires not so much a knowledge of Pascal as a very careful analysis of what tasks need to be done and in what order.

By now, I probably sound like a broken record (a broken CD?) on this issue, but the best way to avoid or minimize logic errors is to keep your code as simple and as compartmentalized as possible.

Failure to Use VAR Parameter When Needed

This is probably the most common error involving subroutines. Remember, there are two ways to pass a variable to a subroutine: by value and by reference. Any variables that are to be changed by a subroutine must be passed to it as VAR parameters—that is, passed by reference. Otherwise, Pascal makes a copy of the variable and passes the copy to the subroutine. No changes made in the copy have any effect on the original variable itself. The following code, for example, does not use VAR parameters and has no effect on the variables a, b, and c.

```
VAR a, b, c : INTEGER;
PROCEDURE AddTwoNumbers(a,b,c : INTEGER);
   BEGIN
      c := a + b
   END;
BEGIN { main body of program }
   a := 1;
   b := 1;
   c := 0;
   AddTwoNumbers(a,b,c)
END;
```

To correct this code, the word VAR has to be put in the procedure declaration before, at least, the c variable, which is the only one that is supposed to be changed by the subroutine. The new code would be as follows:

```
VAR a, b, c : INTEGER;
PROCEDURE AddTwoNumbers(a,b : INTEGER;
                        VAR c: INTEGER);
   BEGIN
      c := a + b
   END;
BEGIN { main body of program }
   a := 1;
   b := 1;
   c := 0;
   AddTwoNumbers(a,b,c)
END;
```

Loop Exit Condition Never Reached

This is the *endless loop* that we've already seen. What usually happens is one of two things: either (a) a counter variable is not increased on each pass through the loop, leading to a constant value for the counter and no exit from the loop; or (b) a *continue* variable controls the exit from the loop, and the programmer forgets to prompt the user for input into this variable, as in *WRITE(' Continue (Y/N)? ');*.

You may think that forgetting to prompt the user for input is a preposterous mistake for anyone to make, and it probably is. But wait until you've made this mistake yourself a few times; it won't seem quite so preposterous.

Loop Executes Wrong Number of Times

Unless this error involves a counter variable (see above), there are two main possibilities here: either the loop never executes when it should execute at least once, or it executes at least once when, under some conditions, it should never execute.

The solution is to remember the key difference between WHILE and REPEAT loops. A WHILE statement evaluates its loop control variable before going through the loop each time. If the control variable does not satisfy the loop condition when the program first reaches the loop, then the statements in the loop will never execute. A REPEAT statement, on the other hand, evaluates the control variable at the end of each loop, so no matter what the initial value of the control variable, a REPEAT loop will always execute at least once.

Using Borland Pascal's Integrated Debugger

Now that you are familiar with the issues involved in debugging, as well as with some of the most common bugs, you are in for a treat. The integrated debugging capabilities in Borland Pascal and Turbo Pascal 7 (as well as in previous versions of Turbo Pascal) make it much easier to find bugs and correct them than with most Pascal compilers.

Borland/Turbo Pascal's integrated debugger is what is called a "high level" debugger, in that it works with the statements of a high-level language—in this case, Pascal. Turbo Pascal also provides some facilities for low-level debugging, in which you go through a series of machine-language statements and directly inspect CPU registers and memory locations. Low-level debugging is, however, not relevant to most programming tasks, so we will not discuss it here. Full high-level and low-level debugging support is provided by Borland's Turbo Debugger, which works with Turbo C and C++ as well as with Turbo Pascal. Borland's Turbo Assembler also provides low-level debugging for assembly language programs.

Borland/Turbo Pascal provides four main tools for debugging: the ability to step through a program one line at a time; the ability to watch the values of variables as the program runs; the ability to change a variable's value in the middle of running a program to find out what effect the change will have; and the ability to set *break-points* at which the program will stop its run, so that you can inspect its results up to that point.

The Debug Menu

Debugging operations are performed from the Debug menu and its submenus, as well as with speed keys. The four options on the Debug menu are (1) Evaluate/Modify, which lets you inspect and/or change the value of a variable at a certain point in the program; (2) Watches, which opens a submenu that lets you add, edit, and delete watches on variables; (3) Toggle Breakpoint, which lets you insert and remove breakpoints in your program code; and (4) Breakpoints, which opens a dialog box that lets you add, delete, and view breakpoints in your program code.

Normally, the values of variables that you see in the Evaluate/Modify dialog box and the Watch window are easy to understand. However, if you want the values displayed in a different format, you can add one of the *format specifiers* listed in Table 14.2. To add a format specifier, you key in the name of the variable, a comma, and then the format specifier, as in **MyCharacter,C** where **MyCharacter** is an ASCII character and **C** is the format specifier.

TABLE 14.2: Format Specifiers for Use in Debugging

Format Specifier	Resulting Format
C	Character. Displays nonprinting control characters (e.g., Enter) on the screen with special display characters.
D	Decimal. Displays all integer values in decimal (normal, base 10) form.
$, H, or X	Hexadecimal. Displays all integer values in hexadecimal (base 16) with the $ prefix.
F*n*	Floating point. Displays real numbers with *n* significant digits.
P default	Pointer. Displays pointers (memory addresses) in segment:offset format instead of the default format, which is Ptr(segment, offset).
R names	Record. Displays record and object field names along with their values.

Watching a Variable

Probably the most important thing you can do with Turbo Pascal's integrated debugger is to put a watch on one or more variables in your program. This allows you to monitor the values of the variables as your program progresses without the need to insert extra debugging statements into your code. Before continuing, close any open windows in Turbo Pascal by selecting Clear Desktop from the System menu (the menu is opened by pressing *Alt+spacebar*). Then, open a new file window and enter and save the program shown in Listing 14.4. Be sure to include the bugs.

Listing 14.4

```
PROGRAM Listing14_4;

  { Illustrates stepping and tracing through a program with
    the Turbo Pascal integrated debugger. }


USES CRT, MyUtils;

VAR
   continue : CHAR;
   a, b,
   result   : INTEGER;


PROCEDURE AddTwoNumbers(a, b: INTEGER; VAR result: INTEGER);
   BEGIN
   result := a + b   { missing semicolon }
   WRITELN;
   WRITELN(' The sum of ', a, ' and ', b, ' is ', result, '.');
   pause
   END;

PROCEDURE MultiplyTwoNumbers(a, b: INTEGER; VAR result: INTEGER);
   BEGIN
   result := a * b;
   WRITELN;
   WRITELN(' The product of ', a, ' and ', b, ' is ', result, '.');
   pause
   END;


{ main body of program }
```

```
BEGIN
   CLRSCR;
   continue := 'Y';
   WRITELN(' This is a program that adds and then multiplies');
   WRITELN(' two numbers. You will first be prompted to enter');
   WRITELN(' the two numbers to add and multiply. Then, the');
   WRITELN(' AddTwoNumbers procedure will calculate the sum of');
   WRITELN(' the two numbers and pause so that you can see the');
   WRITELN(' result. Then, the MultiplyTwoNumbers procedure will');
   WRITELN(' calculate the product of the two numbers and pause');
   WRITELN(' again so that you can see the result.');
   WRITELN;
   WRITELN(' After this process is complete, the program will ask');
   WRITELN(' if you want to run the add and multiply routines again.');
   WRITELN(' If you do, type Y at the prompt; otherwise, type N.');
   pause;
   REPEAT
      CLRSCR;
      WRITELN;
      WRITE(' Enter the first number: ');
      READLN(a);
      WRITE(' Enter the second number: ');
      READLN(b);
      AddTwoNumbers(a,b,result);
      MultiplyTwoNumbers(a,b,result);
      WRITE(' Do another (Y/N)? ');

   { The programmer forgot to include a Readln statement to get input,
     resulting in an endless loop. In addition, without a Readln
     statement to pause the program for input, the "Do Another?" prompt
     goes by so fast that it is virtually invisible. }

   UNTIL UPCASE(continue) <> 'Y'
END.
```

The menu-driven way to add a watch is to choose Add Watch from the Watches submenu, but the most efficient way is to position the cursor on the name of the variable you want to watch, then press *Ctrl+F7*. This opens up the Add Watch window as shown in Figure 14.1. Use this technique to put a watch on the continue variable in Listing 14.4.

FIGURE 14.1:

The Add Watch dialog box

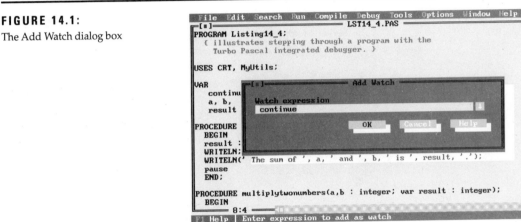

Listing 14.4 has two fairly common bugs. The first, a missing semicolon in the *Add-TwoNumbers* subroutine, is caught when you compile the program. The second bug is more subtle. It will not generate either a compile-time or a run-time error, but will send your program into an endless loop because the value of the loop control variable *continue* never changes. In the next section, we will see how to use the watch window while stepping through a program one line at a time.

Stepping through a Program

Turbo Pascal offers two ways to step through your program. The first method, called *stepping*, executes a single line of code at a time; if the line calls a subroutine, this method simply treats the subroutine as if it were a single statement. You step through a line of code by pressing the *F8* function key; each time you press it, another line of your program is executed. The second method, *tracing*, is similar to stepping except that when a line has a subroutine call, the subroutine is executed a line at a time. Tracing is done by pressing the *F7* function key. In Figure 14.2, we are stepping through Listing 14.4.

FIGURE 14.2:

Stepping through Listing 14.4

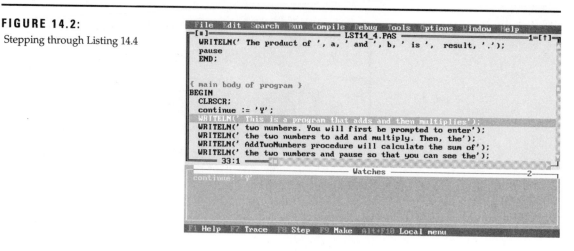

Note that the screen is now divided into two windows: the file window, which contains your program code, and the watch window, which contains the names of variables you are watching and their current values. Sometimes, when you have not yet run the program or a variable is hidden inside a subroutine, a variable will have the message "Cannot access this symbol" or "Unknown identifier" next to it. If you wish to make the screen a little neater, you can choose the Tile option from the Windows menu, although this won't affect how anything works.

The watch window shows that the current value of the *continue* variable is 'Y', indicating that the loop should continue to execute. Keep pressing the *F8* key, one press at a time, to step through the program until you get to the line that begins with UNTIL, as shown in Figure 14.3. At various points, you will be prompted to enter numbers or press a key.

Note that although we have completed the loop, the value of *continue* is still 'Y', and we were given no opportunity to change it inside the loop. Thus, we have found the bug that caused the endless loop.

Deleting a Watch

Now that we have found the bug, we do not need the watch on the *continue* variable any more. With the highlight bar in the watch window on the *continue* variable, open the Debug menu and select the Watches option to move the cursor to the watch

FIGURE 14.3:

Using the watch window to find the loop error

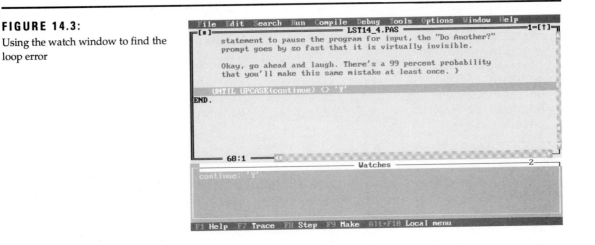

window. Then, just highlight the watch you want to delete and press the *Delete* key on your keyboard. Then, enter the bug-fixed version of the program, as shown in Listing 14.5.

Listing 14.5

```
PROGRAM Listing14_5;

   { Illustrates stepping and tracing through a program with
     the Turbo Pascal integrated debugger. }


USES CRT, MyUtils;

VAR
   continue : CHAR;
   a, b,
   result   : INTEGER;


PROCEDURE ExplainProgram;
   BEGIN
   CLRSCR;
   WRITELN(' This is a program that adds and then multiplies');
   WRITELN(' two numbers. You will first be prompted to enter');
   WRITELN(' the two numbers to add and multiply. Then, the');
   WRITELN(' AddTwoNumbers procedure will calculate the sum of');
```

```
WRITELN(' the two numbers and pause so that you can see the');
WRITELN(' result. Then, the MultiplyTwoNumbers procedure will');
WRITELN(' calculate the product of the two numbers and pause');
WRITELN(' again so that you can see the result.');
WRITELN;
WRITELN(' After this process is complete, the program will ask');
WRITELN(' if you want to run the add and multiply routines again.');
WRITELN(' If you do, type Y at the prompt; otherwise, type N.');
pause
END;



PROCEDURE AddTwoNumbers(a, b: INTEGER; VAR result: INTEGER);
   BEGIN
   result := a + b;
   WRITELN;
   WRITELN(' The sum of ', a, ' and ', b, ' is ', result, '.');
   pause
   END;

PROCEDURE MultiplyTwoNumbers(a, b: INTEGER; VAR result: INTEGER);
   BEGIN
   result := a * b;
   WRITELN;
   WRITELN(' The product of ', a, ' and ', b, ' is ', result, '.');
   pause
   END;


{ main body of program }
BEGIN
   continue := 'Y';
   ExplainProgram;
   REPEAT
      CLRSCR;
      WRITELN;
      WRITE(' Enter the first number: ');
      READLN(a);
      WRITE(' Enter the second number: ');
      READLN(b);
```

```
    AddTwoNumbers(a,b,result);

    MultiplyTwoNumbers(a,b,result);

    WRITE(' Do another (Y/N)? ');
    READLN(continue);
  UNTIL UPCASE(continue) <> 'Y'
END.
```

Notice one other interesting thing about Listing 14.5, apart from the fact that the bugs have been corrected. The lines that explain the program to the user have been bundled into their own subroutine. When you have multiple WRITELN statements as we do here, bundling them into a subroutine makes it easier to step through the program. Instead of having to step through each line one at a time, you simply press *F8* and the *ExplainProgram* routine executes all at once.

Tracing into Subroutines

Sometimes, the bug you want to locate is in a subroutine. In this situation, tracing through a subroutine is helpful. In the previous example, when you stepped through a program by pressing the *F8* key, the internal details of subroutines were skipped, or *stepped over*. When the highlight was on a line with a call to a subroutine, pressing *F8* executed the subroutine in a single step, and then moved the highlight down to the next line.

Pressing *F7* has the same effect as pressing *F8* except when the line contains a subroutine call. Then, *F7* takes you line-by-line through the subroutine itself, just as *F8* takes you line-by-line through the main program. This process is shown in Figure 14.4, where we are tracing through Listing 14.5.

Using Evaluate/Modify

The Evaluate/Modify option in the Debug menu allows you to inspect and, if desired, to change the values of variables at any desired point in your program. To see how this works, do the following:

1. Begin stepping through Listing 14.5 by pressing the *F8* key. When you are prompted to enter numbers for the program, enter 20 for *a* and 25 for *b*.

2. Stop when the highlight is on the line containing the *MultiplyTwoNumbers* subroutine.

3. With the highlight on the *MultiplyTwoNumbers* subroutine, open the Debug menu and pick Evaluate/Modify. The Evaluate/Modify dialog box opens up. (See Figure 14.5.)

FIGURE 14.4:

Tracing into a subroutine

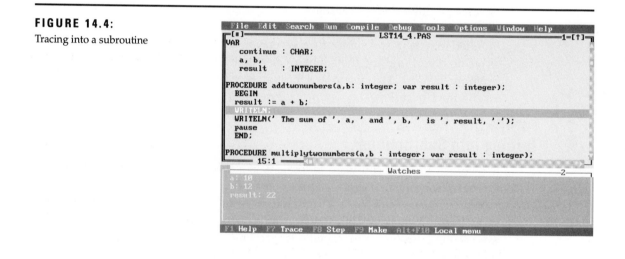

FIGURE 14.5:

Using the Evaluate and Modify dialog box

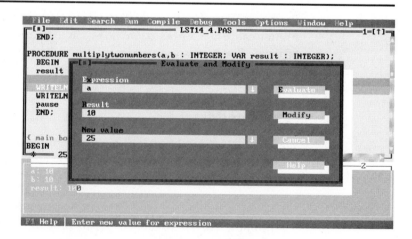

4. In the "Expression" blank of the dialog box, enter **a**. The number 20 is displayed in the "Result" blank because that is the current value of the variable *a*.

5. Tab to the "New value" blank and enter the number **1000**. Then press *Enter* to change *a* to the new value. Press *Escape* to exit from the dialog box.

6. Continue stepping through the program by pressing *F8*. With the value of *a* changed to *1000*, the *MultiplyTwoNumbers* procedure reports that the product of *a* and *b* is *25000*.

The primary use for Evaluate/Modify is to let you play "what if" with the values of variables: by changing the value of a variable in the middle of a program, you can see what the effect would be if it had that value.

Setting Breakpoints

Setting a breakpoint is like putting a stop sign in your code; in fact, "brakepoint" would be a more appropriate spelling. When you run the program, it will run up to the breakpoint and then stop. At that time, you can inspect the values of variables and anything else in the current state of the program. You insert a breakpoint in a program by moving the cursor to the line where you want to insert the breakpoint and then pressing *Ctrl+F8*. To remove a breakpoint, you move the cursor to the line containing the breakpoint and then press *Ctrl+F8* a second time.

The primary advantage of breakpoints over stepping through a program is that, in certain cases, breakpoints can be more efficient. If you want to inspect variables at a point toward the end of a long program, it would be time-consuming to step to that point one line at a time. Inserting a breakpoint allows you to go directly to the place you want to inspect.

FIGURE 14.6:

Using the Breakpoints dialog box

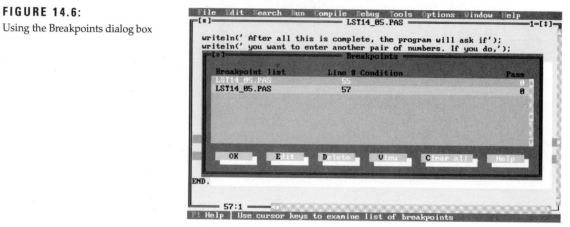

You can use the Breakpoints option in the Debug menu to open the Breakpoints dialog box, from which you can view a list of the current breakpoints in your program, as shown in Figure 14.6. You can also add and delete breakpoints by using this dialog box, but it is more practical to do it with the *Ctrl+F8* speed key method.

CHAPTER
FIFTEEN

Graphics in Turbo Pascal

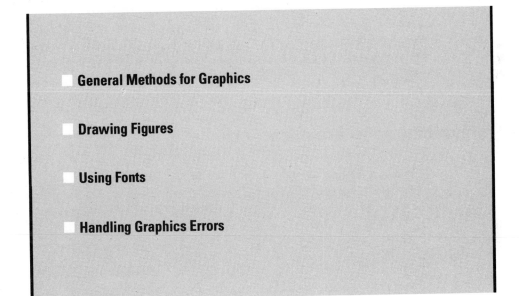

- **General Methods for Graphics**

- **Drawing Figures**

- **Using Fonts**

- **Handling Graphics Errors**

In this chapter, we turn to an area that can simultaneously be the most fun, the most frustrating, and the least portable in Borland Pascal and Turbo Pascal: graphics programming.

Although it is a general-purpose programming language, Borland/Turbo Pascal also provides extensive support for graphics programming on the IBM PC and compatible computers. The problem is that graphics programming relies so heavily on the specific hardware features provided by each computer, that there is almost no portability in graphics code from one type of computer to another. Even worse, there is no official standard for graphics programming, so each Pascal compiler tends to handle graphics in its own unique way—if at all.

That's the bad news, but there is some good news: the basic ideas of graphics programming are pretty much the same in every programming language and on every computer platform. If you are working with another Pascal compiler or on a computer that is not a PC, you won't be able to use your Turbo Pascal graphics code, but you will have a good understanding of how to write graphics code in the other language.

General Methods for Graphics

In order to understand graphics programming in Turbo Pascal, you must first understand the basic elements of graphics in any language. So far, we have worked exclusively in *text mode*. This means that the PC's screen is normally set up to display 25 lines of text with 80 characters per line. If you have an EGA or VGA monitor and video adapter, your monitor may be able to display more than this.

By the way, a video adapter is a part of your computer (usually an add-in board) that controls how text and graphics are displayed on your computer's screen. The original video adapter in the IBM PC, the IBM Monochrome Adapter, supported only text. Soon thereafter, the Hercules Graphics Adapter was introduced and created a de facto standard for monochrome graphics on the PC. IBM itself introduced the Color Graphics Adapter (CGA), which provided color graphics on color (RGB) monitors, but text was fuzzy and somewhat hard to read. More recently, the Enhanced Graphics Adapter (EGA), Video Graphics Array (VGA), and IBM 8514 Graphics Card standards have brought even better support for color graphics while providing sharp, easy-to-read text displays.

Limitations of Text Mode

ASCII characters displayed on the screen are predefined by your PC's hardware, in particular by its video adapter. When you include extended ASCII characters, such as box- and line-drawing characters, you can do some fairly interesting things in text mode. There are, however, three significant limitations.

The first limitation is that you cannot vary the size of the characters displayed on-screen at the same time. Because the size and shape of the characters are controlled by your video adapter and monitor, they all will occupy the same amount of space on the screen so they can fit into the monitor's 25-line by 80-column grid. This does have an important advantage: it makes screen elements in text mode very easy to manipulate. Every line has the same height and every character has the same width. If we want to move up or down one line, we know exactly how far to go; ditto for moving left or right. However, if you want to make *some* text elements larger or smaller than others, you cannot do it.

The second limitation is that you cannot vary the shape of the characters displayed on the screen. Everything comes out in the same typeface, which (theoretically) is easy to read but is not visually interesting. If you want to put some text in a plain font while other characters are in Gothic font, and still others are in Helvetica, you simply cannot do it.

The third limitation is that although you can draw boxes with extended ASCII characters, you cannot draw much else. You can only use the 256 predefined ASCII characters, and only in the 2,000 (25 times 80) text character positions on your screen.

Advantages and Disadvantages of Graphics

These limitations—as well as some of the advantages that go with them—are absent when you work in graphics mode. Instead of 25 lines, each 80 characters wide, you work with tiny dots on the screen, called *pixels* (picture elements). Even in character mode, pixels are present; they are used to form the characters that appear on the screen. Text characters themselves are predefined patterns of pixels. However, because the video adapter provides built-in support for ASCII characters, it constructs them out of pixels automatically, and neither the user nor the programmer has to deal with the problem of construction. Working in graphics mode, however, provides you with the ability to manipulate individual pixels that you do not have available in text mode.

The tremendous advantage of this approach is that you can display literally anything you want to on the screen: fancy text fonts, bar charts, animation, and so forth. The main disadvantage is that creating a graphics screen requires you to provide far more information than a text screen does. Instead of 2,000 text positions, now you must deal with the total number of pixels on the screen.

The arrangement and number of pixels on the monitor's screen is called the *resolution* of the monitor and video adapter. With a Hercules Graphics Adapter, this is 720 pixels wide by 348 pixels high, or 250,560 pixels; the Hercules adapter is said to have a resolution of 720 × 348. Although other factors affect how characters and images appear on the screen, the general rule is that the higher the resolution (the more pixels), the sharper the images on the screen. What is usually called the resolution of a monitor and video adapter is, in fact, its maximum resolution; one or more lower resolutions usually are available as well.

With a color monitor and video adapter, pixels can be any of the colors in the available *palette*. With a monochrome monitor, pixels are either on (lit up) or off (dark). The combination of a particular resolution and a particular color palette is called a graphics mode. When your program first sets up the computer to run graphics, it must tell the video adapter and monitor which of the available graphics modes should be used.

Graphics Drivers

Each different video adapter has different ways of handling graphics. Because of this, a program must be able to work with all or most of the currently used video adapters. However, to include support for all video adapters in every program would make the programs far bigger than necessary. Because of this, Turbo Pascal provides a separate *driver* file for each popular video adapter. When a Turbo Pascal program is run by the user, the program can detect which video adapter is installed in the computer, and it uses the appropriate video driver.

This means, of course, that the required video drivers must be available to the program. Turbo Pascal provides six different video drivers, each of which will work with one or more of the currently popular video adapters. These driver files all have the extension .BGI in their file names, and are normally found in the BGI directory created by the Turbo Pascal installation program. Other drivers for specific video cards are often available from the manufacturers of the video cards.

When you distribute a Turbo Pascal–compiled program that uses graphics, you must include copies of all these video drivers with the program. In addition, if you use special text fonts in graphics screens—as you almost certainly will—you must include copies of the font files. Turbo Pascal's video driver files are listed in Table 15.1; the font files are listed in Table 15.2.

One other point needs to be mentioned. As a conscientious computer user, you know that you cannot legally make copies of Turbo Pascal itself and distribute the copies to other people. However, this restriction does not apply to the video drivers and font files. You are free to copy these files and distribute them with your programs. Not only is this legal, of course, but it is the only solution that makes sense: if every user needed to have Turbo Pascal in order to run graphics programs written in Turbo Pascal, then it would be extremely impractical to write programs that included graphics.

TABLE 15.1: Video Driver Files Included with Turbo Pascal 7

Driver File Name	Video Adapters Supported
ATT.BGI	AT&T 6300 (400-line)
CGA.BGI	IBM CGA, MCGA, and compatibles
EGAVGA.BGI	IBM EGA, VGA, and compatibles
HERC.BGI	Hercules Monochrome and compatibles
IBM8514.BGI	IBM 8514 and compatibles
PC3270.BGI	IBM 3270 PC

TABLE 15.2: Font Files Included with Turbo Pascal 7

Font File	Font Provided
GOTH.CHR	Stroked Gothic
LITT.CHR	Stroked small character
SANS.CHR	Stroked sans serif
TRIP.CHR	Stroked Triplex

*Note: Unlike standard bit-mapped fonts, which are stored as patterns of pixels, stroked fonts are stored as a set of line segments. These segments are called *strokes*.

Setting Up the Screen for Graphics

Making your program set up the monitor and video adapter for graphics is quite similar to making it open and close files. In the beginning, you call the *InitGraph* procedure, which initializes your graphics hardware and puts your computer screen in graphics mode, normally with the maximum resolution available. When your work with graphics is finished, you call the *CloseGraph* procedure to return your computer screen to text mode.

InitGraph takes three parameters: the video driver to be used, the graphics mode (that is, the screen resolution and color palette) to be used, and the path name of the directory where the program can find the video driver files. You will need to have two integer variables in your program to represent the video driver and the graphics mode.

Although you have the option of specifying which video adapter to use, normally this does not make much sense. If you use *InitGraph* and specify the Hercules Monochrome video driver, then your program will not be able to work with any other video adapters. Fortunately, Turbo Pascal's Graph unit, which contains most of Turbo Pascal's graphics routines, has a predefined constant named *detect* that tells *InitGraph* to automatically detect which video adapter is being used and to load the appropriate driver. Table 15.3 lists the names and corresponding integers for Turbo Pascal's graphics drivers.

TABLE 15.3:   Graphic Driver Constants in Turbo Pascal 7

Constant Name	Corresponding Integer Value
Detect	0
CGA	1
MCGA	2
EGA	3
EGA64	4
EGAMono	5
IBM8514	6
HercMono	7
ATT400	8
VGA	9
PC3270	10

To use *detect,* you assign it to the graphic driver variable as shown in Listing 15.1. If you do not specify a value for the graphics mode, *InitGraph* uses the highest-resolution mode available for your video adapter and monitor.

Listing 15.1

```
PROGRAM Listing15_1;


   { Demonstrates fonts, text sizes, directions, and text
     justification modes that are predefined in the BGI. }

USES CRT, GRAPH;

CONST
   gd : INTEGER = detect;

VAR
   gm : INTEGER;

BEGIN
   INITGRAPH(gd, gm, 'c:\bp\bgi');
   OutText('A picture is a model of reality.');
   OutText('  Press any key ...');
   REPEAT UNTIL keypressed;
   CLOSEGRAPH
END.
```

The first thing Listing 15.1 does is to name the CRT and Graph units in the program's USES statement. Then, the graphics driver variable, called *gd,* is created as a typed constant. You should recall from Chapter 5 that a typed constant is actually a variable with a preset initial value. In this case, we have set the value of *gd* to *detect.* The variable to represent graphics mode, *gm,* is declared as an integer variable in the VAR section.

In the action part of the program, the first line is a call to *InitGraph.* Because we set the value of the graphics driver variable to *detect, InitGraph* automatically detects the type of graphics hardware in use and chooses the appropriate driver. The graphics mode variable *gm* is set to the highest-resolution mode available.

Finally, the third parameter tells *InitGraph* where to find the graphics driver files. This is most likely to be the \bp\bgi directory on your c drive. If you have installed the files somewhere else, you should substitute the appropriate path name for 'c:\bp\bgi' in Listing 15.1.

After setting up the computer in graphics mode, the program uses the Graph unit's *OutText* routine to display text on the screen. The Pascal WRITE and WRITELN routines can be used only in text mode, so Turbo Pascal provides *OutText* as an approximate equivalent to the WRITE routine. Next comes a REPEAT loop to pause the program until the user presses a key. Finally, a call to *CloseGraph* shuts down graphics mode and returns the computer to text mode. The result of running Listing 15.1 is shown in Figure 15.1.

Note that this pattern of setting up graphics with *InitGraph* and shutting it down with *CloseGraph* is part of every program that uses graphics.

FIGURE 15.1:

Displaying text in graphics mode

A picture is a model of reality. Press any key ...

Handling Graphics Errors

The program in Listing 15.1 is fine as far as it goes. However, it is unable to cope with situations in which the necessary video driver cannot be found and where, as a result, the graphics hardware cannot be initialized. Listing 15.1 simply assumes that the video drivers will be found in the directory that the program specifies—an assumption that in real-life situations is sometimes not justified.

A solution to this problem is shown in Listing 15.2, which incorporates error-checking into its graphics initialization. A string variable *dpath* is set up with an initial empty value; in this case, the call to *InitGraph* will succeed if the video driver is found in the same directory as the program itself. If not, a REPEAT loop keeps going until the call to *InitGraph* succeeds.

Listing 15.2

```
PROGRAM Listing15_2;


{ Demonstrates how to build error-checking into the graphics
  initialization. This is essential, because many PCs still do
  not have graphics capabilities. Note that the program uses
  GraphResult, a function from the Graph unit that tells if the
  InitGraph routine was successful in initializing the graphics
  hardware: GraphResult works just like IORESULT, which is used
  to determine if a file was opened successfully. GrOK and
  GrFileNotFound are constants defined in the Graph unit; if
  the call to InitGraph is successful, then GraphResult returns
  a value of GrOK; if the required graphics driver cannot be
  found, then it returns a value of GrFileNotFound. }


USES CRT, GRAPH;

CONST
   dpath  : STRING = '';

TYPE
   string80 = STRING[80];

VAR
   gd,
   gm,
   gerror : INTEGER;

BEGIN
   CLRSCR;
   REPEAT
      gd := detect;
      INITGRAPH(gd, gm, dpath);
      gerror := GRAPHRESULT;
      IF gerror <> grOK
         THEN BEGIN
            WRITELN(' Graphics error: ', GraphErrorMsg(gerror));
            IF gerror = GrFileNotFound
               THEN BEGIN
                  WRITELN(' Cannot find graphics driver. Please');
                  WRITE(' enter directory path for the driver: ');
                  READLN(dpath);
```

```
                    WRITELN
                    END
                ELSE HALT(1)
            END
    UNTIL gerror = grOK;

    OutText('A picture is a model of reality.');
    OutText('  Press any key ...');
    REPEAT UNTIL keypressed;
    CLOSEGRAPH
END.
```

Immediately after the call to *InitGraph*, we check a built-in variable called *Graph-Result* and assign its value to an integer variable *gerror*. *GraphResult* works the same way for graphics as *IOResult* works for input-output operations. If the graphics operation is a success, then *GraphResult* returns a value of 0; otherwise, it returns an error code that indicates what problem was encountered. The *GraphResult* value 0 can also be referred to by the identifier *GrOK*, which is used to control the loop. The values and identifiers of various graphics errors are shown in Table 15.4.

TABLE 15.4: GraphResult Error Values

Constant	Value	Problem Detected
grOK	0	No problem
grNoInitGraph	−1	Graphics not yet initialized
grNotDetected	−2	Graphics hardware not found
grFileNotFound	−3	Cannot find video driver file
grInvalidDriver	−4	Invalid driver file
grNoLoadMem	−5	Not enough RAM for graphics
grNoScanMem	−6	Out of RAM in scan fill
grNoFloodMem	−7	Out of RAM in flood fill
grFontNotFound	−8	Font file not found
grNoFontMem	−9	Not enough RAM to load font
grInvalidMode	−10	Invalid graphics mode for driver selected
grError	−11	Generic graphics error
grIOError	−12	Graphics I/O error
grInvalidFont	−13	Invalid font file
grInvalidFontNum	−14	Invalid font number

Like the value of *IOResult*, the value of *GraphResult* is a slippery thing, liable to change without notice. Therefore, we need to store the value of *GraphResult* in the *gerror* variable immediately after the call to *InitGraph*.

If an error is detected, an IF statement is activated. The first thing it does is use Turbo Pascal's *GraphErrorMsg* function with the error code returned by *Graph-Result*; this displays an informative error message on the computer screen. If the problem is that the driver cannot be found in the current directory, it prompts the user to enter a new value for the *dpath* variable. If the driver is found in this directory, then the loop terminates. If the problem is something else, such as not enough memory, then the program simply halts.

Everything else in Listing 15.2 is the same as in Listing 15.1, with an important exception. In 15.2, the graphics driver is not initialized at the beginning of the program as a typed constant; instead, it is included in the REPEAT loop so that it is reinitialized by a call to DETECT before each call to *InitGraph*. This is because a call to *InitGraph*, if unsuccessful, clears the value of the graphics driver variable; if the variable is not reset to the correct value, then the next call to *InitGraph* will fail because it cannot find the graphics hardware that corresponds to the now-incorrect value of the graphics driver variable. This is a bug typical of many loop situations: a particular statement needs to be in (or out of) the loop, but it is currently somewhere else.

Manipulating Items on the Screen

Working in graphics mode is different from working in text mode in some fundamental ways. Because text and art in a graphics screen can be any size and screen resolutions can vary, there is no straightforward way to position items on the screen.

In graphics, everything is calculated in terms of pixel coordinates. The topmost, leftmost pixel has coordinates of 0,0; the bottommost, rightmost pixel, at the lower-right corner of the screen, has coordinates that vary depending on the video adapter and graphics mode in use. In CGA graphics, for example, the resolution is 320 pixels horizontally and 200 pixels vertically (320×200); therefore, because the coordinate numbers start with 0,0, the bottom-right pixel has coordinates of 319,199. With Hercules graphics (resolution 720×348), the bottom-right pixel has coordinates of 719,347.

These differences in the number of pixels in different computer screens mean that it is extremely impractical to use *absolute* coordinates to position items in a graphics screen. For example, suppose that you are writing your program on a PC with a Hercules graphics card, which provides a screen resolution of 720×348. You find that a particular item looks very good when you place it at the pixel coordinates of 350,300—at the bottom center of the screen. If a user then runs your program on a PC with a CGA video adapter, the screen will not display properly because both pixel coordinates are beyond the limits of the CGA display's resolution (320×200).

This means that, most of the time, you position items by using relative instead of absolute coordinates. This is probably the most difficult aspect of graphics programming; next to this, learning how to use graphics drawing routines is a piece of cake. Turbo Pascal's Graph unit provides two functions that enable you to use relative coordinates: *GetMaxX* and *GetMaxY*. A call to *GetMaxX* gives you the number of the maximum x-axis coordinate, while a call to *GetMaxY* gives the maximum y-axis coordinate. No matter what kind of adapter or graphics mode is in use, these functions enable your program to find out the pixel-dimensions of the screen and to position items accordingly, as in:

```
VAR
    gd, gm,
    maxX, maxY : integer;
BEGIN
    gd := detect;
    InitGraph(gd, gm, 'c:\bp\bgi');
    maxX := GetMaxX;
    maxY := GetMaxY;
    OutTextXY(maxX div 2, maxY div 2, 'Centered text.');
    { ... other details of program }
    CloseGraph
END.
```

When you need to position several items on the screen at the same time, sometimes you have to do some fairly tricky arithmetic with *maxX* and *maxY* to get your items positioned properly. The big advantage, however, is that once the items are positioned with this method, they will be in the same relative position on any PC screen with any video adapter and any graphics mode.

Handling Text

The most obvious thing to learn first, in a chapter on graphics, would be how to draw pictures on the computer screen. However, even in graphics mode, text is more fundamental, because some graphics screens will contain only text and most graphics screens will contain at least some text.

OutText and OutTextXY

The most basic text-manipulation routines in graphics mode are *OutText* and *OutTextXY*. Both of these routines work like the WRITE procedure instead of WRITELN; they do not move the cursor down to the next line of text, because in graphics mode there is no predefined "next line" on the screen. *OutText*, which we saw in Listings 15.1 and 15.2, displays a text string at the current (invisible) cursor position. In doing so, it uses the current values for text font, size, direction, and justification; these values can be changed by calls to *SetTextStyle* and *SetTextJust*, as we will see in the next section.

OutTextXY, as you might guess, allows you to display text at the pixel coordinates specified by x and y, whether or not this is the same as the current cursor position. *OutTextXY* is used in the *GWrite* and *GWriteln* routines in Listing 15.3. Enter and run this listing, which gives you a demonstration of the different fonts, text sizes, and text directions available.

Listing 15.3

```
PROGRAM Listing15_3;


   { Demonstrates fonts, text sizes, directions, and text
     justification modes that are predefined in the BGI. }

USES CRT, GRAPH;

CONST
   x         : INTEGER = 10;
   y         : INTEGER = 10;
   lmargin = 10;

   BkSpc     = #8;
   enter     = #13;
```

```
   space   = #32;

TYPE
   string80 = STRING[80];

VAR
   gd,
   gm,
   maxX,
   maxY    : INTEGER;
   name    : STRING;
   FilePath : string80;

PROCEDURE FindFiles(VAR gd, gm: INTEGER;
                    VAR filepath:String80);

   VAR
      gerror: INTEGER;


   BEGIN (* Procedure FindFiles *)
      CLRSCR;
      REPEAT
      gd := detect;
      INITGRAPH(gd, gm, FilePath);
      gerror := GRAPHRESULT;
      IF gerror <> grOK
         THEN BEGIN (* Error Found *)
               WRITELN(' Graphics error: ', GraphErrorMsg(gerror));
               IF gerror = GrFileNotFound
                  THEN BEGIN  (* Prompt *)
                      WRITELN(' Cannot find graphics driver. Please');
                      WRITE(' enter directory path for the driver: ');
                      READLN(FilePath);
                      WRITELN
                      END    (* Prompt *)
                  ELSE HALT(1)
               END  (* Error Found *)
      UNTIL gerror = grOK;
   END; (* Procedure FindFiles *)


PROCEDURE Init(VAR maxX, maxY : INTEGER);
   BEGIN
   maxX := GetMaxX;
```

```
      maxY := GetMaxY
      END;

PROCEDURE HomeCursor(VAR x, y: INTEGER);
   BEGIN
   x := 10;
   y := 10
   END;


PROCEDURE GWrite(VAR X, Y : INTEGER; gtext : STRING);
   { corresponds to WRITE }
   BEGIN
   OutTextXY(X,Y,gtext);
   x := x + textwidth(gtext)
   END;

PROCEDURE GWriteln(VAR X, Y : INTEGER; gtext : STRING);
   { corresponds to WRITELN }
   BEGIN
   OutTextXY(x, y, gtext);
   y := y + TextHeight('M');
   x := lmargin;
   END;


PROCEDURE Gpause;
   VAR
      ch : CHAR;
   BEGIN
      SetTextJustify(LeftText, TopText);
      GWriteln(x, y, '');
      Gwriteln(x,y, 'Press any key ...');
      REPEAT UNTIL keypressed;
      ch := READKEY;
      GWriteln(x,y, '');
   END;

PROCEDURE GpauseXY(VAR x, y : INTEGER);
   VAR
      ch : CHAR;
   BEGIN
      SetTextStyle(TriplexFont, HorizDir, 2);
      SetTextJustify(LeftText, TopText);
      GWriteln(x, y, '');
```

```
        Gwriteln(x,y, 'Press any key ...');
        REPEAT UNTIL keypressed;
        ch := READKEY;
        GWriteln(x,y, '');
    END;


PROCEDURE ShowFontsAndSizes(VAR x, y : INTEGER);
    BEGIN
        GWrite(x, y, 'This is the default font, size 1. ');
        Gpause;

        SetTextStyle(TriplexFont, HorizDir, 2);
        Gwrite(x, y, 'This is the triplex font, size 2. ');
        Gpause;

        SetTextStyle(SmallFont, HorizDir, 4);
        GWrite(x,y,'This is the "small" font, size 4. ');
        Gpause;

        SetTextStyle(SansSerifFont, HorizDir, 3);
        GWrite(x,y,'This is the Sans-serif font, size 3. ');
        Gpause;

        SetTextStyle(GothicFont, HorizDir, 4);
        GWrite(x,y,'This is the Gothic font, size 4. ');
        Gpause;

        ClearDevice;
        HomeCursor(x,y)
    END;

PROCEDURE ShowJustAndDir(VAR x, y : INTEGER;
                             maxX, maxY : INTEGER);
    VAR
        xpos, ypos : INTEGER;
    BEGIN
        SetTextStyle(TriplexFont, HorizDir, 2);
        GWriteln(x, y, 'This is horizontal text, left-justified. ');
        Gpause;
        x := maxX div 3;
        y := y + TextHeight('M');

        SetTextJustify(LeftText, BottomText);
        OutTextXY(x, y, 'Left, bottom-justified');
```

```
       delay(1000);

       SetTextJustify(CenterText, CenterText);
       y := y + TextHeight('M');
       OutTextXY(x, y, 'Center, center-justified.');
       delay(1000);

       SetTextJustify(RightText, TopText);
       y := y + TextHeight('M');
       OutTextXY(x,y, 'Top, right-justified');
       delay(1000);

       x := maxX - maxX div 6;
       y := maxY;
       SetTextStyle(TriplexFont, VertDir, 7);
       SetTextJustify(LeftText,BottomText);
       OutTextXY(x,y, 'Vertical');
       delay(1000);

       SetTextStyle(TriplexFont, HorizDir, 2);
       y := maxY - maxY div 4;
       Gpause;
       ClearDevice;
       HomeCursor(x,y)
    END;


BEGIN
    gd := DETECT;
    FindFiles(gd, gm,FilePath);
    Init(maxX, MaxY);
    ShowFontsAndSizes(x,y);
    ShowJustAndDir(x,y, maxX, maxY);
    CLOSEGRAPH
END.
```

OutTextXY, as you can see in Listing 15.3, takes three parameters: two integers representing the x (horizontal) and y (vertical) pixel coordinates at which you want text displayed, and a string that contains the text to be displayed. There is a lot of information in Listing 15.3, so let's take it one item at a time.

Fonts

The first result of running Listing 15.3 is shown in Figure 15.2, which shows different predefined text fonts and sizes in Turbo Pascal. When you use *OutText* or *OutTextXY*, the text is displayed with the current text font, direction, and size. In the first example we saw in Listing 15.1 and Figure 15.1, this was fairly unimpressive: small text at the top of the screen. In Listing 15.3, however, we use the *SetTextStyle* routine to change from the default settings to fonts and sizes that are a little more interesting.

FIGURE 15.2:

Different fonts and sizes
of text in graphics mode

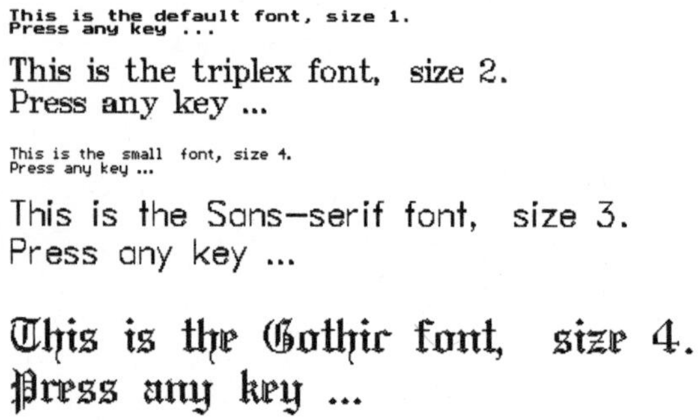

This is the default font, size 1.
Press any key ...

This is the triplex font, size 2.
Press any key ...

This is the small font, size 4.
Press any key ...

This is the Sans—serif font, size 3.
Press any key ...

This is the Gothic font, size 4.
Press any key ...

The *SetTextStyle* routine takes three parameters: the font style to be used, the direction of the text (horizontal or vertical), and a magnification factor from 1 to 10. All three parameters are of type word, which is a special integer type. However, Turbo Pascal provides predefined names for the font styles and the directions, so you need not worry about remembering which number stands for a particular type font or text direction. These names are shown in Table 15.5.

The text font, direction, and size that you set with *SetTextStyle* remain in effect until you change them with another call to *SetTextStyle* or until graphics mode is shut down with a call to *CloseGraph*.

Notice that the *ShowFontsAndSizes* routine ends with a call to the *ClearDevice* routine. Because CLRSCR can be used only with text-mode screens, the Graph unit provides *ClearDevice* to blank the screen as a graphics counterpart of CLRSCR.

TABLE 15.5: Constants for Text Fonts and Directions

Constant	Value
DefaultFont	0 (8 × 8 pixel bit-mapped font)
TriplexFont	1 (stroked fonts)
SmallFont	2
SansSerifFont	3
GothicFont	4
HorizDir	0 (left to right)
VertDir	1 (bottom to top)
UserCharSize	0 (user-defined character size)

Text Justification

Text justification is something that may have surprised you when you ran Listing 15.3. When we are working in text mode, the terms *left-justified, center-justified,* or *right-justified* have meanings that do not seem to apply in graphics mode. When we say that something is left-justified, we mean that it is against the left edge of the screen, while center-justified items are in the center of the screen and right-justified items are against the right edge of the screen.

In the *ShowJustAndDir* routine of Listing 15.3, however, things don't work that way. First, we call *SetTextJustify* to tell Turbo Pascal to left-justify text horizontally and bottom-justify it vertically. Then, we would normally expect the text to appear at the bottom-left corner of the screen. In graphics mode, however, text is justified not relative to the screen as a whole but relative to the current cursor position. A left-justified item will appear to the right of the current location, while a center-justified item will be centered on the current location and a right-justified item will be to the left of the current location. The results are shown in Figure 15.3.

The first text item, which says that "This is horizontal text, left-justified," seems fine: it is against the left edge of the screen. The next three items, however, are puzzling. "Left, bottom-justified" appears not on the left side of the screen, but in the center; "Center, center-justified" appears a little below and to the left of the first item; and "Top, right-justified" appears below and to the left of "Center, center-justified."

This is horizontal text, left–justified.

Press any key ...

Left, bottom–justified
Center, center–justified.
Top, right–justified

Press any key ...

Vertical

The fact that each text item appears below the preceding one is no mystery. Before displaying the second and third items with *OutTextXY*, we move the current cursor location down by a distance equal to a "line" of text in the current font and size. This is done by changing the y (vertical) coordinate: to the original y coordinate, we add the height of a capital letter. Because the y axis increases as we go from the top to the bottom of the screen, this moves the cursor location down. This is the standard method for moving the cursor down a line in graphics mode.

However, the horizontal position of the text items is confusing until you notice that all three items are positioned in relation to the same horizontal location. The left-justified item is positioned to its right, the center-justified item is centered on it, and the right-justified item is to its left.

Vertical justification works in the same odd way, even though this fact is not quite as clear in Figure 15.3. A top-justified item appears below the current cursor position, a center-justified item appears at the same level, and a bottom-justified item appears above the current cursor position. The text justifications that you can use with *SetTextJustify* are shown in Table 15.6.

TABLE 15.6: Text Justification Constants

Constant	Value
Horizontal justification	
LeftText	0 (text appears to right of cursor)
CenterText	1 (text centered on cursor location)
RightText	2 (text appears to left of cursor)
Vertical justification	
BottomText	0 (text appears above cursor location)
CenterText	1 (text centered on cursor location)
TopText	2 (text appears below cursor location)

The *ShowJustAndDir* routine also provides several examples of the sort of travails you must go through to position items on the screen. Most of these positioning operations involve changing the value of the x or y coordinate by relating it to *maxX* or *maxY*, the maximum x and y coordinates of the screen. (Remember that *maxX* and *maxY* are variables that *we* defined, and they are not predefined variables in Turbo Pascal. They get their values from calls to *GetMaxX* and *GetMaxY*.) There really is no formula for this kind of positioning; it is partly a matter of experience, and partly a matter of trial and error.

Graphics Versions of WRITE and WRITELN

Another trick that we introduced in Listing 15.3 was to create *GWrite* and *GWriteln*, which are graphics-mode versions of WRITE and WRITELN. *OutText* and *OutTextXY* are fine as far as they go, but these routines give us a more familiar and flexible way to display text on the screen. Both routines take three parameters: two integers for the x and y coordinates at which the text is to be displayed, and the text string itself.

GWriteln displays text at the specified cursor location (using the current settings for font, size, and justification). It is designed to work only with horizontal text. After the text has been displayed, *GWriteln* moves the cursor down by a "line" and moves it back to the left margin, just the same as WRITELN does in text mode. *Lmargin* itself is a constant x-coordinate value of 10, which is just a little over from the far-left edge of the screen.

GWrite does the same thing as *OutText*, except that it allows you to specify the cursor location at which the text should be displayed. In fact, the main reason to create *GWrite* was to have a parallel graphics-mode routine for WRITE in the same way as we have one for WRITELN.

Getting User Input

Because we probably will use the routines from Listing 15.3 in the future, we should add them to the MyUtils unit that we created in Chapter 10. Add the new routines to the MyUtils unit so that the unit now contains everything shown in Listing 15.4. Then open the Compile menu, and change the Destination to "Disk." Compile the unit, change the Compile Destination back to "Memory," and make sure that the new MyUtils unit is in a directory where Turbo Pascal can find it (one of the directories listed for units in the Options/Directories dialog box).

Listing 15.4

```
Unit MyUtils;  { Listing 15.4: utility routines, including graphics. }


INTERFACE
{ =================== PUBLIC section of unit =================== }

USES CRT, GRAPH;

TYPE
   GoodChars = set of char;   { used with the GetGoodChar procedure }

CONST
   YNchars       : GoodChars = ['Y', 'y', 'N', 'n'];

   backspace     = #8;
   enter         = #13;
   space         = #32;

   x             : INTEGER = 10;
   y             : INTEGER = 10;
```

```
    lmargin     = 10;


TYPE
    string80 = STRING[80];


PROCEDURE Pause;    { accepts any key }

PROCEDURE GetGoodChar(GoodOnes:GoodChars; var InChar:char);

PROCEDURE GetGoodInt(MinNum, MaxNum: integer; var InNum:integer);

PROCEDURE GFilesLoc(VAR Gdriver,GMode:INTEGER;GPath:STRING);

PROCEDURE HomeCursor(VAR x, y: INTEGER);

PROCEDURE GWrite(VAR X, Y : INTEGER; gtext : STRING);
    { corresponds to WRITE }

PROCEDURE GWriteln(VAR X, Y : INTEGER; gtext : STRING);
    { corresponds to WRITELN }

PROCEDURE Gpause;

PROCEDURE GpauseXY(VAR x, y : INTEGER);

PROCEDURE GRead(VAR x, y : INTEGER; VAR gtext: STRING);



IMPLEMENTATION

{ ==================== PRIVATE section of unit ==================== }

VAR
    Gdriver,
    Gmode,
    maxX,
    maxY : INTEGER;

    Gtext: STRING;


PROCEDURE Pause; { Pauses the program until user presses a key. }
```

```
VAR
   Proceed : char;
BEGIN
   Writeln;
   Write(' Press any key to continue ... ');
   Proceed := readkey;
   Writeln; Writeln
END;


PROCEDURE GetGoodChar(GoodOnes:GoodChars; var InChar:char);

   {An error-trapping substitute for "readln" to get character
    input from the keyboard. This procedure takes two parameters:
    a set of "acceptable" characters for input, and a variable
    parameter that is the actual character input. If the input
    character is not in the set of acceptable characters, this
    procedure returns to the original screen position and waits
    for the user to enter an acceptable character.}

   VAR
      markX, markY  : byte;
   BEGIN
      repeat
         BEGIN
            markX := whereX;
            markY := whereY;
            Readln(InChar);
            if not (InChar in GoodOnes) then
               BEGIN
                  gotoXY(markX, markY);
                  ClrEOL
               END
         END
      until InChar in GoodOnes
   END;




PROCEDURE GetGoodInt(MinNum, MaxNum: integer;  var InNum: integer);

   {An error-trapping substitute for "readln" to get integer
    input from the keyboard. This procedure takes two parameters:
    a set of "acceptable" integers for input, and a variable
```

parameter that is the actual integer input. If the input
integer is not in the set of acceptable integers, this
procedure returns to the original screen position and waits
for the user to enter an acceptable integer.}

```pascal
VAR
    markX, markY  : byte;
    LoopControl   : integer;

BEGIN
    repeat
        BEGIN
            markX := whereX;
            markY := whereY;

            {$I-}
            Readln(InNum);
            {$I+}
            LoopControl := ioresult;

            if (LoopControl <> 0) then
                BEGIN
                    gotoXY(markX, markY);
                    ClrEOL
                END;

            if (inNum < MinNum) or (inNum > MaxNum) then
                BEGIN
                    gotoXY(markX, markY);
                    ClrEOL
                END
        END
    until (LoopControl = 0) and (InNum >= MinNum) and (InNum <= MaxNum)
END;


PROCEDURE GFilesLoc(VAR Gdriver,Gmode:INTEGER;GPath:STRING);
            {Procedure to Locate the Path of BGI Files}

    VAR
        gerror: INTEGER;


    BEGIN (* Procedure GFilesLoc *)
        CLRSCR;
```

```
      REPEAT
         Gdriver := detect;
         INITGRAPH(Gdriver, Gmode, GPath);
         gerror := GRAPHRESULT;
         IF gerror <> grOK
            THEN BEGIN (* Error Found *)
               WRITELN(' Graphics error: ', GraphErrorMsg(gerror));
               IF gerror = GrFileNotFound
                  THEN BEGIN  (* Prompt *)
                     WRITELN(' Cannot find graphics driver. Please');
                     WRITE(' enter directory path for the driver: ');
                     READLN(GPath);
                     WRITELN
                     END     (* Prompt *)
                  ELSE HALT(1)
               END  (* Error Found *)
      UNTIL gerror = grOK;
   END; (* Procedure GFilesLoc *)

PROCEDURE HomeCursor(VAR x, y: INTEGER);
   BEGIN
   x := 10;
   y := 10
   END;


PROCEDURE GWrite(VAR X, Y : INTEGER; gtext : STRING);
   { corresponds to WRITE }
   BEGIN
   OutTextXY(X,Y,gtext);
   x := x + textwidth(gtext)
   END;

PROCEDURE GWriteln(VAR X, Y : INTEGER; gtext : STRING);
   { corresponds to WRITELN }
   BEGIN
   OutTextXY(x, y, gtext);
   y := y + TextHeight('M');
   x := lmargin;
   END;

PROCEDURE Gpause;
   VAR
      ch : CHAR;
   BEGIN
```

```
      SetTextJustify(LeftText, TopText);
      GWriteln(x, y, '');
      Gwriteln(x,y, 'Press any key ...');
      REPEAT UNTIL keypressed;
      ch := READKEY;
      GWriteln(x,y, '');
   END;

PROCEDURE GpauseXY(VAR x, y : INTEGER);
   VAR
      ch : CHAR;
   BEGIN
      SetTextStyle(TriplexFont, HorizDir, 2);
      SetTextJustify(LeftText, TopText);
      GWriteln(x, y, '');
      Gwriteln(x,y, 'Press any key ...');
      REPEAT UNTIL keypressed;
      ch := READKEY;
      GWriteln(x,y, '');
   END;

PROCEDURE GRead(VAR x, y : INTEGER; VAR gtext: STRING);
   VAR
      ch : CHAR;
   BEGIN
      gtext := '';
      REPEAT
      ch := READKEY;
      IF ch <> enter
         THEN BEGIN
         GWrite(x, y, ch);
         gtext := gtext + ch
         end
      UNTIL ch = Enter
   END;


END.    { of the "MyUtils" unit }
```

Here are the new graphics routines in the MyUtils unit:

- *GFilesLoc*, which locates the graphics files needed for the other graphics routines.

- *HomeCursor*, which repositions the graphics cursor at the top-left corner of the screen.

- *GWrite*, which displays text at a specified position on the screen.

- *GWriteln*, which displays text at a specified position on the screen, and then moves the cursor down one line and back to the left edge of the screen.

- *Gpause*, which pauses the program and displays a "Press any key" message at the current cursor position.

- *GpauseXY*, which pauses the program and displays a "Press any key" message at a cursor position that you specify.

- *GRead*, a graphics equivalent of the READ procedure, which gets keyboard input from the user, displays it on the screen, and loads it into a string variable.

The new version of MyUtils also adds some constant names for keys, as well as predefined x, y, and left-margin coordinates. But the routine we have not seen in action is *GRead*, which works in graphics mode almost the same as READ works in text mode.

GRead takes three parameters: two integers that represent the x and y coordinates where text input will be echoed to the screen, and a text string variable into which the input gets loaded. We first initialize the text variable to make sure that it is empty. Then we set up a REPEAT loop that continues until the user presses the *Enter* key.

Inside the REPEAT loop, each input character is loaded into a local variable *ch*. If the input character is not the *Enter* key, then it is echoed to the screen and added to the current contents of the text variable. Note, by the way, that we can use the plus sign ("+") with text strings in almost the same way that we can use it with numbers. We keep adding new input characters to the text string until an input character is the *Enter* key, at which point we drop out of the loop and the routine terminates. Listing 15.5 provides a demonstration of *GRead*, the on-screen results of which are shown in Figure 15.4.

Listing 15.5

```
PROGRAM Listing15_5;

    { Demonstrates how to get keyboard input from the
      user. The fundamental routine used is GRead from
      the MyUtils unit; this new routine is defined in
      Listing 15.4. }

USES CRT, GRAPH, MyUtils;

VAR
    gd,
    gm,
    maxX,
    maxY : INTEGER;
    GPath,
    name : STRING;

PROCEDURE InitSettings(VAR maxX, maxY : INTEGER);
    VAR
        ViewPort : ViewPortType;
    BEGIN
        maxX := GetMaxX;
        maxY := GetMaxY;
        SetTextStyle(TriplexFont, HorizDir, 3);
        SetLineStyle(SolidLn, O, ThickWidth);
        GetViewSettings(ViewPort);
        WITH ViewPort DO
            Rectangle(O,O, maxX, maxY)
    END;

PROCEDURE GetUserInput(VAR x, y : INTEGER);
    VAR
        username : STRING;
    BEGIN
        GWrite(x, y, 'Please enter your name: ');
        GRead(x,y, username);
        GWriteln(x,y, '');
        GWrite(x,y, 'Your name is ');
        GWrite(x, y, username);
        GWriteln(x, y, '.');
        Gpause
```

```
    END;

PROCEDURE Congrats(VAR x, y : INTEGER);
    BEGIN
        x := lmargin;
        y := maxY - maxY div 4;
        GWriteln(x,y, 'What a nice name!');
        gpause
    END;

BEGIN
    gd := DETECT;
    GFilesLoc(gd,gm,GPath);
    InitSettings(maxX, maxY);
    Homecursor(x,y);
    GetUserInput(x,y);
    SetLineStyle(DashedLn, 0, ThickWidth);
    Line(lmargin, maxY div 2, maxX, maxY div 2);
    delay(1000);
    Congrats(x,y);
    CLOSEGRAPH
END.
```

FIGURE 15.4:

Screen result from a run of
Listing 15.5

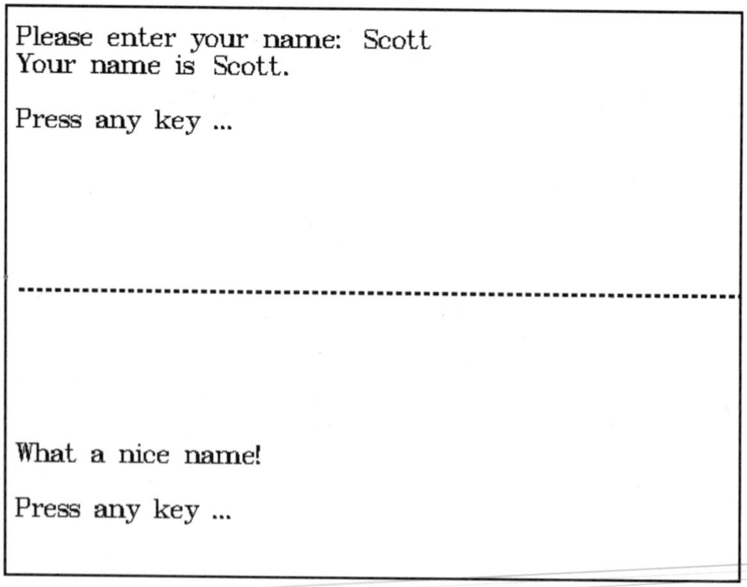

```
Please enter your name: Scott
Your name is Scott.

Press any key ...




-------------------------------------------------------------




What a nice name!

Press any key ...
```

Listing 15.5 has another notable feature. It uses a variable called *ViewPort* to hold the dimensions of the screen, and then calls Turbo Pascal's *Rectangle* graphics routine to draw a box around the screen window. *ViewPort* is defined as being of the data type *ViewPortType*, which is a predefined record type in the graph unit that holds the screen dimensions in its fields. A call to *GetViewSettings* loads the current screen dimensions into the *ViewPort* variable, which is then used to draw the rectangle.

Drawing Figures

Creating images is where graphics programming really shows its power. Turbo Pascal has 19 different drawing routines, most of which we will not have the space to examine in this book. However, let's look at a few of the most important. Four are demonstrated in Listing 15.6, and the result of running Listing 15.6 is shown in Figure 15.5.

Listing 15.6

```
PROGRAM Listing15_6;

    { Demonstrates four Turbo Pascal drawing routines. Also
      shows how to position multiple graphics items on the
      screen. }

USES CRT, GRAPH, MyUtils;

CONST
    gd : INTEGER = detect;

VAR
    gm,
    maxX,
    maxY : INTEGER;
    GFile: STRING;

PROCEDURE InitSettings(VAR maxX, maxY : INTEGER);
    VAR
       ViewPort : ViewPortType;
    BEGIN
       maxX := GetMaxX;
       maxY := GetMaxY;
```

```
    SetTextStyle(TriplexFont, HorizDir, 3);
    SetTextJustify(CenterText, CenterText);
    SetLineStyle(SolidLn, 0, ThickWidth);
    GetViewSettings(ViewPort);
    WITH ViewPort DO
    Rectangle(0,0, maxX, maxY)
  END;


PROCEDURE DrawLine(maxX, maxY : INTEGER);
  VAR
    rightborder,
    bottomborder : INTEGER;
  BEGIN
    rightborder := maxX div 2;
    bottomborder := maxY div 2;
    OutTextXY(rightborder div 2, bottomborder div 5, 'Line');
    Line(x, bottomborder div 3, rightborder - 10, bottomborder div 3);
  END;


 PROCEDURE DrawCircle(maxX, maxY : INTEGER);
  VAR
    leftborder,
    bottomborder : INTEGER;
    radius       : WORD;
  BEGIN
    leftborder := maxX div 2;
    bottomborder := maxY div 2;
    SetLineStyle(SolidLn, 0, NormWidth);
    OutTextXY(leftborder + maxX div 4, bottomborder div 5, 'Circle');
    Circle(leftborder + maxX div 4, bottomborder div 2, 50)
  END;


PROCEDURE DrawArc(maxX, maxY : INTEGER);
  VAR
    topborder,
    rightborder,
    x, y        : INTEGER;
    radius,
    startangle,
    endangle    : WORD;
  BEGIN
    topborder := maxY div 2;
    rightborder := maxX div 2;
    OutTextXY(maxX div 4, topborder + maxY div 10, 'Arc');
```

```
        Arc(maxX div 4, maxY - maxY div 5, 0, 180, 50)
    END;

PROCEDURE DrawBox(maxX, maxY : INTEGER);
    VAR
        leftborder,
        topborder,
        x1, y1, x2, y2 : INTEGER;
    BEGIN
        leftborder := maxX div 2;
        topborder := maxY div 2;
        OutTextXY(maxX - maxX div 4, topborder + maxY div 10, 'Box');
        x1 := leftborder + maxX div 10;
        y1 := topborder + maxY div 5;
        x2 := maxX - maxX div 10;
        y2 := maxY - maxY div 10;
        Rectangle(x1, y1, x2, y2)
    END;

BEGIN
    GFilesLoc(gd,gm,GFile);
    InitSettings(maxX, maxY);
    DrawLine(maxX,maxY);
    DrawCircle(maxX,maxY);
    DrawArc(maxX,maxY);
    DrawBox(maxX,maxY);
    x := lmargin;
    y := maxY - maxY div 6;
    GpauseXY(x, y);
    CLOSEGRAPH
END.
```

In order, Listing 15.6 draws and labels a line, a circle, an arc, and a rectangle. Each is positioned in its own quadrant of the screen, an exercise which requires the programmer to do some more fiddling around with relative screen coordinates.

The *DrawLine* routine positions a line and its label in the top-left quadrant of the screen. To position it correctly, we use integer variables to represent the right and bottom borders of the quadrant. Turbo Pascal's *Line* routine itself takes four parameters: the x and y coordinates where the line begins, and the x and y coordinates where the line ends. The style and thickness of the line itself is set in the *Init-Settings* routine with a call to Turbo Pascal's *SetLineStyle* routine.

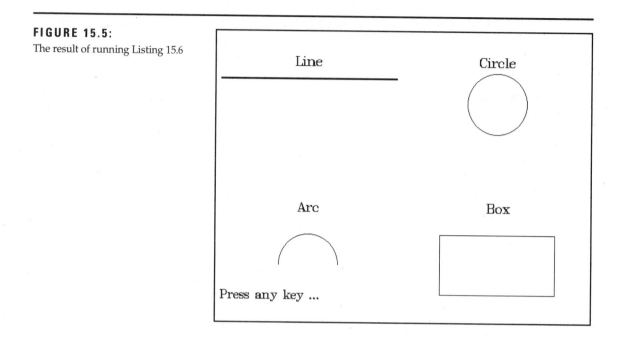

The *DrawCircle* routine positions the circle and its label in the top-right quadrant of the screen, using the same scheme as in *DrawLine* for setting up borders and positioning the items. The Turbo Pascal *Circle* routine itself takes three parameters: the x and y coordinates of the center of the circle, and a word-type number that is the radius of the circle. As usual, x and y are relative coordinates, and the circle is drawn with the current line style and thickness.

In the *DrawArc* routine, Turbo Pascal's *Arc* routine takes five parameters: two integers for the x and y coordinates of the center of the arc, two word-type numbers for the starting and ending angles of the arc, and one word-type number for the radius of the arc. The starting angle of 0 indicates that the arc starts at the three o'clock position and then moves counter-clockwise around its center point for 180 degrees, ending up at the nine o'clock position. Arcs are always drawn in this fashion: counter-clockwise with 0 degrees at three o'clock, 90 degrees at 12 o'clock, 180 degrees at nine o'clock, and 270 degrees at six o'clock. (Of course, you can draw an arc with any starting and ending angle you choose, such as a starting angle of 77 and an ending angle of 121.)

In the *DrawBox* routine, we set up four relative coordinates as integer variables for the four corners of the box drawn by Turbo Pascal's *Rectangle* routine. The four statements assigning values to x1, y1, x2, and y2 are not actually necessary: they are included simply to make the *Rectangle* statement easier to read.

Automatically Adjusting Screen Coordinates

As noted earlier, one of the thorniest problems in handling graphics is trying to adjust the screen coordinates for all the different types of graphics screens that your program might encounter. There is a trick you can use that, though not totally foolproof, will handle most such cases and automatically adjust the graphics coordinates for you.

Simply, we want to create a Borland/Turbo Pascal function that will automatically adjust graphics coordinates for us. This function (actually, two versions of the same function, one for X and one for Y coordinates) is demonstrated in Listing 15.7.

Listing 15.7

```
PROGRAM Listing15_7;

    { Demonstrates functions to convert X and Y coordinates
      for graphics on any screen. The GrafX and GrafY functions
      let you write your code as if all graphics screens are 1,000
      pixels wide and 1,000 pixels high. The functions get the
      maximum X and Y coordinates of the user's screen and convert
      your "1,000 x 1,000" coordinates to the appropriate values. }

uses crt, graph, myutils;

CONST
    dpath  : STRING = 'c:\bp\bgi';

TYPE
    string80 = STRING[80];

VAR
    gd,
    gm,
```

```
    gerror : INTEGER;
    MaxX, MaxY : integer;


FUNCTION GrafX( XCoord: integer) : integer;
    { Normally, MaxX would be passed to the function as a parameter.
      However, MaxX stays the same throughout any given session with
      a program using this function, and passing MaxX as a parameter
      would (a) make the source code less clear and (b) introduce an
      additional chance for passing the wrong value as the MaxX para-
      meter. For those three reasons, MaxX is imported "directly" into
      the function and is not passed as a parameter. The same  applies
      to the GrafY function, which is identical to GrafX except that
      it adjusts the Y coordinate. }
    VAR
        TempX : real;
    BEGIN
        TempX := MaxX / 1000;
        TempX := ( (XCoord * TempX) + 0.5 );
        GrafX := round(TempX);
    END;

FUNCTION GrafY( YCoord: integer) : integer;
    VAR
        TempY : real;
    BEGIN
        TempY := MaxY / 1000;
        TempY := ( (YCoord * TempY) + 0.5 );
        GrafY := round(TempY);
    END;

PROCEDURE StartGraphicsScreen;
    BEGIN
    CLRSCR;
    REPEAT
        gd := detect;
        INITGRAPH(gd, gm, dpath);
        gerror := GRAPHRESULT;
        IF gerror <> grOK
            THEN BEGIN
                WRITELN;
                WRITELN(' Graphics error: ', GraphErrorMsg(gerror));
```

```
            IF gerror = GrFileNotFound
               THEN BEGIN
                   WRITELN(' Cannot find graphics driver.');
                   WRITE(' Enter path for the driver: ');
                   READLN(dpath);
                   WRITELN
                   END
               ELSE BEGIN
                   pause;
                   HALT(1)
                   END
            END
      UNTIL gerror = grOK;
      MaxX := GetMaxX;
      MaxY := GetMaxY;
      END;

PROCEDURE ShutDownGraphicsScreen;
   BEGIN
   OutTextXY( GrafX(50),GrafY(800),
               ' Shutting down graphics, press any key ...');
   REPEAT UNTIL Keypressed;
   CLOSEGRAPH
   END;

BEGIN
   StartGraphicsScreen;
   OutTextXY( GrafX(250), GrafY(200),
               'Coordinates automatically adjusted.');
   ShutDownGraphicsScreen;
END.
```

The GrafX and GrafY functions allow you to assume that all graphics screens are 1,000 pixels wide and 1,000 pixels high. When you pass a pair of X,Y coordinates to these two functions, they use the MaxX and MaxY values to automatically convert your 1,000 x 1,000 numbers into the correct values for the user's graphics adapter and screen.

Incorporating Graphics Drivers and Fonts in a Program

Normally, a Turbo Pascal (or Turbo C++) program that uses graphics and type fonts must have the graphics driver and font files on the disk with the program. If you have Borland Pascal, these files are found in your BP\BGI directory. They have the extensions .BGI (for the graphics drivers) and .CHR (for the font files). When the user runs your program, these files must be available to it—meaning, most likely, that they must be distributed on the same floppy disk as the program itself.

But there's another way to accomplish the same thing. Listing 15.8 incorporates the BGI video drivers and fonts into the compiled *.EXE file. As a result, the compiled program is bigger but you need not include all the *.BGI and *.CHR files on the disk.

To compile and link this program, you must first create object-code (*.OBJ) versions of the BGI graphics driver and font files. You can do this by using the BINOBJ.EXE utility distributed with Turbo Pascal, but it's easier simply to do it as follows:

1. Make sure that your current DOS path includes the directories where BINOBJ.EXE and MAKE.EXE are located (probably \BP\BIN).

2. Find the directory where the file BGILINK.MAK is located; in Borland Pascal, this is C:\BP\EXAMPLES\DOS\BGI.

3. With that directory as the current directory, type this at the DOS prompt: **make -fBGILINK.MAK**. This will invoke the MAKE.EXE program, which will follow the instructions contained in BGILINK.MAK. It will create a unit for the graphics driver files (BGIDRIV.TPU) and the font files (BGIFONT.TPU). Note that these units are named in the USES statement at the top of the listing.

4. Copy *.TPU to \BP\UNITS directory.

5. With these two "extra" units available, you can incorporate the graphics driver and font files into Listing 15.8.

6. If you want to use this technique with other programs, note that the graphics drivers and fonts must be "registered" in the listing's source code. These techniques are also demonstrated in BGILINK.PAS, which is an example program distributed with Borland Pascal and Turbo Pascal.

Listing 15.8

```
PROGRAM Listing15_8;

    { Demonstrates how to link graphics drivers and fonts
      into a program's .EXE file so that the driver and font
      files don't need to be included on the program disk. Before
      you can compile and run this program, you must follow the
      instructions in this chapter for creating the BGIDRIV and
      BGIFONT units. The techniques used in this listing are
      identical to those used in the Borland/Turbo Pascal demo
      program BGILINK.PAS. }

USES CRT, GRAPH, BGIDRIV, BGIFONT, MyUtils;

{ Link the graphics drivers and fonts into the listing's .EXE
file }
PROCEDURE AbortDriver( fontname: STRING );
    BEGIN
    WRITELN( Fontname, ': ', GraphErrorMsg( GraphResult ) );
    HALT;
    END;

PROCEDURE RegisterDrivers;
    BEGIN
        IF RegisterBGIDriver( @CGADriverProc ) < 0
           THEN AbortDriver( 'CGA' );
        IF RegisterBGIDriver( @EGAVGADriverProc ) < 0
           THEN AbortDriver( 'EGA/VGA' );
        IF RegisterBGIDriver( @HercDriverProc ) < 0
           THEN AbortDriver( 'Herc' );
        IF RegisterBGIDriver( @ATTDriverProc ) < 0
           THEN AbortDriver( 'AT&T' );
        IF RegisterBGIDriver( @PC3270DriverProc ) < 0
           THEN AbortDriver( 'PC 3270' );
    END;

PROCEDURE AbortFont( FontName: string );
    BEGIN
    WRITELN(FontName, ': ', GraphErrorMsg( GraphResult ) );
    HALT;
    END;

PROCEDURE RegisterFonts;
    BEGIN
```

```
      IF RegisterBGIFont( @TriplexFontProc ) < 0
         THEN AbortFont( 'Triplex' );
      IF RegisterBGIFont( @SmallFontProc ) < 0
         THEN AbortFont(  'Small' );
      IF RegisterBGIFont( @SansSerifFontProc ) < 0
         THEN AbortFont( 'Sans Serif' );
      IF RegisterBGIFont( @GothicFontProc ) < 0
         THEN AbortFont( 'Gothic' );
      END;

PROCEDURE init;
   VAR
       gd, gm, gerror : INTEGER;
       Graphics: BOOLEAN;
   BEGIN
   RegisterDrivers;
   RegisterFonts;
   Graphics := TRUE;
   gd := Detect;
   InitGraph(gd,gm,'');
   gerror := GraphResult;

   IF gerror <> grOk
      THEN BEGIN
           Graphics := False;
           HALT
           END;
   END; { of init procedure }

PROCEDURE shutdown;
   BEGIN
   CloseGraph;
   END;

{ Main body of the program }
BEGIN
   Init;
   OutText('A picture is a model of reality.');
   OutText('  Press any key ...');
   REPEAT UNTIL keypressed;
   ShutDown
END.
```

Accessing DOS Services

- **Fundamentals of System Programming**

- **Processor Architecture**

- **Using Turbo Pascal DOS Routines**

- **Running a DOS Shell**

Any program in any high-level programming language uses services that are provided by the computer's operating system. For example, when a program needs to open a file or display a text string on the screen, it normally sends a request to the operating system to perform the service. The operating system, in turn, sends the appropriate instructions through the computer's BIOS (Basic Input-Output System) to the disk drive or monitor, and the file is opened or the text is displayed on the screen.

When a program uses operating system services in this way, you as the programmer do not need to know any of the details of how the services are provided. This approach, however, does not allow you to work directly with the computer's operating system, BIOS, and hardware. If you want to perform an operation for which there is no predefined routine in the programming language, then you simply cannot do it.

Borland Pascal and Turbo Pascal 7 provide four main methods by which you can directly use services provided by the computer's operating system and BIOS. Because they are not part of standard Pascal, these methods are located in a separate unit called the DOS unit. Although they all provide access to DOS services, they vary considerably both in the amount of sophistication required to use them—and in the *danger* they present to the careless or inexperienced programmer. These four methods are:

1. Using the *MsDos* procedure to access DOS functions directly.

2. Using the *Intr* procedure to access BIOS services directly through software interrupts.

3. Using predefined DOS unit procedures and functions that access DOS and BIOS services.

4. Using the *Exec* procedure to suspend the current program and run an external program, including DOS itself.

We will look at three of these methods in this chapter. To understand how they work, however, you must first know something about the architecture of the PC's microprocessor, as well as how it works with the BIOS and operating system to provide services to application programs such as those you write in Turbo Pascal.

Fundamentals of System Programming

Before you can understand how to use Turbo Pascal's DOS and BIOS routines (particularly the *MsDos* and *Intr* routines), you must have at least a minimum understanding of the architecture of the Intel 80x86 family of microprocessors, which are used in PCs. You must also understand hardware and software interrupts, know the functions provided by DOS and the PC's BIOS, and be able to figure out hexadecimal numbers when you see them.

Processor Architecture

The central processing unit of a PC is normally a member of the Intel 80x86 family of microprocessors: an 8086, 8088, 80286, 80386, or 80486. The 8086, 8088, and 80286 chips are manufactured by many different chip makers, but the 80386 and 80486 are made only by Intel. PCs can also use 80x86-compatible chips such as the NEC V-20 (compatible with the Intel 8086) or chips that are compatible with the Intel 80386 and 80486.

Although there are significant differences between these classes of microprocessors, they do have some characteristics in common. First, they all can perform the same basic operations performed by the 8086 chip, which was the first chip in the line. Second, each chip contains a variety of *registers* for on-chip storage of data that the processor needs to carry out its work. Each register can hold 16 bits of data, and each register has a different task to perform. The 8086 chip's registers are shown in Figure 16.1. Later members of the 80x86 family also have these registers.

General-Purpose Registers

The *general-purpose* registers AX, BX, CX, and DX are used for temporary storage of data that is being used in calculations. Most data, most of the time, is stored in the computer's random-access memory. For this data to be used in calculations, however, it must be transferred to the microprocessor over a communication channel called the *data bus*. While it is "at" the microprocessor being used in a calculation, each small piece of data is held in one of these registers.

FIGURE 16.1:

Registers in the 8086 microprocessor

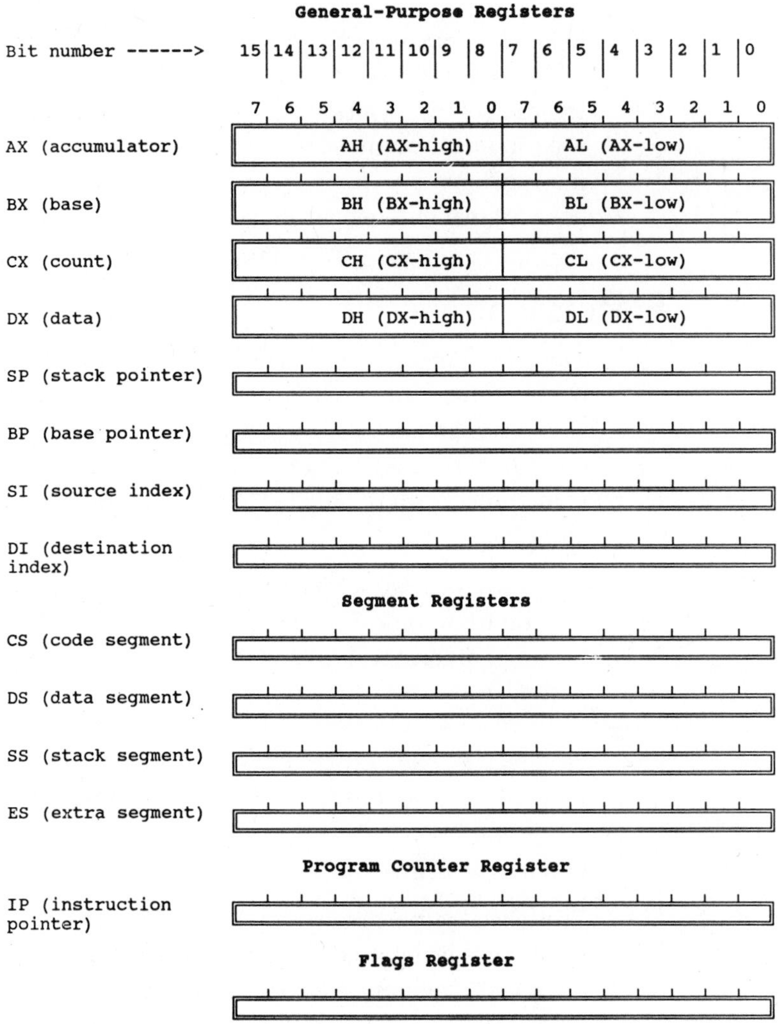

General-Purpose Registers

```
Bit number ------>   15 14 13 12 11 10 9  8  7  6  5  4  3  2  1  0

                      7  6  5  4  3  2  1  0  7  6  5  4  3  2  1  0

AX (accumulator)     ┌──────────────────────┬──────────────────────┐
                     │      AH (AX-high)     │      AL (AX-low)      │
                     └──────────────────────┴──────────────────────┘

BX (base)            ┌──────────────────────┬──────────────────────┐
                     │      BH (BX-high)     │      BL (BX-low)      │
                     └──────────────────────┴──────────────────────┘

CX (count)           ┌──────────────────────┬──────────────────────┐
                     │      CH (CX-high)     │      CL (CX-low)      │
                     └──────────────────────┴──────────────────────┘

DX (data)            ┌──────────────────────┬──────────────────────┐
                     │      DH (DX-high)     │      DL (DX-low)      │
                     └──────────────────────┴──────────────────────┘

SP (stack pointer)   ┌─────────────────────────────────────────────┐
                     └─────────────────────────────────────────────┘

BP (base pointer)    ┌─────────────────────────────────────────────┐
                     └─────────────────────────────────────────────┘

SI (source index)    ┌─────────────────────────────────────────────┐
                     └─────────────────────────────────────────────┘

DI (destination      ┌─────────────────────────────────────────────┐
index)               └─────────────────────────────────────────────┘
```

Segment Registers

```
CS (code segment)    ┌─────────────────────────────────────────────┐
                     └─────────────────────────────────────────────┘

DS (data segment)    ┌─────────────────────────────────────────────┐
                     └─────────────────────────────────────────────┘

SS (stack segment)   ┌─────────────────────────────────────────────┐
                     └─────────────────────────────────────────────┘

ES (extra segment)   ┌─────────────────────────────────────────────┐
                     └─────────────────────────────────────────────┘
```

Program Counter Register

```
IP (instruction      ┌─────────────────────────────────────────────┐
pointer)             └─────────────────────────────────────────────┘
```

Flags Register

```
                     ┌─────────────────────────────────────────────┐
                     └─────────────────────────────────────────────┘
```

The reason it is important for you to know about these registers is that Turbo Pascal's *MsDos* and *Intr* routines require you to load data into specific registers. If you know what the registers are, you will have a better understanding of what you are doing when you use these routines.

The AX, BX, CX, and DX registers have another important feature: each can be treated either as a single 16-bit (word) register or as two 8-bit (byte) registers. Thus, they can be used to store either a single 16-bit piece of data or two separate 8-bit pieces of data. For example, you can load a single 16-bit piece of data into the AX register, or you can load separate 8-bit pieces of data into the AL (AX-low) and AH (AX-high) registers.

You can store any kind of data in these registers, but in general, they are used in the following ways:

- *The AX register* is used to store operands and results in arithmetic operations, such as addition and subtraction. It also can be used to hold the number of a DOS routine from Turbo Pascal's *MsDos* procedure.

- *The BX (base) register* holds memory addresses and is used to find addresses in memory in relation to a *base* address. It also can be used in arithmetic operations.

- *The CX (count) register* is used as a counter for loop control and other repeated program operations. It also can be used in arithmetic operations.

- *The DX (data) register* is used to store some of the results of multiplication and division operations. It also can be used for general data storage and to hold the addresses of I/O devices.

Segment Registers

In order to handle a full megabyte of random-access memory, the 8086 divides memory into 64K segments. To find a location in memory, it combines the starting address of the appropriate segment with an *offset* that indicates a location within that segment. This is very similar to dividing street addresses into "blocks": for example, you can have an offset address of "22" in the 100 block of Maple Street (122 Maple Street), in the 200 block of Maple Street (222 Maple Street), and so forth.

In the same way, the 8086 combines a segment address (the "block") with an offset address (the house number) to identify a specific address in the PC's memory. The segment registers are used to hold the starting addresses of specific segments used by your program:

- *The CS (code segment) register* contains the starting address of the code segment, which contains the instructions from the program that is currently being run. This is used with the instruction pointer from the IP register to find the next program instruction that should be carried out.

- *The DS (data segment) register* contains the starting address of the data segment, which contains data being used by the current program.

- *The SS (stack segment) register* contains the starting address of the stack segment, which holds return addresses for subroutines, variables passed to subroutines, and other data that needs to be stored temporarily during a program run.

- *The ES (extra segment) register*, as its name implies, contains the starting address of an *extra segment*, which is used for miscellaneous data storage during a program run.

Offset Registers

Just as the segment registers contain starting addresses of specific segments in memory, the offset registers contain the "street addresses" of locations within those segments. The offset registers are as follows:

- *The SP (stack pointer) register* contains the address of the current top of the stack. When a subroutine is called, its return address and local variables are placed on the stack. If it calls another routine before terminating, then the return address and local variables of the second routine are placed on the stack *on top of* the corresponding information for the first routine. The top of the stack is the location in memory where the next stack data will be placed. As subroutines finish their work and terminate, their data is removed from the stack in reverse order—that is, the last routine called has its data removed first, then the second to last routine, and so forth.

- *The BP (base pointer) register* is also used for holding addresses of locations in the stack segment.

- *The SI (source index) and DI (destination index) registers* are used to hold miscellaneous addresses in memory. They also are used for string instructions (move and compare) that allow high-speed manipulation of the data in entire blocks of memory.

Instruction and Flags Registers

The other two registers are the *IP (instruction pointer) register* and the *Flags register*. The IP register contains the memory address of the next program instruction to be carried out; the instruction is, of course, somewhere in the code segment. The Flags register has 16 bits available to indicate the status of various processor operations and to handle control functions.

Turbo Pascal's *MsDos* and *Intr* routines allow you to send data to each of these registers through a predefined *registers* data type in the DOS unit. We will look at how to use this data type when we discuss the *MsDos* and *Intr* routines, below.

The Idea of Interrupts

The idea of an interrupt is a familiar one. Suppose that you are performing some task, such as shaving your cat, and the phone rings. As a result, you put the cat down and start talking on the telephone. The telephone ring was an *interrupt:* a signal that you should stop what you are doing temporarily and do something else for a while. When the second task—in this case, talking on the telephone—is finished, then you go back to what you were doing when you were interrupted.

A PC interrupt is almost exactly the same: it signals to the microprocessor that it should stop what it is doing temporarily and do something else that is more urgent. The 80x86 family of microprocessors allows both *hardware* and *software* interrupts. When it receives an interrupt, the processor saves the contents of its registers, handles the task requested by the interrupt, puts the saved information back in the registers, and returns to what it was doing when it received the interrupt.

The 8086 supports 256 different interrupts, numbered 0 to 255 (or 00H to FFH in hexadecimal numbering, which we'll discuss below). Each interrupt requests that the processor carry out a different routine, and the 32-bit (segment plus offset) memory addresses of these routines are located in the PC's *interrupt vector table,* which occupies the first 1K (1,024 bytes) of RAM. Turbo Pascal's DOS unit provides a procedure, *SetIntVec*, that allows you to tamper with the contents of the interrupt vector table, but it is extremely foolish to do so unless you are highly experienced and very careful.

The most common use of interrupts in Turbo Pascal is to call DOS functions, such as those to get disk information or to terminate a program. However, Turbo Pascal also provides high-level routines for many of these functions, so direct use of interrupts is often unnecessary. For a list of specific DOS interrupts, see your DOS manual.

Hexadecimal Notation

If you look at your DOS manual, you will probably notice that the numbers of DOS interrupts are given in both "Hex" and standard decimal notation. That's because if you want to do low-level programming in Turbo Pascal (or any other language), you must have at least some familiarity with hexadecimal arithmetic.

If you went to school in the last 20 years, since the time when the "new math" substituted number theory for such arcane and useless skills as addition and subtraction, you already know the basic ideas behind hexadecimal (even if you can't add or subtract). Our everyday arithmetic uses base 10, but hexadecimal uses base 16. Thus, the first 16 numbers in each base are as shown in Table 16.1.

Table 16.1 also shows the binary numbers that correspond to the first 16 decimal and hexadecimal numbers. This is the primary reason for the use of hexadecimal numbers. Recall that the main principle of the PC's operation is the on/off switch, and binary numbers can be used to represent sequences of on/off switches.

There are 16 possible combinations of four bits, and one hex digit can be used to stand for each of the combinations, thereby providing a convenient shorthand for the corresponding binary numbers. Thus, a 32-bit segment:offset address in memory can be written in hex in only eight digits—for example, as 0CE8:0DBA instead of 0000110011101000:0000110110111010.

The most important aspect of this is simply to be *aware* of hex notation. The numbers of DOS functions and 8086 interrupts are often given in hex notation, and if you mistake it for decimal notation, you will probably call the wrong function or use the wrong interrupt. Hex numbers are *usually*, but not always, preceded by a dollar sign or followed by an uppercase "H". Thus, *$23* and *23H* both denote hex 23.

TABLE 16.1: Decimal, Hexadecimal, and Binary Numbers

Decimal	Hexadecimal	Binary
0	0	0000
1	1	0001
2	2	0010
3	3	0011
4	4	0100
5	5	0101
6	6	0110
7	7	0111
8	8	1000
9	9	1001
10	A	1010
11	B	1011
12	C	1100
13	D	1101
14	E	1110
15	F	1111

Even if a number is not specially marked with a dollar sign or an "H", you should stay alert for the possibility that it is in hex instead of decimal notation.

To indicate that a number in a Turbo Pascal program is in hex rather than decimal, you must use the dollar sign not the "H" (for example, $23).

How to Use the MsDos Procedure

Turbo Pascal's *MsDos* procedure, defined in the DOS unit, provides one way to make a direct call to functions provided by the MS-DOS operating system. This is somewhat trickier than using those functions indirectly through ordinary Pascal commands, but it gives you more flexibility in using them.

To use the *MsDos* procedure, you need to know three things: first, about processor registers, which we looked at earlier in this chapter; second, about the various functions that DOS offers, which we will look at in the next section; and third, about the DOS unit's predefined *registers* data type.

The registers data type is a record type that mirrors the structure of the 8086 registers. It is defined as follows:

```
registers = RECORD
   CASE INTEGER OF
   0 :(AX,BX,CX,DX,BP,SI,DI,DS,ES, Flags: WORD);
   1 :(AL, AH, BL, BH, CL, CH, DL, DH: BYTE)
   END;
```

As you can see, the registers type is a variant record type that allows you to load data either 16 bits or 8 bits at a time. Generally, you do not have to worry about this; when you load a value into a field (for example, AH), Turbo Pascal picks the appropriate variant of the record type for you. If you are using a version of Turbo Pascal prior to version 4, of course, then you have no DOS unit and must declare the registers data type in your program.

To call a DOS function with the *MsDos* procedure, you must first create a registers-type variable in your program. Then, you load the number of the desired DOS function into field AH of your register variable and load any other data needed by the function into the appropriate fields. You then call the *MsDos* routine, which loads the information from the register variable into the actual processor registers and then executes DOS interrupt $21, which is the interrupt to carry out a DOS service. The service is carried out, and when appropriate, the results are loaded back into the fields of the register variable for use by your Turbo Pascal program. This process is illustrated in Listing 16.1.

Listing 16.1

```
PROGRAM Listing16_1;


   { Demonstrates the use of the Turbo Pascal MsDos procedure. In
      this program, we use the DOS "string output" function to display
     ·a text string on the screen. The function number is loaded into
      field AH (AX-high) of the "regs" variable, while the segment
```

address of the text string is loaded into field DS of regs and the offset address is loaded into field DX of regs. The MsDos routine then calls the DOS function, loading the parameters from the "regs" variable into the actual processor registers. }

```
USES CRT, DOS, MyUtils;

CONST
    message : STRING = ' Hello, Pascal programmer!$';

VAR
    regs : Registers;

BEGIN
    CLRSCR;
    regs.ah := $9;        { Number for DOS string output function }
    regs.ds := Seg(message);
    regs.dx := Ofs(message[1]);
    MsDos(regs);
    pause
END.
```

The first thing done by Listing 16.1, of course, is to name the DOS unit in a USES statement. Then, it creates a typed string constant to be displayed on the screen and declares a variable of the registers data type. After clearing the screen, it loads DOS function number 9 (which, in this case, is the same number in hex or decimal) into field AH of the *regs* variable. DOS function 9 is the function to send a text string to the default output device—in this case, to the screen.

Before the processor can display the string, of course, it must know where to find it. Therefore, the next step is to load the string's segment address into field DS (corresponding to the data segment register) and its offset address into field DX (corresponding to the general-purpose data register). Calling the *MsDos* routine with the *regs* variable copies the data from *regs* to the actual processor registers and carries out DOS function 9, displaying the string on the screen. For information about specific DOS functions, you should consult your DOS manual, or the *ABC's of DOS 5*, by Alan R. Miller (1991 SYBEX).

The Turbo Pascal Intr Procedure

Turbo Pascal's *Intr* procedure gives you more flexibility than *MsDos*, which is used simply to call DOS functions. *Intr* gives you the ability to generate a software interrupt for a variety of purposes, *including* to call a DOS function. Because of the *Intr* procedure's specialized nature, however, we will not discuss it any further in this book.

The program begins by loading the number of the DOS function (hex 30) into the AH field of the register-type variable *regs*. Then, the Turbo Pascal *Intr* procedure is called with *$21* (as the interrupt number) and the *regs* variable. This transfers the function number from the AH field of the *regs* variable to the AH register in the PC's processor, then executes interrupt *$21*. This is the pattern for calling DOS functions in any language, whether it is Turbo Pascal or assembly language: first load the function number into register AH, then call interrupt *$21*.

Using Turbo Pascal DOS Routines

Although it gives you the flexibility to call DOS functions when needed, Turbo Pascal also provides predefined DOS routines that often make it unnecessary to use *MsDos* or *Intr* to access DOS functions and software interrupts directly. These routines, which are described in your Turbo Pascal manuals, do the low-level work for you so that you can concentrate on what your program is trying to accomplish.

Listing 16.2 demonstrates the use of several of these predefined routines to display a file directory on the PC screen.

Listing 16.2

```
PROGRAM Listing16_2;


    { Demonstrates the use of Turbo Pascal's predefined
      DOS routines. In this program, we use the FindFirst
      and FindNext routines to display a file directory.
      We also use the GetFAttr procedure to prevent directory
      names from being included in our on-screen file list. }

USES CRT, DOS, MyUtils;

TYPE
```

```
      string5  = STRING[5];
      string12 = STRING[12];

VAR
   fileword   : string5;
   filespec,
   filename   : string12;
   dirsize    : LONGINT;
   numfiles   : INTEGER;

PROCEDURE init(VAR dirsize : LONGINT; VAR numfiles: INTEGER);
   BEGIN
   dirsize := 0;
   numfiles := 0
   END;

FUNCTION DrNo(filesfound : searchrec) : BOOLEAN;
   VAR
      f    : FILE;
      attr : WORD;
   BEGIN
      ASSIGN(f, filesfound.name);
      GetFAttr(f, attr);
      IF (attr AND Directory) = 0
         THEN DrNo := TRUE
         ELSE DrNo := FALSE
   END;

PROCEDURE GetFileSpec(VAR filespec : string12);
   BEGIN
      CLRSCR;
      WRITELN;
      WRITELN('   Please enter a file specification for');
      WRITELN('   file names to display. For example:');
      WRITELN('   ------------------------------------');
      WRITELN('   *.*  = display all files');
      WRITELN('   *.pas = display all pascal source code files');
      WRITELN('   *.doc = display all Microsoft Word documents');
      WRITELN;
      WRITE('   Enter a file specification: ');
      READLN(filespec);
      IF filespec = '' THEN filespec := '*.*';
   END;

PROCEDURE DisplayDir(filespec : string12);
```

```
VAR
   filesfound : searchrec;
BEGIN
   findfirst(filespec, anyfile, filesfound);
   CLRSCR;
   WRITELN;
   WRITELN(' Files found in the current directory: ');
   WRITELN(' ------------------------------------');
   WRITELN;
   WHILE DosError = 0 DO
      WITH filesfound DO
         BEGIN
         IF DrNo(filesfound)
            THEN BEGIN
               WRITELN(' ',name:12, ' .......... ', size, ' bytes');
                  dirsize := dirsize + size;
                  numfiles := numfiles + 1
                  END;
         findnext(filesfound)
         END;
   IF numfiles = 1
      THEN fileword := 'file' ELSE fileword := 'files';
   WRITELN;
   IF numfiles = 0
      THEN WRITELN(' No matching files were found.')
      ELSE BEGIN
            WRITE(' ',dirsize, ' bytes in ', numfiles);
            WRITELN(' ', fileword, '.');
            END
   END;


BEGIN
   init(dirsize, numfiles);
   getfilespec(filespec);
   DisplayDir(filespec);
   pause
END.
```

The first task performed by the program is to initialize the *dirsize* and *numfiles* variables: *dirsize* indicates the total number of bytes in the files displayed, while *numfiles* indicates the number of files displayed. Note, however, that *dirsize* will be smaller than the actual amount of disk space occupied by the files because each file, even a file with nothing in it, must take up a minimum amount of disk space.

The *GetFileSpec* routine then prompts the user to enter a specification for the file names to be listed in the directory; this follows the standard DOS rules for wildcards—for example, "*.*" indicates that all files should be displayed, "*.pas" indicates that only files whose names end in ".pas" should be displayed, and so forth.

The *DisplayDir* routine then uses Turbo Pascal's predefined *FindFirst* procedure to find the first file matching the user's specifications. Just in case the user has asked to see all of the files, it uses the predefined *GetFAttr* procedure in the *DrNo* routine to filter out names of directories; this is done to make the file list easier to read. *DisplayDir* then uses the predefined *FindNext* procedure to find the next matching file, and continues the process until all the matching files in the directory have been found and their names displayed on the screen.

FindFirst takes three parameters: the file specification that was entered by the user in *GetFileSpec*, an attribute that tells it which files to include in the search, and a variable of type *SearchRec*. *FindNext*, which is always used after *FindFirst*, takes the variable as its only parameter. In this case, we have specified *AnyFile* as the attribute, which means that all files matching the specification will be included in the search.

FindFirst and *FindNext* use a predefined data type from the DOS unit called *SearchRec*, which is set up as follows:

```
SearchRec = RECORD
            Fill : ARRAY[1..21] OF BYTE;
            Attr : BYTE;
            Time : LONGINT;
            Size : LONGINT;
            Name : STRING[12]
            END;
```

Listing 16.2 also illustrates a trick that you can use to display varying text on the screen depending on the situation. In this case, the word "file" is used in the directory display if only a single matching file is found; but the plural "files" is used if there is more than one file found.

How to Use the Exec Procedure

Exec is at once the most powerful and the easiest tool provided by the DOS unit. It allows you to suspend the current program temporarily, exit to DOS and run other programs (memory permitting), and then to return to your original program. The *Exec* procedure takes two parameters: the name and directory path of DOS's command interpreter COMMAND.COM, and the name of the external program to be executed.

There's only one hitch in using *Exec*: you must have some extra memory available to run the outside programs. Normally, a Turbo Pascal program reserves all extra DOS memory up to 640K for the heap—that is, the place where it stores dynamic variables. This means that *no* extra memory is left over for running outside programs with *Exec*. To change this, you must use the *$M* compiler directive to reduce the amount of memory reserved for the heap; if your program does not use dynamic variables at all, you can reduce this to zero. The *$M* compiler directive takes three parameters: the amount of memory reserved for the stack, the minimum amount of memory reserved for the heap, and the maximum amount of memory reserved for the heap. Thus, for a 16K stack and no memory reserved for the heap, you would write the directive at the top of your program as {**$M 16384, 0,0**}.

You should also call the *SwapVectors* routine before and after calling *Exec* to safeguard the integrity of your interrupt vector table.

Running External Programs

Listing 16.3 illustrates how to use *Exec* to run an outside program—in this case, an internal DOS command. An internal DOS command is an operating system command that is kept resident in memory, as opposed to external DOS commands such as *format*, which must be read from disk each time they are used.

Listing 16.3

```
PROGRAM Listing16_3;

    { Demonstrates the use of EXEC to suspend the current program
      and run a DOS command. }

USES CRT, DOS, MyUtils;

{ Insert compiler directive to specify the amount of memory
  reserved for the heap, thereby leaving some memory for the
  external program to run. In this case, the stack is set at
  16384 bytes (the default setting), while the minimum and
  maximum sizes of the heap are both set at 0. }
{$M 16384, 0, 0}

 BEGIN
   CLRSCR;
   swapvectors;
   EXEC('c:\command.com', '/c dir *.pas');
   swapvectors;
   pause
END.
```

The program first uses the *$M* compiler directive to limit the amount of heap memory, in this case, to zero. It then calls *SwapVectors* to protect the interrupt vector table and executes *Exec*. *Exec* itself takes the name and path of COMMAND.COM; here, it is in the root directory of the C drive. It also takes the name of the outside program to run. Here, this outside program is the internal DOS command *dir*, so—because it is an internal DOS command—it must be preceded by "/c". After running the *dir* command, the program returns the user to the calling Pascal program. *Swap-Vectors* is called again and the program terminates.

This is, of course, only a very simple example of what you can do with *Exec*. Next, let's look at an even more powerful use of *Exec*: this time to exit to a DOS shell that lets you run any program or programs (memory permitting), and then return to the calling Pascal program.

Running a DOS Shell

Running a DOS shell with *Exec* is even simpler than running a specific external program. Instead of specifying the name of the outside program when you call *Exec*, you specify an empty string ' '. This takes you directly to the DOS prompt, where, subject to memory limitations, you can execute any program you wish.

CHAPTER Seventeen

Elementary Data Structures

- 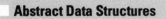 **Abstract Data Structures**

- **Array-Based Data Structures**

- **Linked Stacks and Queues**

In earlier chapters, we have looked at some simple data structures, such as records, static lists, and dynamic lists with pointers. In this chapter, we will look at some more advanced data structures that put even more power at your fingertips. In the next chapter, we will look at some methods ("algorithms") for manipulating information in these and other data structures.

Once we go beyond simple data structures that are predefined in Pascal, such as arrays, the distinction between data structures and algorithms becomes somewhat artificial. A data structure is defined by (1) a specific way of arranging data, and (2) a set of operations performed on the data that make it behave in a certain way. Without the proper set of algorithms, the data structure is incomplete—just as an automobile without a person who knows how to drive it is only an inert pile of metal and glass.

Abstract Data Structures

The data structures we will look at in this chapter are stacks and queues, which are often used in real-life programming situations. Both are lists that can hold any type of data item except a file type.

Abstract Stacks

A *stack* is a list in which all insertions and deletions are made at one end of the list, commonly called the "top" of the list. This is very much like a stack of trays in a cafeteria; the last tray put on top of the stack is the first one removed. For this reason, stacks are also referred to as *last-in-first-out* (or LIFO) lists. Adding an item to a stack is called *pushing* it onto the stack, while deleting an item from a stack is called *popping* it off the stack.

Thus, consider the example shown in Figure 17.1. The sequence of events is as follows:

1. At Step One, the stack is empty. We push the first item, A, onto the empty stack.

2. At Step Two, we push B and C onto the stack. B is added first, going on top of A, and C is added next, going on top of B.

FIGURE 17.1:

Adding and deleting items from a stack

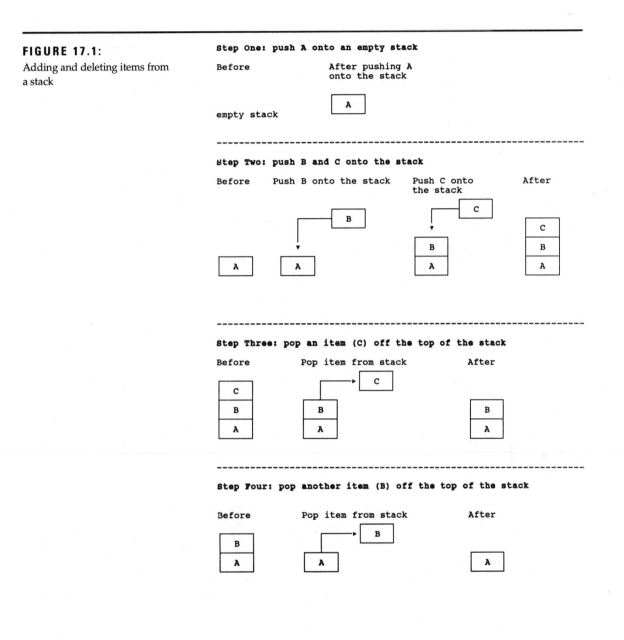

Step One: push A onto an empty stack

Before   After pushing A onto the stack

empty stack

Step Two: push B and C onto the stack

Before   Push B onto the stack   Push C onto the stack   After

Step Three: pop an item (C) off the top of the stack

Before   Pop item from stack   After

Step Four: pop another item (B) off the top of the stack

Before   Pop item from stack   After

FIGURE 17.1:
Adding and deleting items from a stack (continued)

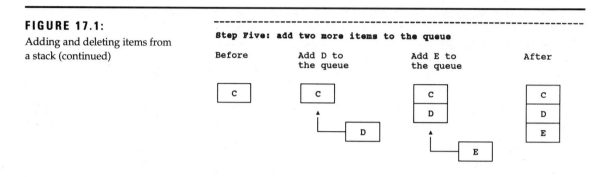

3. At Step Three, we pop an item off the top of the stack. Because C was the last item added to the stack, it is on the top, and hence it is the item first in line to be popped (last in first out).

4. At Step Four, we pop another item from the top of the stack. Because B was added to the stack before C, it is now at the top of the stack and gets popped.

5. At Step Five, only item A is left in the stack. We now push two new items, D and E, onto the top of the stack in the same way that, before, we added B and C. If any more items are popped from the stack, they will be popped in the order opposite to that in which they were added—that is, they will be popped in the order E, D, A.

Notice that at this stage, we are describing stacks as an abstract data type. Not a single word has been said about arrays, pointers, or any other detail of how stacks can be implemented in Pascal. The description we have given could be implemented in any language, using a variety of structured data types.

The most familiar application of stacks is one to which we referred in Chapter 11: *the stack* (which is an area in your PC's memory that Turbo Pascal reserves for local variables and return addresses of subroutines) is also *a* stack, which pops off those variables and addresses in last-in-first-out order. Stacks also can be used for a variety of arithmetic operations.

Abstract Queries

Unlike a stack, which is a last-in-first-out list, a *queue* is a first-in-first-out list. In a queue, all insertions are made at the back of the list and all deletions are made at the front. This works the same way as a line at an airline ticket counter. When new passengers arrive, they join the line at the end. People who arrived earlier, however, leave the line at the front as they get their tickets. Perhaps because queues are more familiar, there are no special terms to describe adding items to queues and deleting items from queues. The operation of a queue is shown in Figure 17.2. The sequence

FIGURE 17.2:

Adding and deleting from a queue

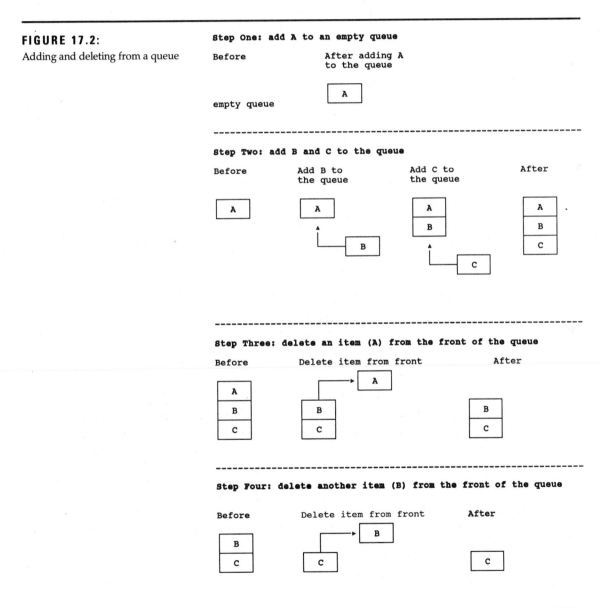

431

FIGURE 17.2:

Adding and deleting from a queue (continued)

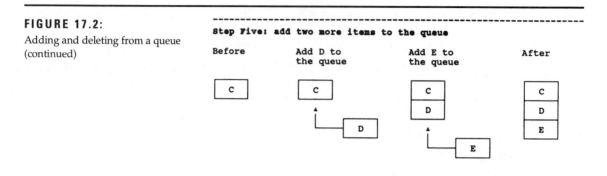

of events is as follows:

1. At Step One, the queue is empty. We add a single item, A, to the queue.

2. At Step Two, we add items B and C to the queue. However, because a queue is a first-in-first-out list, we picture the situation differently. Instead of being added to the "top," as with a stack, the new items are added to the end of the queue, just like new passengers lining up at an airline ticket counter.

3. At Step Three, we delete an item from the queue. Because A was the first item added to the queue, it is also the first item to be deleted.

4. At Step Four, we delete another item from the queue. Because B was the next item added after A, it is the next item to be deleted from the queue. Only item C, the last item added, is left in the queue—still "waiting in line."

5. At Step Five, we add two more items (D and E) to the back of the queue, one after the other. If the items currently in the queue were to be deleted, they would be deleted in the order C, D, E.

As was the case with stacks, we have said nothing about the specific way queues are to be implemented. We could use either static or dynamic data structures, depending on the situation and the programming language. In what follows, we will see how to implement stacks and queues using both static and dynamic data structures.

Because queues are so familiar in everyday life, they have many applications. A typical application would be to simulate the operation of a stoplight at a traffic intersection.

Static Data Structures

Static stacks and queues are implemented in Pascal by using arrays. Because the size of arrays is fixed at compile time, it is necessary to make the arrays as large as the stacks and queues are ever going to be, and to include special routines to check for full stacks and queues.

Array-Based Stacks

Let's look at how to use arrays to implement a stack. The first thing to decide is precisely what data structure we will use to implement our stack. We know in advance that we are going to use an array, but we also need a way to keep track of the top of the stack so that we know where to add the next item. Consider Figure 17.3, which shows a stack implemented with a five-slot array. We know that we should add the first item in slot 1, but after that, the program must have some kind of counter so that it can determine which slot is next.

FIGURE 17.3:
A stack implemented in an array

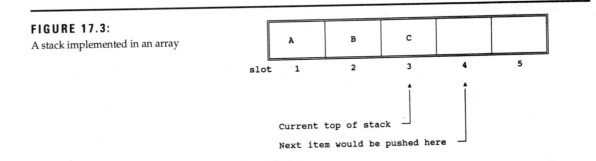

Suppose that we have three items A, B, and C in the stack. A counter variable attached to the stack would inform the program that the current top of the stack is at slot 3, meaning that a pop would delete an item from slot 3 and a push would add a new item to slot number 4. The same counter variable could also be used to indicate when the stack was full or empty.

As we discussed in Chapter 8, the record data type is the usual way to bring items of different data types together in the same data structure. We can thus define our stack data structure as follows:

```
CONST Max = 5;

TYPE
   Stack = RECORD
             stackitem : ARRAY[1..Max] OF item;
             stacktop  : 1..Max
             END;
```

Note that, just as we did in Chapter 8, we have included a counter field, *stacktop*, to keep track of a certain position in the array—in this case, the top of the stack. Given this stack data structure, we can now move on to identify the subroutines we will need to manipulate our stack. They are:

- *Init*, a procedure to initialize the stack

- *Push*, a procedure to push items onto the top of the stack

- *Pop*, a procedure to pop items from the top of the stack

- *FullStack*, a function to indicate when the stack (that is, the array in which the stack is implemented) is full

- *EmptyStack*, a function to indicate when the stack (that is, the array in which the stack is implemented) is empty

FullStack and *EmptyStack* are not strictly necessary, because we can test for a full or empty stack merely by looking at the stack record's counter field. In fact, all of the routines we will create are quite simple, and could be written out wherever they are needed in the program. However, this spotlights two important benefits of structured programming.

First, suppose that instead of creating these procedures and functions, we simply inserted the relevant code wherever it was needed. If we later decided to make any change in our program—such as changing the stack from a static to a dynamic list—we would virtually have to rewrite the whole program. Every place where an item was pushed onto the stack or popped from the stack would have to be recoded. By packaging this code in subroutines, however, we need to change only the subroutines themselves. The changes will take effect automatically wherever the subroutines are called in the program.

Second, it's easier to see what is happening in the program when we use simple names such as push, pop, empty, and full for blocks of code. Instead of having to look at the code and figure out what it does each time, we can see at a glance that it does a "pop" or it checks to see if the stack is full. Listing 17.1 shows how to set up a stack using these ideas.

Listing 17.1

```
PROGRAM Listing17_1;

    { Demonstrates the use of a stack. In this case, the
    program prompts the user to enter enough characters
    to fill up the stack, then pops them off the stack
    in reverse order. }

USES CRT, MyUtils;

CONST
    Max = 5;
    space = ' ';
TYPE
    stack = record
            stackitem : ARRAY[1..Max] of CHAR;
            stacktop  : 0..Max
            END;
VAR
    list    : stack;
    item    : CHAR;

PROCEDURE init(VAR list : stack);
    VAR
        counter : INTEGER;
    BEGIN
        CLRSCR;
        FOR counter := 1 TO max DO
            list.stackitem[counter] := space;
        list.stacktop := 0
    END;

FUNCTION full(list : stack) : BOOLEAN;
    BEGIN
        IF list.stacktop = max
            THEN full := TRUE
            ELSE full := FALSE
```

```
    END;

FUNCTION empty(list : stack) : BOOLEAN;
    BEGIN
    Empty := (list.stacktop = 0)
    END;

PROCEDURE push(item : CHAR; VAR list : stack);
    BEGIN
        WITH list DO
        BEGIN
            IF full(list) { test FOR full stack }
            THEN BEGIN
                WRITELN(' Sorry, full stack!');
                exit
                END;
            stacktop := stacktop + 1;
            stackitem[stacktop] := item
        END
    END;


PROCEDURE pop(VAR item : CHAR; VAR list : stack);
    BEGIN
        WITH list DO
            BEGIN
                IF empty(list)
                THEN BEGIN
                    WRITELN(' Sorry, stack is empty!');
                    exit
                    END;
            item := stackitem[stacktop];
            stackitem[stacktop] := space;
            stacktop := stacktop - 1
        END
    END;


PROCEDURE PushItemsOnStack(VAR list : stack);
    VAR
        newitem : CHAR;
        counter : INTEGER;
    BEGIN
        FOR counter := 1 TO max DO
            BEGIN
            WRITE(' Enter a character to push onto the stack: ');
            readln(newitem);
```

```
            push(newitem, list);
            WRITELN
            END
    END;

PROCEDURE PopItemsOffStack(VAR list : stack);
    VAR
        counter : INTEGER;
    BEGIN
        CLRSCR;
        WRITELN(' The stack items are popped off in reverse order');
        WRITELN(' because a stack is a last-in-first-out list.');
        WRITELN;
        WRITE(' Items popped from the stack: ');
        FOR counter := 1 TO max DO
            BEGIN
            delay(700);
            pop(item, list);
            WRITE(item, ' ')
            END
        END;

BEGIN
    init(list);
    PushItemsOnStack(list);
    PopItemsOffStack(list);
    pause
END.
```

Inside Listing 17.1

The program begins by calling *Init*, which fills up the stack with space characters and sets the *stacktop* field to zero. It then calls the *PushItemsOnStack* routine, which prompts the user to enter characters for the stack and calls the *Push* routine to push each one onto the top of the stack.

At this point, you might be wondering why the code for *Push* wasn't simply included in the *PushItemsOnStack* routine—as well as why the code for *Pop* wasn't included in the *PopItemsOffStack* routine. This is an example of separating different tasks into different subroutines. The main purpose of the *PushItemsOnStack* routine is to get input from the user, while the main purpose of the *PopItemsOffStack* routine is to display output for the user. Thus, these routines should be insulated from the details of how the push and pop operations actually take place. We can change our stack data structure, along with the *Push* and *Pop* routines, without having to make any changes in the *PushItemsOnStack* and *PopItemsOffStack* routines.

Because the stack is a record type, the *Push* routine uses the WITH notation to simplify references to the stack's fields. The first thing it does is to determine if the stack is full by calling the *Full* function. If the *stacktop* field is equal to the maximum number of entries in the stack, then the *Full* function returns a value of true; otherwise, it returns a value of false.

Notice that although the *Full* and *Empty* functions perform the same basic operations, *Full* is coded with an IF statement, while *Empty* assigns the Boolean value of *(list.stacktop = 0)* to itself. This illustrates the equivalence of these two methods.

If the stack is not full, then the *Push* routine's next move is to add 1 to the *stacktop* field, thereby moving up one slot in the array. In this slot, it loads the value to be pushed onto the stack.

The *PopItemsOffStack* procedure calls *Pop* to get values from the stack. The *Pop* routine does essentially the same things as the *Push* routine, merely in reverse. It first checks to see if the stack is empty, because, obviously, it cannot pop anything from the stack if there's nothing to be popped. If the stack is not empty, then it assigns the value in the current top of the stack to the item parameter and then subtracts one from the *stacktop* field, moving the top of the stack down one slot in the array.

Array-Based Queries

Queues are a bit more complicated than stacks. In stacks, we need only keep track of one end of the list: the top. It is at this end that all insertions and deletions are made in the list. With queues, on the other hand, insertions are made at the rear of the list and deletions are made at the front. This means that, at minimum, our queue-handling routines must keep track of two ends of the list instead of just one.

Let's consider a "first draft" of a data structure for holding a queue. We know that we must keep track of both ends of the list, so the natural move is simply to upgrade our stack data type with an additional field:

```
CONST Max = 5;
TYPE
   queue = RECORD
```

```
queueitem : ARRAY[1..Max] of CHAR;
front,
rear      : 0..Max
END;
```

We would then use this data type for our queue, exactly as we used the stack type. The front would start out in slot 1 of the array, with the rear set to 0 (which isn't a slot in the array) to distinguish it from the front in the starting, empty position. Operations with this queue data structure are shown in Figure 17.4, which assumes a five-slot queue.

After adding four items to the queue, the front field of the queue record contains the value 1, indicating which array slot contains the next value that would be deleted from the queue. The rear field contains the value 4, indicating the current

FIGURE 17.4:

First draft of a queue implemented in an array

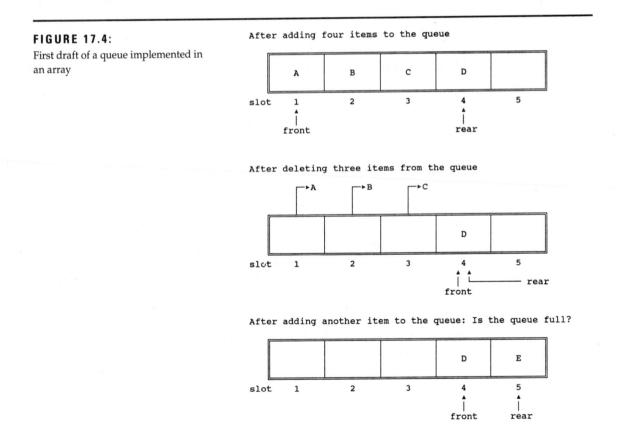

rear end of the queue. The next insertion would be made at slot number 5, filling the queue. Each time we make an insertion, we simply add 1 to the value of the rear field, until we arrive at the maximum size of the queue (that is, the number of slots in the array).

So far, so good. The fact that the queue can be filled up was expected, because we are using arrays. However, the next step in Figure 17.4 begins to raise a problem. We deleted three items from the queue, in first-in-first-out order, just as we should. This leaves only one item in the queue at slot number 4, which is now both the front and the rear of the queue. Next, however, we add another item to the queue, and it goes into slot number 5. The queue is not full—there are three open slots earlier in the array—but it seems as if we have no place to go.

Obviously, something has to be done. We could simply make the array very large, allowing the queue to creep down toward the end of the array as insertions and deletions were made during a program run. This solution, however, would be terribly wasteful in terms of array space. A better approach would be somehow to allow the queue to "double back" to the beginning when it reaches the end of the array. That solution is shown in Figure 17.5.

This approach is conventionally referred to as using a "circular" array, even though there is really no such thing as a circular array. What we are actually doing is using the *mod* operator so that, when the rear of the queue arrives at the last slot in the array, it doubles back to the first slot.

We discussed the mod operator in Chapter 5, but this is a good place for a recap. Mod ("modulus") returns a value equal to the remainder left by integer division. For example, 3 goes into 10 three times, with a remainder of 1, so 10 mod 3 = 1. Likewise, 2 goes into 10 five times, with no remainder, so 10 mod 2 = 0.

In the case of our array-based queue, we will set up the routine to add a new item to the queue so that it does not simply add 1 to the rear, but instead, adds 1 to (rear mod max), where max is the highest slot in the array. Thus, here is where the next item would be placed in several situations, with max = 5:

- If rear = 0 (the situation at the start of the program), then (rear mod max) + 1 = (0 mod 5) + 1 = 1.

- If rear = 3, then (rear mod max) + 1 = (3 mod 5) + 1 = 4.

- If rear = 5, then (rear mod max) + 1 = (5 mod 5) + 1 = 1.

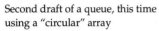

FIGURE 17.5:

Second draft of a queue, this time using a "circular" array

After adding four items to the queue

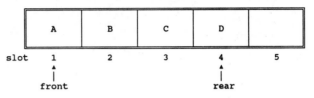

After deleting three items from the queue

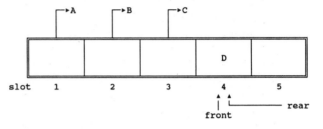

After adding another item to the queue: Is the queue full?

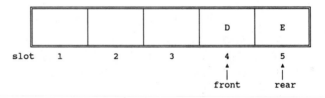

After adding another item to the queue. Instead of simply adding 1 to the (slot) number of the rear of the queue, the AddToQueue routine uses the mod operator to make the next rear-slot number equal to (rear mod max) + 1. In this case, rear = 5, so (rear mod max) = 0 and (rear mod max) + 1 = 1.

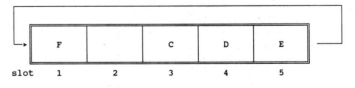

There's only one other problem that needs to be solved—a problem we conveniently glossed over in Figure 17.5. What happens if the queue *really is* full: that is, if rear = 5 so that (rear mod max) + 1 = 1, but slot 1 is still occupied by another item? We need some way to detect when the array really is full so that we will not accidentally "add" a new value to a full queue and thereby erase a previously entered value.

To solve this problem, we simply add a counter field to the record that defines the queue data structure. When this counter field contains a value equal to max, then we know that the queue is full. This data structure is shown in Listing 17.2, which also contains the framework for a program to manipulate a queue.

Listing 17.2

```
PROGRAM Listing17_2;

    { Framework for a program to create and manipulate an
      array-based queue. }

USES CRT, MyUtils;

CONST
   Max = 5;
TYPE
   queue = RECORD
             queueitem : ARRAY[1..Max] of CHAR;
             Qcount,
             front,
             rear      : 0..Max
             END;
VAR
   list    : queue;
   item    : CHAR;


PROCEDURE Init(VAR list : queue);
   BEGIN
   END;

FUNCTION Empty(VAR list : queue) : BOOLEAN;
   BEGIN
   END;

FUNCTION Full(VAR list : queue) : BOOLEAN;
```

```
        BEGIN
        END;

    PROCEDURE AddToQueue(item : CHAR; VAR list : queue);
        BEGIN
        END;

    PROCEDURE DeleteFromQueue(VAR item : CHAR; VAR list : queue);
        BEGIN
        END;

    { ------------------------------------------------------------ }
    {                    MAIN BODY OF PROGRAM                      }
    { ------------------------------------------------------------ }
    BEGIN
    END.
```

Just as with our stack program in Listing 17.1, we need routines to initialize the queue, to add and delete items, and to determine if the queue is empty or full. The details of these routines are shown in Listing 17.3.

Listing 17.3

```
PROGRAM Listing17_3;

    { Demonstrates a program to create and manipulate an
    array-based queue. }

USES CRT, MyUtils;

CONST
    Max = 5;
TYPE
    queue = RECORD
            queueitem : ARRAY[1..Max] of CHAR;
            Qcount,
            front,
            rear      : 0..Max
            END;
VAR
    list    : queue;
    item    : CHAR;

PROCEDURE Init(VAR list : queue);
```

```
      BEGIN
         WITH list DO
            BEGIN
            Qcount := 0;
            front := 1;
            rear := 0
            END
      END;

FUNCTION Empty(VAR list : queue) : BOOLEAN;
   BEGIN
      Empty := (list.Qcount = 0)
   END;

FUNCTION Full(VAR list : queue) : BOOLEAN;
   BEGIN
      Full := (list.Qcount = max)
   END;

PROCEDURE AddToQueue(item : CHAR; VAR list : queue);
   BEGIN
      WITH list DO
         IF full(list)
            THEN WRITELN(' Sorry, queue is full.')
            ELSE BEGIN
                 Qcount := Qcount + 1;
                 rear := (rear mod max) + 1;
                 Queueitem[rear] := item;
                 END
   END; { of AddToQueue routine }

PROCEDURE DeleteFromQueue(VAR item : CHAR; VAR list : queue);
   BEGIN
      WITH list DO
         IF empty(list)
            THEN WRITELN(' Sorry, queue is empty.')
            ELSE BEGIN
                 Qcount := Qcount - 1;
                 item := Queueitem[front];
                 front := (front mod max) + 1
                 END
   END;

PROCEDURE AddItems(VAR list : queue);
   VAR
```

```
   counter : CHAR;
   Qpos    : INTEGER;
BEGIN
   Qpos := list.rear;
   WRITELN(' Now adding items to the queue ...');
                 WRITELN(' ------------------------------');
   FOR counter :=  'a' TO 'e' DO
      BEGIN
      addtoqueue(counter, list);
      Qpos := (Qpos mod max) + 1;
      WRITELN(' Item ', counter, ' added at position ', Qpos, '.');
      delay(1000)
      END;
   WRITELN; WRITELN
END;


PROCEDURE DeleteItems(VAR list : queue);
   VAR
      counter : CHAR;
      Qpos    : INTEGER;
   BEGIN
      Qpos := 0;
      WRITELN(' Now deleting items from the queue ...');
      WRITELN(' ------------------------------------');
      FOR counter := 'a' TO 'e' DO
         BEGIN
         deletefromqueue(item, list);
         Qpos := (Qpos mod max) + 1;
         WRITELN(' Item ', counter, ' deleted from position ', Qpos, '.');
         delay(1000)
         END
   END;


{ ---------------------------------------------------------------- }
{                    MAIN BODY OF PROGRAM                          }
{ ---------------------------------------------------------------- }
BEGIN
   CLRSCR;
   Init(list);
   AddItems(list);
   DeleteItems(list);
   pause
END.
```

445

Inside Listing 17.3

The first task performed by Listing 17.3 is to initialize the queue. This means setting the *Qcount* and *rear* fields to 0 and setting the front field to 1.

The *AddItems* routine then fills up the queue by calling *AddToQueue* five times, each time adding a letter to the queue. The *AddToQueue* routine first checks to make sure that the queue is not full. If not, then it increases the *Qcount* by 1 each time an addition is made; the front of the queue remains the same unless a deletion is made, so *AddToQueue* needs to change only the *rear* field of the queue record; in doing so, it uses the *mod* scheme that was described above.

After the *AddItems* routine has filled up the queue, the *DeleteItems* routine removes items from the queue in first-in-first-out order, as it should. It calls the *DeleteFrom-Queue* routine. *DeleteFromQueue* first checks to make sure that the queue is not empty. If it is not, then *DeleteFromQueue* subtracts 1 from the *Qcount* field, copies the value from the front slot into a parameter, and increases the value in the *front* field by the mod approach, just as it did with the *rear* field. The letters are displayed on the computer screen as they are deleted from the queue.

Dynamic Data Structures

As we have seen, static data structures can be used to create stacks and queues. However, because of the limitations of static variables, this approach tends to waste memory. It also imposes special requirements on the programmer to guard against *full list* conditions, and the array-based implementation of queues is slightly more complicated than we would probably like it to be.

These problems disappear when stacks and queues are implemented in dynamic linked lists. New nodes can be created as they are needed, and a counter field is no longer required. Linked data structures, of course, present their own problems, but are often a better choice than arrays for stacks and queues.

Because operations with pointers are sometimes a little complex, a brief recap is in order here. A pointer is a variable that contains the memory address of another variable and can be used to refer to that variable. If *MyPtr* is a pointer to a record variable with a field *item* that contains a character, then:

- *MyPtr* contains the memory address of a record variable.

- *MyPtr*^ is the record variable itself.

- *MyPtr*^*.item* is the item field of the record variable; this item field is itself a character variable.

- If the record variable is in a linked list, then it has at least a *next* field containing a pointer to the next record. In that case, *MyPtr*^*.next* is itself a pointer, and points either to the next record or to NIL, which indicates that there is no next record.

If you need further review on pointer operations, you should refer back to Chapter 11.

Linked Stacks

Before we discuss how to code linked stacks, it would be a good idea to have a clear picture of what we will be doing. In Figure 17.6, we can look at what actually happens in each step of pushing items onto a linked stack and popping them off.

Figure 17.6 assumes that we will create a stack of items (as yet unspecified) in a singly linked list. As was the case when we looked at stacks in arrays, all insertions and deletions are made at the head of the list, called the *top*. A pointer identifies the top of the stack.

In an empty stack, the *stacktop* pointer points to NIL. When we add a new item to the stack, we use the *New* procedure (see Chapter 11 if you're hazy on this) with a temporary pointer to set aside the appropriate amount of memory on the heap and point the temporary pointer at that memory location. We copy the values we want into the new item and point the *stacktop* pointer at it, setting the next field of the new item to NIL.

It's when we add another item to the stack that things get really interesting. We first call *New* again to create a dynamic variable of the appropriate type. Then we load values into the variable and set its next pointer to point to the current top of the stack. Finally, we repoint the *stacktop* pointer at the new item, which becomes the new top of the stack.

FIGURE 17.6:

Operations with a linked stack

Empty stack

Push item onto empty stack: set stacktop pointer to point to new stack node created with New; set next pointer of new node to NIL.

Push second item onto the stack: set next pointer of newly-created stack node to current top of stack; then set stacktop pointer to point to the new node, which now occupies the top of the stack

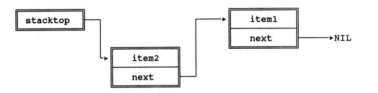

Pop an item from the stack: use a temporary pointer variable to point to the old top of the stack, then point the stacktop pointer at old top item's "next" item, which is the new top of the stack.

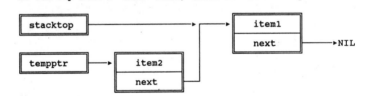

To pop an item from the stack, we reverse this process. We use a temporary pointer to keep track of the item currently on top of the stack, then we repoint the *stacktop* pointer at the next item after the current top item. Note that it is important to do this in the correct order. If we first repointed the *stacktop* pointer, we would then have lost track of the item that had been at the top of the stack. By assigning its location to a temporary pointer as our first step, however, we keep track of the item at the original top of the stack. Finally, we copy the values out of this item and use *Dispose* with the temporary pointer to free up the heap space occupied by the item.

Listing 17.4 demonstrates the Pascal code version of these stack operations.

Listing 17.4

```pascal
PROGRAM Listing17_4;

    { Demonstrates how to set up a linked stack by using pointers.
      Uses the MyUtils unit created in Chapter 10. }

USES CRT, MyUtils;

CONST
    space = ' ';

TYPE
    nodeptr   = ^stackitem;
    stackitem = RECORD
                   item  : CHAR;
                   next  : nodeptr
                   END;
VAR
    item     : CHAR;
    stacktop : nodeptr;

PROCEDURE Init(VAR stacktop : nodeptr);
    BEGIN
       stacktop := NIL
    END;

FUNCTION Empty(stacktop : nodeptr) : BOOLEAN;
    BEGIN
       Empty := (stacktop = NIL)
    END;

PROCEDURE Push(item : CHAR; VAR stacktop : nodeptr);
    VAR
       TempNode : nodeptr;
    BEGIN
       New(TempNode);
       TempNode^.item := item;
       TempNode^.next := stacktop;
       stacktop := TempNode
    END;

PROCEDURE Pop(VAR item : CHAR; VAR stacktop : nodeptr);
```

```
VAR
    TempNode : nodeptr;
BEGIN
    IF Empty(stacktop)
        THEN BEGIN
            WRITELN(' Sorry, stack is empty.');
            exit
            END
        ELSE BEGIN
            item := stacktop^.item;
            TempNode := stacktop;
            stacktop := stacktop^.next;
            Dispose(Tempnode)
            TempNode := NIL
            END
END;

PROCEDURE PromptUserForItems(VAR stacktop : nodeptr);
    VAR
        item,
        continue : CHAR;
    BEGIN
        continue := 'Y';
        CLRSCR;
        WRITELN(' Pushing items onto the stack ...');
        WRITELN(' -------------------------------');
        REPEAT
            WRITELN;
            WRITE(' Enter a letter to push onto the stack: ');
            READLN(item);
            push(item, stacktop);
            WRITELN;
            WRITE(' Do another (Y/N)? ');
            READLN(continue);
        UNTIL UPCASE(continue) <> 'Y'
    END;

PROCEDURE PopItemsOffStack(VAR stacktop : nodeptr);
    VAR
        item : CHAR;
    BEGIN
        CLRSCR;
        WRITELN;
        WRITELN(' Popping items off the stack ...');
        WRITELN(' -------------------------------');
```

```
      WHILE stacktop <> NIL DO
         BEGIN
         pop(item, stacktop);
         WRITE(space, item);
         delay(1000)
         END;
      WRITELN
   END;




{ ---------------------------------------------------------------- }
{                       MAIN BODY OF PROGRAM                        }
{ ---------------------------------------------------------------- }
BEGIN
   CLRSCR;
   init(stacktop);
   PromptUserForItems(stacktop);
   PopItemsOffStack(stacktop);
   pause
END.
```

Inside Listing 17.4

Listing 17.4 first defines a data type for items in the stack, along with a pointer type for those items. Each item will contain a character as its *content* and a pointer to the next item in the list. Then, in the VAR section, we declare a global variable, *item*, for getting characters in and out of the stack, as well as a static pointer variable, *stacktop*, to point to the item at the top of the stack.

The *Init* routine's only purpose is to set the *stacktop* pointer to NIL. However, this is very important because the program uses the *stacktop* pointer's NIL value to determine if the stack is empty.

The *PromptUserForItem* routine is called next, and asks the user to enter characters to be pushed onto the top of the stack. It calls the *Push* routine, which uses Pascal's *New* procedure to create a dynamic stack node on the heap. Into this node, it then loads the character entered by the user. It points the new node's next pointer to the current top of the stack, then repoints the *stacktop* pointer toward the new node, so that the new node is now at the top of the stack. Back in the *PromptUserForItem* routine, we then cycle through a REPEAT loop until the user decides that enough items have been pushed onto the stack.

The *PopItemsOffStack* routine sets up a WHILE loop to pop items off of the stack until the end of the stack is reached. Note that we used a WHILE loop instead of a REPEAT loop to cover the possibility of there being *no* items in the stack, in which case nothing could be popped off. On each pass through the loop, the *Pop* routine is called.

The *Pop* routine creates a temporary (local) pointer to point to the top of the stack. It then checks to see if the stack is empty; if so, it exits back to the calling routine. If the stack is not empty, then it loads the value from the top node into the item parameter (which is standing in for the global variable *item*) and points the temporary pointer at the top node. It takes the value of the top node's next field and loads it into the *stacktop* pointer, thereby pointing the *stacktop* pointer at the next node and making it the new top of the stack. Finally, it calls *Dispose* to free up the heap memory occupied by the popped stack node and sets the temporary pointer to NIL.

The last step, which sets the temporary pointer to NIL, is probably not necessary because the pointer will cease to exist as soon as the *Pop* routine terminates. However, any time you are in doubt, play it safe and set unassigned pointers to NIL.

As each letter is popped off the stack, the *PopItemsOffStack* routine displays it on the screen. As you will see when you run the program, letters are popped off the stack in reverse order, because a stack—regardless of its implementation details—is a last-in-first-out list.

Linked Queues

Just as we did with linked stacks, we will begin our discussion of linked queues by drawing a picture so that we can have a code-free idea of what we are doing. Figure 17.7 shows the operations we will be doing with linked queues.

Linked queues are slightly more complicated than linked stacks. Because insertions are made at one end (the rear) and deletions are made at the other end (the front), we need two pointers to keep track of the front and rear nodes of the queue. There are other ways to solve this problem—for example, with a circularly linked queue.

When the queue is empty, both the front and rear pointers are set to NIL. To add an item to the empty queue, we use the Pascal *New* procedure to create a new node variable on the heap. We load the appropriate values into the node variable's fields and set its next pointer to NIL. We then point both the front and rear pointers at the new node, which is the only node in the queue.

FIGURE 17.7:

Operations with a linked queue

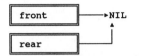

Empty queue

Add item to queue: create new dynamic node by using New, then point both the front and rear pointers at the new node.

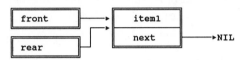

Add a second item to the queue: create new dynamic node by using New, then point the next pointer of the current rear node at the new node; finally, point the rear pointer at the new node, whose next pointer should be set to NIL.

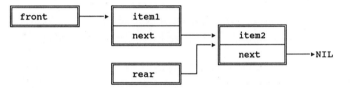

Delete an item from the queue: use a temporary pointer variable to point to the old front node. Then point the front pointer at the "next" node after the old front of the queue. Copy the value(s) out of the old front node and call Dispose to free up the heap memory it occupied.

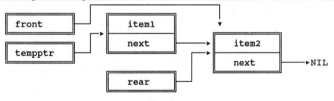

To add items to a *non*empty queue, we create a node variable on the heap. After loading its fields with the desired values, we set the next field of the current rear node to point to the new node, then repoint the rear pointer to point to the new node. As in other cases, the order of these operations is very important: if we had changed the rear pointer first, then we would have had no simple way to find the old rear node and could not have linked the new node into the list. Finally, we set the next field of the new rear node to NIL. Notice that because insertions are made at the rear, no changes had to be made in the front pointer.

To delete an item, we first use a temporary pointer to keep track of the old front node of the queue. Then we load the value from the next field of the old front node into the front pointer, thereby repointing it at the node after the old front node. We copy the values out of the old front node and then call *Dispose* to free up the heap memory that it occupied. Notice that because deletions are made at the front, no changes had to be made in the rear pointer.

Listing 17.5 demonstrates the Pascal code version of these queue operations.

Listing 17.5

```pascal
PROGRAM Listing17_5;

    { Demonstrates a linked-list implementation of a queue.
      Uses the MyUtils unit that was created in Chapter 10. }

USES CRT, MyUtils;

CONST
    space = ' ';

TYPE
    nodeptr = ^node;
    node    = RECORD
                item  : CHAR;
                next  : nodeptr
                END;

VAR
    item   : CHAR;
    front,
    rear   : nodeptr;

PROCEDURE Beep;
    { Causes the PC's speaker to emit a short beep. Intended
      as a preview of Chapter 19. }
    BEGIN
        sound(100);
        delay(150);
```

```
          nosound
       END;

PROCEDURE Init(VAR front, rear : nodeptr);
       BEGIN
       front := NIL;
       rear := NIL
       end;

PROCEDURE AddNode(item : CHAR; VAR front, rear : nodeptr);
       VAR
          TempNode : nodeptr;
       BEGIN
          New(TempNode);
          TempNode^.item := item;
          TempNode^.next := NIL;
          IF front = NIL
             THEN BEGIN
                    front := TempNode;
                    rear := TempNode
                    END
             ELSE BEGIN
                    rear^.next := TempNode;
                    rear := TempNode
                    END
       END;

PROCEDURE DeleteNode(VAR item : CHAR; VAR front, rear : nodeptr);
       VAR
          TempNode : nodeptr;
       BEGIN
          TempNode := NIL;
          IF front = NIL
             THEN BEGIN
                    WRITE(' Sorry, queue is empty.');
                    exit
                    END
             ELSE BEGIN
                    TempNode := front;
                    item := front^.item;
                    front := front^.next;
                    IF front = NIL THEN rear := NIL;
                    Dispose(TempNode);
```

```
                    TempNode := NIL;
                    END
        END;

PROCEDURE PromptUserForItems(VAR front, rear : nodeptr);
    VAR
        item,
        continue : CHAR;
    BEGIN
        continue := 'Y';
        CLRSCR;
        WRITELN(' Now adding items to the queue ...');
        WRITELN(' --------------------------------');
        REPEAT
           WRITE(' Enter a letter to add to the queue: ');
           READLN(item);
           WRITELN;
           WRITELN(' Adding ', item, ' to the queue. ');
           delay(500);
           AddNode(item, front, rear);
           WRITE(' Add another item (Y/N)? ');
           READLN(continue);
           WRITELN;
        UNTIL UPCASE(continue) <> 'Y';
        WRITELN
    END;

PROCEDURE DisplayItemsOnScreen(VAR item : CHAR;
                                  VAR front, rear : nodeptr);
    BEGIN
        CLRSCR;
        WRITELN(' Now deleting items from the queue ...');
        WRITELN(' -------------------------------------');
        WHILE front <> NIL DO
           BEGIN
           deletenode(item, front, rear);
           WRITE(space, item);
           beep;
           delay(1000)
           END;
```

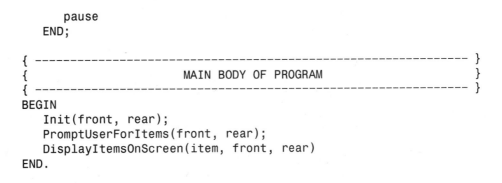

```
      pause
   END;

{ ------------------------------------------------------------ }
{                    MAIN BODY OF PROGRAM                       }
{ ------------------------------------------------------------ }
BEGIN
   Init(front, rear);
   PromptUserForItems(front, rear);
   DisplayItemsOnScreen(item, front, rear)
END.
```

Inside Listing 17.5

Listing 17.5 begins by initializing the queue. In this case, all that is required is to set the front and rear pointers to NIL. The *PromptUserForItems* routine is then called, setting up a REPEAT loop to prompt the user for one or more values to add to the queue.

Once the user has entered a letter to be added to the queue, the *AddNode* procedure is called. *AddNode* calls *New* to create a new node variable on the heap, loading the letter into the new node's item field and setting the new node's next field to NIL because this node will be the new rear of the queue. The routine then checks to see if the queue is empty; if so, it points both the front and rear pointers at the new node. If the queue is not empty, then the routine links the new node to the end of the list by pointing the current rear node's next field at it. It then repoints the rear pointer at the new node.

Back in the *PromptUserForItems* routine, the user is asked if he or she wishes to enter another item in the queue. Depending on the answer, the REPEAT loop either will run again or terminate.

Once the queue is loaded up, we are ready to delete its nodes one at a time and view the result. The *DisplayItemsOnScreen* routine sets up a WHILE loop (in case the queue is empty). The loop calls the *DeleteNode* procedure.

DeleteNode uses a temporary pointer to keep track of the current front node. It then loads the letter from the front node into the item parameter and loads the value from the current front node's next field into the front pointer, thereby repointing it at the next node in the queue. If the previous front node was the only node in the list, and the list is now empty, then the front pointer will now be NIL, and an IF statement sets the rear pointer to NIL as well. The routine then calls *Dispose* to free up the heap memory occupied by the old front node and, as an added safety measure, resets the temporary pointer to NIL.

Back in the *DisplayItemsOnScreen* procedure, the value from the deleted node is displayed on the screen. At the same time, a *Beep* procedure is called to sound a short tone each time a letter is displayed on-screen; this is a "preview of coming attractions" for Chapter 19. *Beep* uses the Turbo Pascal *Sound* procedure, which takes the desired sound frequency as a parameter and causes the speaker to emit a tone until the *NoSound* procedure is called.

CHAPTER Eighteen

Elementary Algorithms

- The Idea of an Algorithm

- Evaluating the Efficiency of Algorithms

- Searching and Sorting Algorithms

In this chapter, we will discuss *algorithms:* step-by-step recipes that tell a computer (or a person) what to do in certain situations. In the broadest sense of the term, algorithms have been an integral part of every chapter we have seen so far. In programming, however, the term is often used more narrowly, to refer to some fairly well-known recipes that have been thoroughly tested in practice. Here, we will look at several such recipes, with the understanding that there is much more to be learned than we can present in the short space we have here.

The Idea of an Algorithm

Before we discuss particular algorithms, however, we should get a better idea of what an algorithm is. The word is derived from the name of a Persian mathematician, Abu Ja'far Mohammed ibn Musa al Khowarizmi, who lived in the Middle Ages, around 800 C.E. An algorithm specifies a precise and totally unambiguous series of steps that will produce a certain result. Thus, an algorithm must have the following characteristics:

1. It must consist of a *finite* series of steps; that is, the conditions in which it will stop running must be clearly defined and must eventually be reached.

2. Each step must be *precise;* there can be no ambiguity about what is supposed to be done at any point in the running of the algorithm.

3. It must terminate in a reasonable amount of time—that is, it must be *efficient.*

4. It must produce the desired results at least under any foreseeable or probable conditions of use—that is, it must be *effective.*

The characteristics of an algorithm make it ideal for giving instructions to a computer, which takes everything literally and does exactly what it is told to do. Hence, the following is an example of an algorithm, in pseudocode rather than Pascal:

```
counter = 0
computer screen line = 5
repeat loop until counter = 10
   begin loop
         counter := counter + 1
```

```
        display counter value at screen column 0.
        screen line := screen line + 1
end loop
```

Efficiency of Algorithms

One of the important features of an algorithm is that it be as efficient as possible. This means that it should run as *fast* as possible and require as little computer *memory* as possible—two goals that are often in conflict.

Consider sequential search, which we looked at in Chapters 8 (for arrays) and 11 (for linked lists). To use this algorithm, you specify a *target* value that you want to look for in the list. The algorithm starts its search at the beginning of the list and compares each value to the target. If the value matches, then the search ends. Otherwise, the algorithm moves down to the next item in the list and does another comparison. It continues this process until it either finds the target value in the list or reaches the end of the list.

Observe that in the version of sequential search we have discussed so far, two operations are done at each position in the list—not just one. The first operation is to determine if the target value has been found. The second is to determine if the end of the list has been reached. Later in this chapter, we will see how to improve on this situation.

For small lists, sequential search is fast enough. It is faster in the array-based version than it is in the linked-list version, but the array-based version will normally require more memory. Thus, we face a trade-off: we can make the algorithm run faster by putting our list in an array, but this means a larger memory requirement. We can reduce the algorithm's memory needs by putting our list in a linked list, but this will cause somewhat slower performance.

Best, Worst, and Average Performance

Another aspect of algorithm performance is how the speed of the algorithm varies with the number of items it has to process. In the case of sequential search, the amount of time it takes to find an arbitrary item in a list varies directly with the size of the list. There are three cases we need to consider:

- *Best-case performance*, which is the number of operations that the algorithm will have to perform under ideal conditions;

- *Worst-case performance*, which is the number of operations that the algorithm will have to perform under the most unfavorable set of conditions; and

- *Average-case performance*, which is the average number of operations that the algorithm will have to perform when all cases are considered.

Notice that these three points refer only to how many operations the algorithm must perform—*not* to how fast it will run. How fast it runs will depend on many factors that cannot be controlled by the programmer, such as the speed of the user's machine. However, the more operations an algorithm has to perform for an input of a certain size, the slower it will run. A more efficient algorithm, which has to do fewer operations for an input of the same size, will run faster on any computer.

As an example, let's look at sequential search to determine its approximate efficiency in searching a list of n items—ignoring, for the moment, the extra end-of-list test at each position. In the best case, the target item will be found at the first position in the list, so the algorithm will need to make only one comparison. In the worst case, the target item will not be found in the list, so the algorithm will make n comparisons and have nothing to show for it.

The average case is a little more complicated. Assume that values are distributed randomly throughout the list: that is, that the target value has an equal chance of being at any position in the list. The target value might be at the first position, or the last, or any position in between. The algorithm might have to make one comparison, two, three, or any number of comparisons up to n. Therefore, using some math that we won't discuss here, the average number of comparisons is

$$\frac{1+2+3+..+n}{n} = \frac{n+1}{2}$$

This is about half the number of comparisons for a worst-case, unsuccessful search. (If you are interested in learning how to do these calculations, see any book on discrete mathematics, such as *Discrete Mathematics* by Richard Johnsonbaugh or *Concrete Mathematics* by Graham, Knuth, and Patashnik.)

As you can see, the performance of sequential search varies directly with the number of items in the list to be searched. Not all algorithms are like this. A few algorithms take the same time regardless of how many items are in the list; for example,

```
VAR
    List : ARRAY[1..50000] OF CHAR;
BEGIN
    WRITELN(List[n])
END;
```

Of course, this is a trivial algorithm, but it is one that pops up occasionally in programs. On the other hand, some algorithms have much slower worst-case performance than sequential search. For example, *Quicksort*, which we will look at later in this chapter, has a worst-case performance of n^2. This means that if one list is 10 times the size of another, then in the worst case it will take 100 times as long to sort the bigger list. (What makes *Quicksort* valuable is that it gives excellent best-case and average-case performance.)

"Big O" Notation

We've talked about how algorithm performance varies with the number of items to be processed, but it would make things easier if we had a simple way to refer to levels of efficiency. This is provided by "Big O" notation. Here, we will simply explain Big O notation enough so that you can understand it when you see it, but we will skip the mathematical details. If you want to develop a deeper understanding of Big O notation, see any of the books on discrete mathematics that were mentioned earlier.

The best way to proceed is with an example. Consider a list containing $>n$ items and some (unspecified) search algorithm that we will call F. Assume that *f(n)* is the number of operations that have to be performed by F in dealing with n items, and $g(n)$ is some function of n, such as $5n$ or n^2. Then, using Big O notation, we say that the algorithm *F is O(g(n))* ("F is Big O of g(n)") if there is some constant c such that

$$|f(n)| <= (c * |g(n)|)$$

This *sounds* a lot more complicated than it really is. Suppose that function g(n) is "n squared," so that g(n) = n^2. Then if our algorithm is O of g(n),— that is, O of n^2— it means simply that as n (the number of items in the list) increases, the number of operations that the algorithm must perform will grow *no faster* than n^2. Thus, the worst-case performance of *Quicksort*, which varies with the square of the number of items in the list, is O of n^2, meaning that with a list of n items the number of operations done by *Quicksort* grows proportionately to n^2 or slower than that. The worst-case performance of sequential search, which varies directly in proportion to the number of items in the list, is O of n, meaning it varies in proportion to n with a list of n items.

Table 18.1 shows the levels of algorithm efficiency that are commonly expressed in Big O notation, from most efficient (Big O of 1) to least efficient (Big O of n factorial).

TABLE 18.1: Common "Big O" Efficiency Ratings of Algorithms (from Most Efficient to Least Efficient)

Big O Notation	How Performance Varies with n[*]
O(1)	Constant (the best: size of n doesn't matter)
O(lg n)[**]	Logarithmic
O(n)	Linear
O(n lg n)	N log n (common with "divide and conquer" algorithms)
O(n^2)	Quadratic
O(n^3)	Cubic
O(mn)[***]	Exponential
O($n!$)	Factorial (the absolute worst!)

[*] n is the number of items that must be handled by the algorithm.

[**] Logarithms normally use 10 as a base; Lg n means Log of n to the base 2, and is commonly used in computer science.

[***] m is a nonnegative constant integer greater than 1.

Tips for Fine-Tuning Algorithms

Algorithm efficiency is important, but it is not equally important in every situation. If you have a simple program to display some text on the computer screen, then it is silly to spend too much time worrying about how efficiently you do it.

Likewise, a routine that is called only once in a program run can probably be as inefficient as you please: if it takes five seconds to run, then it's too bad but it's not a disaster. On the other hand, a routine that is called 1,000 or 1,000,000 times in a program run had better be as efficient as possible: if *it* wastes five seconds on a task that should take only a fraction of a second, then your program could still be running next week! (Turbo Profiler, which is included with Turbo Pascal Professional, can help you determine where you should concentrate your efforts.)

The point is that you should concentrate your optimization efforts where they will do the most good. There are two areas where efficiency is most important:

1. In routines that will be called very often during a run of the program. If one of these routines wastes time, then its inefficiency will be multiplied by the number of instances where it is called in the program.

2. In routines that handle user input and output. Users (PC users in particular) expect almost instant response when they do something on the computer. A routine that takes user input and displays a response on the screen should be as efficient as you can make it. If the user is forced to wait more than a second for a response, he or she will probably start pressing keys to see if your program is working properly—an action that could itself interfere with the operation of your program. (If some delay is unavoidable, then your program should display a message on-screen that says "Processing. Please wait..." or something similar.)

If you focus on these areas, you do not need to spend too much time worrying about the efficiency of other parts of your program.

Searching Algorithms

Now we will examine two searching algorithms and do an analysis of each. First, we will look at an improved version of sequential search that does only half as many operations as the version we saw earlier. Second, we will look at an algorithm called *binary search* that is more difficult but is also much faster than sequential search.

Sequential Search with a Sentinel Node

As noted earlier, our current version of sequential search does two operations at each position in the list:

- First, it compares the item at that position to the search target.

- Second, if the item is not equal to the target, then the search determines if the end of the list has been reached.

If we were certain that the target value was in the list, then we could leave out the second operation (the end-of-list test) and our algorithm would run twice as fast because it would have to do only half the number of operations.

To pull off this trick, we use what is called a *sentinel node*. At the very beginning of our search, we take the target value and insert it at the end of the list. Then we can omit the end-of-list test because we know that the search will terminate when the target value is found. At the same time, we know that if it is found at the last position in the list, then the target value was not really in the list at all—but that our sentinel node was reached. This method is illustrated in Listing 18.1.

Listing 18.1

```
PROGRAM Listing18_1;

    { Demonstrates sequential search of a linked list with a
      sentinel node at the end. This is faster than "plain"
      sequential search because it does fewer operations. }

USES CRT, MyUtils;

TYPE
    CharPtr = ^CharRec;
    CharRec = RECORD
                Letter : CHAR;
                Next   : CharPtr
              END;
VAR
    ListHead,
    ListTail : CharPtr;

PROCEDURE init(VAR ListHead, ListTail : CharPtr);
    BEGIN
        ListHead := NIL;
```

```
        ListTail := NIL;
        CLRSCR;
    END;

PROCEDURE FillList(VAR ListHead, ListTail : CharPtr);
    VAR
        counter : CHAR;
    BEGIN
        FOR counter := 'a' TO 'z' DO
            BEGIN
                IF ListHead = NIL
                    THEN BEGIN
                        NEW(ListHead);
                        ListHead^.letter := counter;
                        ListHead^.next := NIL;
                        ListTail := ListHead;
                        END
                    ELSE BEGIN
                        NEW(ListTail^.next);
                        IF ListHead = ListTail
                            THEN ListHead^.next := ListTail^.next;
                        ListTail := ListTail^.next;
                        ListTail^.letter := counter;
                        ListTail^.next := NIL;
                        END
        END
    END;

PROCEDURE SearchList(ListHead: CharPtr; VAR ListTail: CharPtr);
    VAR
        currptr : CharPtr;
        target  : CHAR;
        counter : INTEGER;

    BEGIN
        currptr := ListHead;
        counter := 1;
        WRITE(' Enter a letter for which to search: ');
        READLN(target);
        IF currptr = NIL
            THEN WRITELN(' Sorry. The list is empty.')
            ELSE BEGIN
                New(ListTail^.next);        { new node for sentinel }
                ListTail := ListTail^.next; { point tail at new node }
                ListTail^.letter := target; { load sentinel value }
```

```
            ListTail^.next := NIL;
            WHILE target <> currptr^.letter DO
                  BEGIN
                  counter := counter + 1;
                  IF currptr^.letter <> target
                     THEN currptr := currptr^.next
                  END;
            IF currptr = ListTail
               THEN WRITELN(' Sorry, target not found in list.')
               ELSE BEGIN
                  WRITE(' Target found at node #', counter);
                  WRITELN(' of list.')
                  END
            END;
       pause
    END;

{ main body of program }
BEGIN
    init(ListHead, ListTail);
    FillList(ListHead, ListTail);
    SearchList(ListHead, ListTail);
END.
```

In Listing 18.1, we create a linked list of characters from 'a' to 'z'. The *Init* procedure simply sets the head and tail pointers of the list to NIL, then clears the screen. The *FillList* procedure actually creates the list, creating and linking nodes to hold the letters.

It is the *SearchList* procedure that is of greatest interest here. This procedure takes both the head and tail pointers of the list as parameters. Because the head pointer won't be changed by the procedure, it is passed by value. The tail pointer, on the other hand, will be changed when we add the new sentinel node at the end of the list, so it is passed as a VAR parameter.

The *SearchList* procedure first sets a temporary pointer to point at the head of the list and initializes a counter variable, just as in the version of sequential search we saw in Chapter 11. It then prompts the user to enter a letter as a search target. If the head pointer equals nil, then the procedure tells the user that the list is empty. Otherwise, it creates a new node, points the tail pointer at the new node, and loads the target value into that node. This is our sentinel node.

Having completed this preparatory work, the *SearchList* procedure goes into the search loop. In the old version of the routine, the WHILE statement had to have two tests to make sure that the loop would eventually terminate: one to determine if the current list item matched the target value, and one to determine if the end of the list had been reached. However, we now know for sure that the target value will be found by the end of the list, so we don't need an end-of-list test to make sure that the loop terminates. Whenever the target value is found, the program drops out of the loop.

If the loop ends with the current pointer equal to the tail pointer, we know that the search routine has gone all the way to the sentinel node without previously finding the target value in the list. Hence, the target was not in the list. If the loop ends and the current pointer is *not* equal to the tail pointer, then we know that the target *was* found in the list because the loop ended before arriving at the sentinel node.

By reducing the number of operations that must be performed each time the search routine goes through the loop, we have made this search algorithm somewhat faster. Observe, however, that this version of sequential search is still $O(n)$—that is, its running time is directly proportional to the number of items in the list. If one list is 10 times larger than another, then its worst-case search time will still be 10 times longer, even though it will take *less* time in both cases than with the old sequential search routine.

Are there any ways to search a list more efficiently? Yes, indeed. In the next section, we will look at binary search, which gives $O(lg\ n)$ performance.

Binary Search

The next search algorithm to examine is called *binary search*. Unlike sequential search, binary search requires that the list already be in order by the search field: for example, if you are searching for a student record by last name, then the records must be in sorted order by last name. For lists that *are* already in order, binary search provides much faster performance than sequential search.

Binary search is what is called a "divide and conquer" algorithm. Instead of trying to search the whole list at once, you break it up into smaller pieces and determine which piece will contain the search target if it is in the list. Then you apply the same method to the new, smaller list (which is one-half of the original list) to get a list that is still smaller. You continue the process of narrowing the list until you either run out of list items or run into the target value.

Two versions of the binary search algorithm are shown in Listing 18.2. The first, *BSearch1*, continues to divide the list until it arrives at a single item, but does not check until then to find out if the target has been found. The second, *BSearch2*, checks at each loop to see if the target value has been found.

Listing 18.2

```
PROGRAM Listing18_2;

   { Demonstrates two versions of binary search. }

USES CRT, MyUtils;

CONST
   max = 8;

TYPE
   list = RECORD
            entry : ARRAY[1..max] of INTEGER;
            count : 0..max
            END;

VAR
   choice,
   target,
   position   : INTEGER;
   found      : BOOLEAN;
   SearchList : list;
   Again      : CHAR;

{ ------------------------------- }
{ MAIN-LEVEL PROCEDURE DECLARATION }
{ ------------------------------- }
PROCEDURE FillList(VAR searchlist: list; max: INTEGER);
   VAR
      counter : INTEGER;
   BEGIN
      for counter := 1 to Max do
      searchlist.entry[counter] := counter;
```

```
          searchlist.count := max
   END;

{ ------------------------------ }
{ MAIN-LEVEL PROCEDURE DECLARATION }
{ ------------------------------ }
PROCEDURE BSearch1(VAR SearchList: list; target: INTEGER;
                   VAR position: INTEGER; VAR found: BOOLEAN);
   { "Nonchecking" binary search. This does not check at
     each loop to determine if the target has been found }
   VAR
      high,
      low,
      middle     : INTEGER;
   BEGIN
      high := SearchList.count;
      low := 1;
      while high > low do
      BEGIN
      middle := (high + low) div 2;
      IF target > SearchList.entry[middle]
         THEN low := middle + 1
         ELSE high := middle
      END;
   IF high = 0
      THEN found := FALSE
      ELSE found := (target = SearchList.entry[high]);
   position := high
   END;

{ ------------------------------ }
{ MAIN-LEVEL PROCEDURE DECLARATION }
{ ------------------------------ }
PROCEDURE BSearch2(VAR SearchList:list; target:INTEGER;
                   VAR position:INTEGER; VAR found:BOOLEAN);
   { "Checking" version that determines at each loop whether
     or not the target has been found. }

   VAR
      high,
      low,
      middle     : INTEGER;
   BEGIN
      high := SearchList.count;
      low := 1;
```

```
        found := FALSE;
        while (not found) and (high >= low) do
        BEGIN
        middle := (high + low) div 2;
        IF target = SearchList.entry[middle]
           THEN found := TRUE
           ELSE IF target < SearchList.entry[middle]
              THEN high := middle - 1
              ELSE low := middle + 1
        END;
        position := middle
   END;


{ ------------------------------- }
{ MAIN-LEVEL PROCEDURE DECLARATION }
{ ------------------------------- }
PROCEDURE GetKey(VAR key:INTEGER);
   BEGIN
      CLRSCR; WRITELN; WRITELN;
      WRITE('Enter the number for which to search: ');
      READLN(key)
   END;


{ ------------------------------- }
{ MAIN-LEVEL PROCEDURE DECLARATION }
{ ------------------------------- }
Procedure InList(found:BOOLEAN; position:INTEGER; VAR Again:CHAR);
   BEGIN
       CLRSCR;
       IF found THEN
          BEGIN
          WRITE('The searched-for item was found at position ');
          WRITELN(position, '.');
          pause;
          CLRSCR
          END
       ELSE
          BEGIN
          WRITELN('The searched-for item was not found in this list.');
          pause
          END;
       WRITE(' Would you like to do another? (Y/N): ');
       READLN(Again);
       IF UPCASE(again) = 'Y'
          THEN BEGIN
```

```
                CLRSCR;
                WRITELN;
                WRITELN
                END
      END;


PROCEDURE DisplayMenu(VAR choice:INTEGER);
   { displays a menu on the screen }
      BEGIN
         CLRSCR; WRITELN; WRITELN;
         WRITELN('                    Search Operations Menu');
         WRITELN('                    ================================');
         WRITELN('                    1. BSearch1 ("non-checking" search)');
         WRITELN('                    2. Binary2 (checks if target found)');
         WRITELN('                    3. Quit'); WRITELN;
         WRITE('                Enter your choice (1/2/3): ');
         READLN(choice)
      END;

PROCEDURE DoChoice(choice:INTEGER);
   BEGIN
      CASE choice OF
         1 : BSearch1(SearchList,target,position,found);
         2 : BSearch2(SearchList,target,position,found);
         3 : HALT
         END
   END;




{ ------------------------------------------------------------------ }
{                     MAIN BODY OF PROGRAM                            }
{ ------------------------------------------------------------------ }
BEGIN
   Again := 'Y';
   FillList(SearchList,Max);
   REPEAT
      GetKey(target);
      DisplayMenu(choice);
      DoChoice(choice);
      InList(found,position,again)
   UNTIL UPCASE(again) <> 'Y'
END.
```

BSearch1 takes four parameters: a list to be searched, a target value, a variable representing the position in the list where the target is found, and a Boolean variable for whether or not the target value has been found. The list, remember, must be in sorted order. The number of items in the list is assigned to the *high* variable, while the *low* variable is set to 1.

A WHILE loop begins the divide-and-conquer part of the routine. It divides the list into two parts, a high part and a low part, by picking a middle position. If the target value is higher in the order than the item in the middle position, then the low variable is set to be one above the middle position. If the target is lower than or equal to the item in the middle position, then the high variable is set to the middle position.

The same process is repeated with the high and low positions getting closer each time, until the two finally come together at some position in the list. If the target value is in the list, it will be in this position. Otherwise, the search is unsuccessful.

BSearch2 works the same way as *BSearch1*, except that at each pass through the loop, it tests the value at the middle position to determine if it matches the target value, in which case the target has been found.

The difference between *BSearch1* and *BSearch2* is that if the target value is found early in the search, then *BSearch2* will require fewer operations than *BSearch1*. However, *BSearch2* also makes twice as many comparisons as *BSearch1*, so in the average and worst cases, it is actually *less* efficient.

Both methods, however, are more efficient for sorted lists than sequential search. Binary search is $O(lg\ n)$, which Table 18.1 shows is faster than sequential search, which is $O(n)$.

Sorting Algorithms

Now we will look at sorting algorithms. These algorithms are used to put list items in order. Some sorting algorithms, such as *Insertion Sort*, are very simple but have average-case performance that is $O(n^2)$. They are suitable for small lists of a few hundred items or less. Other sorting algorithms, such as *Quicksort*, are faster, with average-case performance that is $O(n \lg n)$. These, however, are generally more difficult to code correctly and should be used only where a large number of items must be sorted. In certain circumstances, you can even do some *really* tricky things to get speed approaching $O(n)$, but we won't discuss those here.

Most sorting algorithms also excel in dealing with either array-based lists or linked lists—but not both. Insertion sort is a simple general-purpose sorting routine that can be used either with arrays or linked lists. *Quicksort* is a more powerful routine that does not do very well with linked lists but is very fast in sorting arrays.

Insertion Sort

Insertion sort is perhaps the most familiar of all sorting methods. It is the method that most people use to sort a hand of cards: keep each item in its proper position in a sorted sublist, adding new items one at a time to the sorted sublist. When a new item is inserted in the sorted part of the list, higher-ranking items are moved to the right. When all the items have been added to the sorted sublist, then the original list has been completely sorted. This method is illustrated in Listing 18.3.

Listing 18.3

```
PROGRAM Listing18_3;

   { Demonstrates Insertion Sort with a linked list. }

USES CRT, MyUtils;

TYPE
   nodeptr = ^node;
   node    = RECORD
               item  : CHAR;
               next  : nodeptr
               END;
VAR
   head, tail: nodeptr;

PROCEDURE Init(VAR head, tail: nodeptr);
   BEGIN
      CLRSCR;
      head := NIL;
```

```
        tail := NIL
    END;


PROCEDURE TraverseList(VAR head: NodePtr);
    VAR
        TempPtr : nodeptr;
    BEGIN
        CLRSCR;
        WRITELN(' Now traversing the list from head to tail ...');
        tempptr := head;
        WHILE TempPtr <> NIL DO
            BEGIN
            WRITELN(' Current node contains: ', TempPtr^.item, '.');
            delay(500);
            TempPtr := TempPtr^.next
            END;
        pause
    END;

PROCEDURE addnode(VAR head, tail : nodeptr; newitem: CHAR);
    BEGIN
    IF head = NIL
        THEN BEGIN
            NEW(head);
            head^.item := newitem;
            head^.next := NIL;
            tail := head;
            END
        ELSE BEGIN
            NEW(tail^.next);
            IF head = tail
                THEN head^.next := tail^.next;
            tail := tail^.next;
            tail^.item := newitem;
            tail^.next := NIL;
            END
    END;

PROCEDURE CreateLinkedList(VAR head, tail: NodePtr);
    VAR
        counter : CHAR;
    BEGIN
        CLRSCR;
        FOR counter := 'z' DOWNTO 'a' DO
```

```
        BEGIN
        WRITELN(' Now adding ', counter, ' to the list.');
        delay(500);
        AddNode(head, tail, counter)
        END
    END;

PROCEDURE InsertionSort(VAR head: NodePtr);
    VAR
        LocalTailPtr,
        TempPtr1,
        TempPtr2,
        TempPtr3 : nodeptr;
    BEGIN
        CLRSCR;
        WRITELN(' Now running Insertion Sort! ... ');
        IF head <> NIL
            THEN BEGIN
                LocalTailPtr := head;
                WHILE LocalTailPtr^.next <> NIL DO
                    BEGIN
                    TempPtr1 := LocalTailPtr^.next;
                    IF TempPtr1^.item < head^.item
                        THEN BEGIN
                            LocalTailPtr^.next := TempPtr1^.next;
                            TempPtr1^.next := head;
                            head := TempPtr1
                            END
                        ELSE BEGIN
                            TempPtr3 := head;
                            TempPtr2 := TempPtr3^.next;
                            WHILE TempPtr1^.item > TempPtr2^.item DO
                                BEGIN
                                TempPtr3 := TempPtr2;
                                TempPtr2 := TempPtr3^.next
                                END;
                            IF TempPtr1 = TempPtr2
                                THEN LocalTailPtr := TempPtr1
                                ELSE BEGIN
                                    LocalTailPtr^.next := TempPtr1^.next;
                                    TempPtr1^.next := TempPtr2;
                                    TempPtr3^.next := TempPtr1
                                    END
                            END
                    END
            END
```

```
            END;
        pause
    END;

{ ------------------------------------------------------------ }
{                   MAIN BODY OF PROGRAM                        }
{ ------------------------------------------------------------ }
BEGIN
    Init(head, tail);
    CreateLinkedList(head, tail);
    TraverseList(head);
    InsertionSort(head);
    TraverseList(head);
END.
```

The program in Listing 18.3 first creates a linked list of letters. In the list, the letters are in reverse alphabetical order, from 'z' to 'a'. It then traverses the list, displaying the order of the letters on the computer screen.

The *Insertion Sort* procedure, of course, is the star of the show. It first checks to make sure that the list is not empty, then sets up a WHILE loop to move node-by-node down to the end of the list. It moves to the next node, and if the letter in this node comes before the head node letter in the alphabet (as we know that it does), then it shuffles the link pointers to move the next node to the head of the list. If not, it creates two more temporary pointers and moves them down the list until they reach the location where the node should be inserted. This process is repeated until every item in the list is in its proper location and the list is completely sorted.

Even this simple sorting routine has its share of details, so you should study Listing 18.3 until you are sure you understand how *Insertion Sort* works.

Quicksort

Quicksort, which really is quick most of the time when it comes to sorting arrays, was invented by C. Antony Hoare, an Oxford University computer scientist who has won just about every award that his profession and the computer industry can bestow. *Quicksort* is a classic example of a divide-and-conquer sorting algorithm. Just as a large and complex program can be coded more efficiently when you divide it into smaller, simpler subroutines, so a large array-based list can be sorted more efficiently (most of the time) when you divide it into smaller lists.

Quicksort works by dividing (partitioning) a list into two parts. It does so by selecting a *pivot* location that is midway between the beginning and the end of the list; hopefully, the value in this location will be midway between the lowest and highest values in the list. It then scans through the whole list and puts all the items that are less than the pivot into one sublist and all the items that are greater than or equal to the pivot into another sublist.

Notice that the original list is now partly sorted: all the items less than the pivot are in one sublist, and all the items greater than or equal to the pivot are in the other sublist. If we were to put the two sublists back together at this point, the original list would be closer to being sorted than it was before.

This operation is repeated until each sublist contains only a single element. The sublists are then put back together, one step at a time, until the original list has been reconstituted—this time, in completely sorted order. Listing 18.4 illustrates the use of *Quicksort*.

Listing 18.4

```
PROGRAM Listing18_5;
    { Demonstrates the Quicksort algorithm for sorting arrays. }

USES CRT, MyUtils;

CONST
    ListSize = 26;

TYPE
    List = ARRAY[1..ListSize] OF CHAR;

VAR
    LetterList : list;
    i          : integer;

{ -------------------------------- }
{ MAIN-LEVEL PROCEDURE DECLARATION }
{ -------------------------------- }
PROCEDURE LoadUpList(VAR LetterList : list);
    VAR
        counter : CHAR;
        listpos : INTEGER;
    BEGIN
        CLRSCR;
```

```
     WRITELN(' Now loading the list in reverse alphabetical order,');
     WRITELN(' from "z" to "a" ...');
     listpos := 1;
     FOR counter := 'z' DOWNTO 'a' DO
        BEGIN
        LetterList[listpos] := counter;
        listpos := listpos + 1
        END;
     delay(1000);
     WRITELN;
     WRITELN(' List now loaded in reverse alphabetical order!');
     pause
  END;

{ ------------------------------- }
{ MAIN-LEVEL PROCEDURE DECLARATION }
{ ------------------------------- }
PROCEDURE TraverseList(VAR LetterList : list);
   VAR
      counter : INTEGER;
   BEGIN
      CLRSCR;
      WRITELN(' Now traversing the letter list ...');
      delay(1000);
      FOR counter := 1 TO ListSize DO
         BEGIN
         WRITELN(' Current node contains ', LetterList[counter], '.');
         delay(500)
         END;
      pause
   END;

{ ------------------------------- }
{ MAIN-LEVEL PROCEDURE DECLARATION }
{ ------------------------------- }
PROCEDURE Quicksort(VAR LetterList: list; Low,High: integer);

   { ------------------------------- }
   { Local procedure                 }
   { ------------------------------- }
   { Under Quicksort }
   { ------------------------------- }
   PROCEDURE sort(l,r: INTEGER);
      VAR
         i,j : INTEGER;
```

```
        x,y : CHAR;
    BEGIN
    i:=l;
    j:=r;
    x:=LetterList[(l+r) DIV 2];    { pivot value in array }
    REPEAT
        WHILE LetterList[i] < x DO i := i+1;
        WHILE LetterList[j] > x DO j := j-1;
        IF i <= j
            THEN BEGIN
                y := LetterList[i];
                LetterList[i] := LetterList[j];
                LetterList[j] := y;
                i := i + 1;
                j := j - 1;
                END;
    UNTIL i > j;
    IF l < j THEN sort(l,j);  { the sort routine calls itself:   }
    IF i < r THEN sort(i,r)   { a typical example of recursion.   }
    END;


{ ----------------------------------- }
{ Main body of higher-level procedure }
{ ----------------------------------- }
{ Procedure name: Quicksort           }
{ ----------------------------------- }
BEGIN
CLRSCR;
WRITELN(' Now sorting the list with Quicksort ...');
sort(Low,High);
WRITELN;
WRITELN(' WHOOSH !!!!');
WRITELN(' The list has been sorted! Pretty fast, eh? ');
pause
END;


{ --------------------------------------------------------------- }
{                     MAIN BODY OF PROGRAM                        }
{ --------------------------------------------------------------- }
BEGIN
    LoadUpList(LetterList);
    TraverseList(LetterList);
    quicksort(LetterList, 1, ListSize);
    TraverseList(LetterList)
END.
```

In most respects, Listing 18.4 is just like Listing 18.3. The major differences are that it has an array-based list instead of a linked list, and, of course, it has *Quicksort* instead of *Insertion Sort*. The array-based list is loaded up with letters in reverse alphabetical order. Then, *Quicksort* is called to put them in normal alphabetical order.

Quicksort takes three parameters: the list itself, the array index for the beginning slot, and the array index for the ending slot. It calls a local routine called *Sort*, which does the actual work of sorting. *Sort* picks a location in the middle of the array and uses the value it contains (x) as the pivot.

Using two WHILE statements, *Sort* then scans forward through the array until it gets to a value that is greater than or equal to x, and scans backward until it finds another value that is less than or equal to x. If the array slot of the first value (the value which is greater than or equal to the pivot) is lower than the slot containing the second (which is less than or equal to the pivot), then the routine flip-flops the two items so that the one in the second slot gets moved into the first slot and the one in the first slot gets moved into the second.

This process continues until all the items less than the pivot are moved to one side of the array and all those greater than or equal to the pivot are moved to the other side of the array. The process then repeats within each sublist (that is, each section of the array) until one-item lists are reached, at which point the array is in sorted order.

The *Quicksort* routine is complicated by the fact that, although we have been talking about sublists as if they were physically separate, all of the sorting goes on inside the array that is being sorted. Items are shuffled back and forth in the array until they finally end up in the correct order. This makes things more difficult to code, but it has the advantage of needing very little extra memory beyond the array itself.

As with *Insertion Sort*, you should examine Listing 18.4 carefully until you are sure that you understand how it works. Then, try to create your own implementation of *Quicksort*.

CHAPTER
NINETEEN

Sound and Music Programming

- Sound Effects in Turbo Pascal

- Music Programming in Turbo Pascal

Creating programs that work is one thing; creating programs that are *interesting to use* is something extra. One way to add zip to your programs is by using sound effects and music. A program can beep when the user makes an error, play an anthem when the user saves a file, or make an "exploding" noise when the user opens an on-screen window.

MS-DOS PCs are not designed with computer games and sound effects in mind, so an ordinary PC's sound and music capabilities are somewhat limited. However, Turbo Pascal has features that let you take advantage of what PCs *can* do. With a little imagination, experimentation, and practice, you can create some interesting sound effects. With some sheet music and a basic understanding of the notes, you can even make a PC play melodies.

In this chapter, we will show how to create simple sound effects and explain the basics of PC music.

Making Sounds in Turbo Pascal

Like so much else in computing, the PC's speaker works on the principle of an on/off switch. It is either on, in which case it is making a sound at a particular frequency, or it is off, in which case it is quiet.

The basic tools that Turbo Pascal provides to manipulate the PC's speaker are the *Sound*, *NoSound*, and *Delay* procedures. All are part of the CRT unit. *Sound* takes a single parameter for the frequency of the tone you want to make. Middle C, for example, is 512 Hertz (cycles per second), while the note (C) one octave lower has a frequency of 256 Hertz and the note (C) one octave higher has a frequency of 1024 Hertz.

The *Sound* routine works together with the *NoSound* routine. Once you have turned on the PC's speaker and made it emit a tone, it will continue to emit that tone until you either turn it off with the *NoSound* routine or call the *Sound* routine again with a different frequency. Normally, you will use Turbo Pascal's *Delay* procedure to make the tone continue for a specific amount of time before *NoSound* is called. *Delay* takes a single parameter, the number of milliseconds (thousandths of a second) that it is intended to work.

A typical use of these routines would be as follows:

```
SOUND(256);
DELAY(1000);
NOSOUND;
```

This causes the PC's speaker to emit a 256-Hertz tone (Low C) for 1,000 milliseconds, or 1 second. After 1 second has passed, the call to *NoSound* turns off the speaker, and it is silent until it is activated again by another call to *Sound*.

These tools are fairly basic, but as we'll see in the next section, you can use them to create some surprisingly good sound effects. One word of caution: any time you use the *Sound* routine in your program, you *must* make a call to *NoSound* later on in the program to turn the speaker off again. If you forget to do this, you might end up in a situation in which the only way to make the speaker shut up would be to reboot your computer.

Sound Effects

Although the sound effects you can create on the PC are not very impressive compared to those on more game-oriented machines like the Commodore Amiga, you can still make some interesting sounds if you use your imagination. Here, we will look at a few examples.

Beep

The first sound effect we will look at is one that we have already seen—without much comment—in Chapter 17: a short "beep." This sound effect is demonstrated by Listing 19.1.

Listing 19.1

```
PROGRAM Listing19_1;

   { Demonstrates how to make the speaker emit a beep. }

USES CRT, MyUtils;

VAR mynum : integer;
```

```
PROCEDURE beep;
   BEGIN
      SOUND(150);
      DELAY(400);
      NOSOUND
   END;

BEGIN
   CLRSCR;
   WRITE(' Enter a number from 1 to 5: ');
   READLN(mynum);
   IF (mynum < 1) or (mynum > 5)
      THEN BEGIN
            beep;
            WRITELN(' You didn''t enter a number from 1 to 5!');
            pause
            END
      ELSE BEGIN
            WRITELN(' Congratulations! You followed instructions!');
            pause
            END
END.
```

For the beep tone, we want a fairly low-pitched sound, so a frequency of 150 is just about right. Moreover, a beep should be short, so the *Delay* routine is told to run for 400 milliseconds, or four-tenths of a second. After the delay, a call to *NoSound* turns off the speaker.

Listing 19.1 shows a typical application of a beep: alerting the user to an error. It is simple but effective.

Buzz

A buzzing sound is similar to a beep in that it is low-pitched, but it lasts longer and is more uneven. Listing 19.2 shows how to create a buzzing sound.

Listing 19.2

```
PROGRAM Listing19_2;

    { Demonstrates how to create a buzzing sound. }

USES CRT;
```

```
PROCEDURE Buzz;
   VAR
      counter : integer;
   BEGIN
      FOR counter := 1 TO 30 DO
         BEGIN
            SOUND(100);
            DELAY(30);
            NOSOUND;
            DELAY(30)
         END
   END;

BEGIN
   Buzz
END.
```

Because the buzz tone must be uneven, we want to alternate sound with silence. We set up a FOR loop to keep the buzz going while this process is taking place. The speaker emits a low tone (at 100 Hertz) for 30 milliseconds; then is silent for 30 milliseconds; and then repeats the same sequence of sound and silence, for a total of 30 times in the counter loop. This makes the buzz continue for 1.8 seconds.

Bouncing Ball

For a bouncing ball sound effect, we want to alternate between low and high tones as the ball bounces, goes up, and then comes back down. Each time it bounces, it bounces a little lower, so the bouncing tones get closer together on each bounce. This is illustrated in Listing 19.3. The high and low tones are specified in integer parameters that are passed to the *BouncingBall* routine. We used a WHILE loop instead of a FOR loop because we wanted to change the counter variable by more than 1 on each pass through the loop.

Listing 19.3

```
PROGRAM Listing19_3;

   { Demonstrates a bouncing ball sound effect. }

USES CRT;
VAR
   high, low : INTEGER;
```

```
PROCEDURE BouncingBall(high, low : INTEGER);
    VAR count : INTEGER;
    BEGIN
    count := 20;
    WHILE count > 1 DO
        BEGIN
        SOUND(low - count * 2);
        DELAY((count *500) DIV 20);
        NOSOUND;
        DELAY(100);
        SOUND(high);
        DELAY((count * 500) div 15);
        NOSOUND;
        DELAY(150);
        count := count - 2
        END
    END;

BEGIN
    BouncingBall(350,200)
END.
```

The bouncing ball loop is a little more complicated than the buzzing loop. Because the tones and their duration must change on each pass through the loop, we need some way to control these factors. The most obvious way is to make the tone frequency and duration depend in some way on the value of the counter variable, which itself changes automatically on each pass through the loop.

On the first pass through the loop, the first tone sounds at the "low" frequency minus two times the current counter variable. Because the counter variable decreases from its original value of 20 on each pass through the loop, the value of 2 * *counter* becomes smaller and smaller. Because it is subtracted from the low value to get the sound frequency of the first tone, this means that on each pass, the tone becomes higher, since a smaller number is subtracted from it. At the same time, the *duration* of the tone also becomes shorter as the value of *(count * 500) DIV 20* decreases.

The high frequency itself stays the same, although the duration of the second, higher tone in the loop does become shorter on each pass through the loop. There is nothing very scientific about the mathematical formulas used to control the frequency and duration of tones in the loop: you just have to experiment until you discover a sound sequence you like.

Bombs Away

This sound effect is similar to the one used in television war dramas when a plane drops its bombs. It takes three parameters: a high frequency, a low frequency, and an "altitude" integer variable that is used to control the duration of the tones. It is illustrated in Listing 19.4.

Listing 19.4

```pascal
PROGRAM Listing19_4;

    { Demonstrates a "bombs away" sound effect. }

USES CRT;

VAR
    high, low, altitude : INTEGER;

PROCEDURE BombsAway(high, low, altitude: INTEGER);
    VAR count : INTEGER;
    BEGIN
        count := low;
        WHILE count <= high DO
                BEGIN
                SOUND(count);
                DELAY((altitude DIV count) * 75);
                count := count + 10
                END;
        NOSOUND;

        SOUND(40);
        DELAY(500);
        NOSOUND;
        DELAY(100);

        SOUND(40);
        DELAY(500);
        NOSOUND;
        DELAY(100);

        SOUND(40);
        DELAY(500);
        NOSOUND;
        DELAY(100);
```

```
            SOUND(40);
            DELAY(3000);
            NOSOUND
       END;

BEGIN
    BombsAway(1200, 200, 500)
END.
```

As the loop begins (again, a WHILE loop so that we have more flexibility in changing the counter variable), the counter is set at the low frequency value. The first tone is at this low frequency, lasting for a duration that is determined by dividing the altitude by the counter value, and multiplying the result by 75 to make the tone last longer. The counter variable is then increased by 10. On each pass through the loop, the counter value becomes bigger, so the pitch of the tone becomes higher and the length of the tone becomes shorter as *altitude DIV count* decreases. The loop finally ends when the counter is no longer less than or equal to the high value. A call to *Nosound* is made after the loop ends to shut down the PC's speaker.

Red Alert

This sound effect simulates an alarm, such as the ones that always go off in space operas when a hostile ship is approaching. It simply alternates a high-pitched sound with a low-pitched sound until the user presses a key as shown in Listing 19.5.

Listing 19.5

```
PROGRAM Listing19_5;

    { Demonstrates "red alert" alarm sound effect. }

USES CRT;

PROCEDURE RedAlert(high, low: INTEGER);
    VAR ch : CHAR;
    BEGIN
       CLRSCR;
       WRITE(' Press any key to terminate red alert ... ');
       REPEAT
          SOUND(high);
          DELAY(400);
          SOUND(low);
```

```
            DELAY(400)
        UNTIL Keypressed;
        ch := Readkey;
        NOSOUND
    END;

BEGIN
    RedAlert(350,200)
END.
```

A REPEAT loop is used because we want the tones to sound at least once. Outside the loop, we use a WRITE statement to put a message on the screen telling the user how to terminate the sound. This step is very easy to forget because it has nothing to do with generating the sound, but it is also very important: if a user starts the sound and does not know how to turn it off, extremely angry phone calls about the situation will result.

Note that we called *Readkey* to clear the keyboard buffer after the user presses a key. In normal programming situations, when the user presses a key that is not relayed into a variable, the character resulting from the keypress can still be in the keyboard buffer and can cause unpredictable malfunctions. Calling *Readkey* as we have done here clears the keyboard buffer.

Music

The PC's speaker may not sound as good as your CD player, but at least it can carry a tune. By using the *Sound* procedure with the frequencies of musical notes, you can make your PC play any tune you like.

Listing 19.6 introduces many of the basic concepts of music programming with Borland Pascal.

Listing 19.6

```
PROGRAM Listing19_6;

    { Demonstrates how to play a simple tune. }

USES CRT;

CONST
```

```
    sbrk      = 30;
    lbrk      = 60;
    enote     = 150;
    qnote     = 300;
    hnote     = 600;
    dot_hnote = 900;
    wnote     = 1200;

    { octave below Middle C }
    c1 = 256; c1s = 271; d1 = 287; d1s = 304; e1 = 323; f1 = 342;
    f1s = 362; g1 = 384; g1s = 406; a1 = 431; a1s = 456; b1 = 483;

    { octave containing Middle C }
    c2 = 512; c2s = 542; d2 = 575; d2s = 609; e2 = 645; f2 = 683;
    f2s = 724; g2 = 767; g2s = 813; a2 = 861; a2s = 912; b2 = 967;

    { octave above Middle C }
    c3 = 1024; c3s = 1085; d3 = 1149; d3s = 1218; e3 = 1290; f3 = 1367;
    f3s = 1448; g3 = 1534; g3s = 1625; a3 = 1722; a3s = 1825; b3 = 1933;
PROCEDURE Off;
    BEGIN
    NOSOUND;
    DELAY(notebrk)
    END;


BEGIN
    SOUND(e1);
    DELAY(qnote);
    off;

    SOUND(e1);
    DELAY(qnote);
    off;

    SOUND(e1);
    DELAY(hnote);
    off;
{ ------------------- }
    SOUND(e1);
    DELAY(qnote);
    off;

    SOUND(e1);
```

```
    DELAY(qnote);
    off;

    SOUND(e1);
    DELAY(hnote);
    off;
{ -------------------- }
    SOUND(e1);
    DELAY(qnote);
    off;

    SOUND(g1);
    DELAY(qnote);
    off;

    SOUND(c1);
    DELAY(qnote);
    off;

    SOUND(d1);
    DELAY(qnote);
    off;
{ -------------------- }
    SOUND(e1);
    DELAY(dot_hnote);
    NOSOUND;
    DELAY(qnote);
END.
```

The first thing we have to do is to set up a group of constants to use in our program. Here are the constants used in Listing 19.6:

- *Sbrk* and *Lbrk* are amounts of time between notes.

- *Enote* is the amount of time for an eighth note.

- *Qnote* is the amount of time for a quarter note.

- *Hnote* is the amount of time for a half note.

- *Dot_hnote* is the amount of time for a dotted half note.

- *Wnote* is the amount of time for a whole note.

- Individual note names contain, first, the letter of the note; second, the octave number; and third, an "s" if the note is sharp. Only sharps are recognized in our table of note names, and this causes no problem because any flat note is the sharp note of the note below it—for example, B-flat is A-sharp.

The listing also includes a short "off" procedure to insert breaks between notes. This is included simply to avoid writing *NoSound*; *Delay(notebrk)* over and over. The comment lines indicate the separate bars of the tune.

Creating the Music Unit

As helpful as our table of note names may be, it would be a terrible pain in the neck if we had to put it into every program that used music. The obvious solution is the correct one: we will put the musical notes into a unit that any program can use if it needs to play music. The music unit is shown in Listing 19.7.

Listing 19.7

```
UNIT Music; { Listing 19.7 }

INTERFACE

CONST

    sbrk      = 30;
    lbrk      = 60;
    enote     = 150;
    qnote     = 300;
    hnote     = 600;
    dot_hnote = 900;
    wnote     = 1200;

{ =============== TABLE OF MUSICAL NOTE FREQUENCIES ============== }
{ This table has mnemonic names for the frequencies of musical
  notes. It covers three octaves: the octave containing Middle C,
  the octave below Middle C, and the octave above Middle C. The
  note frequencies are taken from the book Science & Music by
  Sir James Jeans.

  There is one thing to be careful about in using this table.
  Some programs use the text strings 'f1', 'f2', etc. to
  denote the function keys on the PC's keyboard. If you are
```

adding music to a program that uses the function keys, you
should make sure that the function keys are named in some
other way, for example, f_1 for the F1 function key. This
will prevent the program from becoming confused about which
item (a function key or a musical note) a particular 'f1',
etc. identifies. }

{ octave 1, below Middle C }
c1 = 256; c1s = 271; d1 = 287; d1s = 304; e1 = 323; f1 = 342;
f1s = 362; g1 = 384; g1s = 406; a1 = 431; a1s = 456; b1 = 483;

{ octave 2, containing Middle C }
c2 = 512; c2s = 542; d2 = 575; d2s = 609; e2 = 645; f2 = 683;
f2s = 724; g2 = 767; g2s = 813; a2 = 861; a2s = 912; b2 = 967;

{ octave 3, above Middle C }
c3 = 1024; c3s = 1085; d3 = 1149; d3s = 1218; e3 = 1290; f3 = 1367;
f3s = 1448; g3 = 1534; g3s = 1625; a3 = 1722; a3s = 1825; b3 = 1933;

```
TYPE
    string3 = STRING[3];

    noteptr = ^note;
    note    = RECORD
                freq,
                dur,
                brk  : integer;
                next : noteptr
                END;

IMPLEMENTATION

END.
```

As you should recall from Chapter 10, a unit has three parts: an INTERFACE section, which contains material that is accessible to any programs that use the unit;
an IMPLEMENTATION section, which contains material that is private to the unit
and cannot be seen by calling programs; and an optional section to initialize the
values of variables used by the unit.

Although a unit most often is used to hold subroutines, we can also use it to hold publicly accessible constants in its INTERFACE section. Therefore, we simply declare our note names (along with the note durations) as constants in the INTERFACE section of the unit. We also include a TYPE section with a note data type for a linked list of musical notes.

There is one thing to be careful about when using this unit. If you are creating constant names that will represent function keys, the natural name for the F1 key is 'f1'. However, this name is used by the table of musical notes to stand for the note F in octave 1; likewise for 'f2' and 'f3'. If your program uses music, you should use some other names for the function keys, such as 'f1key' for the F1 function key.

The music unit allows the programmer to embed musical notes in the source code of a program. One thing it does not do, however, is allow the user of a program to enter the names of musical notes into variables at the keyboard. You cannot simply prompt the user to enter the name of a musical note and then play that note. To get the note from the user, you would need to use a string variable, because the note names are text strings. If you try to play this note, however, you cannot use the *Sound* routine because it requires a parameter of the integer data type. Thus, a user cannot type 'c2' at the keyboard and expect the computer to sound Middle C.

CHAPTER TWENTY

Object-Oriented Programming

- **Methods and Encapsulation**

- **Virtual Methods and Polymorphism**

- **Dynamic Object Variables and Pointers**

Version 5.5 of Turbo Pascal introduced a new way of thinking about and structuring Pascal programs: *object-oriented programming.* Borland Pascal and Turbo Pascal 7 further extend the object-oriented capabilities of Turbo Pascal, as well as adding Turbo Vision, a library of object routines for use in your own programs. With the tools that Turbo Pascal offers for this powerful approach, you can—in complex programming projects—create better structured, more flexible, and easier to modify programs in less time. You do not have to use Turbo Pascal's object-oriented features if you do not want to (and for smaller programs, they are not always appropriate), but they are there when you need them.

Object-oriented programming is based on an idea that should be familiar by now. In Chapter 17, we saw that any sophisticated data structure, such as a stack, includes two things:

- A particular arrangement of data items, such as an array or a linked list.

- A set of operations that manipulates those data items, such as the *Push* and *Pop* routines used with a stack.

Without *Push* and *Pop* routines, an array is just an array. When you add those routines, you create a stack data structure. If, instead, you add the routines appropriate for a queue, then you turn the array into a queue. In standard Pascal, however, there is no way to *weld* the routines right into the data structure—no way to create a stack, queue, or other data structure that is smart enough to take care of itself and does not need outside routines to help it.

That kind of intelligent data structure is the essence of object-oriented programming. Instead of having a passive array on which external routines operate to create a stack or other data structure, object-oriented programming lets us create a "smart" data structure that contains *within itself* everything it needs to behave as it should. For example, instead of passing a stack to the *Push* routine to add an item, you send a message to the stack object to add an item to itself—an operation that it knows how to do. What makes this tricky is that it involves a totally new way of structuring and thinking about our programs.

Object-oriented programming originally came out of ideas in the Simula programming language of the 1960s. Most of the research work that developed the object-oriented approach, however, was done at Xerox Corporation's Palo Alto Research Center (PARC) in a 10-year project that developed Smalltalk, the first truly and completely object-oriented programming language. Xerox PARC is perhaps most famous for developing the "Xerox Star" microcomputer and its icon-based screen interface, which provided the inspiration for Microsoft Windows and the Apple Macintosh. The difficulty of creating such a screen interface was a key motivation in the development of object-oriented programming techniques, even though object-oriented programming has no necessary connection with icon-based screen displays.

Borland Pascal traces its object-oriented heritage from Xerox PARC's original work on Smalltalk through Apple's Object Pascal and AT&T's C++ programming languages. It takes the best features of each, prunes what is redundant or of questionable value, and builds them into standard Pascal as added features that you can use or ignore as you wish.

Consider the following problems:

- You have a customer billing system and you want to create several different customer data types. They are all basically the same, but each differs from the others in some minor detail.

- You are creating a program with on-screen windows and menus. Although there are several different types of each, you want them all to perform certain operations in the same ways.

- You create a library of Turbo Pascal routines and distribute precompiled units containing those routines, but you want users to be able to modify your routines without having the Pascal source code.

Object-oriented programming has a clean, logical solution to all of those problems. In a customer billing system, for example, you can create a single *parent* customer data type that contains basic customer information such as name, address, and account number. Based on this parent type, you can then create as many specialized customer types as you need, *without* repeating any code from the parent type. Each specialized data type, called a *child* of the parent type, inherits all of the features of the parent type and can add its own new features. It can even cancel out parent features that do not apply to it. Extending the parent-child metaphor, a type that is derived from an earlier object type is called its *descendant,* while the earlier object type, likewise, is called the descendant type's *ancestor.*

Because these object data types inherit the characteristics of their ancestor types, you can extend the capabilities of already-compiled units of object routines even if you do not have the source code. You simply create new object types as descendants of already existing object types, and then add new features or cancel inherited features as needed. Procedures designed to work with ancestor object types will work with their descendant object types as well.

Objects and Object-Oriented Programming

That's the general idea of objects. Now let's take a look at the specifics. Object-oriented programming introduces several new concepts:

- *Objects,* which look similar to records but contain their own procedures and functions, called "methods."

- *Object types,* which define particular object data types and their capabilities.

- *Encapsulation,* which binds procedures and functions into a data structure with the data they process.

- *Messages,* which are instructions sent to objects that tell them to carry out their built-in methods.

- *Inheritance,* by which the characteristics of an object type are passed along to its descendant object types.

- *Polymorphism,* the ability of different objects to respond in their own unique ways to the same program command.

- *Extensibility of code,* by which already compiled units of object types can be used as a basis for creating and using new object types that were unknown at compile time.

Appropriately enough, the fundamental concept in object-oriented programming is that of an *object*. An object looks very much like a Pascal record, except that it has its own procedures and functions. Consider Listing 20.1, which shows a conventional structured programming approach to loading values into a student record. (Before running Listing 20.1 or any of the listings in this chapter, make sure that your printer is connected and ready to print.)

Listing 20.1

```
PROGRAM Listing20_1;

    { Shows standard structured programming techniques for
      entering data into a student record and displaying the
      data. }

USES CRT, MyUtils;

const
    formfeed = #12;

TYPE
    string15 = STRING[15];
    studentrec = RECORD
                    fname,
                    lname : string15;
                    GPA         : REAL;
                    END;
VAR
    student : studentrec;

PROCEDURE init(var student : studentrec);
    BEGIN
        WITH student DO
            BEGIN
                fname      := space;
                lname      := space;
                GPA        := 0.00
            END
    END;

PROCEDURE FillRecord(var student : studentrec);
    BEGIN
        WITH student DO
            BEGIN
                WRITE(' Enter the student''s first name: ');
                READLN(fname);
                WRITE(' Enter the student''s last name: ');
                READLN(lname);
                WRITE(' Enter the student''s current GPA: ');
```

```
            READLN(GPA);
        END
    END;

PROCEDURE SendHonorsLetter(student : studentrec);
    VAR
        letterfile: TEXT;
        counter   : INTEGER;
    BEGIN
        ASSIGN(letterfile, 'prn');
        REWRITE(letterfile);
        FOR counter := 1 TO 10 DO WRITELN(letterfile);
        WRITELN(letterfile, 'Dear Mr./Ms. ', student.lname, ':');
        WRITELN(letterfile);
        WRITELN(letterfile, 'Your grade point average is over 3.5. This');
        WRITELN(letterfile, 'means that you will graduate cum laude from');
        WRITELN(letterfile, 'this institution. Congratulations.');
        WRITELN(letterfile);
        WRITELN(letterfile, 'Sincerely,');
        WRITELN(letterfile);
        WRITELN(letterfile, 'V. Wormer');
        WRITELN(letterfile, 'Dean of Students');
        WRITELN(letterfile, formfeed);
        CLOSE(letterfile)
    END;

PROCEDURE DisplayInfo(student : studentrec);
    BEGIN
        CLRSCR;
        WITH student DO
            BEGIN
            WRITELN(' The student''s name is: ', fname, space, lname, '.');
            WRITELN(' The student''s GPA is: ', GPA:0:2, '.');
            IF GPA > 3.5 THEN SendHonorsLetter(student);
            pause
            END;
    END;

BEGIN
    CLRSCR;
    init(student);
    fillrecord(student);
    pause;
    displayinfo(student)
END.
```

The student record itself uses the RECORD data type to bind together two string fields (for first name and last name) with a real-number field for grade point average. Routines are defined to initialize the record, load it with data, and then display the data on the computer screen. If the student's GPA is over 3.5, then a letter of congratulations is printed.

It is in the main body of the program that we will see the most dramatic change when we go from structured to object-oriented programming. In Listing 20.1, the program clears the screen and then passes the student record variable to the *Init* routine, which initializes its data fields with "blank" values. The variable is then passed to the *FillRecord* routine, which loads name and GPA information into its data fields. Finally, it is passed to the *DisplayInfo* routine, which takes the information in its data fields and displays it on the computer screen.

Through all this, the student record variable is a passive spectator that has things "done to it," like a hospital patient lying on a cart who gets wheeled from one examining room to the next. Poked, prodded, and (we imagine) slightly humiliated by all this, the student record variable nonetheless provides what we need. There is, however, a neater way to do the same thing.

Methods and Encapsulation

The neater way is to declare the student record type as an *object type* instead of a record type. This allows us to include all the procedures and functions needed to manipulate the data in the object itself—an approach called *encapsulation* because it creates a hermetically sealed object "capsule" that includes all the data fields and methods it needs. To declare an object type, you simply use the Turbo Pascal reserved word OBJECT and then list the fields and methods of the object, in much the same way as you would do with a standard record-type declaration:

```
TYPE
studentrec = OBJECT
             fname,
             lname : string15;
             GPA   : REAL;
             PROCEDURE init;
             PROCEDURE fillrecord;
```

```
PROCEDURE SendHonorsLetter;
PROCEDURE DisplayNameAndGPA;
END;
```

All the data fields must be listed in the type definition *before* any methods are listed, as in the example above. One quirk of object-type declarations is that the last method or field declaration before the END must be followed by a semicolon; this is the only place in Pascal where a semicolon must be used right before an END.

Of course, this type declaration does not create an object, any more than declaring a record type creates any records. To create an object, you must declare a variable of the object type:

```
VAR
    student : studentrec
```

At some point, either before or after you declare the object variable, you must spell out the details of the object's methods, just as you would with any other subroutines. There are, however, two key differences:

- First, the name of each method must be preceded by the name of the object type. When we declare the details of our *Init* method for the *studentrec* object type above, for example, we would write the subroutine header as studentrec.init to make it clear that the subroutine is a method in the *studentrec* object type.

- Second, the header for a method does not have to take an object variable itself as a parameter. For example, in the *Init* declaration from Listing 20.1 (which uses standard structured programming), the record variable must be declared as a parameter because it is passed to the *Init* subroutine. With an object type, however, the *Init* routine is *part of* the object variable, so it automatically "knows" which variable it should initialize—that is, itself. Therefore, instead of *Init(student: studentrec)* as in Listing 20.1, the declaration can be simply *studentrec.init*, with no parameters.

The best way to understand these concepts is to look at a simple example, as shown in Listing 20.2. This is exactly the same program as in Listing 20.1, but with a crucial difference: it is coded using object-oriented techniques.

Listing 20.2

```
PROGRAM Listing20_2;

    { Shows object-oriented approach to entering data into a
      student record (an object) and displaying the data.
      Principal feature demonstrated: ENCAPSULATION. }

USES CRT, MyUtils;

const
    formfeed = #12;

type
    string15 = STRING[15];
    studentrec = OBJECT
                fname,
                lname : string15;
                GPA    : REAL;
                PROCEDURE init;
                PROCEDURE fillrecord;
                PROCEDURE SendHonorsLetter;
                PROCEDURE DisplayNameAndGPA;
                END;

PROCEDURE studentrec.init;
    BEGIN
    fname    := space;
    lname    := space;
    GPA      := 0.00
    END;

PROCEDURE studentrec.FillRecord;
    BEGIN
    CLRSCR;
    WRITE(' Enter the student''s first name: ');
    READLN(fname);
    WRITE(' Enter the student''s last name: ');
    READLN(lname);
    WRITE(' Enter the student''s current GPA: ');
    READLN(GPA);
    END;

PROCEDURE studentrec.SendHonorsLetter;
    VAR
```

```
      letterfile: TEXT;
      counter   : INTEGER;
   BEGIN
      ASSIGN(letterfile, 'prn');
      REWRITE(letterfile);
      FOR counter := 1 TO 10 DO WRITELN(letterfile);
      WRITELN(letterfile, 'Dear Mr./Ms. ', lname, ':');
      WRITELN(letterfile);
      WRITELN(letterfile, 'Your grade point average is over 3.5. This');
      WRITELN(letterfile, 'means that you will graduate cum laude from');
      WRITELN(letterfile, 'this institution. Congratulations.');
      WRITELN(letterfile);
      WRITELN(letterfile, 'Sincerely,');
      WRITELN(letterfile);
      WRITELN(letterfile, 'V. Wormer');
      WRITELN(letterfile, 'Dean of Students');
      WRITELN(letterfile, formfeed);
      CLOSE(letterfile)
   END;

PROCEDURE studentrec.DisplayNameAndGPA;
   BEGIN
   CLRSCR;
   WRITELN(' The student''s name is: ', fname, space, lname, '.');
   WRITELN(' The student''s GPA is:  ', GPA:0:2, '.');
   IF GPA > 3.5 THEN SendHonorsLetter;
   END;

VAR
   student : studentrec;

BEGIN
   student.init;
   student.fillrecord;
   student.displaynameandGPA
END.
```

In most of the program code, the differences seem fairly minor. Instead of declaring *studentrec* as a record type, we declare it as an object type. We include as methods in the object type all of the procedures that were formerly separate from the student record: this is an example of encapsulation. When we get to declaring the details of the methods, again, everything looks pretty much the same. The *Init* method initializes the object's data fields with a "blank" value, the *FillRecord* method loads data into the data fields, the *DisplayNameAndGPA* method shows the name and GPA on the screen, and if the GPA is over 3.5, then the *SendHonorsLetter* prints a congratulatory letter.

It is when we arrive at the main body of the program that the dramatic difference becomes clear. Instead of passing the student record variable to the *Init* routine, which would then initialize it (as in Listing 20.1), we send a message to the variable and tell it to initialize itself. It knows how to do this because it has a built-in *Init* method. We then tell the variable to get some data from the user and load the data into its fields. Finally, we tell it to display its data on the screen and, if appropriate, send a congratulatory letter to the student.

Note how we called the methods in the object: by using the name of the object variable (not the object type), a dot, and then the name of the method. The variable name tells the program which object *variable* is to get a message, and the method name tells the variable which of its *methods* it should use.

In this simple example, we can see that object-oriented programming gets rid of the traditional passive data structures that we saw in structured programming. In their place, it puts active, intelligent data structures that know how to do every task that they will be called on to perform.

Which Methods to Include

This leads to a key principle of object design: *make sure that your object type has all the methods it needs to manipulate the data in its fields.* It is possible in Turbo Pascal (but not in most other languages that support object-oriented programming) to access an object's fields directly. For example, instead of sending a message to the student variable to use its *Init* method, you could initialize its fields as follows:

```
student.fname := space;
student.lname := space;
student.GPA := 0.00;
```

As you might suspect, you can also use the WITH notation, just as you can with a record variable:

```
WITH student DO
    BEGIN
    fname      := space;
    lname      := space;
    GPA        := 0.00
    END;
```

Now, if *student* were a record variable, there would be nothing wrong with this: indeed, it would be the only way to initialize the record's data fields. But *student* is *not* a record variable: it is an object that has built-in methods to handle any task involving its data fields. A major benefit of encapsulation is that it allows us to hide even more information inside various compartments of the program. Just as using global variables in a subroutine without declaring them as parameters violates the principle of information hiding and must be avoided whenever possible, so too any attempt to manipulate an object's fields without using its methods violates the same principle and must be avoided.

The key to preserving the integrity of your object variables is to make sure that your object-type definition includes *all* the methods that the object will need to manipulate the data in its fields. If one or more methods are left out of your object type definition, then you will have no choice but to manipulate object fields directly, which you do not want to do.

Obviously, which methods an object will require depends on the purpose of the object. Our student object variable needs methods to initialize its fields, to load them with data, to report that data to the screen, and to print out a letter when appropriate. A stack object variable would also need an *Init* method, and methods to do pushes and pops.

Because you can create descendant object types and add methods that are not in their ancestor types, you can even do this with precompiled libraries of objects, as we will see in the next section.

Inheritance

In this section, we will discuss how to create and use descendant object types that are derived from already-existing object types. Just as human children inherit characteristics from their parents—hair color, height, and so forth—Pascal objects inherit fields and methods from their parent objects, as well as from all their other ancestor objects up the line.

The first thing we want to do is put the object and method declarations from Listing 20.2 into a unit. Listing 21.3 shows how to do this.

Listing 20.3

```
UNIT my_objs;   { Listing20.3 }

    { Demonstrates how to move object types into a unit for
      re-use in other programs. }

INTERFACE

USES CRT, MyUtils;

CONST
    formfeed = #12;

TYPE
    string15 = STRING[15];
    studentrec = OBJECT
                fname,
                lname : string15;
                GPA            : REAL;
                PROCEDURE init;
                PROCEDURE fillrecord;
                PROCEDURE SendHonorsLetter;
                PROCEDURE DisplayNameAndGPA;
                END;

IMPLEMENTATION

PROCEDURE studentrec.init;
    BEGIN
    fname      := space;
    lname      := space;
    GPA        := 0.00
    END;

PROCEDURE studentrec.FillRecord;
    BEGIN
    CLRSCR;
    WRITE(' Enter the student''s first name: ');
    READLN(fname);
    WRITE(' Enter the student''s last name: ');
    READLN(lname);
```

```
    WRITE(' Enter the student''s current GPA: ');
    READLN(GPA);
    END;

PROCEDURE studentrec.SendHonorsLetter;
    VAR
        letterfile: TEXT;
        counter   : INTEGER;
    BEGIN
        ASSIGN(letterfile, 'prn');
        REWRITE(letterfile);
        FOR counter := 1 TO 10 DO WRITELN(letterfile);
        WRITELN(letterfile, 'Dear Mr./Ms. ', lname, ':');
        WRITELN(letterfile);
        WRITELN(letterfile, 'Your grade point average is over 3.5. This');
        WRITELN(letterfile, 'means that you will graduate cum laude from');
        WRITELN(letterfile, 'this institution. Congratulations.');
        WRITELN(letterfile);
        WRITELN(letterfile, 'Sincerely,');
        WRITELN(letterfile);
        WRITELN(letterfile, 'V. Wormer');
        WRITELN(letterfile, 'Dean of Students');
        WRITELN(letterfile, formfeed);
      close(letterfile)
    END;

PROCEDURE studentrec.DisplayNameAndGPA;
    BEGIN
    CLRSCR;
    WRITELN(' The student''s name is: ', fname, space, lname, '.');
    WRITELN(' The student''s GPA is:  ', GPA:0:2, '.');
    IF GPA > 3.5  THEN SendHonorsLetter;
    END;

END.
```

Once you have keyed in Listing 20.3, save it as MY_OBJS.PAS. Go into Turbo Pascal's Compile menu and set the Destination option to "Disk." Then, compile the unit and copy the compiled .TPU file to your Turbo Pascal program directory (probably C:\BP\BIN or C:\BP\UNITS). Finally, go back into the Compile menu and set the Destination option back to "Memory."

You can see in Listing 20.3 that, from the standpoint of creating a unit, there is nothing unusual about setting up a unit with object types. The object type definition itself goes in the INTERFACE section of the unit, while the details of the methods go in the IMPLEMENTATION section, just as you would expect.

The trick comes in Listing 20.4, a program that uses the object type and method definitions in the unit. In this program, we create a *GradStudentRec* object type that is a descendant of the *StudentRec* object type. To do this, we simply include the identifier *StudentRec* in parentheses after the word OBJECT in the object type definition.

Listing 20.4

```
PROGRAM Listing20_4;

  { Shows how the creation of descendant object types saves
    considerable programming work. Principal features shown:

  INHERITANCE, whereby an object type automatically includes
                 fields and methods from its ancestor types; and

  OVERRIDING, whereby an object type can (but does not have to)
                 replace methods from ancestor types with more ap-
                 propriate methods for itself. }

USES CRT, MyUtils, my_objs;

TYPE
    gradstudentrec = OBJECT (studentrec)
                    PhDcandidate : BOOLEAN;
                    PROCEDURE init;
                    PROCEDURE FillRecord;
                    PROCEDURE SendHonorsLetter;
                    END;

PROCEDURE gradstudentrec.init;
    BEGIN
    CLRSCR;
    studentrec.init;
    PhDcandidate := FALSE;
    WRITELN(' The PhDcandidate field has been initialized to false.');
    pause
```

```
    END;

PROCEDURE gradstudentrec.fillrecord;
    VAR candidate : CHAR;
    BEGIN
    studentrec.fillrecord;
    WRITE(' Is the student a Ph.D. candidate (Y/N)? ');
    READLN(candidate);
    IF UPCASE(candidate) = 'Y'
        THEN PhDcandidate := TRUE
        ELSE PhDcandidate := FALSE
    END;

PROCEDURE gradstudentrec.SendHonorsLetter;
    VAR
        letterfile: TEXT;
        counter   : INTEGER;
    BEGIN
        ASSIGN(letterfile, 'prn');
        REWRITE(letterfile);
        FOR counter := 1 TO 10 DO WRITELN(letterfile);
        WRITELN(letterfile, 'Dear Mr./Ms. ', lname, ':');
        WRITELN(letterfile);
        WRITELN(letterfile, 'Your grade point average is over 3.5. This');
        WRITELN(letterfile, 'means that you will receive your Ph.D. "with');
        WRITELN(letterfile, 'distinction" from this institution.');
        WRITELN(letterfile, 'Congratulations.');
        WRITELN(letterfile);
        WRITELN(letterfile, 'Sincerely,');
        WRITELN(letterfile);
        WRITELN(letterfile, 'V. Wormer');
        WRITELN(letterfile, 'Dean of Students');
        WRITELN(letterfile, formfeed);
        CLOSE(letterfile)
    END;

VAR
    gradstudent : gradstudentrec;

BEGIN
    gradstudent.init;
    gradstudent.fillrecord;
    gradstudent.displaynameandGPA;
```

```
    pause
END.
```

Notice that we declared three methods in the *GradStudentRec* object type: *Init, Fill-Record*, and *SendHonorsLetter*. Because these methods have the same names as methods in their ancestor type, they *override* the methods from the ancestor type. If we create a variable of type *GradStudentRec* and send it a message to initialize itself, it will use its own *Init* routine; likewise for the other methods.

The *DisplayNameAndGPA* method did not have to be changed, so we did not have to declare it in *GradStudentRec* at all. Because it is part of the *StudentRec* object type, it is inherited by the *GradStudentRec* object type.

Another trick demonstrated by Listing 20.4 is that in an object type's methods, you can make explicit calls to the methods of ancestor types by using the dot notation with the name of the ancestor type. In the *GradStudentRec.Init* method, for example, there is no need to repeat the code that gets the student name and GPA, because this code is part of the ancestor type *StudentRec*. Instead, we simply include an explicit call to *StudentRec*'s *Init* routine *inside* the *GradStudentRec*'s *Init* routine. When this line of code is reached, *StudentRec.init* executes just like any other subroutine. The rest of the *GradStudentRec.init* routine then gets the information that is unique to the *GradStudentRec* type. The same trick is used in the *GradStudentRec.fillrecord* method.

In summary, to override a method from an ancestor object type, you simply declare a new method in the descendant object type with *the same name* as the method in the ancestor type. To add a new method or field, as we did with the *PhDCandidate* field in the *GradStudentRec* type, simply add it to the descendant type declaration.

Note one very important point: only *methods* can be overridden, *not* data fields. The data fields of an ancestor type are an ineradicable part of all its descendant types, and they cannot be changed. If you have some descendant types that will need a certain field and others that will not need it, you should simply leave that field out of the ancestor type.

Once you have keyed in Listing 20.4, compile and run it. You will see that, as advertised, the *GradStudentRec* methods collect the information and process it as needed—that is, with one exception.

Virtual Methods and Polymorphism

The exception is the *GradStudentRec.SendHonorsLetter* method, which does not seem to execute at all. Instead, we get the letter from the ancestor *StudentRec* object type! Something is clearly going wrong.

The problem is that the *DisplayNameAndGPA* method, which calls the *SendHonorsLetter* method, is *inherited* from the ancestor object type. When the program is compiled, the *DisplayNameAndGPA* method is given the memory address of the *SendHonorsLetter* method that it should use. Because the copy of *DisplayNameAndGPA* we are using is part of the *StudentRec* object type, it naturally uses the *SendHonorsLetter* method that is *also* part of the *StudentRec* object type. Because everything is determined at compile time, this is called an example of *early binding:* the method call is *bound* to a certain copy of the *SendHonorsLetter* method when the program is compiled, and this cannot be changed later on when the program is run. Methods that are bound at compile time are called *static methods* because they cannot be changed after compilation.

The obvious solution to the problem is to put a new method declaration for *DisplayNameAndGPA* into the *GradStudentRec* object type. Then, when the program is compiled, this method is part of the *GradStudentRec* type, so it is bound to the appropriate copy of the *SendHonorsLetter* method. This solution is demonstrated in Listing 20.5.

Listing 20.5

```
PROGRAM Listing20_5;

   { Shows a static-method solution to the problem of the inherited
     "DisplayNameAndGPA" method calling the ancestor object type's
     "SendHonorsLetter" routine instead of the current object type's
     "SendHonorsLetter" routine. This approach requires more code
     than the virtual method solution in Listings 20.6 and 20.7. }

USES CRT, MyUtils, my_objs;

TYPE
   gradstudentreс = OBJECT (studentrec)
                    PhDcandidate : BOOLEAN;
                    PROCEDURE init;
                    PROCEDURE FillRecord;
```

```
                    PROCEDURE SendHonorsLetter;
                    PROCEDURE DisplayNameAndGPA;
                    END;

PROCEDURE gradstudentrec.init;
   BEGIN
   CLRSCR;
   studentrec.init;
   PhDcandidate := FALSE;
   WRITELN(' The PhDcandidate field has been initialized to false.');
   pause
   END;

PROCEDURE gradstudentrec.fillrecord;
   VAR candidate : CHAR;
   BEGIN
   studentrec.fillrecord;
   WRITE(' Is the student a Ph.D. candidate (Y/N)? ');
   READLN(candidate);
   IF UPCASE(candidate) = 'Y'
      THEN PhDcandidate := TRUE
      ELSE PhDcandidate := FALSE
   END;

PROCEDURE gradstudentrec.SendHonorsLetter;
   VAR
      letterfile: TEXT;
      counter   : INTEGER;
   BEGIN
      ASSIGN(letterfile, 'prn');
      REWRITE(letterfile);
      FOR counter := 1 TO 10 DO WRITELN(letterfile);
      WRITELN(letterfile, 'Dear Mr./Ms. ', lname, ':');
      WRITELN(letterfile);
      WRITELN(letterfile, 'Your grade point average is over 3.5. This');
      WRITELN(letterfile, 'means that you will receive your Ph.D. "with');
      WRITELN(letterfile, 'distinction" from this institution.');
      WRITELN(letterfile, 'Congratulations.');
      WRITELN(letterfile);
      WRITELN(letterfile, 'Sincerely,');
      WRITELN(letterfile);
      WRITELN(letterfile, 'V. Wormer');
      WRITELN(letterfile, 'Dean of Students');
```

```
      WRITELN(letterfile, formfeed);
      CLOSE(letterfile)
   END;

PROCEDURE gradstudentrec.DisplayNameAndGPA;
   BEGIN
   CLRSCR;
   WRITELN(' The student''s name is: ', fname, space, lname, '.');
   WRITELN(' The student''s GPA is:  ', GPA:0:2, '.');
   IF GPA > 3.5 THEN SendHonorsLetter;
   END;

VAR
   gradstudent : gradstudentrec;

BEGIN
   gradstudent.init;
   gradstudent.FillRecord;
   gradstudent.DisplayNameAndGPA;
   pause
END.
```

This approach will work: if you run the program in Listing 20.5, you will see that the correct copy of the *SendHonorsLetter* method is being used. Notice, however, that apart from the fact that it is in the *GradStudentRec* object declaration, there is *no difference* between the *DisplayNameAndGPA* routine in Listing 20.5 and the corresponding routine in the ancestor *StudentRec* type. This means we are writing the same code all over again.

One of the advantages of object-oriented programming was *supposed* to be that it reduces the amount of code we have to write. If we have to keep rewriting the same methods in each descendant object type just to make sure that they are bound to the appropriate copies of other methods, then it would seem that we should sue somebody for false advertising: interesting as it is, object-oriented programming would not be making good on its promises.

However, there is a better solution than repeating the same method code in each descendant type (or suing somebody): using *virtual methods*, which are not bound at compile time. Declaring a method as *virtual* tells Turbo Pascal that it is unknown at compile time *which* copy of the method will need to be used, and that this decision should be put off until the program is actually run—an approach called *late binding*. This powerful approach also enables an object and its methods to be *polymorphic*— that is, to respond to the same messages in different ways. Polymorphism is one of the most useful features of objects. When an object gets a message to *DisplayNameAndGPA*, it first checks to see which sort of object it is, and therefore, which version of *SendHonorsLetter* to call.

To declare a method as a virtual method, we add the Turbo Pascal reserved word VIRTUAL at the end of the method header in the object type definition. Listing 20.6 shows how we can change the MY_OBJS unit so that it causes *SendHonorsLetter* to become a virtual method.

Listing 20.6

```
UNIT my_objs2;  { Listing20.6 }

   { Changes the unit in Listing 21.3 to make SendHonorsLetter
     a virtual method instead of a static method. Principal
     features illustrated:

        VIRTUAL METHODS, whereby a program can choose at run-time
                        which method should be executed, and
        A CONSTRUCTOR routine, which is absolutely required in any
                        object type that uses virtual methods. An object
                        variable's constructor MUST be called to set up
                        the VMT before any calls are made to the object's
                        other methods. }

INTERFACE

USES CRT, MyUtils;

CONST
   formfeed = #12;

TYPE
   string15 = STRING[15];
   studentrec = OBJECT
                fname,
                lname : string15;
                GPA           : REAL;
                CONSTRUCTOR init;
                PROCEDURE fillrecord;
                PROCEDURE SendHonorsLetter; VIRTUAL;
```

```
            PROCEDURE DisplayNameAndGPA;
            END;

IMPLEMENTATION

CONSTRUCTOR studentrec.init;
   BEGIN
   fname      := space;
   lname      := space;
   GPA        := 0.00
   END;

PROCEDURE studentrec.FillRecord;
   BEGIN
   CLRSCR;
   WRITE(' Enter the student''s first name: ');
   READLN(fname);
   WRITE(' Enter the student''s last name: ');
   READLN(lname);
   WRITE(' Enter the student''s current GPA: ');
   READLN(GPA);
   END;

PROCEDURE studentrec.SendHonorsLetter;
   VAR
     letterfile: text;
     counter   : integer;
   BEGIN
     assign(letterfile, 'prn');
     rewrite(letterfile);
     for counter := 1 to 10 do WRITELN(letterfile);
     WRITELN(letterfile, 'Dear Mr./Ms. ', lname, ':');
     WRITELN(letterfile);
     WRITELN(letterfile, 'Your grade point average is over 3.5. This');
     WRITELN(letterfile, 'means that you will graduate cum laude from');
     WRITELN(letterfile, 'this institution. Congratulations.');
     WRITELN(letterfile);
     WRITELN(letterfile, 'Sincerely,');
     WRITELN(letterfile);
     WRITELN(letterfile, 'V. Wormer');
     WRITELN(letterfile, 'Dean of Students');
     WRITELN(letterfile, formfeed);
```

```
      close(letterfile)
   END;

PROCEDURE studentrec.DisplayNameAndGPA;
   BEGIN
   clrscr;
   WRITELN(' The student''s name is: ', fname, space, lname, '.');
   WRITELN(' The student''s GPA is:  ', GPA:0:2, '.');
   IF GPA > 3.5 THEN SendHonorsLetter;
   END;

END.
```

Notice that there are two key differences between Listing 20.6 and Listing 20.3. First, of course, we have added the word VIRTUAL after the *SendHonorsLetter* method in the object type definition. Second—and this is vitally important—we have a new name for the *Init* routine: instead of being called a procedure, it is now called a CONSTRUCTOR.

Let's review the situation to see why this is so important. When the program is compiled, any calls to static (nonvirtual) methods are given the memory addresses where those methods can be found—an instance of early binding. With virtual methods, however, it is not known at compile time *which* virtual method will be needed by a particular method call: the method call is *not* given the memory address of a virtual method because it is not known which address (that is, the address of which method) will be needed. This means that when the program is compiled, these method calls *do not know where to find* the virtual methods that they are supposed to call. When the program finally is run, we need a way to tell these method calls where to find the methods that they need.

This task is performed by the CONSTRUCTOR routine. When the program is run, an object variable's CONSTRUCTOR routine must be called before any calls are made to the object's virtual methods. The CONSTRUCTOR routine sets up a virtual method table (VMT) that tells the program where to find the object variable's virtual methods. Note that if you fail to put in a call to the CONSTRUCTOR routine before calling a virtual method, your program will crash.

The good news is that all this work is done simply by including the word CONSTRUCTOR. As long as you call a routine designated as an object's constructor, the VMT will be set up automatically. This means that, even though the *studentrec.init* routine in Listing 20.6 does some other work as well, you could have a CON-STRUCTOR routine that did nothing except set up the VMT, as in

```
CONSTRUCTOR AnotherInitMethod;
    BEGIN
    END;
```

A call to this routine will set up the VMT and make it possible for the object variable to use virtual methods, even though it does not do anything else. It's simply the word CONSTRUCTOR that is important in setting up the VMT.

It is so important that it must be repeated: *every* object variable that uses virtual methods *must* have a CONSTRUCTOR method and the program *must* call that method before attempting to use any of the object variable's virtual methods. Failure to abide by this rule can result in disaster.

Now, let's recode the program from Listing 20.5 and make the *SendHonorsLetter* method a virtual method. First, save Listing 20.6 as MY_OBJS2 and compile it to disk. Copy the MY_OBJS2.TPU file to your Turbo Pascal program directory (probably C:\BP\BIN or C:BP\UNITS). Then, key in the program in Listing 20.7. Do not forget to change the compilation destination back to disk, and be sure that you name MY_OBJS2, not MY_OBJS, in the USES clause of Listing 20.7.

Listing 20.7

```
PROGRAM Listing20_7;

    { Changes the program in Listing 21.5 by using virtual methods
      to eliminate the redundant code in the program. Principal
      features demonstrated:

        VIRTUAL METHODS, whereby a program can choose at run-time
                         which method should be executed, and
        A CONSTRUCTOR routine, which is absolutely required in any
                         object type that uses virtual methods. An object
                         variable's constructor MUST be called to set up
                         the VMT before any calls are made to the object's
                         other methods. }




USES CRT, MyUtils, my_objs2;
```

```
TYPE
   gradstudentrec = OBJECT (studentrec)
                     PhDcandidate : BOOLEAN;
                     CONSTRUCTOR init;
                     PROCEDURE FillRecord;
                     PROCEDURE SendHonorsLetter; VIRTUAL;
                     END;

CONSTRUCTOR gradstudentrec.init;
   BEGIN
   CLRSCR;
   studentrec.init;
   PhDcandidate := FALSE;
   WRITELN(' The PhDcandidate field has been initialized to false.');
   pause
   END;

PROCEDURE gradstudentrec.FillRecord;
   VAR candidate : CHAR;
   BEGIN
   studentrec.FillRecord;
   WRITE(' Is the student a Ph.D. candidate (Y/N)? ');
   READLN(candidate);
   IF UPCASE(candidate) = 'Y'
      THEN PhDcandidate := TRUE
      ELSE PhDcandidate := FALSE
   END;

PROCEDURE gradstudentrec.SendHonorsLetter;
   VAR
      letterfile: TEXT;
      counter   : INTEGER;
   BEGIN
      ASSIGN(letterfile, 'prn');
      REWRITE(letterfile);
      FOR counter := 1 TO 10 DO WRITELN(letterfile);
      WRITELN(letterfile, 'Dear Mr./Ms. ', lname, ':');
      WRITELN(letterfile);
      WRITELN(letterfile, 'Your grade point average is over 3.5. This');
      WRITELN(letterfile, 'means that you will receive your Ph.D. "with');
      WRITELN(letterfile, 'distinction" from this institution.');
      WRITELN(letterfile, 'Congratulations.');
      WRITELN(letterfile);
      WRITELN(letterfile, 'Sincerely,');
      WRITELN(letterfile);
```

```
    WRITELN(letterfile, 'V. Wormer');
    WRITELN(letterfile, 'Dean of Students');
    WRITELN(letterfile, formfeed);
    CLOSE(letterfile)
  END;

VAR
  gradstudent : gradstudentrec;

BEGIN
  gradstudent.init;
  gradstudent.FillRecord;
  gradstudent.DisplayNameAndGPA;
  pause
END.
```

In Listing 20.7, we declare the *Init* method as a CONSTRUCTOR method and make *SendHonorsLetter* into a virtual method. Now, because *SendHonorsLetter* is virtual (in both the *studentrec* and *gradstudentrec* object types), its memory address is not bound to the method call in *DisplayNameAndGPA* when the program is compiled. The decision on which version of *SendHonorsLetter* to use is put off until the program is run. When a call is actually made to *SendHonorsLetter* during a program run, the program first checks to see what type of object is making the method call. It then calls the correct *SendHonorsLetter* method for that object type. In the case of Listing 20.7, *SendHonorsLetter* is being called by a *gradstudentrec*-type object, so it gets the version of *SendHonorsLetter* from the *gradstudentrec* object declaration.

By using virtual methods, we can avoid repeating code in descendant object types. Object-oriented programming has made good on its promise to reduce the amount of code we must write.

An Object-Oriented Stack

As one more illustration, let's look at an object-oriented version of a stack. As you may recall, a stack is a list in which all additions and deletions are made at one end of the list. In Chapter 17, we implemented stacks as both arrays and linked lists by using standard structured programming techniques. Here, we will create an array-based stack with object-oriented techniques: the corresponding listing in Chapter 17 is Listing 17.1.

Listing 20.8

```
PROGRAM Listing20_8;

   { Demonstrates an object-oriented implementation of a stack.
     As in Chapter 17, the program prompts the user to enter
     enough characters to fill up the stack, then pops them off
     the stack in reverse order. Note the key difference between
     this stack and the one in Listing 17.1: while the stack in
     Listing 17.1 was a passive array structure on which some
     procedures operate, this stack is an active data structure
     that includes methods so that it can perform the same stack
     operations on itself. Instead of calling a procedure to do
     something to the stack, as in 17.1, we send a message to the
     stack instructing it to do something on its own. }

USES CRT, MyUtils;

CONST
   Max = 5;

TYPE
   { GENERIC LIST OBJECT TYPE }
   { The list type is an abstract object type. This means that
     we never intend to create any variables of the list type
     itself. The list type is created solely as an ancestor type
     for other list object types, such as stacks and queues. We
     will actually create variables of these descendant types.
     Here, we demonstrate a stack object that is a descendant
     of the abstract list type. }
   list = OBJECT
           listitem  : array[1..Max] OF CHAR;
           count     : 0..Max;
           PROCEDURE init;
           FUNCTION full     : BOOLEAN;
           FUNCTION empty    : BOOLEAN;
           END;

   { STACK OBJECT TYPE }
   stack = OBJECT (list)
               { Because the top of the stack will always be
                 the same as the "count" field inherited from
                 the list object type, there is no need for a
                 separate stacktop field. }
               PROCEDURE push(item : CHAR);
```

```
            PROCEDURE pop(VAR item : CHAR);
            END;

{ ----------------------------------------------------------- }
{               METHODS FOR THE LIST OBJECT TYPE              }
{ ----------------------------------------------------------- }
PROCEDURE list.init;
   VAR
      counter : INTEGER;
   BEGIN
      CLRSCR;
      FOR counter := 1 TO max DO
         listitem[counter] := space;
      count := 0
   END;

FUNCTION list.full : BOOLEAN;
   BEGIN
      IF count = max
         THEN full := TRUE
         ELSE full := FALSE
   END;

FUNCTION list.empty : BOOLEAN;
   BEGIN
   Empty := (count = 0)
   END;


{ ----------------------------------------------------------- }
{              METHODS FOR THE STACK OBJECT TYPE              }
{ ----------------------------------------------------------- }
PROCEDURE stack.push(item : CHAR);
   BEGIN
      IF full    { test FOR full stack }
      THEN BEGIN
           WRITELN(' Sorry, full stack!');
           exit
           END
      ELSE BEGIN
           count := count + 1;
           listitem[count] := item
```

```
            END
     END;

PROCEDURE stack.pop(VAR item : CHAR);
     BEGIN
        IF empty
        THEN BEGIN
             WRITELN(' Sorry, stack is empty!');
             exit
             END
        ELSE BEGIN
             item := listitem[count];
             listitem[count] := space;
             count := count - 1
             END
     END;

{ ------------------------------------------------------------- }
{                 VARIABLE DECLARATION SECTION                  }
{ ------------------------------------------------------------- }
VAR
    charlist : stack;

{ ------------------------------------------------------------- }
{  NON-OBJECT PROCEDURES TO DISPLAY RESULTS ON THE PC'S SCREEN  }
{ ------------------------------------------------------------- }
PROCEDURE PushItemsOnStack(VAR charlist : stack);
     VAR
        newitem : CHAR;
        counter : INTEGER;
     BEGIN
        FOR counter := 1 TO max DO
           BEGIN
           WRITE(' Enter a character to push onto the stack: ');
           READLN(newitem);
           charlist.push(newitem);
           WRITELN
           END
     END;

PROCEDURE PopItemsOffStack(VAR charlist: stack);
     VAR
        counter : INTEGER;
        item    : CHAR;
     BEGIN
```

```
      CLRSCR;
      WRITELN(' The stack items are popped off in reverse order');
      WRITELN(' because a stack is a last-in-first-out list.');
      WRITELN;
      WRITE(' Items popped from the stack: ');
      FOR counter := 1 TO max DO
         BEGIN
         delay(700);
         charlist.pop(item);
         WRITE(item, space)
         END
   END;

{ ------------------------------------------------------------- }
{                   MAIN BODY OF THE PROGRAM                    }
{ ------------------------------------------------------------- }
BEGIN
   charlist.init;
   PushItemsOnStack(charlist);
   PopItemsOffStack(charlist);
   pause
END.
```

We first create a generic ("abstract") object type that can serve as an ancestor type for both stacks and queues: we call this abstract type *list*. This type contains the data fields and methods that will be common to all the *list* object types that we plan to create. Having created this ancestor type, all we need to add when we declare the stack object type are methods to push items onto the stack and to pop items off of the stack.

Note that the methods for pushing and popping have to take only a single parameter: the character that is being pushed or popped. It is not necessary to include the stack object as a parameter because, as discussed earlier, the push and pop routines are *part of* the stack object, not external to it. When a call is made to an object's push or pop methods, it automatically knows that it is supposed to do a push or pop on its own *listitem* data field.

As in Listing 17.1, we also include routines to prompt the user for input and then display the results on the computer screen. These routines *are* external to the stack object and, therefore, the object is passed to them as a parameter.

The rest of the stack operations go pretty much as expected. We first tell the stack object *charlist* to initialize itself. Then, we call the *PushItemsOnStack* and *PopItemsOffStack* routines to get input and display it. These routines, in turn, instruct the stack object to push items onto its *listitem* data field and pop them off.

Dynamic Object Variables and Pointers

Although the procedures are a little more complicated, objects can be used with pointers just like any other variables:

```
TYPE
    studentrecptr = ^studentrec;
    studentrec = OBJECT
                    { object fields and methods }
                    END;
VAR
    student : studentrecptr;
BEGIN
    New(student);
    { ... other program statements }
END.
```

With objects, Turbo Pascal extends the *New* procedure so that you can create a dynamic object variable and initialize it in a single step. You can still do things the traditional way, as in

```
New(student);
student.init;
```

but you can also include the initialization method in the call to the *New* procedure, as in

```
New(student, init);
```

In Borland Pascal and Turbo Pascal 7, you can also use *New* as a function as well as a procedure. If *ThisPtr* is a pointer variable of the same type as *ThatPtr*, you can create a dynamic variable, initialize it, and assign it to *Thisptr* as follows:

```
ThisPtr := New(ThatPtr, Init);
```

Turbo Pascal also extends the *Dispose* procedure to do extra work in handling object variables. Because objects are more complicated than other data types, you can now include a shutdown routine called a *Destructor* in your object type definition to handle any special cleanup chores that are needed. The *Dispose* procedure can now call this *destructor* method at the same time as it deallocates a dynamic object variable. If your *destructor* method is called *done*, then it would be written as:

```
Dispose(student, done)
```

CHAPTER TWENTY-ONE

Introducing Turbo Vision

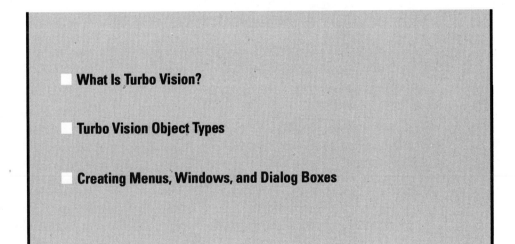

- **What Is Turbo Vision?**

- **Turbo Vision Object Types**

- **Creating Menus, Windows, and Dialog Boxes**

What Is Turbo Vision?

Turbo Vision is the remarkable library of object types included with Borland Pascal and Turbo Pascal 7. By using Turbo Vision, you can incorporate pull-down menus, dialog boxes, mouse support, and a host of other sophisticated features into your applications—all without having to write the code yourself! It's all prepackaged in the Turbo Vision units.

Once you learn to use Turbo Vision, your own programs can have the same professional and easy-to-use screen interface as Turbo Pascal itself. However, learning Turbo Vision is somewhat difficult. Turbo Vision is essentially a specialized I/O (input-output) programming language built on top of Turbo Pascal. This means that the normal Pascal I/O commands you have learned up to now, such as WRITELN, often cannot be used in Turbo Vision programs.

In their place, you will learn completely new ways to display text and get user input through menus, dialog boxes, and windows. Some of these new methods are quite intricate.

Consequently, learning Turbo Vision will require effort and determination on your part—but such effort will produce an equally tremendous benefit at the end. In this chapter, we will be able to introduce only some of the most basic features of Turbo Vision, but they will be enough to get you started. To acquire a fuller understanding of Turbo Vision, you should consult your Turbo Pascal Turbo Vision manual.

Turbo Vision programming requires a solid grasp of both (1) object-oriented programming concepts and (2) operations with pointers and dynamic allocation. If you feel at all insecure about either of these topics, you should review Chapters 11 and 20 before going ahead with this chapter.

There's one other benefit you'll get from Turbo Vision. Writing Turbo Vision programs, you'll use many of the same ideas and techniques used in programming for Microsoft Windows. When and if you decide to write Windows programs— whether with Turbo Pascal for Windows or some other tool—you'll already know many "tricks of the trade."

Structure of Turbo Vision

Turbo Vision is a library of object types that can handle most tasks involved in getting input from the user and displaying output on the screen. Aspects of your program that do not involve I/O tasks can be handled the same way as before: for example, sorting an array or searching through a linked list. Turbo Vision makes changes primarily in the way your program interacts with the user.

The biggest conceptual change in Turbo Vision is that it causes your programs to be *event-driven*. In our previous program examples, we set up menus and prompts that allowed the user to make choices in the program. Our programs were prepared to accept certain kinds of input at certain times, and would not accept such input at any other times. This meant, for instance, that the user could not merely press the *Escape* key at any time to back out of a program task. Instead, he or she had to wait for an appropriate on-screen prompt.

Turbo Vision, however, allows programs to accept and use input in a more flexible way, called "event-driven." An event can be a key press, a mouse click, a request for context-sensitive help, or a message from one part of a program to another. The advantage of this approach is that it does not limit the user to a specific set of menu choices: a Turbo Vision program is ready to perform a wide variety of tasks depending on the event that it detects, and its object types use a special method, *Handle-Event*, to do this.

Basic Turbo Vision Object Types

Turbo Vision is a hierarchy of object types, all of which are descended from a single ancestor object type. Turbo Vision object types divide neatly into two categories: those that are *views* and those that are not views.

A view is anything in the program that can be displayed on the screen. Views are descended from the *TView* object type and include menus, dialog boxes, windows, scroll bars, and text elements. Because Turbo Vision operates in character mode instead of in graphics mode, its views are all rectangular and can draw or redraw themselves very quickly on the screen. Because Turbo Vision views are objects, they have built-in methods that enable them to handle any tasks that come their way.

It is important to remember that in a Turbo Vision program, *only* views are allowed to display anything on the screen. If you try to display text with a WRITELN statement, for example, you will obliterate part of the Turbo Vision screen display, perhaps overwriting a dialog box or part of a window.

Like many Turbo Vision object types, the *TView* object type is very complex, but you can learn its basic features in a fairly short time. Any view must be able to initialize itself, draw itself on the screen, change size or position on the screen if needed, and shut itself down when its work is finished. Turbo Vision view types are shown in Figure 21.1. Ancestor objects are toward the left of the figure, and descendants are connected with their ancestors by horizontal lines.

Turbo Vision object types that are not views are the *TCollection*, *TStream*, *TResource-File*, *TStringList*, and *TStrListMaker* types: these perform a variety of tasks in the background to support view objects.

Creating Pull-Down Menus

The best way to learn Turbo Vision is to jump right in and examine a Turbo Vision program. Listing 21.1 shows how to set up the Turbo Vision desktop, create a status line at the bottom of the screen, and create a menu bar with pull-down menus at the top of the screen.

Listing 21.1

```
PROGRAM Listing21_1;

    { Demonstrates how to set up menus and a status line in
      a Turbo Vision program. Note, however, that none of the
      menu options is implemented yet. The only thing you can
      do at this stage is to exit from the program with Alt-X. }

USES OBJECTS, DRIVERS, VIEWS, MENUS, APP;

CONST
    cmNewWindow = 101;

TYPE
    TMyApp = OBJECT (TApplication)
        PROCEDURE InitMenuBar; VIRTUAL;
```

FIGURE 21.1:

Turbo Vision view types

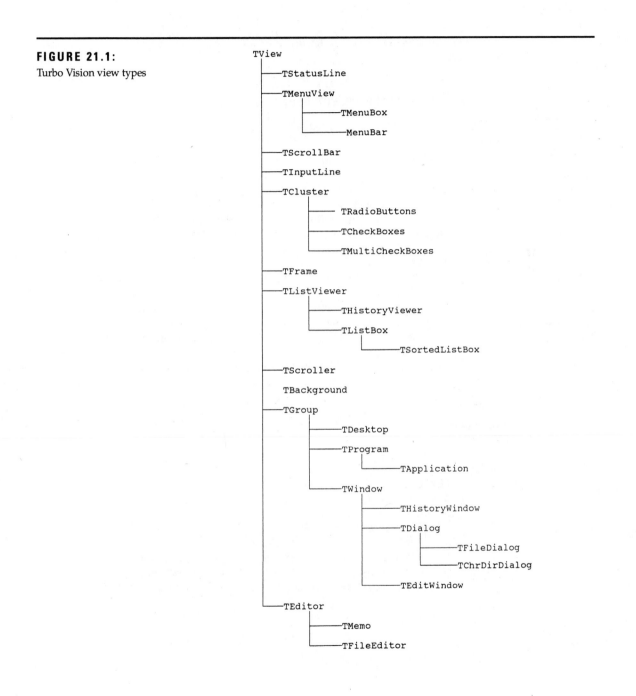

```
    PROCEDURE InitStatusLine; VIRTUAL;
    END;


{ -------------------------------- }
{ METHODS FOR TMYAPP OBJECT TYPE   }
{ -------------------------------- }
PROCEDURE TMyApp.InitMenuBar;
    VAR
        r: TRect;
    BEGIN
        GetExtent(r);
        r.b.y := r.a.y + 1;
        MenuBar := New(PMenuBar, Init(r, NewMenu(
            NewSubMenu('~F~ile', hcNoContext, NewMenu(
                NewItem('~N~ew', 'F4', kbF4, cmNewWindow, hcNoContext,
                NewLine(
                NewItem('Ex~it', 'Alt-X', kbAltX, cmQuit, hcNoContext,
                NIL)))),
            NewSubMenu('~W~indow', hcNoContext, NewMenu(
                NewItem('~N~ext', 'F6', kbF6, cmNext, hcNoContext,
                NewItem('~Zoom', 'F5', kbF5, cmZoom, hcNoContext,
                NIL))),
            NIL))
        )));
    END;


PROCEDURE TMyApp.InitStatusLine;
    VAR
        r: TRect;
    BEGIN
        GetExtent(r);
        r.a.y := r.b.y - 1;
        StatusLine := New(PStatusLine, Init(r,
            NewStatusDef(0, $FFFF,
                NewStatusKey('', kbF10, cmMenu,
                NewStatusKey('~Alt-X~ Exit', kbAltX, cmQuit,
                NewStatusKey('~F4~ New', kbF4, cmNewWindow,
                NewStatusKey('~Alt-F3~ Close', kbAltF3, cmClose,
                NIL)))),
            NIL)
```

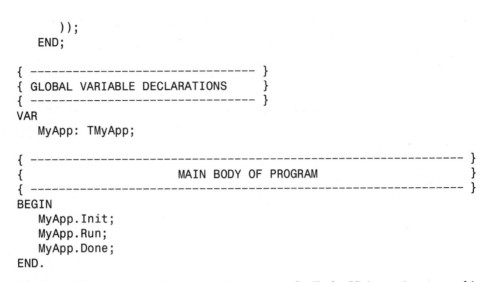

```
        ));
    END;

{ -------------------------------- }
{ GLOBAL VARIABLE DECLARATIONS     }
{ -------------------------------- }
VAR
    MyApp: TMyApp;

{ --------------------------------------------------------- }
{                     MAIN BODY OF PROGRAM                  }
{ --------------------------------------------------------- }
BEGIN
    MyApp.Init;
    MyApp.Run;
    MyApp.Done;
END.
```

The first thing we do in the program is to name the Turbo Vision units we need in the USES clause: in this case, we need object types from the Objects, Drivers, Views, Menus, and App units. We then declare a constant to serve as an intermediary between a menu option to open a window and the actual method in the window object that opens the window.

The only object type that we use in this program is *TMyApp*, which is a descendant of the *TApplication* object type. It has two methods, both of them virtual methods: first, a method to set up a menu bar, and second, a method to set up a status line.

Before we go into the details of setting up the menu bar and status line, however, let's take a quick look at the end of the listing. The main body of the program has three lines in it: *MyApp.Init*, *MyApp.Run*, and *MyApp.Done*. These are all methods that our variable *MyApp*, which is of the *TMyApp* object type, inherited from its ancestor *TApplication*. The point is that the ancestor object type's methods do a tremendous amount of behind-the-scenes work in setting up the Turbo Vision program—work that you as the programmer almost never have to worry about.

Now let's go back to look at *TMyApp.InitMenuBar*, which sets up the menu bar and pull-down menus for our Turbo Vision program. The first thing to ask is: what does a menu bar look like on the screen? Well, it's a rectangle one line high and 80 columns wide. To represent our menu bar on the screen, we declare a variable of type *TRect*, a view that comes from the Objects unit. A *TRect*-type variable is specified by giving the screen coordinates of its upper-left corner (denoted by *a*) and its lower-right corner (denoted by *b*).

When we call the *TView.GetExtent* method, it sets the *TRect* object to include all of the current view: here, the whole Turbo Vision screen. To reduce its height to a single line at the top of the screen, we then reset its *b.y* coordinate (the height of the lower-right corner) so that it is just one line below the *a.y* coordinate (the upper-left corner). This gives us a rectangle that is one line high, at the top of the screen, and extends from the left to the right edge of the screen.

So far, however, it's just a rectangle—not a menu bar. To turn it into a menu bar, we call the *MenuBar* method, and this is one of the places where Turbo Vision starts to get complicated.

Borland Pascal and Turbo Pascal 7 allow you to use the *New* procedure as a function—something that is unheard of in traditional Pascal programming. Remember also that Turbo Pascal allows you to initialize dynamic object variables in the same *New* command that creates them, as in *New(p,init(p))*.

Here, we use *New* as a function to create a dynamic menu bar object with *New(P-MenuBar* (where *PMenuBar* is a predefined pointer type in Turbo Vision) and use *Init(r,NewMenu(* to put the menu bar in the *TRect* variable we have created.

The *NewMenu* part of the call to *Init* is actually what sets up the pull-down menus attached to the menu bar. For each pull-down menu, we call the *NewSubMenu* method. The *NewSubMenu* method takes four parameters: the name of the menu, a constant that indicates the on-screen help (if any) available for this menu, a pointer to the first item in the menu, and a pointer to the next pull-down menu in the menu bar. Notice that *NewSubMenu*, *NewMenu*, and *NewItem* are all functions that return pointers to various menu objects.

In each call to *NewSubMenu* and *NewItem*, the name of the submenu or menu item is a string in single quotes. To highlight a letter in the string, you enclose it in tilde marks—for example, as in '~F~ile' for the File submenu. In each call to *NewItem*, you also use one of Turbo Vision's predefined key constants, such as *kbF4*, to specify that key as a speed key for the menu choice. The command constants, such as *cm-NewWindow*, generally, are not predefined in Turbo Vision and must be defined in your program. The *HcNoContext* in this example shows that we are not making on-screen help information available for these menu choices.

At the end of the method to define a menu bar, we have a bewildering sequence of parentheses and NILs: this is because we have nested menus and menu items several levels deep.

Creating the status line is similar to creating the menu bar. We first define a *TRect* variable and then put the status line into it. Using *PStatusLine*, a predefined Turbo Vision pointer to a status line object, we call *New* as a function to create a dynamic status line variable. The first two parameters, *0, $FFFF*, define help contexts and can be ignored in this example.

Each call to *NewStatusKey* displays a string (which can be an empty string) in the status line and binds a certain key or key combination to a certain command. In this case, *cmQuit* is a predefined Turbo Vision command; we must define the others, as we will do in the listings that follow this one. As before, we end up with a messy but unavoidable sequence of parentheses and NILs.

Until now, we have simply been defining the *TMyApp* object type. It inherits both fields and methods from its ancestor type *TApplication*, and we have added two new methods to set up a menu bar and a status line. We now declare *MyApp*, a variable of this object type, and call its methods in the main body of the program. The result is shown in Figure 21.2.

FIGURE 21.2:

Menu bar and status bar created by Listing 21.1

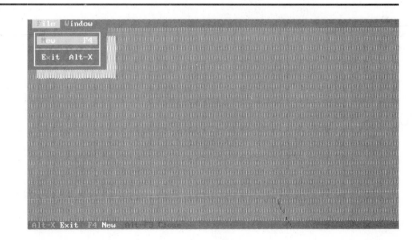

Creating Screen Windows

Now we will look at three main problems: first, how to bind specific commands to items in pull-down menus; second, how to create and open screen windows; and third, how to display text in those screen windows. These operations are illustrated in Listing 21.2. Because of the tremendous amount of detail, we will look only at the most important points in this listing, as we did with Listing 21.1.

Listing 21.2

```
PROGRAM Listing21_2;

   { Demonstrates how to set up commands, open screen windows,
     and display text in the screen windows. }

USES OBJECTS, DRIVERS, VIEWS, MENUS, APP;

CONST
   WinCount: INTEGER =   0;
   cmNewWindow       = 101;

TYPE
   TMyApp = OBJECT (TApplication)
      PROCEDURE HandleEvent(VAR Event: TEvent); virtual;
      PROCEDURE InitMenuBar; virtual;
      PROCEDURE InitStatusLine; virtual;
      PROCEDURE NewWindow;
      END;

   PDemoWindow = ^TDemoWindow;
   TDemoWindow = OBJECT (TWindow)
      CONSTRUCTOR Init(Bounds: TRect; WinTitle: STRING;
                       WindowNo: WORD);
      END;

   PInterior = ^TInterior;
   TInterior = OBJECT (TView)
      CONSTRUCTOR Init(VAR Bounds: TRect);
```

```
      PROCEDURE Draw; virtual;
      END;

{ ------------------------------ }
{ METHODS FOR TINTERIOR          }
{ ------------------------------ }
CONSTRUCTOR TInterior.Init(VAR Bounds: TRect);
   BEGIN
   TView.Init(Bounds);
   GrowMode := gfGrowHiX + gfGrowHiY;
   Options := Options or ofFramed;
   END;

PROCEDURE TInterior.Draw;
   CONST
      Greeting: STRING = 'Hello, new programmer!';
   BEGIN
   TView.Draw;
   WriteStr(4, 2, Greeting,$01);
   END;

{ ------------------------------ }
{ METHODS FOR TDEMOWINDOW        }
{ ------------------------------ }
CONSTRUCTOR TDemoWindow.Init(Bounds: TRect; WinTitle: STRING;
                             WindowNo: WORD);
   VAR
      S: STRING[3];
      Interior: PInterior;
   BEGIN
   Str(WindowNo, S);
   TWindow.Init(Bounds, WinTitle + ' ' + S, wnNoNumber);
   GetClipRect(Bounds);
   Bounds.Grow(-1,-1);
   Interior := New(PInterior, Init(Bounds));
   Insert(Interior);
   END;

{ ------------------------------ }
{ METHODS FOR TMYAPP             }
{ ------------------------------ }
PROCEDURE TMyApp.HandleEvent(VAR Event: TEvent);
   BEGIN
   TApplication.HandleEvent(Event);
   if Event.What = evCommand then
```

```
    BEGIN
    CASE Event.Command OF
        cmNewWindow: NewWindow;
        ELSE
        Exit;
        END;
    ClearEvent(Event);
    END
END;

PROCEDURE TMyApp.InitMenuBar;
    VAR
        r: TRect;
    BEGIN
        GetExtent(r);
        r.b.y := r.a.y + 1;
        MenuBar := New(PMenuBar, Init(r, NewMenu(
            NewSubMenu('~F~ile', hcNoContext, NewMenu(
                NewItem('~N~ew', 'F4', kbF4, cmNewWindow, hcNoContext,
                NewLine(
                NewItem('Ex~it', 'Alt-X', kbAltX, cmQuit, hcNoContext,
                NIL)))),
            NewSubMenu('~W~indow', hcNoContext, NewMenu(
                NewItem('~N~ext', 'F6', kbF6, cmNext, hcNoContext,
                NewItem('~Zo-om', 'F5', kbF5, cmZoom, hcNoContext,
                NIL))),
            NIL))
        )));
    END;

PROCEDURE TMyApp.InitStatusLine;
    VAR
        r: TRect;
    BEGIN
        GetExtent(r);
        r.a.y := r.b.y - 1;
        StatusLine := New(PStatusLine, Init(r,
            NewStatusDef(0, $FFFF,
                NewStatusKey('', kbF10, cmMenu,
                NewStatusKey('~Alt-X~ Exit', kbAltX, cmQuit,
                NewStatusKey('~F4~ New', kbF4, cmNewWindow,
                NewStatusKey('~Alt-F3~ Close', kbAltF3, cmClose,
                NIL)))),
```

```
         NIL)
      ));
   END;

PROCEDURE TMyApp.NewWindow;
   VAR
      Window : PDemoWindow;
      r      : TRect;
   BEGIN
   INC(WinCount);
   r.Assign(0, 0, 32, 7);
   RANDOMIZE;
   r.Move(RANDOM(47), RANDOM(16));
   Window := New(PDemoWindow, Init(r, 'Greeting Window', WinCount));
   DeskTop^.Insert(Window);
   END;


{ -------------------------------- }
{ GLOBAL VARIABLE DECLARATIONS     }
{ -------------------------------- }
VAR
   MyApp: TMyApp;


{ ------------------------------------------------------------------ }
{                  MAIN BODY OF THE PROGRAM                          }
{ ------------------------------------------------------------------ }
BEGIN
   MyApp.Init;
   MyApp.Run;
   MyApp.Done;
END.
```

The first thing you will notice is that we have added two new methods to our *TMy-App* object type: a *HandleEvent* method to get input from the user, and a *NewWindow* method to set up and initialize windows. We also declare a window object type as a descendant of *TWindow*, a predefined Turbo Vision type, and set up a pointer type to point to dynamic window variables.

Here's where you may need to do a quick mental reset. A window is just a frame: it can *contain* something, but it does not come with an interior as standard equipment. If we want something to be in the window, we have to define it ourselves. To that end, we define a *TInterior* object type that can draw itself inside of a window object. We also create a pointer type for this type.

TInterior's constructor method calls the *init* method of its ancestor, *TView*. Using predefined Turbo Vision constants, it also sets up the interior so it can grow, shrink, or move along with the window in which it finds itself.

TInterior's *Draw* method first calls *TView.Draw* to clear the interior of the window, then uses the Turbo Vision *WriteStr* method to display a greeting in the window.

The *TDemoWindow init* method sets up a pointer to connect the window (that is, the frame) with the interior of the window. It then inserts the interior into the frame.

TMyApp.HandleEvent sets up a CASE statement so that it tells the application object which method to execute if it receives a certain command constant: here, only one command constant is defined and it activates the *NewWindow* method.

The *TMyApp.NewWindow* method itself sets up a pointer to the new (dynamic) window object. It then calls the *Assign* method of the *TRect* object to set up a rectangle of a certain size—the size of the window we want. After initializing Turbo Pascal's random number generator, it selects a random location on the screen for the window's upper-left corner, creates a new window with a call to *New*, and displays the window on the screen with a call to the Turbo Vision *Desktop* object's *Insert* method.

The result of all this is shown in Figure 21.3.

FIGURE 21.3:

Creating screen windows in Turbo Vision

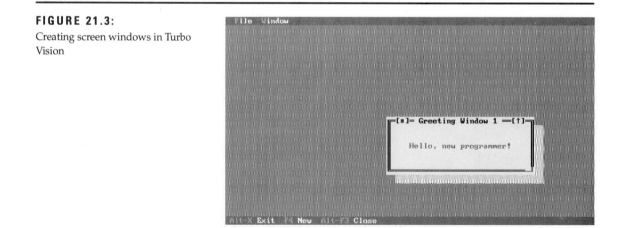

Adding Scroll Bars to Windows

Another thing we can do with screen window objects is to add scroll bars that allow us to move around in the window by using a mouse. Listing 21.3 illustrates how to modify the program in Listing 21.2 so that the on-screen windows have scroll bars. In addition, it displays a text file (Listing 21.3 itself) in the window so that you have enough text to scroll around in.

Listing 21.3

```
PROGRAM Listing21_3;

    { Demonstrates how to add scroll bars to a screen window and
        display a text file in the window. }

USES OBJECTS, DRIVERS, VIEWS, MENUS, APP;

CONST
    SourceFile        = 'list22_3.pas';
    MaxLines          = 200;
    WinCount: INTEGER =   0;
    cmNewWindow       = 101;

{ -------------------------------- }
{ GLOBAL VARIABLE DECLARATIONS     }
{ -------------------------------- }
VAR
    LineCount: INTEGER;
    Lines: ARRAY[O..MaxLines - 1] OF PString;


{ -------------------------------- }
{ OBJECT TYPE DECLARATIONS         }
{ -------------------------------- }
TYPE
    TMyApp = OBJECT  (TApplication)
        PROCEDURE HandleEvent(VAR Event: TEvent); VIRTUAL;
        PROCEDURE InitMenuBar; VIRTUAL;
        PROCEDURE InitStatusLine; VIRTUAL;
        PROCEDURE NewWindow;
    END;

    PInterior = ^TInterior;
    TInterior = OBJECT (TScroller)
```

```
        CONSTRUCTOR Init(VAR Bounds: TRect; AHScrollBar,
                        AVScrollBar: PScrollBar);
        PROCEDURE Draw; VIRTUAL;
        END;

    PDemoWindow = ^TDemoWindow;
    TDemoWindow = OBJECT (TWindow)
        CONSTRUCTOR Init(Bounds: TRect; WinTitle: STRING;
                                    WindowNo: Word);
        PROCEDURE MakeInterior(Bounds: TRect);
        END;

{ ---------------------------------------------------------- }
{ MISCELLANEOUS GLOBAL PROCEDURES NOT TIED TO OBJECT TYPES }
{ ---------------------------------------------------------- }
PROCEDURE ReadFile;
    VAR
        FileToRead: Text;
        LineString: STRING;
    BEGIN
        LineCount := 0;
        Assign(FileToRead, SourceFile);
        {$I-}
        Reset(FileToRead);
        {$I+}
        IF IOResult <> 0
            THEN BEGIN
                Writeln(SourceFile, ' not found.');
                Halt(1);
                END;
        WHILE NOT EOF(FileToRead) AND (LineCount < MaxLines) DO
                BEGIN
                READLN(FileToRead, LineString);
                Lines[LineCount] := NewStr(LineString);
                INC(LineCount);
                END;
        Close(FileToRead);
    END;  { of ReadFile procedure }

PROCEDURE DoneFile;
    VAR
        counter: INTEGER;
    BEGIN
        FOR counter := 0 TO LineCount - 1 DO
            IF Lines[counter] <> NIL
```

```
                THEN DisposeStr(Lines[counter]);
   END;

{ ------------------------------- }
{ METHODS FOR TINTERIOR OBJECT TYPE }
{ ------------------------------- }
CONSTRUCTOR TInterior.Init(VAR Bounds: TRect; AHScrollBar,
                                       AVScrollBar: PScrollBar);

   BEGIN
   TScroller.Init(Bounds, AHScrollBar, AVScrollBar);
   GrowMode := gfGrowHiX + gfGrowHiY;
   Options := Options or ofFramed;
   SetLimit(100, LineCount);
   END;

PROCEDURE TInterior.Draw;
   VAR
      Color: Byte;
      I, Y: INTEGER;
      b: TDrawBuffer;
   BEGIN
      Color := GetColor(1);
      for Y := 0 to Size.Y - 1 do
         BEGIN
         MoveChar(b, ' ', Color, Size.X);
         i := Delta.Y + Y;
         IF (I < LineCount) and (Lines[I] <> nil) THEN
         MoveStr(b, Copy(Lines[I]^, Delta.X + 1, Size.X), Color);
         WriteLine(0, Y, Size.X, 1, b);
         END
   END;

{ --------------------------------- }
{ METHODS FOR TDEMOWINDOW OBJECT TYPE }
{ --------------------------------- }
CONSTRUCTOR TDemoWindow.Init(Bounds: TRect; WinTitle: STRING;
                             WindowNo: Word);
   VAR
      NumString: STRING[3];
   BEGIN
   Str(WindowNo, NumString);
   TWindow.Init(Bounds, WinTitle + ' ' + NumString, wnNoNumber);
```

```
   MakeInterior(Bounds);
   END;

PROCEDURE TDemoWindow.MakeInterior(Bounds: TRect);
   VAR
      HScrollBar, VScrollBar: PScrollBar;
      Interior: PInterior;
      r: TRect;
   BEGIN
   VScrollBar := StandardScrollBar(sbVertical + sbHandleKeyboard);
   HScrollBar := StandardScrollBar(sbHorizontal + sbHandle-
Keyboard);
   GetExtent(Bounds);
   Bounds.Grow(-1,-1);
   Interior := New(PInterior,
                  Init(Bounds, HScrollBar, VScrollBar));
   Insert(Interior);
   END;


{ ------------------------------ }
{ METHODS FOR TMYAPP OBJECT TYPE  }
{ ------------------------------ }
PROCEDURE TMyApp.HandleEvent(VAR Event: TEvent);
   BEGIN
   TApplication.HandleEvent(Event);
   IF Event.What = evCommand THEN
      BEGIN
      CASE Event.Command OF
         cmNewWindow: NewWindow;
         ELSE Exit;
         END;
      ClearEvent(Event);
      END;
   END;

PROCEDURE TMyApp.InitMenuBar;
   VAR
      r: TRect;
   BEGIN
      GetExtent(r);
      r.b.Y := r.a.Y + 1;
      MenuBar := New(PMenuBar, Init(r, NewMenu(
         NewSubMenu('~F~ile', hcNoContext, NewMenu(
            NewItem('~N~ew', 'F4', kbF4, cmNewWindow, hcNoContext,
            NewLine(
```

```
                NewItem('Ex~it', 'Alt-X', kbAltX, cmQuit, hcNoContext,
                    nil)))),
                NewSubMenu('~W~indow', hcNoContext, NewMenu(
                    NewItem('~N~ext', 'F6', kbF6, cmNext, hcNoContext,
                    NewItem('~Z°om', 'F5', kbF5, cmZoom, hcNoContext,
                    nil))),
                nil))
            )));
        END;

PROCEDURE TMyApp.InitStatusLine;
    VAR
        r: TRect;
    BEGIN
        GetExtent(r);
        r.a.Y := r.b.Y - 1;
        StatusLine := New(PStatusLine, Init(r,
            NewStatusDef(0, $FFFF,
                NewStatusKey('', kbF10, cmMenu,
                NewStatusKey('~Alt-X~ Exit', kbAltX, cmQuit,
                NewStatusKey('~F4~ New', kbF4, cmNewWindow,
                NewStatusKey('~Alt-F3~ Close', kbAltF3, cmClose,
                nil)))),
            nil)
        ));
    END;

PROCEDURE TMyApp.NewWindow;
    VAR
        Window: PDemoWindow;
        r: TRect;
    BEGIN
    Inc(WinCount);
    r.Assign(0, 0, 24, 7);
    RANDOMIZE;
    r.Move(RANDOM(55), RANDOM(16));
    Window := New(PDemoWindow, Init(r, 'Window', WinCount));
    DeskTop^.Insert(Window);
    END;

{ -------------------------------- }
{ MORE GLOBAL VARIABLE DECLARATIONS }
{ -------------------------------- }
```

```
VAR
   MyApp: TMyApp;

{ ------------------------------------------------------------- }
{                       MAIN BODY OF PROGRAM                     }
{ ------------------------------------------------------------- }
BEGIN
   ReadFile;
   MyApp.Init;
   MyApp.Run;
   MyApp.Done;
   DoneFile;
END.
```

A key change that we made in this listing was to change the ancestry of our *TInterior* object type. Previously, it was a descendant of the *TView* type. Now, however, it is descended from the *TScroller* type so that we can move around in it by using the scroll bars.

The *ReadFile* and *Done* procedures are not tied to any object type. They open a text file, load it into a window's interior, and shut it down when the window closes. They manage the trick of loading the file into the interior object by creating an array of pointers to text strings; each string holds one line of the file.

The scroll bars themselves are additional dynamic objects that we create in the *TDemoWindow.MakeInterior* method, using predefined Turbo Vision scroll bar object types. The result is shown in Figure 21.4.

FIGURE 21.4:

Adding scroll bars to
a Turbo Vision window

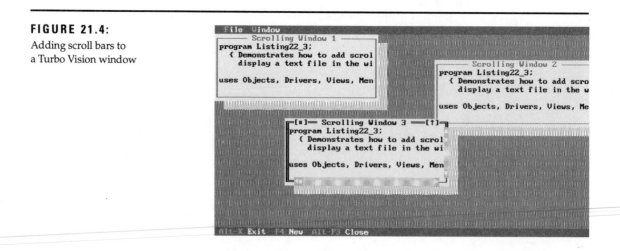

Creating Dialog Boxes

Creating a dialog box involves just as much intricate work as the other things we have done in Turbo Vision, but it proceeds in much the same way. This is illustrated in Listing 21.4.

Listing 21.4

```
PROGRAM Listing21_4;

    { Demonstrates how to set up a dialog box with push buttons,
      check boxes, and radio buttons. }

USES OBJECTS, DRIVERS, VIEWS, MENUS, APP, DIALOGS;

CONST
    WinCount: Integer =    0;
    cmNewWindow      = 101;
    cmSortDialog     = 102;

TYPE
    TMyApp = OBJECT (TApplication)
        PROCEDURE HandleEvent(VAR Event: TEvent); VIRTUAL;
        PROCEDURE InitMenuBar; VIRTUAL;
        PROCEDURE InitStatusLine; VIRTUAL;
        PROCEDURE SortDialog;
        PROCEDURE NewWindow;
        END;

    PDemoWindow = ^TDemoWindow;
    TDemoWindow = OBJECT (TWindow)
        CONSTRUCTOR Init(Bounds: TRect;
                        WinTitle: STRING; WindowNo: WORD);
        END;

    PDemoDialog = ^TDemoDialog;
    TDemoDialog = OBJECT (TDialog)
                END;

    PInterior = ^TInterior;
    TInterior = OBJECT (TView)
                CONSTRUCTOR Init(VAR Bounds: TRect);
```

```
                    PROCEDURE Draw; VIRTUAL;
                    END;

{ TInterior }
CONSTRUCTOR TInterior.Init(VAR Bounds: TRect);
   BEGIN
   TView.Init(Bounds);
   GrowMode := gfGrowHiX + gfGrowHiY;
   Options := Options or ofFramed;
   END;

PROCEDURE TInterior.Draw;
   CONST Greeting: STRING = 'Hello, new programmer!';
   BEGIN
   TView.Draw;
   WriteStr(4, 2, Greeting,$01);
   END;

{ TDemoWindow }
CONSTRUCTOR TDemoWindow.Init(Bounds: TRect;
                            WinTitle: STRING; WindowNo: WORD);
   VAR
      S: STRING[3];
      Interior: PInterior;
   BEGIN
   Str(WindowNo, S);
   TWindow.Init(Bounds, WinTitle + ' ' + S, wnNoNumber);
   GetClipRect(Bounds);
   Bounds.Grow(-1,-1);
   Interior := New(PInterior, Init(Bounds));
   Insert(Interior);
   END;

{ TMyApp }
PROCEDURE TMyApp.HandleEvent(VAR Event: TEvent);
   BEGIN
      TApplication.HandleEvent(Event);
      if Event.What = evCommand then
      BEGIN
         CASE Event.Command OF
               cmNewWindow: NewWindow;
               cmSortDialog : SortDialog
               ELSE
               Exit;
               END;
```

```
        ClearEvent(Event);
        END;
    END;

PROCEDURE TMyApp.InitMenuBar;
    VAR
        r: TRect;
    BEGIN
        GetExtent(r);
        r.B.Y := r.A.Y + 1;
        MenuBar := New(PMenuBar, Init(r, NewMenu(
            NewSubMenu('~F~ile', hcNoContext, NewMenu(
                NewItem('~S°rt', 'F3', kbF3, cmSortDialog, hcNoContext,
                NewItem('~N~ew', 'F4', kbF4, cmNewWindow, hcNoContext,
                NewLine(
                NewItem('Ex~it', 'Alt-X', kbAltX, cmQuit, hcNoContext,
                nil))))),
            NewSubMenu('~W~indow', hcNoContext, NewMenu(
                NewItem('~N~ext', 'F6', kbF6, cmNext, hcNoContext,
                NewItem('~Zoom', 'F5', kbF5, cmZoom, hcNoContext,
                nil))),
            nil))
        )));
    END;

PROCEDURE TMyApp.InitStatusLine;
    VAR
        r: TRect;
    BEGIN
        GetExtent(r);
        r.A.Y := r.B.Y - 1;
        StatusLine := New(PStatusLine, Init(r,
            NewStatusDef(0, $FFFF,
                NewStatusKey('', kbF10, cmMenu,
                NewStatusKey('~Alt-X~ Exit', kbAltX, cmQuit,
                NewStatusKey('~F4~ New', kbF4, cmNewWindow,
                NewStatusKey('~Alt-F3~ Close', kbAltF3, cmClose,
                nil)))),
            nil)
        ));
    END;

PROCEDURE TMyApp.SortDialog;
    VAR
        SDView: PView;
```

```
    Dialog: PDemoDialog;
    r: TRect;
    C: WORD;
BEGIN
r.Assign(20, 6, 60, 19);
Dialog := New(PDemoDialog, Init(r, 'Sorting Algorithms'));

WITH Dialog^ DO
    BEGIN
    { create checkboxes }
    r.Assign(2, 3, 16, 6);
    SDView := New(PCheckBoxes, Init(r,
        NewSItem('~S~creen',
        NewSItem('~F~ile',
        NewSItem('~P~rinter',
        nil)))
    ));
    Insert(SDView);

    { create label for checkboxes }
    r.Assign(2, 2, 10, 3);
    Insert(New(PLabel, Init(r, 'Sort To', SDView)));

    { create radio buttons }
    r.Assign(18, 3, 38, 6);
    SDView := New(PRadioButtons, Init(r,
        NewSItem('~Q~uicksort',
        NewSItem('~I~nsertion Sort',
        NewSItem('~R'dix Sort',
        nil)))
    ));
    Insert(SDView);

    { create label for radio buttons }
    r.Assign(21, 2, 33, 3);
    Insert(New(PLabel, Init(r, 'Algorithm', SDView)));

    { create pushbuttons }
    r.Assign(15, 10, 25, 12);
    Insert(New(PButton, Init(r, '~O~k', cmOK, bfDefault)));
    r.Assign(28, 10, 38, 12);
```

```
        Insert(New(PButton, Init(r, 'Cancel', cmCancel, bfNormal)));
        END;  { of "with Dialog^ do" statement }

    C := DeskTop^.ExecView(Dialog);
    Dispose(Dialog, Done);
    END;

PROCEDURE TMyApp.NewWindow;
    VAR
        Window  : PDemoWindow;
        r       : TRect;
    BEGIN
    Inc(WinCount);
    r.Assign(0, 0, 32, 7);
    RANDOMIZE;
    r.Move(RANDOM(47), RANDOM(16));
    Window := New(PDemoWindow,
                    Init(r, 'Greeting Window', WinCount));
    DeskTop^.Insert(Window);
    END;

VAR
    MyApp: TMyApp;

BEGIN
    MyApp.Init;
    MyApp.Run;
    MyApp.Done;
END.
```

First, we create a dialog box object type that is descended from the predefined *TDialog* object type, along with a pointer to that type. We add an additional item to the File menu and another command constant to the CASE statement in the *Handle-Event* method.

In the dialog box itself, we create rectangles to hold the title of the dialog box. We also use predefined Turbo Vision types to create check boxes, push buttons, and radio buttons in the same way that we created menu items in earlier listings.

When we have finished setting up the dialog box, we insert it into the Turbo Vision *desktop* with a call to the *desktop* object type's *ExecView* method. At this stage, of course, the program is not set up to do any actual sorting in response to the user's actions with the dialog box. The result is shown in Figure 21.5.

FIGURE 21.5:

Creating a dialog box
in Turbo Vision

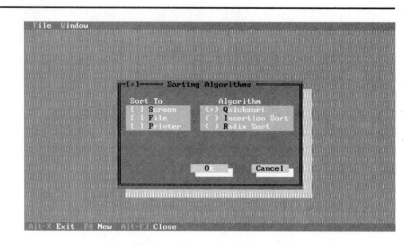

Borland Pascal Only: Browsing Objects

Borland Pascal, BP.EXE, adds two important features to Turbo Pascal 7. The first, which we will discuss in Part IV of this book, allows you to select the "target" of your program—that is, whether it is meant to run in DOS real mode, as a DOS DPMI application, or as a Windows application.

One feature that is valuable in developing real-mode Turbo Vision programs, however, is Borland Pascal's "object browsing" capability. This lets you view a diagram of where an object type fits in the Turbo Vision hierarchy, as well as browse through its methods and their parameters. This feature is not in the plain Turbo Pascal 7 IDE (TURBO.EXE), but only in BP.EXE.

Let's browse one of the object types in Listing 21.4. (If you haven't installed BP.EXE, just follow along even though you won't be able to do the object browsing.)

The object type we'll browse is the *TInterior* type. First, compile the program. Then, move the cursor to the first letter in the word *TInterior* on line 31 (or thereabouts) of the listing. Follow these steps:

1. Open the Search menu (shown in Figure 21.6) and select Objects.

2. The Object Browsing window will open. Press *F5* to zoom it to full-screen status and move the highlight down to *TInterior*, as shown in Figure 21.7.

3. With the highlight on *TInterior*, press *Enter*. A window will open that shows the *TInterior* methods and the parameters they require, as shown in Figure 21.8. Pressing *Enter* again will display the variables used by the *TInterior* methods.

FIGURE 21.6:

The Search menu in
Borland Pascal (BP.EXE)

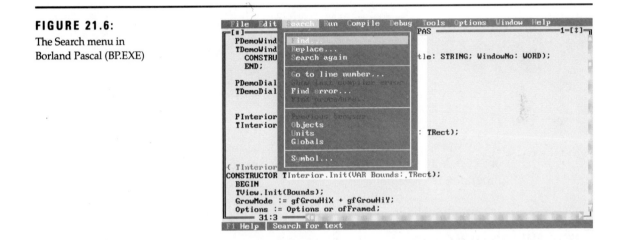

FIGURE 21.7:

The Object Browsing window
with TInterior highlighted

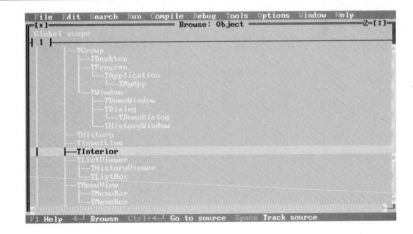

FIGURE 21.8:

A browse window displays the
TInterior methods

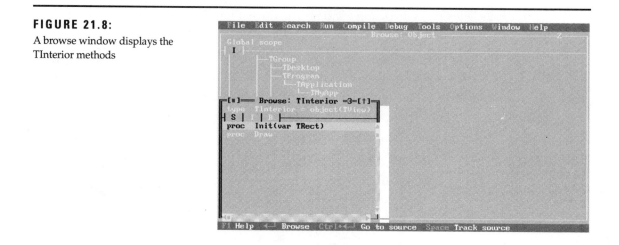

It's easy to see how object browsing can help you make sense out of a complicated
object-type hierarchy. Most simple programs don't really need it, but for larger
programs, it's a valuable tool.

Turbo Vision in Action: "Turbo Resume"

Simple listings of demo programs are nice, but there's no substitute for seeing a
"real" Turbo Vision program in action. To finish our discussion of Turbo Vision,
we'll look at Turbo Resume, a real-world Turbo Vision program that I've stripped
down a little so it's small enough to put in the book.

Unlike other resume programs, which assist you in printing out a paper resume,
Turbo Resume presents your qualifications on the PC's screen—complete with exploding windows, sound effects, graphics, and music. It's like a demo program for
a person.

Listing 21.5

```
PROGRAM Listing21_5;
    { This is "Turbo Resume." Demonstrates a simple but "real-
    life" Turbo Vision application.
    Copyright 1991, 1992 by Scott D. Palmer. }

USES OBJECTS, DRIVERS, VIEWS, MENUS, APP,
    CRT, GRAPH, BGIDRIV, BGIFONT,
    Music, MyUtils;

CONST
    cmObjective      = 101;
    cmExperience     = 102;
    cmJobHistory     = 103;
    cmMiscInfo       = 104;
    cmContactMe      = 105;

    NameFile         = 'name.txt';
    ObjectiveFile    = 'object.txt';
    ExperienceFile   = 'exp.txt';
    JobHistFile      = 'jobs.txt';
    MiscInfoFile     = 'misc.txt';
    ContactMeFile    = 'contact.txt';

    maxlines         = 100;

    CurrentCommand   : INTEGER = 0;
    { A "typed constant" to control the Draw method.
      Command number assignments:
                    1 = Objective
                    2 = Experience
                    3 = JobHistory
                    4 = MiscInfo
                    5 = ContactMe }


    { -------------------------------- }
    { GLOBAL TYPE DECLARATIONS         }
    { -------------------------------- }
    TYPE
```

```
      LineBufArray = array[0..maxlines - 1] of pstring;
      String12     = string[12];


{ ------------------------------ }
{ GLOBAL VARIABLE DECLARATIONS    }
{ ------------------------------ }
VAR
   ObjectiveLineCount, ExpLineCount,
   JobHistLineCount, MiscInfoLineCount,
   ContactMeLineCount                      : INTEGER;

   ObjectiveLines, ExperienceLines, JobHistLines,
   MiscInfoLines, ContactMeLines           : LineBufArray;

   UserName    : STRING;

   { The other global variable is CurrentCommand, which is
     declared as a "typed constant" (i.e., a pre-initialized
     variable) in the CONST section, above. }


{ ------------------------------ }
{ OBJECT TYPE DECLARATIONS        }
{ ------------------------------ }
TYPE

{TYPE FOR APPLICATION OBJECT}
   TMyApp = OBJECT ( TApplication)
     PROCEDURE HandleEvent(VAR Event: TEvent); virtual;
     PROCEDURE InitMenuBar; virtual;
     PROCEDURE InitStatusLine; virtual;
     PROCEDURE Objective;
     PROCEDURE Experience;
     PROCEDURE JobHistory;
     PROCEDURE MiscInfo;
     PROCEDURE ContactMe;
     END;

{TYPE FOR RESUME ITEM WINDOWS}
   PResItemWindow = ^TResItemWindow;
   TResItemWindow = OBJECT (TWindow)
      CONSTRUCTOR Init(Bounds: TRect; WinTitle: STRING);
      PROCEDURE MakeInterior(bounds:trect); virtual;
      END;

{TYPE FOR INTERIOR OF RESUME ITEM WINDOWS}
```

```
    PResItemInterior = ^TResItemInterior;
    TResItemInterior = OBJECT ( Tscroller)
        CONSTRUCTOR Init(VAR Bounds: TRect;
                         ahscrollbar, avscrollbar: pscrollbar);
        PROCEDURE Draw; virtual;
        END;

{*****************************}
{       GLOBAL PROCEDURES      }
{*****************************}
PROCEDURE ReadFiles;
{Initializes the global linecount variable to 0. Opens a file.
Reads it line-by-line into the "lines[]" array of strings, each
time adding 1 to the linecount variable. Finally, closes the
file.}
    VAR
        f : text;
        s : STRING;

    {local procedure under ReadFiles}
    PROCEDURE GetFileData( FileName:string12;
                           VAR LineCount : INTEGER;
                           VAR LineBuffer: LineBufArray);
    BEGIN
        LineBuffer[0] := NewStr('   ');
        LineCount := 1;
        assign(f, FileName);
        {$I-}
        reset(f);
        {$I+}
        IF ioresult <> 0 THEN HALT(1);
        while not eof(f) and (LineCount < maxlines) DO
             BEGIN
             readln(f, s);
             s := '   ' + s;
             LineBuffer[LineCount] := newstr(s);
             inc(LineCount);
             END;
        close(f);
    END;

    {main body of ReadFiles procedure}
    BEGIN
    GetFileData(ObjectiveFile, ObjectiveLineCount, ObjectiveLines);
    GetFileData(ExperienceFile, ExpLineCount, ExperienceLines);
```

```
    GetFileData(JobHistFile,JobHistLineCount,JobHistLines);
    GetFileData(MiscInfoFile,MiscInfoLineCount,MiscInfoLines);
    GetFileData(ContactMeFile,ContactMeLineCount,ContactMeLines);
    END;

PROCEDURE donefiles;
{Just disposes all the pointers in the array of strings
 and deallocates the memory used by them.}
    VAR
        i : INTEGER;
    BEGIN
        FOR i := 0 TO ObjectiveLineCount - 1 DO
            IF ObjectiveLines[i] <> nil
            THEN DisposeStr(ObjectiveLines[i]);
        FOR i := 0 TO ExpLineCount - 1 DO
            IF ExperienceLines[i] <> nil
            THEN DisposeStr(ExperienceLines[i]);
        FOR i := 0 TO JobHistLineCount - 1 DO
            IF JobHistLines[i] <> nil
            THEN DisposeStr(JobHistLines[i]);
        FOR i := 0 TO MiscInfoLineCount - 1 DO
            IF MiscInfoLines[i] <> nil
            THEN DisposeStr(MiscInfoLines[i]);
        FOR i := 0 TO ContactMeLineCount - 1 DO
            IF ContactMeLines[i] <> nil
            THEN DisposeStr(ContactMeLines[i]);
    END;


{ ------------------------------- }
{ METHODS FOR TRESITEMINTERIOR    }
{ ------------------------------- }
CONSTRUCTOR TResItemInterior.Init(VAR Bounds: TRect;
                ahscrollbar, avscrollbar: pscrollbar);
    BEGIN
    Tscroller.Init(Bounds, ahscrollbar, avscrollbar);
    GrowMode := gfGrowHiX + gfGrowHiY;
    Options := Options or ofFramed;
    CASE CurrentCommand of
        1: SetLimit(128, ObjectiveLineCount);
        2: SetLimit(128, ExpLineCount);
        3: SetLimit(128, JobHistLineCount);
        4: SetLimit(128, MiscInfoLineCount);
        5: SetLimit(128, ContactMeLineCount);
        ELSE setlimit(128, 100);
        END;
```

```
        beep;
        END;

PROCEDURE TResItemInterior.Draw;
    VAR
        color : byte;
        i, y  : INTEGER;
        b     : tdrawbuffer;
    BEGIN
    color := getcolor(1);
    FOR y := 0 TO size.y - 1 DO
        BEGIN
        movechar(b, space, color, size.x);
        i:= delta.y + y;
        CASE CurrentCommand of
            1: BEGIN
                IF (i < ObjectiveLineCount)
                    and (ObjectiveLines[i] <> nil)
                THEN movestr(b, copy(ObjectiveLines[i]^,
                                  delta.x + 1, size.x), color);
                writeline(0, y, size.x, 1, b);
                END;
            2: BEGIN
                IF (i < ExpLineCount)
                    and (ExperienceLines[i] <> nil)
                THEN movestr(b, copy(ExperienceLines[i]^,
                                  delta.x + 1, size.x), color);
                writeline(0, y, size.x, 1, b);
                END;
            3: BEGIN
                IF (i < JobHistLineCount)
                    and (JobHistLines[i] <> nil)
                THEN movestr(b, copy(JobHistLines[i]^,
                                  delta.x + 1, size.x), color);
                writeline(0, y, size.x, 1, b);
                END;
            4: BEGIN
                IF (i < MiscInfoLineCount)
                    and (MiscInfoLines[i] <> nil)
                THEN movestr(b, copy(MiscInfoLines[i]^,
                                  delta.x + 1, size.x), color);
                writeline(0, y, size.x, 1, b);
                END;
            5: BEGIN
                IF (i < ContactMeLineCount)
```

```
                              and (ContactMeLines[i] <> nil)
                      THEN movestr(b, copy(ContactMeLines[i]^,
                                        delta.x + 1, size.x), color);
                      writeline(O, y, size.x, 1, b);
                      END;
                   ELSE HALT;
                   END; { of case statement }
              END; { of for..do statement }
          END;


{ -------------------------------- }
{ METHODS FOR TRESITEMWINDOW       }
{ -------------------------------- }

CONSTRUCTOR TResItemWindow.Init(Bounds: TRect;
                  WinTitle: STRING);
   BEGIN
   TWindow.Init(Bounds, WinTitle, wnNoNumber);
   MakeInterior(bounds);
   END;

PROCEDURE TResItemwindow.makeinterior(bounds: trect);
   VAR
      hscrollbar, vscrollbar: pscrollbar;
      interior: PResItemInterior;
      r: trect;
   BEGIN
      vscrollbar := standardscrollbar(sbvertical
                     + sbHandleKeyboard);
      hscrollbar := standardscrollbar(sbhorizontal
                     + sbhandlekeyboard);
      getextent(bounds);
      bounds.grow(-1,-1);
      interior := new(PResItemInterior, init(bounds,
                     hscrollbar, vscrollbar));
      insert(interior);
   END;


{ -------------------------------- }
{ METHODS FOR TMYAPP               }
{ -------------------------------- }
PROCEDURE TMyApp.HandleEvent(VAR Event: TEvent);
   BEGIN
   TApplication.HandleEvent(Event);
   IF Event.What = evCommand THEN
```

```
        BEGIN
        CASE Event.Command OF
            cmObjective: Objective;
            cmExperience: Experience;
            cmJobHistory: JobHistory;
            cmMiscInfo: MiscInfo;
            cmContactMe: ContactMe;
            ELSE Exit;
            END;
        ClearEvent(Event);
        END
    END;

PROCEDURE TMyApp.InitMenuBar;
    VAR
        r: TRect;
    BEGIN
        GetExtent(r);
        r.b.y := r.a.y + 1;
        MenuBar := New(PMenuBar, Init(r, NewMenu(
        NewSubMenu('~R~esume', hcNoContext, NewMenu(
            NewItem('~O·jective', 'Ctrl-F1', kbCtrlF1,
                    cmObjective, hcNoContext,
            NewItem('~E×perience', 'Ctrl-F2', kbCtrlF2,
                    cmExperience, hcNoContext,
            NewItem('~J°b History', 'Ctrl-F3', kbCtrlF3,
                    cmJobHistory, hcNoContext,
            NewItem('~M~iscellaneous Info', 'Ctrl-F4', kbCtrlF4,
                    cmMiscInfo, hcNoContext,
            NewItem('~H°w to contact me', 'Ctrl-F5', kbCtrlF5,
                    cmContactMe, hcNoContext,
            NewLine(
            NewItem('E×~it', 'Alt-X', kbAltX, cmQuit, hcNoContext,
            NIL)))))))),
        NIL))));
    END;

PROCEDURE TMyApp.InitStatusLine;
    VAR
        r: TRect;
    BEGIN
        GetExtent(r);
        r.a.y := r.b.y - 1;
        StatusLine := New(PStatusLine, Init(r,
            NewStatusDef(0, $FFFF,
```

```
                    NewStatusKey('~Alt-R~ Menu', kbF10, cmMenu,
                    NewStatusKey('~Alt-X~ Exit', kbAltX, cmQuit,
                    NewStatusKey('~Ctrl-F1~ Job Objective', kbCtrlF1,
                              cmObjective,
                    NewStatusKey('~Esc~ Close', kbEsc, cmClose,
                    NewStatusKey('', kbAltF3, cmClose,
                    NewStatusKey('~F5~ Zoom', kbF5, cmZoom,
                    NIL)))))),
              NIL)
         ));
      END;


{FOLLOWING ARE METHODS FOR THE MENU CHOICES}

PROCEDURE TMyApp.Objective;
    VAR
        Window : PResItemWindow;
        r      : TRect;
    BEGIN
    CurrentCommand := 1;
    r.Assign(5, 2, 75, 11);
    Window := New(PResItemWindow, Init(r,
                (UserName + ': Objective')));
    DeskTop^.Insert(Window);
    END;


PROCEDURE TMyApp.Experience;
    VAR
        Window : PResItemWindow;
        r      : TRect;
    BEGIN
    CurrentCommand := 2;
    r.Assign(4, 1, 76, 22);
    Window := New(PResItemWindow, Init(r,
                (UserName + ': Experience')));
    DeskTop^.Insert(Window);
    END;


PROCEDURE TMyApp.JobHistory;
    VAR
        Window : PResItemWindow;
        r      : TRect;
    BEGIN
    CurrentCommand := 3;
    r.Assign(4, 2, 76, 20);
```

```
      Window := New(PResItemWindow, Init(r,
                 (UserName + ': Employment History')));
      DeskTop^.Insert(Window);
      END;

PROCEDURE TMyApp.MiscInfo;
   VAR
      Window : PResItemWindow;
      r      : TRect;
   BEGIN
   CurrentCommand := 4;
   r.Assign(5, 2, 75, 11);
   Window := New(PResItemWindow, Init(r,
                 (UserName + ': Miscellaneous Information')));
   DeskTop^.Insert(Window);
   END;

PROCEDURE TMyApp.ContactMe;
   VAR
      Window : PResItemWindow;
      r      : TRect;
   BEGIN
   CurrentCommand := 5;
   r.Assign(5, 2, 75, 20);
   Window := New(PResItemWindow, Init(r,
                 (UserName + ': How to contact me')));
   DeskTop^.Insert(Window);
   END;

PROCEDURE DisplayWelcome;
   VAR
       gd,
       gm,
       ErrCode,
       maxX, MaxY : INTEGER;
       Graphics   : BOOLEAN;
       NameFile   : TEXT;
       NameSize   : INTEGER;

   PROCEDURE anthem;
      BEGIN
      SOUND(c1); DELAY(qnote); NOSOUND; DELAY(sbrk);
      SOUND(f1); DELAY(qnote); NOSOUND; DELAY(sbrk);
      SOUND(f1); DELAY(qnote); NOSOUND; DELAY(sbrk);
      SOUND(f1); DELAY(qnote); NOSOUND; DELAY(sbrk);
```

```
SOUND(g1); DELAY(qnote); NOSOUND; DELAY(sbrk);
SOUND(a1); DELAY(hnote); NOSOUND; DELAY(sbrk);
SOUND(f1); DELAY(hnote); NOSOUND; DELAY(lbrk);
SOUND(g1); DELAY(qnote); NOSOUND; DELAY(sbrk);
SOUND(a1s); DELAY(qnote); NOSOUND; DELAY(sbrk);
SOUND(a1); DELAY(qnote + enote); NOSOUND; DELAY(sbrk);
SOUND(g1); DELAY(enote); NOSOUND; DELAY(sbrk);
SOUND(f1); DELAY(dot_hnote); NOSOUND; DELAY(3 * lbrk);

SOUND(c1); DELAY(qnote); NOSOUND; DELAY(sbrk);
SOUND(f1); DELAY(qnote); NOSOUND; DELAY(sbrk);
SOUND(f1); DELAY(qnote); NOSOUND; DELAY(sbrk);
SOUND(f1); DELAY(qnote); NOSOUND; DELAY(sbrk);
SOUND(a1); DELAY(qnote); NOSOUND; DELAY(sbrk);
SOUND(c2); DELAY(hnote); NOSOUND; DELAY(sbrk);
SOUND(a1); DELAY(hnote); NOSOUND; DELAY(lbrk);
SOUND(c2); DELAY(qnote); NOSOUND; DELAY(sbrk);
SOUND(a1); DELAY(qnote); NOSOUND; DELAY(sbrk);
SOUND(f1); DELAY(qnote + enote); NOSOUND; DELAY(sbrk);
SOUND(a1); DELAY(enote); NOSOUND; DELAY(sbrk);
SOUND(g1); DELAY(dot_hnote); NOSOUND; DELAY(3 * lbrk);

SOUND(f1); DELAY(qnote); NOSOUND; DELAY(sbrk);
SOUND(a1s); DELAY(qnote); NOSOUND; DELAY(sbrk);
SOUND(a1s); DELAY(qnote); NOSOUND; DELAY(sbrk);
SOUND(a1s); DELAY(qnote); NOSOUND; DELAY(sbrk);
SOUND(c2); DELAY(qnote); NOSOUND; DELAY(sbrk);
SOUND(d2); DELAY(hnote); NOSOUND; DELAY(sbrk);
SOUND(a1s); DELAY(hnote); NOSOUND; DELAY(lbrk);
SOUND(c2); DELAY(qnote); NOSOUND; DELAY(sbrk);
SOUND(a1); DELAY(qnote); NOSOUND; DELAY(sbrk);
SOUND(f1); DELAY(qnote + enote); NOSOUND; DELAY(sbrk);
SOUND(a1); DELAY(enote); NOSOUND; DELAY(sbrk);
SOUND(g1); DELAY(dot_hnote); NOSOUND; DELAY(3 * lbrk);

SOUND(c1); DELAY(qnote); NOSOUND; DELAY(sbrk);
SOUND(f1); DELAY(qnote); NOSOUND; DELAY(sbrk);
SOUND(f1); DELAY(qnote); NOSOUND; DELAY(sbrk);
SOUND(f1); DELAY(qnote); NOSOUND; DELAY(sbrk);
SOUND(a1); DELAY(qnote); NOSOUND; DELAY(sbrk);
SOUND(c2); DELAY(hnote); NOSOUND; DELAY(sbrk);
SOUND(f2); DELAY(hnote); NOSOUND; DELAY(lbrk);
SOUND(c2); DELAY(qnote); NOSOUND; DELAY(sbrk);
SOUND(a1); DELAY(qnote); NOSOUND; DELAY(sbrk);
SOUND(g1); DELAY(qnote + enote); NOSOUND; DELAY(sbrk);
```

```
      SOUND(f1); DELAY(enote); NOSOUND; DELAY(sbrk);
      SOUND(f1); DELAY(wnote + qnote); NOSOUND;

      END;

  PROCEDURE NoGraphicsWelcome;
      VAR counter : INTEGER;
      BEGIN
      clrscr;
      window(15,3,75,21);
      WRITELN;
      textcolor(white);
      WRITELN('I---------------------------------------------;');
      WRITE(':');
      FOR counter := 1 TO ( (50 - namesize) div 2 ) DO
WRITE(space);
      WRITE(username);
      FOR counter := 1 TO ( (50 - namesize) div 2 ) DO
WRITE(space);
      WRITELN(':');

      WRITELN('----------------------------------------------');
      WRITELN(':                                            :');
      WRITELN(':                                            :');
      WRITE(':               ');
      textcolor(lightgray);
      WRITE('***** On-line Resume *****');
      textcolor(white);
      WRITELN('              :');
      WRITE(':              ');
      textcolor(lightgray + blink);
      WRITE('     Program loading ...');
      textcolor(white);
      WRITELN('              :');
      WRITELN(':                                            :');
      WRITELN(':                                            :');
      WRITELN('----------------------------------------------');
      WRITELN;
      WRITELN('Including drop-down menus and mouse support');
      textcolor(lightgray);
      WRITELN; WRITELN('TURBO RESUME Copyright 1991, 1992 by
                      Scott D. Palmer.');
      WRITELN('Music Copyright 1992 by Scott D. Palmer');
      anthem;
      pause;
```

```
        window(1,1,80,25);
        clrscr;
        END;

{ *************************************************************** }
{ Procedures to link graphics drivers and fonts into .exe file  }
{*************************************************************** }
PROCEDURE abortdriver( fontname: STRING );
    BEGIN
    WRITELN( Fontname, ': ', GraphErrorMsg( GraphResult ) );
    HALT;
    END;

PROCEDURE registerdrivers;
    BEGIN
        IF RegisterBGIDriver( @CGADriverProc ) < 0
            THEN AbortDriver( 'CGA' );
        IF RegisterBGIDriver( @EGAVGADriverProc ) < 0
            THEN AbortDriver( 'EGA/VGA' );
        IF RegisterBGIDriver( @HercDriverProc ) < 0
            THEN AbortDriver( 'Herc' );
        IF RegisterBGIDriver( @ATTDriverProc ) < 0
            THEN AbortDriver( 'AT&T' );
        IF RegisterBGIDriver( @PC3270DriverProc ) < 0
            THEN AbortDriver( 'PC 3270' );
    END;

PROCEDURE abortfont( FontName: STRING );
    BEGIN
    WRITELN(FontName, ': ', GraphErrorMsg( GraphResult ) );
    HALT;
    END;

PROCEDURE registerfonts;
    BEGIN
    IF RegisterBGIFont( @TriplexFontProc ) < 0
        THEN AbortFont( 'Triplex' );
    IF RegisterBGIFont( @SmallFontProc ) < 0
        THEN AbortFont(  'Small' );
    IF RegisterBGIFont( @SansSerifFontProc ) < 0
        THEN AbortFont( 'Sans Serif' );
    IF RegisterBGIFont( @GothicFontProc ) < 0
```

```
    THEN AbortFont( 'Gothic' );
END;

{local procedure under DisplayWelcome}
PROCEDURE init(VAR maxX, maxY : INTEGER);
    BEGIN
    { ******* Read user's name from name.txt file. ******** }
    Assign(NameFile, 'name.txt');
    {$I-}
    reset(NameFile);
    {$I+}
    IF ioresult <> O THEN HALT;
    readln(NameFile, username);
    NameSize := length(username);

    registerdrivers;
    registerfonts;
    graphics := true;
    gd := Detect;
    InitGraph(gd,gm,'');
    ErrCode := GraphResult;

    IF ErrCode = grOk
        THEN BEGIN
            maxX := GetMaxX;
            maxY := GetMaxY;
            exit
            END
        ELSE BEGIN
            graphics := false;
            END;

    END; { of init procedure }

PROCEDURE openingbox;
    VAR
        counter,
        xx1, yy1, xx2, yy2   : INTEGER;
        color, backcolor : word;

{ local procedure under openingbox }
 PROCEDURE drawbox;
    BEGIN
    color := getcolor;
    setbkcolor(1);
```

```
backcolor := getbkcolor;
setlinestyle(solidln, 0, thickwidth);
counter := 40;
   repeat
      xx1 := maxX div 2 - maxX div counter;
      yy1 := maxY div 2 - maxY div counter;
      xx2 := maxX div 2 + maxX div counter;
      yy2 := maxY div 2 + maxY div counter;
      rectangle(xx1,yy1,xx2,yy2);
      delay(75);
      setcolor(backcolor);
      rectangle(xx1,yy1,xx2,yy2);
      delay(10);
      setcolor(color);
      counter := counter - 2;
   until counter < 4;
xx1 := 0;
yy1 := 0;
xx2 := maxX;
yy2 := maxY;
rectangle(xx1,yy1,xx2,yy2);
END;
{ of drawbox routine under openingbox }

{ local procedure under openingbox}
PROCEDURE Welcome;
   VAR
      left, right,
      top, bottom : INTEGER;
      x, y        : INTEGER;
   BEGIN
   x := 0; y := 0;
   settextstyle(triplexfont, horizdir,5 );
   settextjustify(centertext,centertext);
   left := 0; right := maxX;
   top    := maxY div 10;
   bottom := maxY - maxY div 20;
   y := top;
   setviewport(0, top, maxX, bottom, clipon);
   maxY := GetMaxY;
   outtextXY(maxX div 2,y, username);
   y := y + textheight('M') div 2;
```

```
    outtextXY(maxX div 2,y, '------------------');
    y := y + (textheight('M') div 2);

    settextstyle(gothicfont, 0, 5);
    outtextXY(MaxX div 2, y, 'On-line Resume');
    y := y + textheight('M');

    settextstyle(triplexfont,horizdir,2);
    settextjustify(centertext,centertext);
    outtextXY(maxX div 2, y,
            'With drop-down menus and mouse support');

    y := y + (2 * textheight('M'));
    settextstyle(defaultfont, horizdir, 1);
    outtextXY(maxX div 2, y,
        'TURBO RESUME Copyright 1991, 1992 by Scott D. Palmer');
    y := y + (2 * textheight('M'));
    outtextXY(maxX div 2, y,
            'Music Copyright 1992 by Scott D. Palmer');

    anthem;

    y := bottom - (bottom div 3);
    left := maxX div 5;
    gpauseXY(left,y);
    setviewport(0,0,GetmaxX,GetmaxY, true);
  END;

{ main body of procedure }
BEGIN
    drawbox;
    welcome;
END;

PROCEDURE shutdown;
    BEGIN
    closegraph;
    close(namefile);
    END;

{ main body of DisplayWelcome procedure }
BEGIN
    init(maxX, maxY);
    IF graphics
        THEN BEGIN
```

```
            openingbox;
            shutdown
            END
        ELSE NoGraphicsWelcome
    END;


{ ---------------------------------------------------------- }
{ GLOBAL VARIABLE DECLARATION FOR APPLICATION OBJECT      }
{ ---------------------------------------------------------- }
VAR
    ResumeApp: TMyApp;


{ ------------------------------------------------------------- }
{                    MAIN BODY OF THE PROGRAM                   }
{ ------------------------------------------------------------- }
BEGIN
    DisplayWelcome;
    ReadFiles;
    ResumeApp.Init;
    ResumeApp.Run;
    ResumeApp.Done;
    DoneFiles;
END.
```

The program requires six ASCII files on the disk with it when it runs. These files must have the following names:

NAME.TXT: (job seeker's name)

OBJECT.TXT: (job seeker's job objective)

EXP.TXT: (job seeker's experience/skills)

JOBS.TXT: (job seeker's job history)

MISC.TXT: (misc. info. about job seeker)

CONTACT.TXT: (how to get in touch with the job seeker)

Note that the program violates "Turbo Vision methodology" in one trick it uses. One of the things we wanted was to have an exploding-window sound when the user opens a window. Technically, this type of thing (a call to the "beep" procedure) should be in the window's draw method. However, if it were in the draw method, then the program would beep each time the window was redrawn—first, when it opened up, then again any time it was moved or resized. The solution was to put the beep into the window type's *Init* method, which is only called when the window is first opened. This is mildly illegal but is not known to be fattening.

Graphic Driver and Font Files

Normally, a Borland/Turbo Pascal program that uses graphics and type fonts must have the graphics driver and font files on the disk with the program. This program uses the technique explained at the end of Chapter 15 to incorporate the graphics driver and font files into the program's .EXE file.

Units Used

Turbo Resume requires the MyUtils and Music units. The MyUtils unit was created in Chapter 10 and had new routines added to it in Chapters 15 and 19. The Music unit was created in Chapter 19.

By studying the listing, you'll get an idea of the real power in Turbo Vision—power that even Turbo Resume doesn't use completely. And if you want a programming job when you've finished this book, you can use Turbo Resume yourself!

PART III

Windows Programming with Borland Pascal

The Windows Programming Environment

22

- **Event-Driven Programming**

- **Memory Management**

- **Using Borland Pascal for Windows**

Before we get into the specifics of programming with Borland Pascal for Windows, we need to take a brief look at the Windows programming environment, as well as how Windows applications differ from standard DOS application programs. We'll also take a tour of the Borland Pascal for Windows Integrated Development Environment (IDE) as it appears in Borland Pascal 7. If you have Turbo Pascal for Windows instead of Borland Pascal, your IDE might differ slightly from what appears in this book.

Microsoft Windows is commonly referred to as a *graphic user interface* (GUI), and the implication is that its most important feature is what you see on the PC's screen. The GUI aspect of Windows is indeed important, but it is arguably the least important feature that Windows has to offer.

The fact is that Windows provides a complete operating environment in which application programs can run, offering features that are not available in the MS-DOS operating system. These features include:

- **A queued, event-driven architecture:** an environment in which hardware and software events, such as key presses and mouse clicks, are intercepted by Microsoft Windows, which then sends the appropriate instructions ("messages") to the desired application program in its window.

- **Multitasking:** the ability to run multiple programs at the same time, all sharing the PC's memory, processor, and other system resources.

- **Interprocess communication:** the ability to exchange data between different programs while they are running, either under the user's control or under Windows' control.

- **Device-independent graphics:** a single graphics device interface, under the control of Windows, which insulates application programs from the details of the device used for graphics output whether it is a printer, plotter, Hercules monochrome screen, VGA color screen, or some other device unknown at the time the application program was written.

- **A graphic user interface:** a screen display in which the user issues commands by pointing at on-screen pictures and clicking or dragging the mouse.

Each of these features has significant implications for the way in which Windows programs must be structured and written. Let's take a closer look at each.

A Queued, Event-Driven Architecture

When a standard application program runs under MS-DOS, it gains exclusive control of and access to the PC's system resources memory, keyboard, screen, ports, and so on. Any input, such as a key being pressed by the user, is passed by MS-DOS directly to the application. If the application is not prepared to receive input at that time, the input might or might not get lost.

Consider a traditional Turbo Pascal program running under MS-DOS. It accepts input from the keyboard primarily through READLN and related procedures. If you have set up a menu, for example, you might have a series of statements like the following in your code:

```
WRITELN(' Main Menu');

WRITELN(' ');

WRITELN(' 1. Create');

WRITELN(' 2. Edit');

WRITELN(' 3. Quit');

WRITELN;

WRITE(' Enter your choice (1/2/3): ');

READLN(menuchoice);
```

If your program has reached this READLN or another input statement when the user decides to press a key, everything works fine. However, if your program is busy doing something else, then the key press goes into DOS's keyboard buffer and might or might not be used by your program.

A Windows program, however, is different. Because more than one program may be running at the same time, Windows must intercept input events and route them to the correct application program in a usable format. Hence, Windows monitors *all* the sources of input events to programs. When such an event occurs, Windows generates a message, such as *wm_KeyDown* for a key press, and this message goes into a message queue for the appropriate application program. When the program is ready for input, it reads its messages from the input queue provided by Windows.

Likewise, when the program needs to create output, whether displaying something on the screen or printing a document, it sends a message to Windows, which then carries out the request by using the appropriate hardware device. A Windows application, therefore, must be able to both (1) understand input messages that it receives from Windows and (2) generate the appropriate output messages to send to Windows when it wants to do something.

Significantly, because all input events are intercepted and managed by Windows, and Windows provides an insulating layer between the program and the hardware on which it's running (a traditional operating system function), different versions of Windows could theoretically be created to run on radically different hardware platforms, from PCs to mainframes.

Multitasking

Windows can run multiple application programs at the same time, meaning that system resources must be shared by all the active programs and by Windows. The screen is only the most obvious of these resources: Windows limits each application's use of the screen to the application's own window and "client area," which is the area inside the window. Likewise, Windows schedules different programs' access to the PC's processor, allocates and deallocates memory for applications and their data, and controls interactions between the different programs. An example of this type of situation is shown in Figure 22.1.

This means that a Windows application must not attempt to access any of these devices (processor, memory, screen, and so on) directly. For example, in order to display text on the screen, an application must go through Windows to make sure that the text is displayed in the application's client area, not in another window or on the Windows desktop. Likewise, an application should not try to directly manipulate data in processor registers, because it would almost certainly interfere with Windows' concurrent use of the processor with other applications.

This differs considerably from standard DOS programs, which typically have exclusive access to the processor, the screen, all memory not used by DOS or TSR programs, and all other system resources. "Ill-behaved" DOS programs such as

FIGURE 22.1:

Windows manages multiple concurrent programs in different windows

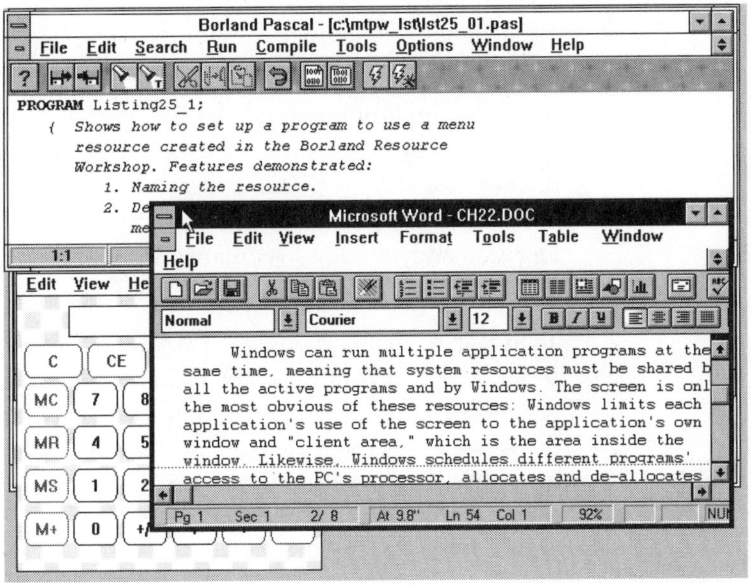

WordPerfect, which also have Windows versions, achieve considerable performance gains in slower machines by bypassing DOS/BIOS calls and writing directly to the hardware (such as the screen). However, such ill-behaved programs normally cannot be multitasked under Windows; in addition, their faster performance is less of an issue with the high-end PCs needed to run Windows in the first place.

Memory Management

Another aspect of the multitasking situation is how Windows handles PC memory. In effect, multitasked programs under Windows are all "resident" programs that can be popped up on the screen at any time. Under DOS, the order of resident programs in memory is static; that is, they cannot be shuffled and moved around in the PC's memory. Once a program and its data areas occupy a certain part of memory, they must remain there until the program is unloaded. Moreover, resident DOS programs must be unloaded in an order opposite to that in which they were loaded: if you load a print spooler, a macro program, SideKick, and a word processor, you must unload the word processor first, then SideKick, then the macro program, and then the print spooler.

Windows applications suffer from no such limitations. They can be loaded and unloaded in any order, and Windows itself takes care of allocating and managing memory for each one. This means, however, that Windows applications must not access memory directly. If you write a program that sets up a pointer to a memory location, and Windows reorganizes the allocation of memory, then your pointer will no longer point to the correct memory address of the data you need.

To manage dynamic memory, Windows uses "handles." Every object in a Windows program and in Windows itself has a handle, which is a special kind of pointer (represented as a number) that is managed by Windows. Programs, windows, icons, devices, and the client areas inside windows are all referred to by their handles. But never fear: Borland Pascal "handles the handles" behind the scenes, so that in your own code, you can use traditional Pascal pointers and operations such as the NEW and DISPOSE procedures.

Another aspect of Windows' memory management is its ability to let more than one program share the same module of compiled code. For example, you might have two copies of the same program running in different windows, or two different programs that can use the same import/export routines. In both of these cases, Windows would keep one copy of the shared code in memory, making it available to all applications that needed it. In the case of the import/export routines, the shared code would be called a *dynamic link library* (DLL), a special kind of .EXE file that can be created in Borland Pascal. DLLs can be loaded and unloaded as they are needed.

Interprocess Communication

"Interprocess communication" means that Windows applications can exchange data with each other either under the user's control or behind the scenes under Windows' control.

The most obvious form of interprocess communication is the Windows Clipboard, a feature already familiar to users of memory-resident utility programs under DOS. The Clipboard allows the user to select a block of text (or graphics) from one window, copy it to a buffer area in memory, and then paste it from the buffer into another window. Under DOS, this type of feature is supported by programs such as SideKick, which can pop up over an application's screen and copy material from the screen. The Windows Clipboard is not limited to copying the currently displayed screen of information; however, information copied to the Clipboard must be in one of several special formats (which we will examine later in this book).

The more sophisticated type of interprocess communication is called *dynamic data exchange* (DDE). This is a feature through which two applications in different windows are able to send information back and forth to each other without the user's direct intervention. For example, a Windows spreadsheet in one window might update a copy of a worksheet in a Windows word processing document that is in another window.

DDE is not the easiest thing in the world to implement, but, as usual, Borland Pascal does its best to hide the messy details. As with the Clipboard, the information to be exchanged must be in a standard format, and the cooperating applications must know how to start, conduct, and terminate the exchange by sending the appropriate messages. Because DDE is complicated and requires lengthy explanation, it's one subject we won't cover in this book, which is an overview of Borland Pascal 7.

Device–Independent Graphics

Another way that Windows insulates application programs is by providing a common *graphics device interface* (GDI) that programs can use regardless of the output device to which they are sending information.

That's very abstract, but in practice it's quite simple. Under DOS, programs must be equipped with a different software driver for every hardware device to which they might need to send output. That much is familiar even to users of word processing packages, who must specify the type of monitor and printer they have when they first install the software. Likewise, Turbo Pascal and Turbo C++ programmers are familiar with the need to include all the appropriate .BGI (Borland Graphics Interface) drivers for different types of video adapters and screen displays; in addition to your program itself, you'll typically include (on the diskette) drivers for IBM monochrome, Hercules graphics, CGA, EGA, and VGA video equipment.

Windows makes all this unnecessary. Because Windows insulates application programs from the underlying hardware, the programs can simply write to the Windows GDI. Windows then formats the output appropriately and routes it to the desired output device, such as a video display, printer, plotter, or modem. When each user installs Windows, the Windows program itself sets up all the drivers needed for a particular hardware configuration; application programs no longer need to worry about them.

Graphic User Interface

Finally, Windows provides a graphic user interface by which the user can interact with application programs. This means that application programs

- must be able to respond to mouse clicks and movements as well as keyboard input;

- must use Windows-standard GUI screen objects, such as dialog boxes, buttons, menus, and scroll bars; and

- must respond to input events in Windows-standard ways—for example, by opening a menu in response to a mouse click on the menu name.

Borland Pascal for Windows makes it easy to do all of these things with the predefined objects in its ObjectWindows class library. Object types that are defined in ObjectWindows already contain most of the required Windows behaviors, so you can simply "inherit" them in your own application programs and modify them as needed.

Programming in Windows

The key to Windows programming with Borland Pascal is to understand the relation between the Windows Application Programming Interface (API) and Object-Windows. Windows provides hundreds of different functions that can be used by application programs. These functions, originally designed to work with the C programming language and Microsoft's Windows SDK, are often complex and difficult to deal with in writing a program.

ObjectWindows provides an easier way of approaching the multitude of functions in the Windows API. Because object types inherit data fields and methods from their ancestor types, the object types in ObjectWindows provide all of the Windows features needed, so that you can concentrate on developing new features that are unique to your application program. To use a particular object type defined in ObjectWindows, you simply

- declare the relevant ObjectWindows unit in a USES clause, and

- define a new object type as a descendant of the ObjectWindows object type.

The new type inherits all the fields and methods of the ObjectWindows type. You can add new fields and methods, or override methods, from the predefined type so that the new object type fits your program's needs. You don't need to worry about defining methods for basic Windows behaviors or screen objects; those are already taken care of for you by the predefined object type.

The result is twofold. First, you have a much easier time dealing with the Windows API, because Borland Pascal and ObjectWindows do most of the work for you. Second, you can develop your programs in object-oriented Borland Pascal without needing to be concerned about many of the program details that would take up a great deal of time if you were working in C or assembly language and making calls directly to the API.

The Borland Pascal for Windows IDE

Until recently, if you wanted to do Windows programming, you had two main choices. You could use the C programming language with the Microsoft Windows SDK, which are flexible but difficult, or you could use end-user packages such as ObjectVision, Visual BASIC, and Toolbook, which are easy but not as flexible as some applications require. There was no middle ground.

Borland Pascal for Windows solves that dilemma. It provides full high-level support for all the Windows functions—both in the user interface and behind the scenes—but it does so through familiar Pascal constructs that mask much of the complexity of the Windows API. At the same time, it provides much more programming flexibility than end-user packages.

The IDE Main Window

Once you've installed Borland Pascal for Windows, you start it up from within Windows by opening the BPW program group and double-clicking on the BPW icon. The BPW program group also includes icons for the Borland Resource Workshop, Turbo Debugger for Windows, and a variety of programming utilities, but those are beyond the scope of our current discussion. For now, just start Borland Pascal for Windows. The opening screen is shown in Figure 22.2.

The first screen you see is the "main window" of the Borland Pascal for Windows IDE. This allows you to interactively develop, test, and debug your Windows programs, and works almost exactly like the IDE in the standard DOS version of Turbo Pascal.

As is standard in Windows programs, the top line of the window gives the name of the program. The next line down is the menu bar. Underneath that is the SpeedBar, which contains buttons that you can click with the mouse: these are shortcuts for sequences of menu operations.

Within this main IDE window, you can open or create multiple "child" windows that contain source code files. These windows can be moved and resized as you

FIGURE 22.2:

The BPW main window

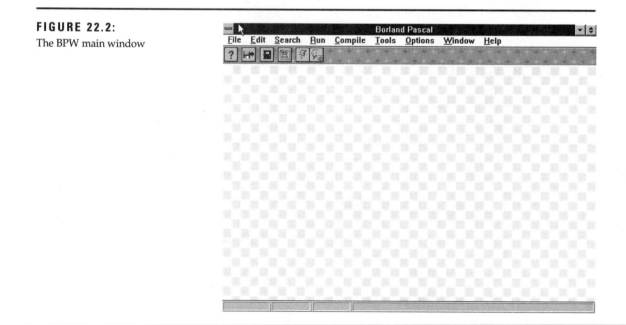

wish. The main difference of all these windows is that they follow the standard Windows user interface guidelines. As in Figure 22.2, each window has devices at the top right to zoom the window to full screen (by using the mouse to click on the up-arrow button) or reduce it to an icon (by clicking on the down-arrow button). When a window is zoomed to full-screen status, the up button also contains a down arrow: this will restore the window to its former size and position instead of reducing it all the way down to an icon.

Likewise, as in Figure 22.3, each window has a device at the top left that opens a menu to switch to other windows or reduce the current window to an icon.

The window-control menu has seven menu options: Restore, Move, Size, Minimize, Maximize, Close, and Switch To; they perform the following operations:

- *Restore:* If a window has been minimized (reduced to an icon), this restores it to its previous size and position on the screen.

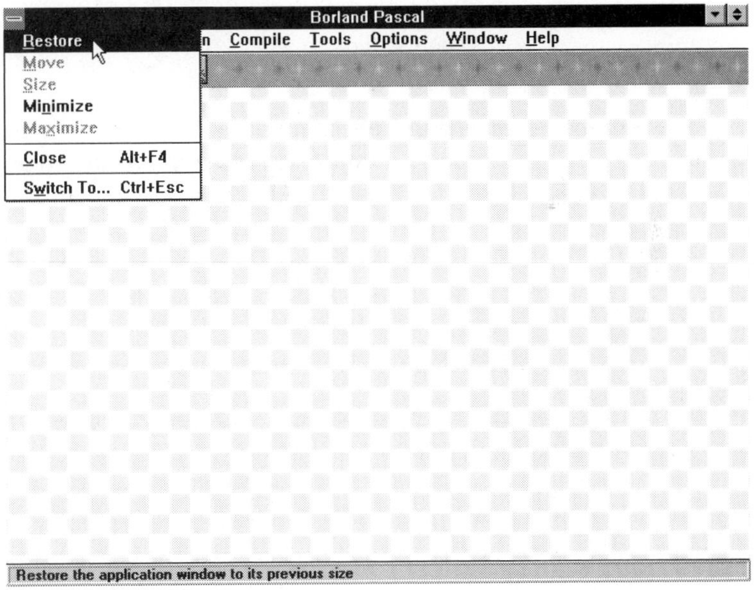

FIGURE 22.3:

The window-control menu

=	Borland Pascal	▼ ⏷
Restore	n Compile Tools Options Window Help	
Move		
Size		
Minimize		
Maximize		
Close Alt+F4		
Switch To... Ctrl+Esc		

Restore the application window to its previous size

- *Move:* This allows you to move a window around on the screen by using the cursor (arrow) keys on the keyboard. After selecting this option, you use the cursor keys to move the window to its new location, then press *Enter*. The move operation is performed more easily, however, by grabbing the window's top border with the mouse and dragging the window.

- *Size:* This allows you to resize a window by using the cursor keys; the method is the same as for moving a window. This operation is easier to perform with the mouse: to resize a window vertically, you simply grab its bottom border and drag it up or down; to resize a window horizontally, you grab its right border and drag it left or right.

- *Minimize:* This shrinks a window to an icon on the screen.

- *Maximize:* This zooms a window to take up the entire screen.

- *Close:* This closes the current window. If the current window is Borland Pascal's main window, it closes down Borland Pascal, releasing the PC resources used by the program; as shown on the menu, you can also use *Alt+F4* as a speed key to perform the close operation. Note that this is different from minimizing the Borland Pascal main window, which leaves the program still open and running—simply in the background and shown on the screen as a icon.

- *Switch To:* This opens a Microsoft Windows task list of programs that are currently running. It allows you to switch temporarily to another program without shutting down Borland Pascal.

Because the main window is simply a "desktop" on which other windows can be opened, it lacks some of the features that are in editing windows. You can open an editing window by selecting the New option from the File menu. The result is shown in Figure 22.4. Notice that several new icons have appeared in the SpeedBar.

Apart from its scroll bars, and from the fact that you enter text into it, the editing window has the same features as the main window (minus the menus, of course). There's the window-control button at the top left, the name of the window (currently noname00.pas) in the center of the top border, and zoom/minimize buttons at the top right. There is one difference in the Window Control menu: instead of "Switch To," which allows you to switch from Borland Pascal to another program, the menu has "Next," which allows you to switch from the current editing window to another one.

FIGURE 22.4:

An editing window

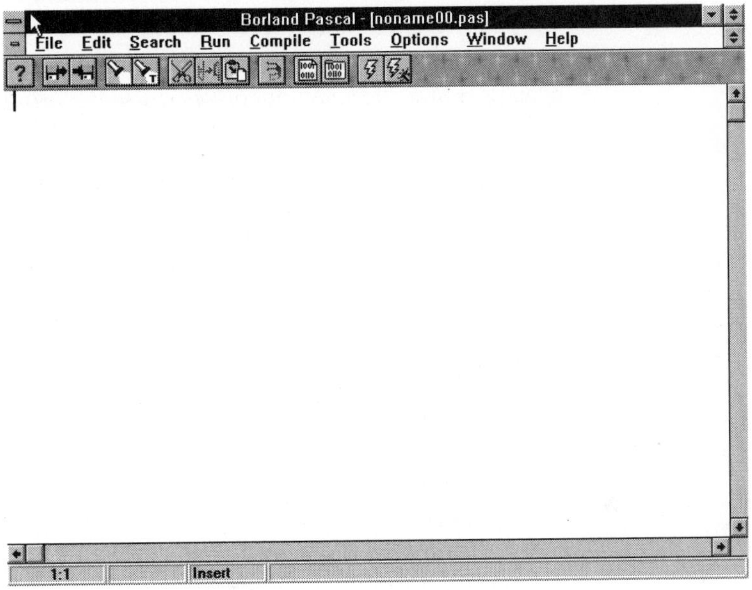

A Quick Demonstration

Now that we have an editing window open, it's a good time for a demonstration of how simple it is to write Windows programs with Borland Pascal for Windows. Enter Listing 22.1 in the "noname00.pas" editing window and, from the File menu, save it as LST22_01.PAS. You don't need to add the .PAS extension: Borland Pascal uses that unless you specify otherwise.

Listing 22.1

```
{Listing 22.1: The "Hello" program
in Borland Pascal for Windows}

PROGRAM Listing22_1;

USES WINCRT;

BEGIN
   WRITELN('Hello, new Windows programmer!');
END.
```

Once you've entered and saved this program, open the Compile menu from the top-line menu bar and select Compile. A dialog box will appear that gives you information about the progress of the compilation process. In this case, of course, the process is almost instantaneous because the program is so short.

To run the program, just open the Run menu and select Run. The program creates a Windows window and displays the text "Hello, new Windows programmer!" inside, as shown in Figure 22.5.

This particular "Hello" program illustrates the WINCRT unit, which lets you run most standard DOS Turbo Pascal programs under Windows. Except for naming WINCRT, Listing 22.1 is a perfectly ordinary Turbo Pascal program, using a WRITELN statement to display text on the screen. However, the text from the WRITELN statement is routed into the program's window— specifically, into its client area. The window in which it resides can perform all of the expected Windows functions, such as displaying a window-control menu, using scroll bars, and responding to mouse clicks. Although most Borland Pascal for Windows programs are more complex than this one, the principle is the same: Let the predefined types in ObjectWindows handle the details and fill in the blanks while you concentrate on the features you want to add or modify.

FIGURE 22.5:

Result of running Listing 22.1

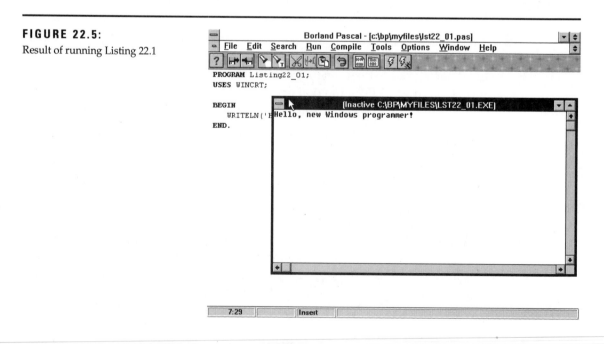

This pattern will be repeated in most of the program listings in this book. Borland Pascal for Windows shields the programmer from unneeded details of the Windows API, doing most of the behind-the-scenes work. It gives you access to low-level Windows function calls when you need them, but you can do most Windows programming in straight object-oriented Borland Pascal with the BPW Object-Windows library.

Using the IDE Menus

The Borland Pascal IDE provides drop-down menus that take care of virtually every normal programming task. You open a menu by using the mouse to click on its name in the menu bar or by pressing the *Alt* key and the underlined letter in the menu name—for example, *Alt+F* to open the File menu.

The IDE also provides speed keys for many operations (such as *Alt+F9* to compile a program file) that are more efficient than going through the menus to achieve the same result. A summary of the IDE menu speed keys appears in Table 22.1, below.

The Borland Pascal menus provide a full range of program development facilities, beyond what is available through the speed keys. The specific features of each menu are discussed below.

File

The File menu, shown in Figure 22.6, allows you to perform the usual file operations. Specific menu choices are as follows:

- *New:* Opens a new, empty edit window in which a new file can be created.

- *Open:* Opens a previously created file in an edit window. This displays the Open File dialog box, as shown in Figure 22.7.

  The dialog box has several parts: boxes that list file names and directories, as well as buttons to perform various operations. With a mouse, you simply click on the part of the dialog box that you want. With the keyboard, you move from one part of a dialog box to another by pressing *Tab* or *Shift+Tab*, and you move *within* part of a dialog box by tapping the appropriate cursor keys. You select a file or directory either by double-clicking on it with the mouse or, from the keyboard, by highlighting it and pressing *Enter*.

TABLE 22.1: The sample table for the Programming Series

Operation	Speed Key	Menu Item
Close/Exit	Alt+F4	File/Exit
Switch To	Ctrl+Esc	Control/Switch To
Close Edit Window	Ctrl+F4	File/Close
Move to next window	Ctrl+F6	Window/Windowname
Undo last edit	Alt+BkSpc	Edit/Undo
Cut selected text, copy to Clipboard	Shift+Del	Edit/Cut
Copy selected text to Clipboard, don't cut	Ctrl+Ins	Edit/Copy
Copy text from Clipboard to cursor position	Shift+Ins	Edit/Paste
Search/repeat search	F3	Search/Search Again
Run program in current window	Ctrl+F9	Run/Run
Compile program in current window	Alt+F9	Compile/Compile
Compile program in current window as well as related files that need to be recompiled	F9	Compile/Make
Display edit windows in "tiled" format	Shift+F5	Window/Tile
Display edit windows in "cascading" format	Shift+F4	Window/Cascade
Open Help Window	F1	Help/Help
Open Help Index	Shift+F1	Help/Index
Open Help on item at cursor location	Ctrl+F1	Help/Topic Search

Near the top of the dialog box is a box where you can enter the name of the file you want to open. You can also enter a file name with wildcard characters, such as ***.pas** or **t*.***, so that only files whose names match the pattern you entered will be displayed in the file list at the lower left.

If you are reopening a file you used previously, you can simply click on the down arrow at the right end of this box to choose from a list of recently used files; from the keyboard, you can press *Alt* and the down-arrow key. Underneath the file name box is displayed the path of the current disk directory, and under that is a list of the files in the current directory that match the wildcard specification in the file name box.

FIGURE 22.6:

The File menu

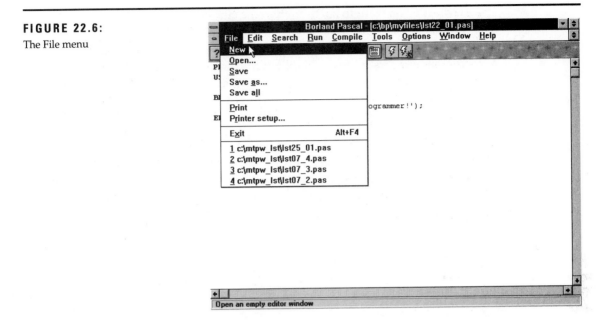

FIGURE 22.7:

The Open File dialog box

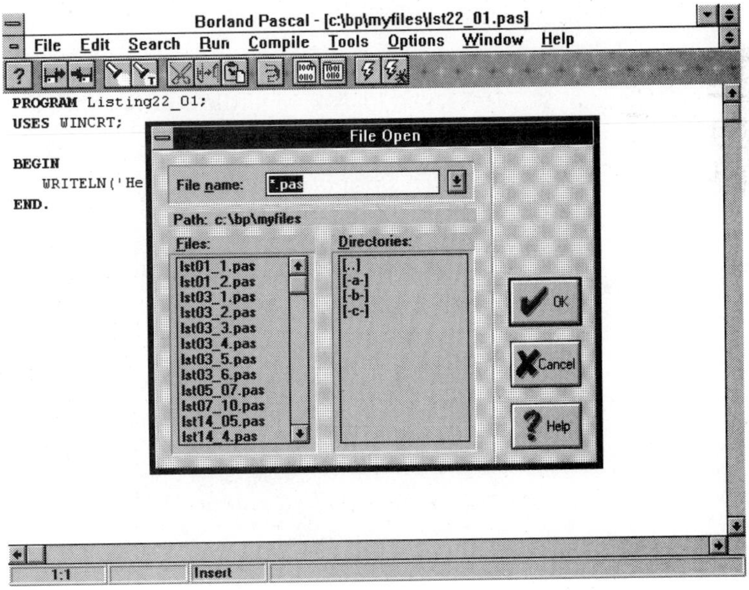

If the file you want to open is not in the current disk directory, then highlight and open the appropriate directory in the Directory box at the right. With the mouse, simply double-click on a directory to open it; with the keyboard, use the *Tab* and cursor keys to highlight the directory, then press *Enter*. As soon as a directory is opened, its files will be displayed in the list on the left.

The three buttons at the right side of the dialog box are standard equipment for every dialog box in Borland Pascal for Windows. Selecting the OK button tells Borland Pascal that it should perform the indicated action—in this case, opening the file whose name is displayed in the file name box. The Cancel button means that you've changed your mind about performing the operation and tells Borland Pascal to close the dialog box without doing anything. The Help button opens a help window with information about the various parts of the dialog box and what you can do with them.

- *Save:* This saves the file in the currently active edit window. If you're saving a new file that hasn't been named yet, Borland Pascal will prompt you to enter a name for the file.

- *Save As:* This allows you to save an existing file under a new file name or in a different directory. It opens up a dialog box that allows you to rename or relocate the file; this dialog box works the same as the Open File dialog box discussed earlier.

- *Save All:* This saves all open files that have been changed since they were last saved to disk, regardless of whether or not they are in the current edit window.

- *Print:* This prints out a hard copy of the file in the current edit window.

- *Printer Setup:* This opens a dialog box that lets you select which printer you want to use to print your program files. One of the advantages of Microsoft Windows is that it has its own printer drivers, so Borland Pascal for Windows does not itself need to include printer drivers for different printers.

- *Exit:* This shuts down Borland Pascal and releases the PC memory that it occupied for use by other programs. The speed key for this is *Alt+F4*; the old speed key, *Alt+X*, is only available through the Alternate user interface definition.

At the bottom of the File menu is a "pick list" of up to five recently used editor files. If you wish to reopen one of these files, you can simply select it like any other menu option, thus bypassing the extra steps involved in using the File Open dialog box.

Edit

The Edit menu provides options that let you cut, copy, and paste selected blocks of text in edit windows. There are two main ways to select a block of text for these operations. With a mouse, you can position the mouse cursor at the beginning of the block of text, hold down the left mouse button, and then simply drag the mouse cursor to the end of the block. This highlights the block of text that has been selected, as shown in Figure 22.8.

An equivalent method with the keyboard is to position the keyboard cursor at the beginning of the text to be selected, hold down the *Shift* key, and then tap the cursor keys until the whole desired text block has been selected.

FIGURE 22.8:

Selecting text in an edit window

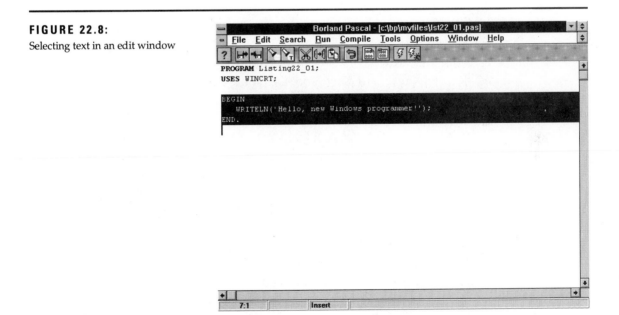

Most of the choices in the Edit menu operate on blocks of text that have been selected in one way or another:

- *Undo:* This reverses the most recent editing change or cursor movement. For example, if you deleted a block of text, choosing Undo would restore the deleted text. Selecting Undo again will not "undo the undo," as in some packages, but will undo the next editing change before the one that was just undone. All editing changes in the current editing session can be undone, but not any changes from previous sessions. Speed key: *Alt+Backspace.*

- *Redo:* This reverses the most recent Undo command. For example, if a block of text was deleted and then restored with Undo, selecting Redo would redelete the block of text. There is no speed key for this operation.

- *Cut:* This deletes a selected block of text and copies it to the Clipboard—an area of memory set aside by Windows. Text can then be pasted from the Clipboard into another edit window or even into another active Microsoft Windows program. Speed key: *Shift+Delete.*

- *Copy:* This copies a selected block of text to the Clipboard but does *not* delete it from the current edit window. It can then be pasted to another location, just as with the Cut command. Speed key: *Ctrl+Insert.*

- *Paste:* This takes whatever is in the Clipboard and copies it to the current location of the keyboard cursor (not the mouse cursor). This operation does *not*, however, delete the contents of the Clipboard, so the same material can be pasted into multiple locations. Speed key: *Shift+Insert.*

- *Clear:* This deletes a selected block of text from the current edit window but does not copy it to the Clipboard—thereby leaving the Clipboard's current contents undisturbed. This operation is equivalent to deleting a selected block of text by pressing the *Delete* key. Speed key: *Ctrl+Delete.*

Search

The Search menu provides a variety of features that allow you to search for text strings, specific locations in your file, and simple programming errors:

- *Find:* This lets you search for a particular text string in the current edit window. Choosing Find opens up the Find Text dialog box, the operation of which is quite standard and works the same as in Turbo Pascal 7.

- *Replace:* This menu choice not only finds a text string for you but lets you replace it with a different text string. It works through the Replace Text dialog box, which is also quite standard and fairly self-explanatory.

- *Search Again:* This menu choice simply repeats whatever search (or search/replace) command you entered last. For example, if you searched for "Writeln", you can repeat the search by using this menu choice—thereby avoiding the extra steps involved in using the Find Text dialog box.

- *Go to Line Number:* This lets you jump directly to a line in a long program file—assuming, of course, that you know the line number to jump to.

- *Show Last Compile Error:* This moves the cursor to the location of the last compilation error (that is, syntax error) that occurred with the current program, even if the error occurred in a different file, such as a unit.

- *Find Error:* This moves the cursor to the location of the last run-time error (for example, file not found) with your current program.

- *Objects:* This opens the BPW Object Browser, which displays a tree diagram of your object hierarchy in programs that use BPW's object-oriented features (that is, programs that are not plain Pascal programs run with the WINCRT unit).

- *Units:* This opens a window that lets you browse through the units used by the current BPW program.

- *Globals:* This opens a window that lets you browse through the global variables and functions available to the current BPW program.

- *Symbols:* This opens a window that lets you browse through the symbols used by the current BPW program.

Run

The Run menu, as you might expect, lets you run your program from within the IDE, and provides features to assist you in testing and debugging it. The menu choices are:

- *Run:* This compiles your program and runs it from within the IDE.

- *Parameters:* This lets you pass command-line parameters to your program, just as if you were starting it from the Windows Program Manager.

Compile

The Compile menu provides various ways of compiling your program—ranging from compiling only the current editor file to recompiling all files linked to the program, whether they need it or not. The menu choices are:

- *Compile:* This compiles the program in the current edit window.

- *Make:* This compiles the file in the current edit window (or the "primary file," if one has been named with the Compile/Primary File menu choice). It also checks any files on which the compiled file depends, such as units, and recompiles them if needed.

- *Build:* This compiles the current editor file or primary file, as well as all files on which it depends—whether or not the other files are up-to-date.

- *Target:* From the BPW development environment, you can (with the appropriate supporting files) compile programs for any of the three platforms supported by Borland Pascal: DOS real mode, DOS protected mode, and Windows. This menu choice lets you specify which platform you want: Windows is the default.

- *Primary File:* This opens a dialog box that lets you specify a "primary file" to be compiled by the Make and Build commands. It is particularly useful when working on large programming projects that involve many linked files.

- *Clear Primary File:* This clears a primary-file specification so that a primary file is no longer specified.

- *Information:* This displays statistics on the last compilation that occurred. It is similar to, but provides more extensive information than, the compilation status dialog box that is displayed while compilation takes place.

Tools

The Tools menu gives you access to programming utilities that are separate from the main BPW IDE. Depending on what you have installed, this menu will normally have options for Turbo Debugger, the Borland Resource Workshop, Winsight, and Turbo Profiler.

Options

The Options menu lets you specify a wide range of preferences for how you want Borland Pascal to work. The menu choices are as follows:

- *Compiler:* This opens a dialog box that lets you set various options for how programs, units, and so forth should be compiled. The Compiler Options dialog box is shown in Figure 22.9.

FIGURE 22.9:

The Compiler Options dialog box

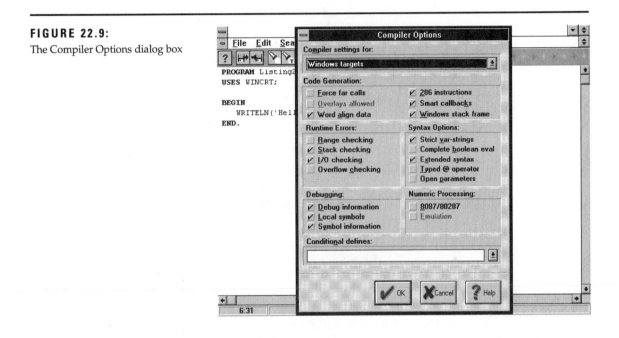

The most important compiler options for program development and debugging are range checking, stack checking, I/O checking, debug information, and local symbols. All of these should be turned on during the program development process to catch errors on compilation and to aid Turbo Debugger. They can be turned off when the final version of the program is compiled; this will produce a smaller .EXE file than if they are turned on. Other features of the Compiler Options dialog box, such as the ability to generate 80x87 code for numeric coprocessors or the ability to change the default sizes of the stack and the heap, will already be familiar to Turbo Pascal programmers.

- *Memory sizes:* This allows you to change the amount of memory that BPW allocates for the stack and the heap in the program you're compiling.

- *Linker:* This opens the Linker Options dialog box, shown in Figure 22.10, with which you can control how your program files are linked.

FIGURE 22.10:

The Linker Options dialog box

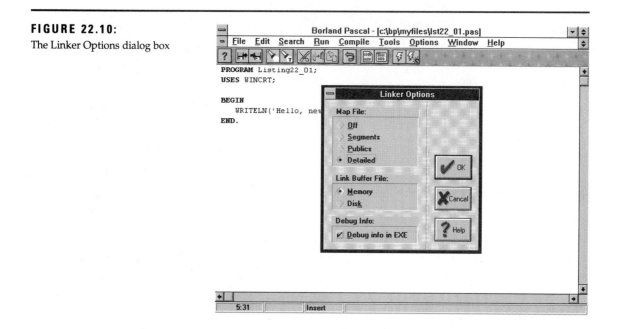

During program development, the Map File option should be "Detailed" to produce a full map file for use with Turbo Debugger for Windows. Likewise, the "Debug info in EXE" box should be checked, but turned off again for compilation of the final version of the program. The Link Buffer feature lets you speed up compilation by using memory (the default) for a link buffer, but you can specify a disk buffer if your program is large and you might run out of memory during compilation.

- *Directories:* This lets you specify the directories where Borland Pascal will put or look for .EXE files and units, include files, object files, and resource files.

- *Browser:* This lets you set options for how the BPW object and symbol browser works and what information is shown.

- *Tools:* This lets you customize the operation and location of BPW tools, such as the Borland Resource Workshop.

- *Environment:* This opens a submenu that lets you set options for the BPW editor, command set, mouse operation, highlighting, and other features.

  It is highly advisable to use the CUA (Command User Axis) command set instead of the "Alternate" command set, even though the latter may be more familiar to users of the non-Windows version of Turbo Pascal. CUA is the standard for user interfaces in Windows programs, so if you use a different interface in Borland Pascal itself, you're defeating the whole purpose of having a standard.

- *Open:* This allows you to load a different set of options than are found in the default configuration file. If you change the options, you can use "Save As" (see below) to save them under a different configuration file name. You can then reload them by loading that file with the Open menu choice.

- *Save:* This saves the current IDE options to the default configuration file.

- *Save As:* This lets you save the current options in a file different from the default configuration file.

Window

The Window menu provides options for arranging windows and icons on the Borland Pascal desktop. The menu choices are as follows:

- *Cascade:* This arranges open windows so that they are "diagonally stacked," with windows overlapping but a portion of each window visible. Speed key: *Shift+F4.*

- *Tile:* This arranges open windows so that they do not overlap, with some of the screen reserved for each window. Speed key: *Shift+F5.*

- *Arrange Icons:* This arranges any icons on the Borland Pascal desktop, just as in Microsoft Windows itself. No speed key.

- *Close All:* This closes all open windows on the Borland Pascal desktop. You will, however, be prompted to save any unsaved files. No speed key.

Help

The Help menu provides a variety of different ways to open Borland Pascal's on-screen help system.

The IDE SpeedBar

Just below the menu bar is the BPW SpeedBar, which has buttons that let you bypass the menus for common tasks. The SpeedBar is shown in Figure 22.4. The buttons, in order, perform the following operations, which we've already explained:

- Help
- Open file
- Save file
- Find text
- Repeat find
- Cut text and copy to Clipboard (available only if a block of text is selected)
- Copy text to Clipboard (available only if a block of text is selected)
- Paste text from Clipboard to cursor position
- Undo last operation
- Compile file in current edit window
- Compile and link current program
- Run current program
- Open Turbo Debugger with current program

ObjectWindows and Other Windows Units

- Units for Windows Programming

- Window and Dialog-Box Object Types

- Using Windows Functions

ObjectWindows (OWINDOWS.TPW) is the library of predefined object types that comes with Borland Pascal for Windows. The great advantage of ObjectWindows is that its object types already include all the basic Windows devices and behaviors. This makes ObjectWindows the single most important feature of Borland Pascal for Windows. All you need to know, as a programmer, is how to use the inherited features and then add the unique features that your own program requires.

To use these predefined types, you simply declare new object types in your program as descendants of the ObjectWindows types, modifying them as needed. If you have already written programs in the DOS version of Turbo Pascal using the Turbo Vision object library, then the ObjectWindows types will seem quite familiar.

All the object types included with ObjectWindows begin with the letter *T*.

ObjectWindows Units

The ObjectWindows object types are organized into several special Borland Pascal *units*. Each unit provides object types for a specific purpose; for example, different units provide Windows-related procedures and functions, specialized data types, and dialog boxes. The units are precompiled, but because they contain object types, it is not necessary to see their source code to create new object types based on them. You simply declare any new object type as a descendant of the predefined object type, then modify it as needed.

OWindows, ODialogs, and Objects

This unit and several other new units replace the unit that was called "WObjects" in the original release of Turbo Pascal for Windows. All the object type, function, variable, and constant declarations in the original WObjects unit were divided up between the smaller units OWindows, ODialogs, and Objects. If you have an earlier version of Turbo Pascal for Windows than the one included in Borland Pascal 7, you should substitute the WObjects unit anywhere a program listing uses the O-Windows, ODialogs, or Objects units.

It's with these units that serious Borland Pascal for Windows applications begin. These units, which form the heart of ObjectWindows, define all the standard object types needed for Windows applications, as well as object types for *collections* and *streams,* which are the object-oriented counterpart of files. Because of their central role, these units must be named by virtually all programs that use any of the special BPW object types—that is, by all programs except DOS applications that have simply been ported to Windows by naming the WinCRT unit (discussed later in this chapter).

WinProcs

The WinProcs unit allows you to call Windows *functions* directly, providing procedure and function headers for every routine in the Windows API. Windows has more than six hundred functions ("function" is the generic term used in Windows to refer to any of its API routines), and the WinProcs unit provides a way for your application to use them directly. When taken along with the WinTypes unit (see below), this gives the complete Borland Pascal implementation of the Windows API.

In general, ObjectWindows will take care of all the underlying details for you. The ObjectWindows object types include *methods* that call Windows API functions; in addition, the object types usually have *data fields* that contain any information that must be passed as parameters to the Windows functions that they call. When a BPW object method calls a Windows function, the required parameters are passed automatically. The most obvious example is a function that must act on a particular window: in order to know what window it should act on, the function must receive that window's *handle* as a parameter when it is called by the application.

WinTypes

The WinTypes unit contains declarations of the Borland Pascal counterparts for the data types used by routines in the Windows API. These include both simple data types and more complex data types (such as records), as well as standard Windows constants for such things as styles, messages, and flags. Data types from this unit that you will see fairly often in BPW programs include:

- *HWnd,* which defines a handle data type for particular window handles.

- *PHandle,* which defines a pointer to a generic Windows handle.

- *THandle,* which defines a generic Windows handle type.

- *THandleTable,* which defines an array of handles.

- *TMDICreateStruct,* which is a record type containing data for the creation of an MDI (Multiple Document Interface) child window.

OStdDlgs

Unlike windows, which provide mostly unstructured interaction with the user, dialog boxes are designed for structured input through buttons and check boxes. The OStdDlgs unit defines two standard types of dialog boxes: *TFileDialog* and *TInputDialog.*

The *TFileDialog* object type allows you to create dialog boxes in which the user can select a file name for saving or loading. The *TInputDialog* object type provides a less structured dialog box that lets the user type in a text response to a query from the program.

OStdWnds

The OStdWnds unit defines two standard types of windows: *TEditWindow* and *T-FileWindow.* A *TEditWindow* provides a simple text-editing window. A *TFileWindow* also provides a simple text-editing window but one that can read from and write to files.

Other BPW Units

Although the ObjectWindows units constitute Borland Pascal's most powerful tool for creating Windows programs, several other units play key roles that are not specifically related to creating Windows objects. These correspond to the units in the DOS version of Turbo Pascal: WinCRT, System, WinDOS, and Strings.

WinCRT

The WinCRT unit, which we already used in the Hello program, is the least complicated of all the units to use. That's because it has only one function: to make it possible for standard Turbo Pascal programs to run as Windows applications. Of course, although these programs are Windows applications in the sense that (1) they run under Windows, and (2) they obey Windows rules for staying in an on-screen window and not hogging the processor, it's really more accurate to call these programs "Windows-compatible" applications, since they don't really take advantage of any of Windows' special features.

You can use the WinCRT unit any time you need to port a DOS-based Turbo Pascal program to Windows and have to do it with a minimum of recoding. The listings in Chapter 3 are a good example: they will compile and run under either DOS Turbo Pascal or Borland Pascal for Windows. The only difference is that DOS programs use the CRT unit in the USES clause, while the Windows programs use the WinCRT unit.

WinCRT does provide most but not all of the standard CRT unit routines, including such standards as CLRSCR, GotoXY, and READKEY. It does lack a few of the less-often-used routines, such as DELAY, so you'll need to do a little modification of non-Windows programs that use these routines.

System

The System unit provides basic Borland Pascal procedures, functions, and definitions that are used by virtually all programs. It is automatically linked to every BPW program when it is compiled, so you never need to explicitly name the System unit in a USES clause.

WinDOS

The WinDOS unit provides a variety of routines for working with MS-DOS and handling files; it corresponds to the DOS unit in standard Turbo Pascal. When using BPW you should provide for as many of these operations as possible to be handled by calls to Windows functions instead of directly through the DOS unit. For example, although the WinDOS unit (like the DOS unit) has routines and data types for manipulating processor registers and software interrupts, these activities can interfere with the operation of other Windows applications that may be running concurrently with your program.

Strings

The Strings unit provides support for the use of *null-terminated strings,* a new string type that is required by the Windows API.

In standard Turbo Pascal, a string is treated as an array of characters with the first position (array[0]) containing the current length of the string. It has a maximum size of 255 characters and can occupy from 1 to 256 bytes of PC memory. A null-terminated string, on the other hand, has no length byte to indicate where the string ends. Instead, it indicates the end of the string with a NULL (#0) character. This means that it can contain up to 65,535 characters, much more than a standard string.

Like most Windows objects, you access a null-terminated string through a handle to that string. This is more similar to standard DOS Turbo Pascal than it might seem, because when you use a string variable in DOS Turbo Pascal, you are actually performing a pointer operation with the details taken care of by Turbo Pascal itself.

ObjectWindows Object Types

There are several different object types included in ObjectWindows. Each type serves a different kind of function in Windows programming from top-level "abstract" types such as *TApplication,* which are never implemented without modification, to types for windows and dialog boxes.

Top-Level Abstract Object Types

The base object type in ObjectWindows is the *TObject* type. This is an abstract type that serves as the ancestor for all other ObjectWindows types, and, as such, it is never actually implemented in any of your BPW programs. It defines basic *constructor* and *destructor* methods.

TApplication is another abstract object type that serves as the basis for defining your own Windows applications. When you create a Windows program, you'll usually declare the main object type as a descendant of *TApplication,* adding (at least) your own version of the inherited *InitMainWindow* method.

Window Object Types

The window object types in ObjectWindows take care of setting up various types of windows and the controls that operate them. You can also, when needed, create many of the controls yourself if you need to add some special functionality to them. The main window object types are:

- *TWindow*, which serves as the basis for general-purpose windows that can be used to hold or display other things, such as graphics or an application's child windows.

- *TEditWindow*, which serves as the basis for windows that provide basic text entry and editing capabilities, but without the ability to read from or write to files.

- *TFileWindow*, which serves as the basis for windows that provide basic text entry and editing capabilities, and also have the ability to read from and write to files.

Dialog-Box Object Types

The dialog-box object types provide for structured interaction with the user via buttons, check boxes, and other controls. The object types are:

- *TDialog*, an abstract object type that serves as the basis for all Windows dialog boxes. Each *TDialog* object type has an associated resource file that describes the appearance and location of the dialog box's control objects. *TDialog* includes methods to initialize, run, and shut down the dialog box, as well as for other tasks, such as interacting with files.

- *TDlgWindow*, which combines characteristics of both dialog boxes and windows, and can include traditional dialog box elements as well as icons and cursors, which are most often associated with windows.

- *TFileDialog*, a standard dialog box type that prompts the user to select a file to open, edit, or save.

- *TInputDialog*, which defines a dialog box for the input of a single item of text.

Control Object Types

Unlike windows, which have mostly standard control devices, dialog boxes merely provide a backdrop for control devices that you specify. You don't need to define these control devices, of course, because their basic appearance and behaviors are already defined in the ObjectWindows object types; however, you must choose which devices will appear and what text they will display—for example, displaying Yes, No, and Cancel buttons. The basic control object types are:

- *TControl*, an abstract type that serves as the basis for all other Windows control types. This contains the necessary functions for creating controls and processing messages for all its descendant control-device object types.

- *TButton*, which serves as the basis for creating push buttons.

- *TListBox*, which serves as the basis for creating general-purpose Windows list boxes.

- *TComboBox*, which adds editing control to the *TListBox* type.

- *TCheckBox*, which serves as the basis for creating check boxes.

- *TRadioButton*, which serves as the basis for creating radio buttons.

- *TGroupBox*, which serves as the basis for creating *group boxes.* (A group box, usually found within a dialog box, serves to group together several related buttons or controls.)

- *TEdit*, which serves as the basis for text-processing capabilities in an editing control.

- *TScrollBar*, which serves as the basis for creating stand-alone scroll-bar controls. Scroll-bar controls are normally included in window object types (descendants of *TWindow*), so you usually won't need a separate operation to create them.

- *TStatic*, which provides methods to set, query, and clear the text in an output-only ("static") control.

MDI Object Types

Windows defines a standard set of behaviors for setting up multiple documents within a single window. This standard is called the Multiple Document Interface. The ObjectWindows MDI types provide a way to set up and manipulate MDI windows. An MDI application has a main window and one or more child windows, each of which can be opened, closed, moved, resized, or reduced to an icon. The object types are:

- *TMDIWindow*, which serves as the basis for creating the main MDI window.
- *TMDIClient*, which serves as the basis for creating child windows and their client (internal) areas.

Using Windows Functions with ObjectWindows

The *WinProcs* and *WinTypes* units provide all you need to call Windows API functions from Borland Pascal programs. To use a Windows function in a program, you simply call the corresponding Borland Pascal procedure or function from the WinProcs unit. Windows functions typically require that one or more parameters be passed to them when they are called: a typical example is the creation of a Windows *MessageBox* in which you specify the types of buttons (such as Yes, No, and Cancel) and an icon that shows the kind of message box that it is. ObjectWindows takes care of many of these parameters, but you must specify others yourself. (See Figure 23.1 for a diagram showing the object hierarchy of ObjectWindows.)

FIGURE 23.1:

The ObjectWindows hierarchy

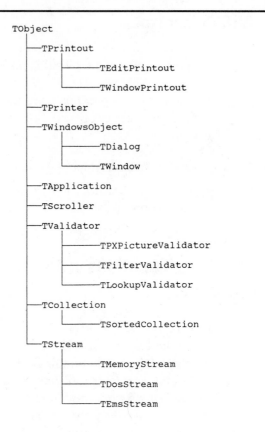

CHAPTER TWENTY-FOUR

Creating and Using a Window

- A Bare-Bones Windows Application

- Responding to Mouse Clicks

- Formatting Data for Display

- Drawing in a Window

24

We've already created one Windows program: the Hello program. However, this program just showed how to run a plain MS-DOS style Turbo Pascal program under Windows. As a result, it was a "Windows program" only by virtue of using the WinCRT unit and running in a window. It didn't really take advantage of the tremendous power that Borland Pascal for Windows puts at your fingertips.

Now that the groundwork has been taken care of, we are ready to get down to some serious Windows programming. In this chapter, we'll look at how to create a more flexible and powerful Windows application than you can create by merely using the WinCRT unit. We'll see how to set up a main window, how to respond to mouse clicks and other input events, how to display text in a window, and how to use some of the predefined object types and methods that are provided in ObjectWindows.

Creating a Bare-Bones Windows Application

The first thing you must do to create a Windows application is to create a main window for that application. In itself, creating a main window is remarkably simple: you simply declare the WOBJECTS unit in a USES clause and inherit what you need. Later, you can define more powerful main-window types, but let's take things one step at a time. The code to set up an application's main window is shown in Listing 24.1, which is a complete, if rather spartan, Windows program in itself.

Listing 24.1

```
PROGRAM Listing24_1;

    { Creates a Windows application and the main window
      of the application. Features demonstrated:
      1. Using the TApplication object type.
      2. Using the inherited InitMainWindow procedure.
      3. Initializing the main window with NEW used
         as a function.
      4. The significance of the main window title. }

USES OWINDOWS;

TYPE
```

```
TMyApp = OBJECT (TApplication)
   PROCEDURE InitMainWindow; VIRTUAL;
   END;

PROCEDURE TMyApp.InitMainWindow;
   BEGIN
   MainWindow := NEW(PWindow, Init(NIL, 'First BPW Program'));
   END;

VAR
   MyApp : TMyApp;

{ Main body of the program }
BEGIN
   MyApp.Init('MyFirst');
   MyApp.Run;
   MyApp.Done;
END.
```

When you enter, compile, and run the program, it should display a screen like that shown in Figure 24.1. A main window should appear, titled "First BPW Program." The basic window-control devices should be present, including maximize/minimize buttons at the top right and a control-menu button at the top left. The actual size and position of the program window may be different from the figure, depending on the type of system you have.

Let's take this program a line at a time, because even though it's a simple program, there's a great deal to notice about it. The first line is a standard Pascal program statement, declaring "Listing24_1" as the program name. The second line (ignoring the comment, of course) is a USES clause that names the OWINDOWS unit. This unit provides three predefined object types that we need to use in this program:

TApplication, which is the object type that controls the behavior of the overall program.

TWindow, which is the object type for the main program window. This object type is used by the inherited method *TApplication.InitMainWindow* unless you override it and specify a different type of window.

PWindow, which is a predefined handle (that is, "pointer") type that can point to an object of type *TWindow*.

FIGURE 24.1:

Running the program in Listing 24.1

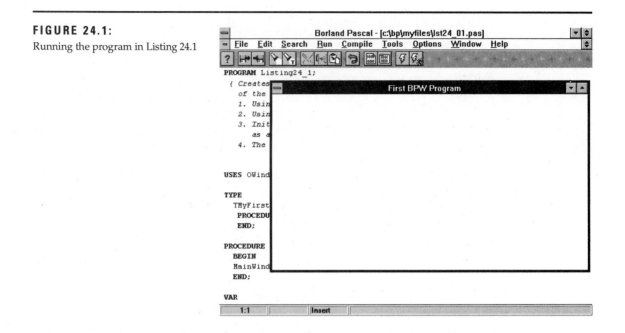

In the TYPE section of the program, we declare *TMyApp* as an object that is a descendant of *TApplication*. This means that it inherits all of *TApplication*'s fields and methods, including *InitMainWindow,* which we override (as you normally will) with a new *InitMainWindow* method. If it is not overridden, the inherited *InitMain-Window* method will produce a generic *TWindow* main window with no title. Note that our new version of the *InitMainWindow* routine is declared as a *virtual* method. Once a method is declared as virtual (as *InitMainWindow* is in the *TApplication* object type), then it must remain a virtual method in all object types that are descended from the base type.

In the *TMyApp.InitMainWindow* method, we assign the title "First BPW Program" to the main window, and thereby to the application task itself. The procedure header is a standard object method header: first it gives the name of the object type that the method goes with, then the name of the method. The body of the method consists of a single line to set up the *MainWindow* variable, which is a predefined pointer type (a handle) that points to the main window object.

Notice that the statement uses Turbo Pascal's extended syntax for the NEW procedure, both using NEW as a function and including a call to the dynamic object's *Init* method. In this case, the *PWindow* parameter is a predefined object type that points to a *TWindow* object. The *TWindow.Init* method takes two parameters itself: first, a handle to the window's parent window, if any, and second, the window title. The first parameter is NIL here because this is the main application window, and therefore, there is no parent window. The second parameter provides the window title that appears in the top border of the application window, as shown in Figure 24.1.

It's worth noting that the main window title doesn't appear only in the top border of the application window. When you call up the Windows task-switching menu, the task for your application is listed under the main window title.

Next in the program comes the VAR section, where we declare a variable of the *TMyApp* object type. And though everyone knows it, it's worth reminding ourselves once more that type declarations, no matter how intricate, do not create any variables of the types declared. The application that we run in this program is not *TMyApp*, which is a data type, but *MyApp*, which is an object variable of that type.

Finally, the main body of the program calls *MyApp*'s INIT, RUN, and DONE methods. We've defined the INIT method, of course, and the RUN and DONE methods are inherited from *TApplication*. The RUN method sets up the application's message loop as a task under Windows. The DONE method disposes of the application's (dynamic) main window object and then shuts down the application.

That may all seem complicated for a program that just opens a window on the screen, but look at what we got for our 17 lines of code. We got a program that runs as a task under Windows, has its own window-control buttons, and has its own window title in the Windows task list. It even has a predefined window-control menu, as shown in Figure 24.2. All in all, that's remarkably little work for a remarkably sophisticated result.

One other point is worth mentioning. If you've tried out the program in Listing 24.1, you know that it can also respond to mouse clicks and drags. When you click the left mouse button on a device, it responds; when you hold down the mouse button and drag the window or one of its borders, the window or border moves just as you would expect. We have not, however, *defined* any methods to respond to mouse input; these are all inherited from the ancestor *TWindow* object that is created by *InitMainWindow*. In the next section, we'll add a method to respond to a left mouse click.

FIGURE 24.2:

MyApp's window-control menu

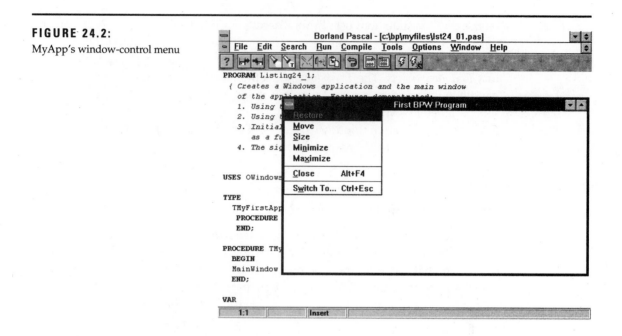

Responding to Mouse Clicks

The program in Listing 24.1 is impressive enough, considering the sophistication of what it does. However, if you click a mouse button when the mouse cursor is in the *middle* of the window—that is, not on one of the window-control buttons or on the border—then nothing happens.

This is because the *TWindow* object type used by *TApplication* includes a method to respond to mouse clicks, but only for left-button clicks and only when the cursor is on a control button or in the window's border. To respond to clicks in the interior of the window—the area called the window's "client area"—we must define our own mouse-click response methods. In this section, we'll look at two ways of doing that. Both ways use the same basic approach—an approach that is in fact used to respond to all Windows messages of all types—but they differ in their results.

Displaying a Message Box in Response to a Mouse Click

The first way of defining mouse-click responses is shown in Listing 24.2. In this program, we set up a method that displays a message box in the window when the click occurs. The code is short but fairly intricate. Therefore, as we did earlier, we'll look at it line by line. First, however, you should enter and run the program to see what it does. Your result should look like Figure 24.3.

FIGURE 24.3:

Displaying a message box in response to a mouse click

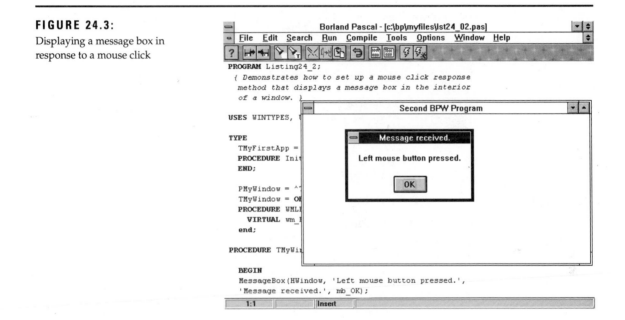

Listing 24.2

```
PROGRAM Listing24_2;

    { Demonstrates how to set up a mouseclick response
      method that displays a message box in the interior
      of a window. }

USES WINTYPES, WINPROCS, OWINDOWS;

TYPE
    TMyApp = OBJECT (TApplication)
```

```
      PROCEDURE InitMainWindow; VIRTUAL;
      END;

   PMyWindow = ^TMyWindow;
   TMyWindow = OBJECT (TWindow)
      PROCEDURE WMLButtonDown(VAR Msg : TMessage);
            VIRTUAL wm_First + wm_LButtonDown;
            end;

PROCEDURE TMyWindow.WMLButtonDown(VAR Msg : TMessage);
   BEGIN
   MessageBox(HWindow, 'Left mouse button pressed.',
            'Message received.', mb_OK);
   END;

PROCEDURE TMyApp.InitMainWindow;
   BEGIN
   MainWindow := NEW(PMyWindow,
      Init(NIL, 'Second BPW Program'));
   END;

VAR
   MyApp : TMyApp;

BEGIN
   MyApp.Init('MySecond');
   MyApp.Run;
   MyApp.Done;
END.
```

Apart from the program name, the first difference between Listing 24.2 and Listing 24.1 is that Listing 24.2 adds the WINTYPES and WINPROCS units to the program's USES clause. We need these because our mouse-click response method, defined later on in the listing, uses Windows API functions and associated ObjectWindows data types: the former are handled by the WINPROCS unit and the latter by the WINTYPES unit.

Next, the declaration of the *TMyFirstApp* object type is the same as in Listing 24.1. This doesn't need to change at all. We begin to see a difference right below it, however, where we declare a pointer (*PMyWindow*) to a new window type (*TMy-Window*). In Listing 24.1, we simply accepted the inherited, generic *TWindow* object type that is used by the *TApplication* object type. Here, though, we want to add features to the main application window, so we define a new window type based on *TWindow* and add our own method to respond to clicks of the left mouse button.

The mouse-click response method itself deserves considerable study. First, the name *WMLButtonDown* indicates that this is intended to override the *TWindow* inherited method of the same name. Because the *TWindow* method that it overrides is virtual, this method must also be virtual. The new *WMLButtonDown* method takes one parameter, *Msg*, which is of the *TMessage* record type. This is a variant record type that has a field for a handle to the window where the mouse click occurs, as well as for the X and Y coordinates of the mouse click inside the window.

After VIRTUAL, the final part of the method header is

```
wm_First + wm_LButtonDown
```

This is called the *extension* of the method header and it tells Turbo Pascal which Windows messages this method is intended to respond to. The first part of the extension, *wm_First*, really doesn't do much of anything. Don't worry about it.

The second part of the extension is the important part, because it tells which Windows message this method responds to. All Windows messages are referred to in BPW by identifiers in the same format:

```
wm_identifier
```

Here, *wm_LButtonDown* is a predefined identifier that says, "This method responds to left-button mouse clicks." If we had used *wm_RButtonDown* instead, the method would respond to right-button mouse clicks.

Now we get to the actual definition of the *TMyWindow.WMLButtonDown* method. The body of the method consists of a single line, which calls the BPW *MessageBox* function. This function creates a *message box* kind of a read-only version of a dialog box. A message box takes four parameters:

1. A **handle** (pointer) to the window (the "parent window") in which the message box is supposed to appear.

2. The **message** to be displayed in the message box. This is a special kind of string used by Windows and the C programming language, called a *null-terminated string*.

3. The **title** of the message box, also in the form of a null-terminated string.

4. One or more **identifiers** that display icons or buttons in the message box.

In this case, *HWindow* is the handle to the parent window. The identifier *HWindow* itself is a predefined window-handle identifier from the OWINDOWS unit that points to whatever window is associated with the mouse click. `'Left mouse button pressed.'` is the message to be displayed in the window, while `'Message received.'` is the window title. Finally, *mb_OK* is a predefined button identifier that displays the OK button in the message box, as shown in Figure 24.3. There is a variety of predefined push-button identifiers that you can use in message boxes and dialog boxes, including such identifiers as *mb_YesNo* (displays Yes and No buttons) and *mb_IconQuestion* (displays a noninteractive question-mark icon).

In most respects, the *TMyFirstApp.InitMainWindow* method is just as it was in Listing 24.1, with the exception that the *MainWindow* function calls NEW with a *PMyWindow*-type window handle instead of the generic *PWindow* window handle. As before, NEW is called as a function and uses extended Borland Pascal syntax to initialize the main window. The rest of the program is the same as Listing 24.1.

Displaying Text in Response to a Mouse Click

Now that we've seen how to create and customize a main application window, let's make our example a little more sophisticated. Instead of displaying a message box when the user clicks the left mouse button, the new application will display a plain-text message at the location of the mouse click inside the window. To see how this works, enter, compile, and run Listing 24.3. After you've clicked the mouse in the window a few times, the result should look like Figure 24.4.

Listing 24.3

```
PROGRAM Listing24_3;

   { Demonstrates how to display text at the location
     of a mouse click. Specific features demonstrated:
     1. The TextOut procedure.
     2. Nullterminated strings vs. regular strings.
```

```
        3. The StrPCopy procedure.
        4. Getting and releasing a device context. }

USES WINTYPES, WINPROCS, OWINDOWS, STRINGS;

TYPE
    TMyThirdApp = OBJECT (TApplication)
        PROCEDURE InitMainWindow; VIRTUAL;
        END;

    PMyWindow = ^TMyWindow;
    TMyWindow = OBJECT (TWindow)
        PROCEDURE WMLButtonDown(VAR Msg : TMessage);
            VIRTUAL wm_First + wm_LButtonDown;
            END;

PROCEDURE TMyWindow.WMLButtonDown(VAR Msg : TMessage);
    VAR
    dc : HDC;
    s  : ARRAY[0..20] OF CHAR;
    BEGIN
    StrPCopy(s, 'Left Button Clicked.');
    dc := GetDC(HWindow);
    TextOut(dc, Msg.LParamLo, Msg.LParamHi, s, strlen(s));
    ReleaseDC(HWindow, dc);
    END;

PROCEDURE TMyThirdApp.InitMainWindow;
    BEGIN
    MainWindow := NEW(PMyWindow,
        Init(NIL, 'Third BPW Program'));
    END;

VAR
    MyThirdApp : TMyThirdApp;

{ main body of program }
BEGIN
    MyThirdApp.Init('MyThird');
    MyThirdApp.Run;
    MyThirdApp.Done;
END.
```

FIGURE 24.4:

Displaying text in a window at the location of a mouse click

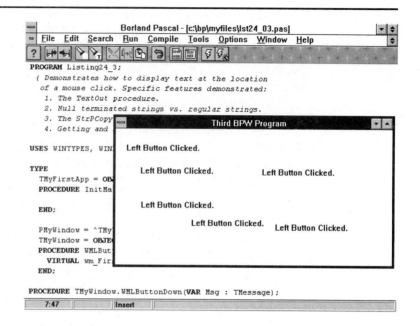

As before, this adds several new wrinkles to the previous program listing. The first is the addition of the STRINGS unit to the USES clause: this is needed to handle the null-terminated string that we will use to display the text in the window. To understand the idea of null-terminated strings, it's useful to contrast them with standard Borland Pascal strings.

In standard DOS Borland Pascal, a string is treated as a special case of an array of characters. Thus, for example, a string of type

```
STRING[20]
```

is really an

```
ARRAY[0..20] OF CHAR
```

The array slots numbered 1..20 are used to store the characters in the string, and the zero slot holds the current length of the array. Thus, if a string of type STRING[20] only held five characters, such as "Susan", then the zero slot would hold the length 5. This is how standard Borland Pascal normally determines where the string ends.

Windows, however, uses a different approach. It uses an ASCII NULL character (#0) to mark the end of the string. Thus, for example, a string with "Susan" in it would actually be a character array containing 'S', 'u', 's', 'a', 'n', #0. This is a more important difference than you might think, and it can get you into trouble if you forget it, as we'll see in Listing 24.4 where we *deliberately* forget it.

The declaration of the *PMyWindow* window handle and the *TMyWindow* object type are the same as in Listing 24.3. This is only to be expected, of course, because if we're encapsulating our method details properly, making a minor change in the method should not require any change in the object type declaration.

The details of the *WMLButtonDown* method, however, are very different. As before, it takes a parameter of type *TMessage*, but that's about the only similarity. First, it declares two local variables, *dc* and *s*:

- *dc* is a variable to hold the handle for a *device context* for the text we are going to display in the window. Any text or graphics drawn in a window must have a device context, which serves as the "drawing surface" on which the text or graphic is created. The data type of the variable, HDC, is the Windows equivalent of a Borland Pascal WORD data type, and is the appropriate type for a handle to a device context.

- *s* is a 21-slot array to hold the 20-character string

  ```
  'Left Button Clicked.'
  ```

  The final slot of the array holds the NULL character, which marks the end of the string.

In the main body of the method, the first action is to call the *StrPCopy* function from the STRINGS unit. This function, which is the Pascal equivalent of a standard C language function, copies the standard string 'Left Button Clicked.' into the array *s* and turns it into a null-terminated string.

Next, we create a device context and load its handle into the *dc* variable by calling the *GetDC* function with the current (parent) window's handle. This gets a device context and associates it with the appropriate window so that when the text is displayed, it goes into the correct window.

Next, we call the *TextOut* procedure. This writes the string contained in array *s* (the fourth parameter) to the current cursor location in the window. It takes five parameters:

1. The **device context** on which the text is to be drawn in the window.

2. (and **3.**) The **window coordinates** of the mouse cursor when the click occurs. *Msg*, you may recall, is a *TMessage*-type variant record. Two of its fields, *LParamLo* and *LParamHi*, can be used to get the current mouse position at a mouse click.

4. The **array** containing the null-terminated string to be drawn on the device context.

5. The **length** of the string. Here, we have used the *StrLen* function to return this value; it would have worked just as well simply to use the integer *20* for a 20-character string.

Finally—and this is very important—we release the device context that we called earlier in the method: the two parameters are the handle to the current window and the handle to the device context.

> **NOTE**
>
> Device contexts are analogous to dynamic variables in standard Borland Pascal. When a dynamic variable is no longer needed in a program, you always dispose of it to free up the memory it required. If you fail to do so, your program can run out of memory because most of the memory is allocated to dynamic variables that aren't being used. Likewise, you must dispose of any device context immediately after using it.

The rest of the code in Listing 24.3 is unproblematic and is the same as in Listing 24.2.

Handling Null-Terminated Strings

One important difference between Borland Pascal for Windows and DOS Borland Pascal is BPW's use of null-terminated strings. If you forget the difference between standard Borland Pascal strings and null-terminated strings, your program can have seemingly inexplicable bugs—at least, until you notice that the array of characters you set up doesn't have that extra slot at the end for a null terminator. Listing 24.4 is identical to Listing 24.3 in every respect but the array length, and yet it produces buggy output. If you enter and run the program, your output should look like Figure 24.5.

Listing 24.4

```
PROGRAM Listing24_4;

    { Demonstrates how failure to remember the
      difference between nullterminated strings
      and standard strings can lead to puzzling
      program bugs. }

USES WINTYPES, WINPROCS, OWINDOWS, STRINGS;

TYPE
    TMyApp = OBJECT (TApplication)
        PROCEDURE InitMainWindow; VIRTUAL;
        END;

    PMyWindow = ^TMyWindow;
    TMyWindow = OBJECT (TWindow)
        PROCEDURE WMLButtonDown(VAR Msg : TMessage);
            VIRTUAL wm_First + wm_LButtonDown;
            END;

PROCEDURE TMyWindow.WMLButtonDown(VAR Msg : TMessage);
    VAR
    dc : HDC;
    s  : ARRAY[0..19] OF CHAR;
    BEGIN
    StrPCopy(s, 'Left Button Clicked.');
    dc := GetDC(HWindow);
    TextOut(dc, Msg.LParamLo, Msg.LParamHi, s, strlen(s));
    ReleaseDC(HWindow, dc);
    END;

PROCEDURE TMyApp.InitMainWindow;
    BEGIN
    MainWindow := NEW(PMyWindow,
```

```
        Init(NIL, 'Buggy BPW Program'));
    END;

VAR
    MyBuggyApp : TMyApp;

{ main body of program }
BEGIN
    MyBuggyApp.Init('MyThird');
    MyBuggyApp.Run;
    MyBuggyApp.Done;
END.
```

FIGURE 24.5:

Buggy output from Listing 24.4

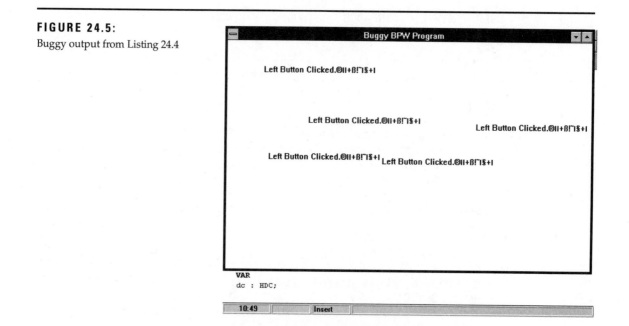

Now, because I've pointed out the bug, it should be obvious. The array *s* is now only a 20-character array: big enough to hold the string 'Left Button Clicked.' but *not* big enough to hold that string plus a NULL character to terminate the string. In this case, the extra characters displayed to the right of the 'Left Button Clicked' message are just whatever characters happen to be in the next memory locations after the string is supposed to end. (Note, however, that if the string had been only 19 characters—for example, 'Left Button Clicked', omitting the period—then everything would be fine, because the 20-slot array would have an empty slot at the end to hold the string-terminating NULL. But failing to remember the extra slot for the NULL can lead to incorrect output.)

Displaying Data in a Window

We've already created a simple Windows application, complete with predefined menu and a message box. Now, let's make it display informative icons in a message box, add file-save protection to your applications, and display graphic data in a window.

Let's start by trying some different features in the dialog box (actually a "message box"). Though that message box simply informs the user that the left mouse button has been pressed and displays an OK push-button, we can make some useful changes quite easily.

One of the simplest things to do is to enhance the dialog box by adding an icon to show the user what kind of dialog box it is. For example, a dialog box that asks the user for information might display a question mark, a warning box might display a stop sign, or a box that provides information might show an "I" for "Information."

Let's make a simple change. Enter and run Listing 24.5, which enhances the message box from Listing 24.2. Notice that the only difference is the addition of a new identifier in the *TMyWindow.WMLButtonDown* method. When it calls the predefined *MessageBox* method to create the dialog box, it adds the identifier *mb_IconExclamation* to the identifier for the OK push button. The result is shown in Figure 24.6.

FIGURE 24.6:

Adding an icon to the "Left mouse button pressed" dialog box

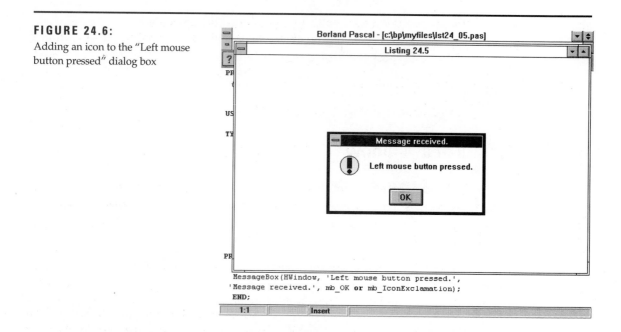

Listing 24.5

```
PROGRAM Listing24_5;

   { Demonstrates how to set up informative icons
     in a dialog box. }

USES WINTYPES, WINPROCS, OWINDOWS;

TYPE
   TMyApp = OBJECT (TApplication)
      PROCEDURE InitMainWindow; VIRTUAL;
      END;

   PMyWindow = ^TMyWindow;
   TMyWindow = OBJECT (TWindow)
      PROCEDURE WMLButtonDown(VAR Msg : TMessage);
         VIRTUAL wm_First + wm_LButtonDown;
         END;

PROCEDURE TMyWindow.WMLButtonDown(VAR Msg : TMessage);
   BEGIN
```

```
   MessageBox(HWindow, 'Left mouse button pressed.',
   'Message received.', mb_OK or mb_IconExclamation);
   END;

PROCEDURE TMyApp.InitMainWindow;
   BEGIN
   MainWindow := NEW(PMyWindow,
   Init(NIL, 'Listing 24.5'));
   END;

VAR
   MyApp : TMyApp;

{main body of program}
BEGIN
   MyApp.Init('Listing24_5');
   MyApp.Run;
   MyApp.Done;
END.
```

Of course, there's no substitute for trying things on your own, but this shows how easy it is to change a message box. BPW provides predefined identifiers for the most common things you want to do in a dialog box; these are shown in Table 24.1. As usual, we've used upper- and lowercase letters to make things easier for you to read. It doesn't matter if you use upper- or lowercase in your BPW programs.

TABLE 24.1: Predefined Identifiers for Use with the MessageBox Function

Identifier	Result
mb_AbortRetryIgnore	Displays push buttons for Abort, Retry, or Ignore in the current operation.
mb_ApplModal	Creates a modal message box.
mb_DefButton1	Makes the first (leftmost) button the default button.
mb_DefButton2	Makes the second button the default button.
mb_DefButton3	Makes the third button the default button.
mb_IconAsterisk	Displays an "I" icon for an information box.
mb_IconExclamation	Displays an exclamation mark icon.
mb_IconHand	Displays a stop sign icon.
mb_IconInformation	Displays an "I" icon for an information box.
mb_IconQuestion	Displays a question mark icon to prompt the user for information.
mb_IconStop	Displays a stop sign icon.

TABLE 24.1: Predefined Identifiers for Use with the MessageBox Function (continued)

Identifier	Result
mb_OK	Displays an OK push button.
mb_OKCancel	Displays OK and Cancel push buttons.
mb_RetryCancel	Displays Retry and Cancel push buttons.
mb_SystemModal	Creates a modal message box that suspends Windows; for use in emergency situations.
mb_TaskModal	Creates a modal message box when no parent window is available. You should specify 0 as the parent window parameter. All top-level windows (tasks) in the application will be suspended.
mb_YesNo	Displays Yes and No push buttons.
mb_YesNoCancel	Displays Yes, No, and Cancel push buttons.

Adding File-Save Protection

Let's look at another example that shows both how to modify push buttons and to remind the user to save work before closing an application. Enter and run the program in Listing 24.6; the result is shown in Figure 24.7.

Listing 24.6

```
PROGRAM Listing24_6;

   { Demonstrates how to set up a dialog box
     that prompts the user to save files when
     closing the window. Also demonstrates how
     to modify the push buttons in a message box. }

USES WINTYPES, WINPROCS, OWINDOWS, STRINGS;

TYPE
   TMyApp = OBJECT (TApplication)
      PROCEDURE InitMainWindow; VIRTUAL;
      END;

   PMyWindow = ^TMyWindow;
   TMyWindow = OBJECT (TWindow)
   FUNCTION CanClose: BOOLEAN; VIRTUAL;
   PROCEDURE WMLButtonDown(VAR Msg : TMessage);
```

```pascal
        VIRTUAL wm_First + wm_LButtonDown;
   END;

FUNCTION TMyWindow.CanClose: BOOLEAN;
VAR
   Reply: Integer;
BEGIN
   CanClose := TRUE;
   Reply := MessageBox(HWindow,
          'Do you want to save your work?',
          'Window content has changed',
           mb_YesNoCancel or mb_IconQuestion);
   IF (Reply = id_Yes) OR (Reply = id_Cancel)
      THEN CanClose := FALSE;
END;

PROCEDURE TMyWindow.WMLButtonDown(VAR Msg : TMessage);
   VAR
   dc : HDC;
   s  : ARRAY[0..20] OF CHAR;
   BEGIN
   StrPCopy(s, 'Left Button Clicked.');
   dc := GetDC(HWindow);
   TextOut(dc, Msg.LParamLo, Msg.LParamHi,
           s, strlen(s));
   ReleaseDC(HWindow, dc);
   END;

PROCEDURE TMyApp.InitMainWindow;
   BEGIN
   MainWindow := NEW(PMyWindow,
   Init(NIL, 'Listing 24.6'));
   END;

VAR
   MyApp : TMyApp;

{main body of program }
BEGIN
   MyApp.Init('Listing24_6');
   MyApp.Run;
   MyApp.Done;
END.
```

FIGURE 24.7:

Adding a file-save dialog box

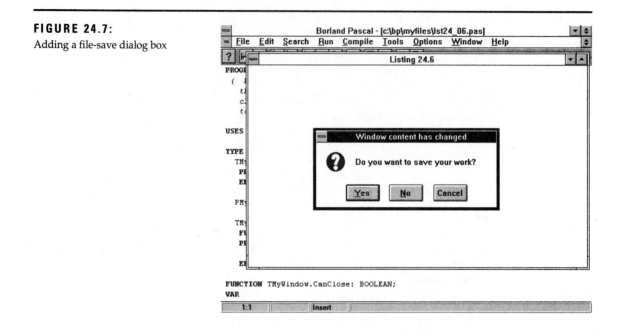

FIGURE 24.7:

Adding a file-save dialog box

Listing 24.6 has several new features that need explaining. The first difference appears in the definition of the *TMyWindow* object type. A new method (a function) has been added called *CanClose*. This is a predefined Boolean function in Object-Windows, but with a twist: *how* it acts is predefined, but the details of *why* it acts are left up to you. If *CanClose* is false, then any attempt to close the current window (of type *TMyWindow*) is canceled; if it's true, then the window can be closed. However, the details of when it is set to false or true are left to be defined by you.

The details of the *CanClose* function are also illuminating. First, we define a local variable called *Reply* of type integer. Then, using the *MessageBox* method as a function, we assign its result to the *Reply* variable.

When *MessageBox* is used in this way, the value it returns depends on which buttons have been put into it. In this case, for example, we have included Yes, No, and Cancel buttons by using the predefined identifier *mb_YesNoCancel*. Clicking on each of these buttons will cause a different value to be assigned to *MessageBox* and, thereby, to the *Reply* variable.

The final line of the *CanClose* method's main body tests the value of the *Reply* variable that was returned by the *MessageBox* function. If the user clicked on either the Yes or the Cancel button, then *CanClose* is set to *false;* otherwise, it remains true and the window is closed.

The identifiers *id_Yes* and *id_Cancel*, as you probably guessed, are predefined ObjectWindows identifiers for the values returned by various push-buttons. Each type of button (see Table 24.1) causes its own particular value to be assigned to *MessageBox*. The buttons' return values are shown in Table 24.2.

TABLE 24.2: Values returned to MessageBox by different types of buttons

Identifier	Meaning
id_Abort	User pressed the Abort button.
id_Cancel	User pressed the Cancel button.
id_Ignore	User pressed the Ignore button.
id_No	User pressed the No button.
id_OK	User pressed the OK button.
id_Retry	User pressed the Retry button.
id_Yes	User pressed the Yes button.

Formatting Data for Display

Another way to display data in a window is to format information and read it into a buffer by using the *WVSPrintF* procedure. You may recall that Windows was originally designed to work with the C programming language: as a result, even Borland Pascal for Windows has a few "C-like" features, and *WVSPrintF* is one place they show up. Along the way, we'll see some new aspects of the *Msg* parameter that we've been using to handle mouse clicks.

To see how *WVSPrintF* works, enter and run Listing 24.7. The output window should look like Figure 24.8. (The actual coordinates, of course, depend on where in the window you click the mouse.)

Listing 24.7

```
PROGRAM Listing24_7;

    { Demonstrates how to format data for display
      by using the WVSPrintF procedure. Specific
      features demonstrated:
      1. How to use the WVSPrintF procedure.
      2. How to format data with WVSPrintF.
      3. The contents of the MSG parameter
         passed with a Windows message. }

USES WINTYPES, WINPROCS, OWINDOWS, STRINGS;

TYPE
    TMyApp = OBJECT (TApplication)
        PROCEDURE InitMainWindow; VIRTUAL;
        END;

    PMyWindow = ^TMyWindow;
    TMyWindow = OBJECT (TWindow)
        FUNCTION CanClose: BOOLEAN; VIRTUAL;
        PROCEDURE WMLButtonDown(VAR Msg : TMessage);
            VIRTUAL wm_First + wm_LButtonDown;
            END;

FUNCTION TMyWindow.CanClose: BOOLEAN;
VAR
    Reply: Integer;
BEGIN
    CanClose := TRUE;
    Reply := MessageBox(HWindow,
            'Do you want to save your work?',
            'Window content has changed',
            mb_YesNoCancel or mb_IconQuestion);
    IF (Reply = id_Yes) OR (Reply = id_Cancel)
        THEN CanClose := FALSE;
END;

PROCEDURE TMyWindow.WMLButtonDown(VAR Msg : TMessage);
    VAR
    dc : HDC;
    s  : ARRAY[0..20] OF CHAR;
    BEGIN
    WVSPrintF(s, 'Click at: %d,%d', Msg.LParam);
```

```
      dc := GetDC(HWindow);
      TextOut(dc, Msg.LParamLo, Msg.LParamHi, s, StrLen(s));
      ReleaseDC(HWindow, DC);
      END;

PROCEDURE TMyApp.InitMainWindow;
   BEGIN
   MainWindow := NEW(PMyWindow,
   Init(NIL, 'Listing 24.7'));
   END;

VAR
   MyApp : TMyApp;

{main body of program }
BEGIN
   MyApp.Init('Listing24_7');
   MyApp.Run;
   MyApp.Done;
END.
```

FIGURE 24.8:

Mouse-click coordinates displayed as formatted with WVSPrintF

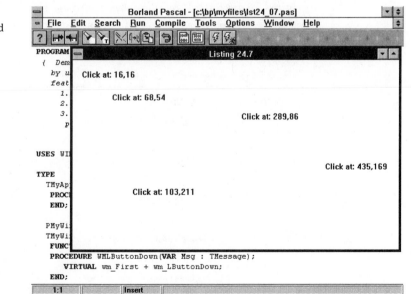

True to the spirit of modular programming, the only differences are in the *W-MLButtonDown* method. As before, the method is defined in such a way that it responds to left-button mouse clicks. It has a local variable, *dc*, for a device context, and another local variable, *s*, which is an array to hold a null-terminated string.

The first line in the main body of the method invokes the *WVSPrintF* procedure, which is similar to the *printf( )* function in C. It takes three parameters:

- A buffer, normally an array, to hold some data.

- A format string that shows how the data should be stored in the buffer.

- A variable that provides the data for the buffer.

The buffer here is *s*, our local character array. The format specification may look familiar if you've programmed in C: *%d* says that the data should be stored in decimal format. In the format string, you can also include other (nonreserved) characters and strings that you want to go with the data: here, we've put in "Click at:" to indicate that the numbers stored (and later displayed) are the coordinates of a mouse click.

Unfortunately, the format specifiers for the data were not documented in the original Turbo Pascal for Windows manuals. The format specifiers are a subset of those used in the C language, and are shown in Table 24.3.

TABLE 24.3:   Predefined data format specifiers for use with WVSPrintF

Specifier	Format
%d	Decimal
%s	String
%c	Char
%i	Integer
%ld	Long signed decimal
%u	Unsigned integer
%lu	Long unsigned integer
%x	Unsigned hex integer
%lx	Long unsigned hex integer

The final parameter in *WVSPrintF* is a variable that holds the data to be put into the buffer. Here, that variable is *Msg.LParam*—one of the fields of the *Msg* parameter that is passed to mouse-click response methods. Previously, we haven't needed to look at this parameter very closely, but now its features become important.

The *Msg* parameter is a record of type *TMessage*, as defined in the OWINDOWS unit. *TMessage* is a variant record type that contains fields for the X and Y coordinates of a mouse click or other user event. *LParam* is a long INTEGER type field (32 bits) that can be subdivided into a low-order part and a high-order part, each of which contains a 16-bit WORD value. Here, we simply load the whole *LParam* value into the buffer, depending on the format specifier to make it display properly.

If you're not familiar with dividing a sequence of bits into low-order and high-order parts, here's an example. Consider the sequence

0000000011111111

This is a 16-bit sequence; however, it can be divided into a low-order part, *00000000*, and a high-order part, *11111111*, each of which has a different value. This means that in a single memory location, you could store any of the following values, depending on how you retrieved the data:

0000000011111111
00000000
11111111

If you can do this, it's obviously more efficient in certain situations.

In the case at hand, *LParam* contains a single 32-bit value that can be split into a low-order part (the X coordinate of the mouse click) and a high-order part (the Y coordinate of the mouse click). We simply load the whole thing into the buffer, then read it out in the format we need.

The next lines simply get a device context, use the *TextOut* procedure to display the text string from the buffer at the coordinates of the mouse click, and release the device context. Everything else in the program is identical to Listing 24.6.

Drawing in a Window

As a final example in this chapter, we'll look at a program to draw lines in a window. While line-drawing itself is not of major importance for most applications, this program does illustrate some key features of Windows programming and provides a jumping-off point for features we'll discuss in later chapters. To get started, enter the program in Listing 24.8.

Listing 24.8

```
PROGRAM Listing24_8;

   { Demonstrates using the mouse to draw in a window.
     Features shown:
     1. Overriding the parent object type's
        CONSTRUCTOR method.
     2. The InvalidateRect method.
     3. The SetCapture and ReleaseCapture methods.
     4. The MoveTo method.
     5. The LineTo method. }

USES STRINGS, WINTYPES, WINPROCS, OWINDOWS;

TYPE
   TMyApp = OBJECT (TApplication)
      PROCEDURE InitMainWindow; VIRTUAL;
      END;

   PMyWindow = ^TMyWindow;
   TMyWindow = OBJECT(TWindow)
      dc: HDC;
      LButtonDown: BOOLEAN;
      CONSTRUCTOR Init(AParent: PWindowsObject;
                       ATitle: PChar);
      FUNCTION CanClose: BOOLEAN; VIRTUAL;
      PROCEDURE WMLButtonDown(VAR Msg: TMessage);
      VIRTUAL wm_First + wm_LButtonDown;
      PROCEDURE WMLButtonUp(VAR Msg: TMessage);
      VIRTUAL wm_First + wm_LButtonUp;
      PROCEDURE WMMouseMove(VAR Msg: TMessage);
      VIRTUAL wm_First + wm_MouseMove;
      END;
```

```
{TMyWindow methods}

CONSTRUCTOR TMyWindow.Init(AParent: PWindowsObject;
                                ATitle: PChar);
    BEGIN
    TWindow.Init(AParent, ATitle);
    LButtonDown := FALSE;
    END;

FUNCTION TMyWindow.CanClose: BOOLEAN;
    VAR
    Reply: INTEGER;
    BEGIN
    CanClose := TRUE;
    Reply := MessageBox(HWindow,
            'Do you want to save your work?',
            'Window content has changed',
            mb_YesNoCancel or mb_IconQuestion);
    IF (Reply = id_Yes) OR (Reply = id_Cancel)
    THEN CanClose := FALSE;
    END;

PROCEDURE TMyWindow.WMLButtonDown(VAR Msg: TMessage);
    BEGIN
    InvalidateRect(HWindow, NIL, TRUE);
    IF not LButtonDown
    THEN BEGIN
        LButtonDown := TRUE;
        SetCapture(HWindow);
        dc := GetDC(HWindow);
        MoveTo(dc, Msg.LParamLo, Msg.LParamHi);
        END;
    END;

PROCEDURE TMyWindow.WMMouseMove(VAR Msg: TMessage);
    BEGIN
    IF LButtonDown
    THEN LineTo(dc, INTEGER(Msg.LParamLo),
                INTEGER(Msg.LParamHi));
    END;

PROCEDURE TMyWindow.WMLButtonUp(VAR Msg: TMessage);
    BEGIN
    IF LButtonDown
    THEN BEGIN
```

```
        LButtonDown := FALSE;
        ReleaseCapture;
        ReleaseDC(HWindow, dc);
        END;
    END;

{TMyApp methods}
PROCEDURE TMyApp.InitMainWindow;
    BEGIN
    MainWindow := New(PMyWindow,
    Init(NIL, 'Listing 24.8'));
    END;

{global object variable for application}
VAR
    MyApp: TMyApp;

{main body of program}
BEGIN
    MyApp.Init('Listing24_8');
    MyApp.Run;
    MyApp.Done;
END.
```

When you run this program, it will open a window on the PC's screen. If you hold down the left mouse button and move the mouse cursor around, it will draw a line in the window, as shown in Figure 24.9. Of course, the line you get will depend on how you move the mouse.

When you release the left mouse button, the line stops. If you click the button again, or move or resize the window, the original drawing disappears, leaving a blank window in which you can enter a new drawing.

There are several new features in Listing 24.8. First, notice that we have added a new Boolean variable, *LButtonDown*: this is needed so that Windows knows if the left mouse button is being held down or not. On the basis of this variable's value, your program knows whether or not to draw a line.

We've also overridden the *Init* method that *TMyWindow* inherits from its predefined ancestor object type, *TWindow*. As such things often are, this is to make a fairly small change. In the definition of the new *Init* method, we simply call the ancestor *Init* method and then set the *LButtonDown* Boolean variable to *false*.

FIGURE 24.9:

Drawing a line in a window

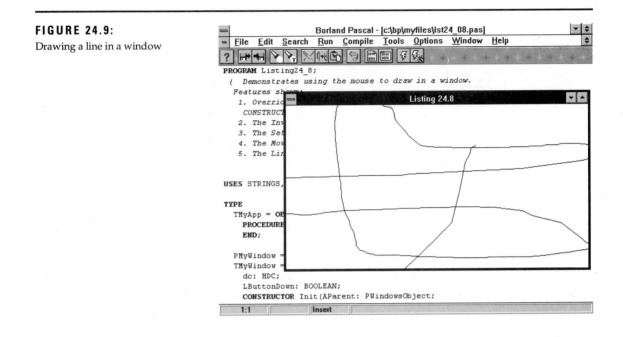

The WMLButtonDown Method

The *WMLButtonDown* method is quite different. It begins by calling *InvalidateRect*, a predefined ObjectWindows routine that operates on an area inside a window. This takes three parameters: a handle to the window in which *InvalidateRect* should work, a *TRect*-type variable indicating the region in the window on which it should work, and a Boolean variable indicating whether or not the region should be erased. In this case, the window handle is of course the current window. The second parameter is set to NIL, indicating that *InvalidateRect* should apply to the entire client area of the window instead of just a region within that client area. The third parameter is set to *true*, indicating that the region should be erased. This is why the previous drawing disappears when you click the left mouse button again.

The *WMLButtonDown* method then sets up an IF statement to see if the mouse button is already depressed. If it is, then you don't want to execute the statements in the THEN part, such as getting a new device context. Without this test, the program would crash almost instantly as it ran out of new device contexts. In the THEN part itself, we first set the *LButtonDown* variable to *true.* Then we call a predefined procedure you haven't seen before: *SetCapture*, which tells Windows that all user input should be restricted to the current window.

The importance of using *SetCapture* is shown in Figure 24.9. Earlier, you may not have noticed, but several of the lines go to the window border, stop, and then reappear at the window border in a different place. This is the result of trying to continue drawing a line outside of the current window. What *SetCapture* does is make sure that all the lines you draw are restricted to the window specified in the program, so that other windows won't be affected even if you move the mouse cursor over their locations on the screen. Later in the program, of course, we'll call *Release-Capture*, which cancels the effect of *SetCapture.*

The next step is to get a device context, which is fairly familiar. Then, we call the (predefined) *MoveTo* method, which moves the mouse cursor to the location of the click. The first parameter is the current device context, while the second and third parameters are the X and Y coordinates of the mouse click—the low- and high-order parts of one of the *Msg* fields, as we saw earlier in this chapter.

WMMouseMove Method

In this program, the mouse doesn't just get clicked and released. As long as the mouse button is held down, we want a line to be drawn from the point at which it was originally pressed to the current location of the mouse cursor. That's what this method does. Notice, in the object type definition near the top of the listing, that this method is set to respond to the Windows message *wm_MouseMove.*

This method first checks to see if the left mouse button is depressed. If it is, it calls the predefined *LineTo* method. This draws a line from the previous location of the mouse cursor to its current location. It takes three parameters. The first parameter is the current device context. The second and third parameters are the X and Y coordinates of the current mouse cursor location. However, *LineTo* requires that these be integers, so we use the *Integer()* function to convert *LParamLo* and *LParamHi* (which are both of type WORD) to integers.

WMLButtonUp Method

Because the mouse button is being held down while drawing in the window, we need a method to take care of things when the button is released. This method is defined so that it responds to the Windows message *wm_LButtonUp*. First, it checks to see if the button has, in fact, been held down—that is, whether or not the *LButton-Down* Boolean variable is set to *true*. If it is, then (because a *wm_LButtonUp* message has just been received by the program) it sets the variable to *false*. It then calls *ReleaseCapture*, which we explained earlier, and releases the device context that was being used for drawing in the window.

Main Body of the Program

The rest of the program is fairly standard. We define an *InitMainWindow* method based on the predefined *InitMainWindow* method in OWINDOWS. Then, we set up an object variable to represent the entire program, and do the usual init-run-done sequence.

CHAPTER TWENTY-FIVE

Getting User Input with Menus and Dialog Boxes

■ Using the Borland Resource Workshop

■ Creating a Menu Resource

■ Creating a Dialog-Box Resource

So far, we've done some remarkable things with remarkably little effort. We've created application programs that run under Windows, respond to mouse clicks, display a predefined window-control menu, and draw text or lines in the window.

One thing we haven't done, however, is add customized menus or dialog boxes to an application. The only menu we've seen so far is the window-control menu that comes predefined with the *CanClose* function.

Preparing a Program to Use a Menu

Setting up menus in Borland Pascal for Windows is quite a bit different from setting them up in a standard Pascal program, though there are some similarities. In most programs, regardless of whether they are in standard Pascal, BASIC, or some other language, a menu structure requires the inclusion of a CASE statement in the program's source code—for example,

```
WRITELN(' Main Menu');
WRITELN(' ');
WRITELN(' 1. Edit');
WRITELN(' 2. Save');
WRITELN(' 3. Quit');
WRITE(' Enter your choice (1/2/3): ');
READLN(menuchoice);
CASE menuchoice OF
    1 : EditFile;
    2 : SaveFile;
    3 : QuitProgram
    ELSE Error
    END;
```

In a Windows program, however, a menu is a *resource* that is defined apart from the main program. There is still the equivalent of a CASE statement in the source code itself, though you'd hardly recognize it. The menu structure itself is defined in a separate file called a *resource file*. Although you can define resources in Borland Pascal itself, the easiest way to do it is to use the Borland Resource Workshop, which is included with the BPW package. Then, by naming the resource at the top of your program and going through a few other gyrations, you get a Windows-compatible drop-down menu in your program.

The basic moves for setting up a program to use a menu are shown in Listing 25.1. We won't be able to run this program until we actually create a menu resource in the Borland Resource Workshop, but we can see how it *will* run when it finally does.

Listing 25.1

```
PROGRAM Listing25_1;

    {  Shows how to set up a program to use a menu
       resource created in the Borland Resource
       Workshop. Features demonstrated:
            1. Naming the resource.
            2. Defining command constants for the various
               menu commands.
            3. Activating the menu with the LoadMenu
               function. }

USES STRINGS, WINTYPES, WINPROCS, OWINDOWS, OSTDDLGS;
{$R MyRes1.res }
CONST
    cm_New   = 101;
    cm_Color = 102;
    cm_Style = 103;
    cm_Thick = 104;
    cm_Help  = 901;
TYPE
    TMyApp = OBJECT(TApplication)
        PROCEDURE InitMainWindow; VIRTUAL;
        END;

    PMyWindow = ^TMyWindow;
    TMyWindow = OBJECT(TWindow)
        dc: HDC;
        LButtonDown: BOOLEAN;
        CONSTRUCTOR Init(AParent: PWindowsObject;
            ATitle: PChar);
        FUNCTION CanClose: BOOLEAN; VIRTUAL;
        PROCEDURE WMLButtonDown(VAR Msg: TMessage);
            VIRTUAL wm_First + wm_LButtonDown;
        PROCEDURE WMLButtonUp(VAR Msg: TMessage);
            VIRTUAL wm_First + wm_LButtonUp;
        PROCEDURE WMMouseMove(VAR Msg: TMessage);
            VIRTUAL wm_First + wm_MouseMove;
        PROCEDURE NewDraw(VAR Msg: TMessage);
```

```
            VIRTUAL cm_First + cm_New;
        PROCEDURE ChangeColor(VAR Msg: TMessage);
            VIRTUAL cm_First + cm_Color;
        PROCEDURE ChangeStyle(VAR Msg: TMessage);
            VIRTUAL cm_First + cm_Style;
        PROCEDURE ChangeThickness(VAR Msg: TMessage);
            VIRTUAL cm_First + cm_Thick;
        PROCEDURE Help(VAR Msg: TMessage);
            VIRTUAL cm_First + cm_Help;
        END;

{TMyWindow methods}
CONSTRUCTOR TMyWindow.Init(AParent: PWindowsObject;
                            ATitle: PChar);
    BEGIN
        TWindow.Init(AParent, ATitle);
        Attr.Menu := LoadMenu(HInstance, 'Linemenu');
        LButtonDown := False;
    END;

FUNCTION TMyWindow.CanClose: BOOLEAN;
    VAR
        Reply: INTEGER;
    BEGIN
        CanClose := TRUE;
        Reply := MessageBox(HWindow,
                    'Do you want to save your work?',
                    'Window content has changed',
                    mb_YesNoCancel or mb_IconQuestion);
        IF (Reply = id_Yes) OR (Reply = id_Cancel)
            THEN CanClose := FALSE;
    END;
PROCEDURE TMyWindow.WMLButtonDown(VAR Msg: TMessage);
    BEGIN
        InvalidateRect(HWindow, NIL, TRUE);
        IF not LButtonDown
        THEN  BEGIN
            LButtonDown := TRUE;
            SetCapture(HWindow);
            dc := GetDC(HWindow);
            MoveTo(dc, Msg.LParamLo, Msg.LParamHi);
            END;
    END;
PROCEDURE TMyWindow.WMMouseMove(VAR Msg: TMessage);
    BEGIN
```

```
        IF LButtonDown
        THEN LineTo(dc, INTEGER(Msg.LParamLo),
                    INTEGER(Msg.LParamHi));
    END;
PROCEDURE TMyWindow.WMLButtonUp(VAR Msg: TMessage);
    BEGIN
        IF LButtonDown
        THEN   BEGIN
               LButtonDown := False;
               ReleaseCapture;
               ReleaseDC(HWindow, dc);
               END;
    END;
PROCEDURE TMyWindow.NewDraw(VAR Msg: TMessage);
    BEGIN
    END;

PROCEDURE TMyWindow.ChangeColor(VAR Msg: TMessage);
    BEGIN
    END;

PROCEDURE TMyWindow.ChangeStyle(VAR Msg: TMessage);
    BEGIN
    END;

PROCEDURE TMyWindow.ChangeThickness(VAR Msg: TMessage);
    BEGIN
    END;

PROCEDURE TMyWindow.Help(VAR Msg: TMessage);
    BEGIN
    END;

{TMyApp methods}
PROCEDURE TMyApp.InitMainWindow;
    BEGIN
    MainWindow := NEW(PMyWindow, Init(NIL, 'Listing 25.1'));
    END;

{global object variable for application}
VAR
    MyApp : TMyApp;
{main body of program}

BEGIN
```

```
    MyApp.Init('Listing25_1');
    MyApp.Run;
    MyApp.Done;
END.
```

Including a Resource File

The first new wrinkle in Listing 25.1 has nothing much to do menus: it's an additional unit, OSTDDLGS, that we declare in the USES clause. This will enable us to create an interactive dialog box with more features than the simple message boxes we've seen so far. We'll return to this when we create a dialog box later in the chapter.

After the USES clause comes a compiler directive that looks very much like one used to insert an "include file"—an older Turbo Pascal programming feature that was replaced by units in versions 4 and later—at that point in the code. In fact, it does insert an include file, but it's an include file of a very special kind. The compiler directive *$R*, when used together with a file name, is called a *resource file directive*, and it names a precompiled resource file that is used by the program. A resource file is a standard type of Windows file that defines characteristics of some windowing object, such as a dialog box, icon, or menu.

We would create a resource file in source-code form and compile it with the Windows Resource Compiler that is included with Borland Pascal. However, it's much easier to accomplish the same goal with the Borland Resource Workshop, as we'll see later in the chapter. In either case, the file will have the same format, since it's a standard Windows resource file. The default file-name extension is .RES.

Note that the resource file directive does not specify a disk directory where the resource file can be found. You can specify a directory path if the file isn't in the current directory. If you don't specify a directory path, then when it compiles the program, Borland Pascal will first look for the resource file in the current directory, then in the directories (if any) you specified in the Resource Directories box that you open from the Options menu.

Defining Command Constants

The next thing in the program that may be unfamiliar (unless you've used Turbo Vision with the DOS version of Borland Pascal) is the CONST section, where we define command constants for the various menu choices:

```
CONST
    cm_New   = 101;
    cm_Color = 102;
    cm_Style = 103;
    cm_Thick = 104;
    cm_Help  = 901;
```

There are a couple of things to notice about this. First, each command constant begins with *cm_*. This marks the identifier as a command constant, just as the prefix *wm_* marks an identifier as corresponding to a Windows message. Object methods that name the *cm_* identifiers in their extensions are *command-response methods*.

Second, each command constant is assigned an integer value. These are the values that we'll assign to the corresponding menu choices when we create the menu resource file. If we wanted to, we could simply use the integer values and forget about defining the command constants. However, defining the command constants makes our code much easier to read, particularly when we get to the extensions for the method headers. The point, however, is that we use the command constants to set up a link between the menu choices defined in the resource file and the method that each one executes.

For example, the value *101* will appear in the resource file next to the menu choice New Drawing. The command constant *cm_New* is defined as having the same value, and this command constant is named in the extension of the method to create a new drawing in the window. Thus, the method is connected—albeit indirectly—to the menu choice that calls it.

Setting Up Command-Response Methods

The *TMyApp* object type definition is the same as in earlier listings, and except for the addition of some new methods, so is the definition of *TMyWindow*. The new methods are the command-response methods that will carry out our menu choices.

Notice that each method header has an extension that begins with *cm_First*, identifying it as a command-response method, and then names the command constant for the particular menu choice. In other respects, however, these method headers are pretty typical of what we've seen so far.

If you look farther down in the listing, you'll see that we've simply put in empty BEGIN..END statements ("stubs") for the details of each method definition. We'll work out those details later on. This way, however, we can get the main framework of the program up and running without needing to define precisely how the methods will work.

Loading the Menu Resource

Just as a file must first be named in the program and then officially "opened," a menu resource must be named in the resource-file compiler directive and then "loaded" with the *LoadMenu* function. Here,

```
CONSTRUCTOR TMyWindow.Init(AParent: PWindowsObject;
                           ATitle: PChar);
   BEGIN
      TWindow.Init(AParent, ATitle);
      Attr.Menu := LoadMenu(HInstance, 'Linemenu');
      LButtonDown := False;
   END;
```

not only initializes the window and the *LButtonDown* variable, but loads the menu resource as well.

The crucial line, of course, is

```
Attr.Menu := LoadMenu(HInstance, 'Linemenu');
```

Let's look at each part of this line in turn.

> **Attr.Menu** The predefined *TWindow* object type, on which our *TMyWindow* type is based, has a field called *Attr* that contains the attributes of any particular instance of that type. The *TWindow.Attr* field is itself a record structure that has fields of its own to hold the different attributes, such as (1) the window's associated text, style, extended style, position, and size; (2) the window's handle; and (3) the window's control ID. One of the fields of *Attr* holds a handle to the window's menus: that field is *Attr.Menu*.

LoadMenu()   This is a Windows API function that returns a handle to a menu resource. It takes two parameters: first, a handle to the program or resource module that contains the menu resource; and second, a null-terminated string that gives the menu's resource ID, which you specify when you create the menu resource. What this line does is to load the menu handle into the *Attr.Menu* field of an object variable of type *TMyWindow*.

HInstance   This is a handle to the menu resource.

'Linemenu'   This is the identifier we're going to assign to the menu resource when we create it in the Borland Resource Workshop.

Nothing else about Listing 25.1 is particularly remarkable, apart from the fact that it won't run until we use the Borland Resource Workshop to create a menu resource. The methods for the specific menu options, at this point, are empty BEGIN..END statements, just as they would be at this stage if we were doing a standard structured program under DOS instead of Windows. We create a *TMyApp*-type variable, just as in Listing 7.4, and then initialize it, run it, and shut it down in the main body of the program.

Starting the Borland Resource Workshop

The next step is to use the Borland Resource Workshop (BRW) to create the menu resource. Before you start the BRW, it will save you some trouble if you write down the menu choices and their corresponding command constants in Listing 25.1. You'll need that information to create the menu resource, and this will save you from needing to switch back and forth between the BRW and Borland Pascal for Windows. In this case, of course, the number of menu choices and command constants is trivial and easy to remember, but when you have got multiple menus and lots of choices, it can be a problem.

To start the BRW, switch to the Windows Program Manager and double-click on the BRW icon in the Borland Pascal program group. The BRW main control screen will appear.

Creating a Menu Resource

There are several different things we can do with the BRW, but at the moment, we're only interested in using the menu editor. (We'll discuss the rest of the BRW and its other features later in the book.) To start up the menu editor, click on File in the top-line menu bar and select New project. The New project dialog box will appear, as shown in Figure 25.1.

In this case, click on the .RES radio button to change the project type to a combined resource file that can include menus, dialog boxes, and other resources. Then click on OK. An empty resource window will appear, as shown in Figure 25.2.

From the Resource menu in the top-line menu bar, select New. The New resource dialog box will appear. In the dialog box, there is a list of resource types that you can create. Scroll down and select MENU, as shown in Figure 25.3. The BRW menu editor will appear, as shown in Figure 25.4.

FIGURE 25.1:

The New project dialog box

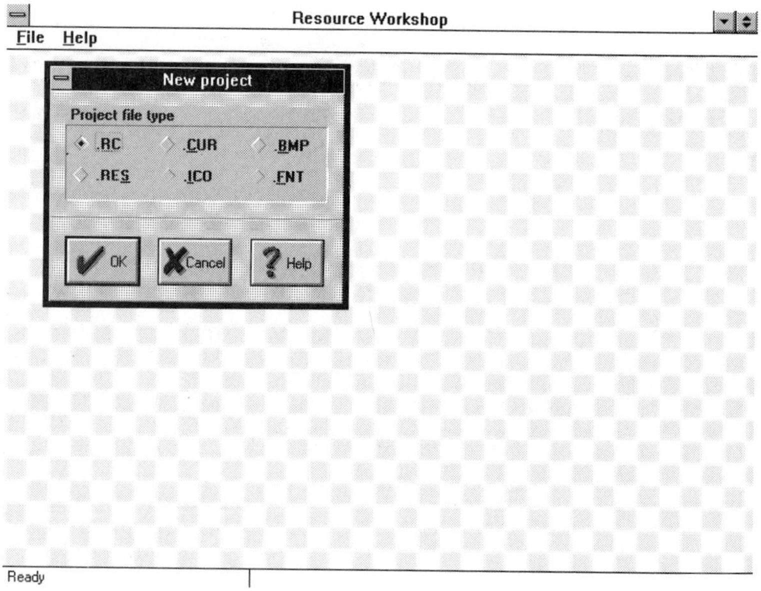

FIGURE 25.2:

Empty resource window opens

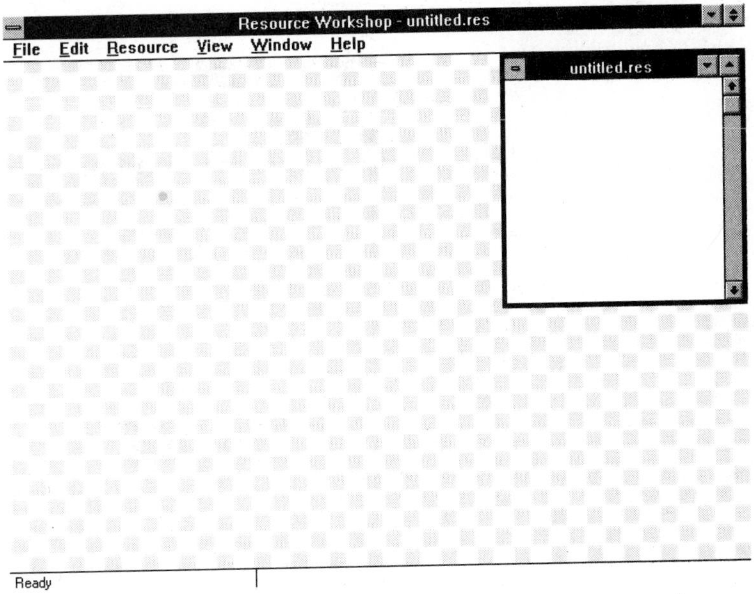

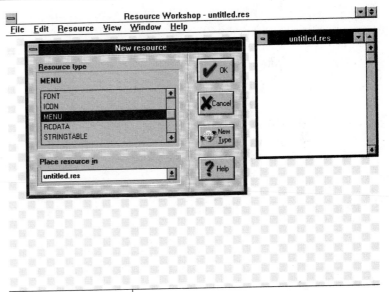

FIGURE 25.3:

Select MENU from the New resource dialog box

FIGURE 25.4:

The BRW menu editor

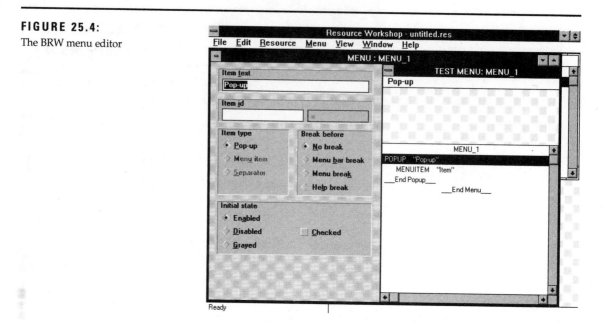

The BRW menu editor is easy once you get the hang of it. Near the top right of the editor window is a "test menu" that shows how your current menu definition will work in a program. Underneath that is a list of the menu choices and the command constants that are associated with them. Near the top left of the window are two blanks, "Item text" and "Item id," where you enter, respectively, the text for each menu choice and the command constant associated with it.

Currently, the menu resource is named, simply, "MENU_1" because we haven't named it yet. Let's fill in the menu choices that will work with the program in Listing 25.1. Follow these steps:

1. Click in the blank under "Item text" or press *Alt+T* to move to that blank. For the menu name, type **&Line** and press *Enter*. Notice that the menu name at the top of the test menu changes to "Line," as does the Pop-up name in the list of menu choices.

2. In the list of menu choices, highlight the line under Pop-up that begins with the word MENUITEM. Press the *Insert* key four times to insert four more lines for menu items.

3. Scroll back up to the first MENUITEM choice in the list.

4. Click in the item text blank and delete the text currently in it. Then type **&New** and press *Enter*. Notice that, as before, your change is reflected in the list of menu choices. The BRW menu editor automatically assigns the command constant 101 to this menu choice because it's the first menu (hence, 100) and the first menu choice (hence, 101). You can change this value if needed.

5. Click on the MENUITEM line under "&New" to highlight it. Then move once again to the item text blank and delete the default text "Item". Type **Change &Color** and press *Enter*.

6. Repeat the same process to fill in the three remaining menu choices: **Change &Style** with item ID = 103, **Change &Thickness** with item ID = 104, and **&Help** with item ID = 901. When you're finished, your screen should look like Figure 25.5.

FIGURE 25.5:

The BRW menu editor with menu choices defined

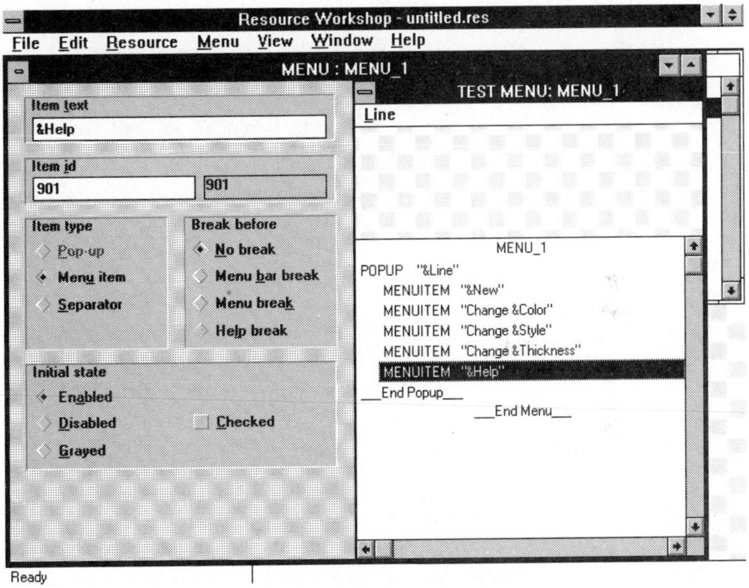

659

To check your work, click on the word "Line" in the test menu. It should display a menu with the choices as you defined them. Now, let's give the menu resource a name and save the whole .RES file. Open the Resource menu and select Rename. The Rename resource dialog box will appear. In the New name blank, type **Linemenu** as shown in Figure 25.6. Then click on OK.

FIGURE 25.6:

Renaming the menu resource

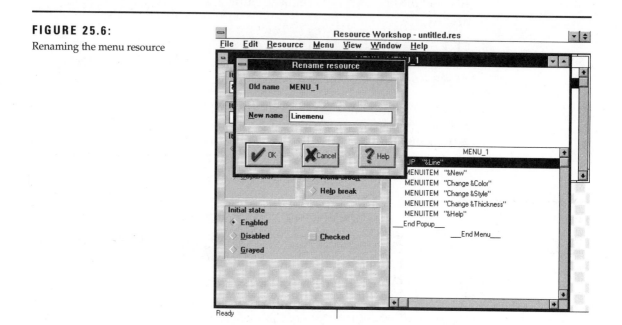

Notice that the name at the top of the menu editor has changed to "Linemenu". Now, open the File menu and save the resource file in your BP\MYFILES directory (or wherever you're keeping your BPW program files) as **myres1**. The .RES extension will be added automatically.

Running the Menu

Now that we've created and saved the menu resource, we can see the result in our program. The program still won't do much of anything—the methods corresponding to the menu choices are still empty—but we can verify that the main program works just fine. After switching back to Borland Pascal for Windows, compile and run Listing 25.1. The result is shown in Figure 25.7.

FIGURE 25.7:

Running Listing 25.1 with a menu resource

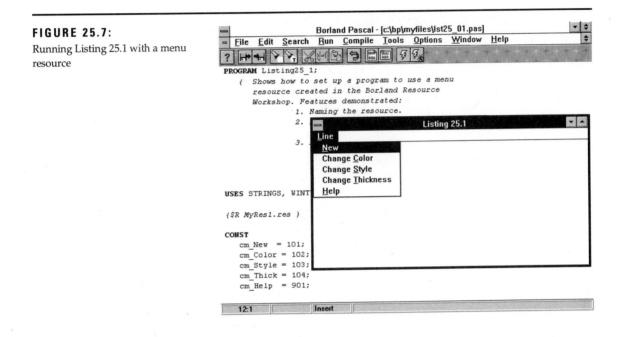

Variations in Menu Formats

The menu we set up in Listing 25.1 was fairly simple, of course, and quite adequate for our purposes. However, there are several other things you can do with menu resources in BPW. Your menus can have submenus that pop open when certain choices are selected, menu choices can be checked or unchecked to indicate the current status of the operations they represent, and menus can have more than one column of choices in a single menu.

Let's look at how we might modify the menus in Listing 25.1 and the *MyRes1.Res* menu resource. We're not going to use these modifications in future chapters, so you might want to save both the listing and the resource file under different names— say, LST25_2.PAS and MyRes1A.Res. The modified listing follows the discussion of these modifications.

Creating Multilevel Menus

The easiest variation is multilevel menus. This allows individual menu choices to activate submenus that pop open just to the right of the original menu. To do this, we'll need to add the appropriate command constants and menu-response methods to Listing 25.1. Then, we'll simply add an indented level of menu choices under one of the existing menu choices in the BRW.

Let's start by changing the name of the menu resource included in the compiler directive statement to MyRes1A.Res, then adding the required code to Listing 25.1 for the added menu choices. We'll create three new menu choices, so we'll need three new command constants in the CONST section of the program. Add them (indented, for clarity) under the *cm_Thick* command constant, as follows:

```
cm_Thin     = 201;
cm_Medium   = 202;
cm_RealThick   = 203;
```

Then, add empty menu-response methods for each of the new menu choices. The code is trivial but is included here for completeness. The method headers should be placed under the header for *TMyWindow.ChangeThickness* in the declaration of the *TMyWindow* object type. The empty method definitions should be placed in the code under the declaration of the details for *TMyWindow.ChangeThickness*.

```
{New menuresponse method headers}
PROCEDURE Thin(VAR Msg: TMessage);
   VIRTUAL cm_First + cm_Thin;
PROCEDURE Medium(VAR Msg: TMessage);
   VIRTUAL cm_First + cm_Medium;
PROCEDURE RealThick(VAR Msg: TMessage);
   VIRTUAL cm_First + cm_RealThick;

{Empty-method definitions}
 PROCEDURE TMyWindow.Thin(VAR Msg: TMessage);
   BEGIN
   END;
PROCEDURE TMyWindow.Medium(VAR Msg: TMessage);
   BEGIN
   END;
PROCEDURE TMyWindow.RealThick(VAR Msg: TMessage);
   BEGIN
   END;
```

The next step is to modify the menu resource. We want to change the menu item "Change &Thickness" from a standard menu choice to a "pop-up" that will open a submenu. There's no direct way to do that in the BRW, so highlight the line with the "Change &Thickness" menu choice and press the *Delete* key to delete it. The line will disappear and the highlight will move to the line above it, "Change &Style."

To insert a new pop-up, press *Ctrl+P* or select "New pop-up" from the BRW Menu menu. A new submenu will appear under the "Change &Style" line, as shown in Figure 25.8.

With the highlight on the new pop-up line, enter "Change &Thickness" in the Item text blank, just as you did for the Line menu pop-up. Then highlight the MENUITEM line under the new pop-up and press the *Insert* key twice to create two new lines for items in the submenu.

FIGURE 25.8:

Inserting a new pop-up menu

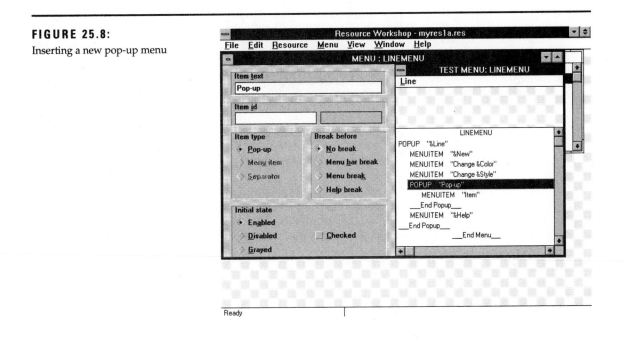

Move the highlight back to the first MENUITEM line of the new pop-up and enter the following values for the three menu items:

- Item text: &Thin; value: 201

- Item text: &Medium; value: 202

- Item text: &Really thick; value: 203

The BRW screen with the new menu items is shown in Figure 25.9, while the result of running the program is shown in Figure 25.10.

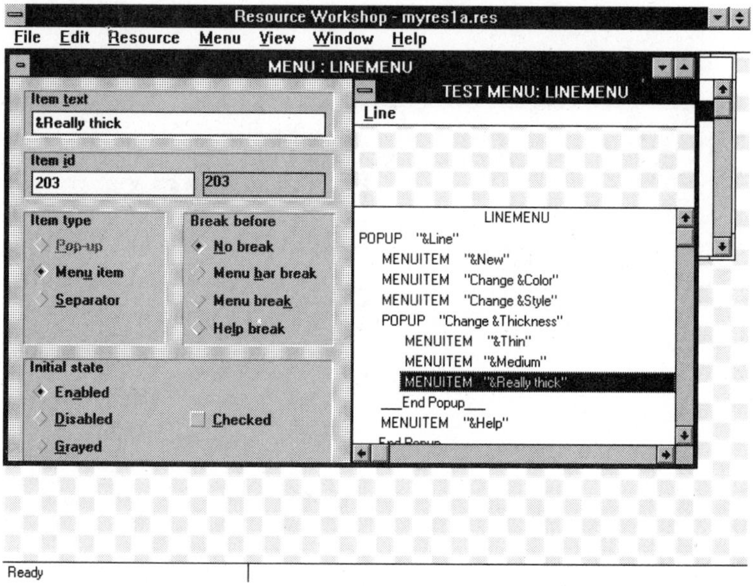

FIGURE 25.9:

Submenu choices added to the LINEMENU resource

FIGURE 25.10:

A submenu added to the BPW program first created in Listing 25.1

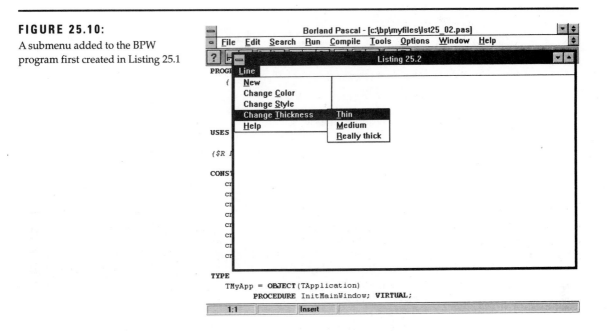

Listing 25.2

```pascal
PROGRAM Listing25_2;

    {  Shows how to set up a program to use multilevel
       menus. }

USES STRINGS, WINTYPES, WINPROCS, OWINDOWS, OSTDDLGS;

{$R MyRes1a.res }

CONST
    cm_New  = 101;
    cm_Color = 102;
    cm_Style = 103;
    cm_Thick = 104;
    cm_Thin      = 201;
    cm_Medium    = 202;
    cm_RealThick = 203;
    cm_Help  = 901;

TYPE
```

```
TMyApp = OBJECT(TApplication)
    PROCEDURE InitMainWindow; VIRTUAL;
    END;

PMyWindow = ^TMyWindow;
TMyWindow = OBJECT(TWindow)
    dc: HDC;
    LButtonDown: BOOLEAN;
    CONSTRUCTOR Init(AParent: PWindowsObject;
        ATitle: PChar);
    FUNCTION CanClose: BOOLEAN; VIRTUAL;
    PROCEDURE WMLButtonDown(VAR Msg: TMessage);
        VIRTUAL wm_First + wm_LButtonDown;
    PROCEDURE WMLButtonUp(VAR Msg: TMessage);
        VIRTUAL wm_First + wm_LButtonUp;
    PROCEDURE WMMouseMove(VAR Msg: TMessage);
        VIRTUAL wm_First + wm_MouseMove;
    PROCEDURE NewDraw(VAR Msg: TMessage);
        VIRTUAL cm_First + cm_New;
    PROCEDURE ChangeColor(VAR Msg: TMessage);
        VIRTUAL cm_First + cm_Color;
    PROCEDURE ChangeStyle(VAR Msg: TMessage);
        VIRTUAL cm_First + cm_Style;
    PROCEDURE ChangeThickness(VAR Msg: TMessage);
        VIRTUAL cm_First + cm_Thick;
    PROCEDURE Thin (VAR Msg: TMessage);
        VIRTUAL cm_First + cm_Thin;
    PROCEDURE Medium (VAR Msg: TMessage);
        VIRTUAL cm_First + cm_Medium;
    PROCEDURE RealThick (VAR Msg: TMessage);
        VIRTUAL cm_First + cm_RealThick;
    PROCEDURE Help(VAR Msg: TMessage);
        VIRTUAL cm_First + cm_Help;
    END;

{TMyWindow methods}
CONSTRUCTOR TMyWindow.Init(AParent: PWindowsObject;
                           ATitle: PChar);
    BEGIN
        TWindow.Init(AParent, ATitle);
        Attr.Menu := LoadMenu(HInstance, 'Linemenu');
        LButtonDown := False;
    END;

FUNCTION TMyWindow.CanClose: BOOLEAN;
```

```
VAR
   Reply: INTEGER;
BEGIN
   CanClose := TRUE;
   Reply := MessageBox(HWindow,
              'Do you want to save your work?',
              'Window content has changed',
              mb_YesNoCancel or mb_IconQuestion);
   IF (Reply = id_Yes) OR (Reply = id_Cancel)
      THEN CanClose := FALSE;
END;


PROCEDURE TMyWindow.WMLButtonDown(VAR Msg: TMessage);
   BEGIN
      InvalidateRect(HWindow, NIL, TRUE);
      IF not LButtonDown
      THEN  BEGIN
            LButtonDown := TRUE;
            SetCapture(HWindow);
            dc := GetDC(HWindow);
            MoveTo(dc, Msg.LParamLo, Msg.LParamHi);
            END;
   END;


PROCEDURE TMyWindow.WMMouseMove(VAR Msg: TMessage);
   BEGIN
      IF LButtonDown
      THEN LineTo(dc, INTEGER(Msg.LParamLo),
                  INTEGER(Msg.LParamHi));
   END;


PROCEDURE TMyWindow.WMLButtonUp(VAR Msg: TMessage);
   BEGIN
      IF LButtonDown
      THEN  BEGIN
            LButtonDown := False;
            ReleaseCapture;
            ReleaseDC(HWindow, dc);
            END;
   END;

PROCEDURE TMyWindow.NewDraw(VAR Msg: TMessage);
   BEGIN
   END;
PROCEDURE TMyWindow.ChangeColor(VAR Msg: TMessage);
```

```
   BEGIN
   END;
PROCEDURE TMyWindow.ChangeStyle(VAR Msg: TMessage);
   BEGIN
   END;
PROCEDURE TMyWindow.ChangeThickness(VAR Msg: TMessage);
   BEGIN
   END;
PROCEDURE TMyWindow.Thin(VAR Msg: TMessage);
   BEGIN
   END;
PROCEDURE TMyWindow.Medium(VAR Msg: TMessage);
   BEGIN
   END;
PROCEDURE TMyWindow.RealThick(VAR Msg: TMessage);
   BEGIN
   END;
PROCEDURE TMyWindow.Help(VAR Msg: TMessage);
   BEGIN
   END;

{TMyApp methods}
PROCEDURE TMyApp.InitMainWindow;
   BEGIN
   MainWindow := NEW(PMyWindow, Init(NIL, 'Listing 25.2'));
   END;
{global object variable for application}
VAR

   MyApp : TMyApp;
{main body of program}
BEGIN
   MyApp.Init('Listing25_2');
   MyApp.Run;
   MyApp.Done;
END.
```

Dialog Resources and Object Types

A dialog box is a special kind of child window that appears inside a main window to receive input from the user. When you plan to implement a dialog box in your

Borland Pascal for Windows program, you need to distinguish between how it appears and what it does:

1. **Appearance:** Including the size and location of explanatory text, check boxes, radio buttons, push buttons, and other controls. Except for a few predefined dialog box types that are included in ObjectWindows (one of which we'll use in this chapter), you'll normally define the appearance of a dialog box in the Borland Resource Workshop's *dialog resource editor.* In most cases, therefore, the appearance definition constitutes an external Windows resource to be used by your program. As with a menu, each object in the dialog box is assigned a specific identifier through which it is linked with the various procedures and methods in your program.

2. **Function:** How the dialog box works, as opposed to how it looks, is entirely up to your BPW program. By linking various methods and procedures with the objects in the dialog box, you control the circumstances under which the dialog box appears and what results it produces when you select its various buttons, boxes, and controls.

Predefined Dialog Box Types

Borland Pascal for Windows—specifically, the OSTDDLGS unit included with the package—defines a few standard dialog box types that you do not need to set up in the BRW. These include the *TInputDialog* and *TFileDialog* types, both of which we'll see in this chapter. The *TInputDialog* type provides for structured entry of a short string of text, and the *TFileDialog* type allows the user to select and save disk files.

Because they are a predefined part of ObjectWindows, you neither need to define the appearance of these dialog box types in the BRW nor set up most of the methods they use. Other than these two types, however, you will need to use the BRW to define the dialog box's appearance, as well as to define most of its methods.

Redrawing a Window

The program we developed in Chapter 24 is fine, except for the fact that it doesn't do anything except let the user draw lines. Even those lines disappear as soon as the window is resized. In this section, we'll see how to make the window redraw its contents when it is resized.

To some extent, we're just teaching the window's client area how to do something that the window already knows how to do for itself. When a window is resized, it automatically redraws itself in the new location with the new coordinates. The drawing inside the window disappears, however, because the window has been given no specific instructions about what to do with its client area when it redraws itself; as a result, it redraws the client area as a blank space.

To make the window redraw its client area, we need to store the area's contents in a buffer so that it can be recreated in the new drawing of the window. This sort of operation will be familiar if you've ever set up a buffer under DOS to save and restore a screen from a suspended DOS application; this is exactly the same thing, merely transplanted to the Windows environment. The technique is shown in Listing 25.3.

Listing 25.3

```
PROGRAM Listing25_3;

{  Demonstrates how to redraw a window's client
   area when the window is resized. Specific
   features demonstrated:
        1. Defining an object type to hold the points in
           a drawing.
        2  Initializing a TCollection.
        3. Using a TCollection to store the points in a
           drawing.
        4. Creating a paint method for the window. }

USES STRINGS, WINTYPES, WINPROCS, OWINDOWS, OSTDDLGS, OBJECTS;

{$R MyRes1.res }

CONST
    cm_New   = 101;
    cm_Color = 102;
```

```
    cm_Style = 103;
    cm_Thick = 104;
    cm_Help  = 901;

{======================================================= }
{========= TYPE DEFINITION SECTION OF PROGRAM ======== }
{======================================================= }
TYPE
    TMyApp = OBJECT(TApplication)
       PROCEDURE InitMainWindow; VIRTUAL;
       END;
    PMyWindow = ^TMyWindow;
    TMyWindow = OBJECT(TWindow)
       dc: HDC;
       LButtonDown: BOOLEAN;
       Points: PCollection;
       CONSTRUCTOR Init(AParent: PWindowsObject;
                        ATitle: PChar);
         DESTRUCTOR Done; VIRTUAL;
         FUNCTION CanClose: BOOLEAN; VIRTUAL;
         PROCEDURE WMLButtonDown(VAR Msg: TMessage);
            VIRTUAL wm_First + wm_LButtonDown;
         PROCEDURE WMLButtonUp(VAR Msg: TMessage);
            VIRTUAL wm_First + wm_LButtonUp;
         PROCEDURE WMMouseMove(VAR Msg: TMessage);
            VIRTUAL wm_First + wm_MouseMove;
         PROCEDURE Paint(PaintDC: HDC;
            VAR PaintInfo: TPaintStruct); VIRTUAL;
         PROCEDURE NewDraw(VAR Msg: TMessage);
            VIRTUAL cm_First + cm_New;
         PROCEDURE ChangeColor(VAR Msg: TMessage);
            VIRTUAL cm_First + cm_Color;
         PROCEDURE ChangeStyle(VAR Msg: TMessage);
            VIRTUAL cm_First + cm_Style;
         PROCEDURE ChangeThickness(VAR Msg: TMessage);
            VIRTUAL cm_First + cm_Thick;
         PROCEDURE Help(VAR Msg: TMessage);
            VIRTUAL cm_First + cm_Help;
         END;

    {object type to save drawing for repainting}
    PDPoint = ^TDPoint;
    TDPoint = OBJECT(TObject)
       X, Y: INTEGER;
       CONSTRUCTOR Init(AX, AY: INTEGER);
```

```
        END;

{=================}
{TMyWindow methods}
{=================}
CONSTRUCTOR TMyWindow.Init(AParent: PWindowsObject;
                          ATitle: PChar);
   BEGIN
   TWindow.Init(AParent, ATitle);
   Attr.Menu := LoadMenu(HInstance, 'Linemenu');
   LButtonDown := FALSE;
   Points := New(PCollection, Init(50, 50));
   END;

DESTRUCTOR TMyWindow.Done;
   BEGIN
   Dispose(Points, Done);
   TWindow.Done;
   END;

FUNCTION TMyWindow.CanClose: BOOLEAN;
   VAR
      Reply: INTEGER;
   BEGIN
      CanClose := TRUE;
      Reply := MessageBox(HWindow,
               'Do you want to save your work?',
               'Window content has changed',
               mb_YesNoCancel or mb_IconQuestion);
      IF (Reply = id_Yes) OR (Reply = id_Cancel)
         THEN CanClose := FALSE;
   END;

PROCEDURE TMyWindow.WMLButtonDown(VAR Msg: TMessage);
   BEGIN
   Points^.FreeAll;
   InvalidateRect(HWindow, NIL, TRUE);
   IF not LButtonDown
   THEN  BEGIN
         LButtonDown := TRUE;
         SetCapture(HWindow);
         dc := GetDC(HWindow);
         MoveTo(dc, Msg.LParamLo, Msg.LParamHi);
         Points^.Insert(New(PDPoint,
                 Init(Msg.LParamLo, Msg.LParamHi)));
```

```
            END;
      END;

PROCEDURE TMyWindow.WMMouseMove(VAR Msg: TMessage);
   BEGIN
   IF LButtonDown
   THEN  BEGIN
         LineTo(dc, INTEGER(Msg.LParamLo),
               INTEGER(Msg.LParamHi));
         Points^.Insert(New(PDPoint,
               Init(INTEGER(Msg.LParamLo),
               INTEGER(Msg.LParamHi))));
         END;
   END;

PROCEDURE TMyWindow.WMLButtonUp(VAR Msg: TMessage);
   BEGIN
   IF LButtonDown
   THEN  BEGIN
         LButtonDown := FALSE;
         ReleaseCapture;
         ReleaseDC(HWindow, dc);
         END;
   END;

PROCEDURE TMyWindow.Paint(PaintDC: HDC;
                  VAR PaintInfo: TPaintStruct);
   VAR
      First: BOOLEAN;
   {local procedure under TMyWindow.Paint method}
   PROCEDURE DrawLine(P: PDPoint); far;
      BEGIN
      IF First
      THEN MoveTo(PaintDC, P^.X, P^.Y)
      else LineTo(PaintDC, P^.X, P^.Y);
      First := FALSE;
      END;
   {main body of TMyWindow.Paint method}
   BEGIN
      First := TRUE;
      Points^.ForEach(@DrawLine);
   END;

PROCEDURE TMyWindow.NewDraw(VAR Msg: TMessage);
   BEGIN
```

```
   Points^.FreeAll;
   InvalidateRect(HWindow, NIL, TRUE);
   END;

PROCEDURE TMyWindow.ChangeColor(VAR Msg: TMessage);
   BEGIN
   END;

PROCEDURE TMyWindow.ChangeStyle(VAR Msg: TMessage);
   BEGIN
   END;

PROCEDURE TMyWindow.ChangeThickness(VAR Msg: TMessage);
   BEGIN
   END;

PROCEDURE TMyWindow.Help(VAR Msg: TMessage);
   BEGIN
   MessageBox(HWindow, 'Not yet implemented',
             'Help', mb_Ok or mb_IconExclamation);
   END;

{================}
{ TDPoint methods}
{================}
CONSTRUCTOR TDPoint.Init(AX, AY: INTEGER);
   BEGIN
   X := AX;
   Y := AY;
   END;

{==============}
{TMyApp methods}
{==============}
PROCEDURE TMyApp.InitMainWindow;
   BEGIN
   MainWindow := New(PMyWindow, Init(NIL, 'Listing 25.3'));
   END;

{=====================================}
{global object variable for application}
{=====================================}
VAR
```

```
MyApp : TMyApp;

{====================}
{main body of program}
{====================}
BEGIN
   MyApp.Init('Listing25_3');
   MyApp.Run;
   MyApp.Done;
END.
```

Defining a Storage Buffer for the Drawing

The first new feature in Listing 25.3 appears in the *TMyWindow* type definition, where we have a new field, *Points*. This field is defined as a *PCollection*, which means that it is a pointer to a variable of type *TCollection*, an object type found in the OBJECTS unit—one of the three units (OWINDOWS, OSTDDLGS, and OBJECTS) derived from the original TPW WOBJECTS unit. A collection is like an object-oriented counterpart of an array, except that it can grow dynamically as needed in increments that you specify. Like an array, it can contain items of pretty much any predefined or user-defined type except file and stream types. Here, we will use it to store the points in a drawing, which we define a little further down in the code as an object type.

The next new wrinkle in the *TMyWindow* object type is the addition of a *Paint* method. This method, which overrides the predefined *Paint* method that is inherited from the *TWindow* object type, is used automatically when Windows sends a message (*wm_Paint*) that the application window needs to redraw its contents. The first parameter, *PaintDC*, is just a device context used by the *Paint* method. The second parameter, *PaintInfo*, is a record type (*TPaintStruct*) defined in the *WinTypes* unit; it contains fields with information to redraw the client area. Most of the fields are used by Windows, but three (*hdc* for the device context, *fErase* to indicate if the background has been redrawn, and *rcPaint* to define the rectangle for redrawing) can be changed by the programmer.

Defining an Object Type to Hold Drawing Points

The next step is to define an object type that can hold the points in the drawing. A drawing can be treated simply as a collection of X,Y coordinate pairs relative to the frame of the window, with each point in the drawing represented by one pair. Thus, and as usual, we define both an object type to hold the points and a corresponding pointer type (*PDPoint*) for the object. The object type (*TDPoint*) has an integer-type field for each coordinate, as well as an *Init* method to load starting values into the fields of each *TDPoint*-type object variable.

Initializing and Disposing of the Point Collection

Before we can use a *TCollection*-type variable to hold the points, of course, we have to create it with a call to NEW. In the *TMyWindow.Init* method definition, we add a line to do just that. Here, in

```
Points := New(PCollection, Init(50, 50));
```

we use NEW as a function to create, initialize, and load a *TCollection* variable into *Points*. The *Init* method of *TCollection* takes two integer-type parameters. The first parameter is the starting size of the collection, in terms of the number of items it can hold. The second is the amount by which the collection will grow when it needs to increase in size.

In this case, we are setting up *Points* to start with 50 slots for drawing points and, when the number of points in a drawing exceeds 50, to increase the size of the collection by 50 slots at a time.

The *TMyWindow.Done* method also has to be changed to dispose of the dynamic *Points* variable when the window closes, just as you would dispose of any dynamic variable when it is no longer needed.

Starting a New Drawing

The next difference occurs in the *WMLButtonDown* method. When we start a new drawing, the old contents of the *Points* buffer must be emptied out to make room for the new drawing. A call to the *FreeAll* method of *Points* (which it inherits from

TCollection) does this for us. Next, as the left mouse button is pressed, the final line in the *WMLButtonDown* method inserts a new point into the *Points* collection, with the X and Y coordinates being taken from the current mouse cursor position (contained in the *Msg.LParamLo* and *Msg.LParamHi* parameters).

As the mouse moves with the left button still held down, the *MouseMove* method draws a line in the window, just as before. The difference is that now, each time it draws another point in the line, it inserts the coordinates of that point into the *Points* collection, which grows as needed to hold all the points in the drawing.

The Paint Method

The next step is to set up a *Paint* method to redraw the window's client area from the data stored in the *Points* collection. As noted earlier, this method takes two parameters: a device context on which the redrawing will be performed, and a *PaintInfo* record with information about how the drawing should be carried out. A local variable, *First*, is defined so that the method knows whether or not the point it's currently processing is the first point in the drawing.

A local procedure, *DrawLine*, actually does the work of recreating the drawing. After this procedure runs once, *First* is set to false. The *MoveTo* and *LineTo* methods work just as before, using the *PaintDC* device context and the point fields from each object in the collection.

In the main body of the *Paint* method, we set the *First* variable to true. Then, we call the *ForEach* method of *Points*, which it inherits from the *TCollection* ancestor type. The *ForEach* method takes a pointer to a procedure (@*DrawLine*) as its parameter. As it traverses the collection, *ForEach* applies the designated procedure to each of the items in the collection. In this case, it executes the *DrawLine* procedure on each pair of X,Y coordinates.

The rest of the program is similar to what we've already seen. If you enter and run the program, draw a line, and then resize the window, you can see the line redrawn in the resized window.

Clearing a Window

Now that we've taught the window how to redraw its client area, we'll show how to implement the first choice ("New Drawing") on the Line menu from the application window created in Listing 25.3. This is a fairly simple operation, and essentially makes explicit what we've already had done for us "behind the scenes" when we start a new drawing.

The relevant code appears in Listing 25.3, and is reproduced below:

```
PROCEDURE TMyWindow.NewDraw(VAR Msg: TMessage);
   BEGIN
   Points^.FreeAll;
   InvalidateRect(HWindow, NIL, TRUE);
   END;
```

This *NewDraw* method is tied to the New menu choice through the *cm_New* command constant that appears in the extension of its heading. First, *NewDraw* clears out all the data in the *Points* collection (by calling *FreeAll*). Then, it calls *Invalidate-Rect* to erase the client area in the window for which the *HWindow* parameter is the window handle. You may recall that the other two parameters are, first, NIL because the window in question has no parent window, and TRUE because we want the client area to be erased.

Creating a Text Input Dialog Box

The other menu items are a little harder to implement because they involve creating a simple dialog box. For our purposes, we will use a *TInputDialog*-type dialog box; this is predefined in the OSTDDLGS unit, which is named in the USES clause of the program. We will create a different instance of this type of dialog box in response to each menu choice. Each will have its own special properties and require its own special methods.

Changing Line Thickness

The first menu choice we will implement is actually the last choice on the menu: "Change Thickness". We do it first because it's the simplest, so the details of creating the dialog box won't be obscured by too many details of performing the menu choice. The implementation of this menu choice is shown in Listing 25.4.

Listing 25.4

```
PROGRAM Listing25_4;

{  Shows how to change the line
   thickness for drawing
   in a window. Specific features demonstrated:
       1. Creating a pen object and a handle to the pen.
       2. The three parameters of the CreatePen function.
       3. Executing a TInputDialog dialog box to get text
          input from the user.
       4. Setting up a method to change pen size. }

USES STRINGS, WINTYPES, WINPROCS, OWINDOWS, OSTDDLGS, OBJECTS;

{$R MyRes1.res }
CONST
    cm_New   = 101;
    cm_Color = 102;
    cm_Style = 103;
    cm_Thick = 104;
    cm_Help  = 901;
{===================================================== }
{ ======== TYPE DEFINITION SECTION OF PROGRAM ======== }
{===================================================== }
TYPE
    TMyApp = OBJECT(TApplication)
        PROCEDURE InitMainWindow; VIRTUAL;
        END;
    PMyWindow = ^TMyWindow;
    TMyWindow = OBJECT(TWindow)
        dc: HDC;
        LButtonDown: BOOLEAN;
        MyPen: HPen;
        PenSize: INTEGER;
        Points: PCollection;
        CONSTRUCTOR Init(AParent: PWindowsObject;
```

```
            ATitle: PChar);
        DESTRUCTOR Done; VIRTUAL;
        FUNCTION CanClose: BOOLEAN; VIRTUAL;
        PROCEDURE WMLButtonDown(VAR Msg: TMessage);
           VIRTUAL wm_First + wm_LButtonDown;
        PROCEDURE WMLButtonUp(VAR Msg: TMessage);
           VIRTUAL wm_First + wm_LButtonUp;
        PROCEDURE WMMouseMove(VAR Msg: TMessage);
           VIRTUAL wm_First + wm_MouseMove;
        PROCEDURE SetPenSize(NewSize: INTEGER);
        PROCEDURE Paint(PaintDC: HDC;
           VAR PaintInfo: TPaintStruct); VIRTUAL;
        PROCEDURE NewDraw(VAR Msg: TMessage);
           VIRTUAL cm_First + cm_New;
        PROCEDURE ChangeColor(VAR Msg: TMessage);
           VIRTUAL cm_First + cm_Color;
        PROCEDURE ChangeStyle(VAR Msg: TMessage);
           VIRTUAL cm_First + cm_Style;
        PROCEDURE ChangeThickness(VAR Msg: TMessage);
           VIRTUAL cm_First + cm_Thick;
        PROCEDURE Help(VAR Msg: TMessage);
           VIRTUAL cm_First + cm_Help;
        END;

    {object type to save drawing for repainting}
    PDPoint = ^TDPoint;
    TDPoint = OBJECT(TObject)
        X, Y: INTEGER;
        CONSTRUCTOR Init(AX, AY: INTEGER);
        END;

{=================}
{TMyWindow methods}
{=================}
CONSTRUCTOR TMyWindow.Init(AParent: PWindowsObject;
                              ATitle: PChar);
    BEGIN
    TWindow.Init(AParent, ATitle);
    Attr.Menu := LoadMenu(HInstance, 'Linemenu');
    LButtonDown := FALSE;
    PenSize := 1;
    MyPen := CreatePen(ps_Solid, PenSize, 0);
```

```
      Points := New(PCollection, Init(50, 50));
      END;

DESTRUCTOR TMyWindow.Done;
   BEGIN
   Dispose(Points, Done);
   DeleteObject(MyPen);
   TWindow.Done;
   END;

FUNCTION TMyWindow.CanClose: BOOLEAN;
   VAR
      Reply: INTEGER;
   BEGIN
      CanClose := TRUE;
      Reply := MessageBox(HWindow,
               'Do you want to save your work?',
               'Window content has changed',
               mb_YesNoCancel or mb_IconQuestion);
      IF (Reply = id_Yes) OR (Reply = id_Cancel)
         THEN CanClose := FALSE;
   END;

PROCEDURE TMyWindow.WMLButtonDown(VAR Msg: TMessage);
   BEGIN
   Points^.FreeAll;
   InvalidateRect(HWindow, NIL, TRUE);
   IF not LButtonDown
   THEN  BEGIN
         LButtonDown := TRUE;
         SetCapture(HWindow);
         dc := GetDC(HWindow);
         SelectObject(dc, MyPen);
         MoveTo(dc, Msg.LParamLo, Msg.LParamHi);
         Points^.Insert(New(PDPoint,
               Init(Msg.LParamLo, Msg.LParamHi)));
         END;
   END;

PROCEDURE TMyWindow.WMMouseMove(VAR Msg: TMessage);
   BEGIN
   IF LButtonDown
   THEN  BEGIN
         LineTo(dc, INTEGER(Msg.LParamLo),
               INTEGER(Msg.LParamHi));
```

```
            Points^.Insert(New(PDPoint,
                    Init(INTEGER(Msg.LParamLo),
                    INTEGER(Msg.LParamHi))));
            END;
      END;

PROCEDURE TMyWindow.WMLButtonUp(VAR Msg: TMessage);
   BEGIN
   IF LButtonDown
   THEN  BEGIN
         LButtonDown := FALSE;
         ReleaseCapture;
         ReleaseDC(HWindow, dc);
         END;
   END;

PROCEDURE TMyWindow.SetPenSize(NewSize: INTEGER);
   BEGIN
   DeleteObject(MyPen);
   MyPen := CreatePen(ps_Solid, NewSize, 0);
   PenSize := NewSize;
   END;

PROCEDURE TMyWindow.Paint(PaintDC: HDC;
                          VAR PaintInfo: TPaintStruct);
   VAR
      First: BOOLEAN;
   {local procedure under TMyWindow.Paint method}
   PROCEDURE DrawLine(P: PDPoint); far;
      BEGIN
      IF First
      THEN MoveTo(PaintDC, P^.X, P^.Y)
      else LineTo(PaintDC, P^.X, P^.Y);
      First := FALSE;
      END;
   {main body of TMyWindow.Paint method}
   BEGIN
      SelectObject(PaintDC, MyPen);
      First := TRUE;
      Points^.ForEach(@DrawLine);
   END;

PROCEDURE TMyWindow.NewDraw(VAR Msg: TMessage);
   BEGIN
   Points^.FreeAll;
```

```
      InvalidateRect(HWindow, NIL, TRUE);
      END;

PROCEDURE TMyWindow.ChangeColor(VAR Msg: TMessage);
   BEGIN
   END;

PROCEDURE TMyWindow.ChangeStyle(VAR Msg: TMessage);
   BEGIN
   END;

PROCEDURE TMyWindow.ChangeThickness(VAR Msg: TMessage);
   VAR
      ThickBuffer: ARRAY[0..5] of CHAR;
      NewSize, ErrorPos: INTEGER;
   BEGIN
      Str(PenSize, ThickBuffer);
      IF Application^.ExecDialog(New(PInputDialog,
            Init(@Self, 'Line Thickness',
            'Input a new thickness:',
            ThickBuffer, SizeOf(ThickBuffer)))) = id_Ok
      THEN BEGIN
            Val(ThickBuffer, NewSize, ErrorPos);
            IF ErrorPos = 0 THEN SetPenSize(NewSize);
            END;
      END;

PROCEDURE TMyWindow.Help(VAR Msg: TMessage);
   BEGIN
   MessageBox(HWindow, 'Not yet implemented',
               'Help', mb_Ok or mb_IconExclamation);
   END;

{================}
{ TDPoint methods}
{================}
CONSTRUCTOR TDPoint.Init(AX, AY: INTEGER);
   BEGIN
   X := AX;
   Y := AY;
   END;

{==============}
{TMyApp methods}
{==============}
```

```
PROCEDURE TMyApp.InitMainWindow;
   BEGIN
   MainWindow := New(PMyWindow, Init(NIL, 'Listing 25.4'));
   END;

{=====================================}
{global object variable for application}
{=====================================}

VAR
   MyApp : TMyApp;

{====================}
{main body of program}
{====================}
BEGIN
   MyApp.Init('Listing25_4');
   MyApp.Run;
   MyApp.Done;
END.
```

Setting Up and Using a Pen

One thing that we haven't seen before, and might not have expected, appears in the new definition of the *TMyWindow* type. We've added a field for a "pen" along with another field for the "pen size." What does this have to do with changing the thickness of lines in the window?

The fact is that whenever you draw in a window, you are using a Windows-style "pen" to do it. If you are happy with thin, solid, black lines, then you can use the default pen (which we've been doing) and not worry about creating your own pen object. However, if you want to change any of the characteristics of the lines you draw, then you must define your own pen or other drawing tool. As you might guess, *HPen* is a handle to a predefined *Pen* drawing tool. To change the thickness of the lines, you change the size of the pen you're using. To accomplish this, we have the *PenSize* field and a new method, *SetPenSize*, both of which are used by the *ChangeThickness* method that is invoked when the user selects the Change Thickness menu option.

Initializing the Pen

It's in the *TMyWindow.Init* method that we actually set up the pen for use. After setting the *PenSize* variable to 1 (the default line thickness), we call the *CreatePen* function to create a dynamic pen object, which we then attach to the *MyPen* handle. In creating the pen, we must specify three parameters:

- *A line style*, represented by one of several predefined ObjectWindows line style constants.

- *A pen size*, which is an integer denoting the size of the pen. The default value is 1.

- *A line color*, which is a 32-bit value denoting the mix of red, green, and blue that makes up the current line color. The default value is 0 (black).

Thus, although the *TMyWindow.Init* method sets up a pen to draw solid, thin, black lines, which is the default value that we were getting before, we can now change one or more of the pen characteristics.

Disposing of the Pen

Just like the *Points* collection, the pen is a dynamic object that must be disposed of when the window is closed. To do this, we insert a new line in the *TMyWindow.Done* method that calls the API *DeleteObject* method to dispose of the pen. We could simply use DISPOSE, but the pen object is more complicated than most dynamic variables, and using *DeleteObject* saves us the extra work of shutting the pen down.

Selecting the Pen

In a way, using a pen in a Windows program is just like using it in real life. Before you can do anything with a pen, you first have to pick it up. We perform this simple but essential job with an extra line in the *WMLButtonDown* method, where we call the *SelectObject* method to position the pen over the appropriate drawing surface—in this case, the device context denoted by the *dc* variable.

Setting the Pen Size

In a certain sense, it's misleading to call what we do in the *SetPenSize* method "setting the pen size." What we actually do is delete the current pen object and then create a new one with the size that has been passed back from the Line Thickness dialog box called from the Change Thickness menu option. First, we call *DeleteObject* to delete the current pen object; then we again call *CreatePen* to make a new pen object with the appropriate characteristics and attach it to the *MyPen* handle.

Using a Dialog Box to Get Input

The *TMyWindow.ChangeThickness* method is where things get just a little confusing. The first thing to understand is that to get data out of a dialog box, you must have something to load the data into while the dialog box is still running. Once the dialog box has shut down, the data is gone. That's why we create a local variable *ThickBuffer*: to get the data from the dialog box. Once the user confirms the information in the dialog box by clicking OK, we take the data from *ThickBuffer*, convert it to its numeric representation, and then, if the string is valid, pass it to the *SetPenSize* method, which does the actual work of changing the pen size.

To run the dialog box, we call the *Application.ExecDialog* method. *Application* is a generic identifier that refers to whatever application is currently running. *ExecDialog*, a method inherited from the *TApplication* object type, takes a pointer to a dialog object as a parameter and executes the associated dialog. Here, we've embedded a call to NEW in the call to *ExecDialog*. NEW creates a dynamic dialog box object of type *TInputDialog*. The associated *Init* method takes five parameters: a pointer to the object itself, a caption for the frame of the dialog box, a prompt telling the user what to do, a buffer (to get the data out of the dialog box), and the size of the data in the buffer. The dialog box is shown in Figure 25.11.

When the user clicks on OK, the dialog box shuts down and the THEN clause is activated. The character data from *ThickBuffer* is converted to an integer and loaded into the global (to *TMyWindow*) *NewSize* variable, with *ErrorPos* indicating if the operation was successful. If it was (if *ErrorPos* = 0), then *SetPenSize* is called. Presto! The line thickness is changed, as shown in Figure 25.12.

FIGURE 25.11:

The Line Thickness dialog box

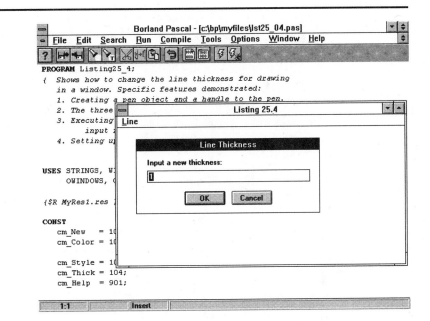

FIGURE 25.12:

The program from Listing 25.4 with a new line thickness

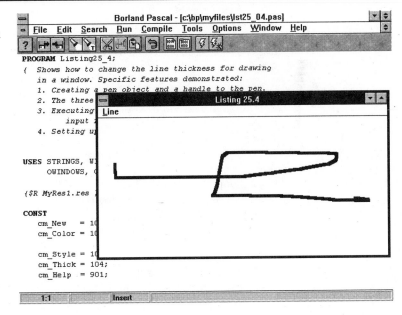

Changing Line Color

Changing line color works essentially the same way as changing line thickness. In Listing 25.5, just as before, we add a new *TMyWindow* field (*PenColor*) to hold the line color, one method (*SetPenColor*) to change the line color, and one method (*ChangeColor*) to run the dialog box. The main difference is that because *PenColor* is a *TColorRef*-type variable, we use the RGB() function in the *SetPenColor* method to make the code a little easier to understand. A naked 32-bit color value, in hexadecimal, is hard to decipher.

Listing 25.5

```
PROGRAM Listing25_5;

{  Shows how to change the color of a line for drawing
   in a window. Specific features demonstrated:
      1. Pen colors.
      2. How to use the RGB() function.
      3. How to use the VAL() function. }

USES STRINGS, WINTYPES, WINPROCS, OWINDOWS, OSTDDLGS, OBJECTS;

{$R MyRes1.res }
CONST
   cm_New   = 101;
   cm_Color = 102;
   cm_Style = 103;
   cm_Thick = 104;
   cm_Help  = 901;
{======================================================= }
{ ======== TYPE DEFINITION SECTION OF PROGRAM ======== }
{======================================================= }
TYPE
   TMyApp = OBJECT(TApplication)
      PROCEDURE InitMainWindow; VIRTUAL;
      END;
   PMyWindow = ^TMyWindow;
   TMyWindow = OBJECT(TWindow)
      dc: HDC;
      ButtonDown: BOOLEAN;
      MyPen: HPen;
      PenSize: INTEGER;
      PenColor : TColorRef;
      Points: PCollection;
```

```
            CONSTRUCTOR Init(AParent: PWindowsObject;
                            ATitle: PChar);
            DESTRUCTOR Done; VIRTUAL;
            FUNCTION CanClose: BOOLEAN; VIRTUAL;
            PROCEDURE WMLButtonDown(VAR Msg: TMessage);
                VIRTUAL wm_First + wm_LButtonDown;
            PROCEDURE WMLButtonUp(VAR Msg: TMessage);
                VIRTUAL wm_First + wm_LButtonUp;
            PROCEDURE WMMouseMove(VAR Msg: TMessage);
                VIRTUAL wm_First + wm_MouseMove;
            PROCEDURE SetPenColor(NewColor: INTEGER);
            PROCEDURE SetPenSize(NewSize: INTEGER);
            PROCEDURE Paint(PaintDC: HDC;
                VAR PaintInfo: TPaintStruct); VIRTUAL;
            PROCEDURE NewDraw(VAR Msg: TMessage);
                VIRTUAL cm_First + cm_New;
            PROCEDURE ChangeColor(VAR Msg: TMessage);
                VIRTUAL cm_First + cm_Color;
            PROCEDURE ChangeStyle(VAR Msg: TMessage);
                VIRTUAL cm_First + cm_Style;
            PROCEDURE ChangeThickness(VAR Msg: TMessage);
                VIRTUAL cm_First + cm_Thick;
            PROCEDURE Help(VAR Msg: TMessage);
                VIRTUAL cm_First + cm_Help;
            END;

        {object type to save drawing for repainting}
        PDPoint = ^TDPoint;
        TDPoint = OBJECT(TObject)
            X, Y: INTEGER;
            CONSTRUCTOR Init(AX, AY: INTEGER);
            END;

{=================}
{TMyWindow methods}
{=================}
CONSTRUCTOR TMyWindow.Init(AParent: PWindowsObject;
                            ATitle:PChar);
    BEGIN
    TWindow.Init(AParent, ATitle);
    Attr.Menu := LoadMenu(HInstance, 'Linemenu');
    ButtonDown := FALSE;
    PenSize := 1;
    PenColor := 0;
    MyPen := CreatePen(ps_Solid, PenSize, PenColor);
```

```
      Points := New(PCollection, Init(50, 50));
   END;

DESTRUCTOR TMyWindow.Done;
   BEGIN
   Dispose(Points, Done);
   DeleteObject(MyPen);
   TWindow.Done;
   END;

FUNCTION TMyWindow.CanClose: BOOLEAN;
   VAR
      Reply: INTEGER;
   BEGIN
      CanClose := TRUE;
      Reply := MessageBox(HWindow,
               'Do you want to save your work?',
               'Window content has changed',
               mb_YesNoCancel or mb_IconQuestion);
      IF (Reply = id_Yes) OR (Reply = id_Cancel)
         THEN CanClose := FALSE;
      END;

PROCEDURE TMyWindow.WMLButtonDown(VAR Msg: TMessage);
   BEGIN
   Points^.FreeAll;
   InvalidateRect(HWindow, NIL, TRUE);
   IF not ButtonDown
   THEN  BEGIN
         ButtonDown := TRUE;
         SetCapture(HWindow);
         dc := GetDC(HWindow);
         SelectObject(dc, MyPen);
         MoveTo(dc, Msg.LParamLo, Msg.LParamHi);
         Points^.Insert(New(PDPoint,
               Init(Msg.LParamLo, Msg.LParamHi)));
         END;
   END;

PROCEDURE TMyWindow.WMMouseMove(VAR Msg: TMessage);
   BEGIN
   IF ButtonDown
   THEN  BEGIN
         LineTo(dc, INTEGER(Msg.LParamLo),
               INTEGER(Msg.LParamHi));
```

```
            Points^.Insert(New(PDPoint,
                    Init(INTEGER(Msg.LParamLo),
                    INTEGER(Msg.LParamHi))));
            END;
    END;

PROCEDURE TMyWindow.WMLButtonUp(VAR Msg: TMessage);
    BEGIN
    IF ButtonDown
    THEN  BEGIN
          ButtonDown := FALSE;
          ReleaseCapture;
          ReleaseDC(HWindow, dc);
          END;
    END;

PROCEDURE TMyWindow.SetPenColor(NewColor: INTEGER);
    BEGIN
    DeleteObject(MyPen);
    CASE NewColor OF
    1: BEGIN
       PenColor := RGB(200,0,0);
       MyPen := CreatePen(ps_Solid, PenSize, PenColor);
       END;
    2: BEGIN
       PenColor := RGB(0,200,0);
       MyPen := CreatePen(ps_Solid, PenSize, PenColor);
       END;
    3: BEGIN
       PenColor := RGB(0,0,200);
       MyPen := CreatePen(ps_Solid, PenSize, PenColor);
       END;
    4: BEGIN
       PenColor := 0;
       MyPen := CreatePen(ps_Solid, PenSize, PenColor);
       END;
    ELSE MyPen := CreatePen(ps_Solid, PenSize, 0)
    END;
END;

PROCEDURE TMyWindow.SetPenSize(NewSize: INTEGER);
    BEGIN
    DeleteObject(MyPen);
    MyPen := CreatePen(ps_Solid, NewSize, PenColor);
    PenSize := NewSize;
```

```
        END;

PROCEDURE TMyWindow.Paint(PaintDC: HDC;
                VAR PaintInfo: TPaintStruct);
    VAR
        First: BOOLEAN;
    {local procedure under TMyWindow.Paint method}
    PROCEDURE DrawLine(P: PDPoint); far;
        BEGIN
        IF First
        THEN MoveTo(PaintDC, P^.X, P^.Y)
        else LineTo(PaintDC, P^.X, P^.Y);
        First := FALSE;
        END;
    {main body of TMyWindow.Paint method}
    BEGIN
        SelectObject(PaintDC, MyPen);
        First := TRUE;
        Points^.ForEach(@DrawLine);
    END;

PROCEDURE TMyWindow.NewDraw(VAR Msg: TMessage);
    BEGIN
    Points^.FreeAll;
    InvalidateRect(HWindow, NIL, TRUE);
    END;

PROCEDURE TMyWindow.ChangeColor(VAR Msg: TMessage);
    VAR
        NewColor,
        ErrorPos: INTEGER;
        ColorBuffer : ARRAY[0..5] OF CHAR;
    BEGIN
        Str(PenColor, ColorBuffer);
        IF Application^.ExecDialog(New(PInputDialog,
            Init(@Self, 'Line Color',
            'Type 1/Red, 2/Green, 3/Blue, 4/Black',
            ColorBuffer, SizeOf(ColorBuffer)))) = id_Ok
        THEN  BEGIN
            Val(ColorBuffer, NewColor, ErrorPos);
            IF ErrorPos = O THEN SetPenColor(NewColor);
            END;
        END;

PROCEDURE TMyWindow.ChangeStyle(VAR Msg: TMessage);
```

```
     BEGIN
     END;

PROCEDURE TMyWindow.ChangeThickness(VAR Msg: TMessage);
   VAR
      ThickBuffer: ARRAY[0..5] of CHAR;
      NewSize, ErrorPos: INTEGER;
   BEGIN
      Str(PenSize, ThickBuffer);
      IF Application^.ExecDialog(New(PInputDialog,
            Init(@Self, 'Line Thickness',
            'Input a new thickness:',
            ThickBuffer, SizeOf(ThickBuffer)))) = id_Ok
      THEN BEGIN
            Val(ThickBuffer, NewSize, ErrorPos);
            IF ErrorPos = 0 THEN SetPenSize(NewSize);
            END;
      END;

PROCEDURE TMyWindow.Help(VAR Msg: TMessage);
   BEGIN
   MessageBox(HWindow, 'Not yet implemented',
            'Help', mb_Ok or mb_IconExclamation);
   END;

{================}
{ TDPoint methods}
{================}
CONSTRUCTOR TDPoint.Init(AX, AY: INTEGER);
   BEGIN
   X := AX;
   Y := AY;
   END;

{==============}
{TMyApp methods}
{==============}
PROCEDURE TMyApp.InitMainWindow;
   BEGIN
   MainWindow := New(PMyWindow, Init(NIL, 'Listing 25.5'));
   END;

{=====================================}
{global object variable for application}
{=====================================}
```

```
VAR
    MyApp : TMyApp;

{====================}
{main body of program}
{====================}
BEGIN
   MyApp.Init('Listing25_5');
   MyApp.Run;
   MyApp.Done;
END.
```

The RGB() function, however, makes it simple. The function takes three parameters, all integers from 0 to 255: first, the intensity of red in the color mix; second, the intensity of green; and third, the intensity of blue. To get pure red, for example, we would use

```
RGB(255,0,0)
```

For pure green, it would be

```
RGB(0,255,0)
```

Unfortunately, the figures in this book are in monochrome, so it's impossible to show here how the colors change. Try it on your own PC, and you'll be impressed with the results.

Changing Line Style

The final menu option lets the user change the *style* of the line being drawn in the window. Borland Pascal for Windows provides several predefined line styles, as listed in Table 25.1.

As when we implemented the menu choices to change line thickness and color, in Listing 25.6 we add a new field (*PenStyle*) to *TMyWindow* to hold the line style (actually the pen style). We then add a new method (*SetPenStyle*) to change the line style and another method (*ChangeStyle*) to run the dialog box. All work in the same way as the methods to change line color. The result is shown in Figure 25.13.

TABLE 25.1: Line Style Constants

Constant	Meaning
ps_Solid	Solid line
ps_Dash	Dashed line
ps_Dot	Dotted line
ps_DashDot	Alternating dashes and dots
ps_DashDotDot	Alternating dashes and pairs of dots
ps_Null	Invisible line
ps_InsideFrame	Used to draw the inside frame of polygons and polylines

Listing 25.6

```
PROGRAM Listing25_6;

{  Shows how to change the style of a line for drawing
   in a window. Specific features demonstrated:
       1. Predefined line styles.
       2. Using a buffer to move data in and out of
          a dialog box. }

USES STRINGS, WINTYPES, WINPROCS, OWINDOWS, OSTDDLGS, OBJECTS;

{$R MyRes1.res }
CONST
    cm_New   = 101;
    cm_Color = 102;
    cm_Style = 103;
    cm_Thick = 104;
    cm_Help  = 901;

{===================================================== }
{ ======= TYPE DEFINITION SECTION OF PROGRAM ======== }
{===================================================== }
TYPE
    TMyApp = OBJECT(TApplication)
       PROCEDURE InitMainWindow; VIRTUAL;
       END;

    PMyWindow = ^TMyWindow;
    TMyWindow = OBJECT(TWindow)
```

```
        dc: HDC;
        ButtonDown: BOOLEAN;
        MyPen: HPen;
        PenSize: INTEGER;
        PenColor : TColorRef;
        PenStyle : INTEGER;
        Points: PCollection;
        CONSTRUCTOR Init(AParent: PWindowsObject;
                         ATitle: PChar);
        DESTRUCTOR Done; VIRTUAL;
        FUNCTION CanClose: BOOLEAN; VIRTUAL;
        PROCEDURE WMLButtonDown(VAR Msg: TMessage);
           VIRTUAL wm_First + wm_LButtonDown;
        PROCEDURE WMLButtonUp(VAR Msg: TMessage);
           VIRTUAL wm_First + wm_LButtonUp;
        PROCEDURE WMMouseMove(VAR Msg: TMessage);
           VIRTUAL wm_First + wm_MouseMove;
        PROCEDURE SetPenColor(NewColor: INTEGER);
        PROCEDURE SetPenStyle(NewStyle: INTEGER);
        PROCEDURE SetPenSize(NewSize: INTEGER);
        PROCEDURE Paint(PaintDC: HDC;
           VAR PaintInfo: TPaintStruct); VIRTUAL;
        PROCEDURE NewDraw(VAR Msg: TMessage);
           VIRTUAL cm_First + cm_New;
        PROCEDURE ChangeColor(VAR Msg: TMessage);
           VIRTUAL cm_First + cm_Color;
        PROCEDURE ChangeStyle(VAR Msg: TMessage);
           VIRTUAL cm_First + cm_Style;
        PROCEDURE ChangeThickness(VAR Msg: TMessage);
           VIRTUAL cm_First + cm_Thick;
        PROCEDURE Help(VAR Msg: TMessage);
           VIRTUAL cm_First + cm_Help;
        END;

    {object type to save drawing for repainting}
    PDPoint = ^TDPoint;
    TDPoint = OBJECT(TObject)
      X, Y: INTEGER;
      CONSTRUCTOR Init(AX, AY: INTEGER);
      END;

{=================}
{TMyWindow methods}
{=================}
```

```
CONSTRUCTOR TMyWindow.Init(AParent: PWindowsObject;
                            ATitle: PChar);
    BEGIN
    TWindow.Init(AParent, ATitle);
    Attr.Menu := LoadMenu(HInstance, 'Linemenu');
    ButtonDown := FALSE;
    PenSize := 1;
    PenStyle := ps_Solid;
    PenColor := 0;
    MyPen := CreatePen(PenStyle, PenSize, PenColor);
    Points := New(PCollection, Init(50, 50));
    END;

DESTRUCTOR TMyWindow.Done;
    BEGIN
    Dispose(Points, Done);
    DeleteObject(MyPen);
    TWindow.Done;
    END;

FUNCTION TMyWindow.CanClose: BOOLEAN;
    VAR
        Reply: INTEGER;
    BEGIN
        CanClose := TRUE;
        Reply := MessageBox(HWindow,
                    'Do you want to save your work?',
                    'Window content has changed',
                    mb_YesNoCancel or mb_IconQuestion);
        IF (Reply = id_Yes) OR (Reply = id_Cancel)
            THEN CanClose := FALSE;
    END;

PROCEDURE TMyWindow.WMLButtonDown(VAR Msg: TMessage);
    BEGIN
    Points^.FreeAll;
    InvalidateRect(HWindow, NIL, TRUE);
    IF not ButtonDown
    THEN  BEGIN
            ButtonDown := TRUE;
            SetCapture(HWindow);
            dc := GetDC(HWindow);
            SelectObject(dc, MyPen);
            MoveTo(dc, Msg.LParamLo, Msg.LParamHi);
            Points^.Insert(New(PDPoint,
```

```
                    Init(Msg.LParamLo, Msg.LParamHi)));
        END;
    END;

PROCEDURE TMyWindow.WMMouseMove(VAR Msg: TMessage);
    BEGIN
    IF ButtonDown
    THEN  BEGIN
        LineTo(dc, INTEGER(Msg.LParamLo),
            INTEGER(Msg.LParamHi));
        Points^.Insert(New(PDPoint,
            Init(INTEGER(Msg.LParamLo),
            INTEGER(Msg.LParamHi))));
        END;
    END;

PROCEDURE TMyWindow.WMLButtonUp(VAR Msg: TMessage);
    BEGIN
    IF ButtonDown
    THEN  BEGIN
        ButtonDown := FALSE;
        ReleaseCapture;
        ReleaseDC(HWindow, dc);
        END;
    END;

PROCEDURE TMyWindow.SetPenColor(NewColor: INTEGER);
BEGIN
    DeleteObject(MyPen);
    CASE NewColor OF
    1: BEGIN
    PenColor := RGB(200,0,0);
    MyPen := CreatePen(PenStyle, PenSize, PenColor);
    END;
    2: BEGIN
    PenColor := RGB(0,200,0);
    MyPen := CreatePen(PenStyle, PenSize, PenColor);
    END;
    3: BEGIN
    PenColor := RGB(0,0,200);
    MyPen := CreatePen(PenStyle, PenSize, PenColor);
    END;
    4: BEGIN
    PenColor := 0;
    MyPen := CreatePen(PenStyle, PenSize, PenColor);
```

```
      END;
   ELSE MyPen := CreatePen(PenStyle, PenSize, 0)
   END;
END;

PROCEDURE TMyWindow.SetPenStyle(NewStyle: INTEGER);
   BEGIN
   DeleteObject(MyPen);
   CASE NewStyle OF
   1: BEGIN
      PenStyle := ps_Solid;
      MyPen := CreatePen(PenStyle, PenSize, PenColor);
      END;
   2: BEGIN
      PenStyle := ps_Dot;
      MyPen := CreatePen(PenStyle, PenSize, PenColor);
      END;
   3: BEGIN
      PenStyle := ps_Dash;
      MyPen := CreatePen(PenStyle, PenSize, PenColor);
      END
   ELSE MyPen := CreatePen(ps_Solid, PenSize, PenColor)
   END;
END;

PROCEDURE TMyWindow.SetPenSize(NewSize: INTEGER);
   BEGIN
   DeleteObject(MyPen);
   MyPen := CreatePen(PenStyle, NewSize, PenColor);
   PenSize := NewSize;
   END;

PROCEDURE TMyWindow.Paint(PaintDC: HDC;
                  VAR PaintInfo: TPaintStruct);
   VAR
      First: BOOLEAN;
   {local procedure under TMyWindow.Paint method}
   PROCEDURE DrawLine(P: PDPoint); far;
      BEGIN
      IF First
      THEN MoveTo(PaintDC, P^.X, P^.Y)
      ELSE LineTo(PaintDC, P^.X, P^.Y);
      First := FALSE;
      END;
   {main body of TMyWindow.Paint method}
```

```
   BEGIN
      SelectObject(PaintDC, MyPen);
      First := TRUE;
      Points^.ForEach(@DrawLine);
   END;

PROCEDURE TMyWindow.NewDraw(VAR Msg: TMessage);
   BEGIN
   Points^.FreeAll;
   InvalidateRect(HWindow, NIL, TRUE);
   END;

PROCEDURE TMyWindow.ChangeColor(VAR Msg: TMessage);
   VAR
      NewColor,
      ErrorPos: INTEGER;
      ColorBuffer : ARRAY[0..5] OF CHAR;
   BEGIN
      Str(PenColor, ColorBuffer);
      IF Application^.ExecDialog(New(PInputDialog,
            Init(@Self, 'Line Color',
            'Type 1/Red, 2/Green, 3/Blue, 4/Black',
            ColorBuffer, SizeOf(ColorBuffer)))) = id_Ok
      THEN  BEGIN
            Val(ColorBuffer, NewColor, ErrorPos);
            IF ErrorPos = O THEN SetPenColor(NewColor);
            END;
   END;

PROCEDURE TMyWindow.ChangeStyle(VAR Msg: TMessage);
   VAR
      NewStyle,
      ErrorPos: INTEGER;
      StyleBuffer : ARRAY[0..5] OF CHAR;
   BEGIN
      Str(PenStyle, StyleBuffer);
      IF Application^.ExecDialog(New(PInputDialog,
            Init(@Self, 'Line Style',
            'Type 1/Solid, 2/Dotted, 3/Dashed',
            StyleBuffer, SizeOf(StyleBuffer)))) = id_Ok
      THEN  BEGIN
            Val(StyleBuffer, NewStyle, ErrorPos);
```

```
               IF ErrorPos = O THEN SetPenStyle(NewStyle);
               END;
     END;

PROCEDURE TMyWindow.ChangeThickness(VAR Msg: TMessage);
   VAR
      ThickBuffer: ARRAY[0..5] of CHAR;
      NewSize, ErrorPos: INTEGER;
   BEGIN
      Str(PenSize, ThickBuffer);
      IF Application^.ExecDialog(New(PInputDialog,
            Init(@Self, 'Line Thickness',
            'Input a new thickness:',
            ThickBuffer, SizeOf(ThickBuffer)))) = id_Ok
        THEN BEGIN
            Val(ThickBuffer, NewSize, ErrorPos);
            IF ErrorPos = O THEN SetPenSize(NewSize);
            END;
     END;

PROCEDURE TMyWindow.Help(VAR Msg: TMessage);
   BEGIN
   MessageBox(HWindow, 'Not yet implemented',
               'Help', mb_Ok or mb_IconExclamation);
   END;

{================}
{ TDPoint methods}
{================}
CONSTRUCTOR TDPoint.Init(AX, AY: INTEGER);
   BEGIN
   X := AX;
   Y := AY;
   END;

{==============}
{TMyApp methods}
{==============}
PROCEDURE TMyApp.InitMainWindow;
   BEGIN
   MainWindow := New(PMyWindow, Init(NIL, 'Listing 25.6'));
   END;
```

```
{=====================================}
{global object variable for application}
{=====================================}
VAR
    MyApp : TMyApp;
{===================}
{main body of program}
{===================}
BEGIN
    MyApp.Init('Listing25_6');
    MyApp.Run;
    MyApp.Done;
END
```

FIGURE 25.13:

A result of changing line style using
Listing 25.6

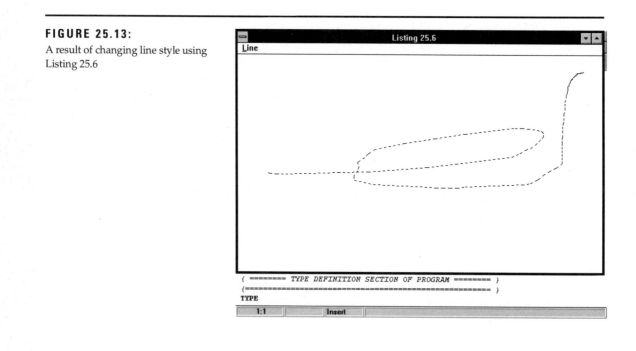

Creating and Using Dialog Resources

- Creating a Dialog Box in the Borland Resource Workshop

- Using a Dialog Resource in a Program

- "Safe" Dialog-Box Execution

In this chapter, we'll show how to create dialog boxes in the Borland Resource Workshop—and, what is far more difficult, how to link them into a source program in Borland Pascal for Windows. First, however, we need to get a better understanding of what Windows resources *are* and what capabilities they make available to the programmer.

What Are Resources?

A Windows resource is an external file that works with your program to define how some of the program's features will appear on screen—including menus, dialog boxes, radio buttons and push buttons, check boxes, icons, and various graphic images. Usually, the resource itself has nothing to do with how these features and devices actually *work:* that part must be defined by you in the source code of your program. There are a few exceptions, where the definition of a resource has a critical impact on how it works, but we'll note those exceptions as we go along.

Like standard program files, a resource file can be in either a source-code or a compiled version. The source-code version of a menu resource file has the extension .RC and is in plain ASCII text, just like most any other program file. The compiled version often has the extension .RES, (for "resource"), as in the examples we'll be looking at.

In this chapter, we'll create a simple application that does nothing but activate a dialog box resource. To activate this resource, we'll also create (in the same .RES file) a simple menu that calls the dialog box. We won't go into any detail about how to write resource files with a text editor; inasmuch as we have the Borland Resource Workshop, writing resource files in that way would be a tremendous waste of time.

Types of Resources

There are seven main types of resources that you'll be dealing with in Windows programs. Some are simpler to create and more widely useful than others, but it's a good idea to be familiar with all of them. The seven types are menus, dialogs, accelerators, bitmaps, icons, cursors, and string tables. Bitmaps, icons, and cursors, though functionally different, are created in basically the same way. All seven main types of resources, as well as a few others, can be created, edited, and compiled in the Borland Resource Workshop.

A complete discussion of Windows resources could easily fill a whole book—as, in one or two cases, it *has*. Here, we'll demonstrate how to write programs with menus and dialog resources, but will simply provide an overview of the other major resource types. For a more detailed tutorial on how to use all kinds of resources in your BPW programs, see the book *Programmer's Introduction to Turbo Pascal for Windows*, published by SYBEX.

Menus

We've already seen an example of a menu resource in Chapter 25, where we created a menu to change the color, style, and thickness of a line drawn in a window. The choices in a menu can be selected by clicking on them with the mouse, and menu choices can cause submenus to pop open alongside the original menu. Apart from accelerators (discussed below), menus are the easiest resource to create and incorporate into a program.

Dialog Boxes

In its ObjectWindows library and associated resource files, Borland Pascal for Windows itself defines two simple *dialog box types*, as we discussed. However, to create more sophisticated dialog boxes, containing a wider variety of control devices such as radio buttons and check boxes, you need to create an external *dialog resource.*

Each screen object in a dialog box, whether it actually does anything or not, is assigned a control ID through which it can be activated (when appropriate) by the program that is using the dialog resource. Nonfunctional parts of the dialog box, such as "static text," which explains the box to the user but doesn't perform any action in the program, are generally all assigned the control ID of –1.

Dialog box resources are not hard to create, but incorporating them into a program is a fairly complicated process. That's why we explain the process in excruciating detail later in this chapter.

Accelerators

Accelerators are "speed keys" or "hotkeys" that let the user bypass the menus to activate a menu choice. A familiar example of an accelerator is the combination *Ctrl+Insert* to copy a block of text to the Windows clipboard; you could open the Edit menu and select Copy instead, but the accelerator saves you keystrokes.

Accelerators are fairly easy to define, and they are entirely optional: it's up to you as the programmer to decide whether you want to associate an accelerator with a menu choice. They are also relatively easy to incorporate into a program, although a couple of special techniques are needed.

Bitmaps

A bitmap, as the name implies, is a binary version of an image. A bitmap can be associated with an action in the program but need not be so associated. If you associate a bitmap with an action, then when the user clicks on the screen image created by the bitmap, the corresponding action will be initiated.

You create a bitmap in the Borland Resource Workshop by using the BRW Bitmap Editor to paint the image, pixel by pixel ("picture elements," the smallest screen elements that can be manipulated by a program), as well as to choose the colors and other characteristics.

Icons

An icon is a small bitmap that is used to represent a minimized window for a file, a program, or any Windows task. You create an icon in the BRW by using the BRW Icon Editor, which is quite similar to the Bitmap Editor, except that icons are generally quite small—measuring either 32×32 pixels or 32×16 pixels.

Cursors

Like an icon, a cursor is a small bitmap that shows the current location of the mouse cursor. The BRW Cursor Editor lets you customize the screen appearance of the cursor so that it looks different in different regions of your program's screen window, when it can be expected to perform different operations.

String Tables

A string table is a resource that can be used to hold text messages for use in your program. Its usefulness is found mainly in situations when you need to change the text displayed by your program without modifying the source code—for example, when you need to produce a foreign-language version.

The Basic Steps in Creating and Using Dialog Resources

The main steps in creating and using dialog box resources are quite simple, even if the details can get a little hairy. In essence, it all boils down to the following steps:

1. Create a dialog resource in the Borland Resource Workshop (or in another resource tool).

2. Include the resource file in your BPW source code using the $R compiler directive.

3. Define an object type to "stand in" for the dialog box resource in your program—much the same as you use a file variable to represent a disk file. This object type will usually be a descendant of *TDialog*, an object type defined in ObjectWindows.

4. If you need to get information out of the dialog box, as you normally will, then define a "transfer buffer" record type to hold the information after the dialog box is closed. One field of the parent window (the window from which the dialog box is called) should be of this type.

5. Initialize the buffer field of the parent window by passing its address to the *TransferBuffer* field of the dialog box object; this is an inherited field from *TDialog*.

6. Execute the dialog, usually by calling the *Execute* method inherited from *TDialog*.

7. Check the transfer buffer for the dialog's return values, and have the program take action based on those values.

In a certain sense, each of these steps is like comedian Steve Martin's famous advice on how to be a millionaire and not pay taxes: "First, get a million dollars." There are numerous tricks and traps along the way. In this chapter, we'll show you how to do it without ending up at the bottom of a pit.

Creating a Dialog Box in the BRW

To begin with, let's get clear on what we will be doing in the Borland Resource Workshop versus what we will be doing in Borland Pascal itself. As mentioned previously, generally the BRW is used only to design the *appearance* of the dialog box, including the locations and types of controls it contains. Our BPW program, on the other hand, defines what each of the dialog box controls *does*: what happens when you select a radio button, check a check box, or click on a push button. There are a few significant exceptions to this rule (such as using the BRW to define the "style" of a radio button, which is a crucial determinant of how it works), but we'll flag each of these exceptions as we get to it.

The other general rule is this: Any dialog box element that you create in the BRW must have a corresponding element in the Borland Pascal program. Thus, for example, the dialog box itself must have a corresponding object type descended from *TDialog*; this object type must contain fields for the dialog box controls (except for the OK and Cancel push buttons) and the appropriate methods to process the data in those fields.

Let's start by creating an empty dialog box. Then, we'll add explanatory text, radio buttons, check boxes, and push buttons.

Creating a Dialog Box

To create a dialog box, you start the BRW by clicking on its icon in the Borland Pascal program group. Then, from the BRW File menu, select New project and choose the .RES file type in the New Project dialog box. As before, open the Resource menu, select New, and choose DIALOG from the list of resource types. The dialog editor will open, as shown in Figure 26.1.

FIGURE 26.1:

The BRW dialog resource editor

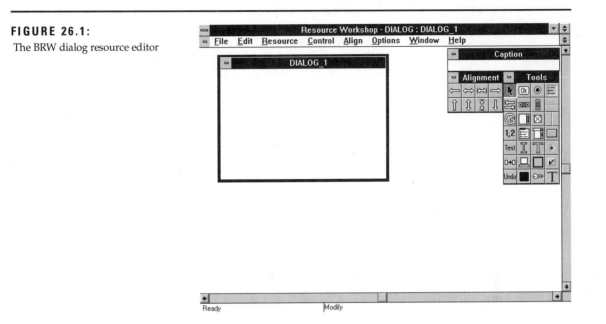

It's worth pausing briefly to look at the different parts of the dialog editor. Along the top of the screen, as usual, is a menu bar from which you can make various selections. The Control, Align, and Options menus are specifically related to dialog boxes, so you'll use those most often. The Control menu, in particular, lets you select dialog box controls such as radio buttons and position them in the dialog box.

At the left side of the screen is the dialog box we're going to create and save as a resource. At the right side of the screen is an array of buttons. Each of these buttons is a speed key for some menu choice in the top-line menu. By and large, you can tell what one of these buttons does by the icon on the button: the button with an "OK" icon is for creating OK push buttons in your dialog box. The button with a big "G" is for putting dialog controls into logical G(roups), and so on. Because it's clearer, we'll generally talk in terms of making menu selections, but you should use the speed buttons as soon as you learn which is which.

First, let's give the dialog window a caption. Double-click on the dialog frame where it says DIALOG_1 and the Window style dialog box will open, as shown in Figure 26.2.

At the top left, type **The Official Do-Nothing Dialog Box** in the Caption blank. Then press *Enter* or click on OK. The caption will appear in the top edge of the dialog box. Note that this is different from assigning a resource ID to the dialog box, which we'll do presently.

Next, we'll add some "static text" to the box. This type of dialog box object doesn't perform any actions, but it provides useful information for the user. From the Control menu, choose Static text. The cursor will turn into a little text icon. Position the cursor near the top of the dialog box, directly under the "D" in "Do-Nothing." Then click the mouse, and the text object will be positioned in the dialog box. If it's not quite in the right place, you can drag it with the mouse, just like any other object. Double-click on the text object and the Static style dialog box will appear, as shown in Figure 26.3.

FIGURE 26.3:

The Static style dialog box

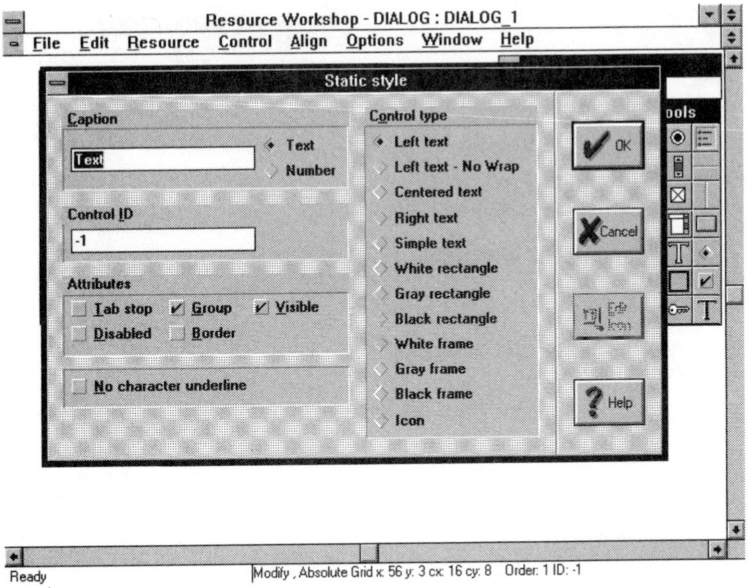

Note that, as befits static text, the dialog editor automatically assigned a control ID of -1 to this object. We can enter the text we want in the blank under Caption. Because "nothing" is the purported goal of our official do-nothing dialog box, let's put in a few words of encouragement appropriate to nothingness. In the blank, enter

```
Nothing is impossible.
```

Then click on OK. The text doesn't look too good right now, because we need to adjust the dimensions and position of the text object.

If you position the mouse cursor over the lower-right corner of the text object, you can drag the corner to change the size of the object, as shown in Figure 26.4. You can then position the mouse cursor in the middle of the text and drag the object to the desired location in the dialog box.

Adjusting the dimensions of the text object

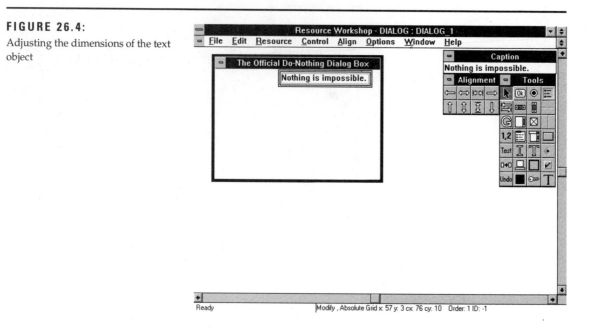

Creating Radio Buttons

The next step is to add some radio buttons to the dialog box. To add a radio button, you select Radio button from the Control menu. The cursor will change into a radio-button icon. Position the cursor toward the left side of the dialog box just under "Nothing is impossible." Then click the mouse to put the radio button in that location.

Next, we'll assign a caption to the radio button. With the cursor inside the radio button object, double-click the mouse. The Button style dialog box will open, as shown in Figure 26.5. Note that since this is the first "active" control we've put in the dialog box, the editor automatically assigns it a control ID of 101.

We need to do two things. First, click in the blank under Caption and enter "Bupkis" as the caption for the radio button. Second, in the Button type list, change the button type to "Auto radio button." This is necessary so that the radio button, once it's in a group of radio buttons, will work as such buttons normally do.

FIGURE 26.5:

The Button style dialog box

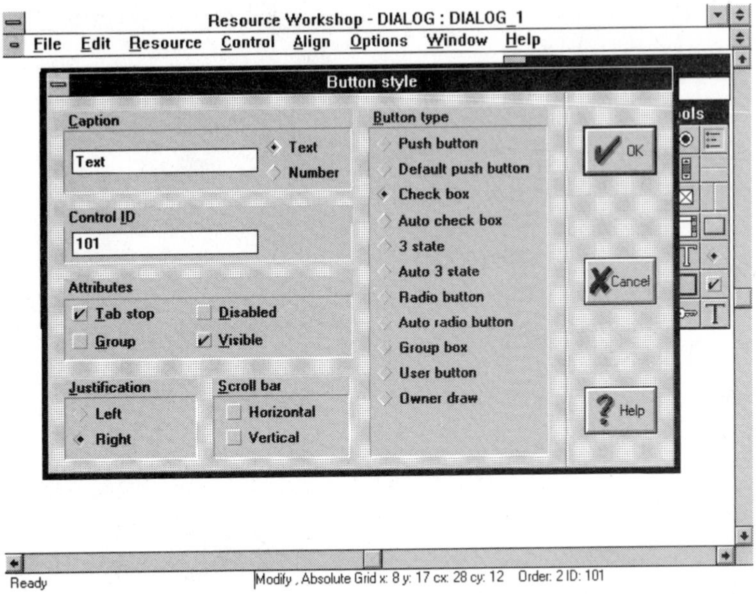

The reason is this. You use radio buttons to let the user select from mutually exclusive alternatives: in our line-drawing program, for example, the user could make the line red, green, blue, or black, but could pick only one color at a time. When the user selects a radio button, you want two things to happen:

1. The selection (called the "focus") should move to that button.

2. All other radio buttons in the same group should be *de*selected.

Unless you make your radio buttons "Auto Radio Buttons," neither of these conditions will be met.

Click on OK and our dialog box will reappear, as shown in Figure 26.6. As before, you'll need to stretch the button object's right edge so that all the text shows on screen.

FIGURE 26.6:

Dialog box with radio button added

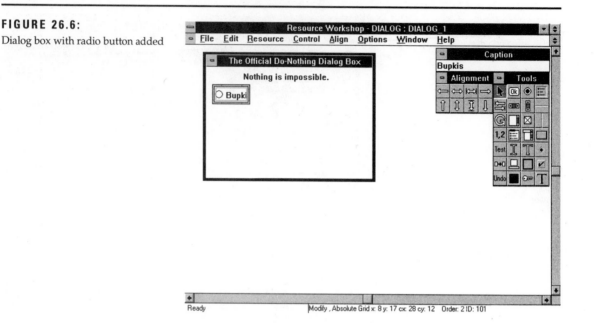

In the same way that you added the Bupkis button, add three more radio buttons on the left side of the box. Don't worry about aligning them precisely; we'll take care of that in a minute. The buttons and values to enter are:

Button Text	Control ID
Nichts	102
Nada	103
Zip	104

When you're finished, the dialog box should look like Figure 26.7.

Grouping Buttons Together

There's one key point we've touched on but haven't explained. Suppose that you have several radio buttons or push buttons in the same dialog box, but that they don't all go together. For example, an all-purpose dialog box for our line-drawing

FIGURE 26.7:

Dialog box with radio buttons

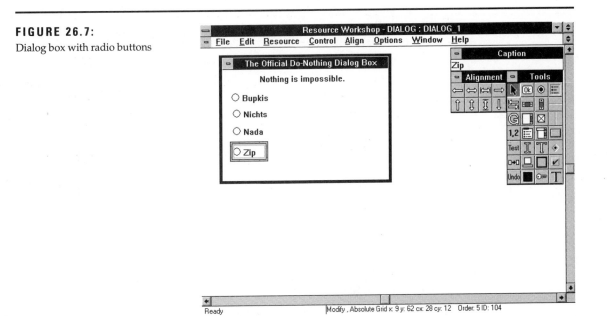

program might have one group of radio buttons for color and another group for line style. When the user selects one color button, all the other color buttons should be deselected, but nothing should happen to the buttons for line style. We need some way to tell the application which buttons go together with which other buttons.

The BRW solves this problem by allowing you to select buttons and then group them together in a single logical group. To do this, select Set groups from the Options menu, or click on the speed button with the big "G". Then position the "G" cursor over the "Bupkis" button object and click on it. It's done! That groups all the radio buttons together. Later, when we create another group, we'll click on *its* first member, thereby separating it from the radio-button group. Note that for this method to work properly, the objects in a group must all be close together on the screen.

To change the cursor back to the standard pointer, click on the "arrow" speed button at the right.

Aligning Buttons

Because the radio buttons are now grouped together, they will work as they should. Moreover, we can now let the BRW position them automatically in the dialog box. To do this, click on the "Bupkis" button object and hold down the *Shift* key. Then click on the other three radio buttons. All four will be enclosed in a box, indicating that they're all selected.

Now, open the Align menu and select Align. The Align controls dialog box will appear, as shown in Figure 26.8.

Under "Horizontal alignment," select "Left sides," and under "Vertical alignment," select "Space equally." Then click on OK. The radio buttons will be aligned perfectly.

Creating Push Buttons

Radio buttons, of course, let the user make choices. But they don't perform any *actions*. To do that, we need to include some push buttons in the dialog box: an OK button and a Cancel button should be adequate. To create the OK button, select the

FIGURE 26.8:

The Align controls dialog box

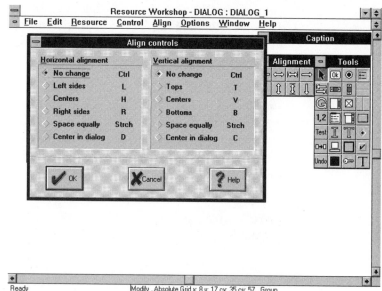

716

speed button that says "OK" on it. Position the cursor toward the right side of the dialog box under "Nothing is impossible" and click to position the button. Then, double-click on the button, and the Button style dialog box will appear. For the text, enter simply **OK**; for the Control ID, a value of 1 (the standard ID for an OK button); and for the button type, accept the default value of "Push button." Click on OK.

Below the OK button, add a Cancel button in the same way, entering 2 as the control ID (the default control ID for a Cancel button). This time, however, choose "Default push button" as the button type in the Button style dialog box.

Just as you did with the radio buttons, you should now put the two buttons in a logical group by selecting the "G" speed button and clicking on the OK button object. (Remember to change the cursor back to an arrow afterwards.) Then, align the two push buttons so that their right edges are together. Your screen should look like Figure 26.9.

FIGURE 26.9:

Dialog box with radio and push buttons

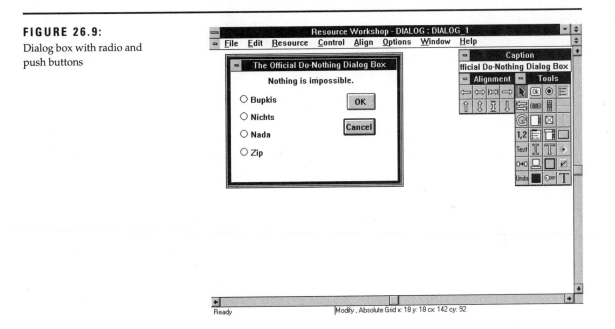

Verifying Groups and IDs

Finally, let's verify that the buttons are grouped properly. From the Options menu, choose Set order. The button objects will be shown with the order in which a *Tab* press would move from button to button, as shown in Figure 26.10. The cursor changes to a "1,2" icon, and you can use it to change the order if you wish. Here, the order is fine, so don't change it.

Saving the Dialog

Now, you should save the dialog in a resource file. First, open the Resource menu and select Rename to change the dialog box's control ID to NOTHING. Then, select Save project from the File menu and save the dialog in your BP\MYFILES directory as NOTHING.RES.

FIGURE 26.10:

Button grouping and order

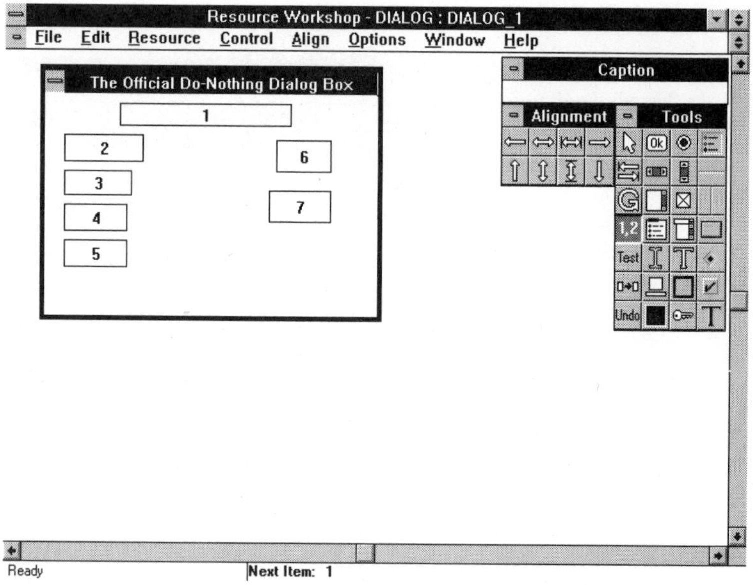

718

Creating a Do-Nothing Menu

We need to do one more thing before we can use this dialog box in a program: we must create a menu that calls the dialog box. Just as we did before, use the BRW menu editor to create a menu with two lines in it: the menu title,

```
Do &Nothing
```

and one MENUITEM,

```
Run &Dialog Box
```

which should have a value of 201. Then save the menu into the same NOTH-ING.RES resource file that contains the Official Do-Nothing dialog box, assigning the menu the name NADAMENU.

Using a Dialog Resource in a Program

Of course, it wouldn't do us much good to create a dialog box—even a "do-nothing" dialog box—unless we could use it in a program. This is a tricky job, even though its broad outlines are pretty clear. To use a dialog box in a program, we have to follow the steps mentioned previously:

1. Include the resource file in the program.

2. Define a *TDialog* descendant object type that will "stand in" for the dialog resource in the program code. The *TDialog* object type is defined in the ODIALOGS unit, which must be added to the program's USES clause.

3. Set up a transfer buffer to move data back and forth between the program and the dialog box.

4. Initialize the transfer buffer by linking it with the *TransferBuffer* field of the *TDialog* descendant object that represents the dialog box in the program.

5. Execute the dialog box, usually with a call to the *Execute* method inherited from *TDialog*.

6. Check the values returned by the dialog box, and make the program take appropriate actions based on those values.

Our discussion of these points will refer to Listing 26.1, which appears below.

Listing 26.1

```
PROGRAM Listing26_1;

{   Illustrates the overall structure of a program that
    uses an external dialog box resource.
    Associated resource file: NOTHING.RES.
        Dialog resources:
            Menu: NadaMenu
            Dialog Box: Nothing   }

USES STRINGS, WINTYPES, WINPROCS, OWINDOWS, OSTDDLGS, OBJECTS,
        ODIALOGS;

{$R Nothing.res }

CONST
    {menu choice identifiers}
    cm_Nada  = 201;

    {dialog botton identifiers}
    id_bupkis = 101;
    id_nichts = 102;
    id_nada = 103;
    id_zip = 104;

{======================================================= }
{ ======== TYPE DEFINITION SECTION OF PROGRAM ======== }
{======================================================= }
TYPE
    TMyApp = OBJECT(TApplication)
        PROCEDURE InitMainWindow; VIRTUAL;
        END;

    { Dialog transfer record }
    ItemTransferBuffer = RECORD
        BupkisBtn,
        NichtsBtn,
        NadaBtn,
        ZipBtn    : WORD;
        END;

    PMyWindow = ^TMyWindow;
    TMyWindow = OBJECT(TWindow)
        DDBuffer : ItemTransferBuffer;
```

```
        CONSTRUCTOR Init(AParent: PWindowsObject;
            ATitle: PChar);
        FUNCTION CanClose: BOOLEAN; VIRTUAL;
        {methods for menu choices}
        PROCEDURE DoNothingMuch(VAR Msg: TMessage);
            VIRTUAL cm_First + cm_Nada;
        END;

    {dialog box type for doing nothing}
    PMyDialog = ^TMyDialog;
    TMyDialog = OBJECT (TDialog)
        BupkisButton,
        NichtsButton,
        NadaButton,
        ZipButton : PRadioButton;
        CONSTRUCTOR Init(AParent: PWindowsObject;
                         ATitle:PChar);

        END;

{=================}
{TMyWindow methods}
{=================}

CONSTRUCTOR TMyWindow.Init(AParent: PWindowsObject;
                           ATitle: PChar);

    BEGIN
    TWindow.Init(AParent, ATitle);
    Attr.Menu := LoadMenu(HInstance, 'NadaMenu');
    with DDBuffer do
        BEGIN
        BupkisBtn := bf_unchecked;
        NichtsBtn := bf_unchecked;
        NadaBtn := bf_unchecked;
        ZipBtn := bf_unchecked;
        END;
    END;

FUNCTION TMyWindow.CanClose: BOOLEAN;
    VAR
        Reply: INTEGER;
    BEGIN
        CanClose := TRUE;
        Reply := MessageBox(HWindow,
                'Do you want to save your work?',
                'Window content has changed',
```

```
                   mb_YesNoCancel or mb_IconQuestion);
        IF (Reply = id_Yes) OR (Reply = id_Cancel)
           THEN CanClose := FALSE;
     END;

PROCEDURE TMyWindow.DoNothingMuch(VAR Msg: TMessage);
     VAR  Dlg: TMyDialog;
          Reply, MyResult: Integer;
     BEGIN
     Dlg.Init(@Self, 'Nothing');
     Dlg.TransferBuffer := @DDBuffer;
     Reply := Dlg.Execute;
     Dlg.Done;

     IF Reply = id_Ok THEN
     IF DDBuffer.BupkisBtn = bf_checked
        THEN MyResult := MessageBox(HWindow,
                 'You get Bupkis',
                 'Event Report',
                 mb_OK or mb_IconExclamation)
     ELSE IF DDBuffer.NichtsBtn = bf_checked
        THEN MyResult := MessageBox(HWindow,
                 'You get Nichts',
                 'Event Report',
                 mb_OK or mb_IconExclamation)
     ELSE IF DDBuffer.NadaBtn = bf_checked
        THEN MyResult := MessageBox(HWindow,
                 'You get Nada',
                 'Event Report',
                 mb_OK or mb_IconExclamation)
     ELSE IF DDBuffer.ZipBtn = bf_checked
        THEN MyResult := MessageBox(HWindow,
                 'You get Zip',
                 'Event Report',
                 mb_OK or mb_IconExclamation)
     ELSE MyResult := MessageBox(HWindow,
                 'You STILL get Zip',
                 'Event Report',
                 mb_OK or mb_IconExclamation);
     END; { of DoNothingMuch routine }

{===================}
{ TMyDialog methods }
{===================}
```

```
CONSTRUCTOR TMyDialog.init(AParent: PWindowsObject;
                           ATitle: Pchar);
   BEGIN
   TDialog.init(aparent, atitle);
   NEW(BupkisButton, initResource(@Self, id_bupkis));
   NEW(NichtsButton, initResource(@Self, id_nichts));
   NEW(NadaButton, initResource(@Self, id_nada));
   NEW(ZipButton, initResource(@Self, id_zip));
   END;

{==============}
{TMyApp methods}
{==============}
PROCEDURE TMyApp.InitMainWindow;
   BEGIN
   MainWindow := New(PMyWindow, Init(NIL, 'Listing 26.1'));
   END;

{=====================================}
{global object variable for application}
{=====================================}
VAR
   MyApp : TMyApp;

{====================}
{main body of program}
{====================}
BEGIN
   MyApp.Init('Listing26_1');
   MyApp.Run;
   MyApp.Done;
END.
```

Include the Resource

The first step is to include the resource file at the top of the source program. As with the menu we created in an earlier chapter, this is done using the $R compiler directive and the name of the resource file. The resource file named must meet one of the following three criteria:

- It must be in the same directory as the source program, or

- It must have a directory path included in the compiler directive, or

- It must be in one of the Resource directories named in the Options/Directories dialog box in Borland Pascal for Windows.

Define Identifiers for Dialog Box Controls

The next step is to define identifiers for the control devices (the buttons, and so on) in the dialog box. As with a menu resource, these identifiers will be used to link the devices in the dialog box resource with the correct methods in the BPW program. Also, as before, we define a command constant identifier to activate the menu choice in the menu resource. This all takes place in the CONST section near the top of the program.

Define a Transfer Buffer

Next, we define a transfer buffer to carry data into and out of the dialog box. When you make a selection in a dialog box, the data that your action creates continues to exist only until the dialog box is destroyed through a call to *TDialog.Done*. Thus, you need this transfer buffer to keep a copy of the data and pass it to the program after the dialog box is closed. This transfer buffer must be a record type with one field (of the appropriate data type) for each control that must pass data out of the dialog box. Here, we define it as *ItemTransferBuffer*, and it has four WORD-type fields (WORD being the appropriate data type for the data created by button and check box selections).

Note that, just below the definition of *ItemTransferBuffer*, the *TMyWindow* type definition has added a new field of its own: *DDBuffer*, a record of type *ItemTransferBuffer* to hold the data passed back from the dialog box.

Define a TDialog Descendant Type

The next step is to define a dialog object type to represent the dialog resource in the program itself. Here, the object type is called *TMyDialog*, descended from *TDialog*. It has four fields, one for each of the four radio buttons in the dialog resource. Also, the fields are of type *PRadioButton*, which means each field can hold a pointer to a *TRadioButton*-type object. There's also a new *TMyDialog.Init* constructor method, which overrides the inherited *TDialog.Init* method, because besides constructing the dialog object we also need it to initialize the button fields and link them to the buttons defined in the dialog resource.

Initialize the Buffer

The next point of interest is the *TMyWindow.Init* constructor method. This starts off by doing two things we've seen before: calling *TWindow.Init* and loading the menu resource into the window's menu *Attr* field. (The explicit call is required before you can override *TWindow.Init* in a descendant type.) Next, however, it initializes the window's buffer field (*DDBuffer*) by assigning the value

```
bf_unchecked
```

to each button field of the buffer, indicating that the buttons should be unselected when the dialog box opens. The other value you might assign—to one button field only—is

```
bf_checked
```

indicating that the particular button is selected, by default, when the dialog box opens.

Of course, it's important to note that at this point, the checked/unchecked information has not yet been loaded into the button resources in the dialog box. We've just put the appropriate values into the corresponding fields of the parent window's transfer buffer.

Initialize the Dialog Box

Next, we define how to initialize the dialog box with the *TMyDialog.Init* constructor method. This begins by calling *TDialog.Init*, which takes care of the handle to the parent window and the title of the dialog. Next, we make four calls to NEW to create four dynamic button objects. Each button object is initialized with a call to *Init-Resource*, which takes two parameters:

- A pointer to the button object being initialized (here, *@Self*).

- The resource ID associated with the button in the external dialog resource. Recall that in the dialog resource, each device had a number assigned to it. In the CONST section of the program, the resource IDs named in *TMy-Dialog.Init* were defined to match those numbers. Thus, for example, the *BupkisButton* field of *TMyDialog* is associated with the *Bupkis* radio button in the NOTHING dialog resource.

Execute the Dialog

The next step is to define how the dialog box will be executed and shut down. This is done by the *TMyWindow.DoNothingMuch* method. If you look back at the original definition of the *TMyWindow* object type, you will note that the *DoNothingMuch* method has the identifier *cm_nada* in its extension, indicating that it responds to the menu command to "Run Dialog Box."

First, this method creates three local variables: *Dlg*, a variable of the correct type to represent a dialog box, and two integer variables, *Reply* and *MyResult*. It then does the following:

1. It calls the *Dlg* variable's *Init* method, which the variable inherits from *TDialog*. This method takes two parameters: first, a pointer to the dialog variable itself (*@Self*), and second, the resource ID of the dialog box (*Nothing*) created in the resource editor. It is through this call to *Dlg.Init* that the dialog object variable is linked to the external dialog resource.

2. It assigns the values in the parent window's transfer buffer field to the *TransferBuffer* field that the dialog variable inherits from *TDialog*. There's more to this move than meets the eye: in addition to transferring the data into the dialog box, it sets up a link that transfers the data *out of* the dialog box and into the buffer when the dialog box is shut down. This is all done behind the scenes, by passing a pointer to the parent window's transfer buffer field into the dialog box's *TransferBuffer* field.

3. It executes the dialog variable by calling the *Execute* method that the variable inherits from *TDialog*. The resulting termination code is assigned to the *Reply* variable.

4. It shuts down the dialog with a call to the variable's inherited *Done* method.

Check the Dialog's Return Values

The next step in this method is to inspect the values passed from the dialog box to the parent window's transfer buffer. Different actions can then be taken based on these values. Here, we've simply set up the program to display a message box indicating which radio button was selected in the dialog box. This is a trivial task, of course, but it shows that the data was successfully transferred out of the dialog box and to the parent window.

Running the Dialog Box Program

The rest of Listing 26.1 is fairly standard. An object variable is declared to represent the application; the variable is initialized, run, and shut down. The results are shown in Figures 26.11 and 26.12.

Adding Check Boxes

You add check boxes to a dialog box in almost the same way as you create radio buttons. Let's add two check boxes to the dialog we created and used in Listing 26.1. Use the BRW to open up the NOTHING dialog in the NOTHING.RES resource file.

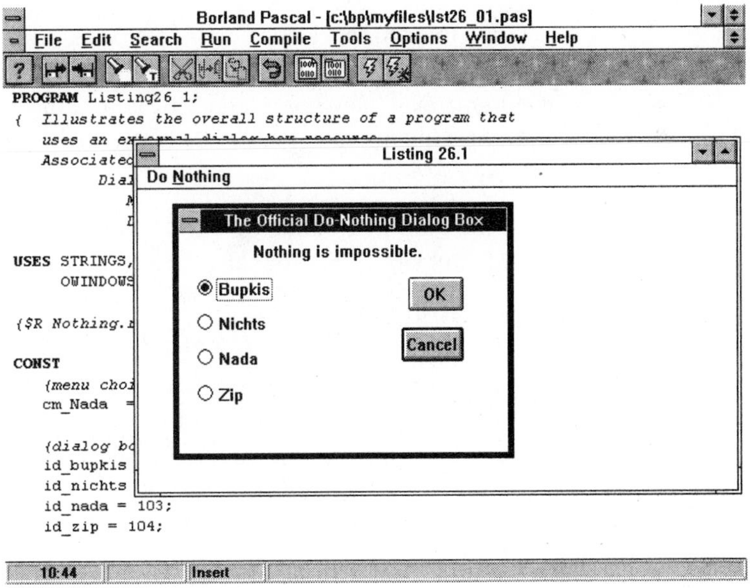

FIGURE 26.11:

The Nothing dialog box used by Listing 26.1

FIGURE 26.12:

Message box used by Listing 26.1

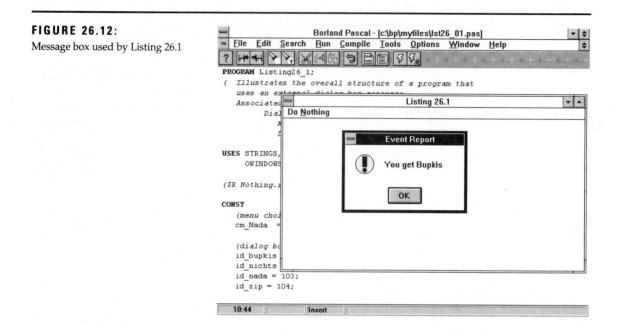

Then select Check box from the Control menu or use the check box speed button at the right; it has a square with an "X" in it.

Position the two check boxes side by side at the lower-right corner of the dialog box. For the first, make the item text "Freberg" and the value 105; for the second, make the item text "Newhart" and the value 106. You can use the Align menu to straighten them out if needed. When you're finished, the dialog box should look like Figure 26.13.

Save the modified dialog box and return to BPW, where we'll make the changes needed in Listing 26.2 so that the program can deal with the check boxes.

Once back in BPW, we need only make very minor changes to handle the check boxes. The first step is in the CONST section of the program, where we must add two new identifiers with the same values as the control IDs of the two check boxes—105 for Freberg and 106 for Rogers. As with other external resources, it's through these identifiers that the check box resources are brought into the program.

FIGURE 26.13:

Positioning a check box in a dialog box

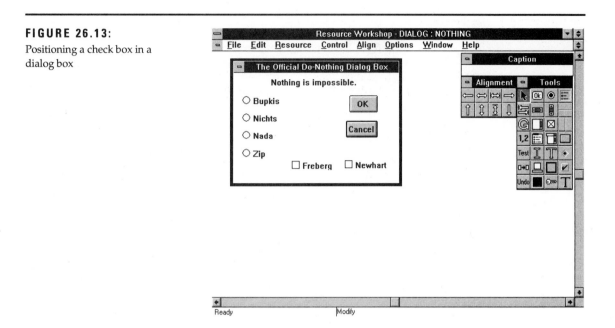

The next step is to add two new fields to the *ItemTransferBuffer* record type—one new field for each check box. Like radio buttons, check boxes have their status indicated by a WORD-type value, so these fields are of the same type as the radio-button fields.

Next, in the definition of the *TMyDialog* object type that stands in for the external resource in the program code, we add two new fields (*Checkbox1* and *Checkbox2*): each field is a pointer to a check box object, just as the radio button fields were pointers to radio button objects.

By now, it shouldn't be hard to guess the next step: we need to add two more lines to the *TMyWindow.Init* method to initialize the two new fields in the parent window's transfer buffer record.

We don't intend that these check boxes have any effect at this time—here, we're just seeing how to set them up. If we did want the program to take some action based on the status of the check boxes (that is, according to whether they were checked or unchecked), we would write some new code in the *TMyWindow.DoNothingMuch* method to take the actions needed. This, however, is simple Pascal programming, and is left to your own imagination. The complete changes are shown in Listing 26.2.

Listing 26.2

```
PROGRAM Listing26_2;

{ Adds check boxes to the dialog box in Listing 26.1.
  Associated resource file: NOTHING.RES.
  Dialog resources:
  Menu: NadaMenu
  Dialog Box: Nothing }

USES STRINGS, WINTYPES, WINPROCS, OWINDOWS, OSTDDLGS, OBJECTS,
     ODIALOGS;

{$R Nothing.res }

CONST
   {menu choice identIFiers}
   cm_Nada  = 201;

   {dialog box identIFiers}
   id_bupkis = 101;
   id_nichts = 102;
   id_nada = 103;
   id_zip = 104;

   id_chkbx1 = 105;
   id_chkbx2 = 106;

{====================================================== }
{ ======== TYPE DEFINITION SECTION OF PROGRAM ======== }
{====================================================== }
TYPE
   TMyApp = OBJECT(TApplication)
      PROCEDURE InitMainWindow; VIRTUAL;
      END;

   { Dialog transfer RECORD }
   ItemTransferBuffer = RECORD
      {radio button fields}
      BupkisBtn,
      NichtsBtn,
      NadaBtn,
      ZipBtn: WORD;

      {check box fields}
```

```
            ChkBox1,
            ChkBox2  : WORD;
            END;

        PMyWindow = ^TMyWindow;
        TMyWindow = OBJECT(TWindow)
            DDBuffer : ItemTransferBuffer;
            CONSTRUCTOR Init(AParent: PWindowsObject;
                ATitle: PChar);
            FUNCTION CanClose: BOOLEAN; VIRTUAL;

            {methods for menu choices}
            PROCEDURE DoNothingMuch(VAR Msg: TMessage);
                VIRTUAL cm_First + cm_Nada;
            END;

        {dialog box type for doing nothing}
        PMyDialog = ^TMyDialog;
        TMyDialog = OBJECT (TDialog)
            BupkisButton,
            NichtsButton,
            NadaButton,
            ZipButton : PRadioButton;
            CheckBox1,
            CheckBox2 : PCheckBox;
            CONSTRUCTOR Init(AParent: PWindowsObject;
                            ATitle:PChar);
            END;

{=================}
{TMyWindow methods}
{=================}

CONSTRUCTOR TMyWindow.Init(AParent: PWindowsObject;
                          ATitle: PChar);
    BEGIN
    TWindow.Init(AParent, ATitle);
    Attr.Menu := LoadMenu(HInstance, 'NadaMenu');
    WITH DDBuffer DO
        BEGIN
        BupkisBtn := bf_unchecked;
        NichtsBtn := bf_unchecked;
        NadaBtn := bf_unchecked;
        ZipBtn := bf_unchecked;
        ChkBox1 := bf_unchecked;
```

```
        ChkBox2 := bf_unchecked
        END
    END;

FUNCTION TMyWindow.CanClose: BOOLEAN;
    VAR
        Reply: INTEGER;
    BEGIN
    CanClose := TRUE;
    Reply := MessageBox(HWindow,
        'Do you want to save your work?',
        'Window content has changed',
        mb_YesNoCancel or mb_IconQuestion);
    IF (Reply = id_Yes) OR (Reply = id_Cancel)
    THEN CanClose := FALSE;
    END;

PROCEDURE TMyWindow.DoNothingMuch(VAR Msg: TMessage);
    VAR
        Dlg: TMyDialog;
        Reply, MyResult: INTEGER;
    BEGIN
    Dlg.Init(@Self, 'Nothing');
    Dlg.TransferBuffer := @DDBuffer;
    Reply := Dlg.Execute;
    Dlg.Done;

    IF Reply = id_Ok THEN
    IF DDBuffer.BupkisBtn = bf_checked
    THEN MyResult := MessageBox(HWindow,
        'You get Bupkis',
        'Event Report',
        mb_OK or mb_IconExclamation)
    ELSE IF DDBuffer.NichtsBtn = bf_checked
    THEN MyResult := MessageBox(HWindow,
        'You get Nichts',
        'Event Report',
        mb_OK or mb_IconExclamation)
    ELSE IF DDBuffer.NadaBtn = bf_checked
    THEN MyResult := MessageBox(HWindow,
        'You get Nada',
        'Event Report',
        mb_OK or mb_IconExclamation)
    ELSE IF DDBuffer.ZipBtn = bf_checked
    THEN MyResult := MessageBox(HWindow,
```

```
            'You get Zip',
            'Event Report',
            mb_OK or mb_IconExclamation)
     ELSE MyResult := MessageBox(HWindow,
            'You STILL get Zip',
            'Event Report',
            mb_OK or mb_IconExclamation);
     END; { of DoNothingMuch routine }


{====================}
{ TMyDialog methods }
{====================}

CONSTRUCTOR TMyDialog.init(AParent: PWindowsObject;
                             ATitle: PChar);
     BEGIN
     TDialog.init(aparent, atitle);
     NEW(BupkisButton, initResource(@Self, id_bupkis));
     NEW(NichtsButton, initResource(@Self, id_nichts));
     NEW(NadaButton, initResource(@Self, id_nada));
     NEW(ZipButton, initResource(@Self, id_zip));
     NEW(CheckBox1, initResource(@Self, id_chkbx1));
     NEW(CheckBox2, initResource(@Self, id_chkbx2))
     END;


{==============}
{TMyApp methods}
{==============}
PROCEDURE TMyApp.InitMainWindow;
     BEGIN
     MainWindow := NEW(PMyWindow, Init(NIL, 'Listing 26.2'));
     END;


{=====================================}
{global object variable for application}
{=====================================}
VAR
     MyApp : TMyApp;


{====================}
{main body of program}
{====================}
```

```
BEGIN
    MyApp.Init('Listing26_2');
    MyApp.Run;
    MyApp.Done;
END.
```

"Safe" Dialog Box Execution

You may have noticed that when we executed the dialog box in Listing 26.2, the technique was different from the one we used in an earlier chapter. In the dialog boxes we created there—all of which were based on predefined ObjectWindows types—we used the *ExecDialog* method of the *Application* object. *Application*, as you will recall, is a predefined variable (like *Self*), which always refers to the current application process. With the appropriate changes made for each different dialog box, the code for executing a dialog box was something like this:

```
IF Application^.ExecDialog(pointer to dialog) = id_OK THEN
    BEGIN ...
```

Because we were using a predefined object type instead of an external dialog box resource, we didn't need to worry about setting up a transfer buffer and getting the data out of the dialog box: that was all handled for us by BPW.

When we created an external dialog resource, however, we did things a little differently. First, in the method that creates and uses the dialog box, we declared a local variable of the appropriate dialog box object type to correspond to the resource. Then, we passed a pointer to the parent window's transfer buffer into the dialog variable's *TransferBuffer* field, thereby initializing it and setting it up to save the data from the dialog box when the dialog was terminated. Finally, after all that setup, we executed the dialog box with a call to its inherited *TDialog.Execute* method. The code looked like this:

```
VAR
    Dlg: TMyDialog;
    Reply, MyResult: Integer;
BEGIN
    Dlg.Init(@Self, 'Nothing');
    Dlg.TransferBuffer := @DDBuffer;
```

```
Reply := Dlg.Execute;
Dlg.Done;

IF Reply = id_Ok THEN
BEGIN ...
```

This is a more direct way to execute a dialog, and it does have the advantage that setting up the transfer buffer is quite straightforward. However, it has one drawback: it lacks the built-in safety features of executing a dialog box with a call to *ExecDialog*. If you're sure that everything is coded properly, then the direct approach is fine.

If there is any doubt, however—particularly when you're just getting started—it's probably better to stick with using *ExecDialog*. This approach lets *ExecDialog* check to make sure that the dialog box was created successfully and executed without errors. If anything goes wrong, *ExecDialog* simply returns *id_Cancel* to your program. Without this safety feature—that is, if an error occurs in a dialog box that you're running with a bare call to *Dialog.Execute*—your program will probably crash.

Setting up the transfer buffer is a little more complicated with this "safe" method, but it's still not terribly difficult. The approach we used earlier won't quite do:

```
IF Application^.ExecDialog(New(PInputDialog,
          Init(@Self, 'Line Color',
          'Type 1/Red, 2/Green, 3/Blue, 4/Black',
          ColorBuffer, SizeOf(ColorBuffer)))) = id_Ok
     THEN  BEGIN ...
```

Here, we've embedded the creation and destruction of the dialog box in the middle of the call to *ExecDialog*, so there's nowhere we can link the dialog's transfer buffer to the buffer record of the parent window. This is something that we absolutely *must* do in the program from Listing 26.2, because we're using an external dialog resource. A step-by-step approach to doing the same thing, however, works fine. We just need to make a slight change in the *TMyWindow.DoNothingMuch* method:

```
PROCEDURE TMyWindow.DoNothingMuch(VAR Msg: TMessage);
   VAR
      Dlg: PMyDialog;
      MyResult: Integer;
   BEGIN
      Dlg := New(PMyDialog, Init(@Self, 'Nothing'));
      Dlg^.TransferBuffer := @DDBuffer;
      IF Application^.ExecDialog(Dlg) = id_OK THEN
      ...
```

Instead of trying to do everything in one fell swoop, we take things one at a time. First, we declare a local dialog box variable, just as we did before. The difference is that *this* time, it's not actually a dialog box variable; instead, it is a *pointer* to that type of dialog box.

Then, using the pointer with a call to NEW, we make it point to a dialog box variable of the appropriate type. We then dereference the pointer (which means that we can now refer to the dialog box variable itself) and, as before, pass the pointer to the parent window's transfer buffer into the dialog variable's *TransferBuffer* field.

After that, the only thing remaining is to execute the dialog, which we can now do either with a (safe) call to *ExecDialog* or a (bold) call to *MyDialog.Execute*. Everything else works the same, and we've bought ourselves a little extra peace of mind.

CHAPTER TWENTY-SEVEN

Integrating Resources into Your Application

- **Specifying Characteristics of Dialog Resources**

- **Setting Up Multiple Transfer Buffers**

- **Running Multiple Dialog Resources**

27

In Chapter 26, we saw how to integrate external dialog resources into a Windows application. Because this is such a daunting task, however, the application in Chapter 26 was deliberately simplified in order to clarify only the main points about using a dialog resource in a program. In the process, certain questions were left unasked:

- What happens if you have more than one dialog box? Can you use the same transfer buffer and dialog object types, or do you need one object type for each dialog resource?

- How do you juggle all the command identifiers and dialog resource identifiers in the program?

- Do you need to have different names for the fields of the transfer buffer, the dialog object fields to which they correspond, and the resource identifiers?

In this chapter, we'll look at a more formal and precise way of specifying the contents of dialog boxes. Then, we'll see how to integrate multiple dialog boxes into a "real" application: in the course of doing so, we will answer these and other questions.

Specifying the Characteristics of Dialog Resources

So far, when we've wanted to create a dialog box, it's been a matter of opening the Borland Resource Workshop and then saying "do this, do that, click on that button," and so on. This kind of specification will indeed produce a dialog box, but it depends on two things:

1. You must be using BRW to create the dialog or other resource. If there's a different tool being used, the do-this-then-do-that kind of guidance is extremely unhelpful.

2. You must have time to work with this type of instruction, which is fine for tutorial purposes, but very inefficient for specifying the characteristics of a dialog resource for an experienced Windows application developer.

It will be much more efficient if we give a more or less formal specification of the characteristics a dialog box (or other resource) should have. When you are creating multiple resources, you need to have such a specification written down anyway to guide your work. Otherwise, you will spend enormous amounts of time switching back and forth between Borland Pascal for Windows and the BRW or other resource tool. Did the resource identifier you defined in the program match the resource ID for the appropriate radio button in the dialog box? What was the value of choice X in menu Y? Having a written, formal specification answers these questions for you. Instead of needing to look at the resource itself in the BRW, you can just look at your specification sheet.

Specifying Resources for a Line-Drawing Program

Now, let's specify some resources for the line-drawing program we developed in an earlier chapter. You may recall that we used predefined BPW dialog box types for the dialog boxes in that application. It was simpler than using external dialog resources, but it seemed fairly artificial. Instead of using radio buttons to make a choice of colors, we asked the user to enter a number; likewise for choosing a line style. The only dialog box where "entering a number" seemed natural was in the one to set line thickness, which can vary over a wide range of numeric values.

Therefore, we'll specify three resources for this application:

1. A menu resource identical to the one we created earlier. This will be shown in Listing 27.1.

2. A dialog resource to change the color of the line being drawn. This will be shown in Listing 27.2.

3. A dialog resource to change the style of the line being drawn. This will be shown in Listing 27.3.

Listing 27.1

```
{specifying a menu resource}
Menu in file MYRES2.RES: resource name = LINEMENU
    Item Text            ID
    &Line                None
    &New                 100
    Change &Color        200
    Change &Style        300
```

```
Change &Thickness        400
&Help                    901
```

Listing 27.2

```
{specifying a dialog resource to change line color}
Dialog in file MYRES2.RES: resource name = CHG_COL
Title: Change Line Color
Static text: New Line Color;
ID = 1
Automatic radio buttons
   left align, space vertically, same size:
ARB text: Red, ID = 201
ARB text: Green, ID = 202
ARB text: Blue, ID = 203
ARB text: Black, ID = 204
Pushbuttons   align right:
PB (pushbutton text): OK, ID = 1
DPB (default pushbutton text): Cancel, ID = 2
```

Listing 27.3

```
{specifying a dialog resource to change line style}
Dialog in file MYRES2.RES: resource name = CHG_STY
Title: Change Line Style
Radio buttons: left align, space vertically, same size.
ARB text: Solid, ID = 301;
ARB text: Dotted, ID = 302
ARB text: Dashed, ID = 303
Pushbuttons   right align:
PB text: OK, ID = 1
DPB text: Cancel, ID = 2
```

Integrating Resources into an Application

There are a few tricks in handling multiple dialog boxes; these go beyond what we saw in the simplified example of Chapter 26. The ideas and techniques are illustrated in Listing 27.4.

Listing 27.4

```
PROGRAM Listing27_4;

{  Shows how to incorporate dialog boxes and
   other resources into a nonvacuous program. }


USES STRINGS, WINTYPES, WINPROCS, OWINDOWS, OSTDDLGS, OBJECTS,
              ODIALOGS;

{$R MyRes2.res }

CONST
    {menu choice identifiers}
    cm_New   = 100;
    cm_Color = 200;
    cm_Style = 300;
    cm_Thick = 400;
    cm_Help  = 901;

    {line color dialog button identifiers}
    id_RedBtn   = 201;
    id_GreenBtn = 202;
    id_BlueBtn  = 203;
    id_BlackBtn = 204;

    {line style dialog button identifiers}
    id_SolidBtn  = 301;
    id_DottedBtn = 302;
    id_DashedBtn = 303;

    {color identifiers}
    red = 1;
    green = 2;
    blue = 3;
    black = 4;

    {style identifiers}
    solid = 1;
    dotted = 2;
    dashed = 3;
```

```
{========================================================= }
{ ======== TYPE DEFINITION SECTION OF PROGRAM ====== }
{========================================================= }
TYPE
    TMyApp = OBJECT(TApplication)
       PROCEDURE InitMainWindow; VIRTUAL;
       END;

    {Line color dialog transfer record}
    ColorTransferBuffer = RECORD
       RedBtn,
       GreenBtn,
       BlueBtn,
       BlackBtn : WORD;
       END;

    {Line style dialog transfer record}
    StyleTransferBuffer = RECORD
       SolidBtn,
       DottedBtn,
       DashedBtn   : WORD;
       END;

    PMyWindow = ^TMyWindow;
    TMyWindow = OBJECT(TWindow)
       ColorBuffer : ColorTransferBuffer;
       StyleBuffer : StyleTransferBuffer;
       dc: HDC;
       LButtonDown: BOOLEAN;
       MyPen: HPen;
       PenSize: INTEGER;
       PenColor : TColorRef;
       PenStyle : INTEGER;
       Points: PCollection;
       CONSTRUCTOR Init(AParent: PWindowsObject;
                        ATitle: PChar);

       DESTRUCTOR Done; VIRTUAL;
       FUNCTION CanClose: BOOLEAN; VIRTUAL;
       PROCEDURE WMLButtonDown(VAR Msg: TMessage);
          VIRTUAL wm_First + wm_LButtonDown;
       PROCEDURE WMLButtonUp(VAR Msg: TMessage);
          VIRTUAL wm_First + wm_LButtonUp;
       PROCEDURE WMMouseMove(VAR Msg: TMessage);
```

```
        VIRTUAL wm_First + wm_MouseMove;
    PROCEDURE SetPenColor(NewColor: INTEGER);
    PROCEDURE SetPenStyle(NewStyle: INTEGER);
    PROCEDURE SetPenSize(NewSize: INTEGER);
    PROCEDURE Paint(PaintDC: HDC;
        VAR PaintInfo: TPaintStruct); VIRTUAL;
    PROCEDURE NewDraw(VAR Msg: TMessage);
        VIRTUAL cm_First + cm_New;
    PROCEDURE ChangeColor(VAR Msg: TMessage);
        VIRTUAL cm_First + cm_Color;
    PROCEDURE ChangeStyle(VAR Msg: TMessage);
        VIRTUAL cm_First + cm_Style;
    PROCEDURE ChangeThickness(VAR Msg: TMessage);
        VIRTUAL cm_First + cm_Thick;
    PROCEDURE Help(VAR Msg: TMessage);
        VIRTUAL cm_First + cm_Help;
     END;

{dialog box type for changing line color}
PColorDialog = ^TColorDialog;
TColorDialog = OBJECT (TDialog)
   RedBtn,
   GreenBtn,
   BlueBtn,
   BlackBtn    : PRadioButton;
   CONSTRUCTOR Init(AParent:PWindowsObject;
                    ATitle:PChar);
   END;

{dialog box type for changing line style}
PStyleDialog = ^TStyleDialog;
TStyleDialog = OBJECT (TDialog)
   SolidBtn,
   DottedBtn,
   DashedBtn   : PRadioButton;
   CONSTRUCTOR Init (AParent:PWindowsObject;
                    ATitle:PChar);
   END;

{object type to save drawing for repainting}
PDPoint = ^TDPoint;
TDPoint = OBJECT(TObject)
   X, Y: INTEGER;
   CONSTRUCTOR Init(AX, AY: INTEGER);
   END;
```

```
{=================}
{TMyWindow methods}
{=================}

CONSTRUCTOR TMyWindow.Init(AParent: PWindowsObject;
                             ATitle: PChar);
    BEGIN
    TWindow.Init(AParent, ATitle);
    Attr.Menu := LoadMenu(HInstance, 'linemenu');
    WITH ColorBuffer DO
        BEGIN
        RedBtn := bf_unchecked;
        GreenBtn := bf_unchecked;
        BlueBtn := bf_unchecked;
        BlackBtn := bf_unchecked;
        END;
    WITH StyleBuffer DO
        BEGIN
        SolidBtn := bf_unchecked;
        DottedBtn := bf_unchecked;
        DashedBtn := bf_unchecked;
        END;
    LButtonDown := FALSE;
    PenSize := 1;
    PenStyle := ps_Solid;
    PenColor := 0;
    MyPen := CreatePen(PenStyle, PenSize, PenColor);
    Points := New(PCollection, Init(50, 50));
    END;

DESTRUCTOR TMyWindow.Done;
    BEGIN
    Dispose(Points, Done);
    DeleteObject(MyPen);
    TWindow.Done;
    END;

FUNCTION TMyWindow.CanClose: BOOLEAN;
    VAR
        Reply: INTEGER;
    BEGIN
        CanClose := TRUE;
        Reply := MessageBox(HWindow,
                'Do you want to save your work?',
```

```
                     'Window content has changed',
                 mb_YesNoCancel or mb_IconQuestion);
        IF (Reply = id_Yes) OR (Reply = id_Cancel)
           THEN CanClose := FALSE;
   END;

PROCEDURE TMyWindow.WMLButtonDown(VAR Msg: TMessage);
   BEGIN
   Points^.FreeAll;
   InvalidateRect(HWindow, NIL, TRUE);
   IF not LButtonDown
   THEN  BEGIN
         LButtonDown := TRUE;
         SetCapture(HWindow);
         dc := GetDC(HWindow);
         SelectObject(dc, MyPen);
         MoveTo(dc, Msg.LParamLo, Msg.LParamHi);
         Points^.Insert(New(PDPoint,
              Init(Msg.LParamLo, Msg.LParamHi)));
         END;
   END;

PROCEDURE TMyWindow.WMMouseMove(VAR Msg: TMessage);
   BEGIN
   IF LButtonDown
   THEN  BEGIN
         LineTo(dc, INTEGER(Msg.LParamLo),
              INTEGER(Msg.LParamHi));
         Points^.Insert(New(PDPoint,
              Init(INTEGER(Msg.LParamLo),
              INTEGER(Msg.LParamHi))));
         END;
   END;

PROCEDURE TMyWindow.WMLButtonUp(VAR Msg: TMessage);
   BEGIN
   IF LButtonDown
   THEN  BEGIN
         LButtonDown := FALSE;
         ReleaseCapture;
         ReleaseDC(HWindow, dc);
         END;
   END;
```

```
PROCEDURE TMyWindow.SetPenColor(NewColor: INTEGER);
BEGIN
   DeleteObject(MyPen);
   CASE NewColor OF
   1: BEGIN
      PenColor := RGB(200,0,0);
      MyPen := CreatePen(PenStyle, PenSize, PenColor);
      END;
   2: BEGIN
      PenColor := RGB(0,200,0);
      MyPen := CreatePen(PenStyle, PenSize, PenColor);
      END;
   3: BEGIN
      PenColor := RGB(0,0,200);
      MyPen := CreatePen(PenStyle, PenSize, PenColor);
      END;
   4: BEGIN
      PenColor := 0;
      MyPen := CreatePen(PenStyle, PenSize, PenColor);
      END;
   ELSE MyPen := CreatePen(PenStyle, PenSize, 0)
   END;
END;


PROCEDURE TMyWindow.SetPenStyle(NewStyle: INTEGER);
   BEGIN
   DeleteObject(MyPen);
   CASE NewStyle OF
   1: BEGIN
      PenStyle := ps_Solid;
      MyPen := CreatePen(PenStyle, PenSize, PenColor);
      END;
   2: BEGIN
      PenStyle := ps_Dot;
      MyPen := CreatePen(PenStyle, PenSize, PenColor);
      END;
   3: BEGIN
      PenStyle := ps_Dash;
      MyPen := CreatePen(PenStyle, PenSize, PenColor);
      END
   ELSE MyPen := CreatePen(ps_Solid, PenSize, PenColor)
   END;
END;
```

```
PROCEDURE TMyWindow.SetPenSize(NewSize: INTEGER);
   BEGIN
   DeleteObject(MyPen);
   MyPen := CreatePen(PenStyle, NewSize, PenColor);
   PenSize := NewSize;
   END;


PROCEDURE TMyWindow.Paint(PaintDC: HDC;
              VAR PaintInfo: TPaintStruct);
   VAR
      First: BOOLEAN;
   {local procedure under TMyWindow.Paint method}
   PROCEDURE DrawLine(P: PDPoint); far;
      BEGIN
      IF First
      THEN MoveTo(PaintDC, P^.X, P^.Y)
      else LineTo(PaintDC, P^.X, P^.Y);
      First := FALSE;
      END;
   {main body of TMyWindow.Paint method}
   BEGIN
      SelectObject(PaintDC, MyPen);
      First := TRUE;
      Points^.ForEach(@DrawLine);
   END;

PROCEDURE TMyWindow.NewDraw(VAR Msg: TMessage);
   BEGIN
   Points^.FreeAll;
   InvalidateRect(HWindow, NIL, TRUE);
   END;


PROCEDURE TMyWindow.ChangeColor(VAR Msg: TMessage);
   VAR
      Dlg: TColorDialog;
      Reply : INTEGER;
   BEGIN
      Dlg.Init(@Self, 'chg_col');
      Dlg.TransferBuffer := @ColorBuffer;
      Reply := Dlg.Execute;
      Dlg.Done;
```

```
            IF Reply = id_OK THEN
                IF ColorBuffer.RedBtn = bf_checked
                THEN SetPenColor(red)
                ELSE IF ColorBuffer.GreenBtn = bf_checked
                THEN SetPenColor(green)
                ELSE IF ColorBuffer.BlueBtn = bf_checked
                THEN SetPenColor(blue)
                ELSE IF ColorBuffer.BlackBtn = bf_checked
                THEN SetPenColor(black)
                {a line for simple error trapping}
                ELSE SetPenColor(black)
        END;


PROCEDURE TMyWindow.ChangeStyle(VAR Msg: TMessage);
    VAR
        Dlg: TStyleDialog;
        Reply : INTEGER;
    BEGIN
        Dlg.Init(@Self, 'chg_sty');
        Dlg.TransferBuffer := @StyleBuffer;
        Reply := Dlg.Execute;
        Dlg.Done;

        IF Reply = id_OK THEN
            IF StyleBuffer.SolidBtn = bf_checked
            THEN SetPenStyle(solid)
            ELSE IF StyleBuffer.DottedBtn = bf_checked
            THEN SetPenStyle(dotted)
            ELSE IF StyleBuffer.DashedBtn = bf_checked
            THEN SetPenStyle(dashed)


            {a line for simple error trapping}
            ELSE SetPenStyle(solid)
        END;


PROCEDURE TMyWindow.ChangeThickness(VAR Msg: TMessage);
    VAR
        ThickBuffer: ARRAY[0..5] of CHAR;
        NewSize, ErrorPos: INTEGER;
    BEGIN
        Str(PenSize, ThickBuffer);
        IF Application^.ExecDialog(New(PInputDialog,
```

```
              Init(@Self, 'Line Thickness',
              'Input a new thickness:',
              ThickBuffer, SizeOf(ThickBuffer)))) = id_Ok
         THEN BEGIN
                 Val(ThickBuffer, NewSize, ErrorPos);
                 IF ErrorPos = 0 THEN SetPenSize(NewSize);
                 END;
         END;


PROCEDURE TMyWindow.Help(VAR Msg: TMessage);
   BEGIN
   MessageBox(HWindow, 'Not yet implemented',
      'Help', mb_Ok or mb_IconExclamation);
   END;

{================}
{ TDPoint methods}
{================}
CONSTRUCTOR TDPoint.Init(AX, AY: INTEGER);
   BEGIN
   X := AX;
   Y := AY;
   END;


{====================}
{Dialog Object Methods}
{====================}
CONSTRUCTOR TColorDialog.Init(AParent:PWindowsObject;
                              ATitle:PChar);
   BEGIN
   TDialog.init(aparent, atitle);
   NEW(RedBtn, initResource(@Self, id_RedBtn));
   NEW(GreenBtn, initResource(@Self, id_GreenBtn));
   NEW(BlueBtn, initResource(@Self, id_BlueBtn));
   NEW(BlackBtn, initResource(@Self, id_BlackBtn));
   END;

CONSTRUCTOR TStyleDialog.Init(AParent:PWindowsObject;
                              ATitle:PChar);
   BEGIN
   TDialog.init(aparent, atitle);
   NEW(SolidBtn, initResource(@Self, id_SolidBtn));
   NEW(DottedBtn, initResource(@Self, id_DottedBtn));
```

```
      NEW(DashedBtn, initResource(@Self, id_DashedBtn));
      END;


{==============}
{TMyApp methods}
{==============}
PROCEDURE TMyApp.InitMainWindow;
   BEGIN
   MainWindow := New(PMyWindow, Init(NIL, 'Listing 27.4'));
   END;

{=====================================}
{global object variable for application}
{=====================================}
VAR
   MyApp : TMyApp;

{====================}
{main body of program}
{====================}
BEGIN
   MyApp.Init('Listing27_4');
   MyApp.Run;
   MyApp.Done;
END.
```

Let's take a look at how this works—leaving aside, of course, the points that we've already covered in previous chapters.

The first new wrinkle is that we've separated the different command and resource identifier constants by their type and by what resources they refer to. This has nothing to do with how well the program will work, but has a lot to do with how easily the program code can be understood.

Setting Up Multiple Transfer Buffers

Each menu choice has its own resource ID, as does each button in each dialog box. Because the dialog boxes have different numbers of buttons, we have defined a separate transfer buffer type for each dialog box. The buffer type for the color-change dialog box is called *ColorTransferBuffer;* it has four fields, one for each of the buttons in the dialog. The buffer type for the style-change dialog box is called *Style-TransferBuffer;* it has three fields, one for each button in its corresponding dialog object type and resource. If the two dialogs had exactly the same type, number, and order of buttons, we could in principle use a single buffer type (and a single buffer field in the parent window) to get data in and out of the dialog boxes. This is a tweak that might produce smaller compiled code size at the price of making the source program a little less clear. As before, the fields in the buffer type are WORDs, which is the appropriate type for the checked/unchecked values of the buttons.

As expected, in the parent window type *TMyWindow*, we have two transfer buffer fields: one for the color dialog box, and one for the style dialog box. We don't need to have a field for the dialog box that changes the line's width, because that dialog box isn't associated with an external dialog resource. Everything else in *TMyWindow* is the same as it was before.

Creating Multiple Dialog Types

Next, we create two different dialog box object types, both descended from *TDialog.* The *TColorDialog* type has four fields of type *PRadioButton*, meaning that each field holds a pointer to a radio button. There's also a constructor *TColorDialog.Init* method; this is needed to call NEW, which creates the buttons as dynamic variables that exist while the dialog is open, and to initialize the button variables with a call to *InitResource*, which we'll discuss in a moment.

The structure of the object type for the style dialog box is identical to that of the color dialog box, except that it has three fields instead of four; these correspond to the three buttons in the style dialog resource.

Initializing Multiple Buffer Fields

The next new feature appears in the constructor method for the *TMyWindow* object type. As before, we call the inherited *TWindow.Init* method from the ancestor type. Then, we use separate WITH statements to initialize each transfer buffer field in a window of this type. Remember that this step has nothing to do with the external dialog resource—at least, not yet. At this point, we're just loading the appropriate values into the buffer fields of the parent window. In the second line of this method, we also use *LoadMenu* to activate LINEMENU, the appropriate menu resource for this application.

The procedures and methods to close a window, to set pen color and style, and to respond to mouse clicks don't change at all from the listing in the earlier chapter. This is a good example of modular programming: we can make changes in a few parts of the program (for example, the dialog boxes and the parts of the program that directly interact with them) and leave the rest of the program as is.

Running Multiple Dialog Resources

The *TMyWindowChangeColor* method, which is invoked in response to a menu choice, has changed quite a bit because it now calls an external dialog resource. It first creates a variable (*Dlg*) of the appropriate dialog object type (*TColorDialog*); this variable will "stand in" for the dialog resource in the program code. We initialize the dialog variable, linking it to the CHG_COL dialog resource in the MyRes2.Res resource file we named at the beginning of the program. As we did in Chapter 26, we then initialize the dialog variable's buttons by loading them with the values from the parent window's transfer buffer; with the same step, we link the transfer buffer to the dialog variable's button fields so that when the dialog is closed, the button values will be copied into the transfer buffer.

The rest of the method is fairly ordinary: the dialog is executed with a call to the variable's *Execute* method, which it inherits from *TDialog*; based on the values in the transfer buffer, the program then executes the *SetPenColor* procedure with the appropriate color parameter. This business of nested IF..THEN..ELSE statements to check the states of radio buttons is a little messy, but there's no straightforward way to use anything that might look neater, such as a CASE statement.

With the expected changes to account for the fact that we're using a different dialog box, the *TMyWindow.ChangeStyle* method is essentially the same as the *ChangeColor* method. The *ChangeThickness* method hasn't changed at all from the earlier chapter, because we're still using a text-input dialog box to prompt the user for a line thickness; this makes sense because of the large number of values that might be entered. In this case, it would be a waste of time and effort to try to cover all the possibilities by using radio buttons.

The *TColorDialog.Init* and *TStyleDialog.Init* methods are, again, essentially the same. Each begins by calling the inherited *Init* method from *TDialog*. Then, each initializes its radio buttons: the first parameter in the NEW statement is the name of the field in the dialog object. The second parameter embeds a call to *InitResource* that links the external button resource (through its resource identifier defined in the CONST section of the program) to the button field in the dialog object type.

CHAPTER TWENTY-EIGHT

Opening and Saving Files and Streams

- Collections and Streams

- File I/O with Streams

28

File handling in Borland Pascal for Windows is not terribly difficult, but it is both different and slightly more complex than file handling in standard DOS Turbo Pascal programs. Some of these differences have to do with the fact that BPW programs must operate in the Windows environment. Others, such as working with files of objects, have nothing much to do with Windows, but come from the nature of object-oriented programming.

In this chapter, we'll look first at files of objects and then at standard text files. The first is inherently a little more complicated than the second, and requires more preparatory discussion of *collections* and *streams*, which are roughly the object-oriented equivalents of arrays and typed files. We'll illustrate the concepts by modifying the program in Listing 27.4, adding the ability to create, save, and load files of objects. Then, to show how you can prepare a BPW program to deal with standard text files, we'll look at the simple text editor object types that are part of ObjectWindows. These object types allow you to incorporate all the basic text-editing tasks (such as entering text, searching for a text string, saving the contents of the window to a text file, and reloading a text file) into your BPW programs with a minimum of extra work.

Collections and Streams

The starting point for understanding collections and streams is to see how they differ from their non-object-oriented counterparts.

Understanding Collections

The best way to understand collections is to contrast them with *arrays,* to which they bear a few similarities. Although arrays are fast, they are inflexible. An array has to be fully defined at compile time, both in terms of the size of the array and in terms of what each array slot will contain; this is necessitated by the requirement that array elements be stored contiguously in main memory. If you need to add items later, or would like to store items of various sizes in an array, you are generally out of luck.

A BPW collection is designed to sidestep these limitations. Just as you can have an array of pointers (for example, to linked lists), you can have an object that *includes* an array of (untyped) pointers to other objects. This is what is meant by "collection."

Of course, using untyped pointers is tricky regardless of whether you're in BPW or doing object-oriented programming. You can't simply use the traditional NEW and DISPOSE routines, because you and the compiler can't be sure how much memory to allocate or deallocate for the referent of an untyped pointer.

To handle such problems, BPW provides the abstract object type called *TCollection*, which serves as an ancestor for other object types. The *TCollection* type has four fields:

Count: This field holds the number of items currently in the collection, up to the current maximum size of the collection.

Delta: If needed, a collection can increase in size at run time. The delta field specifies the size of the increments. For example, you could specify that if the collection needs to expand beyond its initial size, it will grow by 50 slots at a time (that is, delta = 50). Although increasing the size of a collection at run time slows down your program, it can be important to have the possibility to do so. Setting delta to zero means that the collection cannot expand at run time.

Items: This holds a pointer to the array of pointers that is the backbone of the *TCollection* object.

Limit: This is the maximum number of elements that can be contained in the collection. Because of the performance penalty from increasing the size of the collection at run time, it's not a bad idea, when setting the initial limit, to think of the collection as an array that must have enough slots to accommodate any probable number of items.

TCollection also has a large number of methods to manipulate the data in its fields. The most important are:

Init: This is the *TCollection* constructor field. It takes two integer parameters: one for the initial size of the collection (to set an initial value for the *Limit* field) and one for the amount by which the size can change (to set the value for the *Delta* field). If you're still new to collections, the obvious question is: why doesn't the *Init* routine have anything in it about the nature of the objects in the collection? The answer is that the array in the collection holds only *untyped pointers* to the objects that the collection "contains." No matter

757

what those objects are or how big they are, the size of the pointers will always be the same. Thus, the *Init* routine doesn't have to worry about the actual items and it knows how big the pointers will be, since they all occupy the same amount of memory.

Load: This loads items into a collection from a *stream*, which is roughly the object-oriented counterpart of a standard, non-OOP file (see the section on streams later in this chapter). It assumes that the items are descendants of *TObject*, and must be overridden if they are not.

ForEach: This applies a particular procedure (a pointer to which is passed to the method, as its only parameter) to each item in the collection. The items are processed in the order they appear in the collection. The procedure cannot be an object method.

FirstThat and **LastThat:** These methods find an element in the collection based on criteria specified by the user. Each method, if used, returns a pointer to the location of the "found" item matching the criteria, or returns nil if all items fail to match the criteria.

FreeAll: This deletes all items in the collection and deallocates the memory they occupied. Like *Load*, it assumes that it is dealing with descendants of *TObject*.

Done: This not only deletes all items and deallocates the memory (by calling *TCollection.FreeAll*), but it also sets the *Limit* field to zero.

Store: This stores the collection and its constituent items in a stream. This method takes the stream as its only parameter.

Predefined Collection Types

As mentioned earlier, *TCollection* is an abstract type, and is not meant to be used as is. It serves as an ancestor type for both ObjectWindows and user-defined collection types.

Two important *TCollection* descendant types are predefined in ObjectWindows: *TSortedCollection* and *TStrCollection*.

TSortedCollection, which is itself an abstract type, automatically keeps its items sorted. How the items are sorted, and on what field, is determined by the specifics of the descendant type derived from *TSortedCollection*. It includes a *Compare* method that checks the key field (the sort field) of new items as they are added to the collection and inserts them in the correct order. *TSortedCollection* also includes a method for binary search (a *lg n* searching algorithm) to find items in the collection. Duplicate keys are not allowed.

TStrCollection, a descendant of *TSortedCollection*, sets up a sorted list of ASCII text strings.

Understanding Streams

A stream is the file I/O counterpart of a collection; it is simply a collection of objects that is en route to some destination. The destination could be a serial port, expanded memory, or—most likely—a disk file. However, Borland Pascal will not allow you to simply create a typed file of objects. Using a stream solves this problem because the stream itself (that is, the object based on and descended from a *TStream* type) knows that it's dealing with objects and includes *within itself* all the data and methods needed to save and load disk files; the file part itself can still be as "dumb" as ever. In shorthand, you might think of a stream as the sum of

1. a collection of objects

2. information on how to store and load them

3. a disk file

Registering an Object Type for Streaming

Because a stream may have to handle widely different kinds of objects, you have to provide BPW with information about the type of the objects involved before you can send them to a disk file or other device. This is called *registering* the object type with the stream, and uses a predefined BPW procedure, *RegisterType*.

Registering an object type for use with a stream takes a number of steps. The first is the most involved: you need to declare a "stream registration record" that contains information about the stream. Perhaps the most important information contained in this record is the location in memory of the stream's *Load* and *Store* methods, which do much of the hard work associated with opening and saving streams with disk files.

The stream registration record is a predefined BPW type called *TStreamRec*, structured as follows:

```
PStreamRec = ^TStreamRec;
TStreamRec = RECORD
   ObjType: WORD; { an identifier for the type of the object }
   VMTLink : WORD;
   Load : Pointer;    { untyped pointer to the object's LOAD
                        method }
   Store: Pointer;    { untyped pointer to the object's STORE
                        method }
   Next: WORD
   END;
```

It's conventional to name a stream registration record after the object type it registers, substituting an initial "R" for the initial "T." Thus, in Listing 28.1 (later in this chapter), the *TDPoint* object type is registered with a stream registration record named *RDPoint*.

There are really only three fields in the stream registration record that you need to worry about: the *ObjType* field, the *Load* field, and the *Store* field. *ObjType* gets an integer identifier between 0 and 65,535, but BPW reserves the numbers 0..99 for itself, so you shouldn't use numbers in that range. This field is really little more than a placeholder, because the number you use in this field does not need to be referenced anywhere else in your program, nor does it need to be referenced or defined in any of the units or resources that your program uses. All you need to worry about are two things:

- The number you put in the *ObjType* field of a particular stream registration record must be unique; it must not occur elsewhere in your program.

- This number identifies the type of objects that are saved and loaded by reference to this stream registration record. If you change the number and then attempt to load a stream that you saved under a different *ObjType* number, you'll get an unrecoverable application error because BPW won't have any idea of what it's trying to load.

The *Load* and *Store* fields are set up in basically the same way. When you declare an object type that you plan to use in a stream, you must declare *Load* and *Store* methods for that object type. Because the *Load* and *Store* fields contain pointers to those methods, you simply put the pointer addresses in the fields, as in

```
Load : @TDPoint.Load;
Store: @TDPoint.Store;
```

After creating the stream registration record, the second major step to registering an object type for use with a stream is to ensure that your object type contains appropriate *Load* and *Store* methods. *Load* is a constructor method; *Store* is a standard procedure-type method. We'll look at an example in Listing 28.1 later in this chapter.

The third and final step is to make use of the information you provided in the first step, by setting up a procedure that will actually register the stream. This would be something like

```
PROCEDURE RegisterStream;
   BEGIN
   RegisterType(RCollection);
   RegisterType(RDPoint)
   END;
```

This is, in fact, the procedure we'll use in Listing 28.1 to register a stream for saving line drawings. The first line in the BEGIN..END part of the procedure calls the BPW *RegisterType* routine to register the collection that stores the points, while the second line calls the same routine to register the object type of the points themselves.

File I/O with Streams

Let's proceed with an example. Earlier, we created a line-drawing program that could create drawings as well as change line color, style, and thickness. What it could not do was save a drawing to a file and then reload it when needed. Listing 28.1 adds this capability.

Listing 28.1

```
PROGRAM Listing28_1;

{ Shows how to set up the framework for opening
  and saving line drawings to files. Features
  demonstrated:
      1. Modifying an object type for use in
         a stream.
```

```
      2. Setting up a stream registration record.
      3. Registering a stream.
      4. Using standard ObjectWindows FileSave
         and FileLoad dialog boxes.   }

USES STRINGS, WINTYPES, WINPROCS
        OWINDOWS, OSTDDLGS, OBJECTS, ODIALOGS, WINDOS;

{$R MyRes3.res }

CONST
    {menu choice identifiers}
    cm_New     = 101;
    cm_Open    = 102;
    cm_Save    = 103;
    cm_SaveAs   = 104;

    cm_NewDraw = 100;
    cm_Color   = 200;
    cm_Style  = 300;
    cm_Thick   = 400;

    cm_Help      = 901;

    {line color dialog button identifiers}
    id_RedBtn   = 201;
    id_GreenBtn = 202;
    id_BlueBtn = 203;
    id_BlackBtn = 204;

    {line style dialog button identifiers}
    id_SolidBtn  = 301;
    id_DottedBtn = 302;
    id_DashedBtn = 303;

    {color identifiers}
    red = 1;
    green = 2;
    blue = 3;
    black = 4;

    {style identifiers}
    solid = 1;
    dotted = 2;
    dashed = 3;
```

```
{======================================================= }
{ ======== TYPE DEFINITION SECTION OF PROGRAM ======== }
{======================================================= }
TYPE
   TMyApp = OBJECT(TApplication)
      PROCEDURE InitMainWindow; VIRTUAL;
      END;

   {Line color dialog transfer record}
   ColorTransferBuffer = RECORD
      RedBtn,
      GreenBtn,
      BlueBtn,
      BlackBtn : WORD;
      END;

   {Line style dialog transfer record}
   StyleTransferBuffer = RECORD
      SolidBtn,
      DottedBtn,
      DashedBtn   : WORD;
      END;

   PMyWindow = ^TMyWindow;
   TMyWindow = OBJECT(TWindow)
      ColorBuffer : ColorTransferBuffer;
      StyleBuffer : StyleTransferBuffer;

      dc: HDC;
      LButtonDown: BOOLEAN;
      MyPen: HPen;
      PenSize: INTEGER;
      PenColor : TColorRef;
      PenStyle : INTEGER;
      Points: PCollection;

      { NEW }
      FileName: ARRAY[0..fsPathName] OF CHAR;
      NotSaved, IsNewFile : BOOLEAN;

      CONSTRUCTOR Init(AParent: PWindowsObject;
                       ATitle: PChar);
      DESTRUCTOR Done; VIRTUAL;
      FUNCTION CanClose: BOOLEAN; VIRTUAL;
```

```
      PROCEDURE WMLButtonDown(VAR Msg: TMessage);
         VIRTUAL wm_First + wm_LButtonDown;
      PROCEDURE WMLButtonUp(VAR Msg: TMessage);
         VIRTUAL wm_First + wm_LButtonUp;
      PROCEDURE WMMouseMove(VAR Msg: TMessage);
         VIRTUAL wm_First + wm_MouseMove;
      PROCEDURE SetPenColor(NewColor: INTEGER);
      PROCEDURE SetPenStyle(NewStyle: INTEGER);
      PROCEDURE SetPenSize(NewSize: INTEGER);
      PROCEDURE Paint(PaintDC: HDC;
            VAR PaintInfo: TPaintStruct); VIRTUAL;

      { NEW }
      PROCEDURE FileNew(VAR Msg: TMessage);
         VIRTUAL cm_First + cm_New;
      PROCEDURE FileOpen(VAR Msg: TMessage);
         VIRTUAL cm_First + cm_Open;
      PROCEDURE FileSave(VAR Msg: TMessage);
         VIRTUAL cm_First + cm_Save;
      PROCEDURE FileSaveAs(VAR Msg: TMessage);
         VIRTUAL cm_First + cm_SaveAs;
      PROCEDURE LoadFile;
      PROCEDURE SaveFile;

      PROCEDURE NewDraw(VAR Msg: TMessage);
         VIRTUAL cm_First + cm_NewDraw;
      PROCEDURE ChangeColor(VAR Msg: TMessage);
         VIRTUAL cm_First + cm_Color;
      PROCEDURE ChangeStyle(VAR Msg: TMessage);
         VIRTUAL cm_First + cm_Style;
      PROCEDURE ChangeThickness(VAR Msg: TMessage);
         VIRTUAL cm_First + cm_Thick;
      PROCEDURE Help(VAR Msg: TMessage);
         VIRTUAL cm_First + cm_Help;
      END;

   {dialog box type for changing line color}
   PColorDialog = ^TColorDialog;
   TColorDialog = OBJECT (TDialog)
      RedBtn,
      GreenBtn,
      BlueBtn,
      BlackBtn    : PRadioButton;
```

```
          CONSTRUCTOR Init(AParent:PWindowsObject;
                           ATitle:PChar);
          END;

      {dialog box type for changing line style}
      PStyleDialog = ^TStyleDialog;
      TStyleDialog = OBJECT (TDialog)
         SolidBtn,
         DottedBtn,
         DashedBtn   : PRadioButton;
         CONSTRUCTOR Init (AParent:PWindowsObject;
                           ATitle:PChar);
         END;

      {object type to save drawing for repainting}
      PDPoint = ^TDPoint;
      TDPoint = OBJECT(TObject)
         X, Y: INTEGER;
         CONSTRUCTOR Init(AX, AY: INTEGER);

         { NEW }
         CONSTRUCTOR Load(VAR S: TStream);
         PROCEDURE Store(VAR S: TStream);
         END;

{ NEW }
CONST
   RDPoint : TStreamRec
   =  (ObjType : 1111;
      VMTLink :OFS(TypeOf(TDPoint)^);
      Load : @TDPoint.Load;
      Store: @TDPoint.Store);

   PROCEDURE RegisterStream;
      BEGIN
      RegisterType(RCollection);
      RegisterType(RDPoint)
      END;


{=================}
{TMyWindow methods}
{=================}


CONSTRUCTOR TMyWindow.Init(AParent: PWindowsObject; ATitle:
                           PChar);
```

```
BEGIN
TWindow.Init(AParent, ATitle);
Attr.Menu := LoadMenu(HInstance, 'linemenu');
WITH ColorBuffer DO
   BEGIN
   RedBtn := bf_unchecked;
   GreenBtn := bf_unchecked;
   BlueBtn := bf_unchecked;
   BlackBtn := bf_unchecked;
   END;
WITH StyleBuffer DO
   BEGIN
   SolidBtn := bf_unchecked;
   DottedBtn := bf_unchecked;
   DashedBtn := bf_unchecked;
   END;
LButtonDown := FALSE;
PenSize := 1;
PenStyle := ps_Solid;
PenColor := 0;
MyPen := CreatePen(PenStyle, PenSize, PenColor);
Points := New(PCollection, Init(50, 50));

{ NEW }
NotSaved := False;
IsNewFile := True;
RegisterStream;
END;

DESTRUCTOR TMyWindow.Done;
   BEGIN
   Dispose(Points, Done);
   DeleteObject(MyPen);
   TWindow.Done;
   END;

FUNCTION TMyWindow.CanClose: BOOLEAN;
   VAR
      Reply: INTEGER;
   BEGIN
      CanClose := TRUE;

      { NEW }
      IF NotSaved
      THEN  BEGIN
```

```
            Reply := MessageBox(HWindow,
                    'Do you want to save your work?',
                    'Window content has changed',
                    mb_YesNoCancel or mb_IconQuestion);
            IF (Reply = id_Yes) OR (Reply = id_Cancel)
            THEN CanClose := FALSE;
            END
    END;

PROCEDURE TMyWindow.WMLButtonDown(VAR Msg: TMessage);
    BEGIN
    Points^.FreeAll;
    InvalidateRect(HWindow, NIL, TRUE);
    IF not LButtonDown
    THEN   BEGIN
            LButtonDown := TRUE;
            SetCapture(HWindow);
            dc := GetDC(HWindow);
            SelectObject(dc, MyPen);
            MoveTo(dc, Msg.LParamLo, Msg.LParamHi);
            Points^.Insert(New(PDPoint,
                    Init(Msg.LParamLo, Msg.LParamHi)));
            END;
    END;

PROCEDURE TMyWindow.WMMouseMove(VAR Msg: TMessage);
    BEGIN
    IF LButtonDown
    THEN   BEGIN
            LineTo(dc, INTEGER(Msg.LParamLo),
                    INTEGER(Msg.LParamHi));
            Points^.Insert(New(PDPoint,
                    Init(INTEGER(Msg.LParamLo),
                    INTEGER(Msg.LParamHi))));
            END;
    END;

PROCEDURE TMyWindow.WMLButtonUp(VAR Msg: TMessage);
    BEGIN
    IF LButtonDown
    THEN   BEGIN
            LButtonDown := FALSE;
            ReleaseCapture;
```

```
        ReleaseDC(HWindow, dc);
        END;
    END;

PROCEDURE TMyWindow.SetPenColor(NewColor: INTEGER);
BEGIN
    DeleteObject(MyPen);
    CASE NewColor OF
    1: BEGIN
       PenColor := RGB(200,0,0);
       MyPen := CreatePen(PenStyle, PenSize, PenColor);
       END;
    2: BEGIN
       PenColor := RGB(0,200,0);
       MyPen := CreatePen(PenStyle, PenSize, PenColor);
       END;
    3: BEGIN
       PenColor := RGB(0,0,200);
       MyPen := CreatePen(PenStyle, PenSize, PenColor);
       END;
    4: BEGIN
       PenColor := 0;
       MyPen := CreatePen(PenStyle, PenSize, PenColor);
       END;
    ELSE MyPen := CreatePen(PenStyle, PenSize, 0)
    END;
END;

PROCEDURE TMyWindow.SetPenStyle(NewStyle: INTEGER);
    BEGIN
    DeleteObject(MyPen);
    CASE NewStyle OF
    1: BEGIN
       PenStyle := ps_Solid;
       MyPen := CreatePen(PenStyle, PenSize, PenColor);
       END;
    2: BEGIN
       PenStyle := ps_Dot;
       MyPen := CreatePen(PenStyle, PenSize, PenColor);
       END;
    3: BEGIN
       PenStyle := ps_Dash;
       MyPen := CreatePen(PenStyle, PenSize, PenColor);
       END
    ELSE MyPen := CreatePen(ps_Solid, PenSize, PenColor)
```

```
      END;
END;

PROCEDURE TMyWindow.SetPenSize(NewSize: INTEGER);
   BEGIN
   DeleteObject(MyPen);
   MyPen := CreatePen(PenStyle, NewSize, PenColor);
   PenSize := NewSize;
   END;

PROCEDURE TMyWindow.Paint(PaintDC: HDC;
      VAR PaintInfo: TPaintStruct);
   VAR
      First: BOOLEAN;
   {local procedure under TMyWindow.Paint method}
   PROCEDURE DrawLine(P: PDPoint); far;
      BEGIN
      IF First
      THEN MoveTo(PaintDC, P^.X, P^.Y)
      else LineTo(PaintDC, P^.X, P^.Y);
      First := FALSE;
      END;
    {main body of TMyWindow.Paint method}
   BEGIN
      SelectObject(PaintDC, MyPen);
      First := TRUE;
      Points^.ForEach(@DrawLine);
   END;

{ NEW METHODS }
PROCEDURE TMyWindow.FileNew(VAR Msg: TMessage);
   BEGIN
      Points^.FreeAll;
      InvalidateRect(HWindow, NIL, TRUE);
      NotSaved := FALSE;
      IsNewFile := TRUE
   END;

PROCEDURE TMyWindow.FileOpen(VAR Msg: TMessage);
   BEGIN
      IF CanClose
      THEN
         IF Application^.ExecDialog(
            NEW(PFileDialog,
            Init(@Self, PChar(sd_FileOpen),
```

```
                StrCopy(FileName, '*.*')))) = id_OK
        THEN LoadFile;
    END;

PROCEDURE TMyWindow.FileSave(VAR Msg: TMessage);
    BEGIN
        IF IsNewFile
        THEN FileSaveAs(Msg)
        ELSE SaveFile
    END;

PROCEDURE TMyWindow.FileSaveAs(VAR Msg: TMessage);
    VAR Dlg: PFileDialog;
    BEGIN
        IF IsNewFile
        THEN StrCopy(FileName, '');
        IF Application^.ExecDialog(New(PFileDialog,
            Init(@Self, PChar(sd_FileSave), FileName))) = id_Ok
        THEN SaveFile
    END;

PROCEDURE TMyWindow.LoadFile;
    VAR
        TempCollection: PCollection;
        FileToLoad: TDosStream;
    BEGIN
        FileToLoad.Init(FileName, stOpen);
        TempCollection := PCollection(FileToLoad.Get);
        FileToLoad.Done;
        IF TempCollection <> NIL
        THEN  BEGIN
                Dispose(Points, Done);
                Points := TempCollection;
                InvalidateRect(HWindow, NIL, TRUE);
                END;
        NotSaved := False;
        IsNewFile := False;
    END;

PROCEDURE TMyWindow.SaveFile;
    VAR
        FileToSave: TDosStream;
    BEGIN
        FileToSave.Init(FileName, stCreate);
        FileToSave.Put(Points);
```

```
         FileToSave.Done;
         IsNewFile := False;
         NotSaved := False;
    END;

PROCEDURE TMyWindow.NewDraw(VAR Msg: TMessage);
    BEGIN
    Points^.FreeAll;
    InvalidateRect(HWindow, NIL, TRUE);
    END;

PROCEDURE TMyWindow.ChangeColor(VAR Msg: TMessage);
    VAR
        Dlg: TColorDialog;
        Reply : INTEGER;
    BEGIN
        Dlg.Init(@Self, 'chg_col');
        Dlg.TransferBuffer := @ColorBuffer;
        Reply := Dlg.Execute;
        Dlg.Done;

        IF Reply = id_OK THEN
            IF ColorBuffer.RedBtn = bf_checked
            THEN SetPenColor(red)
            ELSE IF ColorBuffer.GreenBtn = bf_checked
            THEN SetPenColor(green)
            ELSE IF ColorBuffer.BlueBtn = bf_checked
            THEN SetPenColor(blue)
            ELSE IF ColorBuffer.BlackBtn = bf_checked
            THEN SetPenColor(black)
            ELSE SetPenColor(black)
    END;

PROCEDURE TMyWindow.ChangeStyle(VAR Msg: TMessage);
    VAR
        Dlg: TStyleDialog;
        Reply : INTEGER;
    BEGIN
        Dlg.Init(@Self, 'chg_sty');
        Dlg.TransferBuffer := @StyleBuffer;
        Reply := Dlg.Execute;
        Dlg.Done;

        IF Reply = id_OK THEN
            IF StyleBuffer.SolidBtn = bf_checked
```

```
            THEN SetPenStyle(solid)
            ELSE IF StyleBuffer.DottedBtn = bf_checked
            THEN SetPenStyle(dotted)
            ELSE IF StyleBuffer.DashedBtn = bf_checked
            THEN SetPenStyle(dashed)
            ELSE SetPenStyle(solid)
      END;

PROCEDURE TMyWindow.ChangeThickness(VAR Msg: TMessage);
   VAR
      ThickBuffer: ARRAY[0..5] of CHAR;
      NewSize, ErrorPos: INTEGER;
   BEGIN
      Str(PenSize, ThickBuffer);
      IF Application^.ExecDialog(New(PInputDialog,
         Init(@Self, 'Line Thickness',
         'Input a new thickness:',
         ThickBuffer, SizeOf(ThickBuffer)))) = id_Ok
        THEN BEGIN
            Val(ThickBuffer, NewSize, ErrorPos);
            IF ErrorPos = 0 THEN SetPenSize(NewSize);
            END;
   END;

PROCEDURE TMyWindow.Help(VAR Msg: TMessage);
   BEGIN
   MessageBox(HWindow, 'Not yet implemented',
      'Help', mb_Ok or mb_IconExclamation);
   END;

{================}
{ TDPoint methods}
{================}
CONSTRUCTOR TDPoint.Init(AX, AY: INTEGER);
   BEGIN
   X := AX;
   Y := AY;
   END;

{ NEW }
CONSTRUCTOR TDPoint.Load(VAR S: TStream);
   BEGIN
      S.Read(X, SizeOf(X));
      S.Read(Y, SizeOf(Y))
   END;
```

```
PROCEDURE TDPoint.Store(VAR S: TStream);
   BEGIN
      S.Write(X, SizeOf(X));
      S.Write(Y, SizeOf(Y))
   END;

{=====================}
{Dialog Object Methods}
{=====================}
CONSTRUCTOR TColorDialog.Init(AParent:PWindowsObject;
                              ATitle:PChar);
   BEGIN
   TDialog.init(aparent, atitle);
   NEW(RedBtn, initResource(@Self, id_RedBtn));
   NEW(GreenBtn, initResource(@Self, id_GreenBtn));
   NEW(BlueBtn, initResource(@Self, id_BlueBtn));
   NEW(BlackBtn, initResource(@Self, id_BlackBtn));
   END;

CONSTRUCTOR TStyleDialog.Init(AParent:PWindowsObject;
                              ATitle:PChar);
   BEGIN
   TDialog.init(aparent, atitle);
   NEW(SolidBtn, initResource(@Self, id_SolidBtn));
   NEW(DottedBtn, initResource(@Self, id_DottedBtn));
   NEW(DashedBtn, initResource(@Self, id_DashedBtn));
   END;

{==============}
{TMyApp methods}
{==============}
PROCEDURE TMyApp.InitMainWindow;
   BEGIN
   MainWindow := New(PMyWindow, Init(NIL, 'Listing 28.1'));
   END;

{====================================}
{global object variable for application}
{====================================}
VAR
   MyApp : TMyApp;
```

```
{====================}
{main body of program}
{====================}
BEGIN
    MyApp.Init('Listing28_1');
    MyApp.Run;
    MyApp.Done;
END.
```

Before you can run Listing 28.1, you need to modify the menu resource in MYRES2.RES so that it includes a File menu and appropriate menu choices. The easiest thing to do in BRW is simply to insert a new popup after the "End Popup" that terminates the "Line" popup. Then, use the cut-and-paste options from the BRW Edit menu to move the Line popup underneath the File popup. Then set up the File popup as follows:

Item Text	ID
&File	None
New	101
Open	102
Save	103
Save As...	104

When you're finished, your screen should look like Figure 28.1. Save the modified resource as MYRES3.RES, which is the resource file named in Listing 28.1.

There are quite a few new features in Listing 28.1, so let's look at them one at a time. We'll start with the easiest: using BPW and ObjectWindows standard routines and types to open and close files.

Opening and Saving Files

BPW makes it fairly easy to open and close files. The parts of the job that require interaction with MS-DOS are handled by the WinDOS unit, which you can see is

FIGURE 28.1:

The menu resource with File menu added

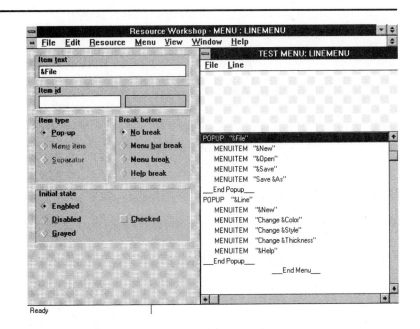

included in Listing 28.1's USES clause at the top of the program. The fancier parts setting up a file-open or file-save dialog box, displaying the contents of the current directory, and letting the user enter a file name are handled by the predefined ObjectWindows type *TFileDialog*, provided in the unit STDDLGS and the resource file STDDLGS.RES.

You might wonder why, if we are using a dialog box whose appearance is defined in STDDLGS.RES, this resource file is not named in Listing 28.1 with a {$R} compiler directive. The reason is that the resource file *is* named by the unit STDDLGS, and we named the unit in the USES clause. This makes STDDLGS.RES available, if indirectly, to the program.

The place where the file-open dialog box puts in an appearance is in the *TMyWindow.FileOpen* method. In that method, we first test the Boolean variable *CanClose* to determine if the current window contents have been changed without having been saved to disk. If they haven't been saved, then we call *Application^.ExecDialog* with a call to NEW and the predefined pointer type *PFileDialog*, which points to a *TFileDialog*-type object. The *Init* method is called in the usual way, and takes three parameters:

@Self (which we've seen before in Chapter 26 under "Execute the Dialog")

PChar(sd_FileOpen) delivers a PCHAR representation of the predefined identifier for the standard dialog box type to open files

StrCopy(FileName, '*.*') copies the file specification *.* into the dialog box's *File Name* field for the list of files to select from. (The *.* means that all files will be displayed. We could just as easily have made it *.PAS, which would have displayed all Pascal source code files, or S*.*, which would have displayed all files whose names begin with the letter *S*.)

If the dialog box executes successfully and returns a value of *id_OK*, this method calls the *TMyWindow.LoadFile* method, which is just a little more complicated. This method first creates two local variables: a pointer to a *TCollection* object to hold the file contents when loaded, and a *TDosStream* object to provide the conduit through which the file will be loaded into the collection. It then initializes the stream variable by calling the predefined method *TDosStream.Init*, which takes two parameters: first, a file name, and second, an "access mode," which denotes the way the stream is being used. Different access mode identifiers are defined for different operations:

Access Mode	Operation
stCreate	Creates file
stOpenRead	Opens read-only file
stOpenWrite	Opens file for writing
stOpen	Opens file for reading and writing

The *TempCollection* variable then gets a pointer to the data loaded from the file, after which the *FileToLoad* variable's inherited *Done* method (from *TDosStream*) is called. The method then checks to see if the file was empty; if it isn't, it disposes of the data in the parent window's *Points* field and then passes the pointer in *TempCollection* to

Points, from which the file's contents are recreated in the window. In order to do this, the predefined *InvalidateRect* routine is called. This routine takes three parameters:

- *HWindow*, a handle to the parent window.
- A *TRect*-type object indicating the region to be updated in the parent window's client area. (Use NIL to indicate the entire client area.)
- A Boolean value indicating whether the region should be erased (true) or not (false) prior to updating.

Finally, the *NotSaved* and *IsNewFile* Boolean variables are set to false to indicate that no changes have (yet) been made in this window's contents.

Saving a file works pretty much the same, and in fact, is a bit less complicated. The only major difference is that it works through three methods instead of two. If the file has already been saved and the user doesn't wish to change the file name, then there's no need to open a dialog box to name the file and specify its directory. Thus, the menu command-response method *TMyWindow.FileSave* first checks to see if the file is a new file that has not been named or saved previously; if so, it calls *TMyWindow.FileSaveAs*, which opens a file-save dialog box (denoted by the standard identifier *sd_FileSave*) so that the user can name the file and specify its location. If the file has already been named or saved, the *FileSave* method calls *TMyWindow.SaveFile*, which simply saves the file under its current name and in its current directory.

Modifying the Object Types

Because we plan to save the contents of the parent window to a disk file, it will be helpful if the parent window has fields to hold the name of the currently loaded file and its status as a not-saved or a new file. We add these fields to *TMyWindow*, which also happens to be the application's main window. The *NotSaved* and *IsNewFile* fields are standard Boolean fields indicating the status of the window contents. When a new file is loaded, when a change is made in an existing drawing, or when a drawing is saved, the methods that carry out these tasks make the appropriate changes in the values of these fields. The *FileName* field is simply a null-terminated array of characters; *fsPathName* is a constant defined in the WinDOS unit and is equal to 79.

Also added to the parent window are all the methods it needs to create, open, and save files.

The parent window isn't the only thing that needs to be modified. The type definition of *TDPoint* also needs new *Load* and *Store* methods so that it knows how to load itself from a file and store itself to a file when called upon to do so. These new methods are actually quite simple:

```
CONSTRUCTOR TDPoint.Load(VAR S: TStream);
   BEGIN
      S.Read(X, SizeOf(X));
      S.Read(Y, SizeOf(Y))
   END;

PROCEDURE TDPoint.Store(VAR S: TStream);
   BEGIN
      S.Write(X, SizeOf(X));
      S.Write(Y, SizeOf(Y))
   END;
```

The *Load* constructor calls the *Read* method of the stream from which the point is being loaded to get the X and Y coordinates that constitute the point. The *Store* method does just the reverse, calling the stream's *Write* method to write the coordinates into the stream.

Initializing and Using Streams

The stream in Listing 28.1 is registered and initialized just as we discussed earlier. First, the program declares a *TStreamRec* to keep track of the object types in the stream, and then a *RegisterStream* method registers both the collection and point types for use with a stream. *RegisterStream* itself is actually called (as opposed to merely being defined) in the parent window's *Init* method, *TMyWindow.Init*.

There's no real way to show in a figure how the program works. Try it out. Draw something in the program's main window, then save it as a file. Clear the window, then reload the file. Your original drawing will reappear.

Using the Windows Multiple-Document Interface

☐ Parts of an MDI Application

☐ Enhancing Child Windows

One thing that almost all Windows applications can do is open multiple windows within the application. This feature is implemented by means of the Windows Multiple-Document Interface (MDI).

Writing an MDI application—that is, an application that can manage multiple child windows—is much easier in BPW than you might imagine. All that's really needed is a type of window that can serve as a containing "frame" to keep track of the different windows inside it and allow the user to perform operations on those windows. ObjectWindows provides this in the *TMDIWindow* type, a descendant of *TWindow*. A *TMDIWindow*-type window keeps pointers to the windows it contains (its child windows) in a linked list that is one of its object fields.

The child windows are not created directly in their parent window (the *TMDIWindow* object) itself. They are actually created in the parent window's client area, which must be a *TMDIClient*-type object, and which the parent window keeps in its *ClientWnd* object field. The client area is very much like the Windows desktop itself. It is in the client area that windows are opened, closed, moved, minimized, rearranged, and so forth.

There is also a variety of standard operations supported by MDI parent windows, such as creating new child windows, cascading or tiling those windows inside the parent's client area, and arranging the icons that represent minimized child windows. Although an MDI window supports these operations, they must be provided with the help of an associated menu resource.

A Simple MDI Application

The preceding gives some of the conceptual background of MDI applications, but there's no substitute for seeing an example. To set up an MDI application, we must first create an appropriate menu resource. Using the BRW (or any other resource editor), create the menu and accelerator resources specified in Listing 29.1. Then, enter the BPW program shown in Listing 29.2.

Listing 29.1

```
Menu resource
&Child windows;  value = none
     &New window;  value = 24339
     &Cascade windows; value = 24337
     &Tile windows;  value = 24336
     Arrange &icons;  value = 24335
     Close &all windows;  value = 24338
Resource file name: MDI_DEMO.RES
name = MDI_MENU
```

Listing 29.2

```
PROGRAM Listing29_2;
{Shows a simple MDI application that can open multiple
 windows, cascade and tile the windows, arrange icons,
 and close all the windows. These features are all pre-
 defined in ObjectWindows. }

{$R MDI_Demo.Res}

USES OWINDOWS, WINTYPES, WINPROCS;

TYPE
   TMDIApplication = OBJECT(TApplication)
      PROCEDURE InitMainWindow; VIRTUAL;
      END;

{This next type declaration is not strictly needed,
 and is included because we are going to extend the
 TMDI_FrameWindow type in Listing 29.3. If we wanted
 to skip this declaration, we could simply use NEW
 with BPW's predefined PMDIWindow pointer type in
 the InitMainWindow method.}

PMDI_FrameWindow = ^TMDI_FrameWindow;
TMDI_FrameWindow = OBJECT(TMDIWindow)
   END;

PROCEDURE TMDIApplication.InitMainWindow;
   BEGIN
```

```
        MainWindow := New(PMDI_FrameWindow,
        Init('Listing 29.2: Simple MDI Demonstration',
            LoadMenu(HInstance, 'MDI_Menu')));
    END;

{global object variable for application}
VAR
    MDI_DemoApp: TMDIApplication;

{main body of program}
BEGIN
    MDI_DemoApp.Init('Listing 29.2');
    MDI_DemoApp.Run;
    MDI_DemoApp.Done;
END.
```

The results of running Listing 29.2 are shown in Figures 29.1 through 29.3. With remarkably few lines of BPW code, we've set up a window that can open and close multiple child windows, rearrange them, and display their icons when they are minimized.

FIGURE 29.1:

Cascading multiple child windows from Listing 29.2

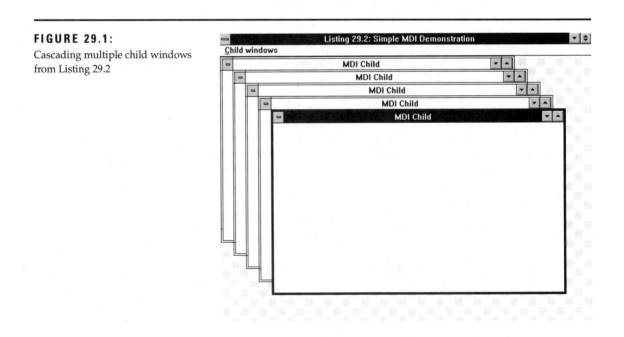

FIGURE 29.2:

Tiled multiple child windows from Listing 29.2

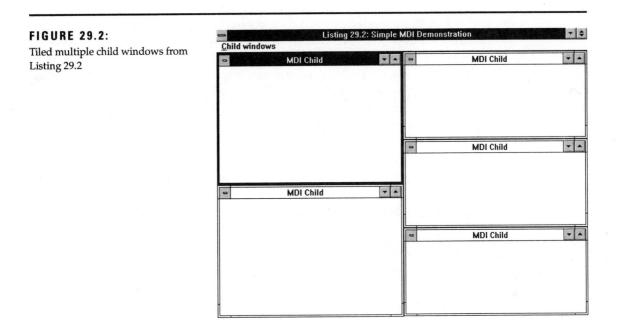

FIGURE 29.3:

Minimized multiple child windows from Listing 29.2

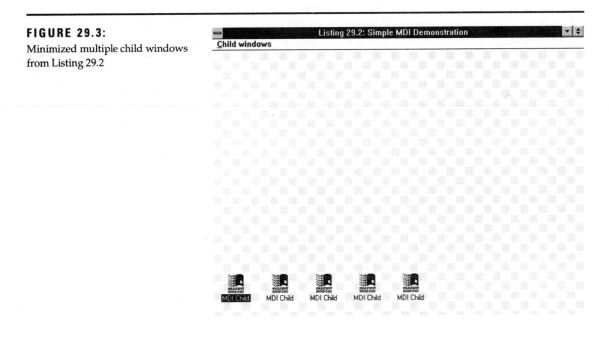

You may notice that all the child windows in the program from Listing 29.2 have the same window title: "MDI Child." Of course, you can modify the BPW program so that each MDI child window gets its own title (often the name of a disk file that the window contains) and exhibits other unique characteristics, but MDI child windows do have certain limitations compared to the parent window:

- They can never extend outside the borders of their parent window.

- They cannot have their own menus—all the operations done on them must be done from the parent window's menu.

Parts of a Simple MDI Application

Let's go through Listings 29.1 and 29.2 step by step. Listing 29.1—the resource specification—will be familiar in some respects but odd in others. In the menu resource, each menu item gets menu text. The values of the menu items, however, are so different from what we've used up to now that you may suspect they're not just random choices.

In fact, the values aren't random choices. These are the values preassigned in BPW to these particular predefined menu operations. Borland Pascal for Windows will do all the work for you in setting up the methods to perform these operations, but only if you know these integer values to include in the menu resource.

In the original version of Turbo Pascal for Windows, these values were documented, but only after a fashion, on page 457 of the *Windows Reference Guide* that came with the package. There were two problems with the documentation: Some of the values given were incorrect, and they were all in hexadecimal notation, which isn't what you need even if they were correct. Table 29.1, below, gives the *correct* values (in decimal notation) to use for these and related menu choices when you set up menus in the BRW (or other resource editor). At the time of this writing, I have not yet had access to the printed manuals for Borland Pascal 7, so it is possible that the errors have been corrected.

TABLE 29.1: Predefined Constants for Standard Menu Choices

	Name	"Official" Value	Decimal Value
Offset Values	cm_First	$A000	40960
	cm_Internal	$FF00	65280
	cm_Reserved	cm_Internal - cm_First	24320
Edit Commands	cm_EditCut	cm_Reserved + 0	24320
	cm_EditCopy	cm_Reserved + 1	24321
	cm_EditPaste	cm_Reserved + 2	24322
	cm_EditDelete	cm_Reserved + 3	24323
	cm_EditClear	cm_Reserved + 4	24324
	cm_EditUndo	cm_Reserved + 5	24325
	cm_EditFind	cm_Reserved + 6	24326
	cm_EditReplace	cm_Reserved + 7	24327
	cm_EditFindNext	cm_Reserved + 8	24328
File and MDI Commands	cm_FileNew	cm_Reserved + 9	24329
	cm_FileOpen	cm_Reserved + 10	24330
	cm_MDIFileNew	cm_Reserved + 11	24331
	cm_MDIFileOpen	cm_Reserved + 12	24332
	cm_FileSave	cm_Reserved + 13	24333
	cm_FileSaveAs	cm_Reserved + 14	24334
	cm_ArrangeIcons	cm_Reserved + 15	24335
	cm_TileChildren	cm_Reserved + 16	24336
	cm_CascadeChildren	cm_Reserved + 17	24337
	cm_CloseChildren	cm_Reserved + 18	24338
	cm_CreateChild	cm_Reserved + 19	24339
	cm_Exit	cm_Reserved + 20	24340

As for the program in Listing 29.2 itself, it begins in the usual way by using the *{$R ..}* compiler directive to include the resource file, then sets up the main object variable for the application itself. The application itself, in spite of the name *TMDIApplication*, is to be a standard-issue *TApplication*-type object, with nothing at all special about it.

The next step is to define a type for the application's main window. This one *does* need to be special, because it must be an MDI window. Ordinarily, in an application this simple, we could omit this step and just make the main window of type *TMDIWindow*, which is all we're really doing anyway. However, this type definition sets the stage for Listing 29.3, where we'll give each child window its own unique window title. The program would work equally well, however, if we omitted the *TMDI_FrameWindow* declaration and, in the *TMDIApplication.InitMainWindow* method, used the predefined *TMDIWindow* as the type for the main application window.

In the *InitMainWindow* method, another difference shows up. Initializing an MDI window is just a little more complicated than initializing a plain *TWindow*-type window. That's because it is known in advance that an MDI window is going to have a menu, so the menu-loading step is included in the call to the window's *Init* constructor method. This method takes two parameters: a null-terminated string, which will be the window title, and a handle to a menu resource, which in this case is returned by the call to *LoadMenu*.

Normally, the child window menu is displayed at the top left of the menu bar. However, if you have other menu popups that you want to appear first, you can change the position of the child window menu by overriding the inherited *TMDIWindow.Init* constructor and explicitly setting the child menu position to something else—for example, so that it will be the third menu in the menu bar, as in

```
CONSTRUCTOR TMDI_FrameWindow.Init(ATitle: PChar; AMenu: HMenu);
   BEGIN
   TMDIWindow.Init(ATitle, AMenu);
   ChildMenuPos := 3
   END;
```

Getting back to Listing 29.2, the next step in *InitMainWindow* is to load the accelerator resource, which is done the same way we've done it before. Then we declare an object variable for the application and run it. That's all there is to it. Most of the work is done for us by BPW and ObjectWindows.

An Enhanced MDI Application

There's so much in BPW's MDI features that a whole book could be devoted to the subject. Let's look at just one more example to show how you can add new features to an MDI application. Listing 29.3 shows an application that sets up each child window with its own unique window title. It also gives a hint of just how much work is going on behind the scenes even in a simple MDI application. The result of running the program is shown in Figure 29.4.

Listing 29.3

```
PROGRAM Listing29_3;

{Shows a slightly more sophisticated MDI application
 in which each child window gets a unique title. }

{$R MDI_Demo.Res}

USES OWINDOWS, WINTYPES, WINPROCS, STRINGS;

TYPE
    TMDIApplication = OBJECT(TApplication)
       PROCEDURE InitMainWindow; VIRTUAL;
       END;

    PMDI_DemoChild = ^TMDI_DemoChild;
    TMDI_DemoChild = OBJECT(TWindow)
       Number: INTEGER;
       CONSTRUCTOR Init(AParent: PWindowsObject;
          ChildNumber: INTEGER);
       END;

    PMDI_FrameWindow = ^TMDI_FrameWindow;
    TMDI_FrameWindow = OBJECT(TMDIWindow)
       FUNCTION CreateChild: PWindowsObject; VIRTUAL;
       END;

CONSTRUCTOR TMDI_DemoChild.Init(AParent:PWindowsObject;
                                   ChildNumber: INTEGER);
    VAR
       TitleStr: ARRAY[0..15] of CHAR;
       ChildNumberStr: ARRAY[0..5] of CHAR;
    BEGIN
       Str(ChildNumber, ChildNumberStr);
       StrCat(StrECopy(TitleStr, 'Window #'), ChildNumberStr);
       TWindow.Init(AParent, TitleStr);
       Number := ChildNumber;
    END;
```

```
FUNCTION TMDI_FrameWindow.CreateChild: PWindowsObject;
    VAR
        ChildNumber: INTEGER;

    {local function under CreateChild method}
    FUNCTION NumberMade(WinPtr:PMDI_DemoChild): BOOLEAN; FAR;
        BEGIN
        NumberMade := ChildNumber = WinPtr^.Number;
        END;

    {main body of CreateChild method}
    BEGIN
        ChildNumber := 1;
        WHILE FirstThat(@NumberMade) <> NIL DO INC(ChildNumber);
        CreateChild := Application^.MakeWindow(NEW(
                        PMDI_DemoChild, Init(@Self, ChildNumber)));
    END;

PROCEDURE TMDIApplication.InitMainWindow;
    BEGIN
        MainWindow := New(PMDI_FrameWindow,
        Init('Listing 29.3: Enhanced MDI Demonstration',
            LoadMenu(HInstance, 'MDI_Menu')));
    END;

{global object variable for application}
VAR
    MDI_DemoApp: TMDIApplication;

{main body of program}
BEGIN
    MDI_DemoApp.Init('Listing 29.3');
    MDI_DemoApp.Run;
    MDI_DemoApp.Done;
END.
```

This is still a simple application by Windows standards, but it is significantly more complex than the program in Listing 29.2. The first thing to notice is that we've added the STRINGS unit to the program's USES clause; that's because we're going to need string-manipulation routines to set up the window titles.

FIGURE 29.4:

An enhanced MDI application with cascading windows

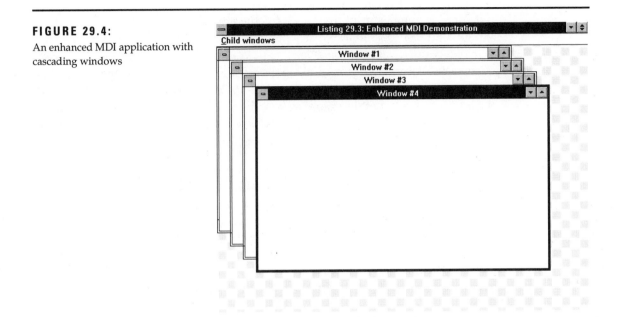

The next new feature is the declaration of a window type—*TMDI_DemoChild*—for the child windows. In this type, we include a field for the window number (because there may be more than one window open in the application) and override the inherited *Init* constructor to include the window number in the title.

Because the child windows will no longer be plain, generic MDI windows, the parent window type *TMDI_FrameWindow* must now have a method to create its child windows. This overrides the *CreateChild* method inherited from the predefined *TMDIWindow* type, which we didn't need to define in Listing 29.2, because we were using it—as well as the MDI child windows—"as is." Here, however, we override it because we're adding a new feature to it. *CreateChild* is a function, and it returns a pointer to the newly created child window. This pointer is added to the parent window's linked list of pointers to child windows.

In the specification of the *TMDI_DemoChild* type's *Init* constructor, we use several routines from the STRINGS unit to concatenate a boilerplate text item with the number of the window. After declaring two local variables to hold the window title and window number, respectively, we call the predefined *Str* routine to convert the window number (passed to *Init* as a parameter) to a string and copy it to the null-terminated string variable *ChildNumberStr*. We then call the *StrCat* routine to concatenate null-terminated strings, using the *StrECopy* routine to copy the desired text into the first eight slots of the *TitleStr* array. *StrCat* then adds the content of *ChildNumberStr* to the end of the value returned by *StrECopy*, and we have our window title. The rest is standard, as we call the *TWindow.Init* routine with the parent-window handle and the child-window title, then assigning the appropriate number to the child window's *Number* field.

Next, we define the details of the parent window's *CreateChild* function. After defining a local variable to hold the number of the child window, we set up a function to get the appropriate window number for us. *NumberMade* takes a pointer to a child window as its argument and returns TRUE if the child window's number field is the same as the current value of the local *ChildNumber* variable. This is actually a pretty tricky move for which the tricky programmers at Borland deserve the credit, and its significance (as well as the reason why the function must be FAR) becomes clear when we get to the main body of the method.

In the main body of the method, we call the *FirstThat* method inherited from the *TWindowsObject* abstract type. This method traverses the child-window linked list of the parent window. At each node in the list, it calls the *NumberMade* function. To the function, it passes the pointer to the current node's corresponding child window as an argument. If the pointer is not NIL, then the end of the list has not yet been reached, and the window number is incremented by 1. The end result is that when the end of the child window list is reached, the window number has been set to the appropriate value.

The function passed to *FirstThat*, however, must be FAR, so that it can access data in another segment. (This is why the *NumberMade* function had the FAR directive in its heading.)

After incrementing the window number, we call the *CreateChild* method with the predefined *Application^.MakeWindow* method to create the child window. The rest of Listing 29.3 should be fairly familiar.

Windows Memory Management with Borland Pascal

- How Windows Organizes Memory

- Using an Application's Local Memory

- Using Windows' Global Memory

Most discussions of Windows tend to focus on its graphic-interface characteristics: how to set up windows and dialog boxes, how to work with bitmaps, and the like. In a way, this is unfortunate, because many of Windows' most impressive and important features never appear on the PC's screen. Windows' memory management capabilities fall into this category.

Borland Pascal for Windows' ability to work with Windows' memory management is equally impressive, even though most of it goes on behind the scenes and doesn't need to concern the programmer. There are times, however, when you'll want to work directly with the Windows memory manager, and BPW provides several ways for you to do that. It also helps a a great deal to understand just how Windows does manage memory, so we'll begin this chapter by covering the basics of Windows memory management. Then, we'll look at how BPW helps you work with the Windows memory manager, both directly and indirectly.

Windows Operating Modes

Windows manages memory in one of three different modes, depending on the hardware that the user has available. Each mode is designed to make maximum use of the memory and processor resources that are available. *Real mode*, the least ambitious, will run on any Windows-capable PC, *standard mode* requires at least an 80286-class PC and a minimum 1 megabyte of RAM, and *enhanced mode* requires an 80386-class PC and at least 2 megabytes of RAM.

Memory Addressing Schemes

In order to understand some of the key differences between real, standard, and enhanced modes, it's necessary to take a brief look at the addressing methods used by different PC processors and how Windows works with these processors.

The most primitive addressing mode was introduced with the original IBM PC and its 8086-class (actually an 8088) processor. This was called *segmented addressing*. Because the 8086 is a 16-bit processor, it was automatically capable of addressing 2 to the 16th power (64K) different memory locations. However, the PC was intended to be able to address a full megabyte of RAM, which meant that some trick would be needed to extend the addressable memory capabilities of the 16-bit processor.

The trick was segmented addressing, which combines two 16-bit logical addresses to give a single 20-bit physical address—enough to cover a full megabyte of RAM. The total address space is divided into 64K segments. The address of any particular item in RAM is given in *segment:offset* form. The first number (usually given in hexadecimal) is the address of the particular 64K memory segment in which the item resides; the second (the offset) is the item's address relative to the beginning of the segment.

A program can get the fastest performance when it keeps the segment address constant and all that changes is the offset address. An address in the same segment (using only the offset address) is called "near," while an address in a different segment is called "far." Within a segment, the offset address can vary up to 64K: from $0000 to $FFFF. We've seen a few examples of near and far method calls in our BPW program listings.

An 8086-class or higher processor has registers to keep track of all the different segments it uses. Segment addresses are kept in the code segment register, the data segment register, the stack segment register, and the extra segment register.

With the introduction of the 80286-class processor came *protected mode*. In protected mode, the segment address no longer refers to a physical memory address where the segment begins, but instead to an address in a "descriptor table" of 24-bit memory addresses in physical memory. The offset address is used with the descriptor table address to derive a 24-bit address in physical memory. This meant, among other things, that the 80286 could directly address up to 16 megabytes (2 to the 24th power) of RAM.

In the 80386-class and later processors, segments were no longer limited to 64K in size; in fact, a segment could now be as large as 4 gigabytes. Descriptor tables were also made more sophisticated so that the 80386 could use virtual memory, up to an almost unimaginable memory size of 64 terabytes.

Real Mode

Real mode is the simplest operating mode of Windows (it was available in versions prior to 3.0) and requires at least an 8086 processor and 640K of RAM. It handles memory in a way that is quite similar to the method used by MS-DOS—one reason that programs developed for Windows real mode can have a hard time adapting to the more sophisticated standard and enhanced modes.

Real mode's segmented-addressing scheme gives it a maximum address space of 1 megabyte, 640K of which is available for DOS applications. As with the other operating modes, real mode sees code and data segments as *fixed* (cannot be moved), *moveable* (can be moved), and *discardable* (can be released when not in use).

In real mode, Windows sets up its global heap as a contiguous area in memory containing both code and data segments, with discardable code segments stacked on top of moveable code and data segments, which in turn are on top of nonmoveable code and data segments.

Standard Mode

Standard mode is somewhat more sophisticated than real mode, and is used automatically by Windows 3.1 when the PC has at least an 80286-class processor and 2 megabytes of RAM. The big advance in standard mode is that Windows uses the protected-mode capabilities of the 80286 (and later) processors. As we saw earlier in the discussion of addressing schemes, a key benefit is that this makes a larger memory space (16 megabytes) available for use by Windows. Windows in standard mode can use both *extended memory* (RAM above 1 megabyte) and *high memory* (which is the first segment in extended memory, normally reserved for other functions) for the *Windows global heap*. To take advantage of high memory, Windows uses HIMEM.SYS or a similar device driver installed in the PC's CONFIG.SYS file.

Enhanced Mode

Enhanced mode is the most advanced operating mode offered in Windows 3.1, and requires at least an 80386-class processor and at least 2 megabytes of RAM. This mode uses the most advanced features of the 80386-class processor (virtual memory addressing and demand paging); the result is that even programs too large to fit into physical memory can be run in this mode.

In addition, enhanced mode uses the "virtual 8086" capabilities of the 80386-class processor to run each multitasked application on its own imaginary 8086 processor. This not only provides extra protection against collisions between separate multitasked applications, but also allows Windows to run as many as 16 standard MS-DOS applications at the same time, with each application getting its own dedicated address space of 640K in memory. (In spite of this, a few MS-DOS applications are so ill-behaved that even Windows 3.1 running in enhanced mode has trouble coping with the mischief they create.)

Even in enhanced mode, Windows sometimes has trouble containing the situation when a multitasked application crashes, and the way in which applications are multitasked is itself not foolproof, though it seems to improve with each new version of Windows.

How Windows Organizes PC Memory

Windows really is a major advance over ordinary MS-DOS, particularly in the area of memory management. Under MS-DOS, PC memory is organized in a hierarchical fashion that is relatively inflexible. At the bottom of PC memory are the BIOS, interrupt vector table, and MS-DOS itself. Above that are device drivers and memory-resident (TSR) programs. Finally, at the top, is the currently loaded application program, which normally takes all remaining memory for itself. The program code segment, the stack, and the heap are restricted to the size initially allocated within the application's allocated memory space; in addition, their locations in memory are fixed (unmoveable).

The practical outcome is relatively inefficient use of memory. In the overall DOS environment, it means that device drivers and TSR programs cannot be unloaded unless all the memory locations above them have been unloaded first; thus, even when they are not being used and are no longer needed, the memory they occupy is still unavailable for other uses. Furthermore, because the dynamic variables on the heap can be unloaded in random order from within an application program's memory space, the heap space that is available will seldom be in a single contiguous segment, and thus may be inadequate for a new large dynamic variable such as an array.

Under Windows, virtually all of these restrictions and inefficiencies disappear. Windows manages all the memory from the point at which MS-DOS loads it into RAM to the end of physical memory; all of this memory is what is called the Windows global heap. In most cases, Windows can rearrange code and data segments for different applications and discard what is not currently needed, so that available memory is used with maximum efficiency.

No Need for MaxAvail

The way in which Windows dynamically reorganizes available PC memory (and uses virtual memory) reduces the need for some routines from the DOS version of Borland Pascal, such as *MaxAvail*, which determines the size of the largest contiguous memory block on the heap. Because Windows automatically compacts heap memory (apart from the exceptions noted earlier), the amount of free heap memory will often be very close to or the same as the amount of contiguous free heap memory.

Fixed versus Moveable Segments

Any Windows application has at least one code segment and at least one data segment, but it can have more if needed. These segments can be either *fixed*, which means that they must stay in the same physical memory location no matter what, or *moveable*, which means that Windows can move them to a different location if needed to make more efficient use of memory. The idea of moveable segments is alien to MS-DOS, which must pretty much leave things wherever they are in RAM as long as they are needed. Because pointers in DOS programs refer to physical memory locations, if a segment belonging to a DOS program were moved, any pointer references to data or instructions in that segment would immediately become invalid.

A Windows application, however, can generally depend on Windows itself to keep pointer references up to date as it moves data and code segments around in memory—because most pointers will be "near pointers"—pointers that refer to an offset address relative to the beginning of the segment. As long as Windows keeps track of where the beginning of the segment is, any near-pointer references will still be valid. "Far pointers," however—pointers that include both a physical segment address and an offset address—will become invalid even under Windows; this is why standard DOS applications must be treated by Windows as fixed rather than moveable. However, the vast majority of segments used in Windows applications are moveable. If you see a resource script for a menu, for example, it will normally be specified as moveable, as in the script for the MDI demonstration menu in Chapter 29 (repeated below):

```
MDI_MENU  MENU LOADONCALL MOVEABLE PURE DISCARDABLE
BEGIN
POPUP "&Child Windows"
   BEGIN
```

```
        MenuItem  "&New Window", 24339
        MenuItem  "&Cascade Windows", 24337
        MenuItem  "&Tile Windows", 24336
        MenuItem  "Arrange &Icons", 24335
        MenuItem  "Close &All Windows", 24338
        END
END
```

NOTE Unless there is a compelling reason to do otherwise, all Windows applications and resources should be made moveable. Applications that require fixed segments interfere with Windows' ability to manage memory efficiently.

Discardable Segments

Another characteristic of Windows memory segments is that they are often *discardable*, meaning that Windows can free up the memory they occupy if they haven't been used for a while. (The data or instructions they contain, of course, can always be reloaded from disk.) To determine which segments to discard, Windows uses an algorithm called "least recently used," which boils down to, "If it hasn't been used for a while, then maybe it's not needed anymore or not needed very often, so let's dump it." Normally, discardable segments will be ones that don't change after being loaded—such as code segments but not data segments.

Also, a discardable segment is *ipso facto* a moveable segment (though a moveable segment is not necessarily a discardable segment). Windows resource specifications will normally be discardable unless you specifically say otherwise.

Borland Pascal and Memory Management

Most of the time, Borland Pascal for Windows will handle all the memory management chores for you. Once in a while, however, you'll need to work with Windows' memory manager directly; BPW makes it easy to do so. For example, you might have an extremely large array that won't fit into the data segment allocated to the program itself. In such a case, BPW provides functions that let you store the large data item in Windows' global heap.

This spotlights, in fact, the main division that you'll encounter in making your applications manage memory: there's the application's local memory, allocated to it by Windows when the program is loaded (the "local heap," set up in the application's data segment) and the global heap, which is all the free memory not being used by Windows or another Windows application.

In general, using local memory results in faster program performance, but its size is limited to 64K. Using global memory, on the other hand, is slower but can provide virtually limitless memory for large data items.

Using the Application's Local Memory

Memory that can only be accessed by a particular application (or a particular instance of an application) is called the application instance's *local heap,* and resides in the application instance's data segment along with the stack and global variables used by the program. Any space in the data segment not used for the stack or global variables is available to the local heap. However, the space is *not* automatically allocated to the local heap by Windows; for that, you must either use the *$M* compiler directive or just set the default heap size in the dialog box called up by the BPW Options/Memory sizes menu choice. (The default heap size is 8,192 bytes.)

If the data segment is fixed, then only the amount of heap memory specified during compilation of the program will be available. However, if the data segment is moveable—certainly the more common situation—then Windows will automatically allocate more heap space if needed, as long as the 64K size limit for local heap memory is not exceeded. In this situation, Windows might also move the data segment, invalidating far pointers to data in the segment—a reason for careful defensive programming.

An important BPW function for working with local heap memory is *LocalAlloc*, a Windows API function that allocates a block of memory from the local heap. It takes one or more flag values as parameters; these flags tell it what characteristics should be assigned to the memory block being allocated—for example, whether or not it is fixed, discardable, and so on. In addition to the flags, the final parameter is the size, in bytes, of the memory block to be allocated. The flag identifiers used with *LocalAlloc* are shown in Table 30.1.

TABLE 30.1:   Local Memory Flags Used with LocalAlloc Function

Identifier	Meaning
lmem_Discardable	Block is discardable. (It must also be moveable.)
lmem_Fixed	Block cannot be moved from its initial memory location.
lmem_Moveable	Block can be moved to a new memory location.
lmem_NoCompact	No other memory blocks should be compacted or discarded in allocating space for this memory block.
lmem_NoDiscard	No other memory blocks should be discarded in allocating space for this memory block.
lmem_ZeroInit	The memory block's contents will be initialized to zero.

Inasmuch as it is a function, *LocalAlloc* returns a value. This value is a handle to the memory block allocated; however, if the allocation attempt was unsuccessful, it returns a value of 0.

The memory block allocated by *LocalAlloc* will be at least as large as the size in bytes passed to the function as a parameter, and it can be larger. To find the exact size of the memory block, you need to use *LocalSize*, a Windows API function that takes the handle to the memory block as a parameter and returns the size in bytes of the memory block (or 0 if the handle is invalid).

Before you can gain access to the data in a local block, however, you must use *Local-Lock*, another Windows API function. This function temporarily makes the block become fixed at its current location in the local heap. *LocalLock* takes a handle to the memory block as its only parameter, and returns a pointer to the block's current location (or NIL if the operation did not succeed). The flip side of *LocalLock* is *Local-Unlock*, which restores the locked (fixed) memory block to its previous status.

When BPW takes care of memory allocation for you, you generally don't have to do anything to clean up afterwards: BPW will do it for you. But when you directly allocate memory, you need to clean up after yourself before shutting down the application. You do this—freeing local memory blocks—by using *LocalFree*, another Windows API function, which can be used not only to deallocate memory blocks at the close of an application, but also to deallocate memory blocks during an application's run if they are no longer needed. *LocalFree* is something like *Dispose* in standard Pascal: it takes a handle to a memory block as a parameter, frees up the memory in the block, and invalidates the handle, which cannot be reused.

Using Windows' Global Memory

Just as BPW allows you to work with an application's local heap memory, it also allows you to work directly with Windows' *global heap memory*, which is shared with other applications. Using global memory is trickier than using local memory, and depending on how much memory is available on the user's machine, it could have a serious impact on the performance of your own and other Windows programs that are running at the same time. For that reason, among others, you need to be extra careful if and when you dip into Windows' global memory. One principle to remember is that the global memory blocks should be freed up as soon as they are no longer needed.

The global cousin of *LocalAlloc* is, sensibly enough, *GlobalAlloc*, which takes one or more flags as parameters plus the size of the desired block in bytes. However, because global memory is inherently more complex than local memory (inasmuch as it must be shared with Windows and other applications), there are more flags than there are for *LocalAlloc*. The most important of these flags are shown in Table 30.2.

Like *LocalAlloc*, *GlobalAlloc* returns a handle to the memory block if the allocation was successful, or 0 if it was not successful. Any time a block is directly allocated in the global heap, no other block is allowed to be moved or discarded; you can use *gmem_NoDiscard* and *gmem_NoCompact* to achieve this result. Also, as with *LocalAlloc*, *GlobalAlloc*

TABLE 30.2: Important Global Memory Flags Used with the GlobalAlloc Function

Identifier	Meaning
gmem_DDEShare	The block can be shared by multiple Windows applications by using dynamic data exchange (DDE). However, the block is discarded when the application that allocated it is closed.
gmem_Discardable	The block can be discarded. This requires that the block also be specified as moveable.
gmem_Fixed	The block cannot be moved to a different memory location.
gmem_Moveable	The block can be moved to a different memory location.
gmem_NoCompact	No other memory blocks should be compacted or discarded in allocating space for this memory block.
gmem_NoDiscard	No other memory blocks should be discarded in allocating space for this memory block.
gmem_ZeroInit	The memory block's contents will be initialized to 0.

will allocate a memory block that is at least the size specified in the final, number-of-bytes parameter. To determine the actual size of the block, you can use the *Global-Size* function, which works in the same way as the *LocalSize* function.

Before working with a global memory block, you should first call *GlobalLock* to fix it at a particular physical memory location. *GlobalLock* takes the handle to the memory block and returns a pointer to its physical location. When they are no longer needed, the memory blocks should be deallocated with a call to *GlobalFree* or *GlobalDiscard*, which work in the same way as the corresponding local-memory functions.

CHAPTER THIRTY-ONE

Using the Clipboard and Dynamic Data Exchange

- Steps in Using the Clipboard

- Setting Up Client and Server Programs

- Using the Dynamic Data Exchange Management Library

In this chapter, we'll see how to exchange data between different Windows applications. There are two ways of accomplishing this task. The first method, in which the data exchange is under the user's direct control, employs the Windows Clipboard to *paste* data—including text, bitmaps, and other formats—from one window to another. The second, which two cooperating applications manage in the background, is called *dynamic data exchange* (DDE), and requires considerable programming sophistication.

Both approaches use some of the memory management routines that we saw in Chapter 30.

BPW and the Windows Clipboard

If you've worked with Windows programs much at all, you're already intimately familiar with the Windows Clipboard. It allows the user to highlight a block of text, copy it into a buffer area in memory, and then copy from that buffer to another window or another location in the same window.

How it all works, however, is a little more complex, even in a BPW program. First, your application must get a pointer to the data that needs to be copied to the Clipboard. Then, it gets a handle to a moveable, global memory block, locks the block in position, and copies the data into the block. It then checks to see if the Clipboard is available; if it is, the application empties the current contents of the Clipboard and copies the data (along with a format identifier) to the Clipboard. Finally, it closes the Clipboard, making the data available for pasting into other windows or other locations in the same window. Retrieving data from the Clipboard is essentially the same process, simply in reverse.

Let's take a look at how to copy data to the Clipboard. Listing 31.1 shows a simple example in which a text string gets copied. The results of running Listing 31.1 are shown in Figures 31.1 and 31.2.

FIGURE 31.1:

Ready to copy text to the clipboard

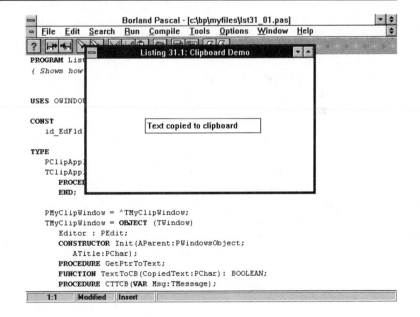

FIGURE 31.2:

Text successfully copied to the clipboard

Listing 31.1

```
PROGRAM Listing31_1;

{ Shows how to copy text to the Windows clipboard. }

USES OWINDOWS, ODIALOGS, WINPROCS, WINTYPES, STRINGS;

CONST
   id_EdFld = 100;

TYPE
   PClipApplication = ^TClipApplication;
   TClipApplication = OBJECT (TApplication)
      PROCEDURE InitMainWindow; VIRTUAL;
      END;

   PMyClipWindow = ^TMyClipWindow;
   TMyClipWindow = OBJECT (TWindow)
      Editor : PEdit;
      CONSTRUCTOR Init(AParent:PWindowsObject;
                       ATitle:PChar);
      PROCEDURE GetPtrToText;
      FUNCTION TextToCB(CopiedText:PChar): BOOLEAN;
      PROCEDURE CTTCB(VAR Msg:TMessage);
         VIRTUAL wm_First + wm_RButtonDown;
      END;

VAR
   PtrToText : PChar;
   TheText: ARRAY[0..30] OF CHAR;

CONSTRUCTOR TMyClipWindow.Init(AParent:PWindowsObject;
                               ATitle:PChar);
   BEGIN
   TWindow.Init(AParent, ATitle);
   Attr.X := 100;
   Attr.Y := 50;
   Attr.W := 400;
   Attr.H := 250;
   Editor := NEW(PEdit,
      Init(@Self, id_EdFld, 'Some text to copy',
      100, 100, 200, 25, 30, FALSE))
   END;
```

```
PROCEDURE TMyClipWindow.GetPtrToText;
   BEGIN
   IF Editor^.GetText(@TheText, 30) <> 0
   THEN PtrToText := @TheText
   ELSE PtrToText := NIL
   END;

FUNCTION TMyClipWindow.TextToCB(CopiedText:PChar): BOOLEAN;
   VAR
      TextGlobalHandle : THandle;
      TextGlobalPtr  : PChar;
   BEGIN
   TextToCB := FALSE;
   IF (CopiedText <> NIL)
   AND (StrLen(CopiedText) > O) THEN
      BEGIN
      TextGlobalHandle := GlobalAlloc(
             gmem_Moveable, StrLen(CopiedText) + 1);
      IF TextGlobalHandle <> O THEN
         BEGIN
         TextGlobalPtr := GlobalLock(TextGlobalHandle);
         IF TextGlobalPtr <> NIL THEN
            BEGIN
            StrCopy(TextGlobalPtr, CopiedText);
            GlobalUnlock(TextGlobalHandle);
            IF OpenClipboard(HWindow) THEN
               BEGIN
               EmptyClipboard;
               SetClipboardData(cf_Text,
               TextGlobalHandle);
               CloseClipboard;
               TextToCB := TRUE
               END
            ELSE GlobalFree(TextGlobalHandle)
            END
         ELSE GlobalFree(TextGlobalHandle)
         END
      END
   END;

PROCEDURE TMyClipWindow.CTTCB(VAR Msg:TMessage);
   BEGIN
   GetPtrToText;
   IF TextToCB(PtrToText)
   THEN Editor^.SetText('Text copied to clipboard')
```

```
    ELSE Editor^.SetText('Clipboard copy failed.')
    END;

PROCEDURE TClipApplication.InitMainWindow;
    BEGIN
    MainWindow :=
          NEW(PMyClipWindow,
          Init(NIL, 'Listing 31.1: Clipboard Demo'))
    END;

VAR
    MyCBApp : TClipApplication;

{main body of program}
BEGIN
    MyCBApp.Init('Listing 31.1');
    MyCBApp.Run;
    MyCBApp.Done
END.
```

Before we get into the details of Listing 31.1, let's zoom in on one specific line in the *TMyClipWindow.TextToCB* function. In the fifth indented BEGIN..END block (the one farthest to the right), the program actually opens the Windows Clipboard and copies the data into it. In doing so, it must inform the Clipboard about the type of data that is going to be copied. That's what is done by the following line of code, which occurs in the middle of the block:

```
SetClipboardData(cf_Text, TextGlobalHandle);
```

This line actually does two things. First, it takes a global Windows handle to the data and passes that handle to the Clipboard. Second—and this is the point we want to focus on—it passes an identifier to the Clipboard showing what kind of data the Clipboard is getting. There are several predefined Windows identifiers indicating the different formats in which the Clipboard can receive data. They are listed in Table 31.1.

TABLE 31.1: Clipboard Data Format Identifiers

Format Identifier	Meaning
cf_Text	Standard text data—i.e., a null-terminated ASCII string, each line of which is delimited by a carriage return/linefeed character.
cf_Bitmap	A Windows-compatible bitmap, such as the ones we created in the earlier chapter on icons and bitmaps.
cf_MetaFilePict	A metafile picture. This is a file containing Windows Graphics Device Interface (GDI) functions together with a data item of type *MetaFilePict*.
cf_SYLK	Data in the Microsoft Symbolic Link format, used for data exchange between Microsoft's Excel, Chart, and Multiplan application packages. This is similar to the cf_Text format, except that the data need not be null-terminated.
cf_DIF	Data in the Data Interchange Format used by the old VisiCalc spreadsheet program. This is also similar to cf_Text but need not be null-terminated.
cf_TIFF	Data in the Tag Image File Format, a popular format for storing graphic images.
cf_OEMText	Text data. This is similar to cf_Text, but instead of ASCII, the data uses the OEM character set.
cf_DIB	A device-independent bitmap beginning with information about the bitmap and then data in the bitmap.
cf_Palette	A Windows handle attached to a color palette, usually used together with cf_DIB to define the palette used by the bitmap.

Steps in Copying to the Clipboard

The essential steps in copying to the Clipboard are somewhat simpler than Listing 31.1 might lead you to believe. First, you must get a pointer to a null-terminated string: that is, a *PChar*-type variable, because like C, BPW treats a pointer to an array of characters the same as it does an array of characters. Thus, a *PChar*-type variable can be thought of as either an array of characters or as a pointer to an array of characters—whichever is more convenient in the current situation.

At any rate, once you have such a pointer, you pass it to a function as a parameter. This function gets a handle to a Windows global memory block and copies the pointer's referenced data into the memory block. It then checks to see if the Clipboard is available. If it is, then the function empties the current contents of the Clipboard, takes the handle to the global memory block, and passes it to the Clipboard. It then closes the Clipboard and, presto, the data is available for pasting.

Inside Listing 31.1

Let's see how these steps apply in Listing 31.1. The first step, as usual, is to declare the relevant BPW units. Then, we define a constant identifier for the edit field that we want to place in the middle of the application window. We'll use this edit field to get the initial text for copying to the Clipboard, then to display a message indicating whether the copy operation was successful, and finally to display text pasted back from the Clipboard. This isn't the only way to do it, of course, but it's probably the simplest that's a real ObjectWindows application.

Let's first go down to the *TMyClipWindow.CTTCB* method, in the bottom third of the listing, to see the overall structure of what's going on. First, the *CTTCB* method calls the *GetPtrToText* method to get a pointer to the text that we want to copy to the Clipboard. Then, it passes that pointer to the *TextToCB* function, which attempts to do the actual copying process. If the process is successful, then it returns a value of TRUE, and the edit field gets a new text string, "Text copied to Clipboard". If the process is unsuccessful (which can happen for a wide variety of reasons), then the new text in the edit field is "Clipboard copy failed."

Now let's go back to the top and look at the details. The definition of the overall application object type is standard stuff. Then, in the object definition of the application's main window, we include a field for the edit object that will contain the text to be pasted to and from the Clipboard. In order to perform the copying and pasting operations, we include three methods: a procedure that gets a pointer to the text in the edit field, a function that actually copies the text to the Clipboard, and a "shell" routine that manipulates both of those methods in response to a right-button mouse click.

Because the pointer to the text and the text-string array are shared by multiple routines, they are declared as global variables.

The *TClipWindow.Init* routine takes care of some basic housekeeping chores. First, it calls the inherited *TWindow.Init* routine to handle all the initialization details that we don't want to bother with. Then, as a cosmetic touch, it sets the position and dimensions of the application's main window. Finally, it initializes the editor field of the main window, creating a new single-line edit object and inserting the phrase "Some text to copy" into it.

The *TClipWindow.GetPtrToText* method calls the *GetText* function that the edit field inherits from its ancestor object type, *TStatic*. The *GetText* function takes two parameters: a pointer to a null-terminated string (in this case, a pointer to the global *TheText* variable) and an integer that denotes the maximum number of characters allowed in that null-terminated string. It copies the text from the edit field into the null-terminated string, and returns as a value the actual number of characters copied. This allows us to test whether the copy was successful by seeing if the return value was zero. If the copy was successful—that is, if the return value of *Get-Text* is not zero—then we assign the address of the null-terminated string to the global *PtrToText* variable. If not, then we set the pointer to NIL.

The Heart of the Operation: The TextToCB Function

The *TMyClipWindow.TextToCB* function is where things really get intricate. It first declares two local variables: one as a handle to pass to the Clipboard, and one as a pointer to manipulate the text string inside the method.

In the main body of the routine, the function first sets itself to FALSE. Then it checks to see if it's received as a parameter a pointer to some actual data. If the *GetPtrToText* operation was successful, this pointer will not be NIL and the length of the text it points to will be greater than zero. If these conditions are both satisfied, it gives us a "green light" to go ahead and try to copy the text to the Clipboard.

The first step is to get a handle to a global memory block, using the *GlobalAlloc* API function that we discussed in Chapter 30. The memory block must be moveable but not discardable, so we simply use the *gmem_Moveable* identifier with *GlobalAlloc* and specify the size as the length of the copied text plus one byte (to allow for the null terminator). If this operation was successful—that is, if we did get a global memory block and assign its handle to *TextGlobalHandle*—then the value of *Text-GlobalHandle* will be non-zero.

If it is non-zero, then we lock the global memory block in position so that it doesn't get moved during the copy operation. (If it moved, then our copied text could end up almost anywhere, with unpredictable results.) We pass the result—a pointer to the memory block—to *TextGlobalPtr*, which will automatically be set to NIL if the operation doesn't succeed.

If the operation was a success, then we call the *StrCopy* routine from the STRINGS unit to copy the text from the *CopiedText* parameter into the global memory block. Once that is done, we can then unlock the memory block in preparation for the final step of passing its handle to the Clipboard.

Before we can pass anything to the Clipboard, however, we must first check to see if the Clipboard is available. If it is in use by another program, the call to *Open-Clipboard* on behalf of this particular application window (*HWindow*) will return a value of FALSE. If not—if the Clipboard is available—then the function calls the Windows API function *EmptyClipboard* to clear the Clipboard of any data it contains from previous copy operations. Then, the *TextToCB* function calls *SetClipboardData* to pass the global memory block's handle to the Clipboard, using one of the data format identifiers we saw earlier in Table 31.1.

Finally, the function closes the Clipboard so that it can be used to copy data to other windows or locations in the same window. This also frees it for use with other Windows applications.

Buried at the end of these IF code blocks are two vital ELSE clauses. What they amount to is this:

- If you don't have a valid pointer to some data, then you can't copy any data to the Clipboard, so you should call *GlobalFree* to release the global memory block and invalidate its handle.

- If, for whatever reason, you can't open the Clipboard, then you can't copy any data to it. Therefore, you should call *GlobalFree* to release the global memory block and invalidate its handle.

Running Listing 31.1

To run Listing 31.1, simply wait for the application main window to open and the text message "Some text to copy" to appear. Then, click the right mouse button with the mouse cursor inside the window border, and the new message "Text copied to Clipboard" should appear. To verify that the text was copied, highlight and delete the text in the edit field. Then, with the text cursor in the edit field, press *Shift+Ins* to paste the original text back from the Clipboard into the edit field.

Pasting Data from the Clipboard

Pasting data from the Clipboard, if you're implementing it in source code, essentially just reverses the process of copying data to the Clipboard. You open the Clipboard with a call to *OpenClipboard*, check the format of the data it contains with *IsClipboardFormatAvailable*, retrieve the data by calling *GetClipboardData*, and close the Clipboard with a call to *CloseClipboard*.

Dynamic Data Exchange

Dynamic data exchange is a very sophisticated Windows capability that allows two applications to exchange data "behind the scenes," without direct intervention or control by the user. DDE is so advanced, in fact, that there aren't yet very many PC applications for it.

However, in outline, DDE is not that hard to understand. DDE is a "protocol"—a convention that tells two cooperating applications what they can expect from each other and how to interpret certain types of messages. In fact, DDE uses a group of Windows messages, all of which begin with the prefix *wm_DDE_*. Through these messages, one application can send data to or request data from another application.

As Windows programming techniques go, using the Clipboard is simple. Dynamic data exchange, on the other hand, is complex and difficult. The difficulty is lessened slightly by Windows 3.1's addition of a "Dynamic Data Exchange Management Library" (DDEML), which takes care of some low-level details for you, and by the DDEML unit included with Borland Pascal for Windows. But DDE is still complicated. Here, we'll discuss the essential techniques for implementing it.

What is DDE?

At bottom, DDE is a set of Windows messages and rules for enabling different Windows programs to exchange data with each other. The program that requests the data is called the client; the program that answers the request is called the server. DDE allows data exchange in both directions, though data normally flows from the server to the client. A program can simultaneously be a server and a client: it can respond to information requests from one program and, at the same time, request information from another program. The exchange of messages and data is called a "conversation" between the two participating programs.

The data can be exchanged in one of two ways: by passing handles to strings (called "atoms," while their handles are of the *TAtom* type), or by passing handles to global memory blocks, which we discussed in Chapter 30. Simple text data can be passed by the former method, while larger or more complex data elements require the latter.

Kinds of DDE Links

There are three main kinds of DDE links between applications: cold, warm, and hot.

- A *cold* link is set up when the client sends out a WM_DDE_INITIATE message, identifying the service and topic it needs. The server receives the DDE request, sends back a message (WM_DDE_ACK) acknowledging it, and the link is established. No data is exchanged until the client sends a WM_DDE_REQUEST message asking for a particular item of information. This is the kind of link used by our example DDE programs in this chapter.

- A *warm* link is set up when the client initiates a conversation as before, but sends a WM_DDE_ADVISE message asking the server to "let it know" if there are any changes in the data. With the WM_DDE_ADVISE message, the server gets a handle to a TDDEADVISE record. In this record is a flags field that indicates, in this case, that the link should be a warm link. No data is sent from server to client unless specifically requested: all that is sent automatically is notification that some of the data has changed.

- A *hot* link is set up when the client initiates a conversation and, by sending a WM_DDE_ADVISE message, asks for changed data automatically to be sent to it from the server. The contents of the TDDEADVISE record's flags field is what distinguishes this type of link from a warm link.

All types of links are terminated if one of the applications shuts down or sends a WM_DDE_TERMINATE message to the other.

Identifying the Data to Exchange

For the client to get the right data from the server, it must identify the data by three strings: the "service" (also called the "application"), the "topic," and the "item." Many of the details of this, as of other aspects of DDE, are simplified somewhat by the use of the DDE Management Library, which is demonstrated in this chapter's client-server programs. To see how this works, enter Listings 31.2 through 31.4 as BPW programs and create the CLIENT.RES resource file as described in Listing 31.5. Remember to save the unit file in Listing 31.2 as DDE_DEFS.PAS.

Listing 31.2

```
UNIT DDE_Defs; { Listing 31.2 }

INTERFACE

CONST
   NumValues = 3;

TYPE
   TDataSample = ARRAY[1..NumValues] OF INTEGER;
   TDataString = ARRAY[0..20] OF CHAR;

CONST
   { service name }
   DataEntryName : PChar = 'DataEntry';

   { topic name }
   DataTopicName : PChar = 'SampledData';

   { item names }
   DataItemNames : ARRAY [1..NumValues]
                         OF PChar = ('DataItem1',
                                     'DataItem2',
                                     'DataItem3');

IMPLEMENTATION
END.
```

Listing 31.3

```
PROGRAM Listing31_3;

{ Server program for DDE demonstration }

USES Strings, WinTypes, WinProcs, OWindows, ODialogs,
     Win31, DDEML, ShellAPI, BWCC, DDE_Defs;

CONST
   M_format = 'Values: %s: %d     %s: %d      %s: %d';

TYPE

{ Type for the application's main window }
  PServerWindow = ^TServerWindow;
  TServerWindow = OBJECT(TWindow)
      Inst       : LONGINT;
      CallBack   : TCallback;
      ServiceHSz : HSz;
      TopicHSz   : HSz;
      ItemHSz    : ARRAY [1..NumValues] OF HSz;
      ConvHdl    : HConv;
      Advising   : ARRAY [1..NumValues] OF BOOLEAN;
      DataSample : TDataSample;

    CONSTRUCTOR Init(AParent: PWindowsObject;
                     ATitle: PChar);
    DESTRUCTOR  Done; VIRTUAL;
    PROCEDURE SetupWindow; VIRTUAL;
    PROCEDURE Paint(PaintDC: HDC;
       VAR PaintInfo: TPaintStruct); VIRTUAL;
    FUNCTION  MatchTopicAndService(Topic, Service: HSz):
       BOOLEAN; VIRTUAL;
    FUNCTION  MatchTopicAndItem(Topic, Item: HSz):
       INTEGER; VIRTUAL;
    FUNCTION  DataRequested(TransType: Word;
       ItemNum: INTEGER; ClipFmt: Word): HDDEData;
       VIRTUAL;
    END;

{ Type for main application object }
  TDDEServerApp = OBJECT(TApplication)
  PROCEDURE InitMainWindow; VIRTUAL;
  END;
```

```
{ Global variable initialized as typed constant }
CONST
   ProgramTitle   : PChar = 'DDE Server';

{ Noninitialized global variable }
VAR
   App: TDDEServerApp;

{ global function }
FUNCTION CallbackProc(CallType, Fmt: Word;
                      Conv: HConv; HSz1, HSz2: HSZ;
                      Data: HDDEData;
                      Data1, Data2: LONGINT):
                      HDDEData; export;
   VAR
      ThisWindow: PServerWindow;
      ItemNum   : INTEGER;
   BEGIN
      CallbackProc := 0;
      ThisWindow := PServerWindow(App.MainWindow);

   { Big CASE statement to control CallBackProc }
   CASE CallType OF

      xtyp_Connect:
         IF Conv = 0
         THEN BEGIN
              IF ThisWindow^.MatchTopicAndService(
                    HSz1, HSz2)
              THEN CallbackProc := 1; { Connected! }
              END;

      { If connection confirmed, record the
        conversation handle as the window's own. }
      xtyp_Connect_Confirm:
         ThisWindow^.ConvHdl := Conv;

      xtyp_AdvReq, xtyp_Request:
         BEGIN
         ItemNum := ThisWindow^.MatchTopicAndItem(HSz1, HSz2);
         IF ItemNum > 0
         THEN CallbackProc :=
              ThisWindow^.DataRequested(CallType, ItemNum, Fmt);
         END;
```

```
    END; { of big CASE CallType statement }

    END; { of CallBack function }


{ TServerWindow Methods }

{ Constructs an instance of the DDE Server Window. }
CONSTRUCTOR TServerWindow.Init(AParent: PWindowsObject;
                                    ATitle: PChar);
    VAR
       i : INTEGER;
    BEGIN
       TWindow.Init(AParent, ATitle);
       Attr.X := 10;
       Attr.Y := 225;
       Attr.W := 600;
       Attr.H := 210;

       Inst      := 0;
       @CallBack := nil;

       RANDOMIZE;
       FOR i := 1 TO NumValues DO
       BEGIN
       DataSample[i]:= RANDOM(1000);
       Advising[i]  := FALSE;
       END;
    END; { of Init constructor }

{ Destroys the DDE Server Window and terminates
  the conversation. }
DESTRUCTOR TServerWindow.Done;
    VAR
       i : INTEGER;
    BEGIN
       IF ServiceHSz <> 0
       THEN DDEFreeStringHandle(Inst, ServiceHSz);

       IF TopicHSz <> 0
       THEN DDEFreeStringHandle(Inst, TopicHSz);

    FOR i := 1 TO NumValues DO
       IF ItemHSz[i] <> 0
```

```
      THEN DDEFreeStringHandle(Inst, ItemHSz[i]);

      IF Inst <> 0
      THEN DDEUninitialize(Inst);

      IF @CallBack <> NIL
      THEN FreeProcInstance(@CallBack);

      TWindow.Done;
   END; { of Done destructor }

{ Initializes the DDEML by registering services
  provided by this application. }
PROCEDURE TServerWindow.SetupWindow;
   VAR
      i : INTEGER;
   BEGIN
      TWindow.SetupWindow;
      @CallBack:= MakeProcInstance(@CallBackProc,
                                 HInstance);
      IF DDEInitialize(Inst, CallBack, 0, 0) = dmlErr_No_Error
      THEN BEGIN
         ServiceHSz:= DDECreateStringHandle(Inst, DataEntryName,
                                            cp_WinAnsi);
         TopicHSz  := DDECreateStringHandle(Inst, DataTopicName,
                                            cp_WinAnsi);

         FOR i := 1 TO NumValues DO
             ItemHSz[i] := DDECreateStringHandle(Inst,
                 DataItemNames[i], cp_WinAnsi);
      IF DDENameService(Inst,
         ServiceHSz, 0, dns_Register) = 0
      THEN BEGIN
          MessageBox(HWindow,
             'Registration failed.',
             Application^.Name,
             mb_IconStop);
          PostQuitMessage(0);
          END;
      END
   ELSE
   PostQuitMessage(0);
   END;

PROCEDURE TServerWindow.Paint(PaintDC: HDC;
                           VAR PaintInfo: TPaintStruct);
```

```
TYPE
   TDataItem = record
                  Name: Pointer;
                  Value: INTEGER;
                  END;
   TData = ARRAY[1..NumValues] OF TDataItem;
VAR
   R: TRect;
   S: ARRAY[0..255] OF CHAR;
   S1: ARRAY[0..512] OF CHAR;
   Len, i: INTEGER;
   Data: TData;
BEGIN
   GetClientRect(HWindow, R);
   InflateRect(R, -10, 0);
   StrCopy(S, M_format);
   FOR i := 1 TO NumValues DO
      BEGIN
      Data[i].Name := DataItemNames[i];
      Data[i].Value := DataSample[i];
      END;
   Len := wvsPrintf(S1, S, Data);
   DrawText(PaintDC, S1, Len, R, dt_WordBreak);
END;

{ Returns True if topic and service match those
  supported by the program. Else, returns False. }
FUNCTION TServerWindow.MatchTopicAndService(
        Topic, Service: HSz): BOOLEAN;
   BEGIN
   MatchTopicAndService := FALSE;
   IF DDECmpStringHandles(TopicHSz, Topic) = 0
   THEN IF DDECmpStringHandles(ServiceHSz, Service) = 0
        THEN MatchTopicAndService := TRUE;
   END;

{ Determines if the topic and item match one supported by this
  program. Returns the item number if a match is found, and
  zero otherwise. }
```

```
FUNCTION TServerWindow.MatchTopicAndItem(Topic, Item: HSz):
     INTEGER;
   VAR
     i : INTEGER;
   BEGIN
   MatchTopicAndItem := 0;
   IF DDECmpStringHandles(TopicHSz, Topic) = 0
   THEN FOR i := 1 TO NumValues DO
        IF DDECmpStringHandles(ItemHSz[i], Item) = 0
        THEN MatchTopicAndItem := i;
   END;

{ Returns the data requested. }
FUNCTION TServerWindow.DataRequested(TransType: Word;
        ItemNum: INTEGER;
        ClipFmt: Word): HDDEData; VAR
     ItemStr: TDataString;   { Defined in DDE_DEFS unit }
   BEGIN
     IF ClipFmt = cf_Text
     THEN BEGIN
        Str(DataSample[ItemNum], ItemStr);
        DataRequested := DDECreateDataHandle(Inst,
              @ItemStr, StrLen(ItemStr) + 1,
              0, ItemHSz[ItemNum], ClipFmt, 0);
        END
     ELSE
     DataRequested := 0;
   END;

{ TDDEServerApp Methods }
PROCEDURE TDDEServerApp.InitMainWindow;
   BEGIN
   MainWindow := New(PServerWindow, Init(nil,
                   Application^.Name));
   END;

{ Main body of server program }
BEGIN
   App.Init(ProgramTitle);
   App.Run;
   App.Done;
END.
```

Listing 31.4

```
PROGRAM Listing31_4;

USES Strings, WinTypes, WinProcs,
     OWindows, ODialogs, Win31, DDEML,
     ShellAPI, BWCC, DDE_Defs;

{$R Client.res}

CONST
{ Resource and command IDs for menu }
    id_Menu  = 'cli_menu';
    cm_Request  = 200;

TYPE
{ Type for application main window }
   PClientWindow = ^TClientWindow;
   TClientWindow = OBJECT(TWindow)
       { data fields }
       Inst: Longint;
       CallBackPtr: ^TCallback;
       ServiceHSz : HSz;
       TopicHSz   : HSz;
       ItemHSz    : ARRAY [1..NumValues] of HSz;
       ConvHdl    : HConv;
       DataSample : TDataSample;
       { methods }
       CONSTRUCTOR Init(AParent: PWindowsObject;
                        ATitle: PChar);
       DESTRUCTOR  Done; VIRTUAL;
       PROCEDURE SetupWindow; VIRTUAL;
       PROCEDURE Paint(PaintDC: HDC;
           VAR PaintInfo: TPaintStruct); VIRTUAL;
       PROCEDURE CMRequest(VAR Msg: TMessage);
           VIRTUAL cm_First + cm_Request;
       PROCEDURE Request(HConversation: HConv);
           VIRTUAL;
    END;

{ Type for application object }
   TDDEClientApp = OBJECT(TApplication)
       PROCEDURE InitMainWindow; VIRTUAL;
       END;
```

```
{ Global variable for application }
VAR
   App: TDDEClientApp;


{ CallBack Procedure for DDEML }
FUNCTION CallbackProc(CallType, Fmt: Word;
        Conv: HConv; hsz1, hsz2: HSZ;
        Data: HDDEData; Data1, Data2: Longint):
        HDDEData; export;
   VAR
      ThisWindow: PClientWindow;
   BEGIN
      CallbackProc := 0;
      ThisWindow := PClientWindow(App.MainWindow);

      CASE CallType of
         xtyp_Register: BEGIN END; { do nothing }
         xtyp_Unregister: BEGIN END; { do nothing }
         xtyp_xAct_Complete: BEGIN END; { do nothing }
         xtyp_Request, Xtyp_AdvData:
            BEGIN
            ThisWindow^.Request(Conv);
            CallbackProc := dde_FAck;
            END;
         xtyp_Disconnect:
            BEGIN
            MessageBox(ThisWindow^.HWindow,
                       'Disconnected!',
                       Application^.Name,
                       mb_IconStop);
            PostQuitMessage(0);
            END;
      END; { of CASE statement }
   END; { of CallBack function }


CONSTRUCTOR TClientWindow.Init(AParent: PWindowsObject;
                               ATitle: PChar);
   VAR
      i : INTEGER;
   BEGIN
      TWindow.Init(AParent, ATitle);
      Attr.Menu := LoadMenu(HInstance, PChar(id_menu) );
      Attr.X := 10;
```

```
        Attr.Y := 10;
        Attr.W := 600;
        Attr.H := 210;

        Inst := 0; { Zero for first call to DDEInitialize }
        CallBackPtr:= NIL;
        ConvHdl    := 0;
        ServiceHSz := 0;
        TopicHSz   := 0;
        FOR i := 1 TO NumValues DO
           BEGIN
           ItemHSz[i]    := 0;
           DataSample[i] := 0;
           END;
     END;

{ Destroys an instance of the Client window. }
DESTRUCTOR TClientWindow.Done;
   VAR
      i : INTEGER;
   BEGIN
      IF ServiceHSz <> 0
      THEN DDEFreeStringHandle(Inst, ServiceHSz);

      IF TopicHSz <> 0
      THEN DDEFreeStringHandle(Inst, TopicHSz);

      FOR i := 1 TO NumValues DO
         IF ItemHSz[i] <> 0
         THEN DDEFreeStringHandle(Inst, ItemHSz[i]);

      IF Inst <> 0
      THEN DDEUninitialize(Inst);

      IF CallBackPtr <> NIL
      THEN FreeProcInstance(CallBackPtr);

      TWindow.Done;
   END;

{ Initializes the use of the DDEML. }
PROCEDURE TClientWindow.SetupWindow;
   VAR
      i : INTEGER;
      InitOK: BOOLEAN;
```

```
    BEGIN
        CallBackPtr := MakeProcInstance(@CallBackProc,
                                        HInstance);

{ Initialize DDE and set up the callback function.
  If the server program is not running, the attempt
  will fail. }
  IF CallBackPtr <> NIL
  THEN BEGIN
        IF DDEInitialize(Inst,
           TCallback(CallBackPtr), AppCmd_ClientOnly,
           0) = dmlErr_No_Error
        THEN BEGIN
            ServiceHSz := DDECreateStringHandle(Inst,
                    DataEntryName, cp_WinAnsi);
            TopicHSz := DDECreateStringHandle(Inst,
                    DataTopicName, cp_WinAnsi);
            InitOK := True;
            FOR i := 1 TO NumValues DO
                BEGIN
                ItemHSz[i]:= DDECreateStringHandle(Inst,
                        DataItemNames[i], cp_WinAnsi);
                InitOK := InitOK and (ItemHSz[i] <> 0);
                END;

            IF (ServiceHSz <> 0)
               AND (TopicHSz <> 0) AND InitOK
            THEN BEGIN
                ConvHdl := DDEConnect(Inst, ServiceHSz,
                                        TopicHSz, NIL);
                IF ConvHdl = 0
                THEN BEGIN
                    MessageBox(HWindow,
                            'Cannot start conversation!',
                            Application^.Name, mb_IconStop);
                    PostQuitMessage(0);
                    END
                END
            ELSE BEGIN
                MessageBox(HWindow, 'Cannot create strings!',
                        Application^.Name, mb_IconStop);
                PostQuitMessage(0);
                END
            END
        ELSE BEGIN
```

```
                MessageBox(HWindow, 'Can''t initialize!',
                        Application^.Name, mb_IconStop);
                PostQuitMessage(0);
                END;
            END;
    END;

{ Repaints the window. }
PROCEDURE TClientWindow.Paint(PaintDC: HDC;
                                VAR PaintInfo: TPaintStruct);
    VAR
        DataItemAmt: ARRAY[0..3] of CHAR;
        i : INTEGER;
    BEGIN
        TextOut(PaintDC, 220, 25, 'Test Data Item 1: ', 18);
        Str(DataSample[1], DataItemAmt);
        TextOut(PaintDC, 340, 25,
                DataItemAmt, StrLen(DataItemAmt));

        TextOut(PaintDC, 220, 50, 'Test Data Item 2: ', 18);
        Str(DataSample[2], DataItemAmt);
        TextOut(PaintDC, 340, 50,
                DataItemAmt, StrLen(DataItemAmt));

        TextOut(PaintDC, 220, 75, 'Test Data Item 3: ', 18);
        Str(DataSample[3], DataItemAmt);
        TextOut(PaintDC, 340, 75,
                DataItemAmt, StrLen(DataItemAmt));
    END;

{ Generate a DDE Request. }
PROCEDURE TClientWindow.CMRequest(VAR Msg: TMessage);
    BEGIN
    Request(ConvHdl);
    END;

PROCEDURE TClientWindow.Request(HConversation: HConv);
    VAR
        hDDETemp : HDDEData;
        DataStr  : TDataString;
        Err, i   : INTEGER;
    BEGIN
        IF HConversation <> 0
        THEN BEGIN
            FOR i := 1 TO NumValues DO
```

```
            BEGIN
            hDDETemp := DDEClientTransaction(NIL,
                       O, HConversation, ItemHSz[i],
                       cf_Text, xtyp_Request, O, NIL);
            IF hDDETemp <> 0
            THEN BEGIN
                DDEGetData(hDDETemp,
                           @DataStr, SizeOf(DataStr), O);
                Val(DataStr, DataSample[i], Err);
                END;
            END;
        InvalidateRect(HWindow, NIL, True);
        END;
    END;

{ Constructs an instance of the DDE Client Window and
  sets it up as the main application window. }
PROCEDURE TDDEClientApp.InitMainWindow;
   BEGIN
   MainWindow := New(PClientWindow,
                     Init(NIL, 'DDE Client'));
   END;

{ Main body of the program }
BEGIN
   App.Init('DDE Client');
   App.Run;
   App.Done;
END.
```

Listing 31.5

```
Resource file name: CLIENT.RES
Menu resource ID: CLI_MENU
POPUP "&DDE"
Menu item "&Get data from server", item ID = 200
```

Inside Listing 31.2

Listing 31.2 is the simplest of the three, so let's start with it. The most important task it performs is to define the names of the service, topic, and items that are available to the client program from the server program. These are defined as *DataEntryName* for the service name, *DataTopicName* for the topic name, and *DataItemNames* for the item names. Both the client and the server programs name this unit in their USES clauses, so they share these names, as well as the other types and constants in the unit.

Inside Listing 31.3

Listing 31.3 is where things start to get complicated. Many of the details will have to be glossed over, but we'll cover all of the essential points. Note, first, that several new units are named in the USES clause, in particular:

- *Win31:* This provides support for new API routines that were added in version 3.1 of Windows. The DDE Management Library is new in Windows 3.1 and uses some of these routines.

- *DDEML:* This unit is designed to serve as the interface between Borland Pascal for Windows and the DDE Management Library.

Next, in the CONST section, we define the format string that will control how the data is displayed in the server window. This is more C than Pascal, but the idea should be familiar. The '%s' indicates that data should be formatted as a string, while the '%d' indicates it should be formatted as a decimal number. When the data items are loaded into the format in the correct order, the format specifiers will display them in the server window.

Next, we define object types for the application main window and the application object itself. The main window type includes fields for the service, topic, and item identifiers requested by a client, as well as other fields indicating the status of a DDE link that has been established. The *ConvHdl* field holds a handle to the DDE link.

The CallBackProc function allows the server to respond to different kinds of client messages. It contains a CASE statement that tells the program what to do for each type of message.

The *TServerWindow.Init* method constructs and initializes the application's main window in a fairly standard way. It also assigns random integer values to the three data items available to the client program. The *TServerWindow.Done* method shuts down the server program, again in a fairly standard way. It also shuts down any DDE links that are currently active. The *SetupWindow* method initializes the DDE Management Library to help run the DDE links.

The *Paint* method displays the data in the server program's window, and is fairly unremarkable.

MatchTopicAndService is a boolean function that returns a value of True if the requested service and topic match those supported by the server program; otherwise, it returns a value of false.

MatchTopicAndItem checks to see if the requested topic and item match one supported by the server program. If they match, the function returns the item number of the item; otherwise, it returns a value of zero.

DataRequested returns the data requested by the client, and can discriminate between different types of requests. The rest of the program is fairly self-explanatory.

Inside Listing 31.4

The client program has some familiar features. First, in the CONST section, we define a resource ID for the application's menu and a command ID for the single menu choice, which requests data from the server. Next, we define types for the program's main window and the application object itself. The client main window has many of the same data fields as the server main window—for example, for the service, topic, and data items to be exchanged.

Similar to the corresponding method in the server program, the *CallBackProc* function contains a CASE statement that keeps track of the status of the DDE link. The *TClientWindow.Init* method assumes that to begin with, no DDE link has been established, and therefore sets the *CallBackPtr* field to NIL and the other data fields to zero.

The *TClientWindow.Done* method checks to see if a DDE link is active, and if so, it frees the handles to the service, topic, and item before shutting down the client program.

The *TClientWindow.SetupWindow* initializes the DDE Management Library and creates handles for the service, topic, and items. The fairly standard *TClientWindow.Paint* method displays the DDE data in the client program's main window.

The *TClientWindow.Request* method is where we really see some action. This method first checks to see if a DDE link has been established—that is, if the method has received a conversation handle *HConversation* as a parameter. If there is a DDE link, the method requests data items from the server one by one, up to the number of values supported (NumValues). It loads the values from the server into a buffer called hDDETemp. It then takes the values from the hDDETemp buffer and copies them to the DataSample array. If you look back at the *TClientWindow.Paint* method, you can see that the *DataSample* array is used (indirectly) to display the DDE-acquired data in the client program's main window.

The rest of the client program is all familiar. To run the DDE demonstration, follow these steps:

1. Create the resource file specified in Listing 31.5 and save it as CLIENT.RES.

2. Compile the DDE_DEFS unit (Listing 31.2).

3. Compile and run the server program (Listing 31.3). Note that this program must be active before you run the client program.

4. Compile and run the client program (Listing 31.4). Your screen should look like Figure 31.3.

FIGURE 31.3:

DDE client program obtains data from server

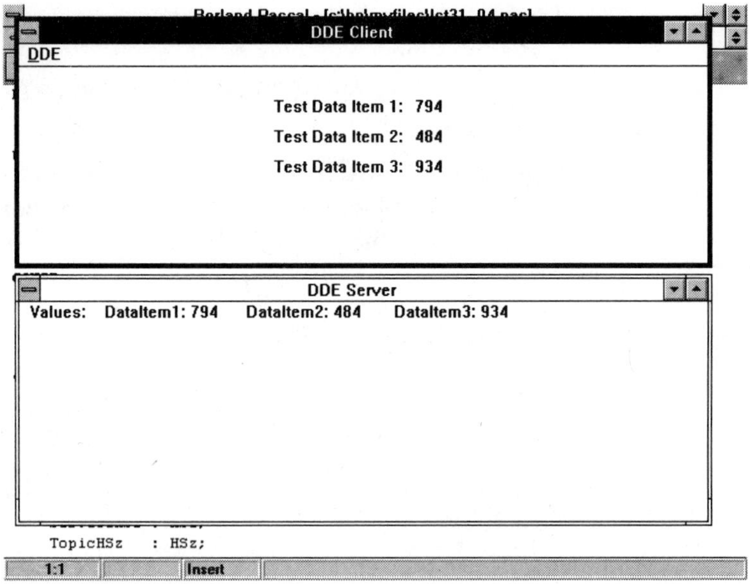

Using the Windows Graphics Device Interface

- What is the Window GDI?

- Important GDI Functions

- Creating Business Graphics

The Windows Graphics Device Interface (GDI) is one of the most important features of Microsoft Windows. Because computer hardware and peripherals (such as monitors, printers, plotters, and so forth) have been developed over the years by many different companies using different techniques, it's a considerable problem to make sure that a program supports at least most of the devices it's likely to meet on a user's desk.

If you've developed graphics programs under the DOS version of Turbo Pascal, then you're already intimately familiar with the problem. In order to make your program work with most of the PC video adapters and monitors available, you had to include all the relevant BGI (Borland Graphics Interface) drivers on the disk along with your program, or else link them into the .EXE file as shown in Chapter 15.

What makes the Windows GDI such a great advance is that you no longer have to worry about what equipment your program will run on. Instead of making your program try to detect the installed graphics hardware and then use the appropriate driver, which must be included, your program simply writes to the Windows GDI. Windows itself then takes care of translating your program's graphics output into the appropriate form—regardless of whether it's being sent to the video monitor, the printer, or some other device. Any device supported by Windows is automatically supported by your program.

This has implications beyond merely saving you the trouble of including drivers with your program for CGA, Hercules, EGA, VGA, and other video modes, and reflects the whole philosophy of Windows. In theory—though not yet in practice, of course—you can develop a Windows program on a PC that will run on any other hardware platform that is capable of running Windows. It could be a PC, a mainframe or minicomputer terminal, a Unix workstation, or even (John Sculley's worst nightmare!) an Apple Macintosh.

In previous chapters, we've already seen some features of the GDI, such as its line-drawing features, pens, line styles, and color support. In this chapter, we'll extend that discussion by looking at some of the most important GDI techniques and features for creating business graphics instead of simply drawing lines in a window.

Basics of Using the GDI

The key element in displaying graphics in a Windows application (as well as for many other Windows tasks) is a device context, also referred to sometimes as a display context. This is the destination to which your program sends its graphics output. Windows itself then takes the graphics output from the device context, translates it, and sends it in the appropriate format to the desired output device.

In earlier chapters, we've discussed three important points about device contexts that are worth reiterating here:

1. Device contexts are a global resource that must be shared by all concurrently running Windows applications. Windows provides a total of five device contexts.

2. You can obtain a device context from Windows by calling the Windows API function *GetDC()*, where the parameter of *GetDC()* is the handle to the window that needs the device context. You then load the handle to the device context into a variable of type HDC, which is a special BPW type for holding device contexts.

3. As soon as the device context is no longer needed, it must be released with a call to the Windows API function *ReleaseDC*. Failure to release a device context means that it will not be available to other programs that need it, or indeed, to other uses of the *GetDC* function in the same program. Once you've used up the five device contexts, your programs can crash if they need any more.

Using the TWindow.Paint Method

One trick that can make drawing graphics somewhat simpler is to use BPW's *TWindow.Paint* method. This method, which you will normally override so that you can customize it to draw the graphics you want, responds to a Windows wm_Paint message and automatically gets and releases a device context when it is called. This device context is automatically passed to the *Paint* method as one of its two parameters: *PaintDC*, which is a handle to a device context, and *PaintInfo*, which is a record of type *TPaintStruct* that contains information needed by the application for using the *Paint* method. Normally, you can ignore the *PaintInfo* parameter and let the ancestor method handle the details.

There's no absolute reason why you need to use the *Paint* method to display your graphics, as long as you remember to do the housekeeping work (for example, getting and releasing device contexts) yourself. In general, however, it's just easier to bundle your graphics routines inside *Paint* unless there's a specific reason to do otherwise. Using the *Paint* method is illustrated in Listing 32.1, below. The result of running the program from Listing 32.1 is shown in Figure 32.1.

Listing 32.1

```
PROGRAM Listing32_1;

{  Shows some of the most important Windows GDI functions
   and how they work. Specific features demonstrated:
   1. Using a Paint method to draw graphics.
   2. The Windows GDI functions Rectangle, Pie,
      and Ellipse.
   3. The Windows GDI function TextOut. }

USES WOBJECTS, WINTYPES, WINPROCS;

TYPE
    Grafapplication = OBJECT (tapplication)
       PROCEDURE InitMainWindow; VIRTUAL;
       END;

    PGrafWindow = ^TGrafWindow;
    TGrafWindow = OBJECT(TWindow)
    CONSTRUCTOR Init(AParent:PWindowsObject;
                     ATitle:PChar);
       PROCEDURE Paint(PaintDC:HDC;
          VAR Paintinfo:TPaintStruct); VIRTUAL;
       END;

PROCEDURE Grafapplication.InitMainWindow;
   BEGIN
   MainWindow := new(PGrafwindow,
          Init(NIL, 'Listing 32.1: Windows GDI Functions Demo'));
   END;

CONSTRUCTOR TGrafwindow.Init(AParent:PWindowsObject;
                                ATitle:PChar);
   BEGIN
   TWindow.Init(AParent, ATitle);
   attr.x := 50;
```

```
        attr.y := 50;
        attr.w := 500;
        attr.h := 400;
        END;

PROCEDURE TGrafwindow.Paint(PaintDC:HDC;
                            VAR Paintinfo:TPaintStruct);

        BEGIN
        Rectangle(PaintDC, 40,40,150,150);
        TextOut(PaintDC, 70,160, 'Square', 6);

        Pie(PaintDC, 180,40,400,120, 375,95,350,60);
        TextOut(PaintDC, 300, 120, 'Pie Slice', 9);

        Ellipse(PaintDC, 40,200,150,310);
        TextOut(PaintDC, 80,320, 'Circle', 6);

        Ellipse(PaintDC, 220,180,450,235);
        TextOut(PaintDC, 320,245, 'Ellipse', 7);

        {draw a line as a "flat" rectangle}
        Rectangle(PaintDC,220,300,450,302);
        TextOut(PaintDC, 325,312, 'Line', 4);

        END;

VAR
    GrafApp : GrafApplication;

BEGIN
    GrafApp.Init('Listing 32.1');
    GrafApp.Run;
    GrafApp.Done
END.
```

The features of Listing 32.1 that are relevant to our discussion of the *Paint* method are as follows. First, *TWindow.Paint* is automatically inherited by our application's main window from its ancestor *TWindow*. However, the inherited method is a generic *Paint* method that won't display customized graphics. That's why normally you will override the inherited *Paint* method with your own version that incorporates the graphics you want to create.

FIGURE 32.1:

The graphics generated by the program in Listing 32.1

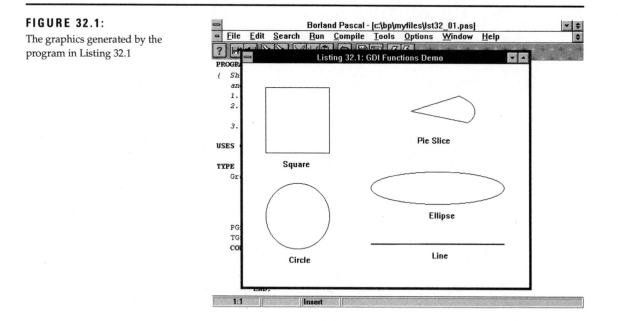

Accordingly, the first step is to declare an explicit *Paint* method in the definition of the application's main window type. To work in the same way as the inherited method (but do different things), the method declaration must have the same header as the inherited method: the two parameters *PaintDC* and *PaintInfo*. It must also be virtual so that the right versions of any *Paint*-related methods get called.

The rest is quite simple. Because the *Paint* method automatically takes care of getting and releasing a device context for its window, you as the programmer are freed to concentrate on the details of generating the graphics you want. Listing 32.1 uses several of the most important predefined graphics routines in the Windows GDI, so let's take a look at each. These routines are provided by Windows itself, not ObjectWindows, but BPW is set up so that you can easily take advantage of them.

Important Windows GDI Functions

Windows has so many functions for the programmer—even just functions related to graphics—that documenting all of them would fill another entire book. Here, we'll just look at some of the most important ones. By using these functions creatively, it's easy to create attractive business graphics in your programs. The specific functions we will look at here are *Rectangle*, *Pie*, *Ellipse*, and *TextOut*. We'll postpone our discussion of *TextOut* until after we've seen how to use Windows fill styles ("hatch styles") to fill in the graphic images.

Rectangle

Rectangle, the first Windows GDI function called in Listing 32.1's *Paint* method, allows you to draw a rectangle by specifying a device context and the coordinates of the rectangle's upper-left and lower-right corners relative to the upper left corner of the parent window. We've made our rectangle a square by giving it equal height and width dimensions, but it doesn't have to be a square. The syntax of the function is:

```
Rectangle(DC: HDC; x1, y1, x2, y2: INTEGER): BOOLEAN
```

In this case, the device context parameter is *PaintDC*, automatically used by the *Paint* method. The upper-left corner is at 40,40 and the lower-right corner is 150,150; thus, the dimensions of the rectangle are 110 by 110. These aren't pixels; they're logical units Windows uses to map your graphics into whatever output device is being used. We'll see how to change the units that Windows uses in calculating coordinates later in the chapter when we discuss mapping modes.

Just as we saw in the earlier line-drawing program, *Rectangle* uses the currently selected pen to do its drawing, so you can change line style, thickness, and color in any way you want. It also uses the currently selected Windows fill style to fill the rectangle, a feature we'll use in the next program listing. If you don't explicitly set up a pen or a brush with a fill style, Windows uses the default pen (which produces a thin black line) and the default fill style (no fill pattern). Also, as a function, *Rectangle* returns a value that you can use to test whether the function was called successfully. If the operation failed, then the function returns a value of 0 (FALSE).

Near the bottom of the source code, we call *Rectangle* one more time. Now, however, we use it to draw a rectangle that is 230 units wide and 2 units high—resulting in a "flat rectangle" that is the same thing as a straight line.

Pie

The next Windows GDI function used in Listing 32.1 is *Pie*, which draws a pie slice with the coordinates you specify. This function is a bit more complicated than *Rectangle*, because it takes more parameters and applies them in a slightly odd way. The declaration syntax of the function is

```
FUNCTION Pie(DC: HDC; x1, y1, x2, y2, x3, y3,
             x4, y4: Integer): BOOLEAN;
```

The first parameter of *Pie* is, as usual, a device context to which the graphics output of the function will be sent. The next four parameters (x1, y1, x2, y2) are the coordinates of the bounding rectangle, which determines the overall size, shape, and position of the pie slice. The next two parameters (x3, y3) are the coordinates of the starting point of the pie's arc—its "crust," so to speak. The final two parameters are the ending point of the pie's arc, counterclockwise from the starting point. Here, the ending point is above and to the left of the starting point, so the pie slice appears as a single slice. If the ending point were below and to the left of the starting point, the graphic image would look like a whole pie with just a slice cut out of it.

Like the *Rectangle* function, *Pie* draws with the currently selected pen and fills the slice with the currently selected fill style. It returns a value of 0 (FALSE) if the operation fails for any reason.

Ellipse

The *Ellipse* function works in a way that is a little less obvious than the *Rectangle* function. With *Ellipse*, you specify the device context, then the coordinates of the upper-left and lower-right corners of the ellipse's bounding rectangle. The function will then draw the biggest ellipse that will fit in the bounding rectangle. If the rectangle is a square, then you'll get a circle for the ellipse; if it's higher than it is wide or wider than it is high, you'll get a corresponding ellipse. The declaration syntax of the function is:

```
FUNCTION Ellipse(DC: HDC; x1, y1, x2, y2: INTEGER): BOOLEAN;
```

Just like the *Rectangle* function, *Ellipse* is drawn with the currently selected pen and filled with the currently selected fill style. Also, it returns a value of 0 if the function call was not successful for any reason.

In Listing 32.1, we used *Ellipse* twice: once with a square bounding rectangle to produce a circle, and once with a nonsquare bounding rectangle to produce what would more often be referred to as an actual "ellipse."

Using Brushes and Fill Styles

The graphic images in Figure 32.1 look fine, but they would be more striking if they were filled in. That little trick is demonstrated by the program in Listing 32.2, which uses Windows brushes and fill styles to fill in the images with different fill patterns. The result of running the program from Listing 32.2 is shown in Figure 32.2.

Listing 32.2

```
PROGRAM Listing32_2;

{ Shows how to use fill styles to fill in Windows
  graphics. Specific features demonstrated:
  1. Using handles to brushes.
  2. Using Windows fill styles for graphic drawings.
  3. Deleting brushes when finished with them. }

USES WOBJECTS, WINTYPES, WINPROCS;

TYPE
    Grafapplication = object (tapplication)
       PROCEDURE InitMainWindow; VIRTUAL;
       END;

    PGrafWindow = ^TGrafWindow;
    TGrafWindow = OBJECT(TWindow)
    CONSTRUCTOR Init(AParent:PWindowsObject;
                     ATitle:PChar);
       PROCEDURE Paint(PaintDC:HDC;
                       VAR Paintinfo:TPaintStruct); VIRTUAL;
       END;

PROCEDURE Grafapplication.InitMainWindow;
   BEGIN
   MainWindow :=
        new(PGrafwindow, Init(NIL,
        'Listing 32.2: Windows GDI Fill Styles Demo'));
   END;
```

```
CONSTRUCTOR TGrafwindow.Init(AParent:PWindowsObject;
                             ATitle:PChar);
   BEGIN
   TWindow.Init(AParent, ATitle);
   attr.x := 50;
   attr.y := 50;
   attr.w := 500;
   attr.h := 400;
   END;

PROCEDURE TGrafwindow.Paint(PaintDC:HDC;
                             VAR Paintinfo:TPaintStruct);
   VAR
      NewBrush,
      OldBrush : HBrush;

   {local procedure under Paint method}
   PROCEDURE DrawBar(x1, y1, x2, y2, BarFillStyle: INTEGER);
      BEGIN
      NewBrush := CreateHatchBrush(BarFillStyle, 0);
      OldBrush := SelectObject(PaintDC, NewBrush);
      Rectangle(PaintDC, x1, y1, x2, y2);
      SelectObject(PaintDC, OldBrush);
      DeleteObject(NewBrush);
      END;

   {local procedure under Paint method}
   PROCEDURE DrawPieSlice(x1,y1,x2,y2,
                          x3,y3,x4,y4, PieFillStyle: INTEGER);
      BEGIN
         NewBrush := CreateHatchBrush(PieFillStyle, 0);
         OldBrush := SelectObject(PaintDC, NewBrush);
         Pie(PaintDC, x1, y1, x2, y2, x3, y3, x4, y4);
         SelectObject(PaintDC, OldBrush);
         DeleteObject(NewBrush);
         END;

   {local procedure under Paint method}
   PROCEDURE DrawEllipse(x1,y1,x2,y2, EFillStyle: INTEGER);
      BEGIN
      NewBrush := CreateHatchBrush(EFillStyle, 0);
      OldBrush := SelectObject(PaintDC, NewBrush);
      Ellipse(PaintDC, x1, y1, x2, y2);
      SelectObject(PaintDC, OldBrush);
      DeleteObject(NewBrush);
```

```
        END;

    {main body of paint method}
    BEGIN
    DrawBar(40,40,150,150, hs_Cross);
    TextOut(PaintDC, 70,160, 'Square', 6);

    DrawPieSlice(180,40,400,120,375,95,350,60,
                 hs_DiagCross);
    TextOut(PaintDC, 300, 120, 'Pie Slice', 9);

    DrawEllipse(40,200,150,310, hs_BDiagonal);
    TextOut(PaintDC, 80,320, 'Circle', 6);

    DrawEllipse(220,180,450,235, hs_FDiagonal);
    TextOut(PaintDC, 320,245, 'Ellipse', 7);

    {draw a line as a "flat" rectangle}
    Rectangle(PaintDC,220,300,450,302);
    TextOut(PaintDC, 325,312, 'Line', 4);

    END;

VAR
    GrafApp : GrafApplication;

BEGIN
    GrafApp.Init('Listing 32.2');
    GrafApp.Run;
    GrafApp.Done
END.
```

The program in Listing 32.2 works the same as the one in Listing 32.1, except that we've added brushes with fill styles to fill in the drawings. This means a slightly more involved *Paint* method, so let's look at it step by step.

The first thing to notice is that, overall, we've created three local procedures inside the *Paint* method. Each local procedure handles drawing one of the different types of figures. This step merely simplifies the overall structure of the *Paint* method, making it easier to see what's going on and less likely to have hidden bugs.

FIGURE 32.2:

Output from running Listing 32.2

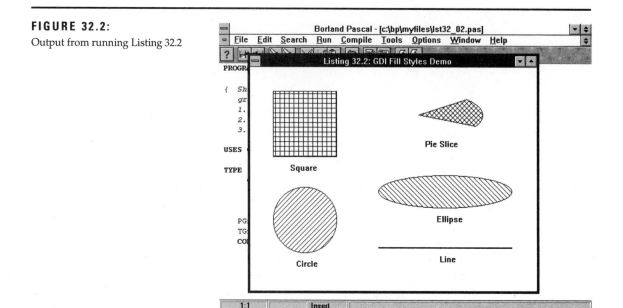

As local variables, we declare two handles to fill styles. The use of these two variables becomes apparent in the first local procedure, *DrawBar*. This procedure takes five parameters:

x1 and *y1*, the coordinates of the upper-left corner of the rectangle being drawn

x2 and *y2*, the coordinates of the lower-right corner of the rectangle being drawn

BarFillStyle, an integer type that can be represented by a predefined fill style identifier

The last parameter is the new twist here. Windows defines a number of different fill styles that you can use. To use a fill style, you have to set up a brush. The fill styles available are listed in Table 32.1.

The main body of the *DrawBar* procedure consists of variations on what we saw in our earlier line-drawing program when we substituted one pen drawing tool for another. First, we call the Windows GDI function *CreateHatchBrush* to get a handle to a new brush tool that uses the fill style specified in the *BarFillStyle* parameter. The

TABLE 32.1: Hatch-Style Fill Identifiers

IDENTIFIER	FILL STYLE
hs_BDiagonal	Backward-slanted (downward to the right) diagonal lines
hs_Cross	Crosses resembling plus signs
hs_DiagCross	Crosses resembling the letter 'x'
hs_FDiagonal	Forward-slanted (upward to the right) diagonal lines
hs_Horizontal	Horizontal lines
hs_Vertical	Vertical lines

second parameter in the call to *CreateHatchBrush* is a *TColorRef*-type number that denotes the color of the fill pattern; here, we've simply let it be *0*, making the lines in the fill pattern black. As a function, *CreateHatchBrush* returns a handle to a brush tool; we assign the handle to the local *NewBrush* variable.

We then call *SelectObject* just as we did in the line-drawing program to substitute one pen tool for another. You may recall that *SelectObject* takes two parameters: a device context, which here is *PaintDC*, and an object, which here is the handle to the new brush tool. It sets up the new brush tool to work in the device context and, simultaneously, kicks out whatever corresponding tool was there before, returning it as the *SelectObject* function's return value. We assign the return value to the local *OldBrush* variable, and we're ready to draw with the new fill style.

The next step is simply to call the *Rectangle* function with the *PaintDC* device context and the appropriate coordinates. Because *NewBrush* is now selected as the "official" drawing tool for *PaintDC*, the *Rectangle* function automatically draws a filled-in figure with the chosen fill style.

Having done our drawing, we immediately switch back to the old brush and, to conserve system resources, dispose of the newly created dynamic brush object with a call to *DeleteObject*.

The other local procedures in the *Paint* method work in exactly the same way as the *DrawBar* procedure, though the parameters vary slightly. In the main body of the *Paint* method, we draw the figures exactly as before, but this time using our local procedures and an assortment of fill styles.

Creating Business Graphics

Borland Pascal for Windows and Windows itself lack some of the more mature capabilities for creating business graphics found in the DOS version of Turbo Pascal. However, by using some fairly simple tricks, you can turn out attractive business graphics with surprisingly little effort.

Here, we'll demonstrate only a simple business graphics program. In a real-world program, of course, you'd provide a front-end part that would get the data for the graphics from the user. Listing 32.3 shows how to use the *Rectangle* and *TextOut* functions to create a simple bar chart. Figure 32.3 shows the result of running the program in Listing 32.3.

FIGURE 32.3:

The bar chart created by the program in Listing 32.3

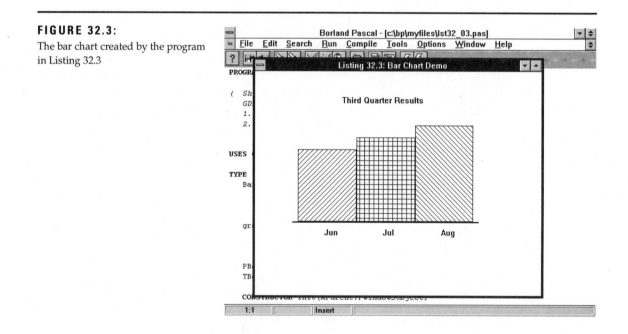

Listing 32.3

```
PROGRAM Listing32_3;

{  Shows how to create a simple bar chart with Windows
   GDI functions. Specific features demonstrated:
   1. Storing bar dimensions in an array.
   2. Creating simple routines to draw and label the
      chart. }

USES OWINDOWS, WINTYPES, WINPROCS;

TYPE
   BarChartapplication = OBJECT (tapplication)
      PROCEDURE InitMainWindow; VIRTUAL;
      END;

   grafdims = RECORD
               x1, y1, x2, y2: INTEGER
               END;

   PBarChartWindow = ^TBarChartWindow;
   TBarChartWindow = OBJECT(TWindow)
      grafbars : ARRAY[0..3] OF grafdims;
   CONSTRUCTOR Init(AParent:PWindowsObject;
                    ATitle:PChar);
      PROCEDURE Paint(PaintDC:HDC;
                      VAR Paintinfo:TPaintStruct); VIRTUAL;
      END;

PROCEDURE BarChartapplication.InitMainWindow;
   BEGIN
   MainWindow :=
        new(PBarChartwindow, Init(
      NIL, 'Listing 32.3: Bar Chart Demo'));
   END;

CONSTRUCTOR TBarChartwindow.Init(AParent:PWindowsObject;
                                 ATitle:PChar);
   BEGIN
   TWindow.Init(AParent, ATitle);
   attr.x := 50;
   attr.y := 50;
   attr.w := 500;
   attr.h := 400;
```

```
        grafbars[0].x1 := 65;
        grafbars[0].y1 := 250;
        grafbars[0].x2 := 385;
        grafbars[0].y2 := 252;

        grafbars[1].x1 := 75;
        grafbars[1].y1 := 130;
        grafbars[1].x2 := 175;
        grafbars[1].y2 := 250;

        grafbars[2].x1 := 175;
        grafbars[2].y1 := 110;
        grafbars[2].x2 := 275;
        grafbars[2].y2 := 250;

        grafbars[3].x1 := 275;
        grafbars[3].y1 := 90;
        grafbars[3].x2 := 375;
        grafbars[3].y2 := 250;
        END;

PROCEDURE TBarChartwindow.Paint(PaintDC:HDC;
                                  VAR Paintinfo: TPaintStruct);
    VAR
       NewBrush,
       OldBrush : HBrush;

    PROCEDURE DrawBar(x1, y1, x2, y2,
                      BarFillStyle: INTEGER);
       BEGIN
       NewBrush := CreateHatchBrush(BarFillStyle, 0);
       OldBrush := SelectObject(PaintDC, NewBrush);
       Rectangle(PaintDC, x1, y1, x2, y2);
       SelectObject(PaintDC, OldBrush);
       DeleteObject(NewBrush);
       END;

    {main body of paint method}
    BEGIN
    Rectangle(PaintDC, grafbars[0].x1, grafbars[0].y1,
              grafbars[0].x2, grafbars[0].y2);
    DrawBar(grafbars[1].x1, grafbars[1].y1,
            grafbars[1].x2, grafbars[1].y2,
            hs_BDiagonal);
```

```
        DrawBar(grafbars[2].x1, grafbars[2].y1,
                grafbars[2].x2, grafbars[2].y2,
                hs_Cross);
        DrawBar(grafbars[3].x1, grafbars[3].y1,
                grafbars[3].x2, grafbars[3].y2,
                hs_FDiagonal);

        TextOut(PaintDC, 120, 260, 'Jun', 3);
        TextOut(PaintDC, 220, 260, 'Jul', 3);
        TextOut(PaintDC, 320, 260, 'Aug', 3);
        TextOut(PaintDC, 150, 40, 'Third-Quarter Results', 21);
        END;

VAR
    BarChartApp : BarChartApplication;

BEGIN
    BarChartApp.Init('Listing 32.3');
    BarChartApp.run;
    BarChartApp.done
END.
```

Including Text with Graphics

The program in Listing 32.3, for the most part, simply applies the features we saw in this chapter's first two listings, adding a minor trick here and there just to make the code simpler. We declare a record type to hold the dimensions of each bar in a multibar chart, then use that type in an array for one of the fields in the parent window. We call a local *DrawBar* routine, just as before, inside the *Paint* method to draw the bars, and then label the bars and the chart as a whole with the Windows GDI *TextOut* function.

The *TextOut* function is not complicated, and it is quite useful. It takes five parameters:

- A handle to a device context (here, *PaintDC*)

- The x and y coordinates where the text string should begin

- The text string itself

- The number of characters in the text string

Using Windows Fonts

One thing we didn't include in the program from Listing 32.3 is very interesting type faces, or fonts, in the text that goes with the bar chart. Frankly, dealing with Windows fonts can be a fairly complex business. Fortunately, there are a few shortcuts. One such shortcut is to avoid using the *CreateFont* function, which takes 14 parameters, and use instead the *CreateFontIndirect* function, which takes only 1 parameter. This technique for using fonts is shown in Listing 32.4. The result of running the program is shown in Figure 32.4.

FIGURE 32.4:

The bar chart with new fonts

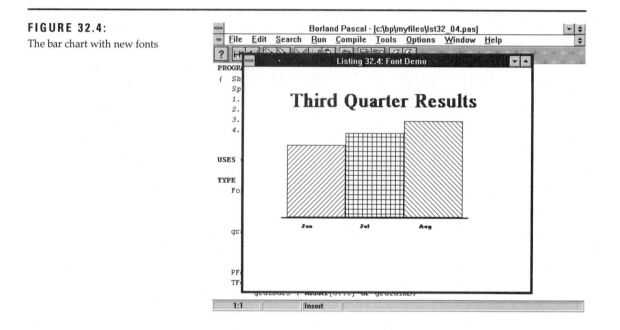

Listing 32.4

```
PROGRAM Listing32_4;

{   Shows how to use predefined Windows fonts.
    Specific features demonstrated:
    1. Using a TLogFont-type record.
    2. Using handles to fonts.
    3. Using the CreateFontIndirect function.
    4. Deleting fonts when finished with them. }
```

```
USES OWINDOWS, WINTYPES, WINPROCS, STRINGS;

TYPE
    FontDemoapplication = object (tapplication)
        PROCEDURE InitMainWindow; VIRTUAL;
        END;

    grafdims = RECORD
                x1, y1, x2, y2: INTEGER
                END;

    PFontDemoWindow = ^TFontDemoWindow;
    TFontDemoWindow = OBJECT(TWindow)
        grafbars : ARRAY[0..3] OF grafdims;
    CONSTRUCTOR Init(AParent:PWindowsObject;
                     ATitle:PChar);
        PROCEDURE Paint(PaintDC:HDC;
                VAR Paintinfo:TPaintStruct); VIRTUAL;
        END;

PROCEDURE FontDemoapplication.InitMainWindow;
    BEGIN
    MainWindow := new(PFontDemowindow,
            Init(NIL, 'Listing 32.4: FontDemonstration'));
    END;

CONSTRUCTOR TFontDemowindow.Init(AParent:PWindowsObject;
                                 ATitle:PChar);
    BEGIN
    TWindow.Init(AParent, ATitle);
    attr.x := 50;
    attr.y := 50;
    attr.w := 500;
    attr.h := 400;

    grafbars[0].x1 := 65;
    grafbars[0].y1 := 250;
    grafbars[0].x2 := 385;
    grafbars[0].y2 := 252;

    grafbars[1].x1 := 75;
    grafbars[1].y1 := 130;
    grafbars[1].x2 := 175;
    grafbars[1].y2 := 250;
```

```
    grafbars[2].x1 := 175;
    grafbars[2].y1 := 110;
    grafbars[2].x2 := 275;
    grafbars[2].y2 := 250;

    grafbars[3].x1 := 275;
    grafbars[3].y1 := 90;
    grafbars[3].x2 := 375;
    grafbars[3].y2 := 250;
    END;

PROCEDURE TFontDemowindow.Paint(PaintDC:HDC;
      VAR Paintinfo: TPaintStruct);
    VAR
      NewBrush,
      OldBrush : HBrush;
      FontInfo : TLogFont;
      OldFont,
      NewFont  : HFont;

    PROCEDURE SetUpFont(FStyle, FWeight,
                        FHeight, FWidth:
                        INTEGER);
      BEGIN
      WITH FontInfo DO
         BEGIN
         lfHeight := FHeight;
         lfWidth := FWidth;
         lfWeight := FWeight;
         lfItalic := FStyle;
         lfUnderLine := 0;
         lfStrikeOut := 0;
         lfQuality := Proof_Quality;
         strPcopy(lfFaceName, 'Tms Rmn');
         END
      END;

    PROCEDURE DrawBar(x1, y1, x2, y2,
                      BarFillStyle: INTEGER);
      BEGIN
      NewBrush := CreateHatchBrush(BarFillStyle, 0);
      OldBrush := SelectObject(PaintDC, NewBrush);
      Rectangle(PaintDC, x1, y1, x2, y2);
      SelectObject(PaintDC, OldBrush);
```

```
      DeleteObject(NewBrush);
      END;

   {main body of paint method}
   BEGIN
   Rectangle(PaintDC, grafbars[0].x1, grafbars[0].y1,
            grafbars[0].x2, grafbars[0].y2);
   DrawBar(grafbars[1].x1, grafbars[1].y1,
          grafbars[1].x2, grafbars[1].y2,
          hs_BDiagonal);
   DrawBar(grafbars[2].x1, grafbars[2].y1,
          grafbars[2].x2, grafbars[2].y2,
          hs_Cross);
   DrawBar(grafbars[3].x1, grafbars[3].y1,
          grafbars[3].x2, grafbars[3].y2,
          hs_FDiagonal);

   SetUpFont(0,700,10,0);
   NewFont := CreateFontIndirect(FontInfo);
   OldFont := SelectObject(PaintDC, NewFont);
   TextOut(PaintDC, 100, 260, 'Jun', 3);
   TextOut(PaintDC, 200, 260, 'Jul', 3);
   TextOut(PaintDC, 300, 260, 'Aug', 3);
   SelectObject(PaintDC, OldFont);
   DeleteObject(newFont);

   SetUpFont(0,1000,50,0);
   NewFont := CreateFontIndirect(FontInfo);
   OldFont := SelectObject(PaintDC, NewFont);
   TextOut(PaintDC, 80, 40, 'Third-Quarter Results', 21);
   SelectObject(PaintDC, oldFont);
   DeleteObject(newFont);
   END;

VAR
   FontDemoApp : FontDemoApplication;

BEGIN
   FontDemoApp.Init('Listing 32.4: Font Demo');
   FontDemoApp.run;
   FontDemoApp.done
END.
```

Depending on your monitor, you may need to use smaller values for the darkness and size parameters of *SetUpFont* and/or change the coordinates to accommodate the text string in *TextOut*.

A font is like any other Windows object. As mentioned previously, you can load a font into your program in one of two ways: with the Windows GDI function *CreateFont* or with the Windows GDI function *CreateFontIndirect*. The syntax for *CreateFont* is

```
CreateFont(Height, Width, Escapement,
   Orientation, Weight: INTEGER;

   Italic, Underline, StrikeOut, CharSet,
   OutputPrecision, ClipPrecision, Quality,
   PitchAndFamily: BYTE;

   FaceName : PChar) : HFont
```

As you can see, giving a full specification of a font's characteristics is no simple business. Fortunately, if you don't want to have to be an expert on fonts, there's an easy way out: use *CreateFontIndirect* instead, and let Windows supply default values for any of the parameters that you're not interested in. The syntax for *CreateFontIndirect* is

```
CreateFontIndirect(LogFont);
```

This is certainly a lot simpler. But, as Nobel laureate economist Milton Friedman often reminds us, there's no such thing as a free lunch (...unless you're a politician). Using *CreateFontIndirect* means that you must declare a variable of type *TLogFont* to hold the font's characteristics, and then pass that variable as a parameter when you call the *CreateFontIndirect* function. *TLogFont* is a predefined record type that's set up as follows:

```
TLogFont = RECORD
   lfHeight: INTEGER;
   lfWidth: INTEGER;
   lfEscapement: INTEGER;
   lfOrientation: INTEGER;
   lfWeight: INTEGER;
   lfItalic: BYTE;
   lfUnderline: BYTE;
   lfStrikeOut: BYTE;
   lfCharSet: BYTE;
   lfOutPrecision: BYTE;
   lfClipPrecision: BYTE;
```

```
    lfQuality: BYTE;
    lfPitchAndFamily: BYTE;
    lfFaceName: ARRAY[0..lf_FaceSize - 1] OF CHAR;
END;
```

You can see that we really didn't "eliminate" any information about the font by using *CreateFontIndirect*. What's the payoff, then? It's simply this: instead of having to specify values for all the different font characteristics by passing each as a parameter to *CreateFont*, you can simply change the fields you want in the *TLogFont* record variable and accept the defaults for all the rest. This not only makes your life easier, but it simplifies your code.

Many of the font characteristics are almost incomprehensible unless you're already familiar with fonts. The ones you're most likely to use are listed in Table 32.2.

The first step in using fonts is to set up (here, in the *Paint* method) a local variable to hold the *TLogFont* information, and two other local variables to hold handles to fonts. We then set up a local procedure that takes as parameters the font characteristics we want to change, and load the values we want into the appropriate fields of the *TLogFont*-type variable *FontInfo*.

A little farther down, we make our first call to the local *SetUpFont* procedure, loading the values we want into *FontInfo*. We then pass the variable as a parameter to *CreateFontIndirect*, which returns a handle to the font. Using *SelectObject* just as we did for pens and brushes, we associate the new font handle with the *PaintDC* device context and "kick out" whatever font was already there into the *OldFont* variable.

TABLE 32.2: Important Font-Characteristic Fields of TLogFont

FIELD	MEANING
lfHeight and lfWidth	Average height and width of the font
lfWeight	The "weight" of the font—i.e., its boldness—in inked pixels per 1000. The value can be from 0 to 1000. Normal boldness is 400.
lfItalic, lfUnderline, and lfStrikeOut	If nonzero, these fields mean that the text should use italic, underlined, or strikeout fonts, respectively
lfCharSet	Denotes one of three predefined Windows font character sets: ANSI_CharSet, OEM_CharSet, or Symbol_CharSet
lfQuality	Denotes the display quality of the font: Default_Quality, Draft_Quality, or Proof_Quality

We then use *TextOut* to display the text we want (the names of months in the quarter), reselect the old font back into the *PaintDC* device context, and dispose of the dynamically created new font by calling *DeleteObject*. As usual, this last step is important so as not to waste system resources.

We then repeat the process to display the title of the bar chart, because we want the title to be larger than the month names; therefore, we have to load different values into *FontInfo*. The rest of the program is standard stuff.

CHAPTER THIRTY-THREE

Creating and Using Dynamic Link Libraries

- How to Set Up a Dynamic Link

- Importing DLL Routines into a Unit

- Using DLL Routines in a Program

A *dynamic link library* (DLL) is an executable module of code and/or data that can be linked to a program at run time. This is a fairly advanced Windows feature, and one that is not needed for many applications. However, it's important to know the basics of what DLLs are and how they are applied, and that's what we will look at in this chapter.

Why Dynamic Link Libraries?

The point of creating dynamic link libraries is that different Windows applications can share the code and data that they contain, thereby economizing on system resources and making it possible to create "standard" libraries that all application programs can use. Windows itself makes use of DLLs to provide Windows functions and resources that need to be available to all Windows applications. Windows fonts, which we saw in Chapter 32, are an example of what DLLs can contain; all libraries used by Windows itself are DLLs.

In some ways, DLLs are a lot like Borland Pascal units, except that they can be shared by all Windows programs (no matter what language they were written in) and can include data as well as subroutines. The benefits are the same: standardized features do not need to be recreated or retyped into each program's source code. The big difference between DLLs and Borland Pascal units is that DLLs are not linked to the program when it is compiled; instead, they are linked as needed at run time. In Windows terminology, a Borland Pascal unit (such as the WinDOS or the WObjects unit) is a "static" rather than a "dynamic" link library.

Another point about DLLs is that they can be written in any source language and used by a BPW program. In a certain sense, of course, this is an obvious point, but it's worth remembering. You can create DLLs in Borland Pascal for use by BPW programs and any other Windows programs; in your BPW programs, you can use DLLs created with Borland Pascal, Borland C++, Microsoft C/C++, or any other Windows-capable programming platform.

How to Set Up a Dynamic Link Library

The best way to understand how DLLs work is to set up a simple one. Listing 33.1 shows a simple dynamic link library that contains a single procedure: *FlipFlop*, a routine that exchanges the values of two character-type variables. Note that Listing 33.1 should be saved under the name FLIPDLL.PAS instead of the usual "listing-filename."

Listing 33.1

```
LIBRARY FlipDLL;

{Listing 33.1: Demonstrates setting up a simple
 dynamic link library.}

{Any units used would be named here. In this case,
none is needed.}

PROCEDURE FlipFlop(VAR vbl1, vbl2: CHAR); EXPORT;
   VAR
      TempVbl: CHAR;
   BEGIN
      TempVbl := vbl1;
      vbl1 := vbl2;
      vbl2 := TempVbl
   END;

EXPORTS FlipFlop  INDEX 1;

BEGIN
END.
```

There's nothing essentially very complex about this listing. At the top is the header, which uses the reserved word *Library* to indicate that this is going to be a dynamic link library instead of a regular BPW program or unit. Then comes the descriptive name of the DLL, which in this case is *FlipDLL*. If any BPW units were needed by the routines in the DLL, the units would be named on the next line.

The details of the routines in the DLL are then spelled out. The headers of the routines end with the directive EXPORT, indicating that they will be exported to another module.

The next part of the DLL specifies the exported routines and gives each an index value. This index value is used in the unit that calls the routine from the DLL; the index identifies the exported routine.

Finally, there is an empty BEGIN..END initialization section, just as you might have with a regular Borland Pascal unit.

You should compile the dynamic link library in Listing 33.1 in preparation for the next step, which is creating a unit to import the DLL routine into a BPW program.

Importing DLL Routines into a Unit

To use a DLL in a BPW program, you must first create a unit that imports the routine from the DLL. This unit is then, in turn, used by your BPW program to gain access to the routines in the DLL. Listing 33.2 shows how to set up a unit that works with the DLL in Listing 33.1.

Listing 33.2

```
UNIT Flip;
INTERFACE
PROCEDURE FlipFlop(VAR vbl1, vbl2: CHAR);
IMPLEMENTATION
PROCEDURE FlipFlop; EXTERNAL 'FlipDLL' INDEX 1;
END.
```

This unit looks almost exactly like any other Borland Pascal unit, but with one key exception. Instead of spelling out the details of FlipFlop in the IMPLEMENTATION section, the unit refers the compiler to an external module which it identifies as *FlipDLL*—the name of our dynamic link library from Listing 33.1. Within that DLL, the unit identifies the appropriate routine by referring to its index value, which in this case is *1*.

In preparation for the final step of running the program that uses the DLL, save the unit under the name FLIP.PAS and compile it.

Using DLL Routines in a Program

The rest of the process is remarkably easy. You don't even need to know, for this step, that the routine you want is in a dynamic link library. All you need to do is name the appropriate unit in a USES clause. Listing 33.3 shows how to use a DLL in a program, and Figure 33.1 shows the result of running the program.

Listing 33.3

```
PROGRAM Listing33_3;

{Demonstrates how a program can use a DLL. }

USES WinCRT, Flip;

VAR
    letter1, letter2: CHAR;

BEGIN
    letter1 := 'a';
    letter2 := 'b';
    WRITELN('Letter #1 is ', letter1, '.');
    WRITELN('Letter #2 is ', letter2, '.');
    FlipFlop(letter1, letter2);
    WRITELN;
    WRITELN('After the FlipFlop routine has run,');
    WRITELN;
    WRITELN('   Letter #1 is now ', letter1, ', and');
    WRITELN('   Letter #2 is now ', letter2, '.')
END.
```

FIGURE 33.1:

Output from running the program in Listing 33.3

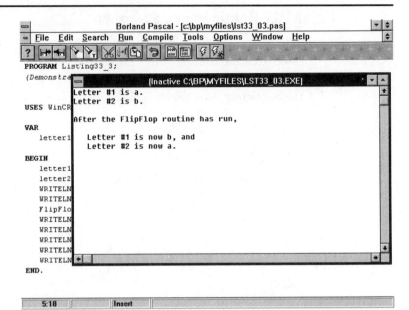

PART IV

Cross-Platform Programming Issues

34

DPMI Programming
with Borland Pascal

- Safe Protected-Mode Programming

- Running a DPMI Application

What on earth is DPMI programming, and why should you care? Those are good questions, but to understand the answers, you have to know a little history.

When Turbo Pascal first appeared—and for several years after that—all PC programs ran in what would later be called "real" mode. In real mode, the programs were compatible with the original 8086-based architecture of the IBM PC. Because of the limitations of the 8086, however, this meant that programs were limited to only 1 megabyte of random-access memory.

With the introduction of the second-generation PC processor, the 80286 chip, a new operating mode was added: protected mode, which theoretically gave programs access to as much as 16 megabytes of memory. However, most programs were unable to exploit this new capability until the 1987 introduction of the Virtual Control Program Interface (VCPI), developed jointly by Phar Lap Software and Quarterdeck Office Systems.

In 1989, Microsoft first made public its own successor to the VCPI standard: the DOS Protected Mode Interface (DPMI). This standard, which was eventually turned over to a software industry group for further development, improved on VCPI by providing more support for features such as virtual memory and safe multitasking.

In order to run a DPMI application, you must have at least an 80286 processor and utility software that provides "DPMI services" to your program. The DPMI server handles memory addresses differently than in DOS real mode (see Chapter 16 for a discussion of memory addressing). A DPMI server uses the segment part of the memory address as an index for a "descriptor table," which contains a 24-bit base segment address. This, together with the offset part of the address, gives the actual memory location of the data or code that the program needs to access.

As you might guess, the details get rather complicated—more complicated, fortunately, than you generally need to worry about in writing DPMI applications with Borland Pascal 7. In fact, the vast majority of real-mode Borland Pascal applications will run without modification as DPMI programs after they are recompiled with the target platform changed from real mode to DPMI. There are just a few important things to remember:

- In order to run a DPMI application, a PC must have the appropriate software to provide DPMI services. This can be a commercially available DPMI server such as Qualitas Software's 386MAX or Quarterdeck Office Systems' QEMM-386.

However, because you can't assume that a user's PC will have a DPMI server, Borland Pascal includes a DPMI server (DPMI16BI.OVL) and a run-time manager (RTM.EXE) that you can include with your DPMI applications. These files should be accessible to your program when it runs.

- Your DPMI programs can access the run-time manager's services though the WinAPI unit, which provides a subset of the Windows 3.1 API to support memory management, dynamic link libraries, and other DPMI features. The WinAPI unit should be named in the USES clause of all your DPMI programs.

- There are certain low-level programming moves that you should either avoid altogether or use with caution in DPMI programming. These are listed in the next section, but in a nutshell, you're safe as long as you're not directly manipulating processor registers or using absolute memory addresses.

- To create a DPMI program, you must be using either Borland Pascal for DOS (BP.EXE) or Borland Pascal for Windows (BPW.EXE). Turbo Pascal 7 (TURBO.EXE) cannot create DPMI programs.

Safe DPMI Programming

Because the DPMI server handles all requests for memory addresses by your application, you can get into trouble if you try to directly access memory locations or processor registers—just the same as you can under Windows. If your program tries to do this, it will be stopped by the DPMI server and a "general protection fault" will occur. This means that the DPMI server halts your program in order to protect any other programs that may be running at the same time. A general protection fault will occur if your program tries to:

- Directly load a value into a processor segment register. These registers can contain only values (selectors, or segment addresses) controlled by the DPMI server. Do not try to directly manipulate values in segment registers with a DPMI application.

- Access memory beyond the end of a segment. This is similar to what can happen in real mode if you attempt to manipulate an address beyond your program's code or data segment. In this case, the DPMI server and run-time manager set the segment size.

- Write data to a code segment. You shouldn't do this even in real mode, though you can get away with it. In DPMI, it's absolutely proscribed and the DPMI server will halt your program if the program tries to do it.

- Dereference a nil pointer. This is a grave programming error even in real mode, but you can sometimes get away with it. In DPMI, it will make the server halt your program.

Running a DPMI Application

As an illustration of how simple Borland Pascal makes it for you to create DPMI programs, we're going to take a real-mode listing from Chapter 3 and simply recompile it in Borland Pascal.

```
PROGRAM Listing34_1;

   { This program, originally developed as a real-mode application
     in Chapter 3, adds two integers. Here, we compile and run it
     almost without modification as a DPMI program. The only change
     is the addition of the WinAPI unit to the USES clause. In this
     program, however, even that change is not necessary, and is made
     simply to illustrate "safe" DPMI programming. It costs nothing
     to name the WinAPI unit, since Borland Pascal has "smart linking"
     and doesn't link anything into the program unless it's required. }

USES CRT, WinAPI;

VAR
   a,b,c : integer;

PROCEDURE Pause;
   VAR
      Proceed : CHAR;
   BEGIN
      WRITELN(' Press any key to continue ...');
      Proceed := READKEY;
      WRITELN; WRITELN
   END;
```

```
PROCEDURE AddTwoNumbers(a,b : integer; VAR c: integer);
   BEGIN
     c := a + b
   END;


BEGIN            { main body of program }
   clrscr;
   c := 0;
   writeln(' The starting value of c is ', c, '.');
   pause;
   a := 1;
   b := 2;
   AddTwoNumbers(a,b,c);
   writeln(' The final value of c is ', c, '.');
   pause
END.
```

Compiling for Protected Mode

Compiling this program as a DPMI application is simplicity itself. From the Compile menu, select Target, as shown in Figure 34.1. The Target dialog box will appear. Select Protected mode, as shown in Figure 34.2. Then compile the program as you normally would.

FIGURE 34.1:

Selecting "Target" from the Compile menu in Borland Pascal

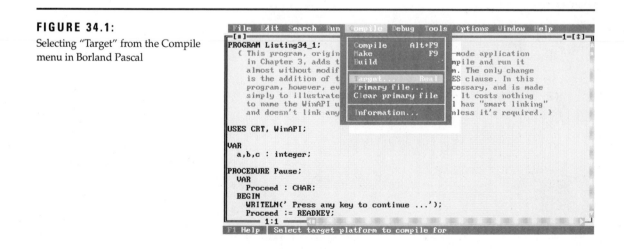

Running the Protected-Mode Program

Make sure that the files DPMI16BI.OVL and RTM.EXE are either in the same directory as your program or on your directory path. Then, run the program just as you would any other DOS program. The result of running the program is shown in Figure 34.3.

FIGURE 34.2:

Selecting "Protected mode" to compile a DPMI program

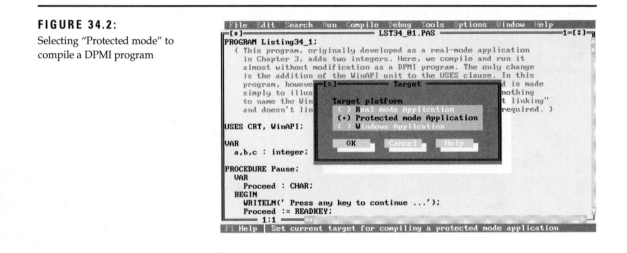

FIGURE 34.3:

Result of running the DPMI program in Listing 34.1

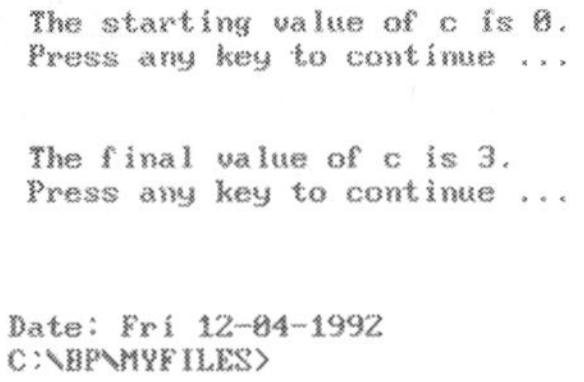

```
The starting value of c is 0.
Press any key to continue ...


The final value of c is 3.
Press any key to continue ...


Date: Fri 12-04-1992
C:\BP\MYFILES>
```

CHAPTER THIRTY-FIVE

Creating DPMI
Dynamic Link Libraries

- **Using a DPMI DLL under DOS**

- **Using a DPMI DLL under Windows**

Another important feature supported by DPMI programming is the use of dynamic link libraries (DLLs), exactly the same as those used in Windows programs. In this chapter, we'll see how to create and use dynamic link libraries in DOS DPMI programs. Then, just to prove we can really do it, we'll take the same dynamic link library we created in Borland Pascal for DOS and use it in a Windows program we'll compile and run in Borland Pascal for Windows.

Creating and Using DPMI DLLs

That introduction sounds ambitious and a little intimidating. But once you understand the concept of dynamic link libraries (as explained in Chapter 33), it's almost a no-brainer to create them in Borland Pascal. It's that easy.

To prove it, we're going to use the very same code we used in Chapter 33, where we demonstrated the use of dynamic link libraries under Windows. The three source code files are Listings 33.1, 33.2, and 33.3, which are now, respectively, Listings 35.1, 35.2, and 35.3. Because they're short listings anyway, we'll repeat them here:

Listing 35.1

```
LIBRARY FlipDLL;

{Listing 35.1: Demonstrates setting up a simple
dynamic link library in Borland Pascal 7 for DOS. Can
be used by DPMI-compatible programs under DOS or Windows.}

{Any units used would be named here. In this case,
none is needed.}

PROCEDURE FlipFlop(VAR vbl1, vbl2: CHAR); EXPORT;
   VAR
      TempVbl: CHAR;
   BEGIN
      TempVbl := vbl1;
      vbl1 := vbl2;
```

```
        vbl2 := TempVbl
    END;

EXPORTS FlipFlop  INDEX 1;

BEGIN
END.
```

Listing 35.2

```
{Listing 35.2: The unit needed to bring the DLL routines
  into a DPMI program, whether under DOS or Windows.}

UNIT Flip;
INTERFACE
PROCEDURE FlipFlop(VAR vbl1, vbl2: CHAR);
IMPLEMENTATION
PROCEDURE FlipFlop; EXTERNAL 'FlipDLL' INDEX 1;
END.
```

Listing 35.3

```
PROGRAM Listing35_3;

{Demonstrates how a program can use a DLL. First, we'll
run this program under DOS/DPMI. Then, we'll change the
WinAPI unit to the WinCRT unit and recompile.}

USES WinAPI, Flip;

VAR
    letter1, letter2: CHAR;

BEGIN
    letter1 := 'a';
    letter2 := 'b';
    WRITELN('Letter #1 is ', letter1, '.');
    WRITELN('Letter #2 is ', letter2, '.');
    FlipFlop(letter1, letter2);
    WRITELN;
    WRITELN('After the FlipFlop routine has run,');
    WRITELN;
    WRITELN('   Letter #1 is now ', letter1, ', and');
    WRITELN('   Letter #2 is now ', letter2, '.')
END.
```

The first step is to compile the DPMI DLL itself. As in Chapter 34, we need to change the Borland Pascal "target" in the Compile menu. If we only wanted to use the DLL in DOS DPMI programs, we could simply change the target to "protected mode." However, Windows programs have some added needs in a DLL. Therefore, to be able to use the DLL in either DOS DPMI or Windows programs, change the target to "Windows." Then follow these steps:

1. Compile the DLL in Listing 35.1 (FLIPDLL.PAS) just as you would any other source code file in Borland Pascal.

2. Change the target to protected mode.

3. Compile the unit in Listing 35.2 (FLIP.PAS) in the same way.

4. Compile and link the program in Listing 35.3 by selecting Make from the Compile menu.

5. Run the program from Listing 35.3. As before, you should make sure that either (a) you have a memory manager loaded that provides DPMI services, or (b) the Borland Pascal files DPMI16BI.OVL and RTM.EXE are available to the program.

The result of running the DPMI program under DOS is shown in Figure 35.1.

FIGURE 35.1:

Result of using the DPMI DLL under DOS

```
Date: Fri 12-04-1992
C:\BP\MYFILES>lst35_3
Letter #1 is a.
Letter #2 is b.

After the FlipFlop routine has run,

    Letter #1 is now b, and
    Letter #2 is now a.

Date: Fri 12-04-1992
C:\BP\MYFILES>
```

Using a DPMI DLL in a Windows Program

Now, let's use the same DLL in a Windows program. Because Windows uses the DPMI standard itself, there is no problem in doing this. First, start Windows and get into Borland Pascal for Windows. Then, recompile the unit in Listing 35.1 (FLIP.PAS), but do NOT recompile the DLL in Listing 35.2. We compiled this once in Borland Pascal for DOS, and that's adequate.

Now, load the program in Listing 35.3. In the USES clause, simply change the WinAPI unit to the WinCRT unit. Then, select Make from the Compile menu. The program should compile without incident. The result of running the program under Windows is shown in Figure 35.2.

FIGURE 35.2:

Running Listing 35.3 under Windows with WinAPI unit changed to WinCRT

CHAPTER THIRTY-SIX

Developing Portable Programs in Borland Pascal

- Problems in Program Portability

- Guidelines for Portable Programming

Developing portable programs is harder than it used to be. A portable program is one that, although written to run on one type of computer, can be moved to a different type of computer with only minimal rewriting of the source code and recompilation on the target platform.

Even a few years ago, most PC programs used basically the same screen interface as that used by dumb terminals attached to a mainframe. If you were writing a Pascal program, you had a reasonable degree of assurance that WRITELN would mean the same and work the same—displaying text on the screen—in any Pascal on any computer. If you wrote a fairly standard Pascal program on a PC, you could with very few changes run the same program on an IBM mainframe, a DEC Vax mini-computer, and many other computers.

Alas, that simple situation no longer exists. A program developed for one environment, such as text-mode MS-DOS, can still be "ported" to a similar environment on another computer. But the arrival of sophisticated graphic interface environments (GUIs) such as Microsoft Windows has meant an exponential increase in the difficulty of porting programs from one machine to another. Text-mode to GUI mode is bad enough; but even the different GUI environments don't handle things in exactly the same ways.

Borland Pascal 7 goes some of the distance toward making this easier, at least for porting applications between DOS and Microsoft Windows. From Borland Pascal for DOS or Borland Pascal for Windows, you can compile programs for any of the three PC target environments: real mode DOS, DPMI DOS, and Windows.

By using the WinCRT unit, you can do a simple port of many DOS Pascal programs to run under Microsoft Windows, as long as the programs don't make much use of hardware-oriented graphics routines or low-level system calls. But this falls far short of making a DOS program into a real Windows program. You'll run into similar problems moving programs between other environments.

"As Portable as Possible"

Given that it's a complicated PC world out there, the most realistic goal is to make programs "as portable as possible"—understanding that even this may sometimes require a lot of recoding when you move from one platform to another. Here are the most important rules for creating maximally portable programs:

Use Clear and Correct Program Design

It's tough enough to port a program when you understand how it works. But if the program is a mish-mash of spaghetti code, poorly planned procedures and functions, global variables altered without being passed as parameters, and no clear divisions in the source code, it'll be easier to toss it out and rewrite it from scratch than to port the old code to a new environment.

Thus, creating a maximally portable program requires careful planning of the design before coding begins. It also demands, in the coding stage, strict adherence to the principles of structured and object-oriented programming—for example:

- Global variables can only be altered by subroutines if they have been passed to those subroutines as parameters.

- Object type definitions must include a sufficient arsenal of methods to perform all required manipulations on the object type's data fields.

- Object fields should not be manipulated by anything but the object's own methods.

Document, Document, Document

Let's face it: programmers like to code. They like to find ingenious solutions for difficult problems. Writing source code documentation is a lot less fun, but it's absolutely necessary for the development of portable programs. This applies whether the programming is done by a single individual or a team. The programmer might understand what-calls-what right after writing the code, but six months later, even he or she might have a hard time figuring it out.

Don't Try to Be Subtle

Ironically, the more subtle and ingenious a programming trick is, the more likely it is that three things will happen:

1. It will have unexpected bugs.

2. A month after coding is complete, nobody, including the original programmer, will understand how the trick works.

3. It will be impossible to port to a different environment.

It's true: coming up with tricky solutions is fun, and can sometimes deliver faster performance and smaller code size than a straightforward approach. But if you want to make your programs portable, then subtlety is not a virtue. Unless it's absolutely necessary to squeeze every last ounce of speed from your code, you should make it as simple and obvious as possible.

Group I/O Functions Together

A lot changes from one environment to another, but nothing changes more than input-output (I/O) functions, which are often completely different. Even between two text-mode Pascal programs on different compilers and hardware platforms, such simple things as opening disk files differ in terminology and in a few details of how they are accomplished.

As much as possible, you should group all I/O subroutines together in your source code file. That will at least give you a head start on the parts that change the most. If you're moving from text-mode to a GUI environment, you'll still have a lot more to do, but you'll know where to start.

Minimize Use of Language Extensions

The final principle is to minimize use of any nonstandard features of a particular Pascal compiler. In the case of Borland Pascal, for example, use record types instead of object types, and avoid using ELSE clauses with CASE statements. Units, by other names, are supported by several Pascal compilers, but include files are supported by virtually all of them.

In general, you should restrict your language syntax to that defined in ANSI or ISO Standard Pascal.

APPENDIX

A

Borland Pascal vs. Borland C++

What are the advantages and disadvantages of Borland Pascal compared to Borland C++?

To some degree, the choice between the two languages depends simply on what you know, what you like, and which language is used where you work. The C and C++ languages are not inherently better than Borland Pascal:

- Just like C and C++, Borland Pascal offers low-level access to the PC's hardware and BIOS.

- Just like Borland C++, Borland Pascal offers full support for object-oriented programming.

- Just like Borland C++, Borland Pascal uses an ObjectWindows library to insulate the programmer from unnecessary details of the Windows API, but provides access to those details whenever they *are* needed.

- Just like Borland C++, Borland Pascal is an "optimizing" compiler that produces small, efficient .EXE files from your source code. The idea that using C or C++ will automatically result in smaller, more efficient .EXE files is a complete myth.

In spite of the similarities, each language does have its own advantages. For example:

- Borland Pascal source code, though it seems impossibly "verbose" to expert C programmers, is generally clearer and easier to understand than the corresponding C code. This is an important advantage, since tricky, nonobvious code is a fertile breeding ground for buggy programs.

- Borland C++ (and C or C++ generally) do handle some situations more easily than Borland Pascal—for example, "operator overloading," which lets you use the same name for different functions. The same thing can be accomplished in Borland Pascal, but it is less straightforward.

- Finally, if the truth be told, there is the simple economic fact: in the job market, C and C++ skills are more in demand than Pascal skills, no matter how well developed.

Your choice between Borland Pascal and Borland C++ (or another C++ package) can be dictated by any or all of these factors. Just remember that in terms of raw programming power, you don't necessarily *have* to move to C or C++ to get what you need: Borland Pascal 7 has it all.

The 10 Most Common
Programming Mistakes in Pascal

1. Unterminated statement (BEGIN, CASE, etc.); too many or too few ENDs. Often result from overly complex source code.

2. Unterminated comment bracket. (Borland Pascal 7's "syntax highlighting" helps catch this error.)

3. Failure to declare global variables as parameters when they are used by a subroutine.

4. Failure to declare global variables as VAR parameters when they must be *changed* by a subroutine.

5. Loop control variable in a WHILE or REPEAT loop never changes its value inside the loop, resulting in an endless loop. Usually results from either (a) the omission of a statement that changes the value of the variable, or (b) the mispositioning of that statement so that it is outside the loop.

6. Confusing the declaration of a data type with the creation of a variable of that type.

7. Failure to initialize variables when needed. This can result in bizarre program behavior that has no obvious connection with the uninitialized variables that are causing the problem.

8. Too much detail at the global level of a program, e.g., (a) declaring too many variables and subroutines as global when they could be local, or (b) having too many lines of code in the main body of the program.

9. Conflict between identifiers, including "unknown identifier" error: usually results from a confusion over the scope of the identifiers.

10. Failure to analyze problems carefully before starting to write code. Usually results in programs that compile but produce incorrect results when they are run.

INDEX

Page numbers in **bold** refer to major listings; page numbers in *italic* refer to program code; page numbers followed by *t* refer to tables; page numbers followed by *f* refer to figures.

Symbols and Numbers

$ (dollar sign), for hex notation, 417
^ (caret)
    for dynamic variable, 271
    for pointer type declaration, 268
(* and *) as comment brackets, 23
* (intersection) operator, 210*t*, 211
↑ (up-arrow symbol), for pointer data type declaration, 269
:= (assignment operator), 46, 131
; (semicolon)
    for compound statements, 36, 37–38, 128, 130
    in object-type declarations, 504
";" (semicolon) expected error message, 351
<> (Does not equal) operator, 140*t*, 212
< (Less than) operator, 140*t*
= (equals) operator, 140*t*
{ } (curly brackets)
    for comments, 23
    for compiler directive, 170
> (Greater than) operator, 140*t*
- (difference) operator, 210*t*, 211
' (quote marks), for text data types, 41
'\0' (null character), 121
80x87 software emulation, 113–114, 115
386MAX (Qualitas Software), 864
8086 microprocessor, registers in, 254, 412*f*
80286 microprocessor, 793, 864
80386 microprocessors, 793, 794

A

abortdriver procedure, *568*
AbortFont procedure, *407*, *568*
absolute pixel coordinates, 380
abstract data structures, **182–184**, **428–432**
    object types, **608**
    queues, **430–432**
    stacks, **428–430**
accelerators, for menu choices, **706**
access function, 199
access mode identifiers, 776
active window, 60, **66**
Add breakpoint (Debug menu), 85
Add watch (Debug menu), 85
Add Watch window, speed key for, 360
AddItems procedure, *444–445*, 446
Addname procedure, *288*
AddNewRecord procedure, *332*
AddNode procedure, *455*, *457*, *476*
AddToQueue procedure, *444*, 446
alarm sound effect, **490–491**
algorithms, **460–482**
    characteristics of, 460
    efficiency of, **461**
    fine-tuning, **464–465**
    performance speed, **461–463**
    for searching, **465–474**
    for sorting, **474–482**
Align control dialog box, 716*f*
alignment of radio buttons, **716**
ancester data types, 44, 513
ancestor object types, 499
    creating, 526
    overriding method from, 513
AND Boolean operator, 138, 138*t*
angle brackets (<>), for set inequality, 212

Key: **bold** = major listing; *italic* = program code; *t* = table; *f* = figure

Key: **bold** = major listing; *italic* = program code; *t* = table; *f* = figure

Key: **bold** = major listing; *italic* = program code; *t* = table; *f* = figure

Key: **bold** = major listing; *italic* = program code; *t* = table; *f* = figure

Key: **bold** = major listing; *italic* = program code; *t* = table; *f* = figure

Key: **bold** = major listing; *italic* = program code; t = table; f = figure

Key: **bold** = major listing; *italic* = program code; *t* = table; *f* = figure

Key: **bold** = major listing; *italic* = program code; *t* = table; *f* = figure

Key: **bold** = major listing; *italic* = program code; *t* = table; *f* = figure

Key: **bold** = major listing; *italic* = program code; *t* = table; *f* = figure

Key: **bold** = major listing; *italic* = program code; *t* = table; *f* = figure

Key: **bold** = major listing; *italic* = program code; *t* = table; *f* = figure

Key: **bold** = major listing; *italic* = program code; *t* = table; *f* = figure

G

Key: **bold** = major listing; *italic* = program code; *t* = table; *f* = figure

Key: **bold** = major listing; *italic* = program code; *t* = table; *f* = figure

Key: **bold** = major listing; *italic* = program code; *t* = table; *f* = figure

Key: **bold** = major listing; *italic* = program code; *t* = table; *f* = figure

Key: **bold** = major listing; *italic* = program code; *t* = table; *f* = figure

M

Key: **bold** = major listing; *italic* = program code; *t* = table; *f* = figure

Key: **bold** = major listing; *italic* = program code; *t* = table; *f* = figure

Key: **bold** = major listing; *italic* = program code; *t* = table; *f* = figure

Key: **bold** = major listing; *italic* = program code; *t* = table; *f* = figure

P

Key: **bold** = major listing; *italic* = program code; *t* = table; *f* = figure

Key: **bold** = major listing; *italic* = program code; *t* = table; *f* = figure

Key: **bold** = major listing; *italic* = program code; *t* = table; *f* = figure

Key: **bold** = major listing; *italic* = program code; *t* = table; *f* = figure

Key: **bold** = major listing; *italic* = program code; *t* = table; *f* = figure

Key: **bold** = major listing; *italic* = program code; *t* = table; *f* = figure

Key: **bold** = major listing; *italic* = program code; *t* = table; *f* = figure

Key: **bold** = major listing; *italic* = program code; *t* = table; *f* = figure

Key: **bold** = major listing; *italic* = program code; *t* = table; *f* = figure

Key: **bold** = major listing; *italic* = program code; *t* = table; *f* = figure

Key: **bold** = major listing; *italic* = program code; *t* = table; *f* = figure

Key: **bold** = major listing; *italic* = program code; *t* = table; *f* = figure

Key: **bold** = major listing; *italic* = program code; *t* = table; *f* = figure

Key: **bold** = major listing; *italic* = program code; *t* = table; *f* = figure

X

Y

Key: **bold** = major listing; *italic* = program code; *t* = table; *f* = figure

Z

SYBEX

FREE BROCHURE!

Complete this form today, and we'll send you a full-color brochure of Sybex bestsellers.

Please supply the name of the Sybex book purchased.

_____

How would you rate it?

_____ Excellent   _____ Very Good   _____ Average   _____ Poor

Why did you select this particular book?

_____ Recommended to me by a friend
_____ Recommended to me by store personnel
_____ Saw an advertisement in _____
_____ Author's reputation
_____ Saw in Sybex catalog
_____ Required textbook
_____ Sybex reputation
_____ Read book review in _____
_____ In-store display
_____ Other _____

Where did you buy it?

_____ Bookstore
_____ Computer Store or Software Store
_____ Catalog (name: _____)
_____ Direct from Sybex
_____ Other: _____

Did you buy this book with your personal funds?

_____ Yes   _____ No

About how many computer books do you buy each year?

_____ 1-3   _____ 3-5   _____ 5-7   _____ 7-9   _____ 10+

About how many Sybex books do you own?

_____ 1-3   _____ 3-5   _____ 5-7   _____ 7-9   _____ 10+

Please indicate your level of experience with the software covered in this book:

_____ Beginner   _____ Intermediate   _____ Advanced

Which types of software packages do you use regularly?

_____ Accounting	_____ Databases	_____ Networks
_____ Amiga	_____ Desktop Publishing	_____ Operating Systems
_____ Apple/Mac	_____ File Utilities	_____ Spreadsheets
_____ CAD	_____ Money Management	_____ Word Processing
_____ Communications	_____ Languages	_____ Other _____

(please specify)

Which of the following best describes your job title?

_____ Administrative/Secretarial _____ President/CEO

_____ Director _____ Manager/Supervisor

_____ Engineer/Technician _____ Other _____
(please specify)

Comments on the weaknesses/strengths of this book: _____

_____

_____

_____

_____

Name _____

Street _____

City/State/Zip _____

Phone _____

PLEASE FOLD, SEAL, AND MAIL TO SYBEX

SYBEX, INC.
Department M
2021 CHALLENGER DR.
ALAMEDA, CALIFORNIA USA
94501

SYBEX

SEAL

Using the Companion Disk

To install the disk, place it in a floppy disk drive and run the program INSTALL, using the Windows Program Manager or File Manager. For complete installation instructions, see the Introduction.

The disk contains the following files:

INSTALL.BAT

LHARC.EXE

LST1_6.LZH

LST7_12.LZH

LST13_18.LZH

LST19_21.LZH

LST22_26.LZH

LST27_33.LZH

LST34_36.LZH

Obtaining a FREE 3½-inch Disk

To receive a 3½-inch disk at no charge, please return the original 5¼-inch disk contained in the envelope and send your written request to

SYBEX Inc.
2021 Challenger Drive
Alameda, CA 94501
ATTN: Order Processing Dept.

Please include your name, address, state, and zip code. Make sure you refer to Reference Number 1151-3 when you order or your request cannot be processed.

Please allow six weeks for delivery.